The YESTERYEAR BOOK
1956 to 1996

Compiled by Kevin McGimpsey
and Stewart Orr.

Special assistance from Horace Dunkley, Peter Mathias, Garry Matthews and Mike Thomas.

Thanks to David Cole, Mike Dukes, Rita Fearnon, Ken Glass, Clare Gouldson, John Gouldson, Darrin Greene, Simon Iredale, Kevin Lam, Tom Mathieson, Ken Noakes, Maureen Quayle, Joe Recchia, Annette Ridgeway, Bob Rusconi, Len Samuel, Roy Sensier, Buddy Styer, Andrew Tallis, Bob Tutt, Maureen Wall, Patrick Williamson, and to the many members of MICA who have submitted information.

© MAJOR PRODUCTIONS LTD., 1996.

Produced by MICA.
Published by Major Productions Ltd.,
13A Lower Bridge Street,
Chester, CH1 1RS
Telephone: 01244 346297
Facsimile: 01244 340437

Photography: David Hughes

Design, Technical Drawings and Typesetting by: Wall St Studios.

Printed in the UK.

ISBN 0 9510885 8 0

INTRODUCTION

It's been our experience that people tend not to read introductions. They like to dive in to the first page, especially of a book such as this and get on with it. This is of course a great pity for the hapless writers, mainly because it is here that the compilers or publishers wish and need to acknowledge the help of those who have had a major contribution to what has effectively become a total rewrite of the original publication of 1993.

Unlike a work of fiction, a factual book such as this requires a huge amount of research and verification. You may be tempted to conclude that so many alterations have been made to this second edition that the first one must have been quite wrong! This is not the case, it is simply that the appearance of the first book prompted so many readers to check their models that significant amounts of new information came to light. Not only that but new information has arrived continuously over the last two years from literally hundreds of collectors the world over. It was all read, noted, discussed and where agreed, incorporated into the following pages.

We would therefore, immediately like to thank all of you who sent in contributions and to acknowledge here your help and enthusiasm. We would especially like to thank Horace Dunkley, Garry Matthews and Peter Mathias for the new copy and amendments, together with Mike Thomas for the overall copy checking, Ken Noakes for his opinions on values, and Buddy Styer for compiling the index.

This second volume now covers forty years of the production of this famous series of model vehicles. Starting with the renowned first series of just sixteen small masterpieces, the range has grown and grown to fill this considerable book. Perhaps the biggest development of recent years, however, has been the widening of the choice of subjects. We now have stagecoaches, racing cars, fire engines, and themed series of vehicles to collect. The chances are that in the future we may be looking at fuselages, hulls and even rocket ships. In any event, display space is likely to be a continuing problem for private collectors and curators alike!

To all of you who have read this far - we hope you enjoy this new book, for that is what it's all about.

Stewart Orr and Kevin McGimpsey

PREFACE

I first met Kevin McGimpsey and Stewart Orr in 1989 and, at the time, when my involvement with Models of Yesteryear was minimal, I was struck by their enthusiasm for and appreciation of this line of sophisticated diecast models.

A few years later, reading this tome covering Yesteryear production over forty years, it is not hard to understand how and why, they, along with thousands of others, avidly and studiously collect this series of models and their venerable history.

This is both a reference guide of extra-ordinary, unsurpassed detail, as well as a subtle glimpse behind the scenes of the development of the range.

In the period of late 1992 until mid 1993, there was a time, under the new ownership of Tyco Toys, of re-assessment of the Yesteryear range. Out of this 'mid life crisis' has come a flowering of the line with a choice of vehicles covering a wider spectrum than before. And what vehicles to collect: increasingly complex and detailed tampo decoration; together with the greater use of diecast components and more attention to detail.

All these new models are included in this book, laid out in the successful, easy to read format pioneered in the earlier publication. Armed with this book, the search and find missions for that elusive model for your collection should be much simpler and more rewarding.

To all of you who read, and perhaps eat and sleep, with this book, I wish you an enjoyable time collecting Yesteryears.

SIMON IREDALE
Manager Tyco International & Collectibles Source Planning. (April 1996)

The YESTERYEAR BOOK
1956 to 1996

Published in 1996

By Kevin McGimpsey and Stewart Orr.

© MAJOR PRODUCTIONS LTD 1996

All rights reserved.

The contents and layout of this book are fully protected by copyright.
No part of this book may be reproduced, stored in a retrieval system or transmitted in any form or by any means, electronic magnetic tape, mechanical, photocopying, recording, or otherwise, without permission in writing from the publishers.

ISBN 0 9510885 8 0

Whilst every care has been exercised in the compilation of the information contained in this book, neither the authors, MICA nor the publishers accept liability for loss, damage, or expense incurred by reliance placed upon the information and the values, which are themselves subject to change caused inter alia by international currency fluctuations, duty charges and international freight levies.

" 'Matchbox' and 'Models of Yesteryear' are the registered trademarks of Matchbox Collectibles, a subsidiary of Tyco Toys Inc. They are the subject of extensive trademark registration (Marca Registrada) and are used with permission."

MATCHBOX TERMINOLOGY

A

APPOINTED STOCKISTS - A term used by Matchbox in 1987 to identify retail shops which sold a good cross section of their diecast products. Appointed Stockists were expected to maintain comprehensive displays and stocks, together with a degree of knowledge about Yesteryears both old and new.

ASTERISKS - Collectors will see small asterisk signs against some of the entries in the schedules. Usually, these are limited to one of the five scarcity ratings which were first used in 'The Collection' publication. Collectors should find that information helpful, particularly because it is linked to the estimated value of a model. The symbol is *

AUSTRALIAN PREMIUM - A term used to describe models that are basically Yesteryear models but which do not bear the Models of Yesteryear legend. An example is the Cobb Stagecoach made from the YSH03 tooling, released by Tyco Croner in late 1995 in Australia. The Models of Yesteryear wording was removed and the packaging made no reference to the range. Australian Premium models do not fall within the scope of this book.

AUTHORISED MATCHBOX COLLECTIBLE CENTRES - Initially established in early 1989 in Australia, by Matchbox Collectibles, these retail shops provide a dedicated service for the Matchbox enthusiast. Their specialist service includes providing valuations, trading and purchasing models, display and sale of obsolete models and sales of new releases. This system has since been extended to the UK, European, North American, New Zealand and South African markets.

B

BASEPLATE - This refers to the chassis and the undersides. The majority of Yesteryear models have diecast baseplates; only a very few have these in plastic. With few exceptions, all pre-1993 Yesteryears have their number and an identifying description cast onto the baseplate. Since 1993, because of 'cross fertilisation' and the interchanging of tools, there has been a greater frequency of Yesteryear numbers and names being tampo printed onto, as opposed to being cast into, the baseplates. Baseplates also normally retain the axles.

See: Chapter on Yesteryear Components.

BASEPLATE DETAILS - In the column headed Baseplate, the reader will find information useful in determining the manufacturer (Lesney, Matchbox or Matchbox Collectibles) the copyright date of the model, the Yesteryear number(s) and the country of manufacture eg LESNEY © 1982 ENGLAND
This information is not to be read literally; it has been recorded as a way of highlighting the important aspects of the baseplate details and to make quick identification easier; consequently the reader will see that instead of spelling out Lesney Products & Co Ltd in full, it has been shortened to read Lesney.

BASEPLATE HOLES - Holes which have been cast either to facilitate fixing the model to giftware items or for painting purposes where the components are located on hooks. The reference 'open' or 'blind' holes indicates whether the hole is intact or has been blanked off, but with the outline still visible.

See: Screwhole

BECKENHAM APPEAL MODELS - Eighteen uniquely recoloured Yesteryears presented to the organiser of the Beckenham Radio Appeal charity. The models were auctioned at Sothebys, London, in 1978 and the proceeds were used to buy a local radio system for Beckenham Hospital. These eighteen models have been classed as Code 4 models. They are seldom seen for sale. In fact, the majority of them are currently in a large collection in the USA. See: Code 4.

BLISTER PACKS - A packaging term which describes a model that has been encased in a thin moulded piece of clear styrene and then glued to a backing card. The system has many advantages to retailers, most notably that the pack can be displayed on racks. Collectors, however, dislike them because if opened, the packaging is damaged. Yesteryear blister packs were only sold in North America.

BODY - For the purposes of this publication the components that make up the majority of the upper part of the model, including: bonnet, boot, roof (where the same colour) and sides.

BOOT - The British term for the rear storage compartment of a car; called a 'trunk' in North America. Not to be confused with a luggage trunk as on the Y11-3 1938 Lagonda.

BOSSES - (1) This relates to a part of a moulding tool (either for plastic or metal parts). Correctly known as an ejector boss - it is a circular piece of metal which moves forward to eject a casting from its mould. It often leaves a circular mark on the casting and these are normally found on the underside of a casting. These marks may be faint, or pronounced depending on the amount of wear in the tool. Hollow bosses occur where the central hole is complete; blind bosses are where the central hole is partially blanked off and solid bosses are bosses with no central hole at all. They can be of interest to a collector as they help to date a model.

(2) Also where metal has been cast as a short tube or collar and projects from the surrounding surface. This was a common practice on baseplates used in the Giftware range, so that the model could be attached to the Giftware items by inserting a screw into the hollow bosses. See: Chapter on Yesteryear Components.

(3) With the introduction of the new packaging in 1993 all range models with few exceptions have two bosses cast on their baseplates to secure the model plastic plinths; even though the plinths were dispensed with all ranges except Great Beers.

BOX TYPES - Throughout this book there are columns headed Box Type. Detailed description of the types are given in a separate glossary.

BRACE - A brace is a piece of metal added to a component to strengthen an area of a casting. They are normally found behind such areas as number plates, or on the inside of wheels. Braces are often added to a tool after pre-production on early runs of models, as it is then that small weaknesses can reveal themselves. The best known example of a brace can be found behind the front bumper of the Y3-1 Tram, on all issues except for the very first issues.

C

CANOPY - A protective top often with an unsupported front edge, eg Y13 Crossley.

CASTINGS - This refers to the metal components used to construct a model. Diecasting is the method of producing a shape by introducing molten metal into a die to produce a cast shape.

CHASSIS - Refers to the lower frame of a vehicle, in vintage vehicles these are also known as chassis frame or side member. For the purposes of this publication the chassis component incorporates the baseplate, mudguards and sometimes the running boards. Yesteryear chassis are usually made from diecast. Some models, such as the YGB16, have part of the chassis made from plastic.

CHINA - New facilities were opened in China for Yesteryear production in 1990 to replace the Macau facilities. Baseplates and boxes continue to reflect the area of manufacture and a column in this publication shows the three areas so far: England, Macau or China.

CHINESE SIX - Six Yesteryears, five of which have pre-1990 liveries, which were made at the China factory and released in July 1991. The models were:
Y2 Bentley in blue
Y4 Duesenberg in silver and blue
Y14 ERA in blue and yellow
Y19 Morris Van - Brasso
Y22 Ford 'A' - Cherry Blossom
Y22 Ford 'A' - Lyons Tea
Their significance was that Matchbox had re-issued obsolete models, similar to the earlier production runs (made in Macau) and had packaged these re-runs in the old style maroon (J2) box marked with 'Made in China', as were the baseplates! Originally the six models were made as a special order for Poland. However, due to political and economic problems, the order was cancelled and the majority were sold through Woolworths and Tescos in the UK. The production run of each model was 5,000.

CHRISTMAS TREASURES (YCC01 and YCC02) - Matchbox Collectibles released their first boxed set of four Austin 7 vans in December 1994. Each model was fitted with a metal 'eye' to enable it to be hung as a Christmas tree decoration. In December 1995 Matchbox Collectibles released a second set.

CODE 1 - "Yesteryear models that have been manufactured in their entirety by Lesney Products, Matchbox Toys Ltd or by Matchbox Collectibles and have been distributed for sale to the general public through retail outlets or by mail order"

CODE 2 - "Yesteryear models that were originally of Code 1 status, but whose livery or decorations have been altered, removed, or replaced by a third party with the full agreement of the said manufacturers; OR where a Code 1 Yesteryear model has not been made available to the general public through retail outlets or directly from Matchbox Collectibles," eg The 'blue' Y12-3 Hoover.

CODE 3 - "Yesteryear models that were originally of Code 1 status but whose livery, or decorations have been altered, removed, or replaced by a third party without the full agreement and the acknowledgement of the manufacturers. NB Matchbox consider that Code 3 models are no longer a part of the Yesteryear range because they no longer control the quality, child safety requirements, packaging standards and the many legal requirements to which their own range models are subjected."

CODE 4 - "Presentation or commemorative Yesteryear models which have been produced under Lesney/Matchbox/Matchbox Collectibles management supervision and which were never intended to be released to the general public through retail outlets".

COLD CAST - An item such as the Christmas tree on the YSC01 Scania was made by this process. A sculptured tree was made from clay. It was then covered in rubber to make a mould. The clay disintegrates. A hard resin substance is then poured into the rubber mould. This makes the 'master', which in turn is covered in rubber to make a further rubber mould. A liquid containing elements of porcelain are poured in. There is no need for applied heat - once the liquid has hardened, the mould is peeled off, leaving the unpainted finished product. The advantages of cold cast are that they have enabled Matchbox Collectibles to bring out loads and vehicle features that, in the past, were simply not done or handled in plastic. All the cold cast loads and features such as those found on the Steam Series (YAS) are hand-painted.

COLLECTION, THE - The first officially Matchbox endorsed publication published in 1985 chronicling the entire range of Yesteryears since 1956. Four supplements, the last one being published in 1991, followed containing information of new releases and updating older published material. Now out of print.

COMPONENTS - A generic term to describe all of the various finished parts used to produce a model.

CONNOISSEUR SET - A limited presentation set of six models which had been in the range during the 1960s and early 1970s. The set was released in 1984, priced at just under £70.00. This price began to fall even though Matchbox offered a Y25 Renault Van 'James Neale' free of charge to retailers who ordered further sets to be given away with a purchase of the set. In recent years the Connoisseur Set has begun to appreciate and are seldom, if ever, seen for sale at less than £95.00. The six models are:
Y1 Model 'T' Ford in black
Y3 Benz Limousine in blue
Y4 Opel in red
Y11 Packard Laudaulet in cream and brown
Y13 Daimler in blue
Y14 Maxwell in cream and green

Each set was presented in a mahogany box and came with a numbered certificate. Matchbox also offered to refund the full purchase price after five years to purchasers who had bought direct from them.

COPYRIGHT DATE - With the exception of some models in the first series and early second series, most Yesteryear models have been given a copyright date on the baseplate, ie a © followed by a date. These numbers record the date that the model was first cast, but not necessarily the year of introduction into the range. A good example being the Y14-3 Stutz Bearcat which was released first in 1974 with 1973 on the baseplate. A sure way in which to determine a pre-production model is to check the baseplate date. Invariably true pre-productions have an incomplete date, eg 197_. It is the policy to complete the date only when Matchbox know the accurate year of release, at which time the tools will be completed to reflect that date. Copyright dates are well sought after variations an example being the Y12 Model 'T' van. The same coloured van was released with several different baseplates. See: Chapter covering copright and registration marks.

CRIMPED - This refers to an early type of axle applied to first series Yesteryears up to 1960. These axles were flattened, or crimped at one end to retain the wheels. Early safety regulations led to the development of 'spun' ends for axles which looked better and had no sharp edges.

D

DECAL - (See Transfer) Decal is an alternative word to transfer. Decals are printed labels which are produced on a special type of paper known as release paper. When wet, this backing paper allows the decal to slide off and be placed on a model.

DIORAMA - This is a modelling term referring to the practice of producing a three dimensional scene in a realistic manner. Matchbox Toys adopted this idea for some of their models in the late 1980s, eg category 'N' style boxes have a cardboard diorama insert.

DIES - Refers to the tools from which model components are cast.

DIFFICULT (D) - One of the five rarity categories used throughout the book described as being not easy to find and with a small price premium.

E

EJECTOR RINGS - See Bosses.
EJECTOR PIN IMPRESSIONS - See Bosses.

ENHANCED - This term was first used by Matchbox to describe the extra detailing given to several of the models first released in the USA as part of the Great Motor Cars of the Century offer in 1989 and 1990. Better use was made of the ever improving tampo printing machines to highlight running boards, sills, strips, door handles, number plates and steering wheels. Although an expensive extra, today's Yesteryears are given extensive degrees of enhancement as the standard finish.

ESTIMATE - See Production Figures.

EXTREMELY RARE (ER) - One of five rarity categories used throughout the book. 'Exceptionally highly priced and very seldomly seen for sale.'

F

FETTLING - This word is used to describe the process by which excess metal (see flashing) is removed from castings by tumbling them in a rotating drum. The abrasive action of this process removes fine metal but leaves the more robust actual casting intact.

FIRE ENGINE SERIES (YFE) - The first six models were released by Matchbox Collectibles during 1994. Promotional literature stated: "Today, six of the most important fire trucks from this golden era have been re-created in the only die-cast collection of its kind. Each model in the collection is faithful to the original and has been seen and approved for historical accuracy by experts at the Fire Brigade Society".
In 1996, the Fire Engine Series had reached number YFE12.

FIRST SERIES - Models of Yesteryear were first produced in 1956 and the range was quickly expanded to produce 16 models by 1961. At that time Lesney decided to adopt a policy of only having 16 models in the range at any one time. Thus new models always replaced older ones which were withdrawn, and these were given the same catalogue numbers. Hence, Yesteryears can be classified into several series. First series models are to be found in box types 'A' to 'D3'.

FORMERS - Made from thin plastic. Moulded to an individual model in two halves which encapsulates the model and fits 'snugly' into the outer card box to prevent damage to the model in transit.

FLASHING - When a component is cast it tends to have, or retain excess metal present either in small cavities, or around its edges, and this is known as Flash, or Flashing. Flashing is normally removed by tumbling the unpainted castings in rotating drums. In some cases the tumbling process fails to remove a piece of flash and it remains evident on the finished model.

FRIDAY AFTERNOON MODELS - See Lunchtime Specials.

G

GIFTWARE - A range of plated Yesteryears first released in 1962. Standard Yesteryear castings were vacuum plated by a Lesney subsidiary, 'Lesney Industries'. As the plated model was to be attached to a trinket box, ashtray or dish etc, the baseplate had to be modified so that screw holes and/or bosses could be incorporated. Often these modified baseplates were used for painted production models. It is possible to buy the gold or silverplated models with or without the giftware item, on the second-hand market.

GRAND MARQUES COLLECTION - A set of six recoloured model cars released by Matchbox Collectibles in 1995. "The six models in this collection recapture motor cars that were not only coveted by the rich and famous of the '20s and '30s ... From the spoked wheels and authentic license plates to the precise colour scheme of the dashboards and coachwork, each model in this collection is crafted in the prized 1:43 scale, the most collectable size of all. It took dozens of components to achieve the precise detailing found in each replica."

GREAT BEERS OF THE WORLD (YGB) - Matchbox Collectibles stated in their publicity literature: "Officially authorised by the creators of World-Class Beers, whose liveries they bear ... precision-crafted model trucks ... the only collection of its kind, available from no other market of collectibles anywhere in the world, at any price." Each model bears a distinctive livery of some of the best known beers. The first six models were released in 1993 as Series I; with six more models as Series II in 1994; six as Series III in 1995 and a further six as Series IV in 1996.

GREAT MOTOR CARS OF THE CENTURY - The collective name used by Matchbox Toys USA to mail order some of the 1989 Yesteryear range in North America.
Twelve models were used, all of which were given new colour schemes, and enhanced detailing. The first four Yesteryears released did not have the self-tapping screwhole in the baseplate, and all twelve models were packaged in a white closed box with minimal black descriptive copy (P). Aiming at a new group of potential collectors, Matchbox Toys USA entered an extensive magazine advertising campaign (which failed) offering the twelve models via mail order only throughout 1989. The twelve models were:
Y2/4   Bentley in blue (no screw hole)
Y4/4   Duesenberg in two-tone blue (no screw hole)
Y11/5 Bugatti in blue
Y14/3 Stutz Bearcat in cream and dark blue
Y16/2 Mercedes Benz in grey and black
Y17/1 Hispano Suiza in two-tone green (no screw hole)
Y18/1 Cord in pale yellow
Y19/1 Auburn in brown and cream
Y20/1 Mercedes Benz in black (no screw hole)
Y24/1 Bugatti T44 in black and red
Y34/1 Cadillac in blue
Y36/1 Rolls Royce in red and black
All twelve models, packaged in standard boxes were later distributed throughout the other major Matchbox markets. The Great Motor Cars of the Century promotion was not repeated once the twelve models had been released. It was a disaster in marketing and sales terms!

GRENODISED - A chemical treatment applied to cast metal components - mainly wheels, which resulted in the metal having a dull grey coloured finish.

H

HERITAGE HORSE-DRAWN VEHICLES (YSH) - Three models based on horse-drawn vehicles. Issued in December 1993 by Matchbox Collectibles, all three models were Special Editions:
YSH01 1900 Gypsy Caravan
YSH02 1886 London Omnibus
YSH03 1875 Wells Fargo Stagecoach

HOOD - A soft material top which may, or may not be folded back. Yesteryear models normally have this component moulded in plastic.

HOT FOILING - The means by which a component can be chromed by applying intense heat to silver coloured foil. An example being the windscreen surround on the Y21 Woody Wagon. Seldom used in recent years, although used on the Y40-1 Mercedes in 1991.

I

INK - The development of tampo-printing in recent years has effectively replaced transfers or decals as a means of decorating models. Tampo-printing uses specialist colour inks and not paint in its process.

ISSUE NUMBER - The first two columns in the schedule are headed ISSUE and YEAR OF RELEASE. These indicate the order in which the models are made and distributed for sale. From the issue number and the model number given at the top of a page, the full nomenclature of the model is obtained, eg Y1-2 - 24 indicates the 1911 Model 'T' Ford car in the Connoisseur Set sold in 1984.

L

LABEL (CLEAR) - Similar at first glance to a transfer and applied by heat and pressure. This form of decoration known as impressal labelling is still used by Matchbox Collectibles when the model's surface is too large or too curved for the tampo printing process. Top quality labels are used with often more than five colours. A good example being the label used to decorate the curved areas of the cab panels of the Y18-2 and Y37-1 steam lorries.

LABEL (PAPER) - Paper labels are used very rarely these days. They were an inexpensive way to decorate a model when there was the need for only one or two colours.

LESNEY PRODUCTS & CO. LTD. - Founded in 1947 by Leslie Smith and Rodney Smith, and later by Jack Odell. The company introduced the Models of Yesteryear range in 1956. Lesney became public in 1960. In 1982 Lesney Products went into receivership. Lesney's assets were transferred into a holding company called Matchbox Toys Ltd., which was bought by Universal Toys in 1982. First series and some of the early second series models were marked Lesney on the baseplate. Later this was expanded to Lesney Products & Co. Ltd. This information has been recorded where relevant throughout the book.

LIMITED EDITION - A term introduced by the Marketing and Sales Departments in the early 1980s to distinguish a model which was released in considerably less than normal quantities and in the range for a relatively short period. An example being the Y5-4 Talbot Van in 'Dunlop' livery. In 1991 Matchbox Toys stated that all models except the Special Limited Edition models, are Limited Editions. The Limited Edition policy ensured that a specific livery or colour scheme of a model could be produced only once in the factory with no successive runs, no matter how popular that model became. This policy has not been adopted by the Matchbox Collectibles Division of Tyco.

LIVERY - A term applicable in this book to commercial vehicles that have been decorated with company logos, eg Y12 'Arnotts' van, or to the overall colour scheme of a model.

LOGO - This term describes the design of a company's trade name or the name of its product. In this case as they appear on a commercial vehicle. A good example of this is the famous logo of 'Coca Cola' as applied to the Y12-3 Ford Model T van.

LUGS - This term is used to describe a protruding piece of a casting, either plastic or metal, which locates, or locks one piece to another. This protrusion is also known less commonly as a tongue.

LUNCHTIME SPECIALS - A colloquial term used to describe models which were made unofficially at the factory by members of the workforce. This practice was at its height during the period just before Lesney went into receivership. Unpainted castings were sprayed in non release colour schemes; tampo printed decoration was applied to the wrong model, or different coloured wheels were used. These models were then removed illegally from the factory and generally sold to collectors. Since the publication of The Collection and due to the diligent work of Matchbox clubs, this unacceptable side of the hobby has been eradicated and few if any of these models are seen for sale.

M

MACAU - Is a Portuguese colony attached to mainland China with production facilities for Matchbox Toys.

MARKETING VARIATION - A change of specification made at the request of Sales & Marketing to stimulate the collectors market, eg the red roofed Y44 Renault and the Taste of France vans YTF02 to YTF06.

MASK SPRAYING - A process by which a second colour can be added to a model. The mask covers all those parts not requiring a second colour. Being a rather inaccurate process, it has a comparatively high rate of failure and therefore rejection. An example of this process appears on the metallic silver and dark blue Duesenberg Y4-4. This process has been replaced by the use of tampo printing, or as in the case of the Y22-1 1930 Ford vans, by substituting a plastic component for the roof of the van body.

MATCHBOX COLLECTIBLES - Originally a subsidiary division of Matchbox Toys Australia, which had been established in the late 1980s to promote and sell the Yesteryear range and the Dinky Collection. In order to simplify the distribution arrangements it was decided to exclude wholesalers and to concentrate on a very limited number of specially vetted shops, which were appointed Authorised Matchbox Collectible Centres. Because of the vastness of the country the majority of the sales were made by mail order. Soon after Tyco took control of the Universal Matchbox group, Matchbox Collectibles became a Tyco international division administered from Australia. Later the arrangement of selling through authorised centres was extended to the UK, Germany and to the USA. In 1993 the administrative headquarters was transferred to New Jersey, USA.

MATCHBOX TOYS - During 1982, when Lesney Products was in receivership, the receivers formed a Holding

Company, namely "Matchbox Toys Ltd". After the purchase later that year for £16.5 million by the Hong Kong toy group "Universal", whose president was Mr David Yeh, the new company was known as the "Universal Matchbox Group." Although it was managed from Hong Kong, research and design for the ranges was still done in England. All major markets: the UK, Australia, the USA and Germany, had their own Matchbox subsidiaries. In October 1992 the Universal Matchbox Group was bought for $US100 million by the American Company Tyco Toys Inc.

MICA - The Matchbox International Collectors Association, the official Matchbox club, founded in 1985 by Stewart Orr and Kevin McGimpsey to promote collector's interests in Matchbox diecast ranges. Members of the Association receive six full colour magazines throughout the year, one every other month.

* MICA UK, Europe & Rest of the World: 13A Lower Bridge Street Row, Chester CH11RS.
* MICA Australia, New Zealand & South Pacific: PO Box 1206 Baulkham Hills, NSW 2153, Australia
* MICA NA United States & Canada: PO Box 28072, Waterloo, Ontario, Canada N2L 6J8

MOBIL This refers to a joint promotion between the Mobil Oil company and Lesney in the 1960s when Yesteryears, some in special Mobil boxes, were given away in exchange for 'purchase' coupons. The models found in the special boxes were the Y2-2 Renault, the Y5-2 Bentley, the Y6-2 Bugatti, the Y8-2 Sunbeam Motorcycle and the Y10-2 Mercedes

MOCK-UP - A very early sample of the proposed model, usually made by a modelmaker from scratch, or by one of the R & D engineers, from available components.

MOULD - An alternative term to describe a casting tool.

N

NEGATIVE VARIATION - On many occasions models have been released missing the specified trim or decoration. A good example being the Y6 AEC Lorry, some of which have been found without silver paint trim to the bonnet handles. Other examples include the Y3 Tanker with one side of the tank tampo printed upside down and the YFE03 Cadillac fire engine with black radiator grille. Negative variations arise due to a form of neglect or lack of quality control, but to be fair to Matchbox, it does not happen very often; especially when one considers the millions of models that leave their factories each year. Few collectors give any due consideration to negative variations, they are more of an oddity and as such fall outside the scope of this publication.

O

OBSOLETE - When a model has been withdrawn from the range, or where a model has been recoloured or reliveried, the earlier model is known as being obsolete.

ODELL - John (Jack) Odell OBE a co-founder of Lesney Products & Co. Ltd., who after the closure of Lesney, founded Lledo Toys Ltd.

ON-PACK OFFER - Where a model has been offered as a promotional item through a redemption coupon offer, eg Y27-1 'Guinness'.

P

PAINTED TRIM - Integral diecast components of the model which have been given a contrasting gold, brass or silver finish which in turn makes the model, not only more realistic but also more attractive. This extra trim was popular up until the late 1960s and was replaced by vacuum plating the said components. Painted trim was applied by hand and examples include radiator shells, side lamps and steering wheels. In recent years Matchbox Collectibles have re-introduced more paint trim to enhance the range, applied in the main by tampo printing.

PASSPORT SCHEME - An incentive scheme first adopted by Matchbox UK in 1988 to encourage the collector to shop in traditional toy shops. Every purchase earned the collector a stamp on a 'passport'. At the end of the year collectors could buy, for a special price, a Framed Cabinet display, that is if they had successfully completed their passports.

PLASTIC TIES - Short pieces of narrow, thin plastic with a thin wire 'spine' used to secure the models onto the cardboard diorama/insert in the main carton/box; eg box types J, J1, and J2.

PLATED PARTS - Plastic components which have been vacuum plated and treated with lacquer to give them a realistic looking metal finish. Such components include headlamps, radiator shell, radiator grille, exhaust pipes, number plates and windscreens. Diecast parts are barrel-plated to have a silver or brass finish. See: Vacuum Plating.

PLINTHS - Made from coloured plastic as issued with, for example, the Taste of France vans. A plastic 'bridge' was fitted to the plinth to give extra protection to the model. Wooden plinths have also been used, eg with the Y1-3 Jaguar in pewter and the YSFE01 Ahrens Fox model.

POLYMER - A nylon based compound, as used for the headlamps on the Y38-1 Rolls Royce 1920 Armoured Car, and the mudguards on the Y2-4 Bentley.

POWER OF THE PRESS (YPP) - Launched by Matchbox Collectibles in 1995 "And now Matchbox pays tribute to the world's greatest newspapers with a unique collection of eight vintage replicas. Each precision engineered model is crafted with a wealth of authentic features...from the real rubber tyres to the intricate interior details. Each is officially authorised by the famous newspaper represented ..."

PRE-PRODUCTION - This term refers to a model or models which have been produced, not for sale, but for evaluation purposes, either to determine how the parts fit or to determine sales potential. Pre-production models often contain differences compared to released models. The most obvious being missing or incomplete copyright dates or Yesteryear numbers.

PRESS-FIT - See Chapter on Yesteryear Components.

PRODUCTION FIGURES - The quantities of models produced at the factory. Some figures provided by Tyco are factory estimates and these are always denoted with an 'E'.

PRODUCTION VARIATIONS - These range from unforeseen production problems at the factory to planned modifications with a view to the long term future of the range. Unforeseen production problems include stop gap short run colour changes, a good example being the Y16-2 Mercedes Benz. In 1981 during production the paint line discovered they had run out of the paint used for the side panels. To maintain production, the factory management substituted a duck-egg blue paint and some 5,000 models with this new paint scheme were produced. Planned variations would include revising the baseplate component so that it could be fitted to several different models. An example being the baseplate which is fitted to the Y22-1 Cherry Blossom model. Two baseplates are associated with this livery with the Yesteryear numbers Y21 and Y22 being common to both. However, the first baseplate shows Y7 whereas the second baseplate has the Y7 reference replaced by Y35. This was a planned production variation as Matchbox knew that the Y7 was to be deleted from the range.

PROGRESSIVE VARIATIONS - These are the most difficult, as well as being the most interesting variations to detect and locate. Progressive variations are casting modifications, to strengthen specific areas of the model. A well known example whereby a model has been strengthened is the Y2 'B' Type Bus. Originally it was produced with four small windows over four large windows. Soon it was found that this area of the model was too fragile and the breakages were commonplace. The engineers made modifications to the tools by inserting extra window frame struts. Throughout the production of a model, improvements or repairs to the tools may be necessary. Such improvements include the addition, or the deletion of extra rivets, locating tabs, stiffening ribs or casting body seams. In some cases, once the first production run of a model has been completed, the factory may note that the tampo decoration has not taken as well as it should have and so the tools are modified to reduce the relief on the tampo printed surface. An example is the Y6-5 Mercedes Benz Lorry which can be found with two types of truck body sides: one with a deep planking effect and the other with a much shallower effect. Only the collector can determine for himself where to draw the line!

PROTOTYPE - Also known as a mock-up. This term can refer to the first model made, often for approval, or for toy shows. It may also be used to describe the first assembled casting of a model.

R

RANGE - The words in the Book to mean the series of models described as 'Yesteryears'.

RARE (R) - One of the five rarity categories used throughout the book 'Seldom seen for sale and with a high premium'.

REAR DOOR TYPES - See Y12-3 Ford van door drawings.

RECOLOUR - On standard range models the manufacturers have over the years relaunched models in new colour schemes. By doing so they can recoup their costs of development and toolmaking over a longer period. In 1990 Matchbox stated a new model would have a maximum of only three recolours during its life. It is unknown whether this policy will be adopted by Matchbox Collectibles.

RESEARCH AND DEVELOPMENT - Presently based in the UK, the Research and Development Department of Tyco Matchbox coordinate the evolution of future range models. In many cases the Project Engineer in the department initiates the choice of subject matter. As a project leader, he arranges for a mock-up or prototype to be made by a modelmaker using information gleaned from car manufacturers' drawings and photographs, or by physically measuring and photographing surviving vehicles found in motor museums or private collections. Once the mock-up has been shown and accepted at the international selection meeting, the Research and Development Department continues to monitor the progress of the model at the factory. Early pre-production samples are sent from the factory and necessary modifications are detailed for the factory engineers to arrange. This checking and modifying may happen several times before the Research and Development engineers are satisfied with the castings. In the meantime new subject matter is being continually investigated for the range in future years. Generally it takes at least two years for the idea of a model to get itself into the Models of Yesteryear range.

REVAMP - This refers to a model having one or more of its main castings substantially altered to produce a noticeably different effect. For example, the Y22 Model A Ford van was given a completely new rear body to resemble a breakdown truck, and renumbered Y7-4.

RIVETED - For the purposes of this book this term refers to the technique of joining components by flattening the head of a protruding pillar of metal after it has been inserted through a locating hole in the part to be joined. The term is also applied to axles where one end of an axle is flattened to secure the wheels. This technique replaced that of crimped axles and more accurately should be called 'spun'.

ROCHFORD - One of the last Lesney factories, based in Essex. It was closed down in 1987 when the production facilities moved to the Far East.

ROOF - A metal top normally with a smooth finish. Some van roofs are 'ribbed', ie a continuous pattern from side to side. Others are 'ridged', ie an interrupted sequence.

S

SCARCE (S) - One of the five rarity categories used throughout the book. Not easy to find and when seen for sale, with a premium.

SCREW HOLE - With the move from Rochford to the Far East for the often lengthy transit period, it became necessary to fix the model in its box in a more secure way. By the time production had been relocated in China the best solution adopted so far, was to screw the model onto the card diorama or plinth. Accordingly, the baseplates were modified to have a small cast hole into which the screw was applied. These holes are not self threaded. It is the application of the self-tapping screw which creates the threads and marks the paintwork!

SECOND SERIES - Refers to models introduced into the Yesteryear range as the original models were withdrawn. The second series of Yesteryears generally occupied the range in the 1960s.

SERIES NUMBER - This heading is to be found in the schedule for models produced from 1993 and denotes the Yesteryear number(s) of the model, eg YTF01. Baseplate components for a particular model in one series can be identical to those in another. It became uneconomical to continue with these series numbers being cast and altered for new models. Instead this information can be tampo printed. An example is the YFE01 Mack fire engine. When it was introduced in 1994 the series number YFE01 was cast on the baseplate. A subsequent production run of the YFE01 had the series number tampo printed.

SHADOW EFFECT - This is a highlighting detail usually to lettering and is made by an extra 'pass' during the tampo process. It is also known as 'drop shadow'. The most noticeable model and livery to reveal shadow effect is the Y12-3 'Suze'.

SMITH - Leslie Smith OBE a co-founder of Lesney Products & Co. Ltd. An honorary member of MICA.

SPECIAL LIMITED EDITION - A term first used by Matchbox Toys in 1985 applied to a model made to an extra high standard, and one that would never appear as a recolour, or revamp in the range. Also compared to range issues and even Limited Editions, the production quota was kept low, eg the Y39-1 Passenger Coach and Horses had a worldwide production of 39,888, compared with about 100,000 for standard models.
This policy has not been adopted by Matchbox Collectibles.

SPRUE - Is the term given to a frame of waste metal, or plastic upon which individual components are cast or moulded. The components are separated from the sprue which is then recycled.

SPUN - A more accurate term than 'riveted' when applied to axles and in recent years to baseplate rivets. Spun axles are axles which have their ends spread by being placed against a rotating surface.

STEAM SERIES (YAS) - Launched by Matchbox Collectibles in 1996.

STRAW BOX - The name given to the range of boxes introduced in 1979. Also referred to as Type 'T'.

T

TAMPO PRINTING - This relatively modern technique for applying decoration, or detailing was first used by Lesney Products in the late 1970s. It is a system whereby coloured inks are printed directly onto the model. Ink is applied to a steel plate with a shallow recess of the design. Excess ink is then wiped off leaving just the ink in the recess. This ink is then picked up onto a soft rubber pad which is pressed hard onto the steel plate. The rubber pad is pressed down onto the surface of the model leaving a permanent impression of the design. Some tampo printing machines have six plates and six rubber pads and so six colour designs can be made in one 'pass' of the tampo printing machine.

TASTE OF FRANCE SERIES (YTF) - A set of six Citroën vans released by Matchbox Collectibles in 1993. One casting was used. Each model was decorated with liveries connected with French produce, such as brandy and cheese.

TILT - This refers to a tilt canopy; which is a canopy that extends over the whole back of a commercial vehicle. The Y13-3 Crossley was the first Yesteryear to feature a tilt canopy.

TONNEAU - A tonneau is a fabric fitting that covers the interior of a car either wholly or partially. It is not another name for a hood. The Y5-1 and Y5-2 Bentleys have tonneaus.

TOOLS - A term given to moulds or dies. Engineers who produce tools are referred to as toolmakers.

TOY FAIR SAMPLE - This phrase refers to the handmade models produced for the annual toy fairs, mainly for the toy trade. Normally six of each model are made and they become much sought after by collectors.

TRANSFER - Also known as decals in the USA. Lesney used waterslide transfers to decorate many of their models in the 1950s and 1960s. With time these had a tendency to alter colour and being fragile by nature many first series models, although mint in every other way, are ruined by poor or damaged transfers. Matchbox Collectibles still use transfers to demonstrate the livery artwork on early prototypes.

TRANSIT SERIES (YET) - A series of buses and trams first released in 1996.

TRIAL RUNS - Refers to models which have been produced to ensure a satisfactory product and to ensure that no defects exist either in the model, or the production process. Trial runs may yield unusual variations. For example, models in the wrong colour often may be used to try out a tampo printing process. Trial run models were as a rule not sold to the consumer, but exceptions can occur.

TWO PART MOULD - Used to produce the wheels for the Yesteryear steam vehicles, the Y23 AEC bus and the Y16 100 Tonner. A mould is made which will produce the required wheel design. The wheel is then placed into a second mould of similar design but has extra room around the circumference to allow for the tyre. Then plastic compound is injected into the mould and forms around the wheel, which, when removed, leaves a wheel complete with a solid tyre.

TYCO TOYS - The American toy company based in New Jersey, USA, which acquired the Universal Matchbox Group on 2nd October 1992 for US $100 million.

U

UNIVERSAL - The Hong Kong toy group headed by Mr. David Yeh that acquired Matchbox in 1982 for £16.5 million.

V

VACUUM PLATING - Used to give a metal effect to plastic components such as radiator shells, headlights, sills or wheel spokes or to diecast components which, when plated, were released as part of the Giftware range. The castings or components were placed in a drum to which a pellet of pure aluminium was added. An electrical flash was then generated to cause the aluminium to attach itself entirely to the components, or the castings. If they were to be finished in silver or chrome, they were sprayed with a clear lacquer, but if the finish was to be gold or brass, then an amber coloured lacquering was applied. Generally pre-1974 Yesteryears were given a brass or silver finish, whereas post 1974 components were given a gold or chrome finish. Although shade differences are many, they are hardly worth further note as they only arise due to the amount of applied lacquer, or to fading since production.

VARIATIONS - An important aspect to the hobby of collecting Models of Yesteryear. A variation occurs when the manufacturer makes a change to the model; which can be from the significant to the insignificant; but in many cases the latter is just as important to collectors as the former. See Marketing Variations, Production Variations, Progressive Variations and Negative Variations.

VERY RARE (VR) - Very occasionally for sale and at a very high price.

W

WEBS - This is a term used to describe a reinforcing brace or strut added to a casting to strengthen it.

WHEELS - See Yesteryear Components.

WHITEWALL TYRES - First introduced during the late 1970s and indicated throughout this publication by (WW) under the column devoted to tyre or wheel detail. Where a model was issued with black or whitewall tyres, this fact is shown by the abbreviation (BW). In some instances, collectors over the years have switched whitewall and blackwall tyres between issues, so beware of persons asking a premium price for a tyre variation.

WHITEWALL WHEELS - First introduced by Matchbox in the early 1990s when press-fit wheels became standard issue. It is less expensive to decorate the wheel flange than to decorate the tyre component. The effect of whitewalling was maintained and whitewall (flanged) wheels are indicated by the abbreviation (WF) in this publication.

WOODGRAIN - This term is used to describe the packaging of the Yesteryear range when they were relaunched in 1974. The new boxes featured a woodgrain effect - hence the name. Also referred to as type 'H' boxes.

Y

YESTERYEAR - The abbreviated name for the Models of Yesteryear range. At the top of each page in this publication just before the models title is a Y (Yesteryear) number, eg Y1-2 1911 Model 'T' Ford. The Y stands for Yesteryear. The first number means it was issued as a number one in the range; the second number indicates that this model was the second number one issue. Collectors often refer to Yesteryear range models as MOY or YY.

Y NUMBER - With the exception of the first series models and some of the earlier second series models, all models incorporate a Y (Yesteryear) number usually on the baseplate, but sometimes the underneath of the roof. Since 1993 the Y number is cast or tampo printed. See: Series Number.

A PAGE AT A GLANCE

INVESTMENT COMMENT:

This gives the original UK retail selling price, quoted in sterling but not in the pounds, shillings and pence which was paid for earlier models. There may be some regional variations in prices. The figures mentioned do not include postage, packaging or insurance costs. The comments on the market situation are subjective and should not be read as anything more than a general guide.

MAIN HEADING AND INFORMATION:

The Y number or Yesteryear number is shown at the top of the page. Also, a brief history of the model and explanations for the variations recorded. The scale of the model is shown.

THE SCHEDULE:

Each model is recorded under headed columns, which name the various 'parts' of a model and other relevant information. The heading descriptions change with the type of model. The Issue column numbers each model variation as it progresses through its production life. Starting when it was first released with a 1 against its year of release. Any amount of issue numbers may or may not appear in one year. Should an issued variation be manufactured in the succeeding year, then the appropriate Issue number will be found adjacent to that year. The information recorded under the Colours column is kept to the basic colours with adjectives to 'subjectively' describe colour shades and tones. In the Rarity column where it is relevant, we use one of five ratings. In most instances these would link with the small asterisks (*) used in the schedule. These indicate the changes on a model, justifying allocating one of the rarity ratings, eg a new colour, a new inscription, or a change in the design of a 'component'.

THE LIVERY:

Usually, this is relevant only to commercial vehicles, ie those with advertising. However, there are a few models, eg racing cars, with a small amount of 'decoration' and these have been recorded. In most instances the lettering has been set-out in upper case (capital) letters. This has been done even when the lettering of the model is in lower case. This presentation should make the description easier to record and to read. Also, the position of the livery on the model vehicle has been indicated and whether it has been produced by tampo printing or by a transfer, or is a label.

DIAGRAMS:

These are not scaled drawings but are accurate enough to give an adequate indication of the various points which need explanation.

NOTES:

This is additional data which may amplify the main text, or which is not suitable for inclusion. For instance, details of the Beckenham Appeal Models. Also, since the release of the 1993/94/95 models, many of which may have been made from existing tools, cross references with other models have been included.

BLACK AND WHITE PHOTOGRAPHS:

These are intended to be used for guide reference identification and should be read in conjunction with the many colour pages in this book.

YESTERYEAR COMPONENTS

In the listings for each model, various terms and phrases are used with reference to axle and wheel types; plastic components, baseplates and screw holes. This chapter has been written to give a fuller and an easy to understand explanation of their "why's and wherefore's".

AXLES

Production of Yesteryears began in late 1955. At their launch in 1956, Lesney's manufacturing methods were rather crude by today's standards. For the manufacture of axles, Lesney and subsequently Matchbox International, made their own from large coils of steel. The earliest types were cut by special machines from mild grey steel. The machines would cut them to precise lengths and they would be finished with a rivet head at only one end. Once the axles and wheels had been fitted to the model, the other end of the axle would be squashed; technically referred to as CRIMPED, to retain the wheels on the axles. This technique gave the squashed (crimped) end of the axles an appearance similar to a small screw-driver blade.

Diagram 1

Y10-1 MERCEDES

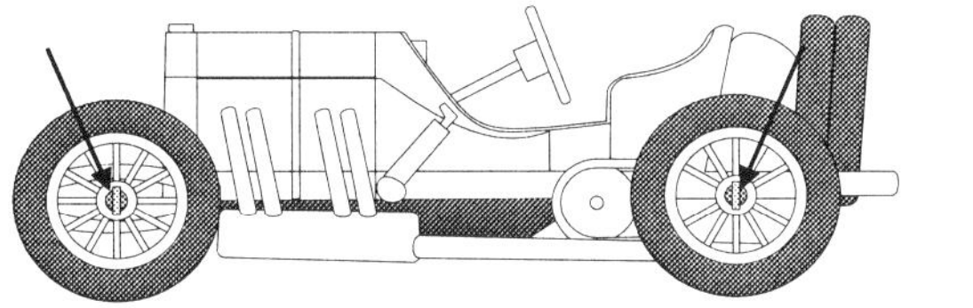

Crimped end *Crimped end*

Lesney's biggest group of customers, in the 50's were children, and soon it became apparent that the crimped ends of the axles were sharp enough to cut skin and were potentially dangerous. This caused such concern at Lesney that an alternative method of retaining wheels on axles had to be devised. The result was axles RIVETED at both ends. Prior to fitting to the models, axles were made in exactly the same way as the crimped types. However, once the axles and wheels had been fitted, a new machine was used to 'rivet' the other end of the axle. Because the axles were being made from mild steel, only a limited amount of pressure could be used for this operation without bending the axles. Consequently one end has a riveted head which is less perfectly formed than the other end; but is sufficient to retain the wheels. Naturally enough, this method is referred to as 'riveted' axles. The new method now complied with safety regulations required for children's toys. See Diagram 2

Diagram 2

Y1-1 ALLCHIN

Riveted end *Riveted end*

Wheels were fitted on riveted axles from late 1957, until mid 1990 when production of Yesteryears had moved to Macau.

Yesteryears were made in England until 1987 and generally axles were made from grey mild steel. However, it is possible to find models with axles with a copper plated finish. This came about purely as a result of Lesney purchasing a batch of steel coils from a different source. The Y5-4 Talbot Van, Y4-4 Duesenberg, Y13-3 Crossley RAF Tender, Y14-3 Stutz, Y16-2 Mercedes and the Y21-2 Ford Tradesmans Woody Wagon are models which had these copper axles fitted on some production runs. In late 1987, total production of Yesteryears was moved to Macau. One noticeable result of this move was that axles were made from a harder type of steel and once they had been cut to length, were then put into a barrel together with chemical compounds. The axles were tumbled by rotating the barrel and at the end of this process emerged with a bright steel finish. This process is known as BARREL-PLATING. In 1986, a new method of fixing the wheels to the axles was used; in which the wheels were press-fitted onto the axles. Initially, this method was only used for the four racing cars; the Y10-4 Maserati, Y11-4 Bugatti, Y14-4 ERA and the Y16-3 Ferrari. The method was used again in 1988 for the Y21-4 BMW car; but it was not until April 1990 that it was adopted for the whole range. The riveted ends disappeared and the ends of the axles were flush with the outside face of the wheel hub centres. (Type A) The axle ends were knurled (milled) to give a barbed surface and the wheels were simply PRESS-FITTED onto the axles. Press-fitted wheels on the same axle cannot be turned independently.

There are two methods of knurling, one which gives a cross-hatch pattern, the other a diagonal pattern. Many wheel moulds were modified so that the axle hole no longer went right through the wheel hub hence the axle end was no longer visible in the centre of the wheel (Type B). See Diagram 8.

Diagram 3

Y21-5 MODEL "TT"

Riveted axle hubs 'free wheel'   *Press-fit wheel to axles. Both wheels and axles rotate together*

This method is still in use and is referred to in the model listings as PRESS-FIT AXLES.
Diagram 3 shows the wheel on the left retained by a riveted axle, whilst the right one is on a press-fit axle; the end of the axle is just visible.

WHEELS & TYRES

Jack Odell, who helped create the Yesteryear range in 1956 was the innovator of pressure fed die-casting; which meant castings could be produced with far more detail than by the then conventional gravity-fed casting process. Pressure casting is achieved when molten metal is forced into the moulds by compressed air; whereas gravity-fed casting is where molten metal flows into the moulds by the force of gravity only. Due to this success with pressure casting, not only were highly detailed 'body' castings produced, but cast spoked wheels were also mass-produced for the first time by a toy manufacturer. The detail was only limited by the skill of the tool makers! Plastic as a material was still in its infancy in 1955; as were plastic moulding machines and so most of the first Yesteryears had metal wheels without the luxury of tyres. The early wheels had either straight spokes or daisy-effect type spokes (see the Y6-1 AEC Lorry). The only models which had wheels without spokes were the small wheels of the Y3-1 Tram, the pony wheels of the Y13-1 Santa Fe locomotive, and Y14-1 Duke of Connaught locomotive. The Y7-1 Four Ton Leyland Van had "solid" (non-spoked) wheels but this was due to the design of the wheels on the actual vehicle. The Y5-1 Le Mans Bentley also had solid wheels, but with a raised design which gave a twenty spoke effect. It was the only model to be fitted with this type of wheel. All subsequent wheels had individual spokes. In 1959, plastic wheels were introduced for models in the "Matchbox" Series range. Final production runs of the Y4-1 Sentinel Steam Wagon, the Y6-1 AEC Lorry and the Y7-1 Leyland Van, due to tool wear of the wheel moulds, were fitted with plastic wheels from that range. Later production runs of the Y3-1 tram had wheels in plastic; but these are exceptions and until 1973, all the other Yesteryear models were fitted with metal wheels. In 1973, production of Yesteryears was suspended by the effects of the "three day week". However during this period, research and development continued apace and when Yesteryears were re-launched in 1974/75, the narrow section metal wheels had been replaced by standardised plastic wheels of a chunkier, wider section design. Trials did take place to produce plastic wheels of the finer pre-1973 design; but this idea was not proceeded with and these wheels were never 'officially' released on completed models; although examples of the Y2-3 Vauxhall, Y3-3 Riley and the Y12-2 Thomas with these wheels do exist. How these models got out of the factory will always remain a mystery, but as they were not meant for general release, are not separately listed in this book. After the first fourteen Yesteryears, the majority of which were commercial vehicles; only cars were featured in the Yesteryear range, known as the 'second series' models until their production was suspended in 1973. All the wheels were metal and with few exceptions were brass plated. They were fitted with hard plastic solid core tyres. Early tyres had a knobbly (coarse) tread pattern; but this design was superseded by a very fine (almost non-existent) tread pattern. With the exception of the Y6-2 Bugatti which has its own particular style of wheels, all of the other wheels were 11mm, or 13mm diameter and were fitted with tyres of a suitable diameter.

Diagram 4 **Y6-2 BUGATTI**

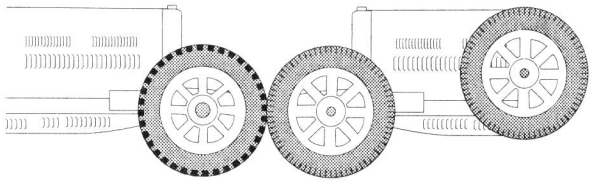

Diagram 4 shows two versions of the Y6-2 Bugatti. Left, model with early wide rims and is fitted with knobbly treaded tyres; right, model with narrow rims is fitted with fine treaded tyres. 11mm diameter wheels were fitted with black tyres; with either knobbly or smooth treaded tyres. The only exceptions to this are first run Y6-2 Bugattis, Y15-1 Rolls Royce Silver Ghosts and Y16-1 Spykers which were fitted with grey knobbly tread tyres. 13mm diameter wheels were only fitted with black tyres with the fine tread pattern. However, a very small quantity of white or grey tyres to fit those larger wheels were produced to test the material compounds for research purposes, but they were not proceeded with and were not 'officially' released. Models are known to exist with these tyres, but how they got out of the factory is not known and have not been included in the listings.

Diagram 5

Y15-1 ROLLS ROYCE

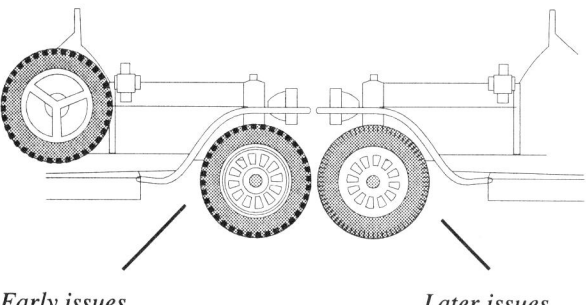

Early issues   *Later issues*

The Y15-1 and Y16-1 are perfect examples of different wheel and tyre designs of the 11mm diameter size. Diagram 5 shows, on the left, a wheel with a wide rim with bolt head detail, split-rim wheels in real life (in silver), fitted with knobbly tread tyres. This design of wheel rim was fairly short lived and was only fitted to the Y15-1 and Y16-1. Whilst all the wheels were meant to have a brass finish, there is one exception. A silver finish was specified for the Y15-1 Rolls Royce and early runs of this model featured silver plated wheels. However, with the introduction of the Y16-1 Spyker, these wheels with their bolt head detail were given a brass finish. On the right of the diagram one can see the more common narrow rim brass plated wheel fitted with fine treaded tyres. The narrow rim wheels can have extended centre hubs on the inside face with two, or four triangular braces between the hub and spokes. The triangular braces can be a large or small design type. Models can be found with any number (up to a maximum of four!!) of wheels with two or four braces. To keep the variation listings within acceptable proportions, these "braced wheels" have not, as, yet been separately listed. Both 11mm and 13mm diameter wheels can be found in bare metal finish. The wheels were meant to have a brass plated finish; but in it's early days, the plating machine could be rather temperamental and break down. Such was the pace of assembly, that quite often there were no plated wheels available and so bare metal ones were fitted rather than halt the assembly process. This non-plating also affected the radiator, windscreen, brake lever and steering wheel (where not painted) components! Again, for logistic reasons, and the fact that models can be fitted with any number or combination of bare metal/plated wheels and components separate listings have generally not been given to models with unplated wheels or components. Finally, wheels can have twelve, twenty four or twenty six spoked configurations and are specified as such in the variation listings. When Yesteryear production resumed in very late 1974 and early 1975, the new wheels were instantly recognisable and they were too large in scale to suit every model in the range. However, the new tooling had been made for these new wheels and tyres and because plastic was cheaper than metal there was no incentive to return to the more true to scale pre-1973 wheels.

Diagram 6

Y6-3 CADILLAC

Pre 1973 solid tyres   *Post 1974 hollow tyres*

The post 1974 wheels were not only of a wider cross section, they also had a raised ridge around the centre of 'the rim' onto which the tyres were fitted. The new tyres were made of a softer plastic compound and are known as "hollow section" tyres, and the hollow internal section fits over the raised ridge on the wheel. All pre-1973 wheels, had a grooved rim which located the solid-core tyres. The post-1974 tyres had three raised lines running the full circumference of the tyre in addition to small "cut-outs" on the edges to represent treads. Post-1974 wheels were of twelve or twenty four spoke patterns and were given either chrome, or gold plated effect; or were left in their original self-coloured state. In 1979, the Y18-1 Cord was introduced to the range. Prior to this, most Lesney made wheels had spokes but research photographs showed that the actual car did not have spoked wheels and so came the introduction of what are known as "SOLID WHEELS". "Solid" is the term used when referring to wheels which represent solid pressed steel wheels, or wheels which are meant to represent the existence of partial, or full diameter hub caps. The Y18-1 Cord also brought about the introduction of "WHITE WALL" tyres. This is shown in the listings as the abbreviation 'WW'. Production models made prior to the Y18-1 Cord were not fitted with solid wheels, or white wall tyres. If you have such a model, its authenticity is doubtful! Also, in passing, the Y18-1 Cord has another claim to fame, in that the 1990 version was fitted with tyres with sidewalls in a lemon colour. This is the only colour variation to date. In late 1987, when Yesteryear production was moved to Macau a much softer, porous type of plastic material was used to produce tyres. However, the nature of the material was not suitable for white wall decoration and the quality of the printing was inferior to the version made in England. With the move to Macau the whitewalling was applied to only one face of the tyre, whereas in England, both sides of the tyre were treated. In 1990, Matchbox introduced the "Great Motor Cars of the Century". A collection of fourteen cars "current" in the range. The poor quality of the whitewalling, unfortunately, was exaggerated by the increased "enhanced detailing" of the rest of the model. To overcome this problem, the wheel moulds were modified to give a flange to one side of each wheel, which provided an ideal surface for the whitewalling effect. All such wheels are fitted with black tyres which is a contradiction in terms of whitewall effect tyres! These are abbreviated in the listings as 'WF'.

Diagram 7

Y4-4 DUESENBERG

White flange *Whitewall tyres*
Black tyres

Diagram 7 shows the flanged wheels on the left; with the previous type of wheel and whitewall tyre on the right, as fitted to the Y4-4 Duesenberg. 1990 also saw the appearance of the Y27-1 Foden Steam Lorry in the livery of Joseph Rank. Early production models had their daisy effect spoked wheels fitted on press-fit axles, with the ends of the axles visible in the centre of the wheel hubs. However, later production models showed no such evidence of the axle ends. The wheel moulds had been modified so that the outside face of the centre hubs were now proud of the wheel rims.

Diagram 8

Y27-1 FODEN

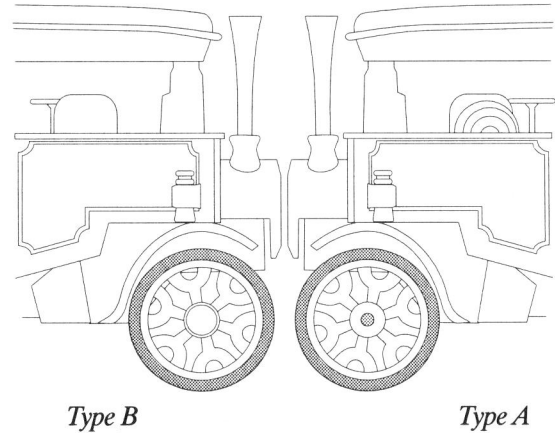

Type B *Type A*

Diagram 8 shows on the right the original wheel with the axle end clearly visible (Type A); whilst the left one has the increased width hub with the axle hole blanked off (Type B). The diagram also shows the wheels fitted with 'solid' tyres. It has already been stated that all post-1974 wheels are made from plastic. However, there are just eight exceptions which do have metal wheels and these are Y12-4 Stevenson's Rocket, Y15-3 Tram, the Y39-1 Passenger Coach and Horses, the Y43-1 Busch Fire Engine, the Y46-1 Merryweather Fire Engine and the three models in the Heritage Horse-drawn Vehicle series (YSH). Finally, all wheel designs which have been introduced since the adoption of the idea of press-fit axles, have the outside face of the hub with no hole for the axle. To many collectors, this gives a much more realistic effect. Not many real vehicles are seen with axles projecting out from the centres of the wheels! 1992 saw the introduction of the then brand new Y64 1938 Lincoln Zephyr. This model introduced yet another type of wheel and tyre. The wheel is a step shaped solid plastic casting. This is also true of the tyre which is made from rubber. However, the tyre can only be fitted to the wheel from the inside face. The chrome hub caps also appear to be separate components; the whole of which is fitted to press-fit axles.

THE CHASSIS/BASEPLATE

In this book these terms are used to describe those 'lower' parts of a model which, on the casting, are associated to each other. Actual vehicles have a chassis framework upon which other components are assembled. The body plus the engine and gear box are mounted above the chassis; whereas the axles with their suspension, the transmission shaft, differential and exhaust pipe are fixed below. Usually with Yesteryear models, the chassis component contains the mudguards; the running boards or cab steps, and where applicable, the suspension, which often are leaf springs, and the baseplate. It is the baseplate which is the subject of the descriptions that follow.
The baseplate shows the lower parts of the engine including the sump; the flywheel housing and gear box; the transmission shaft and differentials and also the exhaust pipe. Steam powered wagons display those components which carry out equivalent operations. Depending upon the type of model and the date when it was made, these features can be cast in full or in limited detail. Perhaps, more significant is the 'inscription' which is cast or tampo printed to show the model type and Yesteryear reference number, the maker's name, eg Lesney, Matchbox Collectibles etc., the first production date with a copyright © or design registration ® sign and where the model was made.

BASEHOLES, BOSSES AND SCREW HOLES

For various reasons a baseplate may have holes cast into it. Firstly, to hang up the model during production, eg during the paint spraying operation. Secondly, because the model was one of those used in the giftware series. There can be one or two holes depending upon the type of giftware 'trinket' to be used, eg an ashtray or a box etc. Thirdly, in 1990, a new box, the 'N' type was introduced. These boxes have cardboard dioramas to the base of which the model is secured by a self-tapping screw into a screwhole; the screw having passed through a small plastic packing and locating plate. Fourthly, in 1993 Matchbox Collectibles produced for the 'Taste of France' series, the 'Q' type box with a plastic plinth onto which the model is mounted. This meant that the baseplate of the Citroen van models have one screw hole and one open boss for the self-tapping screws. A boss is a short cylindrical shaped column which is cast as part of the component to give added strength to an area where a self-tapping screw is to be used.

BASEPLATE LETTERING

Whilst compiling the listings for the Yesteryear models sold under the Matchbox Collectibles name, several points have become apparent in relation to the baseplate lettering. Whilst the majority of models bear the legend MATCHBOX COLLECTIBLES, some, such as the Ford Model 'T' van in "Kirin" or "McDonald's" livery, are spelt COLLECTABLES. The Australian and American spelling of the word uses an 'I', whereas the more usual English spelling has an 'A'. However, both spellings are Queen's English! Also, in the pre-Tyco days, most baseplates bore the copyright symbol © near to the date to show when the design of the vehicle, termed a 'work of art' was first copyrighted. In recent times the registered symbol, either an ® or an R within two brackets has been used. Of course, some models still bear the copyright sign! In compiling this book we have produced, where possible, the relevant symbol under the Baseplate column in the schedule.

COLOURS OF PLASTIC COMPONENTS

From 1986, Matchbox Toys produced Special Limited Edition Models and insisted on authentic liveries for the cars. Prior to 1986, Yesteryears were often referred to as "Toys" by both Lesney and Matchbox. Yesteryears were aimed at the childrens' toy markets and until recent years, children were numerically by far their largest number of customers. Consequently, as far as the cars were concerned, authentic liveries took no part in deciding what colour schemes to use. The attractiveness of colours "in the eyes of children" was the main criteria given to selecting which colours to use. Soon after Lesney began making toys, a Product and Design meeting was held every Monday to discuss which vehicles were to be modelled and what colour schemes were to be adopted. When plastic components became the 'norm' for Yesteryears, Ken Wetton was the senior model maker and part of his week was occupied by dreaming up 'exotic' coloured liveries and plastics to show at the next meeting. Also, early plastics had a tendency to shrink and fade and many different types of self-coloured plastics were experimented with in an attempt to overcome these problems. Both the exotic coloured and experimental plastics resulted in very small quantities (just a dozen or so of each) of unusual coloured plastic components being made by Ken Wetton. These components were not classified as pre-productions; they were not even classified as colour trials. Ken Wetton and the Research & Development team merely referred to them as experimental exercises. They were never meant for 'official' release and were supposed to be destroyed once they had served their purpose. However, by means fair or foul, some of these components did get out of the factory. Some factory employees, realising there was a ready collectors' market for such oddities would produce such items during their lunch breaks, or on a Friday afternoon when production was being wound-down for the weekend. Because of a lack of full records, it is impossible to ascertain what was produced by Ken Wetton and what was produced in lunch times or on Friday afternoons. All we do know is that all so called "exotic" coloured components were not "officially" released onto the market. In the listings within this book, we have referred to "out of the norm" plastic components in the introductory pen-sketches to the models concerned but have not given separate listings to such models. If you are offered one of these models, you can choose whether to purchase or not; but bear in mind a substantial premium will have been placed upon such models.

LIVERIES

When Yesteryears were first introduced, all printed decoration called 'liveries' in this book were applied by means of water-slide transfers. This type of 'logo' decoration was the norm until 1978, when tampo printing was introduced on the Y5-4 Talbot Van in "Liptons Tea" Livery. Tampo printing is, as the term indicates, the printing of details on models by means of printing pads and inks. Initially, tampo printing was restricted to a maximum of four colours, but the rapid increase in precision of this form of printing now allows for many colours to be added with absolute accuracy. Nowadays the key prohibitor for the tampos are the surface to be printed, location and size; in which case a label will be used. Early labels were rather crude. They were usually poor quality paper and the inks were of a watery appearance. The labels were attached by an application of gum, which, with age, tended to lose its adhesive quality and allowed labels to "lift". As the printing methods and adhesives have improved over the years, so the quality of the labels on Yesteryears has improved accordingly and the adhesion is much more secure. Labels are now only used where complex curves are evident.

COLLECTORS' NOTES:

Y _____

ISSUE	YEAR OF RELEASE	COLOURS				BASEPLATE	RARITY	BOX	VALUE

COMMENTS

PLEASE PHOTOCOPY AND SEND TO THE PUBLISHERS WITH YOUR ADDITIONAL INFORMATION; UNCODED ISSUES, MARKET VALUES etc

MODELS OF YESTERYEAR PACKAGING

Before the launch of the Models of Yesteryear series in 1956, it was decided by Lesney Products that the packaging for this range should be similar to the boxes found in their very successful 1-75 series. The package used for the miniature range had been closely based upon a 'Matchbox' with its colourful front and dark blue simulated striker panel. Most young children, especially young boys, hide and preserve their favourite objects such as marbles, chestnuts, and insects within small containers like a matchbox which can be easily carried about, usually in their deepest pocket! The management at Lesney Products had decided to make it easy for children by manufacturing miniature toys which came in their own matchbox. With the resounding success of the "Matchbox" Series range and its miniature matchbox it was decided to launch the new Models of Yesteryear range in a similar matchbox; although bigger to accommodate the larger scale of the models.

These boxes have in themselves become very collectable, although they have developed beyond all recognition from the originals. With the growth of supermarket retailing in the late 1960s, early 1970s it was felt necessary to change the concept of a 'closed in' box to a box which could permanently display its contents. This type of 'see through' box has evolved through various stages.

It is an acknowledged fact that the great majority of Models of Yesteryear collectors not only collect the actual models, but also collect the related boxes. Long gone are the days when collectors threw away the boxes and only kept the models!

PACKAGING DESCRIBED BY TYPE
As used in the individual tables.

LINE DRAWING
This was to contain the first fifteen models in the range as well as three replacement models. It is known as the 'Line Drawing' box because each box front displayed a sketch of the model in black ink on a white background. This drawing was surrounded by a yellow background featuring lettering showing that it was a Model of Yesteryear, made by Lesney in England and its model number. There are three types.

A The end flap of the box has a black number on a deep blue background. Type A category is only known on models Y1-1 to Y9-1. There are two distinct styles of number associated with the Y1-1, Y2-1 and Y3-1. The number can be found in a thin script or a thicker script.

B The end flaps have a blue number in a white circle. Y5-1, Y6-1 and Y7-1 are not known in this category. The Y9-1 line drawing changed to a smaller, angled, view showing more roof detail.

C The end flaps have a red number on a white circle and the model description in white lettering. This box type was also used for the replacement second series models Y4-2, Y6-2 and Y7-2.

PICTURE BOX
Introduced in 1960 - 1961 as a replacement for the 'Line Drawing' box, it can be found with four separate categories. The box had grown to reflect the larger models being introduced. The backgrounds became more pictorial in design.

D1 A coloured illustration of the model on the face of the box on a plain yellow background. The words 'Models of Yesteryear' are found above the picture. The 'Y' number in white and the name of model are on the end flaps. All models within Y1-Y16 have been reported. Within this category some of the end flaps also have the words 'New Model'. Two types of picture are known to exist for the Y3-1 'E' Class Tramcar. The first was a straight side view elevation which also showed the roof detail and blacked out windows. The second was a smaller, lower angle side view showing just the edge of the roof section but with the windows now in detail.

D2 A coloured illustration of the model on the face of the box with a full pictorial background to the model. Some of the end flaps also have the words 'New Model' Y14-1 has not been seen in this category.

D3 A less complicated pictorial background and the title above the model instead of reading 'Models of Yesteryear' now reads 'Matchbox'. Some of the end flaps also have the words 'New Model'. Models Y3-1, Y3-2, Y13-1, Y13-2 are not known in this category.

E The illustration basically remains the same as D3 with a few noted exceptions, i.e. Y6-2 Bugatti colour changes from blue to red and Y7-2 Mercer colour changes from lilac to yellow. In addition the box end flaps now have a picture of the model and 'Matchbox' in red, again with some exceptions, i.e. Y3-2 and Y13-2 exist without 'Matchbox' on the flaps. Some of the end flaps also have the words 'New Model'. Models Y15-1 and Y16-1 and Y1-2 to Y14-2 are known within this category.

(E1) During the period of 1966/67 a subtle change was made to the printing of the boxes. Brighter coloured inks were used; most notably was the use of a much lighter blue to print the box sides. All model boxes were also endorsed with the registered Trade Mark '®' after 'Matchbox'. All end flaps now included 'Matchbox' ® above the picture and some still with 'New Model'.

PINK AND YELLOW

(F) A complete change to MOY packaging came about in 1968. The first 'window' box appeared in the range; because it was thought advantageous for the prospective customer to see the goods inside without having to open the box. These boxes were printed in overall yellow; but with a pink panel on the left side of the front and top of the box. The end flap pictures also had a pinker border and a cellophane window to the front and top panels. The small trademark text under the word 'Matchbox' varied in type face style. The Y9-2 Simplex changed livery at this time, from green to red and gold, and the box was altered to suit. A further development in Models of Yesteryear packaging occurred in the United States. Backing cards reproducing the picture of the model found on the back of the box were glued to it so that retailers could hang the models by these cards on hooks. Another marketing tactic was the introduction of the 'Blister Pack'. Instead of having a box the model was inserted into a stiff clear plastic bubble which was glued to a piece of card showing a picture of the featured model. This type of packaging has never been successful so far as collectors were concerned because the packaging had to be damaged to remove the model.

PURPLE AND YELLOW

(G) Introduced in 1969-1970 as a subtle replacement for the pink and yellow surround window box. Very much the same as category F but the pink areas were now in purple. Models of Yesteryear became a registered Trade Mark so the R appeared and a revised text printed under the description. Although Y2 apparently does not exist, Y1 to Y16 have all been reported.

WOODGRAIN

(H) The Models of Yesteryear range ceased production in 1972. It took the manufacturers two years to overcome the marketing problems incurred by the 'Hot Wheel' revolution from the United States. The re-liveried Models of Yesteryear and some new models began appearing in the retailers during 1974-1975. The old style packaging had been replaced with a new style to be affectionately referred to as the 'Woodgrain' boxes, because of the distinctive end flaps and borders being printed in a dark woodgrain design. There have been various colours and designs reported within the 'Woodgrain' category, the most significant being the changing of the gold colour of the Y Number on the package to a uniform white colour to make it more visible. The front and top faces can be coloured either green or pale blue. All models from the Y1 to Y17 have been reported.

STRAW BOXES

(I) Launched in 1979 and known as 'Straw' boxes by the majority of collectors. These boxes developed further than their predecessors; in so far as a third 'window' was introduced in the rear panel. Two end flap styles exist, the earlier included Y Number and model description along the bottom, the later type had the Y Number included within the thin gold border. The base card inserts were originally finished in a reflective gold. From 1982 these inserts had a matt gold effect. After the Y6-3 Cadillac ceased production, a batch of unboxed models were found at a Lesney warehouse. These were distributed in the Y6-4 Rolls-Royce Fire Engine Straw box. Slight variations have been reported and models from Y1-Y25 exist within this category. A special colour of green was used with the Y12-3 25th Anniversary model; Harrods were allowed to have green printing on their boxes and the Y12-3 Hoover Van had a company logo celebrating 75 years of production printed in the lower front corner. One rare variation appeared on the back of the Y12-3 'Coca Cola' Van box. The 'Joblin' Van was printed in reverse and therefore spelt 'Nilboj'!

RED

(J) Launched in 1983 and known as 'Red', or 'Maroon' boxes. They had a matt finish and lasted until Matchbox moved its production to Macau in 1987. A special colour of green carton was used with the Y29-1 Harrods Walker Electric Van. Models Y1 to Y30 exist in this category with some endorsed with 'Limited Edition'. In 1985 a superior red and maroon box with gold foil lettering was introduced for Special Limited Editions. This box type was used again in 1986. Four boxes appeared in 1986 with a red and gold chequered flag and a racing car in gold. These were issued in the 'Grand Prix' series.

RED 'MADE IN MACAU'

(J1) First issued in 1987 and still printed in red. However, the overall finish of the box took on a gloss finish and a reprinted text to read 'Made in Macau'. To avoid damage during transit the model was held to the box insert with a plastic tie.

RED 'MADE IN CHINA'

(J2) In July 1991, six models were re-released in the then old J1 type box but the text was reprinted to read 'Made in China'. The six models concerned were Y2-4, Y4-4, Y14-4, Y19-3 and two versions of the Y22-1.

The rear of the boxes have a printed $\boxed{\text{CE}}$ and BS5665 concerning Toy Safety Standards.

CONNOISSEUR SET

(K) A polished mahogany presentation box containing six Limited Edition revised livery models. Each box was individually numbered with a gold foil sticker featuring black digits.

GIFT PACK

(L) In this category two, three, four or five Models of Yesteryear were boxed together in a special gift pack. Because the models were also available separately these gift packs have, up to now, never been a desirable addition to collections. This category has still been omitted from the table of known box types with a 'Gift Pack' listing to be made in the future. In 1985 however, a boxed set of three models was released just prior to 'Fathers Day' in the U.K. This set contained the following re-liveried models:- Y11-3 Lagonda in deep red, Y23-1 AEC Omnibus, 'Maples' Y25-1 Renault Type AG Van, 'Duckhams'.

NON-MANUFACTURERS' PACKAGING

(M) These primarily concern the framed cabinets and the Y1-3 pewter Jaguar box which were made by sub-contractors and issued as part of the 'Passport' schemes. One other such box was issued during the mid-1960's and was part of the Mobil Petrol promotional. The colour of the box is orange with a cellophane window which was the only way to determine the contents as there was no descriptive text. The word 'Mobil' was featured on four box panels. Lesney Products supplied a basic range of six second series Models of Yesteryear. Y2-2 1911 Renault Two Seater, Y3-2 1910 Benz Limousine, cream and green, Y5-2 1929 4.5 Litre Bentley, No. 5, Y6-2 1926 Type 35 Bugatti, both blue and red, Y8-2 1914 Sunbeam Motorcycle and Milford Sidecar, Y10-2 1928 Mercedes-Benz 36/220. Often 'Mobil' boxes carry a large premium.

RED WITH CARD DIORAMA 'MADE IN MACAU'

(N) In 1990 a whole 'new look' into packaging design was undertaken as Matchbox and collectors felt a more dramatic and eye catching box was required. The result was not so much a box but a container. The cellophane was replaced by rigid clear plastic which formed the top, front and included the end flaps. The earlier internal fitment and rear window were deleted and the model platform became a diorama background. No variations of this diorama are known, as yet. Two box sizes exist, the larger, only some 10mm extra in height being used for the larger scale models, primarily commercials. Models were now secured by a self tapping screw and support plate onto the diorama insert. Some models have plastic ties for extra security during transit. From 1990 Matchbox implemented a new numbering and livery policy:- (1) "No new model will be issued in more than two liveries after its release livery (three in total)". (2) "A model which is substantially altered by having a new body, or new castings made for it will be re-coloured once only (two in total)". (3) "No new models will be re-coloured or re-liveried within a period of approximately one year". (4) "All new models are to be sold on a Limited Edition basis only". This policy ultimately led to the re-numbering of models well beyond the previous Y30 limit.

RED WITH CARD DIORAMA 'MADE IN CHINA'

(N1) Although identical in construction to the "N" category box, the text print changed from 'Made in Macau' to read 'Made in China'. Not all model numbers have yet been recorded in this category but the range now covers Y1 to Y64.

(N2) 1994 saw the return of the red clear plastic box when Matchbox Collectibles released the Grand Classics Collection. The difference from the N1 boxes was that the box text now featured Matchbox Collectibles and associated copyright and trade mark ownership details.

(N3) A superior 'N2' box in "Corporate" colours e.g. YY027/SA, and YY047/SA.

SPECIAL LIMITED EDITION LARGE RED AND GOLD BOX

(O) This box, first used in 1985 for the Y9-3 Leyland 3 Ton lorry, has led to a number of one off production run models; packaged in these attractive presentations. The use of card insert packing has given way to moulded polystyrene in later boxes.

(O1) In 1992, the Special Limited Edition Y65 1928 Austin 7 Collection was released in a box which differs from the standard 'O' boxes. Finished in red and gold, it is oblong shaped with a fold-over top, which when opened reveals three models on a diorama background. Surprisingly, unlike the end flaps, the top does not 'seal' the box, nor is there a protective plastic insert.

(O2) In 1994 and 1995 the Special 'Christmas Treasures' sets were presented in non standard boxes. These are simple flat white boxes with red (1994) and green (1995) marbled effect tops with gold lettering. The top lifts off to reveal four vans displayed in a green coloured tray, protected with tissue paper and a soft plastic coversheet.

WHITE WITH BLACK PRINTING

(P) In the latter part of 1989, Matchbox Classics (a division of Matchbox Toys U.S.A.) invited collectors to subscribe to twelve enhanced Yesteryear models being marketed in the U.S.A. as "Great Motor Cars of the Century". These models were packaged in a plain white cardboard box with the model description in black printed on one panel of the box only.

MATCHBOX COLLECTIBLES BOXES

(Q) This large box reflects the new era under the auspice of Matchbox Collectibles and has been used for the following series: Taste of France, Great Beers of the World, Power of the Press and the Fire Engine series. The artwork comprising colour-washed line drawings was changed with the introduction of each new series.

(Q1) The same size Q box but with a photograph of the model inside instead of line drawing artwork. First used with the Ronald McDonald charity model of 1995.

(Q2) A slightly larger 'commonality' box, showing on the front panel a black and white drawing of a model car, a pen and two dividers. A basic colour scheme of yellow on cream. The contents are shown by a factory applied label on one end flap. First used with the YSC01-M Scania in 1995.

(Q3) A large box used with models such as the YSFE01 Ahrens Fox or the YSFE02 and YFE08 Leyland Cub. The artwork on this box is an enlarged version of that on the Q box.

(Q4) In 1993 Matchbox released three Special Limited Heritage Horse-drawn carriage models in superior quality boxes; with finely executed coloured drawings depicting the carriages in use and which wrap around the top, the front and the two ends.

(R) A non standard box was used in 1992 for the Special Limited Edition Y66 'Her Majesty's Gold State Coach'. The multi-coloured lettered and decorated cream oblong box has a 'fold-over' top which when opened, reveals the State Coach and four pairs of horses, displayed on a red flock background and with a clear plastic protective envelope.

SUMMARY OF BOX TYPES

A = Line drawing, black number

B = Blue number, white circle

C = Red number, white lettering

D1 = Plain yellow background

D2 = Pictorial background M.O.Y. banners

D3 = Pictorial background Matchbox banners

E = End flap picture

E1 = End flap picture plus "Matchbox ®"

F = Pink and yellow

G = Purple and yellow

H = Woodgrain

I = Straw

J = Red, 'Made in England'

J1 = Red, 'Made in Macau'

J2 = Red, 'Made in China'

K = Connoisseur Set

L = Gift Packs

M = Non-Manufacturers' Packaging

N = Red, 'Made in Macau' Card Diorama

N1 = Red, 'Made in China' Card Diorama

N2 = Red, 'Made in China' Card Diorama and with Matchbox Collectibles details

N3 = As N2 but in corporate colours

O = Large red and gold 'Special Limited Edition'

O1 = Red and Gold with fold-over top

O2 = Christmas Treasures box

P = White with black printing

Q = Matchbox Collectibles 'themed' ranges

Q1 = Regional releases including Charity models

Q2 = Commonality box

Q3 = Ahrens - Fox/Leyland Cub models

Q4 = Heritage Horse-drawn series

R = Non-standard boxes

SUMMARY OF SCARCITY RATINGS

D = DIFFICULT
One of the five rarity categories used throughout the book described as "Being not easy to find and with a small price premium".

S = SCARCE
One of the five rarity categories used throughout the book. "Not easy to find and when seen for sale will have a premium price".

R = RARE
One of the five rarity categories used throughout the book "Seldom seen for sale and with a high premium".

VR = VERY RARE
One of the five rarity categories used throughout the book "Very occasionally seen for sale and at a very high price".

ER = EXTREMELY RARE
One of the five rarity categories used throughout the book. "Exceptionally highly priced and very seldom seen for sale".

THE 1996 MODELS OF YESTERYEAR RANGE

ISSUE	MONTH OF RELEASE	COLOURS				BASEPLATE	RARITY	BOX	PRICE

TO BE COMPLETED AS THE MODELS ARE RELEASED

INTERNATIONAL MARKET VALUES

FOR THE PURPOSES OF THIS EDITION THE FOLLOWING EXCHANGE RATES CAN BE APPLIED:

£1 - AUST $2.20;   £1 - US $1.65;   £1 - DM 2.50

For many, the valuation aspect of the Yesteryear Book will be all important. The values have all been given in sterling for no reason other than the book was written and published in Great Britain. These values are intended as a guide only and have been arrived at after consulting leading international dealers, noting the prices asked at toy shows and recording the realised prices for models sold through auctions. In general the values are a reflection of prices in the leading two Matchbox markets: Australia and Europe, but are just as relevant to other markets such as the USA and Canada.

The authors are aware that even allowing for rising and falling exchange rates, there are many instances when a particular issue will be worth more in one region than the other. For example, in the 1950s and early 1960s Lesney Products exported comparatively small quantities of Yesteryears to Australia. Many of those early Yesteryears have now found their way into Australian collections; due to the work of Australian collectors and dealers who have looked for them in Great Britain, paid for the models in sterling, paid the necessary bank charges, postage and customs duty, which in many cases adds 50% to the original purchase price. In more recent years some models have appeared which have been more popular, or meaningful to the general public in some countries rather than others. This has meant that one country has had more stock of this particular model and that they are more readily available. The Bentley for example was very well received in the UK where it sold in large quantities, and examples today may be less expensive in the UK than in America. The Y12-4 Arnotts is an even more extreme example. These were only released in small numbers in Australia, so any for sale in the UK, and the USA will have been imported at some extra cost.

The prices quoted in this book attempt to accommodate these regional variations. This could mean that a collector will find models offered for sale at less than the prices the authors have quoted. Their response to this is simply that the model in question is, therefore a good buy: In other words, the prices quoted are an indicator, or guide reflecting the scarcity of a model or a specific issue.

The book retains the five scarcity ratings as first used in The Collection and by attaching a value, should prove to be of assistance to the collector. The collector will see that although issues have been asterisked (*) with one of the scarcity ratings, there is often a disparity between the values. This arises more often than not, due to the popularity; or appeal of certain models.

What then is a value? The authors suggest that it is the price, a collector may expect to see a specific model or issue, for sale by a dealer or collector. The model must be in mint condition: no chips, retouches or scratches and it must be boxed. The box must be clean, crisp and devoid of scuffs or tears. The values given in this book are based on the models and their boxes meeting these criteria. Models of a non-factory fresh appearance and boxes being damaged or non-existent will reflect a much lower value. A high standard indeed and it will then be left to the collector to determine whether the model and the box in question are indeed ômint and boxedö. Another way of describing value is the price that one collector would hope to sell a model to another collector. This is not the same as the price the collector would hope to realise by selling to a dealer. Dealers need to make a margin: the difference between the buying price and selling price reflects the paying of any local sales taxes (in the UK 17.5% December 1995), the expenses of advertising and running a shop and, of course, the anticipated net profit on the eventual sale. Collectors should not be surprised or disappointed when selling models to the trade to receive offers that may appear low in comparison with the values shown in the Yesteryear Book. However, dealers are always keen to replenish their stocks with items of good quality and should normally make fair offers. By using the valuations in the Yesteryear Book, collectors will at least have a better idea as to the models worth. When selling models to the trade it is always a good idea to obtain offers from two or three dealers. It is then up to the collector to decide if an offer is fair, and whether to accept it or not.

THE MARKET SINCE 1993

Since the Tyco take-over in 1992 and the creation of the Matchbox Collectibles International Division, the market for older obsolete Models of Yesteryear has been depressed. The market for Models of Yesteryear became unsettled during 1993 and this was partially, not wholly, in response to the new marketing methods instigated by Tyco at that time. Many established collectors stopped buying new releases for three reasons. Firstly, they perceived 1992 as being the end of the era during which the Models of Yesteryear range was owned by either Lesney Products or Universal Matchbox. Secondly, with the brand being exclusively marketed by Matchbox Collectibles, there were long periods in 1993 and 1994 when no models were released. Boredom and apathy crept in and collectors attention turned to other brands. Finally, for many collectors the idea of buying via mail order was a new concept and hard to accept.

Thankfully, many thousands of established collectors stayed with the range, the majority of whom consider that the recent releases are of the very highest quality and although more expensive than, say the issues from the 1991 era, are still good value.

On a positive note, the three Matchbox Collectibles divisions; USA, UK and Australia; now have some 200,000 collectors on their databases, who buy directly by post. Some of these collectors will collect everything offered to them by Matchbox Collectibles, including the Dinky Collection, whilst others will only buy once in a while. The question that can only be answered with time is: "Will new collectors buy earlier releases?" For example, if several thousand 'new' collectors have the first twenty-four Great Beers series, will they be interested in the Y27 'Guinness', the Y26 'Lowenbrau' or the Y13 'Carlsberg'?

Although there has been some increase in the values recorded for the first series, or rarer releases, there have been dramatic increases for the models released in the period 1991 to 1992. The reason being low production runs, poor distribution and as mentioned above, for some collectors, the end of an era. So it appears that some collectors have been prepared to pay the necessary premiums to add to their collection.

INSURANCE & PROBATE

The values shown should make it easier for collectors to obtain sufficient insurance cover. All too often collectors have been faced with lengthy negotiations as to the value of models in their collections. The Yesteryear Book can be used as a reference to confirm the valuation of models. As a rule of thumb, for insurance purposes, the values should be increased by at least a 30% premium. This premium reflects the difficulty of obtaining a particular model on the market. We also hope that collectors will write down their notes on the pages and use the check-list provided. Collectors are encouraged to document prices paid and dates. Armed with this information, a spouse or probate solicitor should be able to make a reasonable estimation as to the value of a collection. As a rule of thumb for probate purposes, the values shown should be decreased by at least 25%. This deduction reflects the difficulty of selling a collection as a whole, quickly.

The authors hope that you will use the valuations as they are intended; as guides to values. They have not been 'set in concrete' and there will be regional anomalies just as there will be differences between two dealers next to each other at a toy show.

How can you help make the next Yesteryear Book better? In two years time, if there is a demand, the authors will publish a new edition of the Yesteryear Book 1956-1998: new issues, releases, added information, revised values and more values for post 1993 releases. Do let us know if you see models for sale, make a note of their prices, whether they sold or not, where seen etc. This will be a further and very exciting source of information to make the book even better. Please write to the publishers: Major Productions Ltd, 13A Lower Bridge Street, Chester, CH1 1RS, England.

INVESTMENT COMMENT

On most pages there is a box entitled 'Investment Comment'. Where known, the authors have included the original price of the featured model. This price is the now defunct recommended retail price set by Lesney/Matchbox Toys or the published price excluding postage and packaging costs from Matchbox Collectibles. There will be obvious regional price differences because of shipping, customs charges and exchange rate fluctuations as previously described.

The Investment Comment is an attempt to forecast models or variations that may perform well in the future. The vast majority of Yesteryear models have growth potential, because they are all eagerly collected and the hobby attracts new collectors continuously - most of them want to collect as many models as they can afford! All of these comments are purely subjective and are an attempt by the authors to draw your attention to informed buying decisions.

THE 1997 MODELS OF YESTERYEAR RANGE

ISSUE	MONTH OF RELEASE	COLOURS				BASEPLATE	RARITY	BOX	PRICE

TO BE COMPLETED AS THE MODELS ARE RELEASED

THE 1998 MODELS OF YESTERYEAR RANGE

ISSUE	MONTH OF RELEASE	COLOURS				BASEPLATE	RARITY	BOX	PRICE

TO BE COMPLETED AS THE MODELS ARE RELEASED

AN INTRODUCTION TO MATCHBOX
A NEW ERA - A NEW BEGINNING

In the early 1990s Tyco Toys Inc. were one of the biggest toy makers in the world. Based in New Jersey in the USA, over a decade of ever increasing profits had led them to look to Europe as their next biggest market. This era had set the stage for toy companies to become world dominating companies or to accept national or even continental status, in other words, to make the big time or take a back seat.

The quick way to make inroads into vast markets is to buy an established company; thus giving the purchaser an instant heritage, brand names, customers and all the infrastructure necessary for modern business.

Matchbox Universal was identified by Tyco as being the ideal candidate for a friendly take-over. It had all the aforementioned qualities; but perhaps best of all, it produced toys in categories that Tyco did not, hence giving them a much expanded range.

Within the wide Matchbox portfolio are the Yesteryear and Dinky brands. Yesteryear has a history under Matchbox stretching back into the 1950s, while the Dinky name, although a recent acquisition by Matchbox in the 1980s, has a legendary past. Both ranges were marketed to quite a different sector from toys; the male adult market. Tyco Toys, originally having been a model railway company, felt that they had an understanding of such a market group.

During the five months from May 1992, Tyco Toys were able to start investigating the Matchbox Universal Group's business. They found that the European distribution system was not quite as good as anticipated and that forecasted sales had not reached the levels expected by Matchbox. However, in October 1992, Tyco signed the final contract with Mr David Yeh, president and major shareholder of Universal Matchbox, purchasing the business for US$100 million.

As invariably happens with merging companies, certain 'sacred cows' are slaughtered and new targets and objectives are set. Miniatures being the pinnacle of the Matchbox line, quite naturally, were the first to come under examination by Tyco. It is necessary to recall that Tyco is a global company, involved in markets as diverse as Mexico, Germany and New Zealand: miniatures were the common denominator. The direction of Yesteryears, and Dinky, would have to wait.

From the end of the 1980s, the demand for Yesteryear products, under Matchbox, at first faltered and, then, started a gradual decline. Other companies had seen the warmth of the reception accredited to the Yesteryear line increase during that decade and decided that they, too, wished to be involved. No longer was Matchbox a sole, high profile player: the Yesteryear line needed serious reassessment.

One of the many avenues charted, was by Matchbox Australia and involved an appraisal of the direct mail market combined with a limited but organised retail presence through bona fide Collector Centres, offering an upgraded service to the consumer. However, by now, full development of the concept would have to wait as the acquisition by Tyco was taking place.

In 1993, Tyco turned the spotlight upon Yesteryear and Dinky, selecting the Australian proposal as how to proceed with the distribution of the line. It was now necessary to finalise the product line preparations with a view to consolidation of the Yesteryear name and, from that, build with a broader customer base, not ignoring the potential for a range expansion a few years ahead.

In July 1993, with 'Collectible' business centres established in Australia, USA and Europe, the company launched a major publicity campaign. Representatives of the press, model periodicals and car publications were interested to see the 1993 range of Yesteryears, the Taste of France series, the first Great Beers series and the three special horse-drawn vehicles. Naturally, during the months of reorganisation it would not have been advisable to leak details of the new ranges of models, so collectors, for the first time in the brand's history, knew nothing of them. Nevertheless, within weeks of the end of the publicity campaign, collectors received information about the new mail order system and details of the new models. Subsequently, between September and December 1993 all of the new models were released, 15 in total! Because the tools had been prepared during the months of the reorganisation it was possible to release three horse-drawn vehicles as Special Editions. Six new models based on the Citroën 'H', originally intended as part of the Dinky Collection, were issued. The other six issues were old models in new colours. Even though they may have made allowances for the problems of reorganisation, collectors reactions were mixed. Whilst many welcomed the issue of any model, others were less happy. Although some would realise that because it helped with the company's cash-flow, the release of old models in new colours were not necessarily welcomed. Some collectors positively disliked the new packaging with the plastic base and protective cover. In consequence, the volume of sales was less than anticipated. However, it was fortunate that the Tyco directors were now convinced that there was a future for the Yesteryear range. Quite naturally, being an American company, they decided that it would be appropriate for the management of the Matchbox Collectibles Division to be located at their headquarters in the USA

Matchbox had long neglected the USA market. Now, perhaps, was the time to give this vast potential another try. The product line would have less of a European imprint and more of a global approach. The Beer Series had been so popular that an expansion of the series was brought about - in 1996, the Series enters "No. 4". The idea of breaking the Yesteryear range down into manageable proportions for the collector evolved further. People would have the choice of selecting specific series to follow. The introduction of the Fire Engine series broadened the appeal, bringing in collectors of fire engines as well as those of diecast. The public sector Transit series also reflects this wider appeal approach.

Another innovation, for the diecast toy market at least, was the publication of the Matchbox Christmas 1994 Catalogue, enabling collectors to acquire models they had 'missed' as well as some new product, strictly from the pages of the catalogue. Another catalogue appeared in 1995.

As we enter 1996, the direction being taken by Matchbox Collectibles with the Yesteryear range remains faithful, yet excitingly rich in the spectrum that it caters to: new tooling, new themed series, existing series expansion; experimental ideas, such as replacing plastic with 'cold cast' as a medium for replicating certain components.

Not least, as a commemoration of the 40th anniversary of Yesteryears, a special eight vehicle collection! No doubt, there will be further 'dramas' within the Yesteryear "life cycle" as we all move towards the new millenium, but, the range now, compared with the past handful of years, radiates with a resolute robustness.

THE NEW NUMBERING SYSTEM

In 1993 with the release of the Taste of France and the Great Beers series, some important changes were noted by collectors. A new numbering system for the Yesteryear range. The Y number had been replaced with three letters, ie YTF for the Taste of France, YGB for the Great Beers series and in 1995 YFE for the Fire Engine models. Although some new models were based on those which were issued in the pre-Tyco days, and because of the new theme and numbering systems, that information could not be added to existing pages of the Book. So a new chapter had really begun!

Using the previous practice, the new number codings were cast onto the baseplates. However, when the Fire Engine series was released and the third series of the Great Beers was being prepared, staff at Tyco noted that there were some basic models common to all these series as well as of the proposed Power of the Press issues, e.g. the Mercedes truck and the Ford AA. To modify the tools and to change the cast information is an expensive and long process. Therefore, it was decided that cast information should be removed and detail replaced with tampo printed data. This process would take a while to implement fully.

1995 saw an important change for Yesteryear collectors. Until that year Matchbox (and Tyco) did not manufacture and issue Code 1 models for individuals and organisations. However, Tyco have stated that such models could be released as Regional Code 1 models. These will be in low production runs of circa 5,000. As most, if not all, such models would be based upon existing castings, they would be distinguished by suffix letters, eg YY027/SA Fullers, released in 1995. The 'S' denotes a special regional model and the 'A' that it is the first of this type. The charity model, YCH01 for 'Ronald McDonald House' is Australia was the first in the Charity Series, hence the YCH coding. At the time of publication, Matchbox Collectibles have planned a YCH02 for the same Australian charity in 1996. These models may well have an element of charity donation nominated by the model's sponsor. For the YCH01, AUS $5.00 was donated for each model sold.

This plate illustrates examples of packaging used by Lesney Products from 1956 to 1979, and demonstrates the growth in size of the models and their cartons. Of special interest are the Type E, blister packs, more usually used in the USA

These later cartons date from 1979 to date and illustrate the use of special boxes for particular models. Of note are the Harrod's boxes and the Mobil carton used during the 1960s

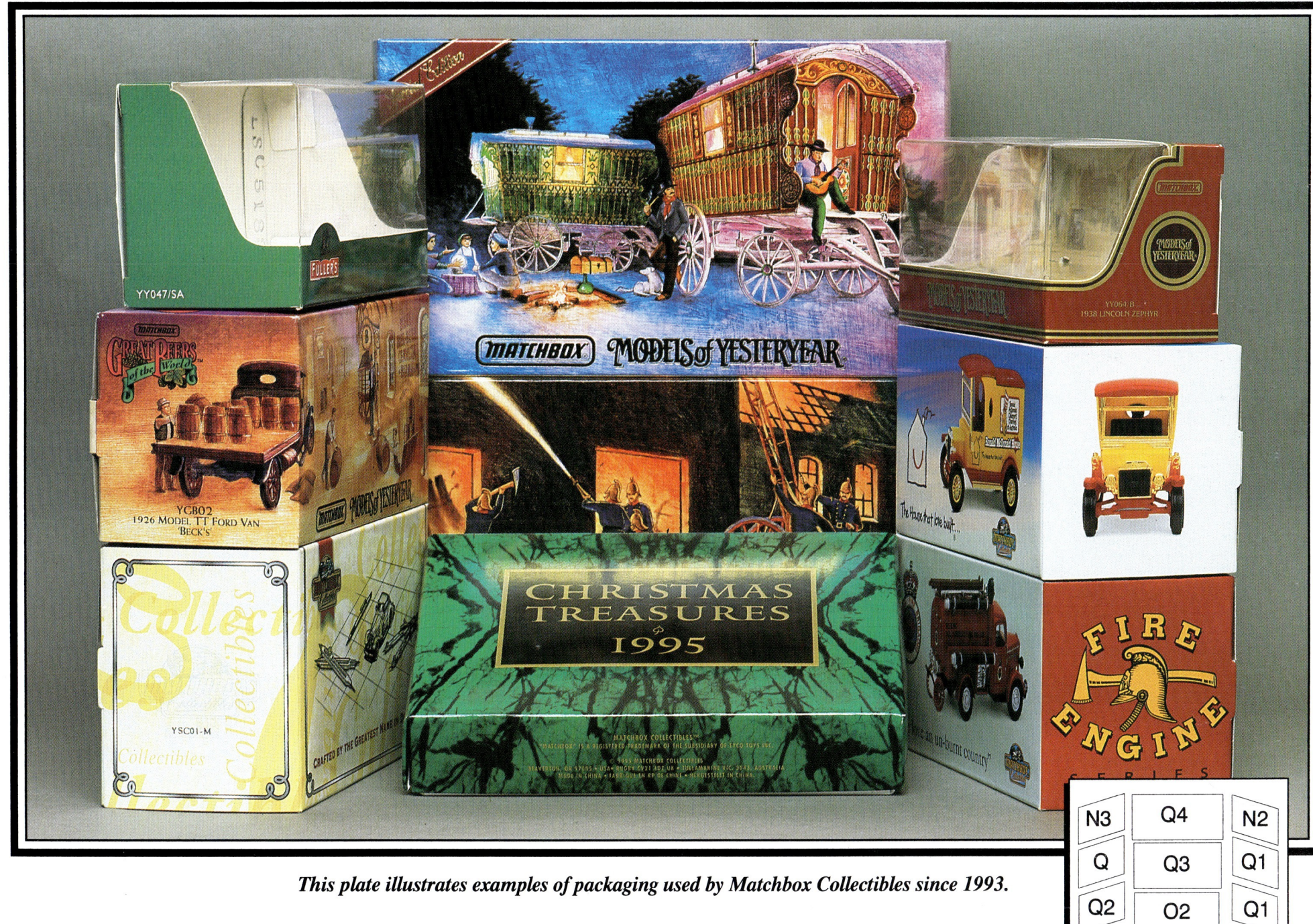

This plate illustrates examples of packaging used by Matchbox Collectibles since 1993.

Shown here are some desirable 'first series' models, Y1-1 to Y6-1, together with examples of the Y4-2 Shand Mason Fire Engine, which to all intents and purposes is a 'first series' release. Note the green boiler door Y1-1 Allchin and the '4 over 4' version of the Y2-1 'B' Type Bus. The Y5-1 Bentley with its grey rear tonneau and silver trim is unusual. All Y6-1 AEC 'Y' lorries are hard to find. This mid-blue issue has only recently come to light.

Further fine examples of the 'first series', Y7-1 to Y12-1. Shown to advantage is this full set of main Y7-1 Four Ton Leyland Lorries. The Y9-1 Showmans Engine in purple continues to be an elusive model. The Y10-1 Mercedes GP in pure white is far scarcer than one might think.

The last of the true 'first series', Y13-1 to Y16-1. The pale green Y13-1 Santa Fe only really stands out when viewed alongside a standard version, quite unlike these examples of a cream coloured and maroon coloured Y16-1 Spyker. Note also the distinctive blue tint of the Y15-1 Rolls Royce model.

The Connoisseurs Collection finally provided the collector with an authentic, Code One, black Model 'T' - it only took some twenty-four years! This plate also clearly shows the differences in colour that exist between the Y1-3 Jaguars in blue or yellow. Note the mixture of plated and unplated components on this Y2-2 Renault.

The most authentic looking Y2-3 Vauxhall is the first version, but the rarest by far is the blue issue with those elusive bright red seats. The Y2-4 Bentley has been the best selling car in the range in recent years. Also on display are the four major colour schemes for the Y3-2 Benz. Note also the varying shades of metallic red applied to the Y3-3 Riley.

Y1-1 1925 ALLCHIN TRACTION ENGINE Scale 1:80

INVESTMENT COMMENT
ORIGINAL PRICE £0.11.5p

Compared to other 'first series' models the Allchain has maintained its value. Issue 1 has shown an increase. All three issues with mid-green boiler doors, still have further potential.

This the first Yesteryear was launched at the British Toy and Hobby Show in 1956. The most prolific variations concern the rear wheel tread pattern types. The early models were fitted with 'straight across' treads; cast at right angles to the edge of the wheel, with a double hub and oval plate on the outside face of the wheel centre. These were soon replaced by rear wheels with diagonally angled treads which give a forward facing chevron pattern. The wheel centres were detailed with or without bolt head detail on the central oval plates. Due to many permutations that could arise for incorrectly fitted wheels, the list has been kept simple, in that angled treads have been confined to forward facing chevron patterns. The last batch of models were fitted with smooth treaded wheels normally associated with the Y11/1 Roller, because the tools had deteriorated and could no longer be used. The flywheel component was painted in black, but this varied to a dark brown and the majority of issues could be found with either colour type although very early issues were fitted with non reinforced spoke braces. Early models also had a completely detailed shackle pin on the towing "eyelet"; whereas later ones did not. The Allchin was withdrawn in 1965.

ISSUE	YEAR OF RELEASE	COLOURS	CAB FLOOR	COLOUR FRONT WHEELS	COLOUR REAR WHEELS	TREAD DESIGN	AXLES	BOILER DOOR	PAINTED TRIM	FLYWHEEL	BASEPLATE	RARITY	BOX TYPE	VALUE	CHECK LIST
1	1956	Mid green body & chassis	9 Slats	Dark red 10 spoke	Dark red 16 spoke	Straight * unpainted	Crimped	Copper	Full gold	6 spoke black	LESNEY No1 ENGLAND	R	A	£200	
2		Mid green body & chassis	9 Slats	Dark red 10 spoke	Dark red 16 spoke	Straight* unpainted	Crimped	Mid green*	Full gold	6 spoke black	LESNEY No1 ENGLAND	VR	A	£350	
3		Mid green body & chassis	9 Slats	Dark red 10 spoke	Dark red 16 spoke	Angled unpainted*	Crimped	Copper	Full gold	6 spoke black	LESNEY No1 ENGLAND	S	A	£90	2 X
4		Mid green body & chassis	9 Slats	Dark red 10 spoke	Dark red 16 spoke	Angled dark red*	Crimped	Copper	Full gold	6 spoke black	LESNEY No1 ENGLAND	S	A/B	£135	
5		Mid green body & chassis	9 Slats	Bright red 10 spoke	Bright red 16 spoke	Angled unpainted	Crimped	Copper	Full gold	6 spoke black	LESNEY No1 ENGLAND		A/B	£90	
6		Mid green body & chassis	9 Slats	Bright red 10 spoke	Bright red 16 spoke	Angled bright* red	Crimped	Copper	Full gold	6 spoke black	LESNEY No1 ENGLAND	S	B/C	£125	
7		Mid green body & chassis	9 Slats	Dark red 10 spoke	Dark red 16 spoke	Angled unpainted	Crimped	Gold	Full gold	6 spoke black	LESNEY No1 ENGLAND		B/C	£90	
8		Mid green body & chassis	9 Slats	Dark red 10 spoke	Dark red 16 spoke	Angled dark red*	Crimped	Gold	Full gold	6 spoke black	LESNEY No1 ENGLAND	S	B/C	£100	
9		Mid green body & chassis	9 Slats	Bright red 10 spoke	Bright red 16 spoke	Angled unpainted	Crimped	Gold	Full gold	6 spoke black	LESNEY No1 ENGLAND		C	£90	
10		Mid green body & chassis	9 Slats	Bright red 10 spoke	Bright red 16 spoke	Angled bright* red	Crimped	Gold	Full gold	6 spoke black	LESNEY No1 ENGLAND	S	C	£125	
11		Mid green body & chassis	9 Slats	Dark red 10 spoke	Dark red 16 spoke	Angled unpainted	Crimped	Mid green*	Full gold	6 spoke black	LESNEY No1 ENGLAND	R	C	£250	
12		Mid green body & chassis	9 Slats	Dark red 10 spoke	Dark red 16 spoke	Angled unpainted	Riveted	Mid green*	Partial gold	6 spoke black	LESNEY No1 ENGLAND	R	C	£250	
13		Mid green body & chassis	9 Slats	Dark red 10 spoke	Dark red 16 spoke	Angled unpainted	Riveted	Gold	Partial gold	6 spoke black	LESNEY No1 ENGLAND		C/D1	£90	
14		Mid green body & chassis	9 Slats	Dark red 10 spoke	Dark red 16 spoke	Angled dark red*	Riveted	Gold	Partial gold	6 spoke black	LESNEY No1 ENGLAND	S	C/D1	£110	
15		Mid green body & chassis	9 Slats	Bright red 10 spoke	Bright red 16 spoke	Angled unpainted	Riveted	Gold	Partial gold	6 spoke brown	LESNEY No1 ENGLAND		C/D1	£90	
16		Mid green body & chassis	9 Slats	Bright red 10 spoke	Bright red 16 spoke	Angled bright* red	Riveted	Gold	Partial gold	6 spoke dark brown	LESNEY No1 ENGLAND	S	C/D1	£110	

DIAGRAM 1

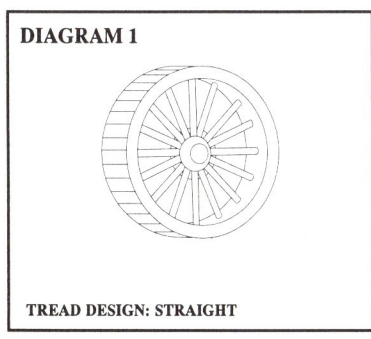

TREAD DESIGN: STRAIGHT

DIAGRAM 2

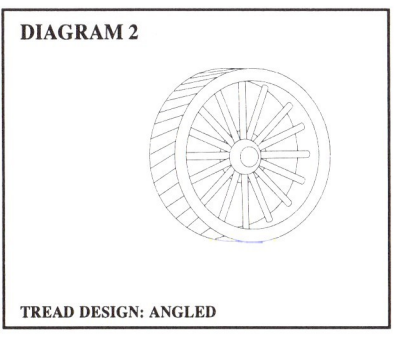

TREAD DESIGN: ANGLED

IDENTIFICATION KEY

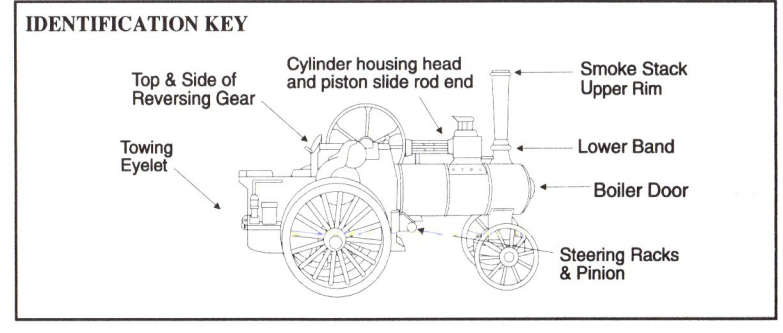

Y1-1 1925 ALLCHIN TRACTION ENGINE CONTINUED SCALE 1 : 80

ISSUE	YEAR OF RELEASE	COLOURS	CAB FLOOR	COLOUR FRONT WHEELS	COLOUR REAR WHEELS	TREAD DESIGN	AXLES	BOILER DOOR	PAINTED TRIM	FLYWHEEL	BASEPLATE	RARITY	BOX TYPE	VALUE	CHECK LIST
17	1963	Mid green body & chassis	11 Slats	Bright red 10 spoke	Bright red 16 spoke	Angled unpainted	Riveted	Gold	Partial gold	6 spoke dark brown	LESNEY No1 ENGLAND		D1	£90	
18		Mid green body & chassis	11 Slats	Bright red 10 spoke	Bright red 16 spoke	Angled bright* red	Riveted	Gold	Partial gold	6 spoke dark brown	LESNEY No1 ENGLAND	S	D1	£110	
19		Mid green body & chassis	11 Slats	Bright red 10 spoke	Bright red 16 spoke	Angled unpainted	Riveted	Silver*	Partial gold	6 spoke dark brown	LESNEY No1 ENGLAND	S	D1	£110	
20		Mid green body & chassis	11 Slats	Bright red 10 spoke	Bright red 16 spoke	Angled bright* red	Riveted	Silver*	Partial gold	6 spoke dark brown	LESNEY No1 ENGLAND	S	D1	£125	
21	1965	Mid green body & chassis	11 Slats	Bright red 10 spoke	Bright red 16 spoke	Smooth* unpainted	Riveted	Gold	Partial gold	6 spoke dark brown	LESNEY No1 ENGLAND	E R	D1	£750	
22		Mid green body & chassis	11 Slats	Bright red 10 spoke	Bright red 16 spoke	Smooth* unpainted	Riveted	Silver	Partial gold	6 spoke dark brown	LESNEY No1 ENGLAND	E R	D1	£750	

NOTES

"Full" gold trim refers to trim applied to the steering racks and pinion, smoke stack and lower band.
Cylinder housing head and piston slide rod end, top and side of reversing gear.
"Partial " gold trim refers when gold is missing from any part.

Y1-2 1911 FORD MODEL 'T' CAR   Scale 1 : 42

INVESTMENT COMMENT
ORIGINAL PRICE £ 0.25p

Still an extremely common model in standard issue. The rarer issues have all dropped in value. However, they still represent good value. The Connoisseurs Set model, Issue 24 has enjoyed some growth and the set is worth acquiring.

Several body modifications were made to this model. Gaps around the rear number plate were filled in and the front number plate was altered so that the digits '3' and '0' were larger. The word 'Ford' on the radiator surround exists in two types and the radiator grille can have one or two horizontal bars. There are at least six different headlight components; but these modifications have not been individually listed as it would make the number of issues over seventy in number. When Yesteryear production began again in 1974/75, Lesney changed the wheel components from narrow ones to wide types. During this period Lesney Products experimented with the colours of the hoods and grilles. These were never intended to be released as production models and colour trial hoods seen include orange, tan, grey and yellow. In 1976 Lesney released to members of an American Matchbox Club, a small batch of all black Y1 models. These Code Two models are very rare but they should not be confused with the all black model released in 1984 as part of the Connoisseurs set. Knowing the scarcity value of the textured black roof component, each roof in the Connoisseurs set had the words 'Limited Edition' cast onto the underside.

ISSUE	YEAR OF RELEASE	COLOURS	HOOD	SEATS	GRILLE	STEERING WHEEL	WHEELS	DIAMETER OF WHEELS	BASE HOLES	WINDSCREEN	BRAKE LEVER	BASEPLATE	RARITY	BOX TYPE	VALUE	CHECK LIST
1	1964	Red body & chassis	Black smooth	Black	Black	Red metal	Brass 12 spoke	13mm	2	Red	Twin*	LESNEY NO Y-1 ENGLAND	R	D2	£130	
2		Red body & chassis	Black smooth	Black	Black	Red metal	Brass 12 spoke	13mm	2	Red	Single	LESNEY NO Y-1 ENGLAND		D2/D3	£20	✓
3		Red body & chassis	Black smooth	Black	Black	Red metal	Brass 12 spoke	13mm	No	Red	Single	LESNEY NO Y-1 ENGLAND		E/E1 ✓	£20	
4	1968	Red body & chassis	Black smooth	Black	Black	Black plastic	Brass 12 spoke	13mm	No	Red	Single	LESNEY NO Y-1 ENGLAND		F / G	£20	
5		Red body & chassis	Black smooth	Black	Black	Black plastic	Brass 12 spoke	11.5mm*	No	Red	Single	LESNEY NO Y-1 ENGLAND	S	F	£45	
6		Red body & chassis	Black textured*	Black	Black	Black plastic	Brass 12 spoke	13mm	No	Red	Single	LESNEY NO Y-1 ENGLAND	R	G	£120	
7	1974	Cream body & red chassis	Black textured*	Bright red	Red	Black plastic	Chrome 12 spoke	10mm	No	Unpainted	Single	LESNEY NO Y-1 ENGLAND	R	H	£120	
8		Cream body & red chassis	Black textured*	Black	Black	Black plastic	Chrome 12 spoke	10mm	No	Unpainted	Single	LESNEY NO Y-1 ENGLAND	R	H	£130	
9		Cream body & red chassis	Black textured*	Black	Red	Black plastic	Chrome 12 spoke	10mm	No	Unpainted	Single	LESNEY NO Y-1 ENGLAND	R	H	£120	
10		Cream body & red chassis	Black textured*	Dark red	Black	Black plastic	Chrome 12 spoke	10mm	No	Unpainted	Single	LESNEY NO Y-1 ENGLAND	R	H	£120	
11		Cream body & red chassis	Black textured*	Dark red	Dark red	Black plastic	Chrome 12 spoke	10mm	No	Unpainted	Single	LESNEY NO Y-1 ENGLAND	R	H	£120	
12		Cream body & red chassis	Dark red textured	Bright red	Red	Black plastic	Chrome 12 spoke	10mm	No	Unpainted	Single	LESNEY NO Y-1 ENGLAND		H	£20	

DIAGRAM 1 TWIN BRAKE LEVER

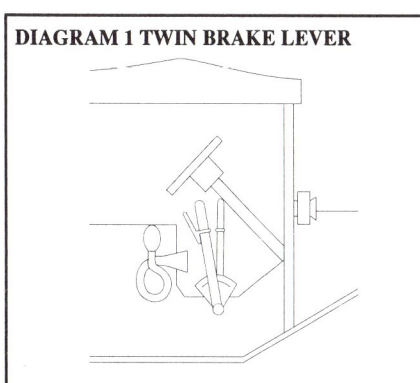

DIAGRAM 2 SINGLE BRAKE LEVER

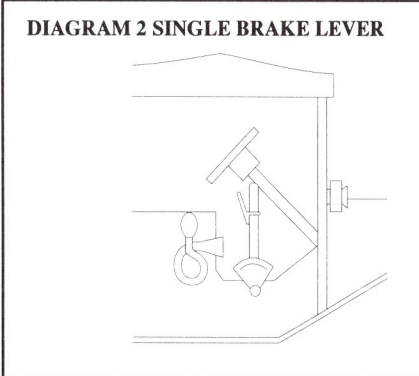

NOTES

1. It is possible to find models with a mixture of white bonnet and cream body or vice versa; all combinations with many various permutations of coloured plastic components may be found.
2. The value of the 1976 all black Code 2 America Matchbox Club model has fallen away in value from £400 plus in the 1980s to between £250 and £300 today.

Y1-2 1911 FORD MODEL 'T' CAR CONTINUED   Scale 1:42

ISSUE	YEAR OF RELEASE	COLOURS	HOOD	SEATS	GRILLE	STEERING WHEEL	WHEELS	DIAMETER OF WHEELS	BASE HOLES	WINDSCREEN	BRAKE LEVER	BASEPLATE	RARITY	BOX TYPE	VALUE	CHECK LIST
13		Cream body & red chassis	Dark red textured	Black	Black	Black plastic	Chrome 12 spoke	10mm	No	Unpainted	Single	LESNEY NO Y-1 ENGLAND		H	£35	
14		Cream body & red chassis	Dark red textured	Black	Red	Black plastic	Chrome 12 spoke	10mm	No	Unpainted	Single	LESNEY NO Y-1 ENGLAND		H	£35	
15		Cream body & red chassis	Dark red textured	Black	Red	Black plastic	Chrome 24 spoke	10mm	No	Unpainted	Single	LESNEY NO Y-1 ENGLAND		H	£20	
16		Cream body & red chassis	Dark red textured	Red	Black	Black plastic	Chrome 24 spoke	10mm	No	Unpainted	Single	LESNEY NO Y-1 ENGLAND		H	£25	
17		Cream body & red chassis	Dark red textured	Red	Red	Black plastic	Chrome 24 spoke	10mm	No	Unpainted	Single	LESNEY NO Y-1 ENGLAND		H	£25	
18		Cream body & red chassis	Dark red textured	Red	Red	Black plastic	Chrome 24 spoke	10mm	No	Brass*	Single	LESNEY NO Y-1 ENGLAND	D	H	£50	
19	1975	White body & red chassis	Dark red textured	Dark red	Dark red	Black plastic	Chrome 12 spoke	10mm	No	Unpainted	Single	LESNEY NO Y-1 ENGLAND		H	£20	
20		White body & red chassis	Dark red textured	Dark red	Dark red	Black plastic	Chrome 24 spoke	10mm	No	Unpainted	Single	LESNEY NO Y-1 ENGLAND		H	£20	
21		White body & red chassis	Mid red textured	Bright red	Bright red	Black plastic	Brass 12 spoke	10mm	No	Unpainted	Single	LESNEY NO Y-1 ENGLAND		H	£35	
22	1976	White body & red chassis	Bright* red textured	Red	Dark red	Black plastic	Chrome 12 spoke	10mm	No	Unpainted	Single	LESNEY NO Y-1 ENGLAND	R	H	£100	
23		White body & red chassis	Bright* red textured	Dark red	Red	Black plastic	Chrome 12 spoke	10mm	No	Unpainted	Single	LESNEY NO Y-1 ENGLAND	R	H	£100	
24	1984	Black body & chassis	Black textured	Fawn	Black	Black plastic	Brass 12 spoke	13mm	No	Black	Single	MATCHBOX © 1984 LIMITED EDITION ENGLAND		K	The Set £95	

NOTES

Y1-3 1936 SS100 JAGUAR

Scale 1:38

INVESTMENT COMMENT
ORIGINAL PRICE £.1.49p
As anticipated Issue 1 has appreciated as has Issue 3. The 1979 issues have "jumped" up considerably. Issue 10 at £50 is low and good value with potential. Issue 14 the pewter model, at £30 is still available through Matchbox Collectibles.

No sooner had production commenced than it was deemed necessary to make three major casting modifications to this model. Firstly, the sidelights on the front wings were virtually doubled in size; the bracing rib behind the front license plate was widened by 1 mm to give it extra strength and finally the wall of the rivet hole in the area of the sump was thickened forming a rim that was proud of the sump. In late 1979 the chassis tools were again modified to include five parallel ribs on the undersides of the running-boards so as to prevent the chassis component sticking to the conveyor belt during the painting process. In 1981 dark green became the standard livery. This was changed to 'Talbot' yellow in 1986, a premature marketing decision as the model was not planned to be changed to yellow until 1987. In all, 1,500 yellow models were made at the Rochford factory, in Essex but only about 100 or so managed to leave the factory. Eventually Matchbox released the remaining balance, the majority ending-up in Germany and the U.S.A. The balance of sprayed yellow castings (unassembled) which were in addition to the 1,500 assembled models. These were then oversprayed in dark green (Issue 11) and the yellow undercoat is obvious. In 1987 with production now in Macau, a darker yellow livery known as 'Sunrise' yellow was issued, along with a plastic diorama. In mid-1991 the production facilities moved to China. The red model (Issue 13) was given greater detail. In late 1991 Matchbox released the model, made entirely out of pewter except for its steel axles, on a wooden plinth, and as part of Matchbox's incentive passport scheme. It cost £16.49 plus £3.50pp within the U.K. In 1994 the red bodied model was re-run as part of the Grand Classic Collection. The shade of red was slightly lighter.

ISSUE	YEAR OF RELEASE	COLOURS	HOOD & SEATS	PLATED PARTS	STEERING WHEEL	WHEELS	AXLES	SIDE LIGHTS	SUMP RIVET HOLE	NUMBER PLATE BRACE	RIBS ON RUNNING BOARD U/SIDE	DIORAMA OR PLINTH	BASEPLATE	RARITY	BOX TYPE	VALUE	CHECK LIST
1	1977	Off white* body & chassis	Black	Chrome	Black	Chrome 24 spoke	Riveted	Small*	Small	Narrow 3mm	None	None	LESNEY © 1977 ENGLAND	R	H	£175	
2		Light cream white body & chassis	Black	Chrome	Black	Chrome 24 spoke	Riveted	Large	Large	Wide 4mm	None	None	LESNEY © 1977 ENGLAND		H	£15	✓
3	1978	Steel grey* body & chassis	Black	Chrome	Black	Chrome 24 spoke	Riveted	Large	Large	Wide 4mm	None	None	LESNEY © 1977 ENGLAND	S	H/I	£125	
4	1979	Steel blue body & chassis	Black	Chrome	Black	Chrome 24 spoke BW	Riveted	Large	Large	Wide 4mm	None	None	LESNEY © 1977 ENGLAND		I	£15	
5		Steel blue body & chassis	Black	Chrome	Black	Chrome 12 spoke BW	Riveted	Large	Large	Wide 4mm	None	None	LESNEY © 1977 ENGLAND		I	£25	
6		Steel blue body & chassis	Black	Chrome	Black	Chrome solid BW	Riveted	Large	Large	Wide 4mm	None	None	LESNEY © 1977 ENGLAND		I	£25	
7		Steel blue body & chassis	Black	Chrome	Black	Chrome 24 spoke BW	Riveted	Large	Large	Wide 4mm	5	None	LESNEY © 1977 ENGLAND		I	£15	
8		Steel blue body & chassis	Black	Chrome	Black	Chrome 12 spoke BW	Riveted	Large	Large	Wide 4mm	5	None	LESNEY © 1977 ENGLAND		I	£25	
9	1981	Dark green body & chassis	Black	Chrome	Black	Chrome 24 spoke BW	Riveted	Large	Large	Wide 4mm	5	None	LESNEY © 1977 ENGLAND		I/J	£8	✓
10	1986	Pale* yellow body & chassis	Black	Chrome	Black	Chrome 24 spoke WW	Riveted	Large	Large	Wide 4mm	5	None	LESNEY © 1977 ENGLAND	S	J	£50	
11		Yellow oversprayed* dark green body & chassis	Black	Chrome	Black	Chrome 24 spoke BW	Riveted	Large	Large	Wide 4mm	5	None	LESNEY © 1977 ENGLAND	D	J	£40	
12	1987	Dark yellow body & chassis	Black	Chrome	Black	Chrome 24 spoke	Riveted	Large	Large	Wide 4mm	5	Diorama	MATCHBOX © 1977 MACAU		J/I	£12	✓
13	1991	Bright red body & chassis	Black	Chrome	Light brown silver spokes	Chrome 24 spoke	Press fit	Large	Large	Wide 4mm	5	None	MATCHBOX © 1977 CHINA		N/I	£20	✓
14	1992	Pewter body & chassis	Pewter	Pewter	Pewter	Pewter 24 spoke	Steel press fit	Large	Large	Wide 4mm	5	Plinth	MATCHBOX CHINA	D	M	£30	
15	1994	Bright red body & chassis	Black	Chrome	Light brown silver spokes	Chrome 24 spoke	Press fit	Large	Large	Wide 4mm	5	Diorama	MATCHBOX CHINA		N 2		

DIAGRAM 1 SIDE LIGHT TYPES

1st TYPE SMALL — Side, Above, Front
2nd TYPE LARGE

DIAGRAM 2 NUMBER PLATE BRACE

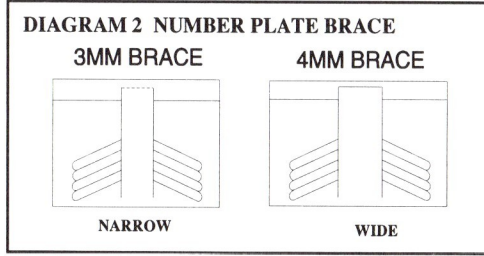

3MM BRACE — NARROW
4MM BRACE — WIDE

DIAGRAM 3 SUMP RIVET HOLE

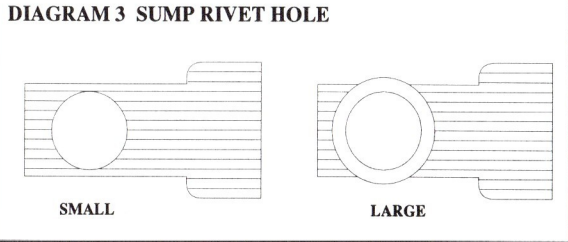

SMALL — LARGE

NOTES

1. BECKENHAM APPEAL MODEL Issued in 1979 in dark green body, black retracted hood, chrome 24 spoke wheels and without the five ribs on the underside of each running board.

2. Issue 9 was also released in Twin and Triple pack gift sets.

INVESTMENT COMMENT
ORIGINAL PRICE £0.11.5p
The rarer issues have been rather static. However, all standard issues have remained on a par with 1992 prices.

Y2-1 1911 "B" TYPE LONDON BUS Scale 1:100

This delicate and well detailed model was first shown to the trade at the 1956 Harrogate Toy Show, and was chosen mainly because Jack Odell's father had been employed as a London bus driver. The first casting did not have guide ribs cast on the bus sides to locate the transfers, Body Type A. Only one further casting modification was necessary which was to the passenger compartment windows. Early models featured four small windows above four large windows. This variant as shown in the diagram is known as the '4 over 4' type. Mass production revealed that the horizontal strut dividing the small and large windows was weak and was prone to breaking. To overcome this problem the tools were modified so that an additional vertical strut was cast in the middle of each of the small windows; - thus creating a variant now known as the '8 over 4' type. Diagram 1. Initially axles were crimped over at one end but these were replaced with both ends being riveted. The driver and steering wheel component was painted in a dark blue, a light blue, or black. Very late production runs featured wheels painted in black.

ISSUE	YEAR OF RELEASE	COLOURS	LOWER DECK CEILING	RADIATOR SHELL	FRONT WHEELS	REAR WHEELS	AXLES	DRIVER STEERING WHEEL	WINDOW DESIGN	BODY TYPE	BASEPLATE	RARITY	BOX TYPE	VALUE	CHECK LIST
1	1956	London transport red body & chassis	Bare metal	Silver	Grenodised 8 spoke	Grenodised 16 spoke daisy	Crimped	Blue	4/4*	A*	LESNEY ENGLAND	ER	A	£400	
2	1956	London transport red body & chassis	Bare metal	Silver	Grenodised 8 spoke	Grenodised 16 spoke daisy	Crimped	Blue	4/4*	B	LESNEY ENGLAND	ER	A	£400	
3		London transport red body & chassis	Bare metal	Silver	Grenodised 8 spoke	Grenodised 16 spoke daisy	Crimped	Light blue	4/4*	B	LESNEY ENGLAND	R	A	£150	
4		London transport red body & chassis	Bare metal	Silver	Grenodised 8 spoke	Grenodised 16 spoke daisy	Crimped	Black	4/4*	B	LESNEY ENGLAND	R	A	£150	
5	1957	London transport red body & chassis	Bare metal	Silver	Grenodised 8 spoke	Grenodised 16 spoke daisy	Crimped	Blue	8/4	B	LESNEY ENGLAND		A/B	£85	
6		London transport red body & chassis	Bare metal	Silver	Grenodised 8 spoke	Grenodised 16 spoke daisy	Crimped	Light blue	8/4	B	LESNEY ENGLAND		A/B	£85	
7		London transport red body & chassis	Bare metal	Silver	Grenodised 8 spoke	Grenodised 16 spoke daisy	Crimped	Black	8/4	B	LESNEY ENGLAND		A/B	£85	
8		London transport red body & chassis	Bare metal	Red	Grenodised 8 spoke	Grenodised 16 spoke daisy	Crimped	Blue	8/4	B	LESNEY ENGLAND		B/C	£85	
9		London transport red body & chassis	Bare metal	Red	Grenodised 8 spoke	Grenodised 16 spoke daisy	Crimped	Light blue	8/4	B	LESNEY ENGLAND		B/C	£85	
10		London transport red body & chassis	Bare metal	Red	Grenodised 8 spoke	Grenodised 16 spoke daisy	Crimped	Black	8/4	B	LESNEY ENGLAND		B/C	£85	
11		London transport red body & chassis	Tan	Red	Grenodised 8 spoke	Grenodised 16 spoke daisy	Crimped	Blue	8/4	B	LESNEY ENGLAND		B/C	£85	
12		London transport red body & chassis	Tan	Red	Grenodised 8 spoke	Grenodised 16 spoke daisy	Crimped	Light blue	8/4	B	LESNEY ENGLAND		B/C	£85	
13		London transport red body & chassis	Tan	Red	Grenodised 8 spoke	Grenodised 16 spoke daisy	Crimped	Black	8/4	B	LESNEY ENGLAND		B/C	£85	✓

DIAGRAM 1 WINDOW DESIGN

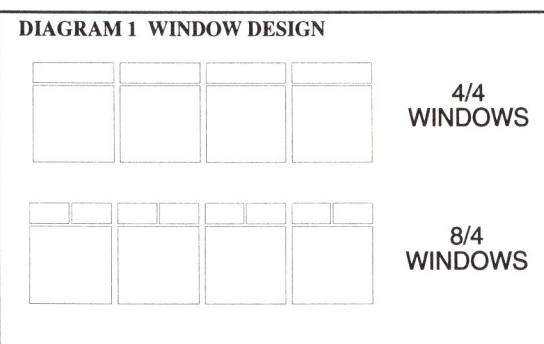

4/4 WINDOWS

8/4 WINDOWS

DIAGRAM 2 BODY TYPES

TYPE A 1st CASTING NO RIBS

TYPE B 2nd CASTING WITH RIBS

LIVERY

Lower panels. Yellow GENERAL
Upper panels. DEWARS in white with black outline.
THE WHISKY in white on red panel on the left WHITE LABEL in white on red panel on the right.
Front destination board. White board with black lettering.
On both sides of board, white PEARS on pale blue panel.
White THE KING OF SOAPS on black.
Rear destination board. White board with black lettering, white NESTLES MILK RICHEST IN CREAM on dark blue to right-hand side.
Stair panel. Yellow OAKEYS WELLINGTON KNIFE POLISH

NOTES

Y2-1 1911 'B' TYPE LONDON BUS CONTINUED Scale 1:100

ISSUE	YEAR OF RELEASE	COLOURS	LOWER DECK CEILING	RADIATOR SHELL	FRONT WHEELS	REAR WHEELS	AXLES	DRIVER STEERING WHEEL	WINDOW DESIGN	BODY TYPE	BASEPLATE	RARITY	BOX TYPE	VALUE	CHECK LIST
14	1959	London transport red body & chassis	Bare metal	Red	Grenodised 8 spoke	Grenodised 16 spoke daisy	Riveted	Blue	8/4	B	LESNEY ENGLAND		B/C	£85	
15		London transport red body & chassis	Bare metal	Red	Grenodised 8 spoke	Grenodised 16 spoke daisy	Riveted	Light blue	8/4	B	LESNEY ENGLAND		B/C	£85	
16		London transport red body & chassis	Bare metal	Red	Grenodised 8 spoke	Grenodised 16 spoke daisy	Riveted	Black	8/4	B	LESNEY ENGLAND		B/C	£85	
17		London transport red body & chassis	Tan	Silver	Grenodised 8 spoke	Grenodised 16 spoke daisy	Riveted	Blue	8/4	B	LESNEY ENGLAND		C/D1	£100	
18		London transport red body & chassis	Tan	Silver	Grenodised 8 spoke	Grenodised 16 spoke daisy	Riveted	Light blue	8/4	B	LESNEY ENGLAND		C/D1	£90	✗
19		London transport red body & chassis	Tan	Red	Grenodised 8 spoke	Grenodised 16 spoke daisy	Riveted	Black	8/4	B	LESNEY ENGLAND		C/D1	£90	✓
20	1961	London transport red body & chassis	Tan	Red	Black* 8 Spoke	Black * 16 spoke daisy	Riveted	Black	8/4	B	LESNEY ENGLAND	S	C/D1	£100	
21		London transport red body & chassis	Tan	Red	Black* 8 spoke	Black*16 spoke daisy	Riveted	Blue	8/4	B	LESNEY ENGLAND	S	C/D1	£100	

INVESTMENT COMMENT
ORIGINAL PRICE £0.15p

All issues are seen as good value. Although not listed individually, models with unplated metal components still attract a premium.

Y2-2 1911 RENAULT TWO SEATER

Scale 1:40

Early models featured a gap between the rear edges of the bonnet and the radiator, Type 1. For subsequent runs the radiator casting was modified to eliminate this gap. Also, very early versions did not have strengthening wing braces cast where the rear wings join the running boards. The other major modification concerns an in-fill between the rear lights and the rear number plate. Although minor variations are associated with spare tyre carrier, for easy listing, these have been restricted to either the early four prong type, or the later three prong type. Originally the steering wheel and column was made in metal and small changes were made to the wheel centre. Although Lesney Products intended that the wheels and other metal parts be brass plated, on many occasions these parts were left unfinished. These have not been listed individually. All issues can have any combination of plated and unplated components fitted. The shades of metallic green can vary from light to dark and although the paint can fade, the lighter shades are more difficult to find.

ISSUE	YEAR OF RELEASE	COLOURS	SPARE TYRE CARRIER	SEATS	RADIATOR CASTING	STEERING WHEEL	PLATED PARTS	REAR WING BRACE	REAR NUMBER PLATE TYPE	WHEELS	BASEPLATE	RARITY	BOX TYPE	VALUE	CHECK LIST
1	1963	Metallic green body & chassis	4 prong	Bright red	Type 1*	Metallic green	Brass	A	1	Brass 12 spoke	LESNEY No2 ENGLAND	R	D1	£50	
2		Metallic green body & chassis	4 prong	Bright red	Type 2	Metallic green	Brass	A	1	Brass 12 spoke	LESNEY No2 ENGLAND		D1	£30	
3		Metallic green body & chassis	4 prong	Bright red	Type 2	Metallic green	Brass	A	2	Brass 12 spoke	LESNEY No2 ENGLAND		D1/D2	£35	
4		Metallic green body & chassis	4 prong	Bright red	Type 2	Metallic green	Brass	B	1	Brass 12 spoke	LESNEY No2 ENGLAND		D1/D2	£30	
5		Metallic green body & chassis	4 prong	Bright red	Type 2	Metallic green	Brass	B	2	Brass 12 spoke	LESNEY No2 ENGLAND		D2/D3	£30	
6		Metallic green body & chassis	3 prong	Bright red	Type 2	Metallic green	Brass	B	2	Brass 12 spoke	LESNEY No2 ENGLAND		D2/D3/E/M	£25	
7	1968	Metallic green body & chassis	3 prong	Bright red	Type 2	Black plastic	Brass	B	2	Brass 12 spoke	LESNEY No2 ENGLAND		D3/E/E1/F/M	£20	✓

DIAGRAM 1 RADIATOR CASTING

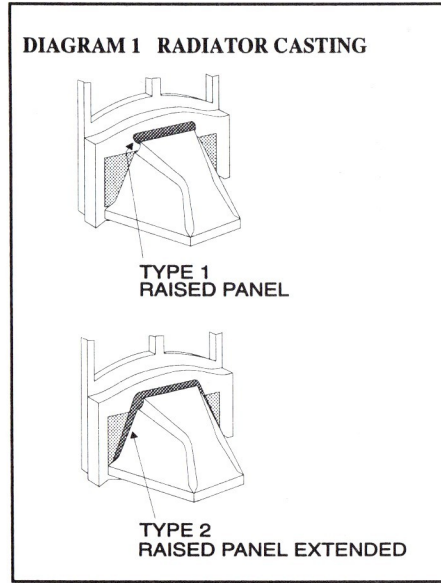

TYPE 1 RAISED PANEL

TYPE 2 RAISED PANEL EXTENDED

DIAGRAM 2 REAR WING BRACE

TYPE A   TYPE B

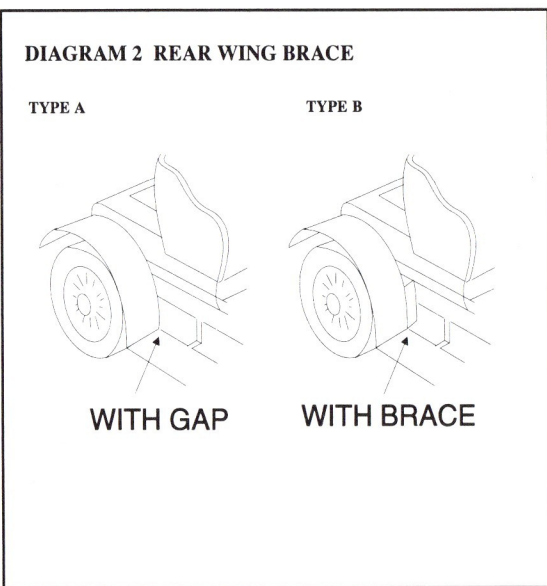

WITH GAP   WITH BRACE

DIAGRAM 3 REAR NUMBER PLATES

TYPE 2   TYPE 1

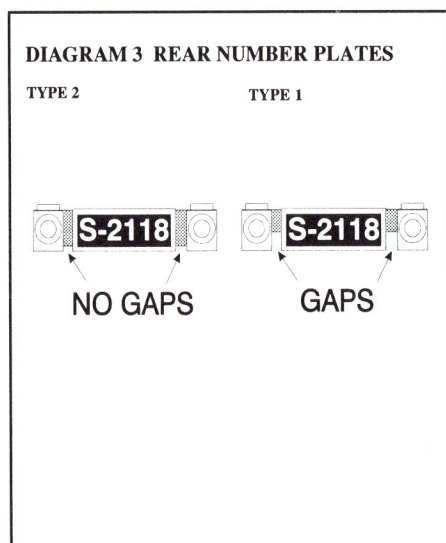

NO GAPS   GAPS

NOTES

Y2-3 1914 PRINCE HENRY VAUXHALL — Scale 1:47

INVESTMENT COMMENT
ORIGINAL PRICE £0.37.5p
Small growth has been noted for Issues 2, 5, 6 and 13. Little potential for the Woodgrain box issues, but watch the earlier issues.

The Vauxhall came to be one of the longest running models in the Yesteryear range. After the early production runs it was necessary to make a strengthening modification to the area of the sidelights (Diagram 1). A more easily recognisable modification was the addition of two floor braces measuring one mm deep and one mm high across the width of the floor. One brace was put in front of the front seat and the other directly behind it, as a securing measure. In 1975 a short run of blue, oversprayed red models were released into the East European market specifically Czechoslovakia, fitted with bright red seats. These red seated models have been found with, or without the floor braces. The colour of the blue models issues 5 to 11 can have a purpley tinge; particulary the chassis. Lesney Products were always experimenting with ways in which to make their models more attractive and tyres were one way in which to make the model more interesting. Colour trial tyres in grey or white have been seen fitted to pre-production Vauxhalls, but it is unlikely that they were ever intended to be released as production models. Grey tyres are found on experimental 26 spoke plastic wheels.

ISSUE	YEAR OF RELEASE	COLOURS	BONNET	PETROL TANK	SEATS	GRILLE	WHEELS	PLATED PARTS	FLOOR BRACES	SPARE WHEEL RIVET	SIDE LIGHTS REINFORCING RIBS	BASEPLATE	RARITY	BOX TYPE	VALUE	CHECK LIST
1	1970	Bright red body & chassis	Silver	Brass	Light cream	Bright red	Brass 26 spoke	Brass	No	Small	No	LESNEY © 1970 ENGLAND		F	£25	✓
2		Bright red body & chassis	Silver	Copper*	Light cream	Bright red	Brass 26 spoke	Brass	No	Small	Yes*	LESNEY © 1970 ENGLAND	V R	F	£150	
3		Bright red body & chassis	Silver	Brass	Light cream	Bright red	Brass 26 spoke	Brass	No	Small	Yes*	LESNEY © 1970 ENGLAND	S	F	£40	
4		Bright red body & chassis	Silver	Brass	Light cream	Black	Brass 26 spoke	Brass	No	Small	Yes*	LESNEY © 1970 ENGLAND	S	H	£40	
5	1975	Dark blue body & chassis	Silver	Copper	Bright red*	Black	Chrome 24 spoke	Brass	No	Small	Yes	LESNEY © 1970 ENGLAND	E R	H	£725	
6		Dark blue body & chassis	Silver	Copper	Bright red*	Black	Chrome 24 spoke	Brass	Yes	Small	Yes	LESNEY © 1970 ENGLAND	E R	H	£725	
7		Dark blue body & chassis	Silver	Brass	Light cream	Black	Chrome 24 spoke	Brass	No	Small	Yes	LESNEY © 1970 ENGLAND		H	£15	
8		Dark blue body & chassis	Silver	Copper*	Light cream	Black	Chrome 24 spoke	Brass	No	Small	Yes	LESNEY © 1970 ENGLAND	S	H	£35	
9		Dark blue body & chassis	Silver	Brass	Light cream	Black	Chrome 24 spoke	Brass	Yes	Small	Yes	LESNEY © 1970 ENGLAND		H	£12	
10		Dark blue body & chassis	Silver	Copper*	Light cream	Black	Chrome 24 spoke	Brass	Yes	Small	Yes	LESNEY © 1970 ENGLAND	S	H	£35	
11		Dark blue body & chassis	Silver	Brass	Light cream	Black	Chrome 12 spoke	Brass	Yes	Small	Yes	LESNEY © 1970 ENGLAND	D	H	£15	
12	1979	Bright red body, black chassis	Silver	Brass	Light cream	Black	Dark red 12 spoke BW	Brass	Yes	Small	Yes	LESNEY © 1970 ENGLAND		I	£10	
13		Orange* red body, black chassis	Silver	Brass	Light cream	Black	Red 12 spoke WW	Brass	Yes	Small	Yes	LESNEY © 1970 ENGLAND	R	I	£100	
14	1984	Lighter red body, black chassis	Silver	Brass	Light cream	Black	Red 12 spoke WW	Brass	Yes	Large	Yes	LESNEY © 1970 ENGLAND		I	£10	✓

DIAGRAM 1 SIDE LIGHTS REINFORCING RIBS

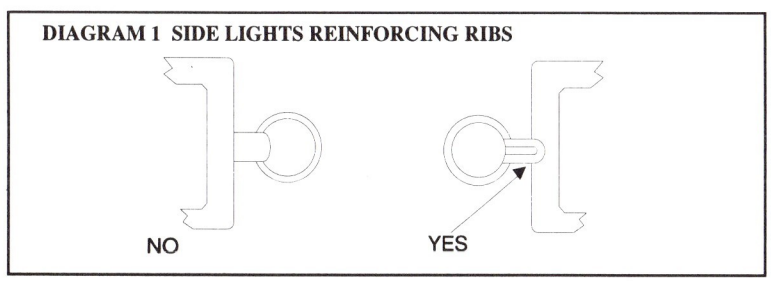

NO — YES

DIAGRAM 2 FLOOR BRACES

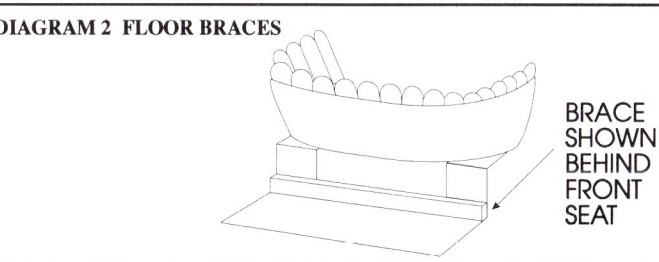

BRACE SHOWN BEHIND FRONT SEAT

NOTES
BECKENHAM APPEAL MODEL
1. 1979 - Yellow body and chassis, bright red seats, chrome 24 spoke wheels, brass petrol tank, front seat braces, and cast sidelight reinforcing rib.
2. Y2-3 seats are the same casting type as used on the Y13-2 Daimler and the colour of the white plastic used can vary from off-white to cream.
3. Issue 12 has black paint oversprayed on dark blue painted chassis/baseplates.

Y 2-4 1930 4½ LITRE BENTLEY

Scale 1:40

INVESTMENT COMMENT
ORIGINAL PRICE £ 3.99p

Values for all issues are climbing steadily, although the earlier green issues have probably been stifled by overproduction. The dark blue Bentley without the threaded screw hole has potential.

This model was the first Yesteryear to use a nylon compound for the mudguards. Prototype models were made entirely in plastic by an Essex based tool making firm in order to test Matchbox's tools. A minor colour variation is associated with early production models (Issue 1) in that the self coloured nylon components did not really match the green body colour; but this was rectified for later issues. When production moved to Macau, a different type of paint was used and consequently (Issue 4) the model was released in a lighter shade of green. The new press-fit axle soon became standard. In 1989 the Bentley in an attractive dark blue was released in the U.S.A. as one of the "Great Motor Cars of the Century" promotion. These were packaged in plain white boxes with black lettering and sold as a mail order item for just under US$20.00. These early blue models were released without cast screw holes and are quite difficult to find on the collectors market. Issues 7 and 8 were released as a range model to all the Matchbox markets. In 1991 a short run of the blue Bentley was made at the new factory in China as one of the "Chinese six". The dark burgundy model was released in December 1991 as part of the 1992 range.

ISSUE	YEAR OF RELEASE	COLOURS	TONNEAU	DASH BOARD	SEATS	BONNET STRAPS	STEERING WHEEL	PLATED PARTS	MUDGUARDS	RADIATOR SHELL	GRILLE	UNION FLAG	WHITE 7	THREADED SCREW HOLE	WHEELS	AXLES	BASEPLATE	RARITY	BOX TYPE	VALUE	CHECK LIST
1	1985	Dark green body & chassis	Black	Mid brown	Mid brown	Mid brown	Black	Chrome	Dark muddy green	Chrome	Chrome	Yes	No	No	Dark green 24 spoke	Riveted	MATCHBOX © 1985 ENGLAND		J	£7	
2		Dark green body & chassis	Black	Mid brown	Mid brown	Mid brown	Black	Chrome	Dark green	Chrome	Chrome	Yes	No	No	Dark green 24 spoke	Riveted	MATCHBOX © 1985 ENGLAND		J	£7	
3		Dark green body & chassis	Black	Light brown	Light brown	Light brown	Black	Chrome	Dark green	Chrome	Chrome	Yes	No	No	Dark green 24 spoke	Riveted	MATCHBOX © 1985 ENGLAND		J	£7	✓
4	1988	Lighter green* body & chassis	Black	Light brown	Light brown	Light brown	Black	Chrome	Dark muddy green	Chrome	Chrome	Yes	No	No	Light green 24 spoke	Riveted*	MATCHBOX © 1985 MACAU	R	J1	£50	
5		Lighter green* body & chassis	Black	Light brown	Light brown	Light brown	Black	Chrome	Dark muddy green	Chrome	Chrome	Yes	No	No	Light green 24 spoke	Press fit	MATCHBOX © 1985 MACAU	D	J1	£25	
6		Lighter green* body & chassis	Black	Light brown	Light brown	Light brown	Black	Chrome	Dark* green	Chrome	Chrome	Yes	No	No	Light green 24 spoke	Press fit	MATCHBOX © 1985 MACAU	D	J1	£25	
7	1989	Dark blue body & chassis	Black	Black	Black	Black	Tan	Chrome	Dark blue	Brass	Gloss black	Yes	Yes	No*	Dark blue 24 spoke	Press fit	MATCHBOX © 1985 MACAU	D	P*	£30	
8	1990	Dark blue body & chassis	Black	Black	Black	Black	Olive green	Chrome	Dark blue	Brass	Gloss black	Yes	Yes	Yes	Dark blue 24 spoke	Press fit	MATCHBOX © 1985 MACAU		N	£10	✓ 2X
9		Dark blue body & chassis	Black	Black	Black	Black	Tan	Chrome	Dark blue	Brass	Gloss black	Yes	Yes	Yes	Dark blue 24 spoke	Press fit	MATCHBOX © 1985 MACAU		N	£10	
10	1991	Dark blue body & chassis	Black	Black	Black	Black	Tan	Chrome	Black	Chrome	Gloss black	Yes	Yes	Yes	Chrome 24 spoke	Press fit	MATCHBOX © 1985 CHINA*	S	J2	£25	
11	1991	Burgundy body & chassis	Black	Black	Mid brown	Black	Tan, black spokes	Chrome	Black	Chrome	Gloss black	No	No	Yes	Chrome 24 spoke	Press fit	MATCHBOX © 1985 CHINA		N1	£15	✓

NOTES

1. Total production of the lighter green Bentley (Macau) was 5079.
2. Total production of the dark blue Bentley was 24,444.
3. Factory errors have resulted in some of the dark blue Bentley models not having the white 7. These are negative variations.
4. Cross over models have been reported with dark green bodies and lighter green chassis.

INVESTMENT COMMENT
ORIGINAL PRICE £ 0.11.5p
Still the most common of all the First Series and prices are presently good value. Issue 2 and 5 are still worth seeking out. As with all early Yesteryears, overseas markets such as Australia and New Zealand attract a premium on all values.

Y3-1 1907 LONDON 'E' CLASS TRAMCAR   Scale 1:130

There are several easily recognisable modifications to the casting of the Tram, caused in the main by wear and tear to the tools. The quadrant shaped opening under the stairs was eventually filled in as flashing was partially filling the opening. See diagram 1. Issues 1 to 5 have both openings fully open. Issues 6 and 7 have both recesses under the stairs partially filled in whereas Issues 8 onwards have the area fully filled in. For similar reasons the holes providing access to the upper deck were eventually filled in. See diagram 2. Lesney engineers noted that the cowcatcher was fragile and after Issues 1 and 2, this area was thickened by a strengthening brace. For no known reason, in some instances the baseplate was painted in grey (Issues 2 and 5) and these variants are seldom seen for sale. By 1962 the wheels were changed from an unpainted metal to black plastic. Although the livery decorations remained constant, two different sets of transfers were used. One set has a white background whereas the other is cream/off white. A gold or silver paint was used to highlight the driver's controls and the headlights but due to an oversight, or for cost saving measures, this trim can be partially, or totally omitted.

ISSUE	YEAR OF RELEASE	COLOURS	ROOF	ACCESS TO UPPER DECK	LIGHTS	WHEELS	RECESS UNDER STAIRS	COW CATCHER TYPE	DRIVERS CONTROL	BASEPLATE COLOUR	BASEPLATE	RARITY	BOX TYPE	VALUE	CHECK LIST
1	1956	London Transport red body	Cream	Open	Silver	Grenodised solid	Yes	Grey thin*	Gold	Black	LESNEY No3 ENGLAND	R	A	£125	
2		London Transport red body	Cream	Open	Silver	Grenodised solid	Yes	Grey thin*	Gold	Grey*	LESNEY No3 ENGLAND	V R	A	£250	
3		London Transport red body	Cream	Open	Silver	Grenodised solid	Yes	Grey thick	Gold	Black	LESNEY No3 ENGLAND		A	£100	
4		London Transport red body	Cream	Open	Gold	Grenodised solid	Yes	Grey thick	Gold	Black	LESNEY No3 ENGLAND		A	£100	
5		London Transport red body	Cream	Open	Silver	Grenodised solid	Yes	Grey thick	Gold	Grey*	LESNEY No3 ENGLAND	V R	A	£250	
6		London Transport red body	Cream	Open	Silver	Grenodised solid	Partial fill in	Grey thick	Gold	Black	LESNEY No3 ENGLAND		B/C	£75	✔
7		London Transport red body	White	Open	Silver	Grenodised solid	Partial fill in	Grey thick	Gold	Black	LESNEY No3 ENGLAND		B/C	£65	
8		London Transport red body	White	Open	Gold	Grenodised solid	Fully filled in	Grey thick	Gold	Black	LESNEY No3 ENGLAND		B/C	£65	
9		London Transport red body	Cream	Open	Gold	Grenodised solid	Fully filled in	Grey thick	Gold	Black	LESNEY No3 ENGLAND		B/C	£65	
10		London Transport red body	Cream	Closed	Gold	Grenodised solid	Fully filled in	Grey thick	Gold	Black	LESNEY No3 ENGLAND		B/C	£65	
11		London Transport red body	White	Closed	Gold	Grenodised solid	Fully filled in	Grey thick	Gold	Black	LESNEY No3 ENGLAND		B/C/D1	£65	
12	1962	London Transport red body	White*	Open*	Gold	Black plastic solid	Fully filled in	Grey thick	Gold	Black	LESNEY No3 ENGLAND	S	D1/D2	£70	
13		London Transport red body	Cream	Open*	Gold	Black plastic solid	Fully filled in	Grey thick	Gold	Black	LESNEY No3 ENGLAND	D	D1/D2	£70	
14		London Transport red body	Cream	Closed	Gold	Black plastic solid	Fully filled in	Grey thick	Gold	Black	LESNEY No3 ENGLAND		D1/D2	£70	
15		London Transport red body	White*	Closed	Gold	Black plastic solid	Fully filled in	Grey thick	Gold	Black	LESNEY No3 ENGLAND	D	D2	£75	
16	1965	London Transport red body	White*	Closed	Gold	Black plastic solid	Fully filled in	White thick*	Gold	Black	LESNEY No3 ENGLAND	D	D2	£125	✔

DIAGRAM 1 RECESS OPENING UNDER STAIRS

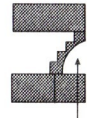

THIS AREA 'OPEN'   THIS AREA 'CLOSED'

DIAGRAM 2 ACCESS TO UPPER DECK

OPEN

DIAGRAM 3 COW CATCHER TYPE

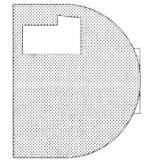

THIN   THICK
VIEWED FROM UNDERNEATH

LIVERY
Transfers
Upper panels. BEST SUNDAY PAPER, NEWS OF THE WORLD, WORLD'S RECORD SALE in dark blue on white or cream panel.
Lower panels. LONDON TRANSPORT in yellow.
End panels. BUY LESNEY TOYS in black on white square below stairs.
Destination Boards. CITY in black on white with black border.

NOTES

Y3-2 1910 BENZ LIMOUSINE   Scale 1:54

INVESTMENT COMMENT
ORIGINAL PRICE £0.20p
This model has many variations but only a few attract high prices. Issue 6, newly coded, is good value presently, and worth the effort to find.

The Benz was introduced in 1965, phased out in 1972 but re-issued in 1984 as one of the six Yesteryears in the Connoisseur set. On early models (Issues 1, 2 & 3) the headlamps were cast as a separate component to the radiator shell. They were located behind the radiator and because of the design of their arms, could be fixed in either a high or a low position. This was due only to a correct or incorrect assembly! From then onwards the lamps were cast as part of the radiator shell and can only be found in the correct low position. With the exception of the last issue, all Benz models were fitted with three prong tyre carriers. Issue 16 was given runningboard treads highlighted in silver. Some differences have been noted regarding the finish to the black roof component. This finish can vary between matt and satin, but not shiny enough to be termed a glossy finish. There are two types of running board. Type A has a deep casting groove. Type B is inset rather than cast on top. Other variations include five different side lamp castings. Several hard to find interim colour combinations exist, and very rare pre-production colour trial models also exist, the most attractive one being the metallic purple variant as shown in the 1991 Matchbox Models of Yesteryear Calendar. As the grilles and seats are very easily inter-changeable these have been recorded as one issue. It should be noted that the grilles are also the same size and shape as used on the Y9 Simplex and the Y12 Thomas Flyabout. The 1970 issues have also been seen fitted with experimental grey tyres, but they were never officially released.

ISSUE	YEAR OF RELEASE	COLOURS	ROOF	SEATS	GRILLE	STEERING WHEEL	WHEELS	PLATED PARTS	SPARE TYPE CARRIER	REAR WING INFILL WEB	TWO HOLES IN BASEPLATE	BASEPLATE	RARITY	BOX TYPE	VALUE	CHECK LIST
1	1965	Cream body & chassis	Dark green	Green or red	Green or red	Cream metal	Brass 12 spoke	Brass	3 prong	Open*	Yes	LESNEY © ENGLAND	R	E	£75	
2		Cream body & chassis	Dark green	Green or red	Green or red	Cream metal	Brass 12 spoke	Brass	3 prong	Cast	Yes	LESNEY © ENGLAND		E	£40	
3		Cream body & chassis	Chartreuse yellow*	Green or red	Green or red	Cream metal	Brass 12 spoke	Brass	3 prong	Cast	Yes	LESNEY © ENGLAND	V R	E/E1	£250	
4	1969	Light green body & chassis	Dark green*	Green or red	Green or red	Light green metal	Brass 12 spoke	Brass	3 prong	Cast	Yes	LESNEY © ENGLAND	V R	E/E1/F	£250	
5		Light green body & chassis	Chartreuse yellow	Green or red	Green or red	Light green metal	Brass 12 spoke	Brass	3 prong	Cast	Yes	LESNEY © ENGLAND		E1/F	£40	
6		Light green body & chassis	Chartreuse yellow	Green or red	Green or red	Light green metal	Brass 12 spoke	Brass	3 prong	Open*	Yes	LESNEY © ENGLAND	R	E1/F	£100	
7		Light green body & chassis	Chartreuse yellow	Green or red	Green or red	Black plastic	Brass 12 spoke	Brass	3 prong	Cast	Yes	LESNEY © ENGLAND		F	£40	
8		Light green body & chassis	Black*	Green or red	Green or red	Light green metal	Brass 12 spoke	Brass	3 prong	Cast	Yes	LESNEY © ENGLAND	S	F	£125	
9		Light green body & chassis	Black*	Green or red	Green or red	Black plastic	Brass 12 spoke	Brass	3 prong	Cast	Yes	LESNEY © ENGLAND	S	F	£125	
10	1970	Dark metallic green body & chassis	Chartreuse yellow*	Green or red	Green or red	Black plastic	Brass 12 spoke	Brass	3 prong	Cast	Yes	LESNEY © ENGLAND	V R	F	£250	
11		Dark metallic green body & chassis	Black	Green or red	Green or red	Black plastic	Brass 12 spoke	Brass	3 prong	Cast	Yes	LESNEY © ENGLAND		F/G	£25	✔
12		Dark metallic green body & chassis	Black	Green or red	Green or red	Black plastic	Brass 12 spoke	Brass	3 prong	Cast	No*	LESNEY © ENGLAND	S	G	£35	
13	1984	Black body & chassis with dark blue side panels	Matt black	Light tan	Dark brown	Black plastic	Silver 12 spoke	Silver	4 prong	Cast	No	MATCHBOX © 1984 LIMITED EDITION ENGLAND		K	The Set £95	

DIAGRAM 1 HEADLAMP POSITIONS

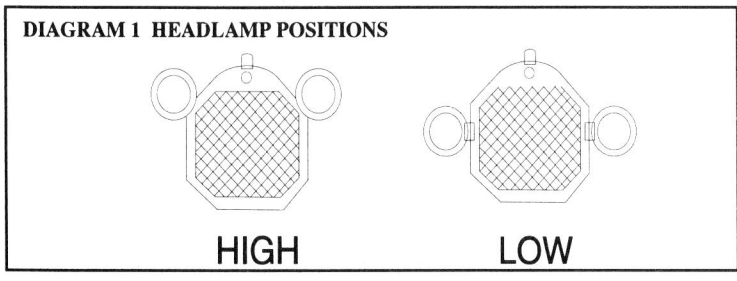

HIGH   LOW

DIAGRAM 2 REAR WING INFILL WEB

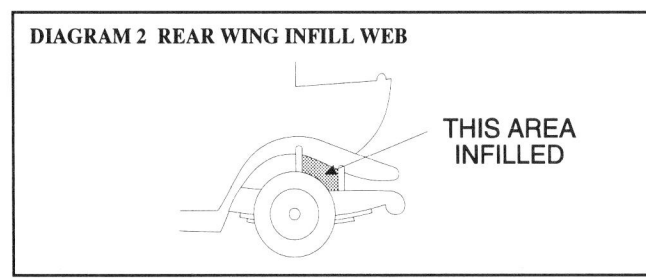

THIS AREA INFILLED

NOTES
1. Some issues 1-12 can be found with only one hole in the baseplate.
2. An example of Issue 6 in chipped condition sold for £90 at the 3rd MICA European Convention in 1995.

INVESTMENT COMMENT
ORIGINAL PRICE £0.55p

This model is seen for sale at relatively low prices. There have been small rises in one or two issues, but there appears to be plenty of stock on the market.

Y3-3 1934 RILEY MPH

Scale 1:35

First issued in the U.S.A. in late 1974 and to other markets in 1975; the Riley was one of the new Yesteryears in the relaunched range. Pre-production trial models have been reported with dark red, green and yellow seats, grilles and 26 spoke experimental wheels but is unlikely that any of these were intended to be released as production models. The 'red' model was produced in three distinct shades of red and many models exist with mis-matched red bodies and chassis components. The metallic purple model issues were released primarily in the North American market. When the 'red' Riley was replaced by the blue, extra decoration in the form of a door transfer was added. The number '3' is hard to find and the number '9' is no more than an upside down '6' (a negative variation)!

ISSUE	YEAR OF RELEASE	COLOURS	SEATS	GRILLE	DOOR DECALS	WHEELS	PLATED PARTS	BASEPLATE	RARITY	BOX TYPE	VALUE	CHECK LIST
1	1974	Metallic purple body & chassis	Black*	Black*	N/A	Chrome 12 spoke	Chrome	LESNEY © 1973 ENGLAND	V R	H	£280	
2		Metallic purple body & chassis	Black*	Black*	N/A	Chrome 24 spoke	Chrome	LESNEY © 1973 ENGLAND	V R	H	£280	
3		Metallic purple body & chassis	White	White	N/A	Chrome 24 spoke	Chrome	LESNEY © 1973 ENGLAND		H	£30	
4		Metallic purple body & chassis	White	White	N/A	Chrome 12 spoke	Chrome	LESNEY © 1973 ENGLAND		H	£30	
5	1975	Ruby red body & chassis	White	White	N/A	Chrome 12 spoke	Chrome	LESNEY © 1973 ENGLAND		H	£25	
6		Ruby red body & chassis	White	White	N/A	Chrome 24 spoke	Chrome	LESNEY © 1973 ENGLAND		H	£20	
7		Dark red body & chassis	White	White	N/A	Chrome 24 spoke	Chrome	LESNEY © 1973 ENGLAND		H	£15	
8		Dark red body & chassis	White	White	N/A	Chrome 12 spoke	Chrome	LESNEY © 1973 ENGLAND		H	£25	
9		Light red body & chassis	White	White	N/A	Chrome 24 spoke	Chrome	LESNEY © 1973 ENGLAND		H	£15	
10		Light red body & chassis	White	White	N/A	Chrome 12 spoke	Chrome	LESNEY © 1973 ENGLAND		H	£15	
11		Light red body & chassis	White	White	N/A	Red 12 spoke*	Chrome	LESNEY © 1973 ENGLAND	D	H	£40	
12	1979	Mid blue body & chassis	White	White	Black 6	Chrome 24 spoke (BW)	Chrome	LESNEY © 1973 ENGLAND		I	£10	✓
13		Mid blue body & chassis	White	White	Black 3*	Chrome 24 spoke	Chrome	LESNEY © 1973 ENGLAND	S	I	£40	
14		Mid blue body & chassis	White	White	Black 6	Chrome 12 spoke*	Chrome	LESNEY © 1973 ENGLAND	D	I	£30	
15	1980	Mid blue body & chassis	White	White	Black 6	Red 12 spoke*	Chrome	LESNEY © 1973 ENGLAND	D	I	£30	

NOTES
1. BECKENHAM APPEAL MODEL 1979. Pale brown body and dark brown chassis, white seats and grille, chrome 24 spoke wheels.

Y3-4 1912 FORD MODEL 'T' TANKER
Scale 1:35

BP. The Y3 Tanker is largely based upon the Y12 Ford Model 'T' Van and used the same chassis, windscreen, radiator assembly and wheels. As a result of this doubling up of standard components, Lesney removed the No. Y12 designation from the baseplate as it was to be used for both the Y12 and the Y3 concurrently. Many variations of the 'BP' logo, caused by the temperamental tampo printing process, have been recorded. The most notable paint variation is Issue 4 which has the tank filler caps with painted black tops instead of gold. Models which were fitted with brass or copper coloured cab roofs were not intended for release and are classified as 'Friday afternoon' models. Finally, the 'BP' tanker was also released in 1982 in a five model gift set. (Issue 3).

ZEROLENE. The 'Zerolene' was an incentive model given by Matchbox (Lesney) to their retailers who had ordered a poor selling five model gift set, of which 50,000 had been produced. Retailers were encouraged to sell these sets and give the Zerolene away free! Many retailers did this; but those who didn't sold them for three times the price of a standard 1982 Yesteryear. In total, 35,000 Zerolene models were released, 20,000 for the UK market and the majority of the balance to the European market. Baseplates were painted with either a matt or gloss black finish. A short final run were fitted with the wheels normally associated with the next livery; 'Express Dairy'.

A : BP (BRITISH PETROLEUM)

ISSUE	YEAR OF RELEASE	COLOURS	ROOF	SEAT	WINDSCREEN/ RADIATOR	WHEELS	PLATED PARTS	TANK FILLER CAPS	"BP" LOGO	No. Y12 CAST ON BASE	BASEPLATE	RARITY	BOX TYPE	VALUE	CHECK LIST
1	1981	Dark green body, bright red tank, glossy black chassis	White	Black plastic	Gold	Red 12 spoke	Gold	Gold	With black shadow effect	Yes*	LESNEY © 1978 ENGLAND	V R	I	£125	
2		Dark green body, bright red tank, glossy black chassis	White	Black plastic	Gold	Red 12 spoke	Gold	Gold	With black shadow effect	No	LESNEY © 1978 ENGLAND		I	£10	
3		Dark green body, bright red tank, glossy black chassis	White	Black plastic	Gold	Red 12 spoke	Gold	Gold	No shadow effect	No	LESNEY © 1978 ENGLAND		I / L	£10	✓
4		Dark green body, bright red tank, glossy black chassis	White	Black plastic	Gold	Red 12 spoke	Gold	Black*	No shadow effect	No	LESNEY © 1978 ENGLAND	S	I	£60	
5		Dark green body, bright red tank, glossy black chassis	White	Black plastic	Gold	Gold* 12 spoke	Gold	Gold	No shadow effect	No	LESNEY © 1978 ENGLAND	D	I	£25	
6		Dark green body, bright red tank, glossy black chassis	White	Black plastic	Gold	Chrome* 12 spoke	Gold	Gold	With black shadow effect	No	LESNEY © 1978 ENGLAND	D	I	£25	

B : ZEROLENE

ISSUE	YEAR OF RELEASE	COLOURS	ROOF	SEAT	WINDSCREEN/ RADIATOR	WHEELS	PLATED PARTS	TANK FILLER CAPS	"BP" LOGO	No. Y12 CAST ON BASE	BASEPLATE	RARITY	BOX TYPE	VALUE	CHECK LIST
1	1982	Bright green body, tank, glossy black chassis*	White	Black plastic	Gold	Gold 12 spoke	Gold	Gold	N/A	No	LESNEY © 1978 ENGLAND	D	I	£40	
2		Bright green body, tank, matt black chassis*	White	Black plastic	Gold	Gold 12 spoke	Gold	Gold	N/A	No	LESNEY © 1978 ENGLAND	S	I	£40	
3		Bright green body, tank, glossy black chassis*	White	Black plastic	Gold	Red* 12 spoke	Gold	Gold	N/A	No	LESNEY © 1978 ENGLAND	D	I	£80	

DIAGRAM 1 Y12 CAST ON BASE

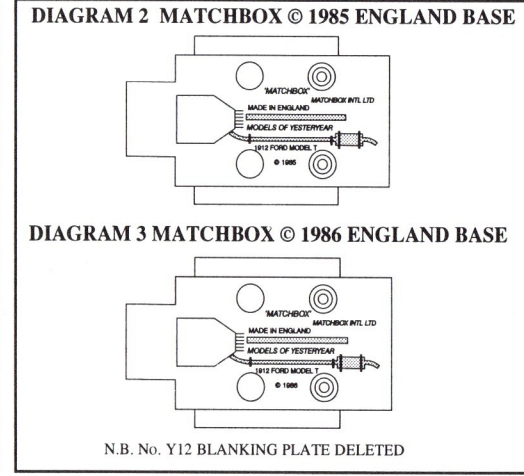

"No.Y12" BASE

Y NUMBER BLANKED OUT

DIAGRAM 2 MATCHBOX © 1985 ENGLAND BASE

DIAGRAM 3 MATCHBOX © 1986 ENGLAND BASE

N.B. No. Y12 BLANKING PLATE DELETED

LIVERY BP
Tampo
Tank sides. Gold B.P.
Lower body sides. White BRITISH PETROLEUM COMPANY LTD.
Cab sides. White 2603.
Cab doors. White 12 mph.
Roof header board. Black MOTOR "BP" SPIRIT

LIVERY ZEROLENE
Tampo
Tank sides. White ZEROLENE STANDARD OIL FOR MOTOR CARS.
Cab sides. White STANDARD OIL COMPANY
Cab doors. White No. 7
Roof header board. Black STANDARD OIL COMPANY.

INVESTMENT COMMENT
ORIGINAL PRICE Y3-4 BP & ZEROLENE £2.49p

BP Issue 1 is occasionally found for sale. Issue 4 with matt black filler caps is still desirable but do check its authenticity.
ZEROLENE Prices represent good value presently. Expect to pay more in the future. Still regarded as being a high profile model.

NOTES

Y3-4 1912 FORD MODEL 'T' TANKER (CONTINUED) Scale 1:35

EXPRESS DAIRY. Released in April 1983, the 'Express Dairy' was rumoured to be another short run model. This was not the case, with 90,000 being released to an eager market. The newly formed Matchbox Company used the model to send out 25,000 questionnaires of which they received back some 7,000. As part of a deal with Express Dairy, Matchbox agreed to change the wheels to red and all such models went to Express Dairy who used them for their own promotion to the dairy trade.

CARNATION. The 'Carnation' tanker was released in June 1984 and was the first Yesteryear to bear a different tampo printed design on either side of the cab. There were few significant variations and issues 5 and 6 were fitted with baseplates normally associated with the Y12-4 'Imbach'; the only difference being that the words 'Limited Edition' were deleted, and the cab steps reverted to full length running boards.

C : EXPRESS DAIRY

ISSUE	YEAR OF RELEASE	COLOURS	ROOF	SEAT	WINDSCREEN / RADIATOR	WHEELS	PLATED PARTS	TANK FILLER CAPS	BASEPLATE	RARITY	BOX TYPE	VALUE	CHECK LIST
1	1983	Blue body, glossy black chassis	White	Black plastic	Gold	Gold 12 spoke	Gold	Gold	LESNEY © 1978 ENGLAND		I	£8	✓
2		Blue body, glossy black chassis	White	Tan* plastic	Gold	Gold 12 spoke	Gold	Gold	LESNEY © 1978 ENGLAND	D	I	£25	
3		Blue body, glossy black chassis	White	Black plastic	Gold	Red * 12 spoke	Gold	Gold	LESNEY © 1978 ENGLAND	D	I	£20	
4		Blue body, glossy black chassis	White	Black plastic	Gold	Chrome 12 spoke	Gold	Gold	LESNEY © 1978 ENGLAND		I	£10	

D : CARNATION

ISSUE	YEAR OF RELEASE	COLOURS	ROOF	SEAT	WINDSCREEN / RADIATOR	WHEELS	PLATED PARTS	TANK FILLER CAPS	BASEPLATE	RARITY	BOX TYPE	VALUE	CHECK LIST
1	1984	Cream body, plum red tank & chassis	Cream	Black plastic	Gold	Bright red 12 spoke (W W)	Gold	Plum red	LESNEY © 1978 ENGLAND		J	£8	✓
2		Cream body, plum red tank & chassis	Cream	Pinky tan* plastic	Gold	Bright red 12 spoke (W W)	Gold	Plum red	LESNEY © 1978 ENGLAND	S	J	£30	
3		Cream body, plum red tank & chassis	Cream	Black plastic	Gold	Bright red 24* spoke (W W)	Gold	Plum red	LESNEY © 1978 ENGLAND	D	J	£20	
4		Cream body, plum red tank & chassis	Cream	Black plastic	Gold	Gold* 12 spoke	Gold	Plum red	LESNEY © 1978 ENGLAND	D	J	£20	
5	1986	Cream body, plum red tank & chassis	Cream	Black plastic	Gold	Bright red 12 spoke (W W)	Gold	Plum red	MATCHBOX © 1985 ENGLAND		J	£10	
6		Cream body, plum red tank & chassis	Cream	Black plastic	Gold	Plum* red 12 spoke (W W)	Gold	Plum red	MATCHBOX © 1985 ENGLAND	D	J	£15	

LIVERY EXPRESS DAIRY
Tampo
Tank sides. EXPRESS DAIRY in white.
Cab sides and lower body. BRANCHES ALL OVER LONDON EST 1864 in white.
Cab doors. White 163 and 12 MPH
Header board. White EXPRESS DAIRY on blue panel.
White coachlining.

LIVERY CARNATION
Tampo
Tank sides. CARNATION FARM PRODUCTS in white.
Cab doors. Red CARNATION FARM PRODUCTS COMPANY
Offside cab. One cream and two red carnations.
Near side cab. THE NAME STANDS FOR QUALITY in red.
Header board. Cream CARNATION on pale red panel.

INVESTMENT COMMENT
ORIGINAL PRICE, EXPRESS DAIRY & CARNATION £3.50p
Express Dairy. Overproduction still means there is little chance of growth. However, Issue 3 with red spoked wheels has risen a little since 1992/1993. Beware of wheel switching.
Carnation. Still a popular model although values are just steady.
NOTES

Y3-4 1912 FORD MODEL 'T' TANKER (CONTINUED) Scale 1:35

MOBILOIL. The 'Mobiloil' tanker was issued in 1985 as a Limited Edition of 80,000. The only notable variation is the colour of plastic seat. The original price in 1985 was £3.99.

CASTROL. The 'Castrol' tanker was originally to have been released one year earlier. It was released in August 1986 replacing the 'Carnation' tanker as the standard range model. During its time in the range, three different baseplates were used and the total production run was 109,000. The original price in 1986 was £3.99. The three baseplate types are still eagerly sought by variation collectors.

E : MOBILOIL

ISSUE	YEAR OF RELEASE	COLOURS	ROOF	SEAT	RADIATOR & WINDSCREEN	WHEELS	PLATED PARTS	TANK FILLER CAPS	BASEPLATE	RARITY	BOX TYPE	VALUE	CHECK LIST
1	1985	Bright red cab doors & bonnet, dark blue tank & body, glossy black chassis	Dark blue	Black* plastic	Gold	Dull red 12 spoke	Gold	Dark blue	LESNEY © 1978 ENGLAND	D	J	£20	
2		Bright red cab doors & bonnet, dark blue tank & body, glossy black chassis	Dark blue	Pinky tan plastic	Gold	Dull red 12 spoke	Gold	Dark blue	LESNEY © 1978 ENGLAND		J	£8	✓
3		Bright red cab doors & bonnet, dark blue tank & body, glossy black chassis	Dark blue	Pinky tan plastic	Gold	Dull red 24* spoke	Gold	Dark blue	LESNEY © 1978 ENGLAND	D	J	£15	

F: CASTROL

ISSUE	YEAR OF RELEASE	COLOURS	ROOF	SEAT	RADIATOR	WINDSCREEN	WHEELS	PLATED PARTS	TANK FILLER CAPS	BASEPLATE	RARITY	BOX TYPE	VALUE	CHECK OIST
1	1986	Dark green body & tank, gloss black chassis	White	Dark tan*	Gold	Gold	Maroon 12 spoke	Gold	Dark green	LESNEY © 1978 ENGLAND	D	J /L		£15
2		Dark green body & tank, gloss black chassis	White	Pinky tan	Gold	Gold	Maroon 12 spoke	Gold	Dark green	LESNEY © 1978 ENGLAND		J		£10
3		Dark green body & tank, gloss black chassis	White	Black*	Gold	Gold	Maroon 12 spoke	Gold	Dark green	LESNEY © 1978 ENGLAND	S	J		£20
4		Dark green body & tank, gloss black chassis	White	Pinky tan	Chrome*	Gold	Maroon 12 spoke	Gold	Dark green	LESNEY © 1978 ENGLAND	S	J		£20
5		Dark green body & tank, gloss black chassis	White	Pinky tan	Gold	Gold	Gold* 12 spoke	Gold	Dark green	LESNEY © 1978 ENGLAND	D	J		£15
6		Dark green body & tank, gloss black chassis	White	Pinky tan	Gold	Gold	Maroon 12 spoke	Gold	Dark green	MATCHBOX © 1985 ENGLAND		J		£10
7		Dark green body & tank, gloss black chassis	White	Pinky tan	Gold	Gold	Dull red 12 spoke	Gold	Dark green	MATCHBOX © 1985 ENGLAND		J	✓	£10
8		Dark green body & tank, gloss black chassis	White	Pinky tan	Gold	Gold	Gold 12 spoke	Gold	Dark green	MATCHBOX © 1986 ENGLAND	S	J		£20
9		Dark green body & tank, gloss black chassis	White	Pinky tan	Gold	Chrome*	Gold 12 spoke	Gold	Dark green	MATCHBOX © 1986 ENGLAND	D	J		£15
10		Dark green body & tank, gloss black chassis	White	Pinky tan	Gold	Chrome*	Chrome *12 spoke	Gold	Dark green	MATCHBOX © 1986 ENGLAND	D	J		£15

LIVERY MOBILOIL
Tampo
Tank sides MOBIL OIL in dark blue with white outline; with white ovals with red gargoyles each side.
Tank rear end. White oval with blue coachlining surrounding blue VACUUM OIL COMPANY LTD above GARGOYLE, above black outlined red gargolye above blue LONDON
Cab sides. White VACUUM OIL COMPANY LTD
Cab doors. White 5 within white circle.
Roof header board. White outlined dark blue MOBIL OIL

LIVERY CASTROL
Tampo
Tank sides and rear end. White outlined CASTROL, with white REGD above gold MOTOR OIL
Cab sides. Gold WAKEFIELD MOTOR OIL
Cab doors. Gold ESTD 1899.
Roof header board. Red CASTROL within red coachlines.

DIAGRAM 1

"MATCHBOX © 1986 ENGLAND LIMITED EDITION" BASE

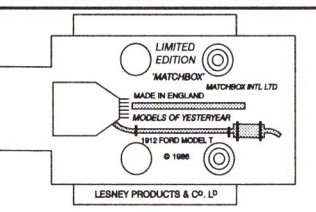

Y3-4 1912 FORD MODEL 'T' TANKER (CONTINUED) Scale 1:35

RED CROWN. The 'Red Crown' tanker was released as a Special Limited Edition model in December 1986. New features were the plastic tank side hoarding panels. A new component for the cab roof was incorporated along with a horizontal oval shaped cab window instead of the normal vertical oval type. Three different baseplates were used during production. Total production was 70,000.

SHELL. The 'Shell' model was released in September 1989 as the standard range Y3 for 1990. The factory experienced difficulties when it came to matching the yellow components; pre-production examples seen, have cabs of a different shade to the tanks. The red ink used for the tampo design on the header board can often appear to be pink which is due to the background colour showing through an application of weak red ink. Total production of the 'Shell' livery was 46,728.

G : RED CROWN

ISSUE	YEAR OF RELEASE	COLOURS	ROOF	SEAT	WINDSCREEN RADIATOR	WHEELS	COMPONENTS	TANK FILLER CAPS	HOSE HOLDALLS	BASEPLATE	RARITY	BOX TYPE	VALUE	CHECK LIST
1	1986	Bright red body & side hoardings, glossy black chassis	Bright red smooth	Black plastic	Gold	Gold 12 spoke	Gold	Bright red	Brass	MATCHBOX © 1986 LIMITED EDITION ENGLAND		J	£12	✓
2		Bright red body & side hoardings, glossy black chassis	Bright red smooth	Black plastic	Gold	Gold 12 spoke (B W)	Gold	Bright red	Brass	LESNEY © 1978 ENGLAND*	D	J	£20	
3		Bright red body & side hoardings, glossy black chassis	Bright red smooth	Black plastic	Gold	Gold 12 spoke	Gold	Bright red	Brass	MATCHBOX © 1985 ENGLAND*	R	J	£30	
4		Bright red body & side hoardings, glossy black chassis	Bright red smooth	Black plastic	Gold	Gold 12 spoke	Gold	Bright red	Brass	MATCHBOX © 1986 ENGLAND*		J	£12	

H : SHELL

ISSUE	YEAR OF RELEASE	COLOURS	ROOF	SEAT	WINDSCREEN RADIATOR	WHEELS	COMPONENTS	TANK FILLER CAPS	HOSE HOLDALLS	BASEPLATE	RARITY	BOX TYPE	VALUE	CHECK LIST
1	1989	Yellow body, gloss black chassis	White	Black plastic	Gold	Red 12 spoke	Gold	Yellow	Black	MATCHBOX © 1986 MACAU		J 1	£10	✓

LIVERY RED CROWN
Tampo
Hoarding panels. RED CROWN GASOLINE in white with company logo in red, white and blue in centre roundel.
Rear of tank. RED CROWN GASOLINE in red with company logo in red, white and blue on white circle with blue ring edging.
Cab sides. STANDARD OIL COMPANY (CALIFORNIA) in white.
Cab doors. White 18 in a white circle.

LIVERY SHELL
Tampo
Tank sides. SHELL MOTOR SPIRIT with black shadow effect and Shell logo in red with black outlining.
Tank end. As tank sides but in oval shape with the shell logo in the centre.
Cab sides. SHELL - MEX LTD in red with black shadow effect with KINGSWAY. LONDON, W.C.2 in red below with red coachlining.
Header board. SHELL in red within red coachline.

INVESTMENT COMMENT
ORIGINAL PRICE, RED CROWN & SHELL £8.99p
Red Crown Good steady growth due to a relatively low production run.

SHELL Surprisingly little or no interest in this, the last Y3 tanker made in the 1980s.
NOTES

Y4-1 1928 SENTINEL STEAM WAGGON Scale 1:100

INVESTMENT COMMENT
ORIGINAL PRICE £0.11.5p

The value of this model has suffered from the number of models coming onto the market in the last few years from 'retiring collectors'. All values are depressed but should pick up.

The Sentinel had a production life of a mere five years, and was based on a Sentinel which delivered flour to an Enfield bakery, quite close to the Lesney factory. The model was only produced in a deep blue with waterslide decals applied; the colour of which can vary between a yellow and an orange. In common with all early Yesteryears the first versions of the Sentinel had axles, crimped at one end to retain the wheels. The metal wheels were grenodised; a chemical solution which turned the metal a dull grey colour. To comply with safety regulations the axles were later replaced by ones with a single head; the other end once in place and holding the wheels would be spun over. By 1959/1960 the dies for the wheels were worn out, so black plastic wheels being used on the "Matchbox" Series miniatures were used. Gold trim was applied to brighten up what the retailers had termed a drab little model. Normally the small box on the right hand side of the chassis was painted gold; but some left the factory without this trim. This was not deliberate but instead a lapse on the part of a Lesney employee. As a 'negative' variation it has not been given a special monetary premium. The amount of trim to the chimney rim can vary.

ISSUE	YEAR OF RELEASE	COLOURS	CHIMNEY	CHIMNEY RIM	BOX	FRONT WHEELS	REAR WHEELS	AXLES	ROOF SUPPORTS	BASEPLATE	RARITY	BOX TYPE	VALUE	CHECK LIST
1	1956	Blue body, black cab interior & chassis	Black	Gold	Black	Grenodised 8 spoke	Grenodised 16 spoke daisy	Crimped	3	LESNEY ENGLAND		A	£80	
2		Blue body, black cab interior & chassis	Black	Gold	Gold	Grenodised 8 spoke	Grenodised 16 spoke daisy	Crimped	3	LESNEY ENGLAND		A	£80	✓
3		Blue body, black cab interior & chassis	Black	Gold	Gold	Grenodised 8 spoke	Grenodised 16 spoke daisy	Riveted*	3	LESNEY ENGLAND	D	A / B	£125	
4	1959/60	Blue body, black cab interior & chassis	Black	Gold	Gold	Black plastic* solid 24 tread	Black plastic* solid 24 tread	Riveted	3	LESNEY ENGLAND	V R	B	£150	

LIVERY
Transfers
Cab front, body sides and tail gate. Yellow SAND & GRAVEL SUPPLIES. All within red coachline.

NOTES
1. Models with the centre roof support missing are the result of this support being broken off during production.
2. The Yesteryear number, No.4, is to be found on the unpainted segment beneath the chimney stack forward of the front axle.

Y4-2 1905 SHAND MASON HORSE DRAWN FIRE ENGINE Scale 1:63

INVESTMENT COMMENT
ORIGINAL PRICE £0.20p
This classic model remains the most desirable of the early Yesteryears. The model in standard form passed the £100 mark in the mid-1980s and prices have held their own in recent years. Good growth noted for issues 6, 7 and 8. Still a must for any collection.

Due to the premature deterioration of the Y4-1 Sentinel tooling the Shand Mason became the first 'replacement' Yesteryear model. Originally it was going to be the first Y16 model! Main casting changes concerned the rear footplate, ashcan and slats; the raised relief to the hose locker sides and the horse to body draw bar. A minor casting modification was also made to the boiler. Originally this component was hollow but later the chimney was blocked off some 0.25 inches from the top. Models have been reported missing the brass plating finish to the boiler/pump component (Issues 6-14). Genuine firemen were made in black plastic and generally speaking early crew were trimmed in gold; but in time this 'extra' was abandoned. The commonest colours for the metal horses were black or white. Very early releases were given a distinctive grey hue! Also, a small run of models were fitted with 'bronze' coloured horses i.e. a metallic black with gold tints throughout. All of these casting changes, trim detail to the firemen and colours of the horses could result in dozens of permutations. So the listing below has been based upon the more well established issues. The Shand Mason model has always enjoyed huge popularity amongst collectors.

ISSUE	YEAR OF RELEASE	COLOURS	HORSE COLOURS	MANE & TAIL COLOURS	BOILER & PUMP	ASHCAN TO FOOTPLATE	HOSE LOCKER SIDES	HORSE TO BODY DRAWBAR	WHEELS	BLACK PLASTIC CREW	LOGO & TYPE	BASEPLATE	RARITY	BOX TYPE	VALUE	CHECK LIST
1	1960	Fire engine red body	Grey*	Dark grey*	Brass	Type A	Type A	Type 1	Front black 13 spoke rear black 15 spoke	3	KENT Type 1	LESNEY No 4 ENGLAND	E R	C	£600	
2		Fire engine red body	Grey*	White*	Brass	Type A	Type A	Type 1	Front black 13 spoke rear black 15 spoke	3	KENT Type 1	LESNEY No 4 ENGLAND	E R	C	£600	
3*		Fire engine red body	White	Grey	Brass	Type A	Type A	Type 1	Front black 13 spoke rear black 15 spoke	3	KENT Type 1*	LESNEY No 4 ENGLAND	S	C/D1	£175	
4		Fire engine red body	White	Grey	Brass	Type B*	Type A	Type 2*	Front black 13 spoke rear black 15 spoke	3	KENT Type 1	LESNEY No 4 ENGLAND	S	C/D1	£175	
5	1963	Fire engine red body	White*	Grey	Brass	Type A	Type A*	Type 1	Front black 13 spoke rear black 15 spoke	3	LONDON Type 2	LESNEY No 4 ENGLAND	R	D 1	£200	
6		Fire engine red body	White*	Grey	Brass	Type A	Type A*	Type 1	Front black 13 spoke rear black 15 spoke	3	LONDON Type 3	LESNEY No 4 ENGLAND	V R	D 1	£250	
7		Fire engine red body	White*	Grey	Brass	Type A	Type B	Type 2	Front black 13 spoke rear black 15 spoke	3	LONDON Type 3	LESNEY No 4 ENGLAND	V R	D 1/D 2/ D 3	£250	
8*		Fire engine red body	White	Grey	Brass	Type B	Type B	Type 2	Front black 13 spoke rear black 15 spoke	3	LONDON Type 3	LESNEY No 4 ENGLAND	V R	D 2/D 3	£250	✔

DIAGRAM 1 ASHCAN TO FOOTPLATE TYPES

A — 9 FULL & 3 PARTIAL SLOTS
B — 7 FULL SLOTS ONLY
C — MODIFIED ASH-CAN TO FOOTPLATE WEBS 7 FULL SLOTS ONLY

DIAGRAM 2 HOSE LOCKER SIDE TYPES

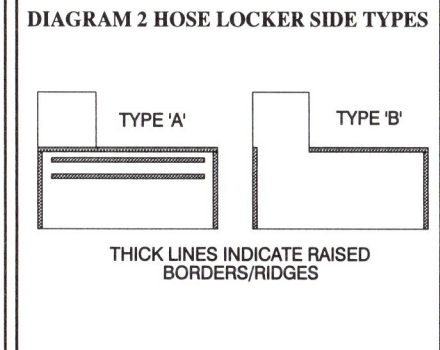

TYPE 'A' TYPE 'B'
THICK LINES INDICATE RAISED BORDERS/RIDGES

DIAGRAM 3 DRAWBAR TYPES

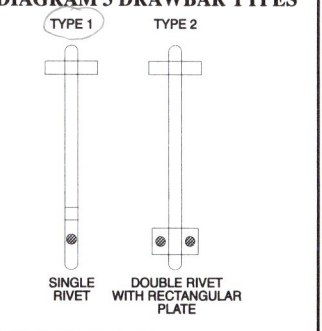

TYPE 1 — SINGLE RIVET
TYPE 2 — DOUBLE RIVET WITH RECTANGULAR PLATE

LIVERY

Transfers
Type 1. "KENT FIRE BRIGADE" on a single line, all in yellow.
Type 2. "LONDON FIRE BRIGADE" on two lines, all in yellow, within double dark blue border, and '72' in yellow on a dark blue panel.
Type 3. "LONDON FIRE BRIGADE" on two lines, all in yellow, within double black border, and '72' in yellow on a black panel.
Type 4. "LONDON FIRE BRIGADE" on two lines, all in yellow, within single gold border and '72' in yellow on black panel.

NOTES

1. The two braces connecting the ashcan to the footplate on Types A and B, can be 1mm or 2mm thick.

Y4-2 1905 SHAND MASON HORSE DRAWN FIRE ENGINE CONTINUED   Scale 1:63

ISSUE	YEAR OF RELEASE	COLOURS	HORSE COLOURS	MANE & TAIL COLOURS	BOILER & PUMP	ASHCAN TO FOOTPLATE	HOSE LOCKER SIDES	HORSE TO BODY DRAWBAR	WHEELS	BLACK PLASTIC CREW	LOGO & TYPE	BASEPLATE	RARITY	BOX TYPE	VALUE	CHECK LIST
9		Fire engine red body	Bronze*	White	Brass	Type B	Type A*	Type 2	Front black 13 spoke rear black 15 spoke	3	LONDON Type 3	LESNEY No 4 ENGLAND	V R	D 2 / D 3	£300	
10		Fire engine red body	Black	White	Brass	Type B	Type B	Type 2	Front black 13 spoke rear black 15 spoke	3	LONDON Type 3	LESNEY No 4 ENGLAND	VR	D 2 / D 3	£300	
11		Fire engine red body	Black	White	Brass	Type B	Type B	Type 2	Front black 13 spoke rear black 15 spoke	3	LONDON Type 3	LESNEY No 4 ENGLAND	S	D 2 / D 3	£175	
12		Fire engine red body	Black	White	Brass	Type B	Type A*	Type 2	Front black 13 spoke rear black 15 spoke	3	LONDON Type 4	LESNEY No 4 ENGLAND	R	D 2 / D 3	£200	
13*		Fire engine red body	Black	White	Brass	Type B	Type B	Type 2	Front black 13 spoke rear black 15 spoke	3	LONDON Type 4	LESNEY No 4 ENGLAND	D	D 2 / D 3	£150	
14*		Fire engine red body	Bronze*	White	Brass	Type C	Type B	Type 2	Front black 13 spoke rear black 15 spoke	3	LONDON Type 4	LESNEY No 4 ENGLAND	D	D 3	£150	

Y4-3 1909 OPEL COUPE

Scale 1:38

INVESTMENT COMMENT
ORIGINAL PRICE £0.22p
Values for standard issues have held steady and Issue 9 with its extremely rare hood window aperture has increased. Always a popular model with collectors especially the early white bodied models.

The Opel was first issued in 1967, phased out in 1976 but then re-issued as part of the Connoisseur set. The white model was fitted with three different baseplate components (see baseplate texts below). The most famous Opels are Issues 9 and 10 fitted with the rear windowed textured tan hood. Fakes have however been seen whereby the rear window has been cut out of the plastic, so check ones seen for sale carefully! Colour trial seats have also been seen; pale blue, green, pink, beige and mauve but unlikely that these were intended to be released as production models. The orange Opel was only issued with the Type C baseplate. The major casting modification was to the axle struts on the rear mudguards; these began as fully open, but with time, a strengthening wedge was added. The orange bodied models can vary from pale to dark orange and the difference is very obvious. All grilles incorporate the Opel logo. Finally it should be noted that the Opel found with the Connoisseur set, was given an enhanced trim and a tan textured hood with rear window. However knowing the value of this component, Matchbox had the foresight to cast 'Limited Edition' on the underside of the hood.

ISSUE	YEAR OF RELEASE	COLOURS	HOOD	BODY PINS	SEAT PINS	HOOD WINDOW	SEATS	GRILLE	WHEELS	REAR MUDGUARD STRUTS	PLATED PARTS	BASEPLATE TYPE	BASEPLATE	RARITY	BOX TYPE	VALUE	CHECK LIST
1	1967	White body & chassis	Tan smooth	Yes	No	No	Maroon	Maroon*	Brass 12 spoke	Open	Brass	A	LESNEY ENGLAND	R	E	£70	
2	1968	White body & chassis	Tan smooth	Yes	No	No	Maroon*	Bright red	Brass 12 spoke	Open	Brass	A	LESNEY ENGLAND	D	E	£30	
3		White body & chassis	Tan smooth	Yes	No	No	Bright red	Bright red	Brass 12 spoke	Open	Brass	A	LESNEY ENGLAND		E/E1	£20	
4		White body & chassis	Tan smooth	Yes	No	No	Bright red	Bright red	Brass 12 spoke	Open	Brass	B	LESNEY ENGLAND		E1/F/G	£20	
5		White body & chassis	Tan smooth	Yes	No	No	Bright red	Bright red	Brass 12 spoke	Open	Brass	C	LESNEY ENGLAND		F/G	£20	✓
6		White body & chassis	Tan smooth	No	Yes	No	Bright red	Bright red	Brass 12 spoke	Open	Brass	C	LESNEY ENGLAND		F/G	£20	
7		White body & chassis	Tan smooth	No	Yes	No	Bright red	Bright red	Brass 12 spoke	Closed	Brass	C	LESNEY ENGLAND		F/G	£20	
8		White body & chassis	Tan smooth	No	Yes	No	Maroon*	Bright red	Brass 12 spoke	Closed	Brass	C	LESNEY ENGLAND	D	F/G	£25	
9		White body & chassis	Tan textured*	No	Yes	Yes*	Bright red	Bright red	Brass 12 spoke	Closed	Brass	C	LESNEY ENGLAND	E R	F/G	£375	
10		White body & chassis	Tan textured*	No	Yes	Yes*	Maroon	Bright red	Brass 12 spoke	Closed	Brass	C	LESNEY ENGLAND	E R	F/G	£300	
11	1975	Orange body & gloss black chassis*	Black textured	No	Yes	Yes	Maroon	Light cream	Chrome 12 spoke	Closed	Brass	C	LESNEY ENGLAND	D	H	£30	
12		Orange body & matt black chassis	Black textured	No	Yes	Yes	Maroon	Light cream	Chrome 12 spoke	Closed	Brass	C	LESNEY ENGLAND		H	£20	
13		Orange body & matt black chassis	Black textured	No	Yes	Yes	Maroon	Light cream	Chrome 24 spoke	Closed	Brass	C	LESNEY ENGLAND		H	£20	
14	1984	Bright red body & dark red chassis	Tan textured	No	Yes	Yes	Ruby red	Black	Gold 12 spoke	Closed	Brass	D	MATCHBOX © 1984 LIMITED EDITION ENGLAND		K	£95 The Set	

DIAGRAM TEXT BASEPLATE TYPES

● BASEPLATE A
"Models of Yesteryear""1909 Opel Coupe" (One Line)
2 hollow bosses, 2 rivets in the sump

● BASEPLATE B
"Matchbox" "Models of Yesteryear" on a raised platform
"1909 Opel Coupe" (One Line)
2 hollow bosses, 2 rivets in sump.

DIAGRAM TEXT BASEPLATE TYPES

● BASEPLATE C
"Matchbox" "Models of Yesteryear" on a raised platform.
"1909 Opel Coupe" (2 Lines) No hollow bosses. Only 1 (one) rivet in the sump.

● BASEPLATE D
"Models of Yesteryear" "Limited Edition" " © 1984"
"1909 Opel Coupe" (1 line) No hollow bosses, one rivet in the sump. "Matchbox", "Made in England" on underside of running boards.

DIAGRAM 1 REAR MUDGUARD STRUTS

'OPEN' V SHAPE — 'HALF CLOSED' V SHAPE

NOTES

INVESTMENT COMMENT
ORIGINAL PRICE £0.49p
Issues 1 and 2 remain "blue chip". An example of Issue 1 was sold for £1,500 in 1994. All other issues have increased slightly, or remained constant.

Y4-4 1930 DUESENBERG MODEL "J" TOWN CAR   Scale 1:43

The final pre-production colour trial run of the red, white and yellow Duesenberg was rejected as being too garish and toy-like by the Lesney management. It was decided to change the colour scheme completely and at the same time revise some of the casting defects that were apparent from the first run, most notably, the roof section. All models were then destroyed with the exception of an estimated four boxes containing 144 models that erroneously left the factory for retail distribution. These extremely rare models have been located in toy shops as far away as Mexico City. The basic Duesenberg model has proved to be a consistent seller and was still in production in 1994. Examples of Issues 10 to 14 have been recorded where the metallic red paint slightly shows through the light green metallic paint because of over spraying previous issue chassis. The powder-blue model as issued in 1989 was first released onto the North American market by Matchbox Toys USA under the banner of 'Great Motor Cars of the Century'. These early enhanced models retailed for about double the normal retail price and were issued in white cardboard boxes with black print. All Y4 Duesenberg models destined for the USA lacked the self-tapping screw hole in the baseplate, and are a sought after variant. Total production of issues 26 to 29 was 26,099. In 1994 the powder blue bodied model was re-run as part of the Grand Classics series.

ISSUE	YEAR OF RELEASE	COLOURS	SIDE PANELS	REAR PANEL	HOOD	REAR WINDOW	SEATS	STEERING WHEEL	WHEELS	AIR HORNS	PLATED PARTS	Y4 ON BUMPER	AXLES	BASEPLATE	RARITY	BOX TYPE	VALUE	CHECK LIST
1	1976	White body orange* red chassis	N/A	N/A	Yellow*	7 mm*	Yellow*	Black	Chrome 24 spoke	Hollow	Chrome	No*	Riveted	LESNEY ENGLAND © 1975	E R	H	£1500	
2		White body orange* red chassis	N/A	N/A	Black*	7 mm*	Black	Black	Chrome 24 spoke	Hollow	Chrome	No*	Riveted	LESNEY ENGLAND © 1975	E R	H	£1500	
3	1976	Metallic dark red body & chassis	N/A	N/A	Black	8 mm	Black	Black	Chrome 24 spoke	Hollow	Chrome	No*	Riveted	LESNEY ENGLAND © 1975	R	H	£70	
4		Metallic dark red body & chassis	N/A	N/A	Black	8 mm	Black	Black	Chrome 24 spoke	Hollow	Chrome	Yes	Riveted	LESNEY ENGLAND © 1975		H	£10	
5		Metallic dark red body & chassis	N/A	N/A	Black	8 mm	Black	Black	Chrome 24 spoke	Solid	Chrome	Yes	Riveted	LESNEY ENGLAND © 1975		H	£15	
6		Metallic dark red body & chassis	N/A	N/A	Black	8 mm	Black	Black	Chrome 24 spoke	Solid	Chrome	No*	Riveted	LESNEY ENGLAND © 1975	R	H	£70	
7		Metallic dark red body & chassis	N/A	N/A	Black	8 mm	Black	Black	Chrome 12* spoke	Solid	Chrome	Yes	Riveted	LESNEY ENGLAND © 1975	D	H	£25	
8		Metallic dark red body & chassis	N/A	N/A	Maroon*	8 mm	Maroon*	Black	Chrome 24 spoke	Solid	Chrome	Yes	Riveted	LESNEY ENGLAND © 1975	R	H	£250	
9		Metallic dark red body & chassis	N/A	N/A	Green*	8mm	Green*	Black	Chrome 24 spoke	Solid	Chrome	Yes	Riveted	LESNEY ENGLAND © 1975	R	H	£100	
10	1979	Light metallic green body & chassis	Lime green*	Lime green*	Green	8 mm	Green	Black	Chrome solid	Hollow	Chrome	Yes	Riveted	LESNEY ENGLAND © 1975	S	I	£80	
11		Light metallic green body & chassis	Lime green*	Lime green*	Green	8 mm	Green	Black	Chrome* 24 spoke	Hollow	Chrome	Yes	Riveted	LESNEY ENGLAND © 1975	S	I	£80	
12		Light metallic green body & chassis	Lime green	Light metallic green	Green	8mm	Green	Black	Chrome solid(BW)	Hollow	Chrome	Yes	Riveted	LESNEY ENGLAND © 1975		I	£10	
13		Light metallic green body & chassis	Lime green	Light metallic green	Green	8mm	Green	Black	Chrome* 24 spoke	Hollow	Chrome	Yes	Riveted	LESNEY ENGLAND © 1975	D	I	£15	
14		Light metallic green body & chassis	Lime green	Light metallic green	Black*	8 mm	Black	Black	Chrome solid	Hollow	Chrome	Yes	Riveted	LESNEY ENGLAND © 1975	D	I	£20	

DIAGRAM 1 PASSENGER CEILING
ISSUES 1&2 ONLY
PASSENGER COMPARTMENT "CEILING"
FRONT

ISSUES 1 & 2
Also; bases have full length lugs to locate front bumper tab.
Front & Rear bumper tabs are not cast with 'Y4' on them. The lug/tab which locates the rear of the body to the baseplate is but 2 mm long (adjacent rear axle).

DIAGRAM 2 PASSENGER CEILING
ISSUES 3 ONWARDS
PASSENGER COMPARTMENT "CEILING"
FRONT

ISSUES 3 ONWARDS
Also; bases have ½ length lugs to locate front bumper tab.
Front & rear bumper tabs have 'Y4' cast on them. The lug/tab which locates the rear of the body to the baseplate is 4 mm long (adjacent rear axle).

NOTES
1. BECKENHAM APPEAL MODEL
Light brown body and brown chassis, black hood, solid air horns, chrome 24 spoke wheels and Lesney baseplate.

Y4-4 1930 DUESENBERG MODEL "J" TOWN CAR CONTINUED   Scale 1:43

ISSUE	YEAR OF RELEASE	COLOURS	SIDE PANELS	REAR PANELS	HOOD	REAR WINDOW	SEATS	STEERING WHEEL	WHEELS	AIR HORNS	PLATED PARTS	Y4 ON BUMPER	THREADED SCREW HOLE	AXLES	BASEPLATE	RARITY	BOX TYPE	VALUE	CHECK LIST
15	1983	Dark brown body & chassis	Dark cream	Dark brown	Cream	8 mm	Cream	Black	Chrome 24 spoke(BW)	Hollow	Chrome	Yes	No	Riveted	LESNEY ENGLAND © 1975		I	£5	
16		Dark brown body & chassis	Dark cream	Dark brown	Cream	8 mm	Cream	Black	Chrome 24 spoke(BW)	Hollow	Chrome	Yes	No	Riveted	MATCHBOX © 1975 ENGLAND		I	£5	
17		Dark brown body & chassis	Dark cream	Dark brown	Cream	8 mm	Cream	Black	Chrome solid (BW)	Hollow	Chrome	Yes	No	Riveted	LESNEY ENGLAND © 1975		I	£5	
18		Dark brown body & chassis	Dark cream	Dark brown	Cream	8 mm	Cream	Black	Chrome solid (BW)	Hollow	Chrome	Yes	No	Riveted	MATCHBOX © 1975 ENGLAND		I	£8	
19		Dark brown body & chassis	Dark cream	Dark brown	Beige	8 mm	Beige	Black	Chrome 24 spoke (BW)	Hollow	Chrome	Yes	No	Riveted	LESNEY © 1975 ENGLAND		I	£8	
20		Dark brown body & chassis	Dark cream	Dark brown	Beige	8 mm	Beige	Black	Chrome 24 spoke (BW)	Hollow	Chrome	Yes	No	Riveted	MATCHBOX © 1975 ENGLAND		I	£8	
21	1983	Dark brown body & chassis	Dark cream	Dark brown	Beige	8 mm	Beige	Black	Chrome solid (BW)	Hollow	Chrome	Yes	No	Riveted	LESNEY © 1975 ENGLAND		I	£8	
22		Dark brown body & chassis	Dark cream	Dark brown	Beige	8 mm	Beige	Black	Chrome solid (BW)	Hollow	Chrome	Yes	No	Riveted	MATCHBOX © 1975 ENGLAND		I	£8	
23	1985	Dark brown body & chassis	Dark cream	Dark brown	Rust brown	8 mm	Rust brown	Black	Chrome 24 spoke (BW)	Hollow	Chrome	Yes	No	Riveted	LESNEY © 1975 ENGLAND		I	£10	
24		Dark brown body & chassis	Dark cream	Dark brown	Rust brown	8 mm	Rust brown	Black	Chrome 24 spoke (BW)	Hollow	Chrome	Yes	No	Riveted	MATCHBOX © 1975 ENGLAND		I J	£10	
25	1986	Metallic silver body, royal blue chassis	Royal blue tampo	Metallic silver	Black	8 mm	Black	Black*	Blue 24 spoke (WW)	Hollow	Chrome	Yes	No	Riveted	MATCHBOX © 1975 ENGLAND		J	£10	✔
26		Metallic silver body, royal blue chassis	Dark blue tampo	Metallic silver	Black	8 mm	Black	Black*	Blue 24 spoke	Hollow	Chrome	Yes	No	Riveted	MATCHBOX © 1975 ENGLAND		J/L	£10	
27	1988	Metallic silver body, darker blue chassis	Dark blue mask	Metallic silver	Black	8 mm	Black	Black*	Blue 24 spoke (WW)	Hollow	Chrome	Yes	No	Riveted	MATCHBOX © 1975 MACAU*	S	J 1	£25	
28	1989	Powder blue body & dark blue chassis	Powder blue	Powder blue	Off white	8 mm	Tan	Light tan, black spokes	Chrome 24 spoke (WW)	Hollow	Chrome	Yes	No*	Riveted	MATCHBOX © 1975 MACAU	S	P*	£25	
29	1990	Powder blue body & dark blue chassis	Powder blue	Powder blue	Off white	8 mm	Tan	Light tan, black spokes	Chrome 24 spoke (WW)	Hollow	Chrome	Yes	Yes	Riveted	MATCHBOX © 1975 MACAU		N	£10	✔
30		Powder blue body & dark blue chassis	Powder blue	Powder blue	Off white	8 mm	Tan	Light tan, black spokes	Chrome 24 spoke (WF)	Hollow	Chrome	Yes	Yes	Press fit	MATCHBOX © 1975 MACAU		N	£10	
31		Powder blue body & dark blue chassis	Powder blue	Powder blue	Off white	8 mm	Tan	Light olive green, black spokes	Chrome 24 spoke (WF)	Hollow	Chrome	Yes	Yes	Press fit	MATCHBOX © 1975 MACAU		N	£10	
32	1991	Metallic silver body, darker blue chassis	Dark blue mask	Metallic silver	Metallic silver	8 mm	Black	Black	Blue 24 spoke (WW)	Hollow	Chrome	Yes	Yes	Press fit	MATCHBOX © 1975 CHINA*	S	J2	£15	
33	1994	Powder blue body and dark blue chassis	Powder blue	Powder blue	Pale off white	8 mm	Light tan	Brown, black spokes	Chrome 24 spoke (WF)	Hollow	Chrome	Yes	Yes	Press fit	MATCHBOX © 1975 CHINA		N 2		

NOTES
Issues 29 to 31 have full width silver painted running boards.
Issue 33 does not have full width silver painted running boards, giving a dark blue edge effect to the running boards both on the outside and next to the chassis.

Y5-1 1929 LE MANS BENTLEY

Scale 1:55

INVESTMENT COMMENT
ORIGINAL PRICE £0.12.5p

This model is one of the more common First Series Yesteryears and there appear to be good opportunities to buy on the second-hand market. Prices are presently good value and now is the time to buy. Values are likely to increase.

The Y5-1 1929 Le Mans Bentley was issued in 1958 and was in the range until 1961. Some realism was afforded this crude model by featuring the rear of the tonneau/folded hood in grey. This was to prove too costly an exercise and was quite quickly omitted. Slight variations in the colour have been noted for the wheels and the unpainted steering wheel. In some instances Lesney used a lacquer which with ageing caused tarnishing to create a pale copper finish. Wheels that appear silver in colour were lacquer free. Although the correct terminology for the wheels is solid; in fact they do have a twenty wire spoke raised relief design.

ISSUE	YEAR OF RELEASE	COLOURS	TONNEAU	FOLDED DOWN HOOD	SEATS/ INTERIOR	GRILLE	RADIATOR SHELL	STEERING WHEEL	WHEELS	PETROL TANK FILLER CAP	AXLES	BASEPLATE	RARITY	BOX TYPE	VALUE	CHECK LIST
1	1958	British racing green body, black chassis	British racing green	Grey*	Red	Silver	Silver	Unpainted silver effect	Unpainted solid	Silver	Crimped	LESNEY No 5 ENGLAND	R	A	£130	
2		British racing green body, black chassis	British racing green	Grey*	Red	Green	Silver	Unpainted silver effect	Unpainted solid	Silver	Crimped	LESNEY No 5 ENGLAND	R	A	£130	
3		British racing green body, black chassis	British racing green	Grey*	Red	Green	Gold*	Unpainted silver effect	Unpainted solid	Gold*	Crimped	LESNEY No 5 ENGLAND	R	A	£150	
4		British racing green body, black chassis	British racing green	British racing green	Red	Green	Gold*	Unpainted silver effect	Unpainted solid	Gold*	Crimped	LESNEY No 5 ENGLAND		A/C	£75	
5		British racing green body, black chassis	British racing green	British racing green	Red	Green	British racing green	Unpainted silver effect	Unpainted solid	British racing green	Crimped	LESNEY No 5 ENGLAND		A/C	£75	
6		British racing green body, black chassis	British racing green	British racing green	Red	Green	British racing green	Unpainted silver effect	Unpainted solid	British racing green	Riveted	LESNEY No 5 ENGLAND		C/D1	£75	
7		British racing green body, black chassis	British racing green	British racing green	Red	Green	Gold	Unpainted silver effect	Unpainted solid	Gold	Riveted	LESNEY No 5 ENGLAND		C/D1	£75	✓
8		British racing green body, black chassis	British racing green	British racing green	Red	Green	Gold	British racing green*	Unpainted solid	Gold	Riveted	LESNEY No 5 ENGLAND	R	C/D1	£100	

IDENTIFICATION KEY

DIAGRAM 1

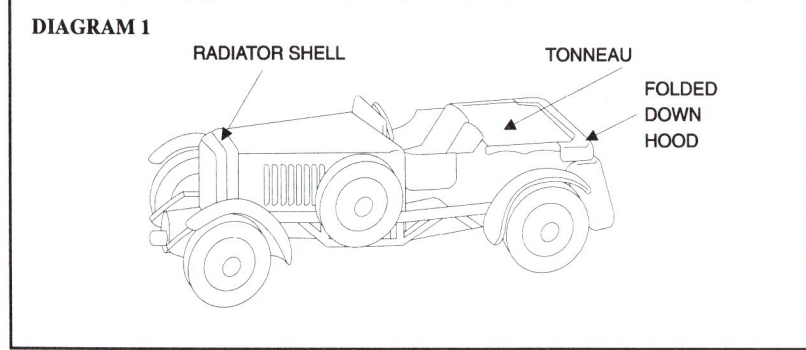

LIVERY

Transfer
"5" in black on white disc both sides, to rear of doors.

NOTES

Y5-2 1929 4½ LITRE BENTLEY — Scale 1:52

INVESTMENT COMMENT
ORIGINAL PRICE £0.15p

An extremely good seller for Lesney Products and even in standard form maintains a higher value than other Second Series models. The rarer issues have dropped a little in recent years but should 'bounce' back.

When the redesigned Bentley model was released there were complaints from the Bentley Owners Club at the 'apple green' or 'candy green', as it is known in the U.S.A., colour scheme. The paint was quickly changed to a more authentic British racing green. Three differently coloured plastic seats and tonneau components were used by Lesney. Modifications were made to the baseplate component, and in all, four different types were used. Initially the baseplate stopped one millimetre short of the front axle. On all later models the baseplate was increased in length to finish in line with the body. To improve the appearance of the model, later models were given a separate radiator. These issues are easy to recognise as the new radiator was silver, in contrast to early issues where it was painted in green, with only the radiator core being painted silver. There was always a Union flag on the body as well as a number on a white disc. Numbers used were '5', '3' and '6'. Prior to the new radiator casting, two holes were let into the baseplate to facilitate mounting the plated version onto various giftware items. Finally a minor modification was made to the rear axle hole area whereby the axle hole flange was made larger to withstand the rigours of the tumbling process. It should be noted that strengthening webs were fitted to the rear spring area of the baseplates on the B, C and D type baseplate components. The Y5-2 Bentley model was also released in Mobil boxes during the mid-1960's as part of a petroleum promotion.

ISSUE	YEAR OF RELEASE	COLOURS	SEATS & TONNEAU	GRILLE	STEERING WHEEL	WHEELS	PLATED PARTS	SEPARATE RADIATOR CASTING	COLOUR OF RADIATOR SHELL	RACING NUMBER	BASEPLATE TYPE	BASEPLATE	RARITY	BOX TYPE	VALUE	CHECK LIST
1	1962	Metallic apple green* body & chassis	Green	Silver	Silver	Silver 24 spoke	Silver	No	Metallic apple green*	Black 5	A	LESNEY No 5 ENGLAND	V R	D1	£275	
2		Metallic apple green* body & chassis	Dark red*	Silver	Silver	Silver 24 spoke	Silver	No	Metallic apple green*	Black 5	A	LESNEY No 5 ENGLAND	V R	D1	£275	
3		British racing green body & chassis	Green	Silver	Silver	Silver 24 spoke	Silver	No	British racing green	Black 5	A	LESNEY No 5 ENGLAND		D1/D2	£45	
4		British racing green body & chassis	Green	Silver	Silver	Silver 24 spoke	Silver	No	British racing green	Black 5	B	LESNEY No 5 ENGLAND		D2	£45	
5		British racing green body & chassis	Darker red*	Silver	Silver	Silver 24 spoke	Silver	No	British racing green	Black 5	B	LESNEY No 5 ENGLAND	D	D2	£60	
6		British racing green body & chassis	Bright red	Silver	Silver	Silver 24 spoke	Silver	No	British racing green	Black 5	B	LESNEY No 5 ENGLAND		D2	£30	
7	1964	British racing green body & chassis	Bright red	Silver	Silver	Silver 24 spoke	Silver	Yes*	Silver	Black 5	B*	LESNEY No 5 ENGLAND	V R	D2/D3	£100	✓
8		British racing green body & chassis	Bright red	Silver	Silver	Silver 24 spoke	Silver	Yes	Silver	Black 5	C	LESNEY No 5 ENGLAND		D3/E/M	£25	
9		British racing green body & chassis	Bright red	Silver	Silver	Silver 24 spoke	Silver	Yes	Silver	Black 3*	C	LESNEY No 5 ENGLAND	D	E/E1	£40	
10	1968	British racing green body & chassis	Bright red	Silver	Silver	Silver 24 spoke	Silver	Yes	Silver	Red 6*	C	LESNEY No 5 ENGLAND	R	E/E1/F	£100	
11		British racing green body & chassis	Bright red	Silver	Silver	Silver 24 spoke	Silver	Yes	Silver	Red 6*	D	LESNEY No 5 ENGLAND	R	F	£100	
12		British racing green body & chassis	Bright red	Silver	Silver	Silver 24 spoke	Silver	Yes	Silver	Black 3*	D	LESNEY No 5 ENGLAND	D	F	£40	
13		British racing green body & chassis	Bright red	Silver	Silver	Silver 24 spoke	Silver	Yes	Silver	Black 5	D	LESNEY No 5 ENGLAND		F	£30	

DIAGRAM 1
TYPE 'A'
BASE PLATE STOPS 3mm FROM CENTRE OF FRONT RIVET. NO HOLES.
TYPE 'A' REAR SPRINGS TO PETROL TANK CASTING

DIAGRAM 2
TYPE 'B'
BASE PLATE STOPS 3mm FROM CENTRE OF FRONT RIVET. 2 HOLES.
TYPE 'A' REAR SPRINGS TO PETROL TANK CASTING

DIAGRAM 3 REAR SPRINGS
TYPE 'A'
GAPS BETWEEN REAR SPRINGS & PETROL TANK

DIAGRAM 4
TYPE 'C'
BASE EXTENDED TO 5.5mm FROM CENTRE OF FRONT RIVET. 2 HOLES.
TYPE 'B' REAR SPRINGS TO PETROL TANK CASTING

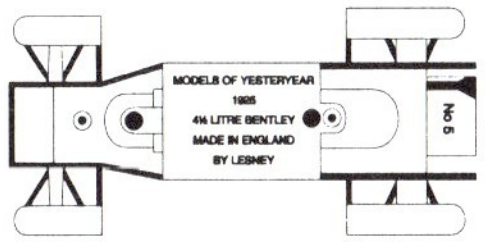

DIAGRAM 5
TYPE 'D'
BASE EXTENDED TO 5.5mm FROM CENTRE OF FRONT RIVET. NO HOLES. CENTRE LINE OF TEXT ON RAISED PLATFORM. REAR RIVET MOVED 6.5mm TO REAR
TYPE 'B' REAR SPRINGS TO PETROL TANK CASTING

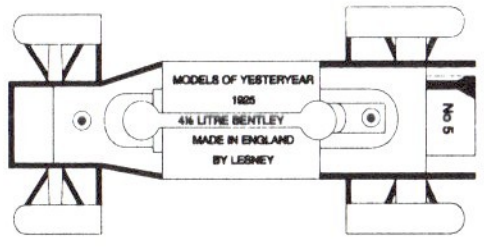

DIAGRAM 6 REAR SPRINGS
TYPE 'B'
NO GAPS BETWEEN REAR SPRINGS & PETROL TANK

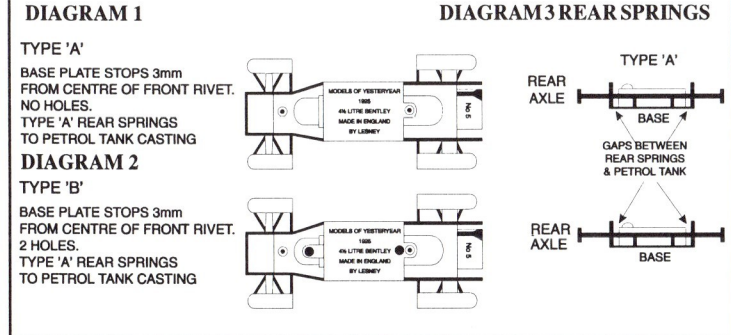

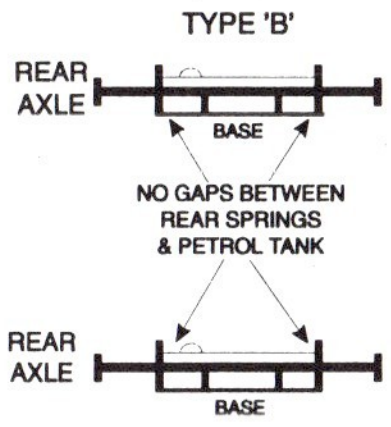

LIVERY
Transfer

Rearside panels. 5 in black or 6 in red or 3 in black on white disc. Doors. Union flag.

NOTES

INVESTMENT COMMENT
ORIGINAL PRICE £0.36p
This model still highlights the extreme differences charged for relatively small casting changes. Most values have remained constant over the last few years. Good value at present.

Y5-3 1907 PEUGEOT

Scale 1:43

Introduced in 1969 and phased out in 1977. Originally shown in the 1969 Collectors Catalogue in a blue livery it was however, introduced into the range in yellow with a black roof having both clear and various tinted windows. These window colour changes were caused by using differently coloured Perspex material. The clear windows are very rare; with distribution going mostly to South Africa. There are no colour variations on the yellow model although a few exist with a black chassis which is often reported as being issued, but, was in fact a preproduction run and was not genuinely issued from the factory. The very first issued model had no rib running down the rear edge of the front seats. (Diagram 1) Another rare variation is the gold body with black roof and base which were made for and exported exclusively to the U.S.A. There are considerable colour variations on the gold version ranging from a light pure gold to a deep orange gold and combinations of different coloured roofs and bodies have been reported. e.g. orange gold roofs on light gold bodies and vice versa. The gold livery can also fade considerably in strong daylight.

ISSUE	YEAR OF RELEASE	COLOURS	ROOF	SEATS	GRILLE	WHEELS	PLATED PARTS	PERSPEX WINDOWS	FRONT SEAT BEAD	BASEPLATE	RARITY	BOX TYPE	VALUE	CHECK LIST
1	1969	Bright yellow body & chassis	Matt black	Bright red	Bright red	Brass 12 spoke	Brass	Dark orange	No*	LESNEY ENGLAND © 1969	R	F	£85	
2		Bright yellow body & chassis	Matt black	Bright red	Bright red	Brass 12 spoke	Brass	Dark orange	Yes	LESNEY ENGLAND © 1969		F	£25	✓
3		Bright yellow body & chassis	Matt black	Bright red	Bright red	Brass 12 spoke	Brass	Pale amber	Yes	LESNEY ENGLAND © 1969		F	£25	
4		Bright yellow body & chassis	Matt black	Bright red	Bright red	Brass 12 spoke	Brass	Clear*	Yes	LESNEY ENGLAND © 1969	V R	F	£150	
5	1975	Orangey gold body & matt black chassis	Orangey gold	Bright red *	Bright red*	Brass 12 spoke*	Brass	Pale amber	Yes	LESNEY ENGLAND © 1969	V R	H	£150	
6		Orangey gold body & matt black chassis	Matt black*	Black	Black	Chrome 12 spoke	Brass	Pale amber	Yes	LESNEY ENGLAND © 1969	S	H	£125	
7		Orangey gold body & matt black chassis	Orangey gold	Black	Black	Chrome 12 spoke	Brass	Pale amber	Yes	LESNEY ENGLAND © 1969		H	£25	
8		Orangey gold body & matt black chassis	Orangey gold	Black	Black	Chrome 12 spoke	Brass	Dark orange	Yes	LESNEY ENGLAND © 1969		H	£25	
9	1976	Light gold body & matt black chassis	Matt black *	Black	Black	Chrome 12 spoke	Brass	Pale amber	Yes	LESNEY ENGLAND © 1969	S	H	£125	
10		Light gold body & matt black chassis	Light gold	Black	Black	Chrome 12 spoke	Brass	Pale amber	Yes	LESNEY ENGLAND © 1969		H	£20	
11		Light gold body & matt black chassis	Light gold	Black	Black	Chrome 12 spoke	Brass	Clear*	Yes	LESNEY ENGLAND © 1969	V R	H	£150	
12	1977/1978	Light gold body & matt black chassis	Light gold	Black	Black	Chrome 24 spoke*	Brass	Clear*	Yes	LESNEY ENGLAND © 1969	V R	H	£150	

DIAGRAM 1 FRONT SEAT BEAD

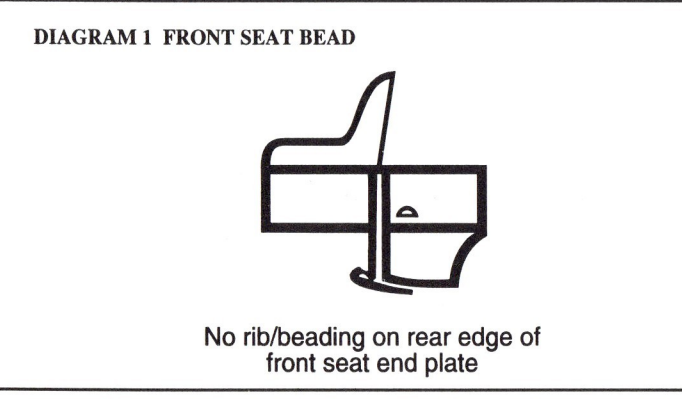

No rib/beading on rear edge of front seat end plate

DIAGRAM 2 FRONT SEAT BEAD

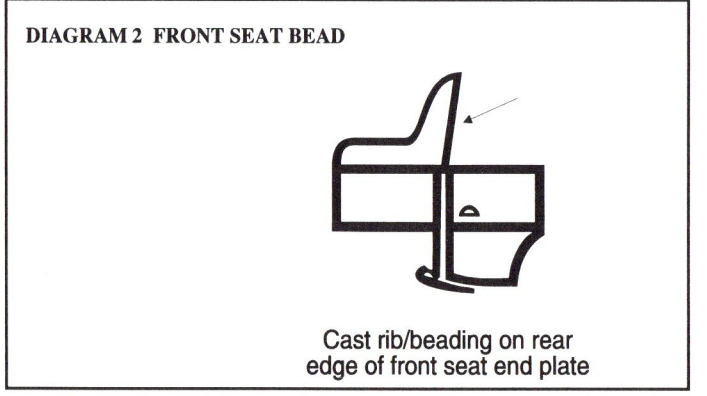

Cast rib/beading on rear edge of front seat end plate

NOTES

Y 5-4 1927 TALBOT VAN

Scale 1:47

LIPTON'S TEA WITH ROYAL CREST. Introduced in 1978 as the first of a new van series. Permission to use the Royal Crest and Cypher on the van had been sought from the Lord Chamberlain's office. Lesney, assumed incorrectly, that this permission would be a mere formality and production of the van began. Rumours began to circulate that there was a problem over the livery and many models were bought and hoarded in case the model proved to be a short run. This was not the case, as several tens of thousands of models with the crest were released. Lesney also encountered teething problems with their newly acquired tampo printing machines. At different times, production models were either given a black shadow effect to the words 'Lipton's Tea' or none at all.

LIPTON'S TEA WITH CITY ROAD. This model bears the revised livery following the refusal by the Lord Chamberlain's office to grant Lesney permission to use the Royal Crest. The tampo printing problems continued, and as with the first livery, several colour types of wheels were fitted to production models. There has been a report of this model with four; not three, rivets in the baseplate It is clear these were pre-production experimental samples only and were never released as production issues.

A : LIPTON'S TEA (WITH CREST)

ISSUE	YEAR OF RELEASE	COLOURS	ROOF	SEAT	WHEELS	PLATED PARTS	LOGO	LIPTON'S TEA SHADOW EFFECT	TOOL BOX LID	BASEPLATE	RARITY	BOX TYPE	VALUE	CHECK LIST
1	1978	Dark green body, matt black chassis*	Matt black	Black	Dark green 12 spoke	Chrome	LIPTON'S TEA	Yes	Brass	LESNEY © 1978 ENGLAND	R	H	£50	
2		Dark green body, glossy black chassis	Matt black	Black	Dark green 12 spoke	Chrome	LIPTON'S TEA	Yes	Brass	LESNEY © 1978 ENGLAND		H	£10	✔
3		Dark green body, glossy black chassis	Matt black	Black	Dark green 12 spoke	Chrome	LIPTON'S TEA	No*	Brass	LESNEY © 1978 ENGLAND	S	H	£40	
4		Dark green body, glossy black chassis	Matt black	Black	Chrome 12 spoke*	Chrome	LIPTON'S TEA	Yes	Brass	LESNEY © 1978 ENGLAND	D	H	£25	
5		Dark green body, glossy black chassis	Matt black	Black	Chrome 24* spoke	Chrome	LIPTON'S TEA	Yes	Brass	LESNEY © 1978 ENGLAND	D	H	£25	

B : LIPTON'S TEA (CITY ROAD)

ISSUE	YEAR OF RELEASE	COLOURS	ROOF	SEAT	WHEELS	PLATED PARTS	LOGO	LIPTON'S TEA SHADOW EFFECT	TOOL BOX LID	BASEPLATE	RARITY	BOX TYPE	VALUE	CHECK LIST
1	1978	Dark green body, glossy black chassis	Matt black	Black	Dark green 12 spoke	Chrome	LIPTON'S TEA	Yes*	Brass	LESNEY © 1978 ENGLAND	R	I	£60	
2		Dark green body, glossy black chassis	Matt black	Black	Olive*green 12 spoke	Chrome	LIPTON'S TEA	Yes*	Brass	LESNEY © 1978 ENGLAND	R	I	£60	
3		Dark green body, glossy black chassis	Matt black	Black	Dark green 12 spoke	Chrome	LIPTON'S TEA	No	Brass	LESNEY © 1978 ENGLAND		I	£10	
4		Dark green body, glossy black chassis	Matt black	Black	Chrome* 12 spoke	Chrome	LIPTON'S TEA	No	Brass	LESNEY © 1978 ENGLAND	D	I	£20	
5		Dark green body, glossy black chassis	Matt black	Black	Chrome* 24 spoke	Chrome	LIPTON'S TEA	No	Brass	LESNEY © 1978 ENGLAND	D	I	£20	
6		Dark green body, glossy black chassis	Matt black	Black	Olive*green 12 spoke	Chrome	LIPTON'S TEA	No	Brass	LESNEY © 1978 ENGLAND	D	I	£20	
7		Dark green body, glossy black chassis	Glossy black*	Black	Olive* green 12 spoke	Chrome	LIPTON'S TEA	No	Brass	LESNEY © 1978 ENGLAND	S	I	£35	

LIVERY LIPTON'S TEA (WITH CREST)

Tampo
Van sides. LIPTON'S TEA in yellow.
Lower van sides. Royal Crest in yellow with yellow BY APPOINTMENT.

LIVERY LIPTON'S TEA (CITY ROAD)

Tampo
Van sides. LIPTON'S TEA in yellow.
Lower van sides. CITY ROAD, LONDON. E.C.1. in yellow with company logo in yellow.

INVESTMENT COMMENT

ORIGINAL PRICE £1.50p

Regarded widely as being the model that sparked the growth of the hobby in the late 70s, the Lipton's Tea with Royal Crest livery was in such demand, which Lesney Products satisfied, that it has not appreciated substantially as many would have expected. The City Road version was a good seller in large quantities and has failed to appreciate significantly. Issue 7, however, is seldom seen for sale.

NOTES

1. Road wheels of a different colour or design to the spare wheel are by and large the result of wheel swapping by private individuals. Treat with suspicion. This note applies to all Talbot Vans.

2. It is difficult to find models with completely 'mint' logos and quality colouring.

Y5-4 1927 TALBOT VAN (CONTINUED)   Scale 1:47

CHOCOLAT MENIER. Introduced in 1979 for the French market initially but made available to all other major markets within fifteen months. Early releases for the French market were packaged in wood grain (H) boxes with an affixed pale blue sticker. Again many different types of wheels were used up by Lesney Products. Although the basic colour of ink used during the tampo printing process was yellow, a short run was produced using an off-white coloured ink. The yellow tampo decoration can be a light or a dark tone. The very last issues were fitted with badly matched lighter blue doors.

TAYSTEE BREAD. Released in May 1980 as part of a redemption offer with the American Bakeries Co. within the U.S.A. Lesney then decided to make it a general release to replace the 'Chocolat Menier'. There is a Code Two version of the Taystee; when American Bakeries discovered that they had run out, they obtained permission from Lesney Products to make new labels and these are instantly recognised by the lack of the white outline around the word 'Taystee'. Wheel variations were plenty, and although the official policy was to fit white wall tyres, all issues have been found with black tyres!

C : CHOCOLAT MENIER

ISSUE	YEAR OF RELEASE	COLOURS	ROOF	SEAT	WHEELS	PLATED PARTS	LOGO	TAMPO DECORATION	TOOLBOX LID	BASEPLATE	RARITY	BOX TYPE	VALUE	CHECK LIST
1	1978/9	Royal blue body, glossy black chassis	Matt black	Black	Chrome 12 spoke	Chrome	CHOCOLAT MENIER	Yellow	Brass	LESNEY © 1978 ENGLAND		H/I	£8	✓
2		Royal blue body, glossy black chassis	Matt black	Black	Chrome 24 spoke*	Chrome	CHOCOLAT MENIER	Yellow	Brass	LESNEY © 1978 ENGLAND	D	H/I	£25	
3		Royal blue body, glossy black chassis	Matt black	Black	Chrome 12 spoke	Chrome	CHOCOLAT MENIER	Off white*	Brass	LESNEY © 1978 ENGLAND	S	I	£20	
4		Royal blue body, glossy black chassis	Matt black	Black	Red 12 spoke*	Chrome	CHOCOLAT MENIER	Yellow	Brass	LESNEY © 1978 ENGLAND	D	I	£25	
5		Royal blue body, glossy black chassis	Matt black	Black	Solid red*	Chrome	CHOCOLAT MENIER	Yellow	Brass	LESNEY © 1978 ENGLAND	D	I	£25	
6		Royal blue body, glossy black chassis	Matt black	Black	Dark green 12 spoke*	Chrome	CHOCOLAT MENIER	Yellow	Brass	LESNEY © 1978 ENGLAND	D	I	£25	

D : TAYSTEE BREAD

ISSUE	YEAR OF RELEASE	COLOURS	ROOF	SEAT	WHEELS	PLATED PARTS	LOGO	TAMPO DECORATION	TOOLBOX LID	BASEPLATE	RARITY	BOX TYPE	VALUE	CHECK LIST
1	1980	Bright yellow body & chassis	Matt black	Black	Red 12 spoke (BW)	Chrome	TAYSTEE	N/A	Brass	LESNEY © 1978 ENGLAND		I	£8	
2		Bright yellow body & chassis	Matt black	Black	Dark red 12 spoke (BW)	Chrome	TAYSTEE	N/A	Brass	LESNEY © 1978 ENGLAND		I	£8	
3	1981	Bright yellow body, glossy black* chassis	Matt black	Black	Red 12 spoke (BW)	Chrome	TAYSTEE	N/A	Brass	LESNEY © 1978 ENGLAND	D	I	£10	✓
4		Bright yellow body, glossy black* chassis	Matt black	Black	Dark red 12 spoke (BW)	Chrome	TAYSTEE	N/A	Brass	LESNEY © 1978 ENGLAND	D	I	£10	
5		Bright yellow body, glossy black* chassis	Matt black	Black	Red solid* (BW)	Chrome	TAYSTEE	N/A	Brass	LESNEY © 1978 ENGLAND	S	I	£25	

LIVERY   CHOCOLAT MENIER

Tampo
Van sides. CHOCOLAT MENIER and diamond in yellow.

LIVERY   TAYSTEE BREAD

Transfers
Van sides. White TAYSTEE on red oval with white surround above black OLD FASHIONED ENRICHED BREAD.

INVESTMENT COMMENT
ORIGINAL PRICE £2.45P

CHOCOLAT MENIER The Menier is still readily available on the second-hand market and standard issues are unlikely to show any immediate growth. However, the scarcer models have jumped up considerably and should be monitored closely.
TAYSTEE Values for the Taystee have fallen. This is surprising. Issue 5, seldom seen for sale, has retained its value.

NOTES
BECKENHAM APPEAL MODEL.
Blue body, dark blue chassis.
Gold tampo printed "Chocolat Menier"
Black seats and roof
Chrome plated parts.

Y5-4 1927 TALBOT VAN (CONTINUED) Scale 1:47

NESTLE'S. This livery was available initially within the United Kingdon. An early short run of black roofed models arising from a mistake at the factory was soon followed by the specified dark grey roof type. These models were generally released onto the European markets. Final issued models were fitted with much lighter grey roofs and these were released onto the Australian market. Although total production figures are unknown, the 'Nestle's' run was relatively short and all three issues attract a premium. Look out for some issued with copper axles!
CHIVERS. The 'Chivers' became the standard range Y5 in 1982 and was the first Talbot van to feature fully brass plated components. No significant variations have been reported although many models have been seen with faultily applied tampo printing. White wall tyres were standard but all issues have been seen with plain black tyres.

E : NESTLE'S

ISSUE	YEAR OF RELEASE	COLOURS	ROOF	SEAT	WHEELS	PLATED PARTS	LOGO	TOOL BOX LID	BASEPLATE	RARITY	IBOX TYPE	VALUE	CHECK LIST
1	1981	Blue body, glossy black chassis	Matt black*	Black	Dark red 12 spoke (WW)	Chrome	NESTLE'S	Brass	LESNEY © 1978 ENGLAND	R	I	£175	
2		Blue body, glossy black chassis	Dark grey*	Black	Dark red 12 spoke (WW)	Chrome	NESTLE'S	Brass	LESNEY © 1978 ENGLAND	D	I	£15	
3		Blue body, glossy black chassis	Pale grey*	Black	Dark red 12 spoke (WW)	Chrome	NESTLE'S	Brass	LESNEY © 1978 ENGLAND	S	I	£45	

F : CHIVERS

ISSUE	YEAR OF RELEASE	COLOURS	ROOF	SEAT	WHEELS	PLATED PARTS	LOGO	TOOL BOX LID	BASEPLATE	RARITY	IBOX TYPE	VALUE	CHECK LIST
1	1982	Cream body, dark green chassis	Cream	Black	Dark red 12 spoke (BW)	Brass	CHIVERS	Brass	LESNEY © 1978 ENGLAND		I	£8	
2		Cream body, dark green chassis	Cream	Black	Red 12 spoke (BW)	Brass	CHIVERS	Brass	LESNEY © 1978 ENGLAND		I / L	£8	✔
3		Cream body, dark green chassis	Cream	Tan*	Red 12 spoke (BW)	Brass	CHIVERS	Brass	LESNEY © 1978 ENGLAND	D	I	£15	
4		Cream body, dark green chassis	Cream	Black	Red 12 spoke (BW)	Chrome*	CHIVERS	Brass	LESNEY © 1978 ENGLAND	D	I	£15	

LIVERY NESTLE'S
Transfer
Van sides. NESTLE'S MILK in white on dark blue oval.
Two gold medallions ONE QUALITY ONLY in white, a red and white Swiss flag, and white THE RICHEST IN CREAM.

LIVERY CHIVERS
Tampo
Van sides. CHIVERS & SONS LTD in green with black surround ESTD 1873 in black on black and cream shield with JAMS JELLIES & MARMALADES, THE ORCHARD FACTORY, HISTON, CAMBRIDGE in green.

INVESTMENT COMMENT
ORIGINAL PRICE NESTLE'S £2.60p   CHIVER'S £2.50p

NESTLE'S Although the UK released variation has fallen in value, reports from Australia are that it has continued to grow in value. An attractive model with relatively low production figures, the Nestle's should come back.
CHIVER'S Remains good value, especially for newer collectors. Issue 3 with tan coloured seat has potential for further growth but beware of fakes.

NOTES

1. There are known to be fakes of Issue 1, Nestle's
2. Issue 2 Chiver's, was released in 1982 as a Limited Edition set of five models.

Y5-4 1927 TALBOT VAN (CONTINUED) — Scale 1:47

WRIGHT'S. This livery was released as a Limited Edition in 1982. At the time of production, which was a period of four weeks, the machinery used to apply the brass effect to the plastic components, such as the lights and wheel spokes, broke down. The official factory specification had been for brass/gold, but a number were produced with chrome effect components. Cross-over variations were inevitable.

EVER READY. The "Ever Ready" model was released in mid 1983 as a replacement for the now obsolete "Chivers". Of interest was the use of three differently coloured plastics to make the seat component. White wall tyres were standard issue. The first issue models were released when the straw (I) type box was still current and models with tan or black seats can be found in these boxes. The second issue was released when the maroon (J) type cartons were current. The final issue in the J type cartons are only seen with black seats.

G : WRIGHT'S

ISSUE	YEAR OF RELEASE	COLOURS	ROOF	SEAT	WHEELS	PLATED PARTS	LOGO	TOOL BOX LID	BASEPLATE	RARITY	BOX TYPE	VALUE	CHECK LIST
1	1982	Dark brown body, beige chassis	Beige	Black	Chrome 12 spoke	Chrome	WRIGHT'S	Brass	LESNEY © 1978 ENGLAND		I	£8	✓
2		Dark brown body, beige chassis	Beige	Black	Gold 12 spoke	Brass	WRIGHT'S	Brass	LESNEY © 1978 ENGLAND	D	I	£10	
3		Dark brown body, beige chassis	Beige	Black	Gold 12 spoke*	Chrome*	WRIGHT'S	Brass	LESNEY © 1978 ENGLAND	S	I	£15	

H : EVER READY

ISSUE	YEAR OF RELEASE	COLOURS	ROOF	SEAT	WHEELS	PLATED PARTS	LOGO	TOOL BOX LID	BASEPLATE	RARITY	BOX TYPE	VALUE	CHECK LIST
1	1983	Dark blue body, glossy black chassis	White	Tan	Chrome 12 spoke (WW)	Chrome	EVER READY	Brass	LESNEY © 1978 ENGLAND		I/J	£8	✓
2	1984	Dark blue body, glossy black chassis	White	Pinky Tan*	Chrome 12 spoke (WW)	Chrome	EVER READY	Brass	LESNEY © 1978 ENGLAND	S	J	£15	
3		Dark blue body, glossy black chassis	White	Black	Chrome 12 spoke (WW)	Chorme	EVER READY	Brass	LESNEY © 1978 ENGLAND		J	£8	

LIVERY WRIGHT'S

Tampo
Van sides. Dark brown WRIGHT'S ORIGINAL over single outlined dark brown COAL TAR SOAP. All above dark brown CLEAN AND HEALTHY FAMILY CARE. All within dark brown oval line. All on pale cream oval. Pale cream WRIGHT LAYMAN & UMNEY LTD.

LIVERY EVER READY

Tampo
Van sides. EVER READY above REGD TRADE MARK all in blue or white rectangle. All on white edged orange panel, with white BATTERIES FOR LIFE!

INVESTMENT COMMENT

ORIGINAL PRICE WRIGHT'S & EVER READY £2.99p

WRIGHT'S A limited edition, but with too high a production run. There has never been and is never likely to be much interest in this model.

EVER READY Little or no progress and a model with little growth potential.

NOTES

Y5-4 1927 TALBOT VAN (CONTINUED)   Scale 1:47

DUNLOP. Designated as a Limited Edition, the 'Dunlop' was one of the first models to be packaged in the new maroon (J) type boxes. A noteable variation was in the colour of yellow plastic used to make the wheels. The paler yellow plastic (Issue 3) was a darker shade than for example the yellow, used in conjunction with the Y12 'Silver Jubilee' model.

ROSE'S. This livery was first released in July 1985. In January 1986 the cream paint normally associated with the 'Chivers' livery was used up to complete a production run at the soon to close Rochford factory. Production continued from the Macau factory for a short while (Issue 6).

I : DUNLOP

ISSUE	YEAR OF RELEASE	COLOURS	ROOF	SEAT	WHEELS	PLATED PARTS	LOGO	TOOLBOX LID	BASEPLATE	RARITY	BOX TYPE	VALUE	CHECK LIST
1	1984	Black body & chassis	Yellow	Tan	Dark yellow 12 spoke	Chrome	DUNLOP	Brass	LESNEY © 1978 ENGLAND		J	£7	
2		Black body & chassis	Yellow	Black*	Dark yellow 12 spoke	Chrome	DUNLOP	Brass	LESNEY © 1978 ENGLAND	D	J	£25	
3		Black body & chassis	Yellow	Tan	Paler* yellow 12 spoke	Chrome	DUNLOP	Brass	LESNEY © 1978 ENGLAND	S	J	£15	
4		Black body & chassis	Yellow	Black*	Paler* yellow 12 spoke	Chrome	DUNLOP	Brass	LESNEY © 1978 ENGLAND	S	J	£25	

J : ROSE'S

ISSUE	YEAR OF RELEASE	COLOURS	ROOF	SEAT	WHEELS	PLATED PARTS	LOGO	TOOLBOX LID	BASEPLATE	RARITY	BOX TYPE	VALUE	CHECK LIST
1	1985	Light cream body, bright green chassis	Bright green	Black	Dark green 12 spoke (BW)	Chrome	ROSE'S	Brass	LESNEY © 1978 ENGLAND		J	£8	✓
2		Light cream body, bright green chassis	Bright green	Tan*	Dark green 12 spoke (BW)	Chrome	ROSE'S	Brass	LESNEY © 1978 ENGLAND	S	J	£20	
3	1986	Very pale cream body, dark green (CHIVERS) chassis	Bright green	Black	Dark green 12 spoke (BW)	Chrome	ROSE'S	Brass	LESNEY © 1978 ENGLAND		J	£8	
4		Very pale cream body, dark green (CHIVERS) chassis	Bright green	Tan*	Dark green 12 spoke (BW)	Chrome	ROSE'S	Brass	LESNEY © 1978 ENGLAND	S	J	£15	
5		Light cream body, bright green chassis	Bright green	Black	Red 12 spoke (BW)*	Chrome	ROSE'S	Brass	LESNEY © 1978 ENGLAND	D	J	£10	
6	1988	Light cream body, bright green chassis	Bright green	Black	Green 12 spoke (BW)	Chrome	ROSE'S	Brass	MATCHBOX © 1978 MACAU*	D	J1	£10	

LIVERY   DUNLOP

Label
Van sides. Black DUNLOP below a tyre, the Union flag pole, lanyard and scroll in black, white, red and blue.

Tampo
Lower van sides. White TYRES & ACCESSORIES.

LIVERY   ROSE'S

Tampo
Van sides. ROSE'S in bright green with black surround over two limes in yellow with green leaves. LIME JUICE CORDIAL in cream with black outline.

INVESTMENT COMMENT

ORIGINAL PRICE DUNLOP & ROSE'S £3.50p

DUNLOP An unexciting design; with little investment potential even though the livery is so well known.

ROSE'S Standard issues still fail to "ignite" any interest; this unfortunate fact is likely to continue.

NOTES

Y5-4 1927 TALBOT VAN (CONTINUED) Scale 1:47

INVESTMENT COMMENT
ORIGINAL PRICE £6.25p

LYLE'S Some interest in this, the last of the 80's liveries, has been recorded. Still has potential with its relatively low production figures and attractive livery.

LYLE'S. Introduced in January 1989 some eighteen months after the Rose's van. Once the tools had been modified to remove the horizontal ridge that had divided the van sides on all previous releases, the extensive design was tampo printed onto the van. Although a Limited Edition, the factory did produce the last run with black spoked wheels instead of the more common gold effect wheels. This was most likely due to the production of the Y14-3 'Kohle & Koks' (which had black twelve spoke wheels in the main) being produced concurrently with the 'Lyle's'. The 'Lyle's' livery was the last of eleven code one logos on the Talbot van issued between 1978 and 1989. The total production of the 'Lyle's' model was 48,966.

K : LYLE'S

ISSUE	YEAR OF RELEASE	COLOURS	ROOF	SEAT	WHEELS	PLATED PARTS	LOGO	TOOLBOX LID	BASEPLATE	RARITY	BOX TYPE	VALUE	CHECK LIST
1	1989	Bright green body, black chassis	White	Tan	Gold 12 spoke	Brass	LYLE'S	Brass	MATCHBOX © 1978 MACAU		J 1	£10	✓
2		Bright green body, black chassis	White	Tan	Black 12 spoke*	Brass	LYLE'S	Brass	MATCHBOX © 1978 MACAU	D	J 1	£25	

LIVERY LYLE'S

Tampo
Van sides. LYLE'S GOLDEN SYRUP in white with black shadow effect and a tin of syrup in gold, green, white and black.
Cab doors. Company logo of a lion in gold, black and white surrounded with ABRAM LYLE & SONS, SUGAR REFINERS in white in black oval with white edging.

NOTES

1. Compare with YGB 10

Y5-5 1929 LEYLAND TITAN BUS

Scale 1:76

SOUTHDOWN. The project engineers from the R & D Department at Matchbox based the Y5 Bus on a Leyland TD1 located at the Chalk Pits Museum in Amberley, Sussex, England. Originally the first livery was to be that of 'Black and White' Whisky and pre-production models were shown in catalogues. Some of these pre-production models have found their way onto the collectors' market. The model attracted some criticism from collectors, concerning the upper deck seat unit that warped at the rear and the inaccurate thickness of the window frames to the driver's cab. Total production 50,868.

ASHTON-UNDER-LYNE. The 'Swan Fountpens' livery was used for the third U.K. passport scheme. Collectors within the United Kingdom were invited to send their remittance plus a fully stamped passport in order to obtain the bus, which only came with the framed cabinet. Later the bus with cabinet was made available to other markets, but at double the price to United Kingdom collectors i.e. around £55.00, it was also released as a range item to all other markets. Models from the early part of the run had Type A top deck seats but the majority featured the modified seats with the extended pillar which reached the ceiling and by doing so prevented the seat warping upwards, Type B. Total production, 9,996.

A : SOUTHDOWN

ISSUE	YEAR OF RELEASE	COLOURS	ROOF	LOWER DECK WINDOW FRAMES	UPPER & LOWER DECK INTERIORS	UPPER DECK REAR SEAT	DRIVERS CAB WINDOW TYPE	WHEELS	PLATED PARTS	GRILLE	STAIRS	SIDE GUARD RAILS	LOGO	BASEPLATE	RARITY	BOX TYPE	VALUE	CHECK LIST
1	1989	Light green body, mid green chassis	Cream	Cream	Fawn	A	1	Solid green	Chrome	Black	Brown	Mid green	ROBIN STARCH	MATCHBOX © 1989 MACAU		J 1	£15	✓

B : ASHTON-UNDER-LYNE

ISSUE	YEAR OF RELEASE	COLOURS	ROOF	LOWER DECK WINDOW FRAMES	UPPER & LOWER DECK INTERIORS	UPPER DECK REAR SEAT	DRIVERS CAB WINDOW TYPE	WHEELS	PLATED PARTS	GRILLE	STAIRS	SIDE GUARD RAILS	LOGO	BASEPLATE	RARITY	BOX TYPE	VALUE	CHECK LIST
1	1990	Blue body, gloss black chassis	Mid blue	Cream	Dark blue	A*	1	Solid dark blue	Chrome	Black	Mid blue	Black	SWAN FOUNTPENS	MATCHBOX © 1989 MACAU	D	Framed cabinet M	£80	
2		Blue body, gloss black chassis	Mid blue	Cream	Dark blue	B	1	Solid dark blue	Chrome	Black	Mid blue	Black	SWAN FOUNTPENS	MATCHBOX © 1989 MACAU		Framed cabinet M	£70	

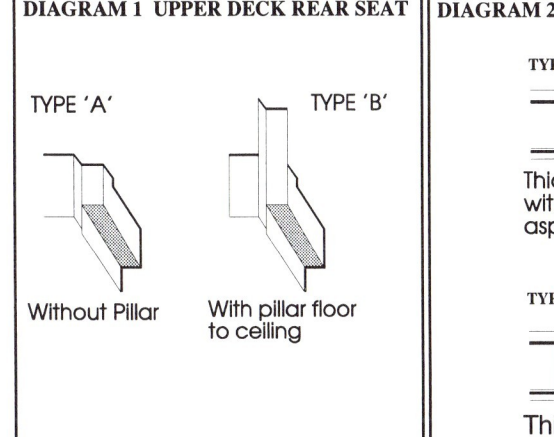

DIAGRAM 1 UPPER DECK REAR SEAT

TYPE 'A' — Without Pillar
TYPE 'B' — With pillar floor to ceiling

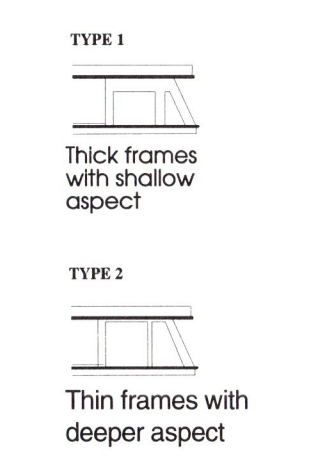

DIAGRAM 2 DRIVERS CAB WINDOW

TYPE 1 — Thick frames with shallow aspect

TYPE 2 — Thin frames with deeper aspect

INVESTMENT COMMENT
ORIGINAL PRICE. SOUTHDOWN £6.25 ASHTON £29.00

SOUTHDOWN Surprisingly this model has languished in the £10 to £15 bracket but certainly one for the future.

ASHTON At one time the framed cabinet model reached in excess of £80. The 'MICA' boxed model now sells for £40, and its value is rising.

LIVERY SOUTHDOWN
Tampo
Upper deck panels. White ROBIN THE NEW STARCH between two birds in brown yellow and red on white discs. All on red panels with yellow surround.
Lower panels. Gold SOUTHDOWN.
Destination boards. White 4. White TARRING DURRINGTON HIGH SALVINGTON.
Number plate. White UF 6473 on black panel.

LIVERY ASHTON-UNDER-LYNE
Tampo
Upper deck panels. SWAN FOUNTPENS in black with white surround. Company logo of a swan in white and black in red shield. All on yellow panel.
Lower panels. Ashton Corporation crest in red, gold and white.
Destination boards.
Front. GARAGE in white on black.
Rear. ASHTON VIA HEYROD in white on black.
N.B. No number plate.

NOTES
1. In 1993 MICA purchased from Matchbox Toys, 750 framed cabinets and permission was given to rebox these Titan buses in replica second series boxes.
2. The passenger vertical handhold bar is bright steel.

Y5-5 1929 LEYLAND TITAN BUS (CONTINUED) Scale 1:76

INVESTMENT COMMENT
ORIGINAL PRICE £8.99p

COVENTRY Some growth has been noted and is a model whose value is likely to gradually creep upwards. The MICA Club model has steadily risen in value and sells for in excess of £35

CITY OF COVENTRY CORPORATION. By the time that the 'Newcastle Brown Ale' livery was released, Matchbox had successfully modified the tools to rectify the points of criticism of the first two Titan buses. The upper deck seating was fitted with a pillar that extended to the upper deck ceiling; Type B. The driver's cab window frames were given a deeper aspect; Type 2. Also on the baseplate some of the prop shaft detail was curtailed to facilitate the baseplate screwhole, to hold the model securely in its box. The copyright date was moved to the rear of the front axle. In 1992 MICA (The Matchbox International Collectors Association) obtained relabelled Titans from Matchbox which were only available to MICA members on a one member one model basis. This was a limited run of 5,000 models and all were purchased by members.

C : CITY OF COVENTRY

ISSUE	YEAR OF RELEASE	COLOURS	ROOF	LOWER DECK WINDOW FRAMES	UPPER & LOWER DECK INTERIORS	UPPER DECK REAR SEAT	DRIVERS CAB WINDOW TYPE	WHEELS	PLATED PARTS	GRILLE	STAIRS	SIDE GUARD RAILS	LOGO	THREADED SCREW HOLE	BASEPLATE	RARITY	BOX TYPE	VALUE	CHECK LIST
1	1991	Maroon body, gloss black chassis	Cream	Fawn	Fawn	B	2	Solid maroon	Chrome	Black	Black	Black	NEWCASTLE BROWN ALE	Yes	MATCHBOX © 1989 CHINA		N 1	£15	✓

LIVERY
Tampo
Upper side panels. NEWCASTLE BROWN ALE in red with a blue star at each end on white panel.
Lower side panels. Multi-coloured City of Coventry Corporation Crest.
Lower window frames. Black CITY OF COVENTRY.
Destination boards. White EARLSDON on a black panel.
N.B. No number plates.

NOTES

1. The passenger vertical handrail is bright steel.

2. Compare with YET 02-M

Y6-1 1916 AEC 'Y' TYPE LORRY Scale 1:100

INVESTMENT COMMENT
ORIGINAL PRICE £0.11.5p

Still the hardest First Series to find especially in perfect condition. Issues 1, 2 and 7 are seldom offered for sale. All other issues exceed the £100 mark, and prices represent good value at present. Expect a premium in overseas markets.

Late pre-production and early releases were painted in a pale blue colour, known as 'duck-egg' blue, but were soon replaced by mid blue and then by a light grey colour. The paint pigment has a tendency to fade to a blueish grey colour and so these have not been given individual codings. Due to oversights at the factory, several runs of the model had bonnet handles which were not painted by the outworkers. These have not been given separate codings. By 1959 the shade of grey had been considerably darkened. Those models are slightly harder to find than the lighter grey ones. The final run saw the need to use black plastic wheels taken from models in the "Matchbox" Series. The transfers used by Lesney were relatively fragile and it is hard to find a model with absolutely perfect ones. Original transfers normally discolour with age.

ISSUE	YEAR OF RELEASE	COLOURS	RADIATOR SHELL	SEAT	DRIVER	STEERING WHEEL	GRILLE	FRONT WHEELS	REAR WHEELS	AXLES	LOGO	BASEPLATE	RARITY	BOX TYPE	VALUE	CHECK LIST
1	1957	Pale blue* body & chassis	Gold	Pale blue	Pale blue	Pale blue	Pale blue	Grenodised 10 spoke	Grenodised 16 daisy	Crimped	OSRAM LAMPS	LESNEY No6 ENGLAND	E R	A	£1600	
2	1957	Mid blue* body & chassis	Gold	Mid blue	Mid blue	Mid blue	Mid blue	Grenodised 10 spoke	Grenodised 16 daisy	Crimped	OSRAM LAMPS	LESNEY No6 ENGLAND	E R	A	£1600	
3		Light grey body & chassis	Silver*	Light grey	Light grey	Light grey	Light grey	Grenodised 10 spoke	Grenodised 16 daisy	Crimped	OSRAM LAMPS	LESNEY No6 ENGLAND	D	A	£110	✓
4	1958	Light grey body & chassis	Gold*	Light grey	Light grey	Light grey	Light grey	Grenodised 10 spoke	Grenodised 16 daisy	Crimped	OSRAM LAMPS	LESNEY No6 ENGLAND	R	A	£120	
5	1958	Dark* grey body & chassis	Silver	Dark grey	Dark grey	Dark grey	Dark grey	Grenodised 10 spoke	Grenodised 16 daisy	Crimped*	OSRAM LAMPS	LESNEY No6 ENGLAND	R	A	£160	
6		Dark* grey body & chassis	Silver	Dark grey	Dark grey	Dark grey	Dark grey	Grenodised 10 spoke	Grenodised 16 daisy	Riveted	OSRAM LAMPS	LESNEY No6 ENGLAND	S	A	£140	
7	1961	Dark* grey body & chassis	Silver	Dark grey	Dark grey	Dark grey	Dark grey	Black solid 24 tread*	Black solid 30 tread*	Riveted	OSRAM LAMPS	LESNEY No6 ENGLAND	E R	A	£1200	

LIVERY

Transfers
Lorry sides. OSRAM LAMPS in white with black surround, and G.E.C. LONDON in white; all within a red border.

NOTES

1. An example of Issue 1 sold for £1900 at an auction in Devizes, Wiltshire, UK. in 1995.

Y6-2 1926 TYPE 35 BUGATTI

Scale 1:48

INVESTMENT COMMENT
ORIGINAL PRICE £0.15p

This once common and inexpensive model has in some cases maintained its value and in other cases has risen. A must for any serious collection and a model with still further scope for value increase.

Issued in 1961 & phased out in 1967, there are no colour variations on either the blue or red models. There are slight differences to the wheel rim sizes and three main types of tyre exist; grey and black knobbly treads and black fine treads. The plated components; steering wheel, brake lever, and road wheels, can be found in unplated/bare metal. Throughout production the seat component remained in black plastic. The racing number transfers, correctly applied, are a red '6' on white background, but odd models have been reported with a red '9' - the number '6' upside down. Black '5' and '3' transfers have also been reported, but the authenticity of these can be doubtful. An early colour trial model was finished in the metallic green of the Y2-2 Renault and was not issued as a regular production model. The petrol filler cap was usually painted gold but this trim can be omitted or can be missing because the model has rubbed against the interior of its box.

ISSUE	YEAR OF RELEASE	COLOURS	RADIATOR GRILLE	STEERING WHEEL	WHEELS	WHEEL RIMS	TYRES	PLATED PARTS	DASHBOARD & FLOOR	BASEPLATE	RARITY	BOX TYPE	VALUE	CHECK LIST
1	1961	French racing blue body, black base plate	Gold	Brass	Brass 8 spoke	Broad 1mm	Grey knobbly*	Brass	Red	LESNEY No6 ENGLAND	R	C	£125	
2		French racing blue body, black base plate	Gold	Brass	Brass 8 spoke	Broad 1mm	Black knobbly	Brass	Red	LESNEY No6 ENGLAND		C/D1/D2	£40	
3		French racing blue body, black base plate	Gold	Brass	Brass 8 spoke	Broad 1mm	Black fine	Brass	Red	LESNEY No6 ENGLAND		D2	£40	
4		French racing blue body, black baseplate	French racing blue*	Brass	Brass 8 spoke	Broad 1mm	Black knobbly	Brass	Red	LESNEY No6 ENGLAND	R	D1/D2	£125	
5		French racing blue body, black base plate	Gold	Brass	Brass 8 spoke	Narrow 0.5mm	Black fine	Brass	Red	LESNEY No6 ENGLAND		D1/D2/M	£40	
6		French racing blue body, black base plate	French racing blue*	Brass	Brass 8 spoke	Narrow 0.5mm	Black fine	Brass	Red	LESNEY No6 ENGLAND	R	D2/D3	£125	
7		French racing blue body, black base plate	Gold	Brass	Brass 8 spoke	Narrow 0.5mm	Black fine	Brass	White*	LESNEY No6 ENGLAND	E R	D3	£400	
8	1965	Italian racing red body, black baseplate	Gold	Brass	Brass 8 spoke	Narrow 0.5mm	Black fine	Brass	White	LESNEY No6 ENGLAND		D3/E/M	£45	
9		Italian racing red body, black baseplate	Red*	Brass	Brass 8 spoke	Narrow 0.5mm	Black fine	Brass	White	LESNEY No6 ENGLAND	S	D3/E	£75	
10		Italian racing red body, black baseplate	Gold	Brass	Brass 8 spoke	Narrow 0.5mm	Black fine	Brass	Black*	LESNEY No6 ENGLAND	ER	E	£450	

LIVERY

Transfers.
Tail sides. Racing number 6 in red on white disc.

NOTES

1. The red model in the box showing a red model attracts an extra premium.

Y6-3 1913 CADILLAC
Scale 1:48

INVESTMENT COMMENT
ORIGINAL PRICE £0.23.5p

Surprisingly, this beautifully engineered model has failed to register interest and prices remain rather subdued. However, the very early issues, although seldom seen for sale, are certainly worthy of any collection.

Issued in 1968 and withdrawn in 1976, this model was subjected to several baseplate modifications; see diagrams on next page. Very early windscreen frames had uniformly thick top bars, but later issues had a backward facing lug. First type hoods had a smooth underside, but all subsequent issues had two small pips on the underside front edge which locate either side of the windscreen lug. Pre-production models have been recorded with experimental grey fine tread tyres and with white or black smooth hoods and matching radiator grilles. Two distinctly different shades of gold were used before the model was released in the metallic green livery. Interim models inevitably emerged during the change of livery/colour, a prime example being Issue 11. During production of the green livery, trials with different types of self coloured plastic were carried out but were not intended to be released. However, models with light green, pale blue, beige and light pink seats and grilles were found on sale in shops in South Africa. Other trial seats and grilles in white, grey and beige have been recorded. In 1981, a batch of green liveried models were found in a Lesney warehouse; which were packaged with other models in Y6-4 1920 Rolls Royce Fire Engine "straw" Type 1 boxes and sold in retail outlets at £1.00 each. It should be noted that the seats & hoods are easily interchangeable.

ISSUE	YEAR OF RELEASE	COLOURS	HOOD	SEATS	GRILLE	HOOD LOCATION PIPS	WINDSCREEN LUG	BODY SIDE CUT OUTS	WHEELS	BASEPLATE TYPE	BASEPLATE	RARITY	BOX TYPE	VALUE	CHECK LIST
1	1968	Light gold body & chassis	Smooth dark red	Dark red	Dark red	No*	No*	No*	13mm Diameter Brass 12 spoke	A	LESNEY ENGLAND	VR	E1	£100	
2		Light gold body & chassis	Smooth dark red	Dark red	Dark red	Yes	No*	No*	13mm Diameter Brass 12 spoke	A	LESNEY ENGLAND	S	E1	£50	
3		Light gold body & chassis	Smooth dark red	Dark red	Dark red	Yes	Yes	No*	13mm Diameter Brass 12 spoke	A	LESNEY ENGLAND	S	E1/F	£50	
4		Light gold body & chassis	Smooth dark red	Dark red	Dark red	Yes	Yes	Yes	13mm Diameter Brass 12 spoke	A*	LESNEY ENGLAND	R	E1/F	£75	
5		Light gold body & chassis	Smooth dark red	Dark red	Dark red	Yes	Yes	No*	13mm Diameter Brass 12 spoke	B	LESNEY ENGLAND	S	E1/F	£50	
6		Light gold body & chassis	Smooth dark red	Dark red	Dark red	Yes	Yes	Yes	13mm Diameter Brass 12 spoke	B	LESNEY ENGLAND		E1/F	£20	
7		Light gold body & chassis	Smooth dark red	Dark red	Dark red	Yes	Yes	Yes	11mm Diameter Brass 12 spoke	C	LESNEY ENGLAND	S	E1/F	£60	
8		Light gold body & chassis	Smooth dark red	Dark red	Dark red	Yes	Yes	Yes	13mm Diameter Brass 12 spoke	C	LESNEY ENGLAND		E1/F/G	£20	
9	1970	Dark gold body & chassis	Textured* dark red	Dark red	Dark red	Yes	Yes	Yes	13mm Diameter Brass 12 spoke	A*	LESNEY ENGLAND	R	F/G	£70	
10		Dark gold body & chassis	Smooth dark red	Dark red	Dark red	Yes	Yes	Yes	13mm Diameter Brass 12 spoke	C	LESNEY ENGLAND		F/G	£20	
11		Dark gold body & chassis	Smooth dark red	Dark red	Dark red	Yes	Yes	Yes	13mm Diameter Brass 12 spoke	D*	LESNEY ENGLAND	D	F/G	£35	✔
12		Dark gold body & chassis	Smooth dark red	Dark red	Dark red	Yes	Yes	Yes	13mm Diameter Brass 12 spoke	E*	LESNEY ENGLAND	S	F/G	£40	

DIAGRAM 1 BODY CUT-OUTS

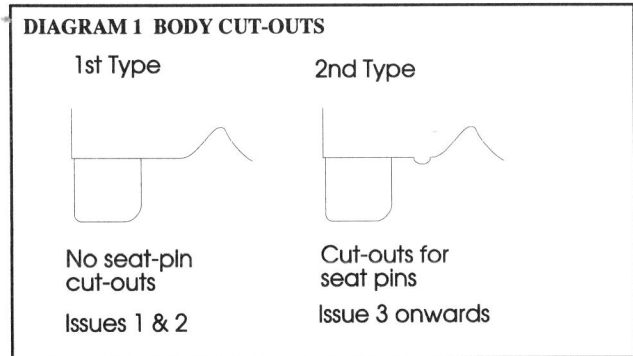

1st Type — No seat-pin cut-outs — Issues 1 & 2

2nd Type — Cut-outs for seat pins — Issue 3 onwards

DIAGRAM 2 WINDSCREEN LUGS AND HOOD PIPS

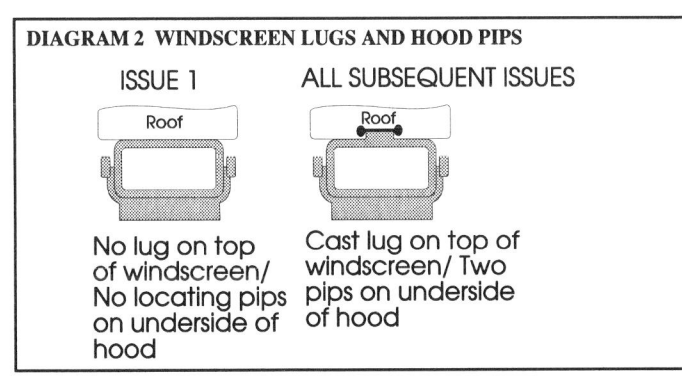

ISSUE 1 — No lug on top of windscreen/ No locating pips on underside of hood

ALL SUBSEQUENT ISSUES — Cast lug on top of windscreen/ Two pips on underside of hood

NOTES
1. All plated parts are in brass effect.
2. Seats and grilles in pink, pale green, or pale blue are colour trial components which were not officially released.

Y6-3 1913 CADILLAC   CONTINUED   Scale 1:48

ISSUE	YEAR OF RELEASE	COLOURS	HOOD	SEATS	GRILLE	HOOD LOCATION PIPS	WINDSCREEN LUG	BODY SIDE CUT OUTS	WHEELS	BASEPLATE TYPE	BASEPLATE	RARITY	BOX TYPE	VALUE	CHECK LIST
13		Dark gold body and chassis	Textured* dark red	Dark red	Dark red	Yes	Yes	Yes	13mm diameter brass 12 spoke	E*	LESNEY ENGLAND	S	F/G	£60	
14		Dark gold body and chassis	Smooth dark red	Dark red	Dark red	Yes	Yes	Yes	13mm diameter brass 12 spoke	F	LESNEY ENGLAND		G	£10	
15		Dark gold body and chassis	Smooth dark red	Bright* red	Dark red	Yes	Yes	Yes	13mm diameter brass 12 spoke	F	LESNEY ENGLAND	R	G	£75	
16		Dark gold body and chassis	Textured* dark red	Dark red	Dark red	Yes	Yes	Yes	13mm diameter brass 12 spoke	F	LESNEY ENGLAND	S	G	£60	
17	1975	Dark gold body and chassis	Textured black	Bright yellow	Bright yellow	Yes	Yes	Yes	Chrome* 12 spoke	F	LESNEY ENGLAND	R	G/H	£100	
18		Metallic green body & chassis	Textured black	Bright yellow	Bright yellow	Yes	Yes	Yes	Chrome* 12 spoke	F	LESNEY ENGLAND	D	H	£15	
19		Metallic green body & chassis	Textured black	Bright yellow	Bright yellow	Yes	Yes	Yes	Chrome* 24 spoke	F	LESNEY ENGLAND		H	£15	
20	1981	Metallic green body & chassis	Textured black	Bright yellow	Bright yellow	Yes	Yes	Yes	Chrome 12 spoke	E	LESNEY ENGLAND		H/I	£15	
21		Metallic green body & chassis	Textured black	Bright yellow	Bright yellow	Yes	Yes	Yes	Yellow* 12 spoke WW	F	LESNEY ENGLAND	D	H/I	£20	

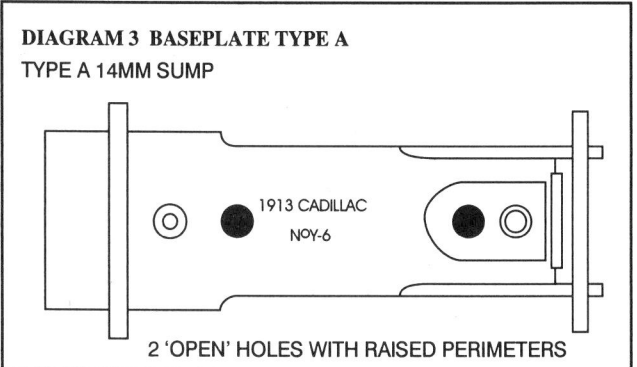

DIAGRAM 3 BASEPLATE TYPE A
TYPE A 14MM SUMP
2 'OPEN' HOLES WITH RAISED PERIMETERS

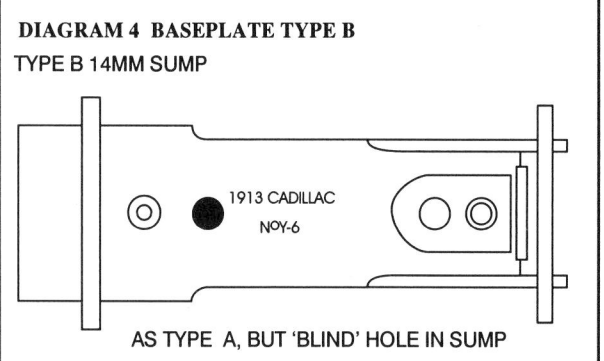

DIAGRAM 4 BASEPLATE TYPE B
TYPE B 14MM SUMP
AS TYPE A, BUT 'BLIND' HOLE IN SUMP

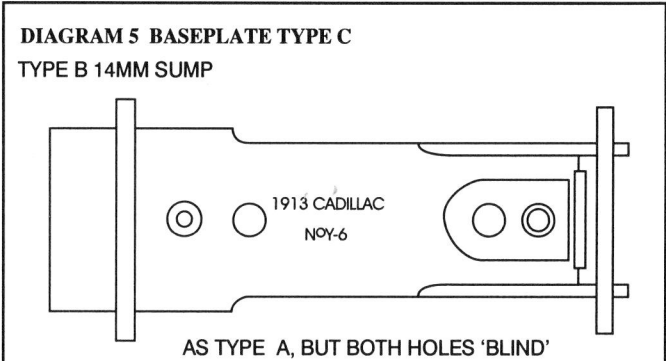

DIAGRAM 5 BASEPLATE TYPE C
TYPE B 14MM SUMP
AS TYPE A, BUT BOTH HOLES 'BLIND'

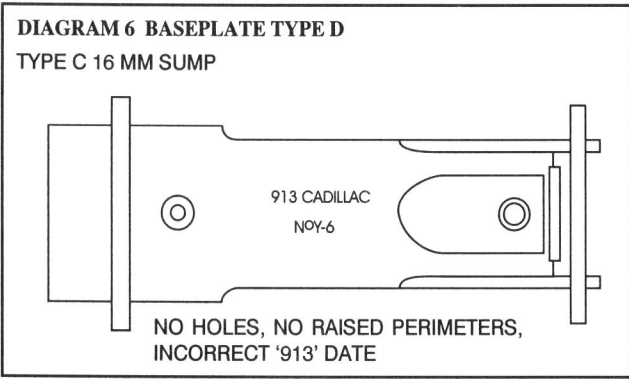

DIAGRAM 6 BASEPLATE TYPE D
TYPE C 16 MM SUMP
NO HOLES, NO RAISED PERIMETERS, INCORRECT '913' DATE

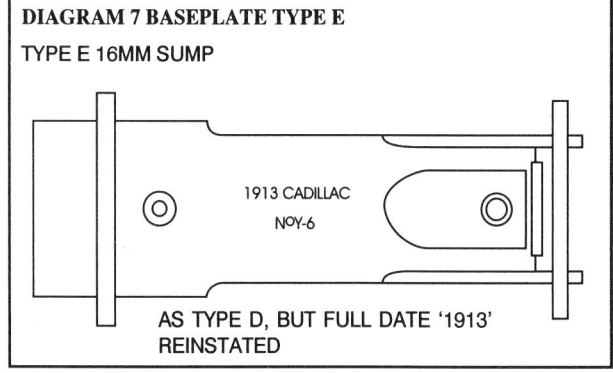

DIAGRAM 7 BASEPLATE TYPE E
TYPE E 16MM SUMP
AS TYPE D, BUT FULL DATE '1913' REINSTATED

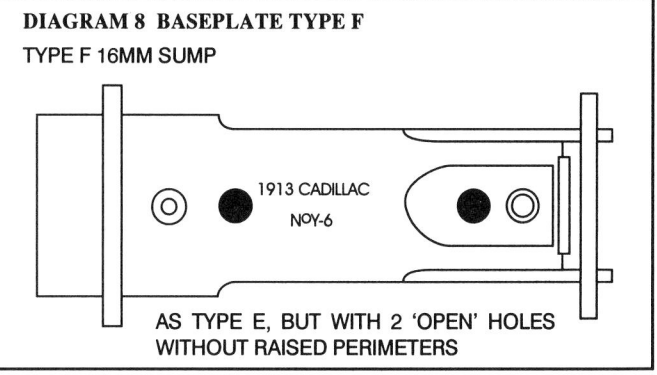

DIAGRAM 8 BASEPLATE TYPE F
TYPE F 16MM SUMP
AS TYPE E, BUT WITH 2 'OPEN' HOLES WITHOUT RAISED PERIMETERS

Y6-4 1920 ROLLS ROYCE FIRE ENGINE — Scale 1:48

INVESTMENT COMMENT
ORIGINAL PRICE £1.49p
Little interest has been recorded since the last publication. Only time will tell if these low value models are "snapped" up by the new generation of fire fighting vehicle collectors. However Issues 14 and 15 often sell for at least £300, and are worth looking for.

This popular model first issued in 1977, was somewhat of a hybrid in that the chassis from the Y7-3 Rolls Royce and the windscreen component from the Y2-3 Vauxhall were used. Pre-production models had matt black chassis; but this livery was not proceeded with, although the 1984 final run did have a glossy black chassis. In 1978, the ladder design was altered to give more prominent, enlarged end lugs. Just before this, the body sides were modified to include two small vertical lugs to indicate the position of the 'Borough Green' labels to the assembly workers. The 1983 issues had a duller, darker red livery than the previous issues and of all the 1983 issues seen so far, it would appear all the chassis' were probably left over from a Y7-3 Rolls Royce car run. The underside of the chassis/baseplates are the same very dark, dull red finish as the cars. Also in 1983, due to tool wear, a new mould was made for the crewmens side seats which resulted in this component being made in plastic. All previous issues had this component in metal. Also in 1983 a limited batch of this model were fitted with bright red front seats, all of which were distributed in West Germany. This variant is now much sought after. Apart from Issue 1 and 17, no great importance has been given to the ladder colours because at the factory these were fitted with no regard to the colour and are so easily interchangeable. This model was withdrawn from the range when production moved to Macau.

ISSUE	YEAR OF RELEASE	COLOURS	DRIVER'S SEAT	CREW MENS SIDE SEATS	PLATED PARTS	WHEELS	LADDERS	LABEL POSITIONING LUGS	BASEPLATE	RARITY	BOX TYPE	VALUE	CHECK LIST
1	1977	Bright red body & chassis	Black plastic	Bronzed metal	Gold	Gold 24 spoke	Type 'A' *White*	Not cast*	LESNEY No Y7 ENGLAND	R	H	£120	
2		Bright red body & chassis	Black plastic	Bronzed metal	Gold	Gold 24 spoke	Type 'A' brown or orangey brown	Not cast*	LESNEY No Y7 ENGLAND	R	H	£100	
3		Bright red body & chassis	Black plastic	Bronzed metal	Gold	Gold 12 spoke	Type 'A' brown or orangey brown	Not cast*	LESNEY No Y7 ENGLAND	R	H	£100	
4		Bright red body & chassis	Black plastic	Bronzed metal	Gold	Gold 12 spoke	Type 'A' brown or orangey brown	Cast	LESNEY No Y7 ENGLAND		H	£15	
5		Bright red body & chassis	Black plastic	Bronzed metal	Gold	Chrome 24 spoke*	Type 'A' brown or orangey brown	Cast	LESNEY No Y7 ENGLAND	D	H/I	£15	
6	1978	Bright red body & chassis	Black plastic	Bronzed metal	Gold	Gold 12 spoke	Type 'B' white, brown, or orangey brown	Cast	LESNEY NoY7 ENGLAND		H/I	£10	✓
7		Bright red body & chassis	Black plastic	Bronzed metal	Gold	Gold 12 spoke	Type 'A' brown or orangey brown	Cast	LESNEY NoY7&Y6 ENGLAND		H/I	£10	
8		Bright red body & chassis	Black plastic	Bronzed metal	Gold	Gold 12 spoke	Type 'B' white, brown, or orangey brown	Cast	LESNEY NoY7&Y6 ENGLAND		H/I	£10	
9		Bright red body & chassis	Black plastic	Bronzed metal	Gold	Chrome 24 spoke*	Type 'B' white, brown, or orangey brown	Cast	LESNEY NoY7&Y6 ENGLAND	D	H/I	£15	
10		Bright red body & chassis	Black plastic	Bronzed metal	Gold	Red 12 spoke	Type 'B' white, brown, or orangey brown	Cast	LESNEY NoY7&Y6 ENGLAND	S	H/I	£20	
11	1983	Darker red body & chassis	Black plastic	Bronzed metal	Gold	Gold 12 spoke	Type 'B' white, brown, or orangey brown	Cast	LESNEY NoY7&Y6 ENGLAND		I	£10	

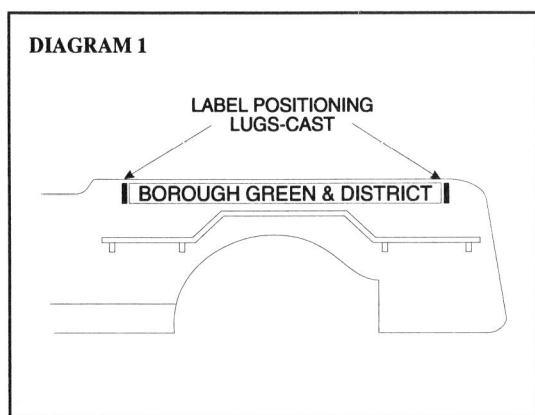

DIAGRAM 1 — LABEL POSITIONING LUGS-CAST — BOROUGH GREEN & DISTRICT

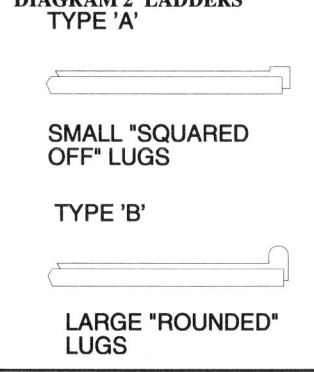

DIAGRAM 2 LADDERS
TYPE 'A'
SMALL "SQUARED OFF" LUGS
TYPE 'B'
LARGE "ROUNDED" LUGS

LADDER TYPES
Ladders. Issue 1 only had a type 'A' ladder in white. Issues 2 to 5 & 7 can have any combination of brown or orangey brown type 'A' ladders. Issues 6 & 8 to 16 can have any combination of white, brown or orangey brown type 'B' ladders. Issue 17 only ever had a white type 'B' ladder.

LIVERY
Labels
Vehicle sides. Yellow BOROUGH GREEN & DISTRICT in red.
N.B. Colours can vary due to either different printing runs or to fading.

NOTES
BECKENHAM APPEAL MODEL
Pale grey body, black chassis.
Gold plated parts.
Brown ladder black seats.

Y6-4 1920 ROLLS ROYCE FIRE ENGINE (CONTINUED)   Scale 1:48

ISSUE	YEAR OF RELEASE	COLOURS	DRIVERS SEAT	CREW MENS SIDE SEATS	PLATED PARTS	WHEELS	LADDERS	LABEL POSITIONING LUGS	BASEPLATE	RARITY	BOX TYPE	VALUE	CHECK LIST
12		Darker red body & chassis	Black plastic	Bronzed metal	Gold	Red 12 spoke*	Type 'B' white, brown, or orangey brown	Cast	LESNEY NoY7&Y6 ENGLAND	D	I	£15	
13		Darker red body & chassis	Black plastic	Bronzed metal	Gold	Chrome 12 spoke*	Type 'B' white, brown, or orangey brown	Cast	LESNEY NoY7&Y6 ENGLAND	D	I	£15	
14		Darker red body & chassis	Bright red plastic*	Bronzed metal	Gold	Gold 12 spoke	Type 'B' white, brown, or orangey brown	Cast	LESNEY NoY7&Y6 ENGLAND	V R	I	£300	
15		Darker red body & chassis	Bright red plastic*	Black plastic	Gold	Gold 12 spoke	Type 'B' white, brown, or orangey brown	Cast	LESNEY NoY7&Y6 ENGLAND	V R	I	£300	
16		Darker red body & chassis	Black plasitc	Black plastic	Gold	Gold 12 spoke	Type 'B' white, brown, or orangey brown	Cast	LESNEY NoY7&Y6 ENGLAND		I	£10	
17	1984	Darker red body gloss black chassis	Black plastic	Black plastic	Gold	Gold 12 spoke	Type 'B' white	Cast	LESNEY NoY7&Y6 ENGLAND		J/L	£10	
18		Darker red body gloss black chassis	Black plastic	Black plastic	Gold	Chrome* 12 spoke	Type 'B' white	Cast	LESNEY NoY7&Y6 ENGLAND	D	J	£15	✔

NOTES

Y6-5 1932 MERCEDES BENZ "L5" LORRY Scale 1:69

INVESTMENT COMMENT
ORIGINAL PRICE £5.75p

Certainly good value at the moment. An attractive livery with Issue 2, the one to find.

STUTTGARTER HOFBRÄU. The introduction of the Mercedes Benz Lorry in June 1988 was a further example of the internationalism of the range with Germany in particular being one of the strongest markets. Several collectors, upon finding the reference number 'YY32' cast onto the underside of the tarpaulin cover support framework and front underside of the body, correctly assumed that the Models of Yesteryear range was soon to be extended beyond Y30! This reference number was used to identify components during manufacture. It should be noted that in 1989 the planking relief of the truck body sides was reduced i.e. made shallower to give a smoother surface for the tampo printing process. Unfortunately the only way to see the difference is to compare an early model with a later one! The Y6-5 model became the basis for the Y41-1 model 'Howaldtswerke A.G.' The second livery, "Holstein" was to have been a 1992 release, but was cancelled. However in 1993 it did appear as YGB06.

A : STUTTGARTER HOFBRÄU

ISSUE	YEAR OF RELEASE	COLOURS	CAB ROOF	SEAT & CAB FLOOR	GRILLE	STEERING WHEEL	WHEELS	PLATED PARTS	TARPAULIN FRAME WORK	TARPAULIN	LOGO	TRUCK BODY 'PLANKING' EFFECT	CAB STEP SUPPORTS	BASEPLATE	RARITY	BOX TYPE	VALUE	CHECK LIST
1	1988	Cream body cab and bonnet. Gloss black cab steps and mudguards. Grey chassis	Cream plastic	Dark grey plastic	Black	Dark grey plastic	Red 6 spoke	Chrome	Dark grey plastic	Cream plastic	STUTTGARTER HOFBRÄU	Deep	Type A	MATCHBOX © 1988 MACAU		J 1	£10	
2	1989	Cream body cab and bonnet. Gloss black cab steps and mudguards. Grey chassis	Cream plastic	Dark grey plastic	Black	Dark grey plastic	Red 6 spoke	Chrome	Dark grey plastic	Cream plastic	STUTTGARTER HOFBRÄU	Deep*	Type B*	MATCHBOX © 1988 MACAU	S	J 1	£15	
3	1989	Cream body cab and bonnet. Gloss black cab steps and mudguards. Grey chassis	Cream plastic	Dark grey plastic	Black	Dark grey plastic	Red 6 spoke	Chrome	Dark grey plastic	Cream plastic	STUTTGARTER HOFBRÄU	Shallow	Type B	MATCHBOX © 1988 MACAU		J 1	£10	✓

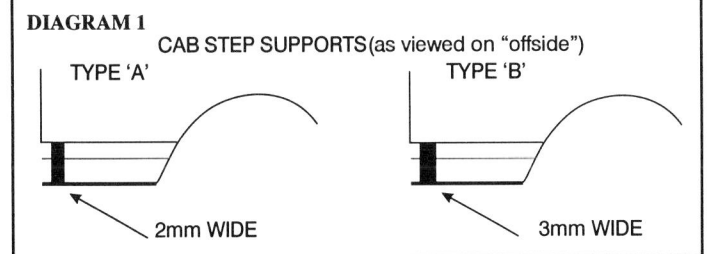

DIAGRAM 1 CAB STEP SUPPORTS (as viewed on "offside")
TYPE 'A' — 2mm WIDE
TYPE 'B' — 3mm WIDE

LIVERY STUTTGARTER HOFBRÄU
Tampo
Truck body sides. Red STUTTGARTER HOFBRÄU with black edging.
Cab doors and tarpaulin. Gold and black company crest.

NOTES
1. Compare with Y41-1, YGB06, YFE05, YGB17, and YPP03.
2. When the planking was reduced, the front of the tarpaulin cover was also changed by adding a 3mm square lug to locate into the square of the rear cab window. This was to prevent the tarpaulin falling off.

Y 7-1 1918 4 TON LEYLAND VAN

Scale 1:100

INVESTMENT COMMENT
ORIGINAL PRICE £0.12.5p

Always a popular model. Be prepared to pay top price for absolutely mint and boxed models. A must for any serious collection.

Issued in 1957 and withdrawn in 1960. In 1970 in Kenya and 1971 in Spain, a small quantity were found with the "By Royal Appointment" centre line of the body transfers omitted. Some were complete transfers with just the lettering and coat of arms omitted; some were two piece transfers with the centre line cut out prior to fixing to the models. Some have the black dividing lines and some do not. Many theories exist for the transfers being in this state, but no official reason exists. The one piece transfers without the centre line lettering were probably pre-production examples made prior to permission being granted by the Lord Chamberlain's office to use the 'By Royal Appointment' logo and coat of arms. The roof of this model commonly suffered from a "pitted" finish caused by problems with the moulds. During the final production run, the supply of the grey metal wheels was exhausted and a concession was given to use the black plastic wheels from the "Matchbox" Series to complete the remaining models.

ISSUE	YEAR OF RELEASE	COLOURS	ROOF	RADIATOR SHELL	FRONT WHEELS	REAR WHEELS	UNDERSIDE OF ROOF	LOGO	AXLES	TRANSFER TYPE	BASEPLATE	RARITY	BOX TYPE	VALUE	CHECK LIST
1	1957	Dark brown* body & chassis	White*	Silver	Grenodised solid	Grenodised solid	Bare metal	W & R JACOB & CO LTD	Crimped	A	LESNEY NO 7 ENGLAND	S	A	£120	
2		Dark brown* body & chassis	Cream	Silver	Grenodised solid	Grenodised solid	Bare metal	W & R JACOB & CO LTD	Crimped	A	LESNEY NO 7 ENGLAND	D	A	£110	
3		Lighter* brown body & chassis	Cream	Silver	Grenodised solid	Grenodised solid	Bare metal	W & R JACOB & CO LTD	Crimped	B*	LESNEY NO 7 ENGLAND	E R	A	£600	
4		Lighter* brown body & chassis	Cream	Silver	Grenodised solid	Grenodised solid	Bare metal	W & R JACOB & CO LTD	Crimped	A	LESNEY NO 7 ENGLAND	S	A	£110	
5	1959	Reddish brown* body & chassis	Cream	Reddish brown	Grenodised solid	Grenodised solid	Bare metal	W & R JACOB & CO LTD	Crimped	A	LESNEY NO 7 ENGLAND	D	A	£110	
6		Reddish brown* body & chassis	Cream	Reddish brown	Grenodised solid	Grenodised solid	Cream	W & R JACOB & CO LTD	Crimped*	A	LESNEY NO 7 ENGLAND	S	A	£110	
7		Reddish brown* body & chassis	Cream	Silver	Grenodised solid	Grenodised solid	Cream	W & R JACOB & CO LTD	Riveted	A	LESNEY NO 7 ENGLAND	D	A	£110	
8		Reddish brown* body & chassis	Cream	Reddish brown	Grenodised solid	Grenodised solid	Cream	W & R JACOB & CO LTD	Riveted	A	LESNEY NO 7 ENGLAND	D	A	£110	
9	1960	Reddish brown body & chassis	Cream	Reddish brown	Black* solid 24 tread	Black* solid 32 tread	Cream	W & R JACOB & CO LTD	Riveted	A	LESNEY NO 7 ENGLAND	E R	A	£900	

LIVERY TYPE A

Transfers
Van body sides. Top line. W & R JACOB & CO LTD in yellow with white shadow.
Centre line. BY ROYAL APPOINTMENT TO HIS MAJESTY THE KING and Royal Crest in yellow with black horizontal coach lines above and below.
Bottom line. BISCUIT MANUFACTURER and associated scroll-work in yellow.

LIVERY TYPE B

Transfers
Van body sides. As type A but BY ROYAL APPOINTMENT TO HIS MAJESTY THE KING and Royal Crest missing. Also the two horizontal black coach lines may or may not be deleted.

NOTES

INVESTMENT COMMENT
ORIGINAL PRICE £0.20p.

As previously forecast, the later yellow models have not only held their market value but have seen an increase. The Mercer remains a popular model with collectors and values should increase further.

Y7-2 1913 MERCER RACEABOUT TYPE 35J   Scale 1:46

Introduced in 1961, this model had a fairly short life of just six years. Originally intended as a replacement for the Y6-1 AEC Lorry, it in fact replaced the prematurely discontinued Y7-1 Leyland van. Pre - production Mercers had No6 cast on the base, but this was changed to No7. The original livery of lilac was superceded after four years by a bright yellow livery. The shade of lilac can vary from almost silver to purplish mauve, due to paint variations or fading; but the bright yellow varied very little. The seats were only made in black plastic. The main casting variations concerned the gap between the front mudguards and the chassis and the addition of strengthening webs to the front springs. Minor alterations were made to the centre boss of the steering wheel and the length of the spotlamp during production. This model suffered from the wheels, gear/brake levers, lamps and steering wheel not being brass plated and models exist with any combination of plated/unplated components. This fact, together with variations in the shade of lilac has resulted in over one hundred permutations. Thus the following issues are based only on the major changes made and assumes all plated components have the correct brass plating effect finish.

ISSUE	YEAR OF RELEASE	COLOURS	RADIATOR SHELL	GRILLE	PLATED PARTS	SPOT LAMP	TYRES	WHEELS	FRONT MUDGUARDS TO CHASSIS	BASEPLATE TEXT	BASEPLATE HOLES	FRONT SPRING WEBS	BASEPLATE	RARITY	BOX TYPE	VALUE	CHECK LIST
1	1961	Lilac body & chassis	Gold	Lilac	Brass	Short	Black knobbly	Brass 12 spoke	Type 1*	3 Lines	None	No*	LESNEY ENGLAND No 7	R	C	£60	
2		Lilac body & chassis	Gold	Lilac	Brass	Short	Black knobbly	Brass 12 spoke	Type 2*	3 Lines	None	No*	LESNEY ENGLAND No 7	S	C	£50	
3		Lilac body & chassis	Gold	Lilac	Brass	Short	Black knobbly	Brass 12 spoke	Type 3*	4 Lines	Two	Yes	LESNEY ENGLAND No 7	D	D1/D2	£50	✓
4		Lilac body & chassis	Gold	Lilac	Brass	Short	Black knobbly	Brass 12 spoke	Type 4	4 Lines	None*	Yes	LESNEY ENGLAND No 7	D	D1/D2	£50	
5		Lilac body & chassis	Gold	Lilac	Brass	Short	Black fine	Brass 12 spoke	Type 4	4 Lines	Two	Yes	LESNEY ENGLAND No 7		D1/D2	£35	
6		Lilac body & chassis	Gold	Lilac	Brass	Short	Black knobbly	Brass 12 spoke	Type 4	4 Lines	Two	Yes	LESNEY ENGLAND No 7		D2/D3	£35	
7	1963	Lilac body & chassis	Gold	Lilac	Brass	Long	Black fine	Brass 12 spoke	Type 4	4 Lines	Two	Yes	LESNEY ENGLAND No 7		D2/D3	£40	
8		Lilac body & chassis	Gold	Lilac	Brass	Long	Black fine	Brass 12 spoke	Type 4	4 Lines	Two	Yes	LESNEY ENGLAND No 7		D2/D3	£35	
9	1965	Yellow body & chassis	Gold	Yellow	Brass	Short*	Black fine	Brass 12 spoke	Type 4	4 Lines	Two	Yes	LESNEY ENGLAND No 7	D	D3/E	£50	✓
10		Yellow body & chassis	Gold	Yellow	Brass	Long	Black fine	Brass 12 spoke	Type 4	4 Lines	Two	Yes	LESNEY ENGLAND No 7		D3/E	£45	
11		Yellow body & chassis	Yellow*	Yellow	Brass	Long	Black fine	Brass 12 spoke	Type 4	4 Lines	Two	Yes	LESNEY ENGLAND No 7	S	E	£50	

DIAGRAM 1 FRONT MUDGUARDS TO CHASSIS TYPES

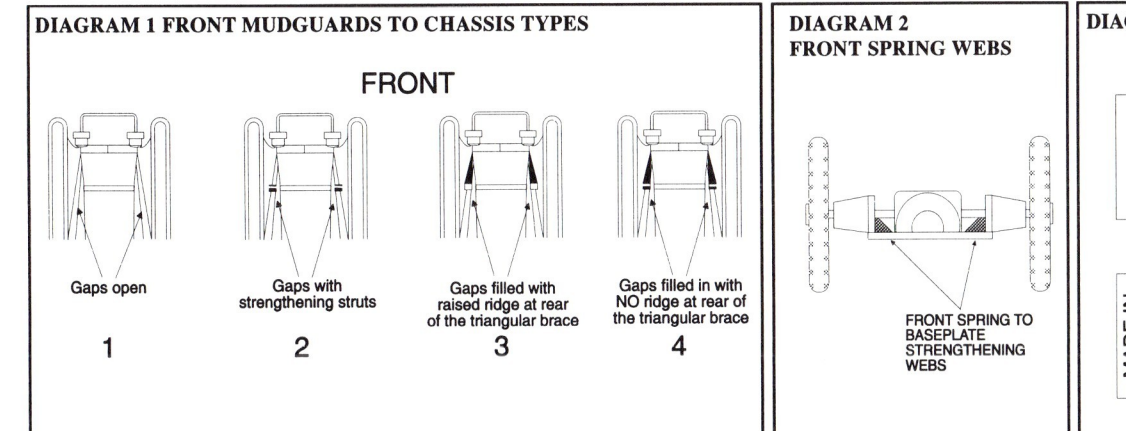

1. Gaps open
2. Gaps with strengthening struts
3. Gaps filled with raised ridge at rear of the triangular brace
4. Gaps filled in with NO ridge at rear of the triangular brace

DIAGRAM 2 FRONT SPRING WEBS

FRONT SPRING TO BASEPLATE STRENGTHENING WEBS

DIAGRAM 3 BASEPLATE TEXT

MADE IN ENGLAND BY LESNEY — NO BASEPLATE HOLES 3 LINE TEXT

Rear of Base

MADE IN ENGLAND BY LESNEY — TWO BASEPLATE HOLES 4 LINE TEXT

DIAGRAM 4 SPOT LAMPS

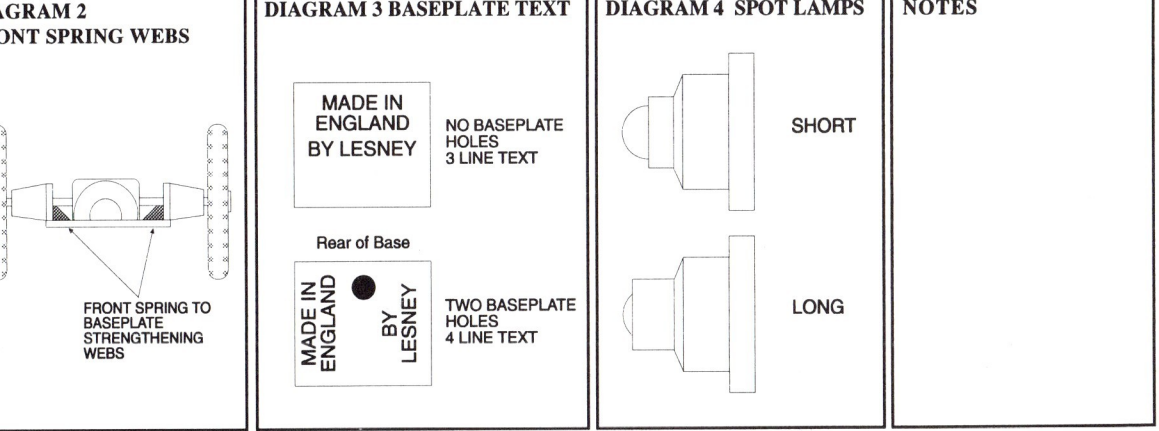

SHORT

LONG

NOTES

Y7-3 1912 ROLLS ROYCE

Scale 1:48

INVESTMENT COMMENT
ORIGINAL PRICE £0.34p

Standard issue models presently represent very good value especially the silver and red models. A good seller for Lesney and Matchbox and worthy of any Yesteryear collection.

Issued in 1968 and phased out of production in 1983, this model is probably the most extensively modified model in the range. Three different spare tyre carriers were used, the second and third types because of the change over of tyre types. Five different modifications were made to the baseplate due to the model being used in the Giftware series and the baseplate being used on the Y6-4 Fire Engine. The roof was altered three times; the first time to change the top surface design and the second to include two small locating lugs on the underside. Grey ribbed roofs with these small lugs (Type C) could have been switched from the giftware models and could be fakes. Differences in the shade of gold bodies and the red of the roofs on Issues 10 to 29 can vary considerably. When the Yesteryear range was relaunched in 1974, many interim versions were found for sale in different countries, but the quantities were very limited and are very rarely seen for sale nowadays. Seats and grilles can have a tendency to fall out and are easily switched, giving rise to even more variations - not necessarily genuine! The majority of Issues 4 and 6 were exported to the USA and were packaged in "blister" packs.

ISSUE	YEAR OF RELEASE	COLOURS	ROOF TYPE	SPARE TYRE CARRIER TYPE	SEATS	GRILLE	WHEELS	PLATED PARTS	BASEPLATE TYPE	BASEPLATE	RARITY	BOX TYPE	VALUE	CHECK LIST
1	1968	Silver body & bonnet, dark red chassis	Dark red A	A	Dark red	Dark red	Brass 12 spoke	Brass	A	LESNEY ENGLAND		E 1	£25	✓
2		Silver body & bonnet, dark red chassis	Dark red A	A	Yellow	Dark red	Brass 12 spoke	Brass	A	LESNEY ENGLAND	V R	E 1	£350	
3	1969	Silver body & bonnet, dark red chassis	Grey A	A	Dark red	Dark red	Brass 12 spoke	Brass	A	LESNEY ENGLAND		E 1	£30	
4		Silver body & bonnet, dark red chassis	Grey B*	A	Dark red	Dark red	Brass 12 spoke	Brass	A	LESNEY ENGLAND	R	E 1/ F	£125	
5		Silver body & bonnet, dark red chassis	Dark red B	A	Dark red	Dark red	Brass 12 spoke	Brass	A	LESNEY ENGLAND		F	£20	✓
6		Silver body & bonnet, dark red chassis	Grey B*	A	Dark red	Dark red	Brass 12 spoke	Brass	B	LESNEY ENGLAND	R	F	£125	
7		Silver body & bonnet, dark red chassis	Dark red B	A	Dark red	Dark red	Brass 12 spoke	Brass	B	LESNEY ENGLAND		F/ G	£20	
8		Silver body & bonnet, dark red chassis	Dark red C	A	Dark red	Dark red	Brass 12 spoke	Brass	B	LESNEY ENGLAND		F/G	£20	
9		Silver body & bonnet, dark red chassis	Dark red C	B*	Dark red	Dark red	Chrome 12 spoke*	Brass	B	LESNEY ENGLAND	S	H	£30	
10	1974	Gold body, silver* bonnet, red chassis	Red C	A	Dark red	Dark red	Brass 12 spoke	N.B. Brass but *copper fire extinguisher*	D	LESNEY ENGLAND	V R	H	£150	
11		Gold body, silver* bonnet, red chassis	Red C	A	Black	Black or dark red	Brass 12 spoke	N.B. Brass but *copper fire extinguisher*	B	LESNEY ENGLAND	V R	H	£150	
12		Gold body, silver* bonnet, red chassis	Red C	A	Black	Dark red	Brass 12 spoke	N.B. Brass but *copper fire extinguisher*	C	LESNEY ENGLAND	R	H	£150	
13		Gold body & bonnet red chassis	Red C	A*	Dark red	Dark red	Brass 12 spoke*	Brass	B	LESNEY ENGLAND	R	H	£150	
14		Gold body & bonnet red chassis	Red C	A*	Black	Black	Brass 12 spoke*	Brass	B	LESNEY ENGLAND	R	H	£125	

DIAGRAM 1 — POSITION OF ROOF LUGS
ROOF LUGS

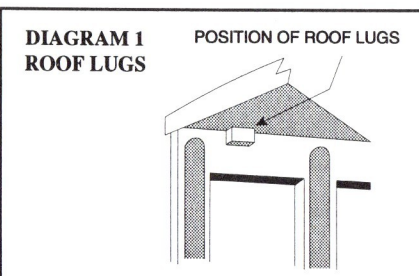

DIAGRAM 2 — SPARE TYRE CARRIER TYPES

TYPE 'A'  FOR ORIGINAL SOLID TYRES NOTE RETAINING TABS

TYPE 'B'  FOR WIDER HOLLOW SECTION TYRES **NO** RETAINING TABS

TYPE 'C'  SOLID CENTRE FOR WIDER HOLLOW SECTION TYRES

BOTH WITH CENTRE 'CUT-OUT' SECTIONS

ROOF TYPES

TYPE A. Smooth.
TYPE B. Ribbed rear section.
TYPE C. Ribbed rear section with roof lugs.

NOTES

BECKENHAM APPEAL MODEL
Lemon body and bonnet. Brown Type C roof and brown.
Type E baseplate.
Dark red seats, black grille and chrome 12 spoke wheels.
Brass plated parts, but copper coloured extinguisher.

Y7-3 1912 ROLLS ROYCE CONTINUED   Scale 1:48

ISSUE	YEAR OF RELEASE	COLOURS	ROOF TYPE	SPARE TYRE CARRIER TYPE	SEATS	GRILLE	WHEELS	PLATED PARTS	BASEPLATE TYPE	BASEPLATE	RARITY	BOX TYPE	VALUE	CHECK LIST
15		Gold body & bonnet, red chassis	Red C	B	Dark red	Dark red	Chrome 12 spoke	Brass	B	LESNEY ENGLAND		H	£20	
16		Gold body & bonnet, red chassis	Red C	B	Black	Black	Chrome 12 spoke	N.B. Brass but brass or copper fire extinguisher	B	LESNEY ENGLAND		H	£20	
17		Gold body & bonnet, red chassis	Red C	B	Black	Black	Chrome 24 spoke	N.B. Brass but brass or copper fire extinguisher	B	LESNEY ENGLAND		H	£18	
18		Gold body & bonnet, red chassis	Red C	A	Dark red	Dark red	Brass 12 spoke*	N.B. Brass but brass or copper fire extinguisher	C	LESNEY ENGLAND		H	£50	
19		Gold body & bonnet, red chassis	Red C	A	Black	Black	Brass 12 spoke*	N.B. Brass but brass or copper fire extinguisher	C	LESNEY ENGLAND		H	£50	
20		Gold body & bonnet, red chassis	Red C	B	Dark red	Dark red	Chrome 12 spoke	Brass	C	LESNEY ENGLAND		H	£12	
21		Gold body & bonnet, red chassis	Red C	B	Black	Black	Chrome 12 spoke	Brass	C	LESNEY ENGLAND		H	£12	
22		Gold body & bonnet, red chassis	Red C	B	Dark red	Dark red	Chrome 12 spoke	Brass	D	LESNEY ENGLAND		H	£12	
23		Gold body & bonnet, red chassis	Red C	B	Black	Black	Chrome 12 spoke	Brass	D	LESNEY ENGLAND		H	£12	
24		Gold body & bonnet, red chassis	Red C	C	Dark red	Dark red	Chrome 12 spoke	Brass	D	LESNEY ENGLAND		H	£12	
25		Gold body & bonnet, red chassis	Red C	C	Black	Black	Chrome 12 spoke	Brass	D	LESNEY ENGLAND		H	£12	
26		Gold body & bonnet, red chassis	Red C	C	Black	Black	Chrome 24 spoke	Brass	D	LESNEY ENGLAND		H	£12	
27		Gold body & bonnet, red chassis	Red C	C	Green*	Green*	Chrome 12 spoke	Brass	D	LESNEY ENGLAND	V R	H	£125	
28		Gold body & bonnet, red chassis	Red C	C	Black	Black	Chrome 12 spoke	Brass	E	LESNEY ENGLAND		H	£12	✓
29		Gold body & bonnet, red chassis	Red C	C	Black	Black	Red 12 spoke	Brass	E	LESNEY ENGLAND	D	H	£35	
30	1979	Yellow body & bonnet, gloss black chassis	Gloss black C	C	Black	Black	Dark or mid red 12 spoke (BW)	Brass	E'	LESNEY ENGLAND		I	£12	✓
31		Yellow body & bonnet, gloss black chassis	Gloss black C	C	Black	Black	Chrome 12 spoke (BW)	Brass	E	LESNEY ENGLAND	D	I	£25	
32		Yellow body & bonnet, gloss black chassis	Gloss black C	C	Black	Black	Chrome 24 spoke (BW)	Brass	E	LESNEY ENGLAND	D	I	£25	

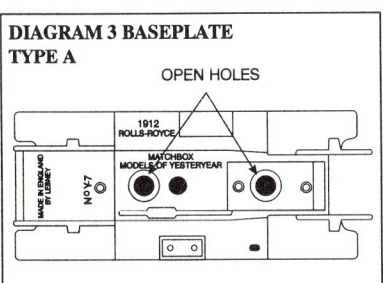

DIAGRAM 3 BASEPLATE TYPE A — OPEN HOLES

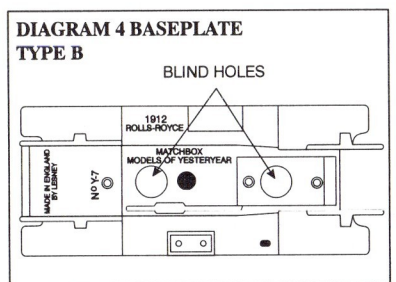

DIAGRAM 4 BASEPLATE TYPE B — BLIND HOLES

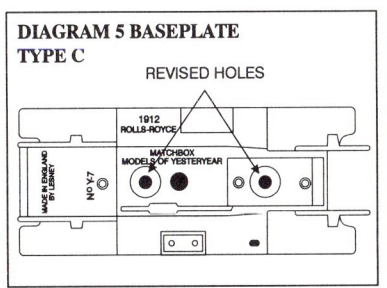

DIAGRAM 5 BASEPLATE TYPE C — REVISED HOLES

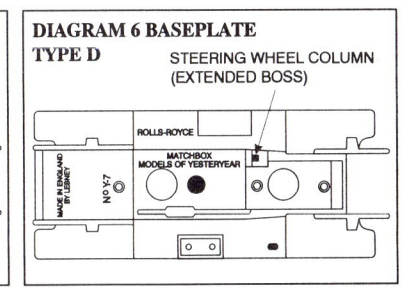

DIAGRAM 6 BASEPLATE TYPE D — STEERING WHEEL COLUMN (EXTENDED BOSS)

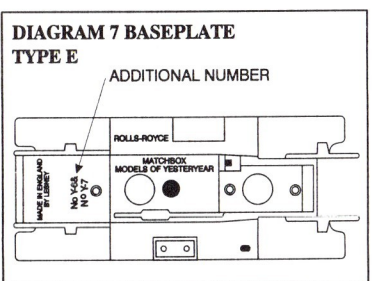

DIAGRAM 7 BASEPLATE TYPE E — ADDITIONAL NUMBER

Y7-4 1930 FORD BREAKDOWN TRUCK   Scale 1:40

BARLOW. Issued in 1985 this model was based upon a breakdown truck which was located in the United States. The Research and Development team at Matchbox Toys used a Y21 Model "A" Ford as the basis for their model. They modified the cab and fitted a simulated canvas roof and opened up the rear to hold a plastic crane jib and hook. Early mock-ups and toy fair samples had modified roofs taken from the Y13 Crossley. They had much larger green hooks and orange painted plastic bumpers. On all production models the front bumper was made in orange plastic whereas the rear bumper was made in metal and painted orange. The box containing the 1985 issue had a gold and red sticker label for the 1986 Calendar offer. With the move of Yesteryear production to Macau, the baseplate was altered and models bearing the Macau baseplate began appearing on the market in mid 1987 and a new type of paint was used. Total production of Issue 4 and 5 was 2,760 models.

SHELL. Introduced in May 1988 as a new standard livery for this model. Modifications were made to the original Y21 and Y22 baseplate by including Y7 as the baseplate component was common to all three models. As was the case with the "Barlow" model the baseplate component continued to have one hole and a further hole through the sump. A well received addition to the range with only one reported variation and generally thought to be a most attractive model.

A : BARLOW MOTOR SALES

ISSUE	YEAR OF RELEASE	COLOURS	ROOF	SEAT FLOOR/DASH	PLATED PARTS	WHEELS	CRANE UNIT/CRANE WINCH	BUMPER	LOGO	BASEPLATE	RARITY	BOX TYPE	VALUE	CHECK LIST
1	1985	Orange body, glossy black chassis	Black plastic	Light brown	Chrome	Orange solid (WW)	Dark green ✓	Orange	BARLOW	MATCHBOX © ENGLAND 1981 Y21		J	£8	✓?
2		Orange body, glossy black chassis	Black plastic	Light brown	Chrome	Orange solid (WW)	Light green*	Orange	BARLOW	MATCHBOX © ENGLAND1981 Y21	S	J	£20	
3		Orange body, glossy black chassis	Black plastic	Light brown	Chrome	Orange solid (WW)	Grass green ✓	Orange	BARLOW	MATCHBOX © ENGLAND1981 Y21		J	£8	✓
4		Bright orange body, glossy black chassis	Black plastic	Rust brown	Chrome	Darker orange solid (WW)	Dull darker green	Orange	BARLOW	MATCHBOX © MACAU* 1981 Y7 Y21 Y22*	S	J1	£20	
5		Bright orange body, glossy black chassis	Black plastic	Rust brown	Chrome	Darker orange solid (WW)	Dark green	Orange	BARLOW	MATCHBOX © MACAU 1981 Y7 Y21 Y22*	R	J1	£25	

B : SHELL

ISSUE	YEAR OF RELEASE	COLOURS	ROOF	SEAT FLOOR/DASH	PLATED PARTS	WHEELS	CRANE UNIT/CRANE WINCH	BUMPER	LOGO	BASEPLATE	RARITY	BOX TYPE	VALUE	CHECK LIST
1	1988	Bright yellow body, glossy black chassis	Black plastic	Rust brown	Chrome	Red solid (WW)	Light grey	Yellow	SHELL	MATCHBOX © MACAU 1981 Y7 Y21 Y22		J	£8	✓
2	1988	Bright yellow body, glossy black chassis	Black plastic	Rust brown	Chrome	Red solid (WW)	Grey*	Yellow	SHELL	MATCHBOX © MACAU 1981 Y7 Y21 Y22	D	J	£10	

LIVERY BARLOW MOTOR SALES
Tampo
Cab doors. BARLOW MOTOR SALES in black with white shadow effect.
QUALITY CARS. ROCKVILLE CONN. EST 1939 in black.
Body panels. WRECKER SERVICE TR5-2538 in black with white shadow effect. 24 HOUR PHONE in black.

LIVERY SHELL
Tampo
Body panels. SHELL in red with black shadow effect and SERVICE STATION in black.
Cab doors. Three dimensional sketch of oil can in red, white on black.

INVESTMENT COMMENT
ORIGINAL PRICE, BARLOW £3.99p
SHELL £4.25p
BARLOW An increasingly popular livery and one with potential. Issue 4 or 5 with Macau baseplates presently valued at £20 have a further growth potential, especially as a mere 2,760 models were made.
SHELL Although few models are seen for sale on the second-hand market, the value has remained static.

Y8-1 1926 MORRIS COWLEY BULLNOSE — Scale 1:50

INVESTMENT COMMENT

ORIGINAL PRICE £0.12.5p

This fragile model has continued to hold its value. It is not easy to find a model in absolutely mint boxed condition: often the dickey seat cover tab has been broken off. Although it is still to reach the £100 mark; it often commands prices in excess of this in the Australian and German markets.

Issued in 1958, this model was enthusiastically received by collectors being the first saloon car in the range. Apart from a minor change to the tan coloured dickey seat cover hinge, the casting remained unchanged for its production life of four years. Whilst the majority of these models have bare metal wheels, the standard wheel finish for this model is silver plating. Many models however were fitted with unplated wheels which have discoloured with age to reveal a copper effect. Either type of wheel finish can be found in all issues. The dickey seat cover is a separate component, and because two distinct tones of tan exist the cover can miss-match the main body colour. In 1988, models were reported with what appeared to be a tow hook, but in fact was part of the casting sprue which had not been removed during the fettling process. All issues had black knobbly tyres.

ISSUE	YEAR OF RELEASE	COLOURS	PAINTED TRIM	RADIATOR / GRILLE	AXLES	WHEELS	BASEPLATE	RARITY	BOX TYPE	VALUE	CHECK LIST
1	1958	Tan body, dark brown chassis	Gold	Gold	Crimped	Silver plated 10 spoke	LESNEY No 8 ENGLAND		A	£90	
2		Tan body, dark brown chassis	Gold	Gold	Crimped	Bare metal 10 spoke	LESNEY No 8 ENGLAND		A/B	£90	
3		Tan body, dark brown chassis	Gold	Gold	Riveted	Silver plated 10 spoke	LESNEY No 8 ENGLAND		B/C	£90	
4		Darker tan body, dark brown chassis	Gold	Gold	Riveted	Bare metal 10 spoke	LESNEY No 8 ENGLAND		C	£90	

NOTES

INVESTMENT COMMENT
ORIGINAL PRICE £0.15p
An unpopular model at its time of release but now one of the more popular Second Series. Values for standard issues fluctuate between £40 and £60. The rarer issues have all increased in value, albeit not dramatically.

Y8-2 1914 SUNBEAM MOTORCYCLE WITH MILFORD SIDECAR   Scale 1:34

When first issued the Sunbeam Motorcycle with Milford sidecar was unpopular with collectors for several reasons; the scale was out of line with the rest of the range and the silver plated finish was deemed quite inappropriate. The model was produced with a green plastic sidecar seat, but a limited number of final production models were finished in black plastic and more often than not showing signs of tool deterioration. The policy at Lesney Products for the changing of colour plastic components once the standard colour had been exhausted was that there was no need for management permission if the factory had a production quota of less than 200 models to finish! Consequently very few of the black seated models were produced and issued. It is now regarded by collectors as being one of the very rare Yesteryear models. The Sunbeam Motorcycle was also used as a promotional item by Mobil. A special box was produced and the model was given away at Mobil petrol stations. The Sunbeam was also considered by Lesney Products in 1981 as being a suitable subject for a special 25th Anniversary Model to celebrate the 'Models of Yesteryear' range, but this never materialised; although trial models in various colours were produced, including green, blue, red, green, white and yellow.

ISSUE	YEAR OF RELEASE	COLOURS	MOTORCYCLE SEAT	SIDE CAR SEAT	FRONT FORKS	WHEELS	SIDECAR AXLE BRACE	BASEPLATE	RARITY	BOX TYPE	VALUE	CHECK LIST
1	1962	Motorcycle & sidecar chrome plated	Black	Dark green	Open*	Unplated 26 spoke	No*	LESNEY No 8 ENGLAND	D	D1/D2	£60	
2		Motorcycle & sidecar chrome plated	Black	Dark green	Closed	Unplated 26 spoke	Yes	LESNEY No 8 ENGLAND		D!/D2/D3/E/E1/F/M	£50	
3		Motorcycle & sidecar chrome plated	Black	Dark green	Closed	Unplated 26 spoke	No	LESNEY No 8 ENGLAND		D1/D2/D3/E/E1/F/M	£50	
4		Motorcycle & side car pale gold plated*	Black	Dark green	Closed	Unplated 26 spoke	Yes	LESNEY No 8 ENGLAND	E R	D3/E/E1	£650	
5		Motorcycle & sidecar chrome plated	Black	Emerald* green	Closed	Unplated 26 spoke	Yes	LESNEY No 8 ENGLAND	V R	E/E1/F	£300	
6	1967	Motorcycle & sidecar chrome plated	Black	Black*	Closed	Unplated 26 spoke	Yes	LESNEY No 8 ENGLAND	V R	F	£400	

DIAGRAM 1 FRONT FORKS

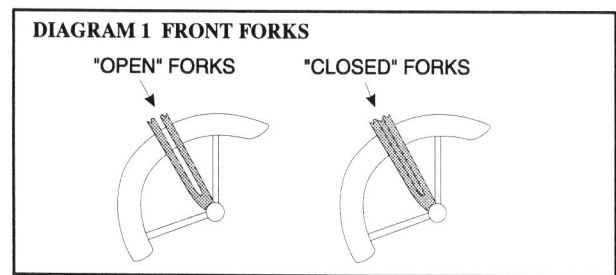

DIAGRAM 2 SIDE CAR AXLE BRACE

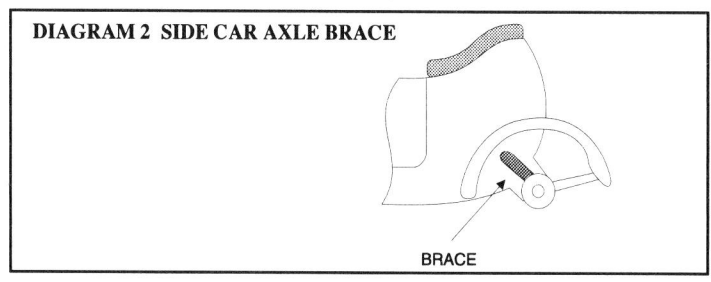

NOTES

INVESTMENT COMMENT
ORIGINAL PRICE £0.36p
Curiously, the Stutz has not attracted much interest and still performs poorly. However, probably due to their attractive colour schemes, Issues 6 and 8 have made gains.

Y8-3 1914 STUTZ TYPE 4E ROADSTER   Scale 1:48

The Stutz was introduced in 1969. There were only two basic colour schemes although earlier red models were in a darker shade than the later production models. Experimental colour trial spare tyre carrier and rear luggage boxes in yellow and red have been recorded but were never officially released. Also pre-production colour trial seats and grilles in grey, purple and orange have also been seen. It should be noted that the hood and seat components are interchangeable with the Y13-3, Y14-2, and the Y26-1. The seats are also interchangeable with the Y25-1 and the Y44-1. The tan textured hood of Issues 3, 4 and 5 do not have the additional lugs, which were added in 1973 so that this component could clip onto the top of the Y13 Crossley windscreens. On genuine textured hoods for this model, there are just two lugs which are near to the front and locate behind the top bar of the windscreen. There are variations to both basic colours, a paler red, lighter or darker bases and bodies. However these do not warrant separate codings.

ISSUE	YEAR OF RELEASE	COLOURS	HOOD	SEATS	GRILLE	WHEELS	PLATED PARTS	PETROL TANK	SPARE TYRE CARRIER	REAR LUGGAGE BOX	BASEPLATE	RARITY	BOX TYPE	VALUE	CHECK LIST
1	1969	Metallic dark red body & chassis	Tan smooth	Green	Green	Brass 12 spoke	Brass	Copper	Black A	Black	LESNEY © 1969 ENGLAND		F / G	£20	✓
2		Metallic dark red body & chassis	Tan smooth	Green	Green	Brass 12 spoke	Brass	Brass*	Black A	Black	LESNEY © 1969 ENGLAND	R	F / G	£60	
3		Metallic dark red body & chassis	Tan textured*	Green	Green	Brass 12 spoke	Brass	Copper	Black A	Black	LESNEY © 1969 ENGLAND	D	G	£35	
4		Metallic dark red body & chassis	Tan textured*	Green	Red*	Brass 12 spoke	Brass	Copper	Black A	Black	LESNEY © 1969 ENGLAND	S	G	£30	
5		Metallic dark red body & chassis	Tan textured*	Pinky red	Maroon*	Brass 12 spoke	Brass	Copper	Black A	Black	LESNEY © 1969 ENGLAND	R	G	£80	
6	1973	Metallic blue body & chassis	Black textured	White	White	Chrome 12 spoke	Brass	Copper	Black B	Black	LESNEY © 1969 ENGLAND		H / L	£20	✓
7		Metallic blue body & chassis	Black textured	Bright red*	Bright red*	Chrome 12 spoke	Brass	Copper	Black B	Black	LESNEY © 1969 ENGLAND	D	H	£45	
8		Metallic blue body & chassis	Black textured	White	White	Chrome 24 spoke	Brass	Copper	Black B	Black	LESNEY © 1969 ENGLAND		H	£20	

DIAGRAM 1 SPARE TYRE CARRIER & REAR LUGGAGE BOX

GENERAL VIEW

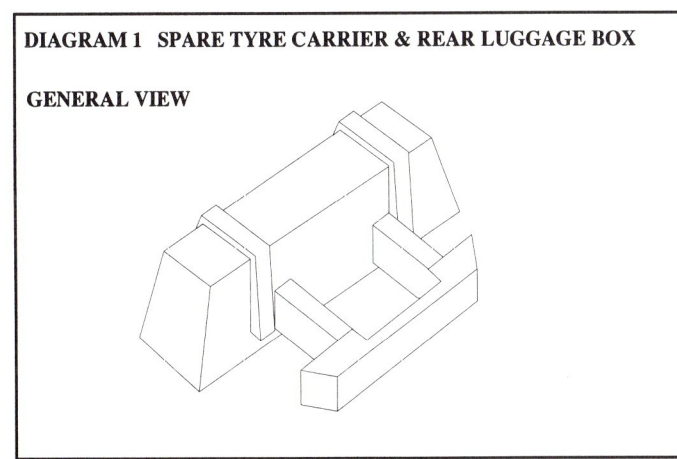

DIAGRAM 2 TYRE CARRIER TYPE

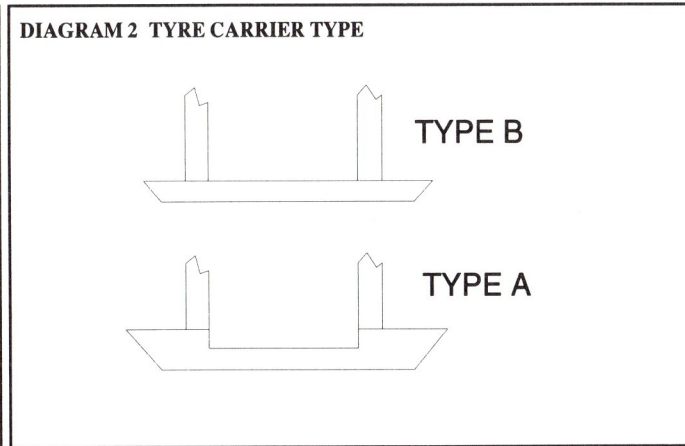

TYPE B

TYPE A

NOTES
1. Issue 6 was also issued in the G5 "Famous Cars of Yesteryear" presentation set.

Y8-4 1945 MG "TC"

Scale 1:35

INVESTMENT COMMENT
ORIGINAL PRICE £1.50p

In 1994 a large quantity of Issue 1 with tan coloured seats was found in a UK wholesalers. With their introduction onto the market the value has decreased. Presently all issues represent good value and all including Issue 1 have growth potential.

The MG "TC" was the first in the series to be modelled on a post-World War II vehicle. Originally released in 1978 it was recoloured three times. Issues 1 to 6 can have the racing number omitted; a negative variation. These have not been given individual codings! From 1981 onwards, both black or white wall tyres were standard issue, but the majority of red models were issued with all black tyres. Many different coloured hoods and seats have been recorded; but beware, roof components are renowned for being switched on this model.

ISSUE	YEAR OF RELEASE	COLOURS	HOOD	SEATS	PLATED PARTS	WHEELS	TRANSFER NO 3	BASEPLATE	RARITY	BOX TYPE	VALUE	CHECKLIST
1	1978	Dark green body & chassis	Tan	Tan*	Chrome	Chrome 24 spoke	Yes	LESNEY © 1977 ENGLAND	S	H	£35	
2		Dark green body & chassis	Tan	Bright red	Chrome	Chrome 24 spoke	Yes	LESNEY © 1977 ENGLAND		H	£15	✓
3		Dark green body & chassis	Tan	Bright red	Chrome	Green* 12 spoke	Yes	LESNEY © 1977 ENGLAND	D	H	£20	
4		Dark green body & chassis	Tan	Bright red	Chrome	Red 12 spoke*	Yes	LESNEY © 1977 ENGLAND	D	H/I	£35	
5		Dark green body & chassis	Tan	Dark* pink	Chrome	Chrome 24 spoke	Yes	LESNEY © 1977 ENGLAND	R	H/I	£50	
6		Dark green body & chassis	Tan	Black*	Chrome	Chrome 24 spoke	Yes	LESNEY © 1977 ENGLAND	S	I	£40	
7	1981	Bright red body & chassis	Tan	Black	Chrome	Chrome 24 spoke (BW)	No	LESNEY © 1977 ENGLAND		I	£10	✓
8		Bright red body & chassis	Rust brown	Black	Chrome	Chrome 24 spoke (BW)	No	LESNEY © 1977 ENGLAND		I	£10	
9		Bright red body & chassis	Tan	Bright* red	Chrome	Chrome 24 spoke (BW)	No	LESNEY © 1977 ENGLAND	D	I	£25	
10		Bright red body & chassis	Tan	Bright* red	Chrome	Chrome* solid	No	LESNEY © 1977 ENGLAND	S	I	£15	
11		Darker red body & chassis	Tan	Black	Chrome	Chrome 24 spoke (BW)	No	LESNEY © 1977 ENGLAND		I	£10	
12		Darker red body & chassis	Rust brown	Black	Chrome	Chrome 24 spoke (BW)	No	LESNEY © 1977 ENGLAND		I	£10	

LIVERY ISSUES 1-6
Transfer
Black racing number 3 on a white disc, both doors.

NOTES
BECKENHAM APPEAL MODEL
Bright red body and chassis with black seats and tan roof.

Y8-4 1945 MG "TC"   CONTINUED   Scale 1:35

ISSUE	YEAR OF RELEASE	COLOURS	HOOD	SEATS	PLATED PARTS	WHEELS	RACING NO 3	BASEPLATE	RARITY	BOX TYPE	VALUE	CHECK LIST
13		Darker red body & chassis	Tan	Bright red*	Chrome	Chrome 24 spoke (B W)	No	LESNEY © 1977 ENGLAND	D	I	£25	
14		Darker red body & chassis	Tan	Pinky tan	Chrome	Chrome 24 spoke (B W)	No	LESNEY © 1977 ENGLAND		I	£15	
15	1983	Blue body & chassis	Tan	Black	Chrome	Chrome 24 spoke (B W)	No	LESNEY © 1977 ENGLAND		I	£12	
16		Blue body & chassis	Tan	Tan	Chrome	Chrome 24 spoke (B W)	No	LESNEY © 1977 ENGLAND		I	£12	
17		Blue body & chassis	Rusty brown	Black	Chrome	Chrome 24 spoke (B W)	No	LESNEY © 1977 ENGLAND		I	£15	
18		Blue body & chassis	Rusty brown	Tan	Chrome	Chrome 24 spoke (BW)	No	LESNEY © 1977 ENGLAND		J	£15	
19	1984	Cream body & dark brown chassis	Tan	Tan	Chrome	Chrome 24 spoke (W W)	No	LESNEY © 1977 ENGLAND		J	£10	
20		Cream body & dark brown chassis	Darker tan	Darker tan	Chrome	Chrome 24 spoke (W W)	No	LESNEY © 1977 ENGLAND		J	£10	
21		Cream body & dark brown chassis	Tan	Pinky tan	Chrome	Chrome 24 spoke (W W)	No	LESNEY © 1977 ENGLAND		J	£10	
22		Cream body & dark brown chassis	Tan	Black	Chrome	Chrome 24 spoke (W W)	No	LESNEY © 1977 ENGLAND		J	£10	
23		Cream body & dark brown chassis	Rusty brown	Tan	Chrome	Chrome 24 spoke (W W)	No	LESNEY © 1977 ENGLAND		J	£10	✓
24		Cream body & dark brown chassis	Rusty brown	Pinky tan	Chrome	Chrome 24 spoke (W W)	No	LESNEY © 1977 ENGLAND		J	£10	

Y8-5 1917 YORKSHIRE STEAM WAGON   Scale 1:61

JOHNNIE WALKER. The Yorkshire Steam Wagon is a further example of Matchbox Toys reverting to the very successful days of the First Series with the inclusion of popular steam driven vehicles. The Yorkshire Wagon was originally scheduled for release in August, but eventually came out in September 1987. Originally the cab roof was to be made in zinc and fixed in place by only two rivets. It was discovered that there were problems with overspraying, so the roof was changed to a self-coloured plastic and ultimately an extra rivet was added. Variations have been recorded; one of the more significant being the colour of ink applied to the side of the canopy. The second concerns the Johnnie Walker figure. Early production models were shown to the trademark owner who raised objections to the walking style of the figure. The figure was then re-positioned so that he did not appear to be goose-stepping. After the first run it was also noticed that the gold tampo print did not adhere well and so the canopies were clear lacquered.
SAMUEL SMITH. This particular livery was originally issued as part of the UK and Eire Passport Scheme; although limited quantities of the model in the Framed Cabinet were made available in Australia and North America - this model was never issued as a separate boxed item. Some 12,000 models were made and sold to collectors at £20.90 including postage and within weeks they began to fetch a premium price.

A : JOHNNIE WALKER

ISSUE	YEAR OF RELEASE	COLOURS	ROOF	SEATS	CANOPY	WHEELS	ROOF SUPPORT BULKHEAD	CAB ROOF RIVETS	BOILER BANDS	LOGO	TAMPO DECORATION	JOHNNIE WALKER FIGURE	BASEPLATE	RARITY	BOX TYPE	VALUE	CHECK LIST
1	1987	Strawberry red body, black chassis	Grey	Black	Creamy brown	Red 6 spoke	Brown	Type A*	Gold	Johnnie Walker	Johnnie Walker Whisky in bright red*	Type 1	MATCHBOX © 1987 MACAU Y8	R	J1	£120	
2		Strawberry red body, black chassis	Grey	Black	Creamy brown	Red 6 spoke	Brown	Type B	Gold	Johnnie Walker	Johnnie Walker Whisky in bright red*	Type 1	MATCHBOX © 1987 MACAU Y8	S	J1	£50	
3		Strawberry red body, black chassis	Grey	Black	Creamy brown	Red 6 spoke	Brown	Type B	Gold	Johnnie Walker	Johnnie Walker Whisky in dark maroon	Type 1	MATCHBOX © 1987 MACAU Y8		J1	£12	✓
4		Strawberry red body, black chassis	Grey	Black	Creamy brown	Red 6 spoke	Brown	Type B	Gold	Johnnie Walker	Johnnie Walker Whisky in light maroon	Type 1	MATCHBOX © 1987 MACAU Y8		J1	£12	
5		Strawberry red body, black chassis	Grey	Black	Creamy brown	Red 6 spoke	Brown	Type B	Gold	Johnnie Walker	Johnnie Walker Whisky in light maroon	Type 2*	MATCHBOX © 1987 MACAU Y8	ER	J1	£400	

B : SAMUEL SMITH

ISSUE	YEAR OF RELEASE	COLOURS	ROOF	SEATS	CANOPY	WHEELS	ROOF SUPPORT BULKHEAD	CAB ROOF RIVETS	BOILER BANDS	LOGO	TAMPO DECORATION	JOHNNIE WALKER FIGURE	BASEPLATE	RARITY	BOX TYPE	VALUE	CHECK LIST
1	1989	Green body black chassis	Light beige	Black	Light beige	Green 6 spoke	Green	Type B	Cream & red	Samuel Smith	N/A	N/A	MATCHBOX © 1987 MACAU Y8	S	M	£70	

DIAGRAM 1 JOHNNIE WALKER FIGURES

TYPE 1 "GOOSE STEP"

TYPE 2 NORMAL GAIT

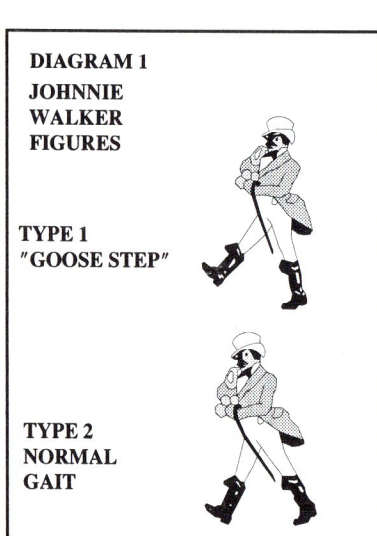

DIAGRAM 2 CAB ROOF RIVETS

TYPE A

UNDERSIDE OF ROOF WITH 2 RIVETS

TYPE B

UNDERSIDE OF ROOF WITH 3 RIVETS

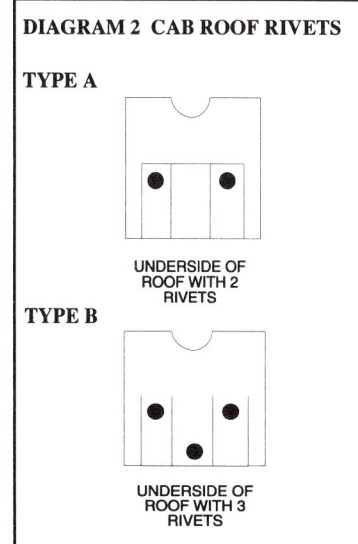

LIVERY JOHNNIE WALKER

Tampo
Canopy sides. Red or maroon JOHNNIE WALKER WHISKY and JOHNNIE WALKER figure in red, gold, black and white.
Wagon sides. KILMARNOCK & LONDON in gold within gold coachlining.
Cab doors. Gold No 7
Front boiler support frame. Gold JOHNNIE WALKER and NV 1108 in white on black.
Gold coachlining.

LIVERY SAMUEL SMITH

Tampo
Canopy sides. Green SAMUEL SMITH. Company logo of three red S's within green shield.
Wagon sides. VICTORIA CORN MILLS SHEFFIELD in cream.
Cab doors. Company logo in red. Cream coachlines.
Front boiler support frame. Cream SAMUEL SMITH.
Gold coachlines.

INVESTMENT COMMENT

ORIGINAL PRICE
JOHNNIE WALKER, £5.25p
SAMUEL SMITH £20.90p

JOHNNIE WALKER The value of Issue 1 has now levelled out between £100 and £150 and there is still potential for further growth. Issue 5 is seldom offered on the market but is worth looking for.
SAMUEL SMITH Good growth has been recorded and has potential for further growth. One to watch closely.

NOTES

Y8-5 1917 YORKSHIRE STEAM WAGON (CONTINUED) Scale 1:61

WILLIAM PRICHARD. This model was released in May 1989. A prototype model had first appeared in the 1989 UK Trade Catalogue which described it as a Y27 1922 Foden Steam Lorry. Originally the Yorkshire Wagon was going to be used for the 'Guinness' livery but when it was discovered that Guinness had not used Yorkshire Wagons, but had used Fodens; they were inter-changed (Y27-1). The prototype model in the catalogue had wheel spokes in a grey-blue whereas eventual colour is off-white. The simulated load of flour sacks had previously been used on the Y27 Spillers lorry. The William Prichard livery was a Limited Edition with a total production of 50,148 models.

FYFFES. The fourth livery on the Y8-5, is of a long and well established U.K. banana importer. Collectors gave it a warm reception and most markets were sold out very quickly. The more fastidious collectors soon noticed 2 different colours of plastic had been used for the cab roof, white and light cream. The white cab roofs were probably a balance left over from the Y32 Sam Smith production run and may be more difficult to find. The baseplate Y number had been changed to Y32 during the Y32 Sam Smith run, but despite the commonality of the base/chassis component to both the Y8 & Y32, all the bases on the Fyffes had only Y32 cast on them.

C : WILLIAM PRICHARD

ISSUE	YEAR OF RELEASE	COLOURS	ROOF	SEATS	CANOPY	LOAD	WHEELS	ROOF SUPPORT BULKHEAD	BOILER BANDS	LOGO	BASEPLATE	RARITY	BOX TYPE	VALUE	CHECK LIST
1	1989	Dark blue body, black chassis	Blue grey	Black	N/A	Sacks off-white	Off-white 6 spoke	Brown	White	WILLIAM PRICHARD	MATCHBOX © 1987 MACAU Y8		JI	£8	✓

D : FYFFES

ISSUE	YEAR OF RELEASE	COLOURS	ROOF	SEATS	CANOPY	LOAD	WHEELS	ROOF SUPPORT BULKHEAD	BOILER BANDS	LOGO	BASEPLATE	RARITY	BOX TYPE	VALUE	CHECK LIST
1	1992	Yellow body navy blue chassis	White*	Black	Light cream	N/A	Light yellow 6 spoke	Brown	Navy blue	FYFFES	MATCHBOX © 1987 CHINA Y32		NI	£10	✓
2		Yellow body navy blue chassis	Light cream*	Black	Light cream	N/A	Light yellow 6 spoke	Brown	Navy blue	FYFFES	MATCHBOX © 1987 CHINA Y32		NI	£10	

LIVERY WILLIAM PRICHARD

Tampo
Wagon sides. White WILLIAM PRICHARD VICTORIA MILLS CARNARVON.
Cab doors. White MILLENIUM FLOUR and IS THE BEST in blue on white sack. All within white coachlining.
Front boiler support frame. White MILLENIUM FLOUR within white coachlining. Four highlighted sacks and black WILLIAM PRICHARD with black coachlines.

LIVERY FYFFES

Tampo
Canopy sides. Blue FYFFES.
White FYFFES BLUE LABEL BRAND on navy blue oval.
Wagon sides with blue coachlines. BANANA MERCHANT in navy blue.
Wagon rear. Fyffes trademark as above.
Cab sides. FYFFES ARE BEST and coachline in navy blue.
Front boiler support frame. Fyffes trademark as above but smaller.
Navy blue coachlines on both ends and front of boiler support frame.

INVESTMENT COMMENT

ORIGINAL PRICE WILLIAM PRICHARD £6.25p
FYFFES £7.95

WILLIAM PRICHARD. This model has failed to inspire much interest, but may improve.
FYFFES Although seldom seen on the second-hand market, values have been surprisingly depressed. However, one to watch.

NOTES
1. Compare with YAS04-M

Y9-1 1924 FOWLER "BIG LION" SHOWMANS ENGINE   Scale 1:80

INVESTMENT COMMENT
ORIGINAL PRICE £0.12.5p
A classic model, the Fowler, has maintained its value. In some instances the rarer issues have even increased in value. Best potential must still be the bright red models packaged in the scarce D3 boxes.

Thought by many collectors to be the most attractive model in the range. It was immensely popular and many thousands were sold, in a production life lasting a decade. The intricacy of the model in addition to its continued popularity has combined to create many hundreds of minor variations relating to the colour, the brass plating, the castings and the painted trim. Colour can generally be said to have become lighter with production ranging from very dark maroon through to a final bright red. The light purple issue has a slight metallic finish, and t
om full to partial. The casting modifications include the roof section; early roof castings have generally three ejector pin impressions on one side of the underside, whereas later castings usually have five impressions; three on one side and two on the other and adjacent to the words 'Lesney Products & Co. Ltd.'. Also, the number (No. 9) was cast on the underneath of the roof and not on the baseplate. Models can be found with many combinations of components and components can be found lacking standard gold trim including the smoke stack and the dynamo shaft end covers.

ISSUE	YEAR OF RELEASE	COLOURS	ROOF	CYLINDER BLOCK	BOILER DOOR	SPIRALLED ROOF SUPPORTS	WHEELS	SMOKE STACK EXTENSION	ROOF ENDS PLATES	FIRE BOX ENDS	NAME PLATE COLOUR	BASEPLATE	RARITY	BOX TYPE	VALUE	CHECK LIST
1	1958	Dark maroon* body & base	Cream	Gold*	Copper	Gold	Yellow 12 spoke front, 18 spoke rear	Black	Cream	Square	Dark maroon	LESNEY ENGLAND	R	A	£200	✓
2		Dark maroon* body & base	Cream	Dark maroon	Copper	Gold	Yellow 12 spoke front, 18 spoke rear	Black	Cream	Square	Dark maroon	LESNEY ENGLAND	S	A	£140	✓
3		Dark maroon* body & base	Cream	Dark maroon	Gold	Gold	Yellow 12 spoke front, 18 spoke rear	Black	Cream	Square	Dark maroon	LESNEY ENGLAND	S	A	£140	
4		Light purple* body & base	Cream	Gold*	Copper	Gold	Yellow 12 spoke front, 18 spoke rear	Black	Cream	Square	Light purple*	LESNEY ENGLAND	V R	A/B	£300	
5		Light purple* body & base	Cream	Light purple*	Copper	Gold	Yellow 12 spoke front, 18 spoke rear	Black	Cream	Square	Light purple*	LESNEY ENGLAND	V R	A/B	£300	
6		Pale maroon body & base	Cream	Pale maroon	Gold	Gold, white or silver bare metal	Yellow 12 spoke front, 18 spoke rear	Black	Gold, white or silver bare metal	Square	Black*	LESNEY ENGLAND	D	B/C	£125	
7		Pale maroon body & base	Cream	Pale maroon	Gold	Gold, white or silver bare metal	Yellow 12 spoke front, 18 spoke rear	Black	Gold, white or silver bare metal	Square	Pale maroon	LESNEY ENGLAND		B/C	£85	
8		Pale maroon body & base	Cream	Pale maroon	Silver	Gold, white or silver bare metal	Yellow 12 spoke front, 18 spoke rear	Black	Gold, white or silver bare metal	Square	Pale maroon	LESNEY ENGLAND		B/C	£85	
9		Pale maroon body & base	Cream	Pale maroon	Silver	Gold, white or silver bare metal	Yellow 12 spoke front, 18 spoke rear	Black	Gold, white or silver bare metal	Square	Black*	LESNEY ENGLAND	D	B/C	£120	
10		Pale maroon body & base	White*	Pale maroon	Gold	Gold, white or silver bare metal	Yellow 12 spoke front, 18 spoke rear	Black	Gold, white or silver bare metal	Square	Pale maroon	LESNEY ENGLAND	D	C/D	£120	

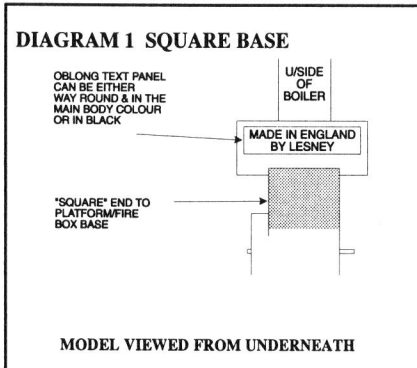

DIAGRAM 1 SQUARE BASE
MODEL VIEWED FROM UNDERNEATH

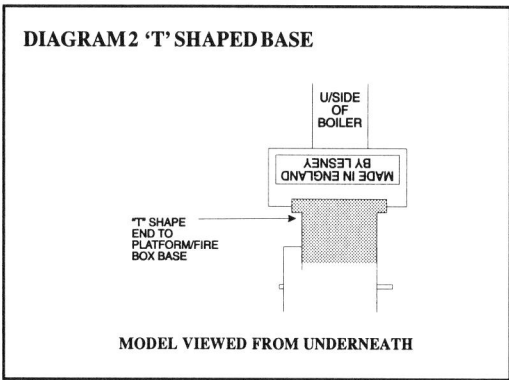

DIAGRAM 2 'T' SHAPED BASE
MODEL VIEWED FROM UNDERNEATH

LIVERY
Transfer
Side fascias of roof. LESNEY'S MODERN AMUSEMENTS in yellow with green shadow effect on maroon or red.
Water tank. Yellow coachlining to front and side panels.
Piston rod housing. Yellow coachlining.
Piston cylinder sides. Yellow and green coachlining. Yellow seven pointed star on red or maroon within a yellow circle.

NOTES
Early issues have detailed hubs, only on the outer face of the rear wheels. So that the wheels could be fitted either way during assembly. Later issues have both faces detailed.

Y9-1 1924 FOWLER "BIG LION" SHOWMAN'S ENGINE (CONTINUED)   Scale 1:80

ISSUE	YEAR OF RELEASE	COLOURS	ROOF	CYLINDER BLOCK	BOILER DOOR	SPIRALLED ROOF SUPPORTS	WHEELS	SMOKE STACK EXTENSION	ROOF ENDS PLATES	FIRE BOX ENDS	NAME PLATE COLOUR	BASEPLATE	RARITY	BOX TYPE	VALUE	CHECK LIST
11	1965	Bright red body & base	Cream	Bright red	Gold	Gold, white or silver bare metal	Yellow 12 spoke front, 18 spoke rear	Black	Gold, white or silver bare metal	Square	Bright red	LESNEY ENGLAND		D1/D2	£100	
12		Bright red body & base	White	Bright red	Gold	Gold, white or silver bare metal	Yellow 12 spoke front, 18 spoke rear	Black	Gold, white or silver bare metal	Square	Bright red	LESNEY ENGLAND		D1/D2	£100	
13		Bright red body & base	White	Bright red	Gold	Gold, white or silver bare metal	Yellow 12 spoke front, 18 spoke rear	Black	Gold, white or silver bare metal	Square	Black*	LESNEY ENGLAND	S	D1/D2	£120	
14		Bright red body & base	White	Bright red	Silver	Gold, white or silver bare metal	Yellow 12 spoke front, 18 spoke rear	Black	Gold, white or silver bare metal	Square	Bright red	LESNEY ENGLAND		D1/D2	£100	
15		Bright red body & base	White	Bright red	Gold	Gold, white or silver bare metal	Yellow 12 spoke front, 18 spoke rear	Black	Gold, white or silver bare metal	'T' shaped*	Bright red	LESNEY ENGLAND		D2/D3	£110	
16		Bright red body & base	White	Bright red	Silver	Gold, white or silver bare metal	Yellow 12 spoke front, 18 spoke rear	Black	Gold, white or silver bare metal	'T' shaped*	Bright red	LESNEY ENGLAND		D3	£110	

NOTES

INVESTMENT COMMENT
ORIGINAL PRICE £0.34p
Issue 1 still represents good value. Issue 20 and 21 with their Macau baseplates are ones to find and have potential for growth.

Y9-2 1912 SIMPLEX

Scale 1:48

Issued in 1968, this is the longest running model to date, spanning some 21 years. A host of minor modifications were made to the front and rear spring areas and are not easily discernible, but more obvious modifications to the rear seat area and the hood locating pins are detailed below. Very early battery box covers had five raised ridges; later covers had finer effect ridges. These main changes were made during the first two years of production with no further changes occurring for the rest of its life. The only exception being a redesigned spare tyre carrier for the introduction of the wide/hollow section tyres. Many different coloured hoods, seats & radiator grilles have been recorded, but these were the results of experimental trials and were not officially released. Slight variations in the shade of dark gold of Issues 7 & 8 are known, but the metallic gold of Issue 9 is unmistakeably lighter than the dark gold. The bright red of Issue 10 can vary to an orangey red, but the darker red livery was much darker than Issue 10.

ISSUE	YEAR OF RELEASE	COLOURS	HOOD	SEATS	GRILLE	PLATED PARTS	BODY TYPE	WHEELS	BATTERY COVER	BASEPLATE	RARITY	BOX TYPE	VALUE	CHECK LIST
1	1968	Lime* green body & chassis	Smooth tan	Bright red	Dark red	Brass	A*	Brass 12 spoke	Type 1	LESNEY ENGLAND	S	E1	£45	
2	1969	Mid green body & chassis	Smooth tan	Bright red	Dark red	Brass	A*	Brass 12 spoke	Type 1	LESNEY ENGLAND	D	E1	£25	
3		Mid green body & chassis	Smooth tan	Bright red	Dark red	Brass	B*	Brass 12 spoke	Type 1	LESNEY ENGLAND	S	E1	£40	
4		Mid green body & chassis	Smooth tan	Bright red	Dark red	Brass	C	Brass 12 spoke	Type 1	LESNEY ENGLAND		E1/F	£20	
5		Mid green body & chassis	Textured dark tan*	Bright red	Dark red	Brass	C	Brass 12 spoke	Type 2	LESNEY ENGLAND	S	E1/F	£30	
6		Mid green body & chassis	Textured pale tan*	Bright red	Dark red	Brass	C	Brass 12 spoke	Type 2	LESNEY ENGLAND	S	F	£40	
7	1970	Metallic dark gold body, metallic dark red chassis	Textured black	Dark red	Dark red	Brass	C	Brass 12 spoke	Type 2	LESNEY ENGLAND		F/G	£35	
8		Metallic dark gold body, metallic dark red chassis	Textured black	Dark red	Dark red	Brass	C	Chrome 12 spoke*	Type 2	LESNEY ENGLAND	S	F/G	£45	
9	1973	Metallic gold* body, bright red chassis	Textured black	Dark red	Dark red	Brass	C	Chrome 12 spoke	Type 2	LESNEY ENGLAND	V R	H	£110	
10	1975	Bright red body & chassis	Textured black	Bright yellow	Bright yellow	Brass	C	Chrome 12 spoke	Type 2	LESNEY ENGLAND		H/L	£20	✓
11		Dark red body & chassis	Textured black	Bright yellow	Bright yellow	Brass	C	Chrome 12 spoke	Type 2	LESNEY ENGLAND		H	£12	
12		Dark red body & chassis	Textured black	Bright yellow	Bright yellow	Brass	C	Red 12 spoke	Type 2	LESNEY ENGLAND		H	£12	
13	1979	Dark red body, glossy black chassis	Textured black	Bright yellow	Bright yellow	Brass	C	Dark red 12 spoke(BW)	Type 2	LESNEY ENGLAND		I	£12	
14		Dark red body, glossy black chassis	Textured black	Bright yellow	Bright yellow	Brass	C	Chrome 12 spoke (BW)	Type 2	LESNEY ENGLAND		I	£12	

DIAGRAM 1 BODY TYPE A
ROOF RETAINING PINS CAST WITH BODY
NO SEAT BRACE

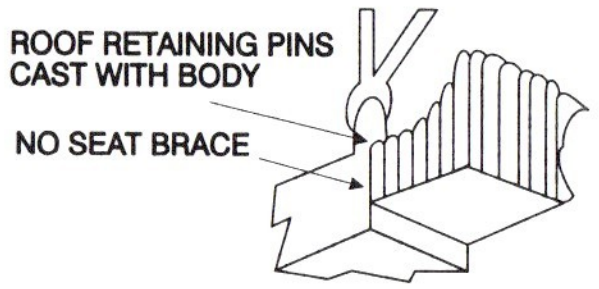

DIAGRAM 2 BODY TYPE B
ROOF RETAINING PINS ATTACHED TO SEAT
NO SEAT BRACE

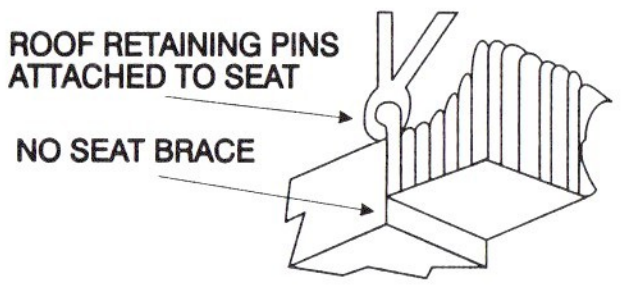

DIAGRAM 3 BODY TYPE C
ROOF RETAINING PINS ATTACHED TO SEAT

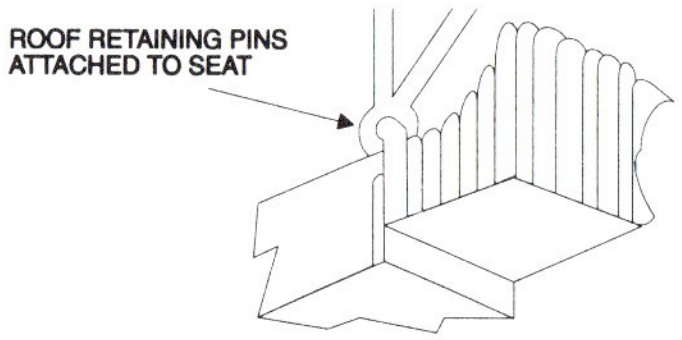

DIAGRAM 4
BATTERY BOX COVER TYPES

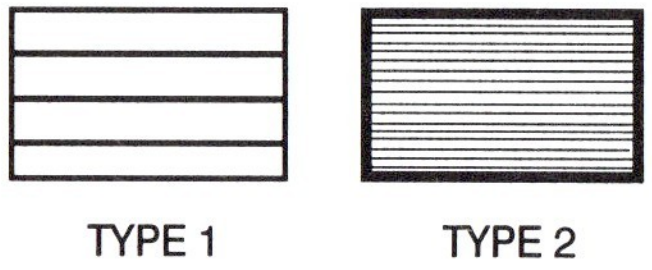

TYPE 1   TYPE 2

NOTES
Webs were added to rear springs from 1970 but transitional models may exist.
Because of the inconsistency in the making of plastics, the colour of the smooth tan roofs vary from light to dark. Also the textured orange yellow of issue 17 can be a light, mid or dark tone.

Y9-2 1912 SIMPLEX   CONTINUED   Scale 1:48

The 1986 re-livery model was issued with a plastic diorama of a contemporary lock-up garage. The Lesney legend was removed from the baseplate. This livery and diorama was used again after production had moved to Macau, but the yellow of the body was darker and the seats were of a darker brown plastic. It was quickly realised that on all Macau models, the whitewall decoration to the tyres was only applied to the outside face of the tyre. Total production of Issues 18 to 21 was 93,000. When studying this listing, it must be remembered that hoods, seats & radiator grilles are easily interchangeable and that the radiator grilles are the same size and design as those fitted to the Y3-2 Benz and Y12-2 Thomas Flyabout.

ISSUE	YEAR OF RELEASE	COLOURS	HOOD	SEATS	GRILLE	PLATED PARTS	BODY TYPE	WHEELS	BATTERY COVER	BASEPLATE	RARITY	BOX TYPE	VALUE	CHECK LIST
15		Dark red body, glossy black chassis	Textured black	Bright yellow	Bright yellow	Brass	C	Chrome 24 spoke (BW)	Type 2	LESNEY ENGLAND		I	£12	
16		Dark red body, glossy black chassis	Textured yellow	Bright yellow	Bright yellow	Brass	C	Dark red 12 spoke (BW)	Type 2	LESNEY ENGLAND		I	£12	✓
17	1983	Dark red body, glossy black chassis	Textured orange yellow	Bright yellow	Bright yellow	Brass	C	Dark red 12 spoke (BW)	Type 2	LESNEY ENGLAND		I	£12	
18	1986	Yellow body & bonnet, glossy black chassis	Textured yellow	Light brown	Black	Brass	C	Gold 12 spoke (WW)	Type 2	ENGLAND		J	£10	
19		Yellow body & bonnet, glossy black chassis	Textured black	Light brown	Black	Brass	C	Gold 12 spoke (WW)	Type 2	ENGLAND		J	£10	✓
20	1988	Darker yellow body & bonnet, glossy black chassis	Textured yellow	Brown	Black	Brass	C	Gold 12 spoke (WW)	Type 2	MATCHBOX MACAU*	R	J1	£35	
21		Darker yellow body & bonnet, glossy black chassis	Textured black	Brown	Black	Brass	C	Gold 12 spoke (WW)	Type 2	MATCHBOX MACAU*	R	J1	£35	

NOTES

BECKENHAM APPEAL MODEL
Powder blue body and chassis.
Yellow seats and grille.
Black textured hood.
Body type C.
Gold 12 spoke wheels.

INVESTMENT COMMENT
ORIGINAL PRICE £14.99p
Presently good value for money and being the first Special Limited Edition, model has potential for the future.

Y9-3 1920 3 TON LEYLAND LORRY

Scale 1:62

Issued in December 1985 the Leyland Lorry will be remembered chiefly for the controversial way in which it was sold within the U.K. The model was made from tooling which was not finally hardened so that only 40,000 units could be produced. This meant that all the tooling costs had to be recovered over that quantity. Because the model was to cater for the collectors market, the retail price was established at £14.99. Each box was individually numbered with a letter prefix and four digits. An added feature was the superior presentation of the box; red in colour with gold foil lettering. The trade in the UK were asked to buy two of each of the three Special Edition commercials for every Leyland they wished to order. In Australia, however, this did not apply, and they ordered 16,000 models. Early versions of the prototypes had a mis-spelling of the word 'Malden'. The tampo-print manufacturers mistakenly changed the spelling of the town to the one situated close to the Rochford factory in Essex i.e. Maldon as they thought the name applied locally and not to the featured town in Surrey, England. Two types of mudguard were fitted. See Diagram 1.

ISSUE	YEAR OF RELEASE	COLOURS	CAB STEPS	SEATS	PLATED PARTS	FRONT MUDGUARD TYPE	WHEELS	BASEPLATE	RARITY	BOX TYPE	VALUE	CHECK LIST
1	1985	Dark green body, black base & bright red chassis	Black	Pale tan	Black	1	Dark green solid	MATCHBOX © 1985 ENGLAND		0	£20	
2		Dark green body, black base & bright red chassis	Black	Mushroom	Black	1	Dark green solid	MATCHBOX © 1985 ENGLAND		0	£20	
3		Dark green body, black base & bright red chassis	Black	White*	Black	1	Dark green solid	MATCHBOX © 1985 ENGLAND	D	0	£40	
4		Dark green body, black base & bright red chassis	Black	Pale tan	Black	2*	Dark green solid	MATCHBOX © 1985 ENGLAND	D	0	£40	
5		Dark green body, black base & bright red chassis	Black	Mushroom	Black	2*	Dark green solid	MATCHBOX © 1985 ENGLAND	D	0	£40	✓

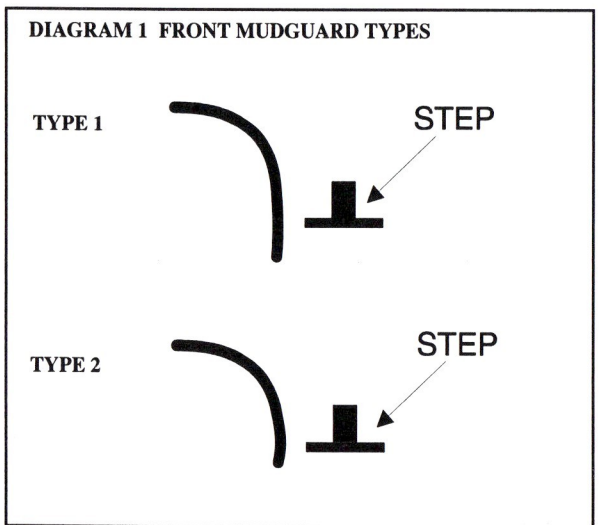

LIVERY

Tampo
Truck sides. A. LUFF & SONS LTD in red with white outline on light brown sculptured background with white outline above LANDSCAPE GARDENERS in white.
White NEW MALDEN - KINGSTON HILL - GUILDFORD SURREY.
Cab doors. White 3 within white coachlining.
Cab rear side panels. White coachlining.
Header board. White A. LUFF & SONS.

NOTES

Y9-4 1936 LEYLAND CUB FIRE ENGINE FK-7
Scale 1:49

INVESTMENT COMMENT
ORIGINAL PRICE £15.95p

This model was not produced in sufficient quantity to satisfy the market and has shown a healthy rise in value. Further growth is possible when new collectors realise that the YFE08 was based on the Y9-4.

Issued in 1989 as a Special Limited Edition, this is undoubtedly one of the finest model fire engines produced by a diecast manufacturer. It is a faithful replica of an actual vehicle owned and preserved by Leyland Motors in Lancashire. The actual vehicles were commissioned in many different forms and served in many fire services around the world. The model was an overnight success and stocks were quickly sold. The chrome trim was to have originally been in brass, but this was thought to spoil the overall appearance and hence was changed to chrome. Production of the model was limited to 41,100 units worldwide. There are no reported variations.

ISSUE	YEAR OF RELEASE	COLOURS	ROOF	SEAT	GRILLE	STEERING WHEEL	FRONT WHEELS	REAR WHEELS	ESCAPE LADDER WHEELS	PLATED PARTS	HOSES	ESCAPE LADDER	BASEPLATE	RARITY	BOX TYPE	VALUE	CHECK LIST
1	1989	Bright red body & chassis with chromed underframe	Textured black plastic	Light brown	Black	Black	Red solid	Red solid (doubles)	Bright red 16 spoke	Chrome	White plastic	Light brown plastic extending 3 piece ladder with top & pulley wheels in white. Brass chains, bright red framework.	MATCHBOX © 1989 MACAU	S	0	£60	✓

LIVERY

Tampo
Rear side panels. LEYLAND in gold with black shadow effect, gold coachline.
Rear side doors. WORKS FIRE SERVICE in gold with black shadow effect with gold coachline
Coachlining. Extensive gold coachlining to the side panels, the doors and to the bonnet side panels.

NOTES
Compare with YFE08.

Y10-1 1908 "GRAND PRIX" MERCEDES — Scale 1:54

INVESTMENT COMMENT
ORIGINAL PRICE £0.12.5p
A steady performer over the last few years and one which has maintained, or increased in value. The white bodied models can still be found on the collectors market; often sold as regular issues by unknowledgeable vendors.

This model which was based on the French Grand Prix winner of 1908 remained in production for five years. It underwent three main casting changes. Early versions were fitted with a seat side panel cast with a two mm vertical strengthening lug. This lug, or bar was later increased in size to give further strength to the fragile side panel during production. A similar strengthening modification was carried out to the rear chassis cross member ; its thickness was increased from one mm to two mm. The third modification involved the exhaust pipes and silencer assemblies. On early castings four connecting webs were cast between these pipes. With time, the top pair was deleted, leaving the lower pair; the rear one of which had a rivet cast to secure the assembly to the body. Earlier issues have dull black underbodies; whereas later models are gloss black. Because the seats were sprayed first and then the body after, some issues can be found with a blemish tinge around the seat edge and floor. Finally, it should be noted that the Y10-1 model is known to have silver, gold, or no trim to the radiator, petrol caps, dashboard tops and oil pump.

ISSUE	YEAR OF RELEASE	COLOURS	SEATS	PLATED PARTS	WHEELS	PAINTED TRIM	SPARE WHEEL RETAINER TYPE	AXLES	SEAT SIDE PANEL TYPE	FOUR EXHAUST WEBS	BASEPLATE	RARITY	BOX TYPE	VALUE	CHECK LIST
1	1958	Cream body, black chassis	Light green*	Yes	Plated 12 spoke	Gold	Thin	Crimped	1*	Yes	LESNEY NO 10 ENGLAND	S	B	£125	
2		White * body, black chassis	Light green*	Yes	Plated12 spoke	Gold	Thin	Crimped	1*	Yes	LESNEY NO 10 ENGLAND	R	B	£220	
3		Cream body, black chassis	Light green*	Yes	Unplated 12 spoke	Gold	Thin	Crimped	1*	Yes	LESNEY NO 10 ENGLAND	S	B/C	£115	
4		Cream body, black chassis	Light green*	No	Unplated 12 spoke	Gold	Thin	Crimped	2	Yes	LESNEY NO 10 ENGLAND	S	B/C	£95	
5		Cream body, black chassis	Light green*	Yes	Plated 12 spoke	Gold	Thin	Crimped	2	No	LESNEY NO 10 ENGLAND	S	B/C	£95	
6		Cream body, black chassis	Dark green	Yes	Plated 12 spoke	Silver	Thin	Crimped	2	No	LESNEY NO 10 ENGLAND		C/D1	£90	
7		Cream body, black chassis	Dark green	Yes	Unplated 12 spoke	Gold	Thin	Riveted	2	No	LESNEY NO 10 ENGLAND		C/D1	£90	
8		Cream body, black chassis	Light green *	Yes	Unplated 12 spoke	Gold	Thin	Riveted	2	No	LESNEY NO 10 ENGLAND	S	C/D1	£95	
9		Cream body, black chassis	Dark green	No	Unplated 12 spoke	Silver	Thin	Riveted	2	No	LESNEY NO 10 ENGLAND		D1	£90	
10		Cream body, black chassis	Dark green	Yes	Plated 12 spoke	Gold	Thick	Riveted	2	No	LESNEY NO 10 ENGLAND		D1	£90	
11		White *body, black chassis	Dark green	Yes	Plated12 spoke	White	Thick	Riveted	2	No	LESNEY NO 10 ENGLAND	R	D1	£180	

DIAGRAM 1 SEAT SIDE PANEL
TYPE 1
2mm WIDE RAISED LUG

TYPE 2
LUG INCREASED IN SIZE

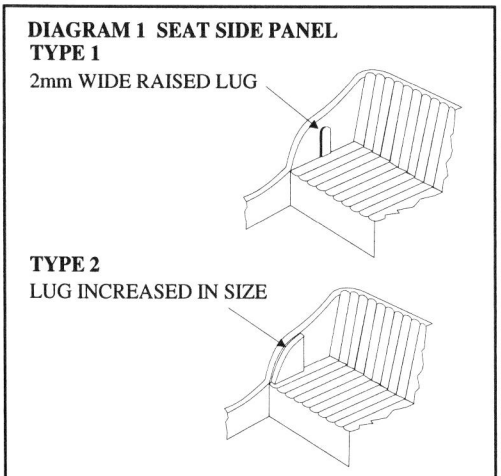

DIAGRAM 2 SPARE WHEEL RETAINER
THIN BRACE - 1mm

THICK BRACE - 2mm

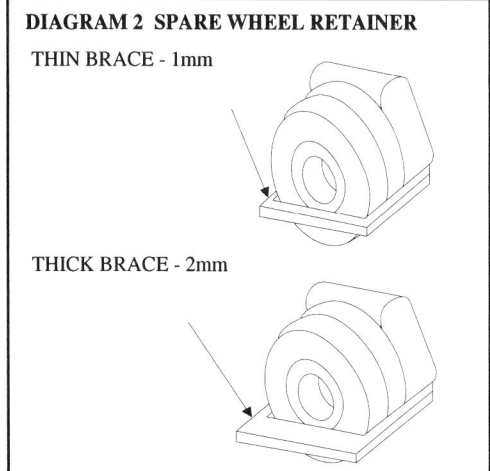

DIAGRAM 3 EXHAUST WEBS
FOUR

TWO

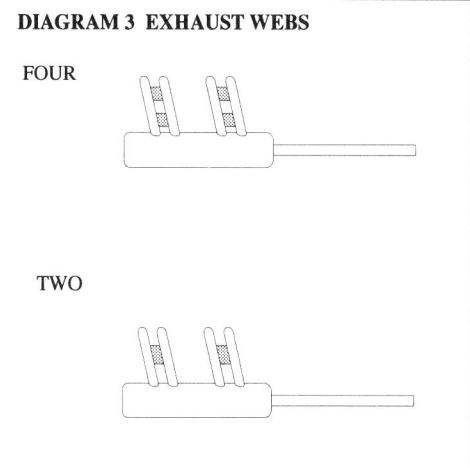

NOTES

Y10-2 1928 MERCEDES BENZ 36-220

Scale 1:52

INVESTMENT COMMENT

ORIGINAL PRICE £ 0.20p

Good progress for Issue 1. All other issues have remained static. The Mercedes remains a good model and don't be surprised if values start to climb rather quickly.

Issued in 1963 and phased out in 1968. Only minor casting variations are known. Earlier versions had two baseplate holes, later models none. Trim can be either silver, or unplated. There are no significant colour variations and any variation from the bright red of the plastic seats is due to fading. Throughout production, black fine treaded tyres were standard issue. Models fitted with grey plastic seats have also been reported, but these are likely to be of pre-production status. The first issue with gloss black seats is regarded by collectors as being one of the rarest Yesteryears and commands a very high premium when seen for sale. The Y10-2 model like the Y5-2 Bentley and the Y8-2 Sunbeam motor cycle was packaged in Mobil boxes and given away by that company in their garage forecourts throughout England, as part of a petroleum promotion.

ISSUE	YEAR OF RELEASE	COLOURS	FOLDED HOOD	SEATS	WHEELS	PLATED PARTS	FLOOR/DASHBOARD	SPARE WHEELS	HOLES IN BASEPLATE	BASEPLATE	RARITY	BOX TYPE	VALUE	CHECK LIST
1	1963	White body & chassis	Black*	Black*	Silver 24 spoke	Silver	Tan	2*	2	LESNEY NO 10 ENGLAND	E R	D1	£1200	
2		White body & chassis	Bright red	Bright red	Silver 24 spoke	Silver	Tan	2*	2	LESNEY NO 10 ENGLAND	D	D1/D2	£50	
3		White body & chassis	Bright red	Bright red	Silver 24 spoke	Silver	Tan	1	2	LESNEY NO 10 ENGLAND		D1/D2/D3	£35	
4		White body & chassis	Bright red	Bright red	Silver 24 spoke	Silver	Tan	2*	None*	LESNEY NO 10 ENGLAND	S	D2/D3/EI	£60	
5		White body & chassis	Bright red	Bright red	Silver 24 spoke	Silver	Tan	1	None	LESNEY NO 10 ENGLAND		D2/D3/EI/M	£30	

NOTES

There have been reports of Y10-2 Mercedes models fitted with smaller diameter wheels.

Y10-3 1906 ROLLS ROYCE SILVER GHOST — Scale 1:51

INVESTMENT COMMENT
ORIGINAL PRICE £0.34p
Surprisingly there has been little, or no activity to report about this popular model. Values represent good value and should begin to show some growth soon.

Introduced in 1969, this was the second Rolls Royce in the range and was the successor to the Y15-1 Silver Ghost. No sooner had production began than two modifications took place. The first one involved the body mould. The tooling allowing the mould to open and close, was altered. This is apparent by a single, central seam on the rear body panel, whereas all bodies from the modified tooling had double seams on the rear body panel (Diagram 1). The baseplate mould was also altered to give more strength to the front springs by widening the axle housings (Diagram 2) and adding small triangular braces to the inside faces (Diagram 3). The 1974 Issue had a new style spare tyre carrier for the new wide hollow section tyres; and it soon became apparent that three distinctly different colours had been applied to the baseplate/chassis component. The first colour a metallic purple; and the second colour a purple red were very similar to the rarer colours of the Y11 Lagonda chassis. The third colour is a ruby red, much darker than the previous two. At the same time Lesneys were experimenting with various types and colours of plastic and the 1974 model has been reported with various coloured plastic components, none of which were officially released. Various wheel types and coloured plastics were fitted to the 1979 issues, but it must be remembered that plastic components on this model can be easily switched.

ISSUE	YEAR OF RELEASE	COLOURS	SEATS	GRILLE	PLATED PARTS	WHEELS	REAR BODY PANEL	FRONT SPRINGS	BASEPLATE	RARITY	BOX TYPE	VALUE	CHECK LIST
1	1969	Metallic lime green body, metallic bronze chassis	Dark red	Dark red	Brass	Brass 12 spoke	A	A	LESNEY © 1969 ENGLAND	S	F	£25	
2		Metallic lime green body, metallic bronze chassis	Dark red	Dark red	Brass	Brass 12 spoke	A	B	LESNEY © 1969 ENGLAND	D	F/G	£20	
3		Metallic lime green body, metallic bronze chassis	Dark red	Dark red	Brass	Brass 12 spoke	B	B	LESNEY © 1969 ENGLAND		F/G	£18	
4	1974	White body, metallic purple chassis	Dark red	Dark red or black	Brass	Chrome 12 spoke	B	B	LESNEY © 1969 ENGLAND		H	£12	
5		White body, metallic purple chassis	Black	Black	Brass	Chrome 12 spoke	B	B	LESNEY © 1969 ENGLAND		H	£12	
6		White body, metallic purple red chassis	Black	Black	Brass	Chrome 12 spoke	B	B	LESNEY © 1969 ENGLAND		H	£12	✓
7		White body, metallic ruby red chassis	Black	Black	Brass	Chrome 12 spoke	B'	B	LESNEY © 1969 ENGLAND		H	£12	
8		White body, metallic ruby red chassis	Black	Black	Brass	Chrome 24 spoke*	B	B	LESNEY © 1969 ENGLAND	D	H	£18	
9		White body, metallic ruby red chassis	Black	Black	Brass	Dark red 12 spoke*	B	B	LESNEY © 1969 ENGLAND	D	H	£18	

DIAGRAM 1 REAR BODY PANEL

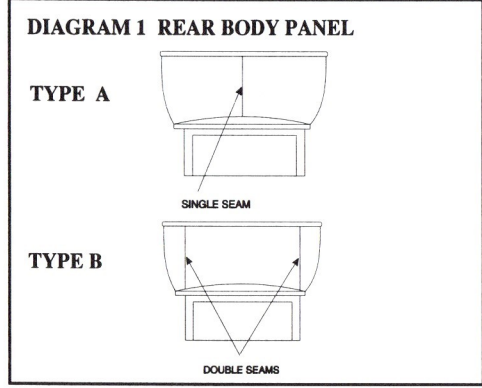

TYPE A — SINGLE SEAM
TYPE B — DOUBLE SEAMS

DIAGRAM 2 FRONT SPRINGS

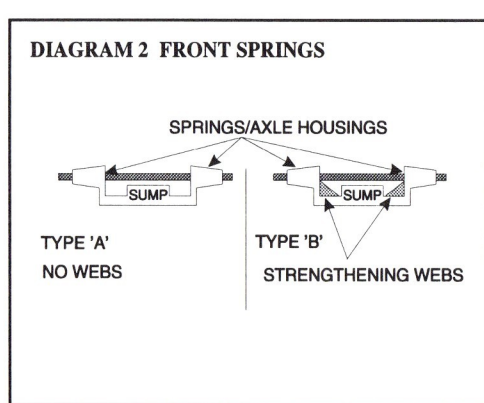

SPRINGS/AXLE HOUSINGS
SUMP
TYPE 'A' NO WEBS
TYPE 'B' STRENGTHENING WEBS

DIAGRAM 3 FRONT SPRINGS

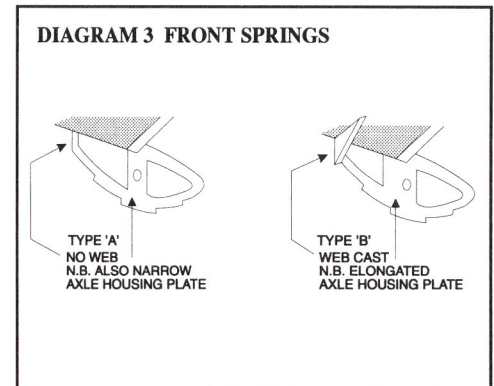

TYPE 'A' NO WEB N.B. ALSO NARROW AXLE HOUSING PLATE
TYPE 'B' WEB CAST N.B. ELONGATED AXLE HOUSING PLATE

NOTES
BECKENHAM APPEAL MODEL.
Silver body & chassis.
Black seats & grille.
Gold 12 spoke wheels (wide plastic type) black tyres. 'B' type rear body panel & 'B' type front springs.

Y10-3 1906 ROLLS ROYCE SILVER GHOST   CONTINUED   Scale 1:51

A final run of the 1979 livery fitted with white seats/floor components are now much sought after. In 1988 when production was moved to Macau, a number of models as per issue 14 were found in the Rochford factory. Rather than destroy these models, they were packaged in the maroon J type boxes and sold exclusively in Australia and therefore will have a premium price in the UK and elsewhere.

ISSUE	YEAR OF RELEASE	COLOURS	SEATS	GRILLE	PLATED PARTS	WHEELS	REAR BODY PANEL	FRONT SPRINGS	BASEPLATE	RARITY	BOX TYPE	VALUE	CHECK LIST
10	1979	Silver body,* metallic ruby red chassis	Black	Black	Brass	Chrome 12 spoke (BW)	B	B	LESNEY © 1969 ENGLAND	R	I	£30	
11		Silver body & chassis	Black	Black	Brass	Dark red 12 spoke (BW)	B	B	LESNEY © 1969 ENGLAND		I	£8	
12		Silver body & chassis	Black	Black	Brass	Chrome 12 spoke (BW)	B	B	LESNEY © 1969 ENGLAND		I	£8	
13	1980	Silver body & chassis	Dark red	Black	Brass	Dark red 12 spoke (BW)	B	B	LESNEY © 1969 ENGLAND		I	£8	
14		Silver body & chassis	Dark red	Black	Brass	Bright red 12 spoke (BW)	B	B	LESNEY © 1969 ENGLAND		I / J / L	£8	✓
15		Silver body & chassis	Dark red	Black	Brass	Chrome 12 spoke (BW)	B	B	LESNEY © 1969 ENGLAND		I	£8	
16		Silver body & chassis	Dark red	Black	Brass	Chrome 24 spoke (BW)	B	B	LESNEY © 1969 ENGLAND		I	£8	
17		Silver body & chassis	Yellow*	Black	Brass	Bright red 12 spoke (BW)	B	B'	LESNEY © 1969 ENGLAND	D	I	£30	
18		Silver body & chassis	Yellow*	Black	Brass	Dark red 12 spole (BW)	B	B	LESNEY © 1969 ENGLAND	D	I	£30	
19		Silver body & chassis	Yellow*	Black	Brass	Chrome 12 spoke (BW)	B	B	LESNEY © 1969 ENGLAND	D	I	£45	
20		Silver body & chassis	Yellow*	Black	Brass	Chrome 24 spoke (BW)	B	B	LESNEY © 1969 ENGLAND	D	I	£50	
21	1983	Silver body & chassis	White*	Black	Brass	Red 12 spoke (BW)	B	B	LESNEY © 1969 ENGLAND	V R	I	£250	

NOTES

Issue 14 was also released in the 1982 Limited Edition pack of 5 models.

Y10-4 1957 MASERATI 250F

Scale 1:35

INVESTMENT COMMENT
ORIGINAL PRICE £4.25p

Although an unpopular addition to the range at the time of release, few are available on the collectors market today and prices continue to rise steadily.

The set of four racing cars was conceived as part of a co-ordinated promotion and was originally intended to promote the sponsorship by Matchbox of an historic car race. However, it soon became clear that the total cost of such a sponsorship would be inordinate and so reluctantly Matchbox had to cancel the promotion. The first 30,000 Maseratis were produced without the full copyright description on the baseplate. Also after the first production run, twelve thousandths of an inch, (Type 2) was added to the rear suspension, in order to remove the amount of lateral rear wheel movement. The finish on the wheels and the exhaust pipes etc. can vary from matt to bright chrome. The total production run of all four issues was 97,000.

ISSUE	YEAR OF RELEASE	COLOURS	WINDSCREEN	SEAT / DASHBOARD	GRILLE	STEERING WHEEL	WHEELS	COCKPIT INTERIOR/EXHAUST PIPES	BRAKE DRUMS / SUSPENSION	BASEPLATE TYPE	BASEPLATE	RARITY	BOX TYPE	VALUE	CHECK LIST
1	1986	Italian racing red body & chassis	Clear perspex	Black plastic	Light grey	Light grey plastic	Bright chrome 24 spoke	Light grey	Light grey	1*	MATCHBOX ENGLAND	D	J	£15	
2		Italian racing red body & chassis	Clear perspex	Black plastic	Light grey	Light grey plastic	Aluminium 24 spoke	Light grey	Light grey	1*	MATCHBOX ENGLAND	D	J	£15	
3		Italian racing red body & chassis	Clear perspex	Black plastic	Light grey	Light grey plastic	Aluminium 24 spoke	Light grey	Light grey	2	MATCHBOX ENGLAND		J	£10	
4		Italian racing red body & chassis	Clear perspex	Black plastic	Light grey	Light grey plastic	Bright chrome 24 spoke	Light grey	Light grey	2	MATCHBOX ENGLAND		J	£10	✓

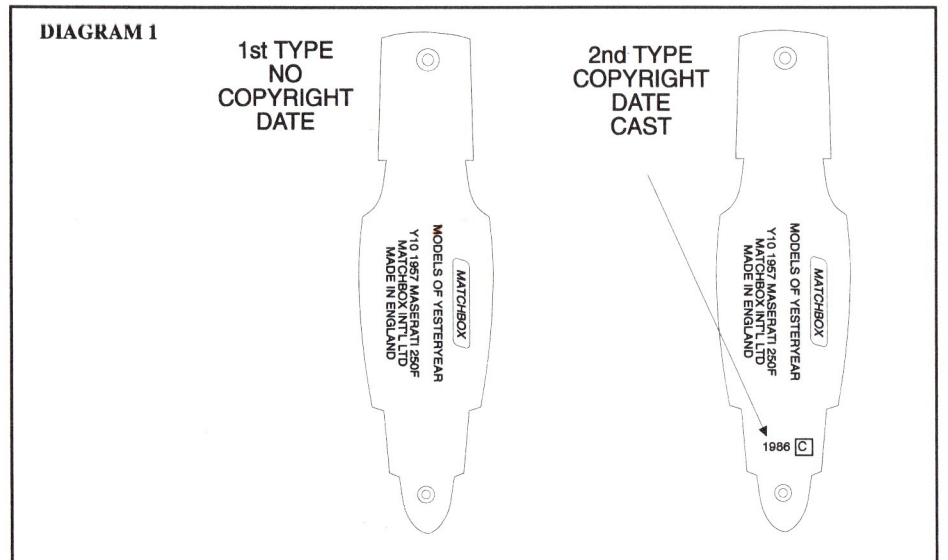

DIAGRAM 1

1st TYPE NO COPYRIGHT DATE

2nd TYPE COPYRIGHT DATE CAST

LIVERY
Tampo
Tail sides and top of the bonnet above the grille.
Racing number. Black 12 on white disc.

NOTES

The rather dumpy looking Y3-4 Ford 'T' Tanker in its various colourful liveries should constitute an easy set to collect, although harder to find are the Zerolene and Red Crown releases. The Y4-3 Opel in orange tends to command more interest than most other 'woodgrain' models.

The Y4-4 Duesenberg was in the range for fifteen years and went through many colour schemes, but it is the first issue that we all want, isn't it? This plate also reveals the two shades of red plastic used on the Y5-2 Bentley and shown on the right are the rare metallic green versions. The often uninteresting Y5-3 Peugeots, however, do throw up some collectable variations. Note the clear window example on the left: when we say clear, we mean clear!

The now defunct Y5-5 Talbot van, with its eleven liveries, makes it a colourful 'sub-range' to collect. The Y5-5 Titan bus should be due for a new livery.

Unlike the Y6-3 Cadillac, Y6-2 Bugattis are eagerly sought after. This comment also applies to the Y7-2 Mercer, especially the later yellow version. The Y7-3 Rolls Royce looked best in its final yellow livery and, there are many roof types to collect.

Note the relatively pale finish to the gold plated Y8-2 Motorcycle. All issues are highly collectable but most especially the late black seated version. The Y8-3 Stutz in blue remains a popular release and the Y8-4 model is still sought after by MG owners. The Y8-5 Yorkshire Steam Wagons make an extremely attractive display. The pale green Y9-2 Simplex on the left is in reality far rarer than its darker green successor.

All three of these Special Limited Editions are excellent models, especially the Y9-4 Leyland Cub Fire Engine. The Y10-2 Mercedes with black seats is extremely rare and only a handful are known to exist. The Y10-3 Rolls Royce models never really looked that attractive and were possibly hindered by their garish colour schemes.

Early Y11-2 Packards, especially with unplated parts, are rarer than their market values would suggest. The famous purple Y11-3 Lagonda on the left is actually very difficult to accurately photograph, but is well illustrated here. The Y11 Bugattis reveal minimal alteration to warrant their change from a Type 35 to a Type 51!

The rather bland Y12-2 Thomas Flyabout did at least produce the famous yellow seated version shown here. The Y12-3 Ford 'T' vans, also shown on the next plate, form an attractive collection in their own right.

Y10-5 1931 DIDDLER TROLLEY BUS

Scale 1:76

INVESTMENT COMMENT
ORIGINAL PRICE £17.49p

An excellent model and subject which as a Special Limited Edition remains a unique casting. Values have recently begun to increase; but further increase is likely to be slow.

Issued in late 1988 as a Special Limited Edition model. The response from both the trade and collectors was such that the model was sold out within weeks of its release, even though the recommended selling price was £17.49. The total production run was 55,000 models worldwide and the model, as with all Special Limited Edition models, was packaged in an attractive red and gold box. The success of this model was in part due to the fact that no other manufacturer had produced a trolley bus since the 1930s. In 1988 the model had the most individual components, of any in the range, thirty-six in all!

ISSUE	YEAR OF RELEASE	COLOURS	ROOF	SEATS	UPPER DECK FLOOR	UPPER DECK WINDOW FRAMES & DECK DIVIDE	SINGLE HEADLAMP	WHEELS	LOGO	SIDELIGHTS & PANTOGRAPH	STAIRS & LOWER DECK FLOORS	BASEPLATE	RARITY	BOX TYPE	VALUE	CHECK LIST
1	1988	London Transport red body black chassis	Light grey	Light brown	Light brown	Cream	Chrome	Solid mid brown	LONDON TRANSPORT	Black	Mid brown	MATCHBOX © 1988 SPECIAL LIMITED EDITION MACAU		0	£25	✓

LIVERY
Tampo
Lower side panels. Gold LONDON TRANSPORT with London Transport insignia on black adjacent to passenger platform.
Label.
Near side upper panel. RONUK in white on dark blue background with gold edging. To the left of light blue panel, dark blue BY FAR THE BEST WAX POLISHES and to the right FOR FLOORS FURNITURE BOOTS & MOTOR CARS.
Off side upper panel. Dark blue insect with red insect, blue JEYES, red KILLS, blue GERMS. All on cream panel.
Front upper quarter panels. A Johnnie Walker advertising panels in black, red, and yellow to the left and right of destination boards.
Destination boards. White 604 HAMPTON CRT VIA MALDEN & KINGSTON on black board.

NOTES

1. The passenger vertical handhold is bright steel.
2. The window glazing is clear perspex.
3. Compare with YET03-M

INVESTMENT COMMENT
ORIGINAL PRICE £0.14p

Still regarded as being one of the harder to find First Series Models. Values have been maintained and still attract a hefty premium in many overseas markets. Always a popular addition to a Yesteryear collection.

Y11-1 1920 AVELING & PORTER STEAM ROLLER   Scale 1:80

This is the most contemporary model of the first series as steam rollers were still in regular use in the 1960's. This sturdy model survived with no casting modifications, but the roof component suffered badly from a rough and sometimes pitted finish, exactly the same as the Y7-1 Leyland van. The three roof supports vary in length somewhat and allow the roof to be above, level, or below the chimney rim. No particular significance has ever been afforded to the variance, but roof supports finished in black or green are noteworthy. As with the Y1-1 Allchin, the flywheels can be finished in black varying from a matt to silk finish (jet black), or in very dark brown varying from a silk to gloss finish; the very dark brown ones having a bronze tinge to them. The wheels were only ever finished in a slightly varying dark red and the rollers and `tyres' were always in bare metal. Different, roller and flywheel moulds resulted in minor differences to the hub designs of these three components. The gold trim is significant in that the first production models had the makers plate on the front of the piston housing painted gold, these variants being exceptionally hard to find. Because of the close proximity of the chimney, it was not easy to paint the makers plate quickly and cleanly, and so this particular piece of trim was deleted early in the model's life. The second reduction in gold trim saw the steering and reversing gear rods on the right hand side of the body not being picked out in gold. Due to the small area of baseplate, the underside of the roof was used for the Lesney legends. After a life of just 5 years, this model was withdrawn from the range in 1963.

ISSUE	YEAR OF RELEASE	COLOURS	ROOF SUPPORTS	FLYWHEEL	MAKERS PLATE	GOLD TRIM	FRONT ROLLERS	REAR WHEELS	ROOF INSCRIPTION	RARITY	BOX TYPE	VALUE	CHECK LIST
1	1958	Mid green	Black	Dark brown*	Gold*	Full	Dark red 10 spoke	Dark red 14 spoke	LESNEY ENGLAND	R	B	£250	
2		Mid green	Black	Dark brown*	Mid green	Full	Dark red 10 spoke	Dark red 14 spoke	LESNEY ENGLAND	S	B	£130	
3		Mid green	Black	Jet black	Mid green	Full	Dark red 10 spoke	Dark red 14 spoke	LESNEY ENGLAND		C/D1	£90	
4	1961	Mid green	Mid green	Dark brown*	Mid green	Partial	Dark red 10 spoke	Dark red 14 spoke	LESNEY ENGLAND	R	C/D1	£130	
5		Mid green	Mid green	Jet black	Mid green	Partial	Dark red 10 spoke	Dark red 14 spoke	LESNEY ENGLAND		C/D1	£90	✓

NOTES

Y11-2 1912 PACKARD LANDAULET   Scale 1:50

INVESTMENT COMMENT
ORIGINAL PRICE £0.25p
A fine Second Series Yesteryear that enjoyed considerable popularity when in the range. Still easy to find and buy at reasonable prices.

Introduced in March 1964 and withdrawn in 1971, this model was resurrected in 1984 to be one of the 6 models in The Connoisseurs Set. Only one major casting change was made, to the base (see diagram) and that was very early in the life of this model. For issues 4,5 and 6 the dashboard was altered by the inclusion of a raised ridge on the front face between the sidelight arms. Slight differences in the 4 prong spare tyre carrier show that several different moulds were used for it's manufacture, but the main difference was the change from 4 prongs to just 3. The 'road' wheels are of the stepped rim variety. Earlier issues have either none or two triangular braces; later issues have four and the 1984 issue can have either none or four braces. See Y15-1 wheel diagrams. The original metal steering wheels and columns were superseded by the black plastic type. This model can have components without plating and models can have any combination of plated and bare metal fittings. The following list has been compiled with all these fittings in the plated state. Models have been reported with experimental grey tyres and colour trial seats in white or bright red; but these were not officially released by the factory. Stocks of the heraldic shield transfers were exhausted before the 5th Issue in vermillion (orangey red) livery was completed; but this transfer was also removed by private individuals to "enhance sales," so beware!

ISSUE	YEAR OF RELEASE	COLOURS	STEERING WHEEL	STEERING COLUMN	SPARE TYRE CARRIER	PLATED PARTS	WHEELS	SEATS	BASEPLATE TYPE	BASEPLATE	RARITY	BOX TYPE	VALUE	CHECK LIST
1	1964	Dark red body & chassis gloss black bonnet	Brass (metal)	Bare steel	4 prong	Brass	Brass 12 spoke	Black plastic	A*	LESNEY ENGLAND	S	D1	£40	
2		Dark red body & chassis gloss black bonnet	Brass (metal)	Bare steel	4 prong	Brass	Brass 12 spoke	Black plastic	B	LESNEY ENGLAND		D1/D2/D3	£22	
3		Dark red body & chassis gloss black bonnet	Brass (metal)	Bare steel	3 prong	Brass	Brass 12 spoke	Black plastic	B	LESNEY ENGLAND		D3/E	£22	
4	✓	Dark red body & chassis gloss black bonnet	Black plastic	Black plastic	3 prong	Brass	Brass 12 spoke	Black plastic	B	LESNEY ENGLAND		E/F	£20	✓✓
5	1971	Orangey* red body & chassis gloss black bonnet	Black plastic	Black plastic	3 prong	Brass	Brass 12 spoke	Black plastic	B	LESNEY ENGLAND	S	F	£30	
6	1984	Cream body & bonnet black roof, very dark brown chassis	Black plastic	Black plastic	4 prong	Brass	Brass 12 spoke	Brown plastic	B	MATCHBOX ENGLAND © 1984		K	£95 The Set	

DIAGRAM 1 BASEPLATE TYPE A

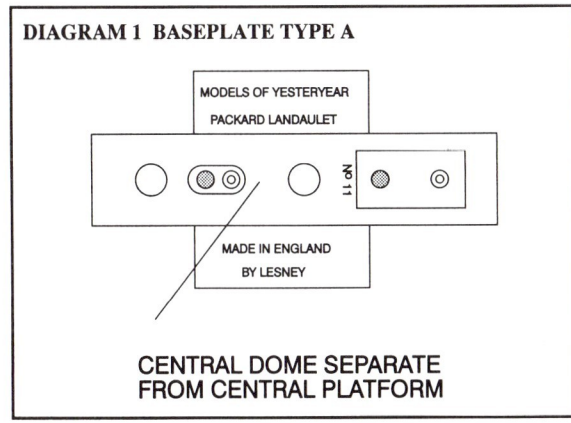

CENTRAL DOME SEPARATE FROM CENTRAL PLATFORM

DIAGRAM 2 BASEPLATE TYPE B

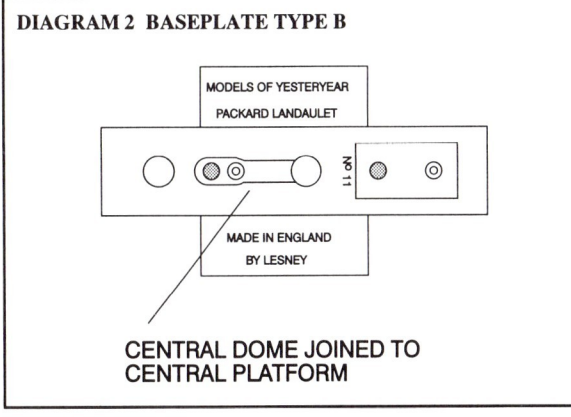

CENTRAL DOME JOINED TO CENTRAL PLATFORM

LIVERY ISSUES 1-5

Transfers
Doors. Heraldic Shield in white with Coat of Arms in gold, green, black and red.

NOTES

1. Type D1 boxes can have a pale yellow background, with the vehicle in a dark red colour similar to the model, or a lighter red vehicle on a slightly orangey background. These are genuine printing variations.

2. The D2 box always attracts a premium

INVESTMENT COMMENT
ORIGINAL PRICE £0.50p

Most of the interest for this model is concentrated on the first four issues. The purple model has increased a little. Most other issues have seen an upward trend, and this must continue!

Y11-3 1938 LAGONDA DROPHEAD COUPE Scale 1:43

First issued in 1972; the first three issues of this model are amongst the most desirable Yesteryears. Issue 1 models were in fact final pre-production models, but as with other Yesteryears, a few of these were distributed with the regular production versions and were put on sale in some toy shops. Casting modifications were made to the bumper tabs and the baseplate was lengthened slightly, before regular production began. However, Issue 1 had unmodified bumpers/baseplate. Issue 2 onwards all had these modifications; see diagram below. The copper finish of Issues 7 to 12 can vary from light to reddish copper. Copper bodied and dark cream bodied models have been reported with left hand drive steering wheels as a result of fitting the dashboard/windscreen component from the Y14-3 Stutz. These are either due to a factory error or, are lunch time/Friday afternoon specials and have been classified as negative variations. Pre-1979 models fitted with solid chrome wheels are forgeries because this type of wheel was not made until 1979, being introduced specifically for the Y18-1 Cord. Dark green plastics have been reported fitted to copper bodied models, but the authenticity of these remain in doubt.

ISSUE	YEAR OF RELEASE	COLOURS	SEATS/ FLOOR	REAR BUMPER TYPE	FOLDED HOOD & LUGGAGE TRUNK	GRILLE	PLATED PARTS	WHEELS	BASEPLATE	RARITY	BOX TYPE	VALUE	CHECK LIST
1	1972	Metallic gold body, metallic purple* chassis	Black	A*	Black	Black	Brass	Brass 24 spoke	LESNEY © 1972 ENGLAND	E R	G	£750	
2		Metallic gold body, dark red* chassis	Black	B	Black	Black	Brass	Brass 24 spoke	LESNEY © 1972 ENGLAND	V R	G	£300	
3		Metallic gold body, strawberry red* chassis	Black	B	Black	Black	Brass	Brass 24 spoke	LESNEY © 1972 ENGLAND	V R	G	£280	
4		Metallic gold body, dark maroon* chassis	Black	B	Black	Black	Brass	Brass 24 spoke	LESNEY © 1972 ENGLAND	D	G	£30	
5	1974	Metallic orange body, metallic gold chassis	Black	B	Black	Black	Brass	Brass* 24 spoke	LESNEY © 1972 ENGLAND	R	H	£75	
6		Metallic orange body, metallic gold chassis	Black	B	Black	Black	Brass	Chrome 24 spoke	LESNEY © 1972 ENGLAND		H	£15	✓
7		Metallic copper body, metallic gold chassis	Black	B	Black	Black	Brass	Chrome 24 spoke	LESNEY © 1972 ENGLAND		H	£15	✓ 2x
8		Metallic copper body, metallic gold chassis	Black	B	Black	Black	Brass	Chrome 12 spoke	LESNEY © 1972 ENGLAND		H	£15	
9		Metallic copper body, metallic gold chassis	Black	B	Black	Black	Brass	Red 12 spoke	LESNEY © 1972 ENGLAND		H	£25	
10		Metallic copper body, metallic gold chassis	Maroon	B	Maroon	Maroon	Brass	Red 12 spoke	LESNEY © 1972 ENGLAND		H	£25	
11		Metallic copper body, metallic gold chassis	Maroon	B	Maroon	Maroon	Brass	Chrome 24 spoke	LESNEY © 1972 ENGLAND		H	£25	
12		Metallic copper body, metallic gold chassis	Bright red*	B	Bright red*	Bright red*	Brass	Chrome 24 spoke	LESNEY © 1972 ENGLAND	R	H	£250	
13	1979	Metallic copper body, gloss black* chassis	Maroon	B	Maroon	Maroon	Brass	Chrome solid (WW)	LESNEY © 1972 ENGLAND	R	H	£100	

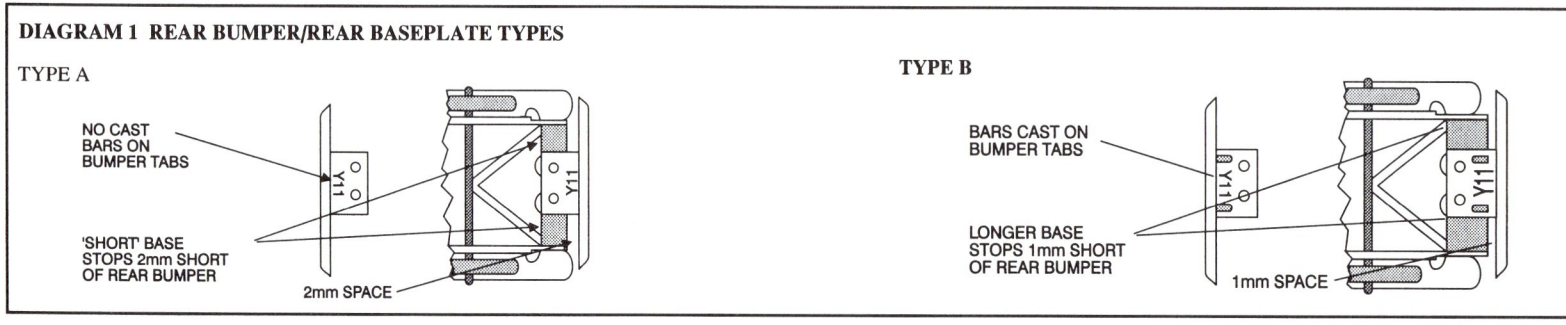

DIAGRAM 1 REAR BUMPER/REAR BASEPLATE TYPES

TYPE A — NO CAST BARS ON BUMPER TABS; 'SHORT' BASE STOPS 2mm SHORT OF REAR BUMPER; 2mm SPACE

TYPE B — BARS CAST ON BUMPER TABS; LONGER BASE STOPS 1mm SHORT OF REAR BUMPER; 1mm SPACE

NOTES
BECKENHAM APPEAL MODEL
White body; grey chassis;
Black seats, floor, folded hood & luggage trunk;
Chrome 24 spoke wheels with black tyres.

Y11-3 1938 LAGONDA DROPHEAD COUPE CONTINUED Scale 1:43

Issues 14 to 21 can have either black or maroon grilles, but these can be easily swapped and no great importance is attached to this fact, as is the case with black or white wall tyres. Three different coloured plastics were used for Issues 14 to 22, maroon, a reddish (Chestnut) brown and black. Issues 23 and 24 were released with rear wing section gaps filled in. The 1985 issues were only available as part of a special Fathers Day triple pack.

ISSUE	YEAR OF RELEASE	COLOURS	SEATS/FLOOR	REAR BUMPER TYPE	FOLDED HOOD & LUGGAGE TRUNK	GRILLE	PLATED PARTS	WHEELS	BASEPLATE	RARITY	BOX TYPE	VALUE	CHECK LIST
14		Dark cream body, metallic gold chassis	Maroon	B	Maroon	Maroon	Chrome but brass bumpers	Chrome 24 spoke (BW)	LESNEY ENGLAND	R	I	£100	
15		Dark cream body, glossy black chassis	Maroon	B	Maroon	Maroon or black	Chrome	Chrome 24 spoke (BW)	LESNEY ENGLAND		I	£15	
16		Dark cream body, glossy black chassis	Maroon	B	Maroon	Maroon or black	Chrome	Chrome 12 spoke (BW)	LESNEY ENGLAND		I	£15	
17		Dark cream body, glossy black chassis	Maroon	B	Maroon	Maroon or black	Chrome	Chrome solid (BW)	LESNEY ENGLAND		I	£10	✓
18		Dark cream body, glossy black chassis	Chestnut brown	B	Chestnut brown	Maroon or black	Chrome	Red 12 spoke (BW)	LESNEY ENGLAND		I	£15	
19		Dark cream body, glossy black chassis	Chestnut brown	B	Chestnut brown	Maroon or black	Chrome	Chrome solid (BW)	LESNEY ENGLAND		I	£10	
20		Dark cream body, glossy black chassis	Chestnut brown	B	Chestnut brown	Maroon or black	Chrome	Chrome 24 spoke (BW)	LESNEY ENGLAND		I	£15	
21		Dark cream body, glossy black chassis	Black*	B	Black*	Black*	Chrome	Chrome solid (BW)	LESNEY ENGLAND	D	I	£35	
22		Dark cream body, glossy black chassis	Black*	B	Black*	Black*	Chrome	Chrome 24 spoke	LESNEY ENGLAND	D	I	£35	
23	1985	Deep red body & chassis	Black	B	Black	Black	Brass	Brass 24 spoke	LESNEY ENGLAND		L	-	
24		Deep red body & chassis	Chestnut brown	B	Chestnut brown	Black	Brass	Brass 24 spoke	LESNEY ENGLAND		L	-	

NOTES

INVESTMENT COMMENT
ORIGINAL PRICE £4.25p

This model has shown little increase in value, although Issue 1 when seen for sale is always at a premium.

Y11-4 1932 BUGATTI TYPE 51

Scale 1:35

The Y11-4 Bugatti Type 51 was released in 1986. Originally Matchbox Toys were going to sponsor a series of vintage and veteran racing car Grand Prix events around the world. However, it soon became clear that the high costs of sponsorship were going to outweigh the benefits of publicity and so Matchbox withdrew. Even so, Matchbox had made the tools for four racers, one of which was the Bugatti Type 51 and the decision to go ahead with the new models was made. After the initial run, two modifications were made to the body casting. The axle housings at the rear were widened by 1mm (Type 2) to reduce the amount of rear wheel movement. The colour of the wheels has been described as being a matt chrome or aluminium. Also the dashboard was kept in place by means of a larger securing lug. All models were fitted with a clear Perspex windscreen. In all 92,000 Bugattis were made at the Rochford Essex factory. Although packaged in a 'J' type box, there was extra black artwork applied to help differentiate the box from standard models.

ISSUE	YEAR OF RELEASE	COLOURS	SEAT	GRILLE	STEERING WHEEL	WHEELS	PLATED PARTS	DOUBLE PETROL CAPS	BONNET STRAPS	RACING NUMBER	DASHBOARD TYPE	REAR AXLE HOUSING TYPE	BASEPLATE	RARITY	BOX TYPE	VALUE	CHECK LIST
1	1986	French racing blue body & chassis	Brown	Black	Grey	Aluminium 8 spoke	Silver grey	Silver grey	Painted brown	4	1*	A*	MATCHBOX © 1986 ENGLAND	R	J	£30	✓
2		French racing blue body & chassis	Brown	Black	Grey	Aluminium 8 spoke	Silver grey	Silver grey	Painted brown	4	2	B	MATCHBOX © 1986 ENGLAND		J	£10	✓

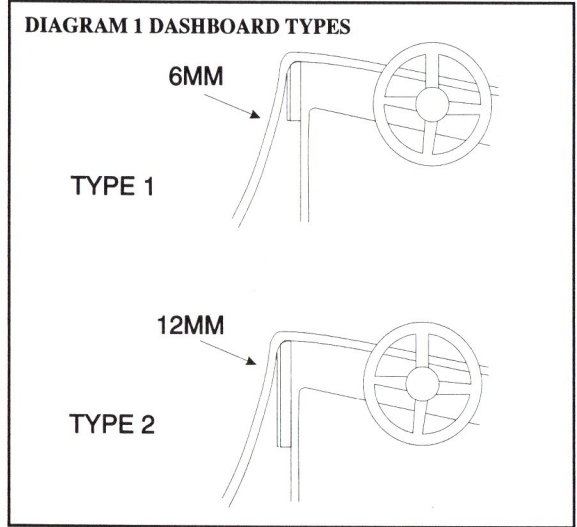

DIAGRAM 1 DASHBOARD TYPES
6MM — TYPE 1
12MM — TYPE 2

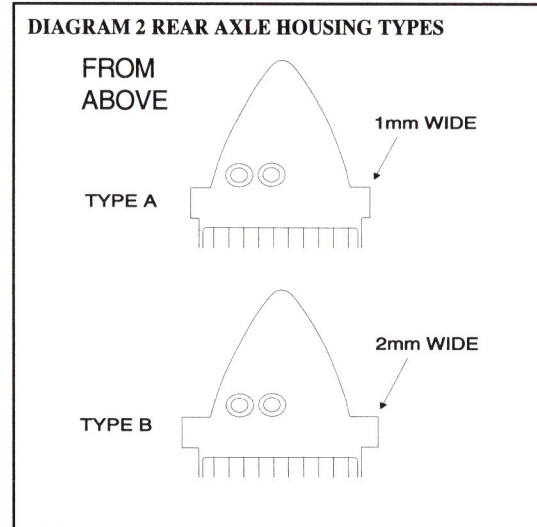

DIAGRAM 2 REAR AXLE HOUSING TYPES
FROM ABOVE
TYPE A — 1mm WIDE
TYPE B — 2mm WIDE

LIVERY
Tampo
Tail sides and on drivers side of the bonnet.
Racing number black 4 on white disc.

NOTES

INVESTMENT COMMENT

ORIGINAL PRICE £6.99p
Seldom seen on the collectors market, this model is presently undervalued. Time will tell....

Y11-5 1924 BUGATTI TYPE 35
Scale 1:35

The Y11-5 Bugatti Type 35 was a modified version of the Y11-4 Type 51. The tail section was modified to have just the one petrol cap; the chassis continued to be made in plastic and the bonnet straps were changed from being painted to ones made in plastic. Originally the Type 35 was sold by Matchbox Toys USA on the American market as one of the twelve "Great Motor Cars of the Century". This issue was not screwed into the box packaging and so the small screw hole unlike the worldwide issue shows no sign of wear to the plastic base, also the model was sold slightly later by Matchbox Toys in standard boxes (N) to all of the major markets. Also the Y11-5 model had detailing to the dashboard with the instrument dials in black, and the rear view mirror and starting handle in silver. Total production was 29,538.

ISSUE	YEAR OF RELEASE	COLOURS	SEAT	GRILLE	STEERING WHEEL	WHEELS	PLATED PARTS	SINGLE PETROL CAP	BONNET STRAPS	RACING NUMBER	DASHBOARD TYPE	REAR AXLE HOUSING TYPE	BASE SCREW HOLE	BASEPLATE	RARITY	BOX TYPE	VALUE	CHECK LIST
1	1990	Pale French racing blue body & chassis	Black	Black	Brown with grey spokes	Chrome 8 spoke	Chrome	Chrome	Brown plastic	6	2	B	Yes	MATCHBOX © 1986 MACAU	D	P* / N	£10	✓

LIVERY

Tampo
Tail sides. Both sides of bonnet and the grille.
Racing number, white 6.

NOTES

INVESTMENT COMMENT
ORIGINAL PRICE £0.14p

This delicate model still tends to lag behind other First Series models but still attracts a premium in the German and Australian markets. Values should begin to increase in the future.

Y12-1 1899 LONDON HORSE DRAWN BUS   Scale 1:100

The London Horse Drawn Bus model was in the Yesteryear range between 1959 and 1966. The red colour for the body never changed throughout. All models were fitted with black sixteen spoke wheels; twelve mm at the front and sixteen mm at the rear. Early models were fitted with lighter brown horses. The most significant casting change related to the method of attaching the horse bar to the underside of the bus body. Initially this was fixed by a single rivet (Type A) but this proved too fragile. Later models were fitted with an additional rectangular plate and two rivets (Type B). Two different lower panel decals were used throughout production: The longer (2.7cms) is duller in colour compared with the shorter (2.6cms). The amount of gold trim was less on Issues 5-8. All drivers were painted in the same colour as the seats. More often than not, the paint on top of the driver's bowler hat wore off due to the tight fitting box. Compared to the other horse drawn model of the time; the Y4-2 Shand Mason, the Y12-1 has not seen dramatic increases in value, possibly because it was a more robust model, no removable parts such as crew and was probably made in much greater numbers. The last issue can be found with a much creamier beige upper deck.

ISSUE	YEAR OF RELEASE	COLOUR	HORSES	HORSE COLLAR	HORSE BAR RIVET TYPE	PASSENGER SEATS	UNDERSIDE PASSENGER DECK	TOP LINE LOWER DECAL	BASEPLATE	RARITY	BOX TYPE	VALUE	CHECK LIST
1	1959	Red body, chassis & horse bar	Brown with white manes & tails	All gold	A*	Beige	Unpainted	Type 1	LESNEY NO 12 ENGLAND	D	B	£90	
2		Red body, chassis & horse bar	Brown with white manes & tails	All gold	A*	Beige	Beige	Type 1	LESNEY NO 12 ENGLAND	D	B	£90	✓ 2X
3		Red body, chassis & horse bar	Brown with white manes & tails	All gold	A*	Beige	Beige	Type 2	LESNEY NO 12 ENGLAND	D	C/D1	£90	
4		Red body, chassis & horse bar	Brown with white manes & tails	All gold	B	Beige	Beige	Type 2	LESNEY NO 12 ENGLAND		C/D1	£70	✓
5		Red body, chassis & horse bar	Dark brown with white manes & tails	Partial gold	A*	Beige	Beige	Type 2	LESNEY NO 12 ENGLAND	D	D1	£90	
6		Red body, chassis & horse bar	Dark brown with white manes & tails	Partial gold	B	Beige	Beige	Type 2	LESNEY NO 12 ENGLAND		D1/D2/D3	£70	
7		Red body, chassis & horse bar	Dark brown with white manes & tails	Partial gold	B	Beige	Unpainted	Type 2	LESNEY NO 12 ENGLAND		D2/D3	£70	
8		Red body, chassis & horse bar	Dark brown with white manes & tails	Partial gold	B	Cream/beige	Cream/beige	Type 2	LESNEY NO 12 ENGLAND		D3	£70	

DIAGRAM 1 HORSEBAR RIVET TYPES

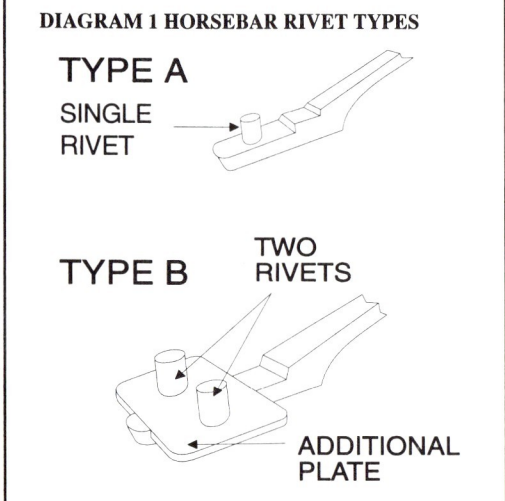

TYPE A SINGLE RIVET

TYPE B TWO RIVETS / ADDITIONAL PLATE

TOP LINE LOWER DECAL TEXT SETTING

TYPE 1 - 'M' of OMNIBUS directly above '&'; 'D' of LIMITED above final 'S' of CROSS
(Shorter and Duller)

TYPE 2 - 'O' of OMNIBUS directly above '&'; 'E' of LIMITED above final 'S' of CROSS
(Larger and Brighter)

LIVERY

Transfers
Upper side panels. White LIPTON'S TEA
Lower side panels. LONDON GENERAL OMNIBUS COMPANY LIMITED above VICTORIA & KING'S CROSS in yellow.
Upper front panels. HUDSON'S SOAP in blue and white, both sides of driver.
Rear upper panel. Blue SANITAS FLUID DISINFECTANT on yellow panel. Red COLMAN'S MUSTARD on yellow panel.
Stairs panel. Yellow PICCADILLY CIRCUS with Heinz and Horlick's advertisements.

NOTES

Y12-2 1909 THOMAS FLYABOUT

Scale 1:48

INVESTMENT COMMENT
ORIGINAL PRICE £0.26.5p
Issue 1 remains "blue chip" and recent dealings indicate that it may well reach the £1,000 mark before too long. Standard issues have remained steady and at present represent good value.

First issued in 1967, this model was not deleted from the range until 1978. During the initial production run some models were fitted with bright yellow seats and grilles and are now part of Yesteryear folk lore. Whilst the seats are the same dimensions as the Y9-2 Simplex, the upholstery pattern is different. Many different coloured plastic components have been reported on this model, but their authenticity is questionable. The listed issues have been based entirely on Matchbox's records. The minor casting differences to the windscreen/sidelights component are due to several different moulds being used, each being very slightly different. The brake lever/spare tyre carrier was redesigned when the wider, hollow section tyres were introduced. Due to this model being used in the plated Gift Ware series, three different types of baseplate were used. The hood locating pins became part of the seat due to the body mounted pins being damaged, or broken during the fettling/tumbling process. The livery can vary from an almost turquoise colour to royal blue. The blue liveried models can also have unplated components. There are also two distinctly different liveries on the 1975 to 1978 issues; the first being a purple red colour, whilst the later colour is a very rich ruby red. It must be noted that the plastic components are easily interchangeable!

ISSUE	YEAR OF RELEASE	COLOURS	HOOD	SEATS	GRILLE	PLATED PARTS	WHEELS	HOOD LOCATERS	BODY TYPE	BASEPLATE TYPE	BASEPLATE	RARITY	BOX TYPE	VALUE	CHECK LIST
1	1967	Metallic blue body & chassis	Tan smooth	Bright yellow*	Bright yellow*	Brass	Brass 12 spoke	Body pins	A	A	LESNEY ENGLAND	E R	E	£900	
2		Metallic blue body & chassis	Tan smooth	Dark red	Dark red	Brass	Brass 12 spoke	Body pins*	A	A	LESNEY ENGLAND	D	E ✓	£25	✓ 2x
3		Metallic blue body & chassis	Tan smooth	Dark red	Dark red	Brass	Brass 12 spoke	Seat pins	B	A	LESNEY ENGLAND		E/F	£20	
4		Metallic blue body & chassis	Tan smooth	Dark red	Dark red	Brass	Brass 12 spoke	Seat pins	B	B*	LESNEY ENGLAND	V R	E/F	£100	
5		Metallic blue body & chassis	Tan smooth	Dark red	Dark red	Brass	Brass 12 spoke	Seat pins	B	C	LESNEY ENGLAND		F	£20	
6		Metallic blue body & chassis	Tan textured*	Dark red	Dark red	Brass	Brass 12 spoke	Seat pins	B	C	LESNEY ENGLAND	D	F/G	£30	
7		Metallic blue body & chassis	Tan textured*	Dark red	Dark red	Brass	Brass 12 spoke	Seat pins	B	A	LESNEY ENGLAND	D	F/G	£30	
8		Metallic blue body & chassis	Black textured	White*	Dark red	Brass	Brass 12 spoke	Seat pins	B	C	LESNEY ENGLAND	D	H	£25	
9	1975	Metallic purple red body & chassis	Black textured	Dark red	Black	Brass	Chrome 12 spoke	Seat pins	B	C	LESNEY ENGLAND		H	£25	
10		Metallic purple red body & chassis	Black textured	White	Black	Brass	Chrome 12 spoke	Seat pins	B	C	LESNEY ENGLAND		H	£20	✓
11		Metallic purple red body & chassis	Black textured	White	Black	Brass	Chrome 24 spoke	Seat pins	B	C	LESNEY ENGLAND		H	£20	
12		Metallic ruby red* body & chassis	Black textured	White	Black	Brass	Chrome 24 spoke	Seat pins	B	C	LESNEY ENGLAND	D	H	£25	
13		Metallic ruby red* body & chassis	Black textured	White	Black	Brass	Chrome 12 spoke	Seat pins	B	C	LESNEY ENGLAND	D	H	£25	

DIAGRAM 1 HOOD LOCATERS - BODY PINS

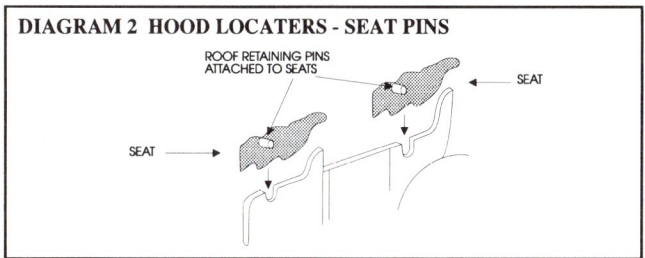

ROOF RETAINING PINS CAST WITH BODY

DIAGRAM 2 HOOD LOCATERS - SEAT PINS

ROOF RETAINING PINS ATTACHED TO SEATS — SEAT
SEAT

DIAGRAM 3 BASEPLATE TYPE A

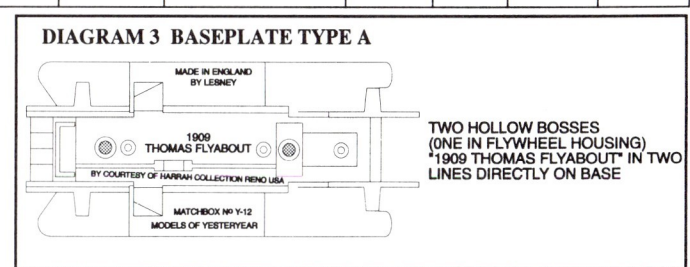

TWO HOLLOW BOSSES (ONE IN FLYWHEEL HOUSING) "1909 THOMAS FLYABOUT" IN TWO LINES DIRECTLY ON BASE

DIAGRAM 4 BASEPLATE TYPE B

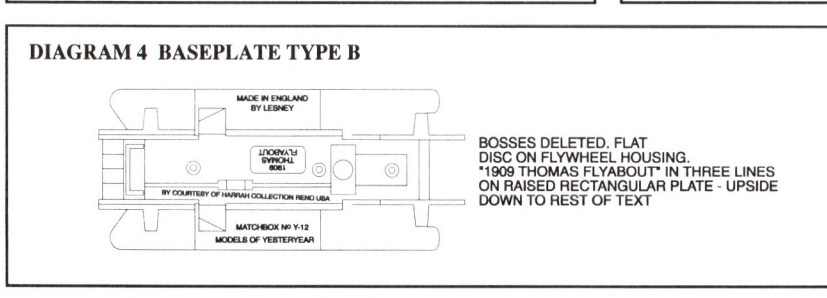

BOSSES DELETED. FLAT DISC ON FLYWHEEL HOUSING. "1909 THOMAS FLYABOUT" IN THREE LINES ON RAISED RECTANGULAR PLATE - UPSIDE DOWN TO REST OF TEXT

DIAGRAM 5 BASEPLATE TYPE C

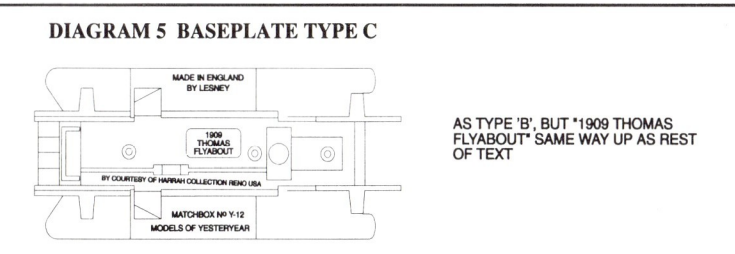

AS TYPE 'B', BUT "1909 THOMAS FLYABOUT" SAME WAY UP AS REST OF TEXT

NOTES

BECKENHAM APPEAL MODEL
Dark green body, bonnet & chassis. White seats, black textured hood, black grille. Hood located on seat pins, chrome 12 spoke wheels with black tyres. 'C' type base.

INVESTMENT COMMENT
ORIGINAL PRICE £1.50p
COCA COLA Issues 1 and 2 seldom come onto the market and the later issues have maintained their values. Always a popular addition to any collection.

Y12-3 1912 FORD MODEL 'T' VAN   Scale 1:35

COCA-COLA. This livery made at the same time as the 'Colman's Mustard' model, was originally made for distribution in the North American market. Subsequent releases were planned for other markets. However Lesney had to quickly modify their marketing strategy when they discovered that Coca-Cola Bottlers, UK Ltd. wanted exceptionally high royalty payments. Although some 'Coca-Cola' models had been released in Germany and Austria, Lesney were forced to halt further production and distribution. Early issues were afforded an extra (fifth) vertical red coach line and these are seldom seen for sale. This fifth line was deleted when the concurrently produced 'Colman's' model revealed a problem. The positioning of the word 'Mustard' made this fifth line redundant and so the tampo plates were modified by removing the line. Therefore, all remaining 'Coca-Cola' models were released with a four line design. Again with regards the rare five line models it has recently been noted that the tampo design of the letters 'C' and 'L' in the word 'Cola' is slightly different from the design of the four line models. In the former, where the top of the letter 'C' intersects the letter 'L' there is a break which allows the off-white of the body to show through. In the latter, there are no breaks. In the main rear lights were red but models can be found with black rear lights. It should be noted that the 2,000 run Coke 75th models made by Bob Brennan in 1980, were never sanctioned by Lesney and although attractive and desirable, are Code 3 models.

A : COCA - COLA

ISSUE	YEAR OF RELEASE	COLOURS	ROOF	SEAT	GRILLE	WHEELS	PLATED PARTS	LIVERY	REAR DOORS	REAR LIGHTS	TAMPO DECORATION	FIVE VERTICAL LINES	BASEPLATE NUMBER	BASEPLATE	RARITY	BOX TYPE	VALUE	CHECK LIST
1	1979	Off white / creamy white body, black chassis	Black	Black	Chrome	Red 12 spoke	Chrome	COCA-COLA	Red type 1	Red	Type 1	Yes*	No Y-12	LESNEY © 1978 ENGLAND	V R	I	£350	
2		Off white / creamy white body, black chassis	Black	Black	Gold	Red 12 spoke	Gold	COCA-COLA	Red type 1	Red	Type 1	Yes*	No Y-12	LESNEY © 1978 ENGLAND	V R	I	£350	
3		Off white / creamy white body, black chassis	Black	Black	Gold	Red 12 spoke	Gold	COCA-COLA	Red type 1	Red	Type 1	No	No Y-12	LESNEY © 1978 ENGLAND		I	£30	✓
4		Off white / creamy white body, black chassis	Black	Black	Gold	Red 12 spoke	Gold	COCA-COLA	Red type 1	Red	Type 2	No	No Y-12	LESNEY © 1978 ENGLAND		I	£30	
5		Off white / creamy white body, black chassis	Black	Tan*	Gold	Red 12 spoke	Gold	COCA-COLA	Red type 1	Red	Type 2	No	No Y-12	LESNEY © 1978 ENGLAND	D	I	£60	
6		Off white /creamy white body, black chassis	Black	Black	Gold	Chrome * 12 spoke	Gold	COCA-COLA	Red type 1	Red	Type 2	No	No Y-12	LESNEY © 1978 ENGLAND	D	I	£60	
7		Off white / creamy white body, black chassis	Black	Black	Gold	Chrome * 24 spoke	Gold	COCA-COLA	Red type 1	Red	Type 2	No	No Y-12	LESNEY © 1978 ENGLAND	D	I	£60	
8		Off white / creamy white body, black chassis	Black	Black	Gold	Gold * 12 spoke	Gold	COCA-COLA	Red type 1	Red	Type 2	No	No Y-12	LESNEY © 1978 ENGLAND	D	I	£70	

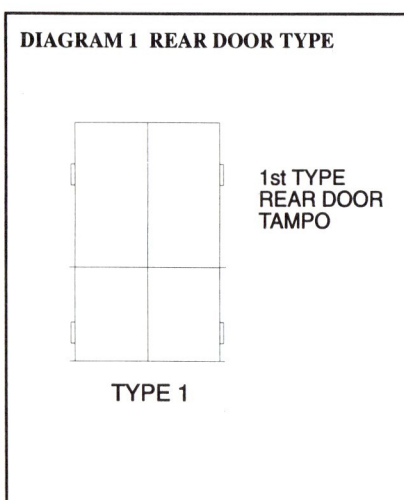

DIAGRAM 1 REAR DOOR TYPE — 1st TYPE REAR DOOR TAMPO — TYPE 1

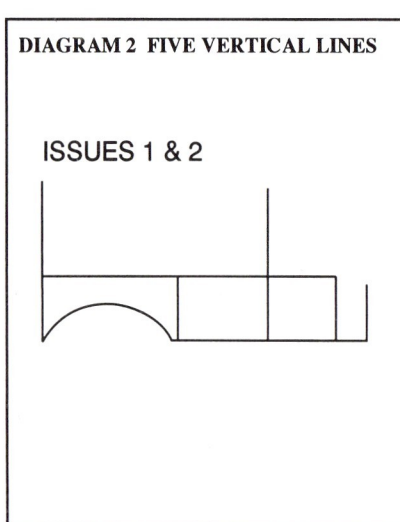

DIAGRAM 2 FIVE VERTICAL LINES — ISSUES 1 & 2

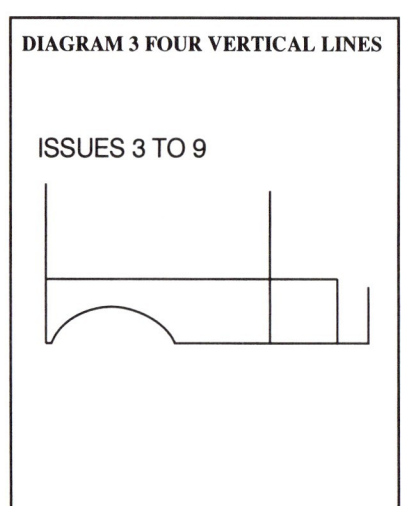

DIAGRAM 3 FOUR VERTICAL LINES — ISSUES 3 TO 9

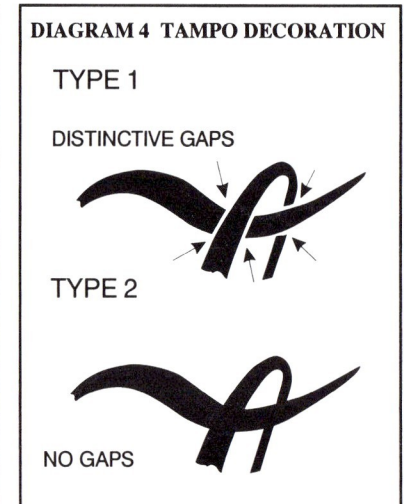

DIAGRAM 4 TAMPO DECORATION — TYPE 1 DISTINCTIVE GAPS — TYPE 2 NO GAPS

LIVERY Coca-Cola
Tampo
Van sides. Black ENJOY above red COCA-COLA above black TRADEMARK and copyright R in black circle.
All within red coachlining including cab doors and sides.

NOTES

Y12-3 1912 FORD MODEL 'T' VAN (CONTINUED) Scale 1:35

COLMAN'S MUSTARD. Launched in 1979 concurrently with the 'Coca-Cola' model, a year after the start of the Y5/4 1927 Talbot Van, the Ford 'T' gave Lesney and later Matchbox the facility to produce a range of liveries, all on the same body. The policy was to use liveries contemporary with the age of the van. One of the more famous and expensive pre-productions was the all white 'Colman's Mustard'. These were tampo trial run models using the painted bodies from the then concurrently produced 'Coca-Cola' model. An excellent reference photograph can be found in the 1991 Matchbox Models of Yesteryear Calendar. In order to use the baseplate component for the production of the Y3 Ford Tanker, the tools were modified so that the number Y12 was removed. It should be noted that throughout production the seats remained black and that the plated parts were in a gold/brass colour.
TAYSTEE. This model has long been regarded as a Code 3. The story dates back to 1979/1980 when 'The American Bakeries Company' placed an order with Lesney for the Y5 Talbot model decorated as a Taystee van. A number of Y12 models were made with the Taystee logo. At the factory it was not immediately noticed that a mistake had been made. Upon being told of the mistake, it was agreed to dispose of the Y12 models by packing them in with standard Y5 Taystee models. Two well-respected dealers state that they received a quantity of Y12 Taystee models with their orders. These were subsequently sold at the standard Yesteryear price at the Gloucester and Windsor swapmeets. Collectors should be aware that genuine labels measure 30mm x 19mm. It is estimated that no more than 200 Y12 'Taystee' vans were produced.

B : COLMAN'S

ISSUE	YEAR OF RELEASE	COLOURS	ROOF	SEAT	GRILLE	WHEELS	PLATED PARTS	LIVERY	REAR DOORS	REAR LIGHTS	BASEPLATE NUMBER	BASEPLATE	RARITY	BOX TYPE	VALUE	CHECK LIST
1	1979	Yellow body, black chassis	Matt black	Black	Gold	Red 12 spoke	Gold	COLMAN'S	Red type 1	Red	Y12	LESNEY © 1978 ENGLAND		I	£10	✓
2		Yellow body, black chassis	Matt black	Black	Gold	Red 12 spoke	Gold	COLMAN'S	Red type 1	Black	Y12	LESNEY © 1978 ENGLAND		I	£10	
3		Yellow body, black chassis	Matt black	Black	Gold	Chrome 12 spoke*	Gold	COLMAN'S	Red type 1	Black	Y12	LESNEY © 1978 ENGLAND	D	I	£25	
4		Yellow body, black chassis	Matt black	Black	Gold	Chrome 24 spoke*	Gold	COLMAN'S	Red type 1	Red	Y12	LESNEY © 1978 ENGLAND	D	I	£25	
5		Yellow body, black chassis	Matt black	Black	Gold	Red 12 spoke	Gold	COLMAN'S	Red type 2*	Black	Y12*	LESNEY © 1978 ENGLAND	D	I	£20	
6		Yellow body, black chassis	Matt black	Black	Gold	Red 12 spoke	Gold	COLMAN'S	Red type 2	Red	None	LESNEY © 1978 ENGLAND		I	£15	
7		Yellow body, black chassis	Matt black	Black	Gold	Gold 12 spoke*	Gold	COLMAN'S	Red type 2	Black	None	LESNEY © 1978 ENGLAND	S	I	£30	
8		Yellow body, black chassis	Gloss black*	Black	Gold	Red 12 spoke	Gold	COLMAN'S	Red type 2	Black	None	LESNEY © 1978 ENGLAND	S	I	£25	

C : TAYSTEE

ISSUE	YEAR OF RELEASE	COLOURS	ROOF	SEAT	GRILLE	WHEELS	PLATED PARTS	LIVERY	REAR DOORS	REAR LIGHTS	BASEPLATE NUMBER	BASEPLATE	RARITY	BOX TYPE	VALUE	CHECK LIST
1*	1980	Yellow body, black chassis	Matt black	Black	Gold	Red 12 spoke	Gold	TAYSTEE	Red type 1	Red	Y12	LESNEY © 1978 ENGLAND	V R	I	£250	

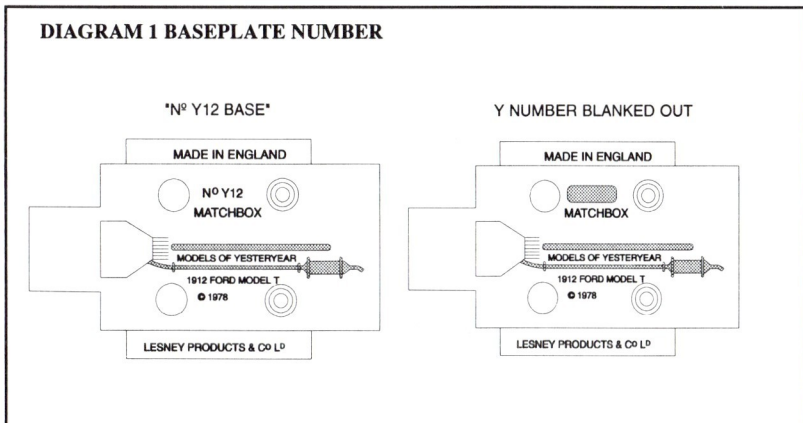

DIAGRAM 1 BASEPLATE NUMBER — "N° Y12 BASE" / Y NUMBER BLANKED OUT

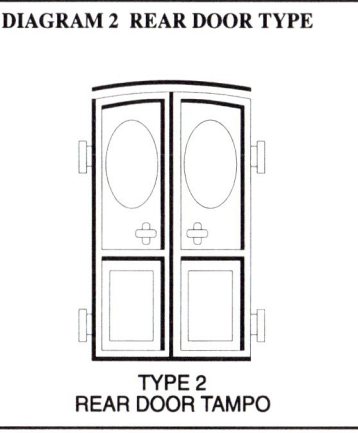

DIAGRAM 2 REAR DOOR TYPE — TYPE 2 REAR DOOR TAMPO

LIVERY COLMAN'S
Tampo
Van sides. Black COLMAN'S above black bull's head in black circle above red MUSTARD.
Red coachlining.

LIVERY TAYSTEE
Transfer
TAYSTEE in white on red oval with white surround, both van sides. OLD FASHIONED ENRICHED BREAD in black both van sides.

INVESTMENT COMMENT
ORIGINAL PRICE COLMAN'S & TAYSTEE £1.50p
Colman's Although it is now 17 years old it is only wheel variations which attract much attention. It should increase in value, but at a slow rate. The one to watch may be Issue 5.

Taystee A new discovery and one to acquire if possible. Great potential.
NOTES
There are so many wheel fakes on the market that few Y12-3 models with wheel variations can be afforded a premium.

Y12-3 1912 FORD MODEL 'T' VAN (CONTINUED) Scale 1:35

SUZE. Lesney decided that the 'Colman's' livery did not appeal to the international market and so the Suze was launched to cater for the European Countries. However, because the demand was so good, the manufacturers quickly made it available in all other markets. With the redesign of the rear doors came the inevitable overlap of both types, with the second type in either red, or black being an eagerly sought after variation. For details on the baseplate numbers, see Y3-4 "BP" tanker.

SMITH'S CRISPS. The crisp manufacturer agreed a redemption offer with Lesney (Matchbox) whereby the public could buy direct, one of the Y12 models for £1.95 plus five coupons. Once the offer was over the model was released as a range model for all the Matchbox markets. The two types of Lesney baseplate were used and the first 2,000 models were released with a black seat. It should be noted that Smith's organised their own promotion with their food retailers and offered as an incentive a privately produced promotional Y12 (Code 3) to those who ordered sufficient quantities of their potato crisps.

D : SUZE

ISSUE	YEAR OF RELEASE	COLOURS	ROOF	SEAT	GRILLE	WHEELS	PLATED PARTS	LOGO	REAR DOORS	REAR LIGHTS	BASEPLATE NUMBER	BASEPLATE	RARITY	BOX TYPE	VALUE	CHECK LIST
1	1980	Yellow body, black chassis	Matt black	Black	Gold	Red 12 spoke	Gold	SUZE	Black type 1	Black	Y12	LESNEY © 1978 ENGLAND		I	£10	
2		Yellow body, black chassis	Matt black	Tan*	Gold	Red 12 spoke	Gold	SUZE	Black type 1	Black	Y12	LESNEY © 1978 ENGLAND	S	I	£25	
3		Yellow body, black chassis	Matt black	Black	Gold	Chrome 12 spoke	Gold	SUZE	Black type 1	Black	Y12	LESNEY © 1978 ENGLAND		I	£10	
4		Yellow body, black chassis	Matt black	Black	Gold	Chrome 24 spoke	Gold	SUZE	Black type 1	Black	Y12	LESNEY © 1978 ENGLAND		I	£10	
5		Yellow body, black chassis	Matt black	Black	Gold	Red 12 spoke	Gold	SUZE	Black type 1	Red*	Y12	LESNEY © 1978 ENGLAND	S	I	£25	
6		Yellow body, black chassis	Matt black	Black	Gold	Red 12 spoke	Gold	SUZE	Black type 2*	Black	Y12*	LESNEY © 1978 ENGLAND	R	I	£35	
7		Yellow body, black chassis	Matt black	Black	Gold	Red 12 spoke	Gold	SUZE	Black type 2	Black	None	LESNEY © 1978 ENGLAND		I	£8	
8		Yellow body, black chassis	Glossy black*	Black	Gold	Red 12 spoke	Gold	SUZE	Black type 2	Black	None	LESNEY © 1978 ENGLAND	S	I	£40	
9		Yellow body, black chassis	Glossy black*	Black	Gold	Red 12 spoke	Gold	SUZE	Red type 2*	Black	None	LESNEY © 1978 ENGLAND	VR	I	£150	

E : SMITH'S CRISPS

ISSUE	YEAR OF RELEASE	COLOURS	ROOF	SEAT	GRILLE	WHEELS	PLATED PARTS	LOGO	REAR DOORS	REAR LIGHTS	BASEPLATE NUMBER	BASEPLATE	RARITY	BOX TYPE	VALUE	CHECK LIST
1	1981	Blue body, black chassis	White	Black*	Gold	Red 12 spoke (WW)	Gold	SMITH'S	White type 1	White	Y12	LESNEY © 1978 ENGLAND	D	I	£20	
2		Blue body, black chassis	White	Tan	Gold	Red 12 spoke (WW)	Gold	SMITH'S	White type 1	White	Y12	LESNEY © 1978 ENGLAND		I	£10	
3		Blue body, black chassis	White	Tan	Gold	Red 12 spoke (WW)	Gold	SMITH'S	White type 1	White	None	LESNEY © 1978 ENGLAND		I	£10	
4		Blue body, black chassis	White	Tan	Gold	Red 12spoke (WW)	Gold	SMITH'S	White type 2	White	None	LESNEY © 1978 ENGLAND		I	£10	
5		Blue body, black chassis	White	Tan	Gold	Red 12 spoke (WW)	Gold	SMITH'S	White type 2	White	Y12*	LESNEY © 1978 ENGLAND	S	I	£20	
6		Blue body, black chassis	White	Black*	Gold	Red 12 spoke (WW)	Gold	SMITH'S	White type 2	White	None	LESNEY © 1978 ENGLAND	D	I	£20	
7		Blue body, black chassis	White	Black*	Gold	Red 12 spoke (WW)	Gold	SMITH'S	White type 2	White	Y12*	LESNEY © 1978 ENGLAND	D	I	£25	

LIVERY SUZE
Tampo
Van sides. Black SUZE with red outline above black A LA GENTIANE. Coachling in black.

LIVERY SMITH'S CRISPS
Tampo
Van sides. Red POTATO CRISPS and white SMITH'S on red, all in white panel. White THE BEST, white 17 in a white circle, white HEAD OFFICE CRICKLEWOOD LONDON and white 58-60 BRINKWAY STOCKPORT. Cab doors. White ALWAYS READY FOR ALL MEALS. Coachlining in white.

INVESTMENT COMMENT
ORIGINAL PRICE SUZE £1.50p SMITH'S £1.95
The Suze was a slow performer during the 1980s, but is now gathering pace and steadily increasing in value. Issue 9 is one to seek. The Smith's Crisps is less common than many other Y12 vans and as such has some growth potential.

NOTES

Y12-3 1912 FORD MODEL 'T' VAN (CONTINUED) Scale 1:35

SILVER JUBILEE. With the imminent anniversary of twenty five years (1956-1981) production of Yesteryears it was decided to celebrate the event with a new Y12 livery. Although undoubtedly much effort went into the design, it turned out rather drab and was not greeted with much enthusiasm. The packaging was the same shape and size of the standard box, but was finished in white with silver and black decoration. The model is described as Y12/45 on the end flaps.

BIRD'S CUSTARD. Launched in 1982 to become the standard Y12 in the range. There were component overlaps for the 'Silver Jubilee' model and a batch of models were fitted with yellow spoked wheels. A much sought after variation is Issue 3 with its metallic paint finish. A factory error caused a final production run to be released with no rear door decoration. This issue has not been included because it is a negative variation. The colour of yellow on the roofs can vary according to the amount of paint applied.

F : 25 YEARS SILVER JUBILEE

ISSUE	YEAR OF RELEASE	COLOURS	ROOF	SEAT	GRILLE	WHEELS	PLATED PARTS	LOGO	REAR DOORS	REAR LIGHTS	BASEPLATE NUMBER	BASEPLATE	RARITY	BOX TYPE	VALUE	CHECK LIST
1	1981	Light green body, dark green chassis	Grey	Black	Chrome	Yellow 12 spoke (W W)	Chrome	25 YEARS	Silver type 1*	Grey	Y12*	LESNEY © 1978 ENGLAND	E R	I	£400	
2		Light green body, dark green chassis	Grey	Black	Chrome	Yellow 12 spoke (W W)	Chrome	25 YEARS	Silver type 2	Grey	Y12*	LESNEY © 1978 ENGLAND	D	I	£20	
3		Light green body, dark green chassis	Grey	Black	Chrome	Yellow 12 spoke (W W)	Chrome	25 YEARS	Silver type 2	Grey	Blank	LESNEY © 1978 ENGLAND		I	£15	✓
4		Light green body, dark green chassis	Grey	Black	Chrome	Chrome 12 spoke (W W)	Chrome	25 YEARS	Silver type 2	Grey	Blank	LESNEY © 1978 ENGLAND		I	£15	
5		Light green body, dark green chassis	Grey	Black	Chrome	Red 12 spoke (W W)	Chrome	25 YEARS	Silver type 2	Grey	Blank	LESNEY © 1978 ENGLAND		I	£15	
6		Light green body, dark green chassis	Grey	Black	Chrome	Yellow 24* spoke (W W)	Chrome	25 YEARS	Silver type 2	Grey	Blank	LESNEY © 1978 ENGLAND	D	I	£20	

G : BIRD'S CUSTARD

ISSUE	YEAR OF RELEASE	COLOURS	ROOF	SEAT	GRILLE	WHEELS	PLATED PARTS	LOGO	REAR DOORS	REAR LIGHTS	BASEPLATE NUMBER	BASEPLATE	RARITY	BOX TYPE	VALUE	CHECK LIST
1	1982	Royal blue body, black chassis	Yellow	Black	Chrome	Red 12 spoke (W W)	Chrome	BIRD'S	Yellow type 2	Yellow	Blank	LESNEY © 1978 ENGLAND		I	£12	
2		Royal blue body, black chassis	Yellow	Tan	Chrome	Red 12 spoke (W W)	Chrome	BIRD'S	Yellow type 2	Yellow	Blank	LESNEY © 1978 ENGLAND		I	£12	✓
3		Metallic* royal blue body, black chassis	Yellow	Black	Chrome	Red 12 spoke (W W)	Chrome	BIRD'S	Yellow type 2	Yellow	Blank	LESNEY © 1978 ENGLAND	R	I	£120	
4		Royal blue body, black chassis	Yellow	Black	Chrome	Yellow 12 spoke (W W)	Chrome	BIRD'S	Yellow type 2	Yellow	Blank	LESNEY © 1978 ENGLAND		I	£35	
5		Royal blue body, black chassis	Yellow	Black	Chrome	Red 12 spoke (W W)	Chrome	BIRD'S	Type 3	Yellow	Blank	LESNEY © 1978 ENGLAND		I	£12	
6		Royal blue body, black chassis	Yellow	Tan	Chrome	Red 12 spoke (W W)	Chrome	BIRD'S	Type 3	Yellow	Blank	LESNEY © 1978 ENGLAND		I	£12	
7		Royal blue body, black chassis	Yellow	Black	Gold*	Red 12 spoke (W W)	Gold*	BIRD'S	Type 3	Yellow	Blank	LESNEY © 1978 ENGLAND	S	I	£50	
8		Royal blue body, black chassis	Yellow	Black	Chrome	Chrome 12 spoke* (W W)	Chrome	BIRD'S	Type 3	Yellow	Blank	LESNEY © 1978 ENGLAND	D	I	£30	

LIVERY 25 YEARS SILVER JUBILEE
Tampo
Van sides. Silver 25 with black highlights. Dark green YEARS, SILVER JUBILEE EDITION. Silver MODELS OF YESTERYEAR 1956 1981 on dark green. Coachlining in silver.
Van doors. Silver coachlining.

LIVERY BIRD'S CUSTARD
Tampo
Van sides. BIRD'S CUSTARD POWDER in white on red panel above white MAKES THE RICHEST CUSTARD WITHOUT EGGS AT HALF THE COST & TROUBLE. THE ORIGINAL & ONLY GENUINE ALFRED BIRD & SONS BIRMINGHAM. All on red panel.
Coachlining in pale yellow.

INVESTMENT COMMENT
ORIGINAL PRICE '25' YEARS £2.49p BIRD'S £2.50p
The Silver Jubilee models although made in prolific numbers have continued to be a popular van, especially in Australia where it enjoys a considerable premium. Issue 6 is rarely seen for sale. The Bird's Custard has also shown growth and should continue to perform steadily. Issue 3 has potential for good growth, having appreciated significantly over the last few years.

Y12-3 1912 FORD MODEL 'T' VAN (CONTINUED) Scale 1:35

CEREBOS. During 1982 whilst the 'Cerebos' van was being produced, a Matchbox employee by mistake attached yellow roof components from the 'Birds Custard' to the bodies of the 'Cerebos'. Although there was a mixture of plated components used, it was reported at the time that the number of yellow roofed Cerebos vans was a mere 500! The early issues were fitted with either all black or white wall tyres.

ARNOTT'S. Originally the 'Arnott's' van was scheduled to be issued on a world wide basis, with Australia receiving theirs six months in advance. With only 18,000 models having been made, Lesney Products were put in the hands of the Receiver. When the newly created Matchbox Company emerged it was felt it was too late to re-run the 'Arnott's' especially because the model was fetching a high premium on the collectors market Within weeks of being landed in Australia, several hundreds were exported back to the UK by dealers and collectors and were selling for £15.00 each. Some 'Arnott's' vans have been found with two labels per side; the extra labels were applied to cover badly applied labels and have been included as separate issues.

H : CEREBOS

ISSUE	YEAR OF RELEASE	COLOURS	ROOF	GRILLE	PLATED PARTS	SEAT	WHEELS	LOGO	REAR DOORS	REAR LIGHTS	BASEPLATE	RARITY	BOX TYPE	VALUE	CHECK LIST
1	1982	Mid blue body, black chassis	Yellow*	Gold	Gold	Black	Red 12 spoke	CEREBOS	White type 2	Yellow	LESNEY © 1978 ENGLAND	R	I	£250	
2		Mid blue body, black chassis	Yellow*	Chrome	Chrome	Black	Red 12 spoke (WW)	CEREBOS	White type 2	Yellow	LESNEY © 1978 ENGLAND	R	I	£250	
3		Mid blue body, black chassis	Yellow*	Gold	Gold	Black	Gold 12 spoke	CEREBOS	White type 2	Yellow	LESNEY © 1978 ENGLAND	R	I	£250	
4		Mid blue body, black chassis	White	Gold	Gold	Black	Gold 12 spoke (BW)	CEREBOS	White type 2	White	LESNEY © 1978 ENGLAND		I	£12	✓
5		Mid blue body, black chassis	White	Gold	Gold	Tan*	Gold 12 spoke (BW)	CEREBOS	White type 2	White	LESNEY © 1978 ENGLAND	S	I	£75	
6		Mid blue body, black chassis	White	Gold	Gold	Black	Red 12 spoke	CEREBOS	White type 2	White	LESNEY © 1978 ENGLAND		I	£12	
7		Mid blue body, black chassis	White	Gold	Gold	Black	Chrome 12 spoke	CEREBOS	White type 2	White	LESNEY © 1978 ENGLAND		I	£12	

I : ARNOTT'S BISCUITS

ISSUE	YEAR OF RELEASE	COLOURS	ROOF	GRILLE	PLATED PARTS	SEAT	WHEELS	LOGO	REAR DOORS	REAR LIGHTS	BASEPLATE	RARITY	BOX TYPE	VALUE	CHECK LIST
1	1982	Orange/red body, black chassis	Gloss black*	Gold	Gold	Black	Gold 12 spoke	ARNOTT'S (single)	Yellow type 2	Black	LESNEY © 1978 ENGLAND	R	I	£175	
2		Orange/red body, black chassis	Matt black*	Gold	Gold	Black	Gold 12 spoke	ARNOTT'S (single)	Yellow type 2	Black	LESNEY © 1978 ENGLAND	S	I	£150	
3		Orange/red body, black chassis	Gloss black*	Gold	Gold	Black	Gold 12 spoke	ARNOTT'S (double)	Yellow type 2	Black	LESNEY © 1978 ENGLAND	S	I	£180	
4		Orange/red body, black chassis	Matt black*	Gold	Gold	Black	Gold 12 spoke	ARNOTT'S (double)	Yellow type 2	Black	LESNEY © 1978 ENGLAND	S	I	£160	

LIVERY CEREBOS
Tampo
Van sides. CEREBOS TABLE SALT in white with gold outline on black with gold border.
SEE HOW IT RUNS! in white and Company logo of a figure of a boy and a chicken in white with black outline.

LIVERY ARNOTT'S BISCUITS
Label
Van sides. ARNOTT'S BISCUITS in yellow/white with black outline above and below.
FAMOUS SAO in cream and red outline, a wheatsheaf and parrot each end on black and yellow background.
Cab doors. No 3 PHONE U6621 WILLIAM ARNOTT LTD. HOMEBUSH in yellow.
Coachlining in yellow.

INVESTMENT COMMENT
ORIGINAL PRICE. £2.49p ARNOTT'S £5.00 (approx)
CEREBOS Even though there have been fakes on the market, Issue 1, 2 and 3 have increased in value. Standard issues have been dormant.
ARNOTT'S A very popular model within the range. Presently excellent value and one to watch closely. Always sells with a premium in Australia and New Zealand.

NOTES
It is now known that a roll of Arnott's labels were stolen within the Rochford factory; models seen with cast rear doors are fakes, or Code 3's.

Y12-3 1912 FORD MODEL 'T' VAN (CONTINUED)   Scale 1:35

HARRODS. Matchbox Toys agreed with Harrods to produce an exclusive 'Harrods' van; which when made was only sold at the Harrods department store in London. Early production runs were fitted with black seats, type two doors and a cream surround to the cab window. A second run, saw the change to tan and in some cases a cream seat and type three doors. The size of the tampo print plates was also reduced so that the cab window surround was in green formed by the body paint below. Although packaged in a standard sized 'straw box' the overprinting was in a distinctive colour of green in accordance with Harrods livery.

SUNLIGHT. Only 12,000 'Sunlight' models were issued by Matchbox. They were released in Germany, Austria and Switzerland in 1983. Within days of release they were changing hands at £13.00 each. Some models were released in standard boxes but with a circular gold and black sticker which stated that the Sunlight was a "Sondermodel Limitierte Auflage" (limited edition). There are fake 'Sunlights' on the market and these have tended to restrict the financial growth of genuine models. On genuine 'Sunlight' labels, there is a clothes line and post to the rear of the girl and an incomplete solid blue panel above the wheel arch, whereas on fake labels, there is no clothes line post to the rear of the girl and the blue panel is complete. No genuine variations on production models have been recorded.

J : HARRODS

ISSUE	YEAR OF RELEASE	COLOURS	ROOF	SEAT	GRILLE	WHEELS	PLATED PARTS	LOGO	UPPER PANELS	REAR DOORS	REAR LIGHTS	SIDE WINDOW BORDERS	BASEPLATE	RARITY	BOX TYPE	VALUE	CHECK LIST
1	1982	Dark green body, black chassis	Dark khaki	Black	Gold	Gold 12 spoke	Gold	HARRODS	Cream	White type 2	Dark khaki	Cream	LESNEY © 1978 ENGLAND		I	£10	
2		Dark green body, black chassis	Light khaki	Black	Gold	Gold 12 spoke	Gold	HARRODS	Dark cream	Type 3	Light khaki	Green	LESNEY © 1978 ENGLAND		I	£10	
3		Dark green body, black chassis	Light khaki	Tan	Gold	Gold 12 spoke	Gold	HARRODS	Dark cream	Type 3	Light khaki	Green	LESNEY © 1978 ENGLAND		I	£10	
4		Dark green body, black chassis	Light khaki	Pale cream*	Gold	Gold 12 spoke	Gold	HARRODS	Dark cream	Type 3	Light khaki	Green	LESNEY © 1978 ENGLAND	S	I	£15	
5		Dark green body, black chassis	Light khaki	Pale Cream*	Gold	Gold 12 spoke	Gold	HARRODS	Beige	Type 3	Light khaki	Green	LESNEY © 1978 ENGLAND	S	I	£15	

K : SUNLIGHT

ISSUE	YEAR OF RELEASE	COLOURS	ROOF	SEAT	GRILLE	WHEELS	PLATED PARTS	LOGO	UPPER PANELS	REAR DOORS	REAR LIGHTS	SIDE WINDOW BORDERS	BASEPLATE	RARITY	BOX TYPE	VALUE	CHECK LIST
1	1983	Yellow* body, black chassis	Matt black	Black	Gold	Red 12 spoke	Gold	SUNLIGHT	N/A	Red type 2	Black	Covered by label	LESNEY © 1978 ENGLAND	S	I	£130	✓

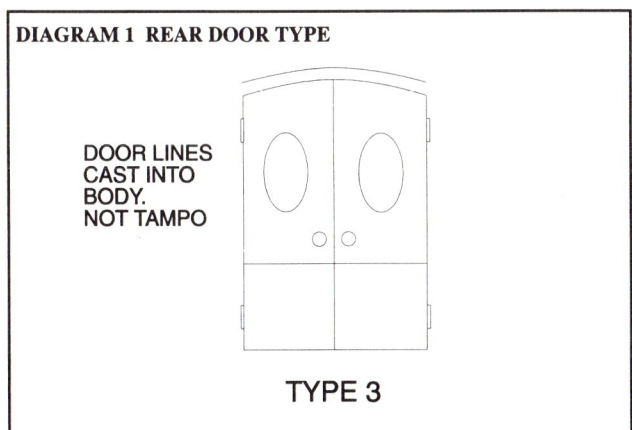

DIAGRAM 1 REAR DOOR TYPE

DOOR LINES CAST INTO BODY. NOT TAMPO

TYPE 3

LIVERY HARRODS
Label
Upper van panels. HARRODS EXPRESS DELIVERY in gold
Lower van panels. MOTOR ACCESSORIES in gold.

LIVERY SUNLIGHT
Label
One piece label with complex design using red, black, yellow, green, light blue, dark blue and white colours featuring SUNLIGHT SEIFE.

INVESTMENT COMMENT
ORIGINAL PRICE. HARRODS £2.99p
SUNLIGHT £4.00
HARRODS The Harrods van certainly peaked in value in the mid-1980s and has contracted in value in recent years. It may increase again.
SUNLIGHT This well documented model has caught everyone off guard by retracting in value within the UK market; although values seem to have been maintained in overseas markets. Good value at present and therefore may be the right time to acquire one.
NOTES

Y12-3 1912 FORD MODEL 'T' VAN (CONTINUED) Scale 1:35

INVESTMENT COMMENT
ORIGINAL PRICE £3.50p
ROYAL MAIL Little to report except that issues 1 and 2 have risen in value. These issues can still be bought at reasonable prices from unwary vendors.

ROYAL MAIL Early releases were made from surplus painted 'Arnotts' vans and this shade of red is easily distinguishable from standard Royal Mail releases. Also these early issues were released with Type 2 doors. There have been many noted variations to the crown, the most common being a crown with two white segments.

L : ROYAL MAIL

ISSUE	YEAR OF RELEASE	COLOURS	ROOF	SEAT	GRILLE	WHEELS	PLATED PARTS	LOGO	REAR DOORS	REAR LIGHTS	BASEPLATE	RARITY	BOX TYPE	VALUE	CHECK LIST
1	1983	Orange*red body, black chassis	Black	Black	Gold	Bright red 12 spoke	Gold	ROYAL MAIL	Yellow type 2	Black	LESNEY © 1978 ENGLAND	V R	I	£250	
2		Orange*red body, black chassis	Black	Black	Gold	Gold 12 spoke	Gold	ROYAL MAIL	Yellow type 2	Black	LESNEY © 1978 ENGLAND	V R	I	£250	
3		Post office red body, black chassis	Black	Black	Gold	Bright red 12 spoke	Gold	ROYAL MAIL	Type 3	Black	LESNEY © 1978 ENGLAND		I	£10	✓
4		Post office red body, black chassis	Black	Black	Gold	Gold 12 spoke	Gold	ROYAL MAIL	Type 3	Black	LESNEY © 1978 ENGLAND		I	£10	
5		Post office red body, black chassis	Black	Black	Gold	Dull red 12 spoke	Gold	ROYAL MAIL	Type 3	Black	LESNEY © 1978 ENGLAND		I	£10	
6		Post office red body, black chassis	Black	Black	Chrome*	Bright red 12 spoke	Chrome*	ROYAL MAIL	Type 3	Black	LESNEY © 1978 ENGLAND	S	I	£30	
7		Post office red body, black chassis	Black	Black	Gold	Chrome 12 spoke	Gold	ROYAL MAIL	Type 3	Black	LESNEY © 1978 ENGLAND		I	£15	
8		Post office red body, black chassis	Black	Black	Gold	Chrome 24 spoke	Gold	ROYAL MAIL	Type 3	Black	LESNEY © 1978 ENGLAND		I	£15	

LIVERY ROYAL MAIL
Transfers
Van sides. Black ROYAL MAIL above gold Royal crown in black and red above GR in gold edged black.

NOTES

Y12-3 1912 FORD MODEL 'T' VAN CONTINUED   Scale 1:35

CAPTAIN MORGAN. This attractive livery was originally produced with a one piece label which covered the entire sides of the van and the cab doors. It was quickly discovered that this label was prone to cracking at the join between the cab doors and the van body. A two piece transfer was designed which proved more substantial. A quick way to distinguish a label from a transfer is to look at the word 'Rum;' on labels, the size of lettering is small whereas with the transfer is much larger.

HOOVER. Matchbox Toys, supplied the Hoover management with 540 'Hoover' vans painted in aqua blue. They were accompanied with a numbered certificate one of which was presented to Queen Elizabeth II by the Hoover Management. A further 20 models without certificates were kept back and given to directors at Matchbox. The blue 'Hoover' is a Code 2 model. The standard livery was in orange. As with the final production 'Captain Morgan' models, many orange 'Hoover' vans incorporate a hole at the rear of the base of the body which was cast to assist the spraying of the Y12 model. A small number of orange 'Hoover' models decorated with a two piece transfer have been reported as existing. These were fakes ie Code 3's.

M : CAPTAIN MORGAN

ISSUE	YEAR OF RELEASE	COLOURS	ROOF	SEAT	GRILLE	WHEELS	PLATED PARTS	LOGO	REAR DOORS	REAR LIGHTS	DECORATION	BASE HOLE AT REAR OF BODY	BASEPLATE	RARITY	BOX TYPE	VALUE	CHECK LIST
1	1983	Black body, black chassis	White	Tan	Gold	Gold 12 spoke	Gold	CAPTAIN MORGAN	Type 3	White	One piece label small RUM	No	LESNEY © 1978 ENGLAND		I	£9	
2		Black body, black chassis	White	Black*	Gold	Gold 12 spoke	Gold	CAPTAIN MORGAN	Type 3	White	One piece label small RUM	No	LESNEY © 1978 ENGLAND	S	I	£50	
3		Black body, black chassis	White	Black*	Gold	Bright red 12 spoke	Gold	CAPTAIN MORGAN	Type 3	White	One piece label small RUM	No	LESNEY © 1978 ENGLAND	S	I	£50	
4		Black body, black chassis	White	Tan	Gold	Gold 12 spoke	Gold	CAPTAIN MORGAN	Type 3	White	Two piece transfer large RUM	No	LESNEY © 1978 ENGLAND		I	£9	✓
5		Black body, black chassis	White	Black*	Gold	Gold 12 spoke	Gold	CAPTAIN MORGAN	Type 3	White	Two piece transfer large RUM	No	LESNEY © 1978 ENGLAND	S	I	£50	
6		Black body, black chassis	White	Tan	Gold	Gold 12 spoke	Gold	CAPTAIN MORGAN	Type 3	White	Two piece transfer large RUM	Yes*	LESNEY © 1978 ENGLAND	R	I	£60	
7		Black body, black chassis	White	Black*	Gold	Gold 12 spoke	Gold	CAPTAIN MORGAN	Type 3	White	Two piece transfer large RUM	Yes*	LESNEY © 1978 ENGLAND	R	I	£60	

N : HOOVER

ISSUE	YEAR OF RELEASE	COLOURS	ROOF	SEAT	GRILLE	WHEELS	PLATED PARTS	LOGO	REAR DOORS	REAR LIGHTS	DECORATION	BASE HOLE AT REAR OF BODY	BASEPLATE	RARITY	BOX TYPE	VALUE	CHECK LIST
1		Orange body, black chassis	Black	Black	Chrome	Black 12 spoke	Chrome	HOOVER	Type 3	Black	N/A	No	LESNEY © 1978 ENGLAND		I	£8	✓
2		Orange body, black chassis	Black	Tan*	Chrome	Black 12 spoke	Chrome	HOOVER	Type 3	Black	N/A	No	LESNEY © 1978 ENGLAND	S	I	£30	
3		Orange body, black chassis	Black	Black	Chrome	Black 12 spoke	Chrome	HOOVER	Type 3	Black	N/A	Yes	LESNEY © 1978 ENGLAND		I	£8	
4		Orange body, black chassis	Black	Black	Chrome	Black 24* spoke	Chrome	HOOVER	Type 3	Black	N/A	Yes	LESNEY © 1978 ENGLAND	D	I	£15	

DIAGRAM 1 BASE HOLE

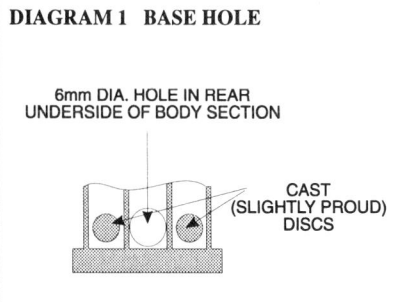

6mm DIA. HOLE IN REAR UNDERSIDE OF BODY SECTION

CAST (SLIGHTLY PROUD) DISCS

DIAGRAM 2 CAPTAIN MORGAN

TRANSFER   LABEL

LIVERY CAPTAIN MORGAN

Labels or Transfers.
Van sides. CAPTAIN MORGAN in white below figure head of Captain Morgan in yellow, black and red, on blue oval with "rope" gold coachlining. CAPTAIN MORGAN RUM DISTILLERS DACRE STREET LONDON SW1 in gold. All within gold "rope" coachlining.
Cab doors. BLACK LABEL in gold above red RUM. All within gold "rope" coachlining.

LIVERY HOOVER

Tampo
Van sides. THE HOOVER IT BEATS AS IT SWEEPS AS IT CLEANS in black. Multi-coloured oval of young girl with a Hoover cleaner. All within black coachlining.
Cab doors. Black SAVES TIME AND LABOR.

INVESTMENT COMMENT
ORIGINAL PRICE CAPTAIN MORGAN & HOOVER £3.50p

CAPTAIN MORGAN Little progress has been recorded but non standard colour seat issues still have potential. Examples with the cast hole in the base of the van bodies are very hard to find.
HOOVER Everyone still wants the Code 2 blue Hoover, presently valued in the region of £800. The orange coloured models still languish in the doldrums.

Y12-3 1912 FORD MODEL 'T' VAN (CONTINUED)   Scale 1:35

PEPSI-COLA. In complete contrast to Coca Cola, 'Pepsi-Cola' welcomed the free publicity this model afforded them and no royalty payments were demanded. Both Lesney © 1978 and Matchbox © 1985 baseplates were used on this model, Issue 4 being the hardest to find. A re-run in 1986 produced models with modified roofs. The roof section had been modified by having two hollow bosses cast on the underside to allow the fitting of the 'Heinz' gherkin. Once the 'Heinz' run was completed, the holes were blanked-off, but the bosses remained. These can be seen by looking through the rear door windows.

MOTOR 100. This was only the second time the Model 'T' Van had been used to celebrate an event not concurrent with the era of the actual vehicle. It was used to celebrate the centenary of the internal combustion engine, an event which was centred on the famous Silverstone racing circuit in England. 2,300 such models were produced with certificates and were sold at Silverstone with all proceeds going to the Motor & Cycle Trade Benevolent Fund charity. After the event, it was released worldwide but without the centenary event certificates. A small quantity of models were issued with the tampo printing reversed!.

O : PEPSI-COLA

ISSUE	YEAR OF RELEASE	COLOURS	ROOF	SEAT	GRILLE	WHEELS	PLATED PARTS	LOGO	REAR DOORS	REAR LIGHTS	BASE HOLE AT REAR	TWO CAB ROOF BOSSES	TAMPO DECORATION	CERTIFICATE	BASEPLATE	RARITY	BOX TYPE	VALUE	CHECK LIST
1	1984	White body, royal blue chassis	Red	Black	Chrome	Chrome 12 spoke	Chrome	PEPSI-COLA	Type 3	Red	Yes	No	N/A	N/A	LESNEY © 1978 ENGLAND		J	£10	
2		White body, royal blue chassis	Red	Black	Chrome	Red 12 spoke	Chrome	PEPSI-COLA	Type 3	Red	Yes	No	N/A	N/A	LESNEY © 1978 ENGLAND		J	£10	
3		White body, royal blue chassis	Red	Black	Chrome	Chrome 24 spoke (WW)	Chrome	PEPSI-COLA	Type 3	Red	Yes	No	N/A	N/A	LESNEY © 1978 ENGLAND		J	£10	
4		White body, royal blue chassis	Red	Black	Chrome	Chrome 12 spoke	Chrome	PEPSI-COLA	Type 3	Red	Yes	No	N/A	N/A	MATCHBOX © 1985* ENGLAND	D	J	£20	
5	1986	White body, royal blue chassis	Red	Black	Chrome	Chrome 12 spoke	Chrome	PEPSI-COLA	Type 3	Red	Yes	Yes	N/A	N/A	MATCHBOX © 1985 ENGLAND		J	£10	✓
6		White body, royal blue chassis	Red	Black	Chrome	Chrome 24 spoke	Chrome	PEPSI-COLA	Type 3	Red	Yes	Yes	N/A	N/A	MATCHBOX © 1985 ENGLAND		J	£10	

P : MOTOR 100

ISSUE	YEAR OF RELEASE	COLOURS	ROOF	SEAT	GRILLE	WHEELS	PLATED PARTS	LOGO	REAR DOORS	REAR LIGHTS	BASE HOLE AT REAR	TWO CAB ROOF BOSSES	TAMPO DECORATION	CERTIFICATE	BASEPLATE	RARITY	BOX TYPE	VALUE	CHECK LIST
1	1985	Metallic bronze body, dark brown chassis	Dark brown	Black	Gold	Dull red 12 spoke	Gold	MOTOR 100	Type 3	Dark brown	Yes	No	Blue water cream land	Yes*	LESNEY © 1978 ENGLAND	D	J	£45	
2		Metallic bronze body, dark brown chassis	Dark brown	Black	Gold	Dull red 12 spoke	Gold	MOTOR 100	Type 3	Dark brown	Yes	No	Blue water cream land	No	LESNEY © 1978 ENGLAND		J	£10	
3		Metallic bronze body, dark brown chassis	Dark brown	Black	Gold	Dull red 12 spoke	Gold	MOTOR 100	Type 3	Dark brown	Yes	No	Blue land cream water*	No	LESNEY © 1978 ENGLAND	VR	J	£400	
4		Metallic bronze body, dark brown chassis	Dark brown	Black	Gold	Gold 12 spoke	Gold	MOTOR 100	Type 3	Dark brown	Yes	No	Blue water cream land	No	LESNEY © 1978 ENGLAND		J	£10	
5		Metallic bronze body, dark brown chassis	Dark brown	Black	Gold	Bright red 12 spoke	Gold	MOTOR 100	Type 3	Dark brown	Yes	No	Blue water cream land	No	LESNEY © 1978 ENGLAND		J	£10	

DIAGRAM 1 UNDERSIDE BODY ROOF BOSSES

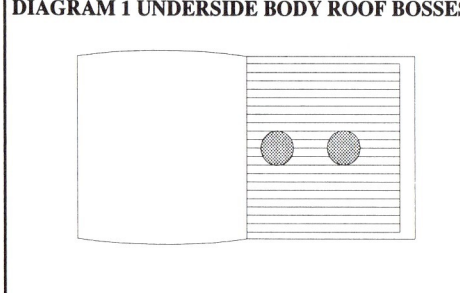

LIVERY PEPSI-COLA
Tampo
Van sides. PEPSI-COLA in red within red coachline.
Cab doors. 12 MPH in red within red coachline.

LIVERY MOTOR 100
Tampo
Van sides. MOTOR 100 in red circling globe of the earth in white & blue. Event details in black lettering around globe.
SILVERSTONE CIRCUIT ENGLAND in black.
Extensive black double coachlining to van body sides and cab doors.

INVESTMENT COMMENT
ORIGINAL PRICE PEPSI £3.99 MOTOR 100 £4.99
The Pepsi-Cola retains its reputation as being a poor performer. Too many models were produced.
Motor 100 Issue 1 has now progressed to £45 and is popular due to the limited quantity of numbered certificates. Issue 3 remains the one to search for but is seldom seen for sale.

NOTES
The metallic bronze body colour of the Motor 100 model can vary from very light to darker shades.

Y12-3 1912 FORD MODEL 'T' PICK UP TRUCK CONTINUED

Scale 1:35

INVESTMENT COMMENT

ORIGINAL PRICE £9.95p

Even though a Special Limited Edition, the Imbach has failed to make much progress.

IMBACH. This was issued as one of the four first Special Limited Editions, all of which were packaged in superior dark red and gold foil printed cartons. Major modifications were made to this model. The running boards were modified, so instead of running the full length between the front and rear mudguards, they appeared only as cab steps. The cab sides and roof section were completely retooled and the truck body was obviously a totally new feature. All other components were identical to the regular Model T Van. The baseplates were cast with the capital words 'Limited Edtion' ie.edition being spelled incorrectly.

Q : IMBACH

ISSUE	YEAR OF RELEASE	COLOURS	ROOF	SEAT	GRILLE	WHEELS	PLATED PARTS	LOGO	CAB DECORATION	BASEPLATE	RARITY	BOX TYPE	VALUE	CHECK LIST
1	1985	Blue body, black chassis	Blue	Tan	Gold	Gold 12 spoke	Gold	G. IMBACH	Red out-line to cab logo	MATCHBOX © 1985 ENGLAND LIMITED EDTION		J	£12	
2		Blue body, black chassis	Blue	Pinky tan	Gold	Gold 12 spoke	Gold	G. IMBACH	Red out-line to cab logo	MATCHBOX © 1985 ENGLAND LIMITED EDTION		J	£12	✓
3		Blue body, black chassis	Blue	Pinky tan	Gold	Red* 12 spoke	Gold	G. IMBACH	Red out-line to cab logo	MATCHBOX © 1985 ENGLAND LIMITED EDTION	D	J	£18	

LIVERY IMBACH

Tampo
Truck sides. G IMBACH KIEGESCHAFT, WOLHUSEN in white.
Cab sides. Company logo I G. in white with dark red shadow effect.
All within a white coachline.

NOTES

Y12-3 1912 FORD MODEL 'T' VAN (CONTINUED) Scale 1:35

INVESTMENT COMMENT
ORIGINAL PRICE £4.25p

Heniz. Of all the issues, the most sought after remains Issue 1, which is virtually a pre-production model. There has been little growth in the standard issues, but issues 8, 11 and 12 are very hard to find and show good potential.

HEINZ. This model was released in 1986, coming after a consumer offer by Heinz as part of their Centenary celebrations. An early batch (1000 boxed models) were sent to Heinz to be used as samples. The boxes had a mis-spelling of the word 'Gherkin' and the tampo printing differed slightly from later production models (Issue 1). As this model had a gherkin mounted on the van body, the roof mould was modified to have two bosses on the underside, complete with holes in which to hold the gherkin in place. Once the 'Heinz' production run was completed (160,000 models) these holes in the roof were blanked off but the underside bosses remained. These bosses can be found on final run 'Pepsi-Cola' and all 'Rosella' models. It should be noted that all 'Heinz' vans were fitted with the gherkin in a bright green plastic with the word 'Heinz' in white lettering both sides. Some models have been found with the gherkin fitted the wrong way round and as a 'negative' variation has not been afforded a coding. Models with the gherkin fitted the wrong way round (stalk at front) are more often than not fitted with the hard to find 1986 bases!! It is not easy to distinguish between black and dark green seats in anything other than very good light and by comparing one with the other.

R : HEINZ

ISSUE	YEAR OF RELEASE	COLOURS	ROOF	SEAT	GRILLE	WHEELS	PLATED PARTS	LOGO	REAR DOORS	REAR LIGHTS	BASE HOLE AT REAR OF BODY	TAMPO DECORATION LARGE ROUNDEL	BASEPLATE	RARITY	BOX TYPE	VALUE	CHECK LIST
1	1986	Grey green body,* dark green chassis	Grey green*	Black	Gold	Bright red 12 spoke	Gold	HEINZ	Type 3	Grey green	Yes	Dark green gherkin, dark red roundel & VARIETIES in thick lettering*	LESNEY © 1978* ENGLAND	VR	J	£300	
2		Pale green grey body, dark green chassis	Pale grey green	Dark green	Gold	Maroon 12 spoke	Gold	HEINZ	Type 3	Pale grey green	Yes	Bright green gherkin in bright red roundel & VARIETIES in thin lettering	MATCHBOX © 1985 ENGLAND		J	£10	
3		Pale green grey body, lighter green chassis*	Pale grey green	Dark green	Gold	Maroon 12 spoke	Gold	HEINZ	Type 3	Pale grey green	Yes	Bright green gherkin in bright red roundel & VARIETIES in thin lettering	MATCHBOX © 1985 ENGLAND		J	£10	
4		Pale green grey body, dark green chassis	Pale grey green	Dark green	Gold	Maroon 12 spoke	Gold	HEINZ	Type 3	Pale grey green	Yes	Bright green gherkin in bright red roundel & VARIETIES in thick lettering	MATCHBOX © 1985 ENGLAND		J	£10	
5		Pale green grey body, dark green chassis	Pale grey green	Black	Gold	Maroon 12 spoke	Gold	HEINZ	Type 3	Pale grey green	Yes	Bright green gherkin in bright red roundel & VARIETIES in thin lettering	MATCHBOX © 1985 ENGLAND		J	£10	
6		Pale green grey body, dark green chassis	Pale grey green	Dark green	Gold	Dark red 12 spoke	Gold	HEINZ	Type 3	Pale grey green	Yes	Bright green gherkin in bright red roundel & VARIETIES in thin lettering	MATCHBOX © 1985 ENGLAND		J	£10	✓
7		Pale green grey body, dark green chassis	Pale grey green	Dark green	Gold	Bright red 12 spoke	Gold	HEINZ	Type 3	Pale grey green	Yes	Bright green gherkin in bright red roundel & VARIETIES in thin lettering	MATCHBOX © 1985 ENGLAND		J	£10	
8		Pale green grey body, dark green chassis	Pale grey green	Dark green	Chrome*	Dull red 12 spoke	Chrome*	HEINZ	Type 3	Pale grey green	Yes	Bright green gherkin in bright red roundel & VARIETIES in thin lettering	MATCHBOX © 1985* ENGLAND	D	J	£25	
9		Pale green grey body, dark green chassis	Pale grey green	Dark green	Gold	Gold 12 spoke	Gold	HEINZ	Type 3	Pale grey green	Yes	Bright green gherkin in bright red roundel & VARIETIES in thin lettering	MATCHBOX © 1985 ENGLAND		J	£10	
10		Pale green grey body, dark green chassis	Pale grey green	Black	Gold	Bright red 12 spoke	Gold	HEINZ	Type 3	Pale grey green	Yes	Bright green gherkin in bright red roundel & VARIETIES in thin lettering	MATCHBOX © 1985 ENGLAND		J	£10	
11		Pale green grey body, dark green chassis	Pale grey green	Dark green	Gold	Maroon 12 spoke	Gold	HEINZ	Type 3	Pale grey green	Yes	Bright green gherkin in bright red roundel & VARIETIES in thin lettering	MATCHBOX © 1986* ENGLAND	S	J	£35	
12		Very pale* green grey body, dark green chassis	Grey green*	Dark green	Gold	Maroon 12 spoke	Gold	HEINZ	Type 3	Grey green*	Yes	Emerald green gherkin in pink roundel & VARIETIES in thin lettering	MATCHBOX © 1986* ENGLAND	R	J	£50	

LIVERY HEINZ

Tampo
Van sides. H. J. HEINZ CO. in red with black surround.
PURE FOOD PRODUCTS in grey on red, 57, VARIETIES in red, and HEINZ in green gherkin with white HEINZ.
Cab doors. Red 15 in black circle. Black coachlining.

NOTES

Y12-3 1912 FORD MODEL 'T' VAN (CONTINUED) Scale 1:35

INVESTMENT COMMENT
ORIGINAL PRICE £5.25p
Very popular with Australian collectors where a premium value is maintained. The continuation of the Y12 in the form of, for example, the YGB14 'Kirin' in 1995, may encourage newer collectors to buy all or some of the Y12 liveried models.

ROSELLA. Released as a Limited Edition in January 1987 the 'Rosella' model was the last of the Y12 Model 'T' Ford van 'earlier' series and was made just before the Rochford factory, Essex, England closed. In an attempt by the factory to use most of the remaining Y12 components, a concession was given to the production line to use the four available baseplate components. As with other Y12 models, a mixture of coloured wheels were also used. Although the 'Rosella' was a slow seller in the United Kingdom, for obvious reasons it was a great seller in Australia and commands a premium price in that market. It should be noted that it may be possible to find Rosella vans fitted with the very dark green seats as fitted to the Heinz van!

S : ROSELLA

ISSUE	YEAR OF RELEASE	COLOURS	ROOF	SEAT	GRILLE	WHEELS	PLATED PARTS	LOGO	REAR DOORS	REAR LIGHTS	BASE HOLE AT REAR OF BODY	UNDERSIDE ROOF BOSSES	BASEPLATE	RARITY	BOX TYPE	VALUE	CHECK LIST
1	1987	Dark blue body, black chassis	Yellow	Black	Gold	Gold 12 spoke	Gold	ROSELLA	Type 3	Yellow	Yes	Yes	MATCHBOX © 1986 ENGLAND		J	£12	✓
2		Dark blue body, black chassis	Yellow	Black	Gold	Gold 12 spoke	Gold	ROSELLA	Type 3	Yellow	Yes	Yes	MATCHBOX © 1986 ENGLAND LIMITED EDITION *	D	J	£30	
3		Dark blue body, black chassis	Yellow	Black	Gold	Dark red 12 spoke	Gold	ROSELLA	Type 3	Yellow	Yes	Yes	MATCHBOX © 1986 ENGLAND		J	£12	
4		Dark blue body, black chassis	Yellow	Black	Gold	Gold 12 spoke	Gold	ROSELLA	Type 3	Yellow	Yes	Yes	MATCHBOX © 1985* ENGLAND	S	J	£40	
5		Dark blue body, black chassis	Yellow	Black	Gold	Gold 12 spoke	Gold	ROSELLA	Type 3	Yellow	Yes	Yes	LESNEY © 1978 ENGLAND		J	£12	
6		Dark blue body, black chassis	Yellow	Black	Gold	Maroon 12 spoke	Gold	ROSELLA	Type 3	Yellow	Yes	Yes	LESNEY © 1978 ENGLAND		J	£12	
7		Dark blue body, black chassis	Yellow	Black	Gold	Bright red 12 spoke	Gold	ROSELLA	Type 3	Yellow	Yes	Yes	LESNEY © 1978 ENGLAND		J	£12	
8		Dark blue body, black chassis	Yellow	Black	Chrome	Chrome 12 spoke	Chrome	ROSELLA	Type 3	Yellow	Yes	Yes	LESNEY © 1978 ENGLAND		J	£12	

LIVERY ROSELLA
Tampo
Van sides. White ROSELLA above white TOMATO SAUCE, PICKLES & CHUTNEY with white ripple lines.
All around multi-coloured parrot. All above gold CASH SALES SERVICE on red panel with gold border.
All within gold coachlining with gold decorations in corners.
Cab sides. White VAN No.7 above gold ROSELLA CONDIMENTS.
Cab doors. Gold TEL JB 2171 and gold coachlining around doors and the oval side windows.

NOTES
Compare with YGB14.

INVESTMENT COMMENT
ORIGINAL PRICE £17.95p

A model that has surprisingly performed poorly perhaps due to too high a production run for a Special Limited Edition. May still be of some interest to railway enthusiasts.

Y12-4 1829 STEPHENSON'S ROCKET

Scale 1:64

During the mid 1980's, Matchbox Toys considered releasing a small range of trains and locomotives, within the Models of Yesteryear range. The project was partially abandoned with the only model to get to production being the Y12 'Rocket'. It was released in December 1987 as a Special Limited Edition with a production run of 60,000 models. A further locomotive model eventually appeared as the load for the Y16-5 Scammell 100 Ton Low Loader.

ISSUE	YEAR OF RELEASE	ENGINE COLOURS	TENDER COLOURS	CHIMNEY STACK	PISTON HOUSING	FRONT WHEELS ENGINE	REAR WHEELS ENGINE	WHEELS TENDER	PLATED PARTS	BASEPLATE, TENDER	BASEPLATE, ENGINE	RARITY	BOX TYPE	VALUE	CHECK LIST
1	1987	Yellow body, black chassis	Yellow body black chassis	White with black top, white bottom	Black	Yellow 12 spoke	Yellow 12 spoke	Yellow 8 spoke	Gold	Y 12 THE ROCKET	MATCHBOX © 1987 LIMITED EDITION MACAU		0	£12	✓

LIVERY

Tampo
ROCKET in black on boiler sides.
Locomotive. Black enhancement to the spokes and to the hubs of the driving wheels with gold enhancement to the boiler bands.
Tender. Black enhancement to panel sides and the water barrel straps.

NOTES

Compare with YAS01-M. ✓

Y12-5 1937 GMC VAN

Scale 1:45

GOBLIN. This new casting was released in August 1988. Some criticism was aired over the ill fitting bonnet, early versions of which were only fitted to the 'Goblin' GMC van. The horizontal cast line on both sides of the body did not interfere with the tampo print and all 'Goblin' vans were issued with Type 1 castings. This casting was altered for the 'Baxters' livery (Type 2). The width of this cast line did not change; it was made less proud. It had always been Matchbox's intention to issue the 'Goblin' with a grey roof. However the factory encountered problems with the mask-spraying of the roof and even though 6,000 grey roofed 'Goblin' vans had been produced, it was decided to produce the majority of models in all over black. A modification was also made to the headlights. All grey roofed models and all early black roofed models were fitted with acorn shaped lights and were fitted to the Goblin (Issue 3) and Baxter's (Issue 2). These were altered to larger conical shaped lights were fitted to the Goblin (Issue 3) and Baxter's (Issue 2). Due to the gloss black paint being an unsuitable base for the grey paint, some grey roofed models started to show hair-line cracks in the paint finish within a couple of years of manufacture; the glossy black paint underneath only serving to make these cracks more obvious.

BAXTER'S. This second livery was released in July 1989. By now the ill-fitting bonnet had been retooled and all subsequent vans were fitted with the Type B bonnets. Problems during the pre-production stage centred around the poor tampo printing of the livery, and so the horizontal casting line on the body sides was reduced in height. This casting modification, Type 2, was incorporated on all subsequent liveries. The 'Baxter's' GMC van was a Limited Edition. Pre-production examples did not have the company's name and address on the bottom edge of the cab doors and had a poor paint finish.

A : GOBLIN

ISSUE	YEAR OF RELEASE	COLOURS	ROOF	SEAT	WHEELS	PLATED PARTS	LOGO	HEADLIGHTS	BONNET TYPE	REAR NUMBER PLATE TYPE	BODY TYPE	BASEPLATE	RARITY	BOX TYPE	VALUE	CHECK LIST
1	1988	Black body, black chassis	Grey*	Cream	Solid chrome	Chrome	GOBLIN	Acorn*	A	Open*	1	MATCHBOX © 1988 MACAU	R	J 1	£50	
2		Black body, black chassis	Grey*	Cream	Solid chrome	Chrome	GOBLIN	Acorn*	A	Closed	1	MATCHBOX © 1988 MACAU	S	J 1	£20	
3		Black body, black chassis	Black	Cream	Solid chrome	Chrome	GOBLIN	Acorn*	A	Closed	1	MATCHBOX © 1988 MACAU	D	J 1	£10	✓
4		Black body, black chassis	Black	Cream	Solid chrome	Chrome	GOBLIN	Streamline	A	Closed	1	MATCHBOX © 1988 MACAU		J 1	£10	

B : BAXTER'S

ISSUE	YEAR OF RELEASE	COLOURS	ROOF	SEAT	WHEELS	PLATED PARTS	LOGO	HEADLIGHTS	BONNET TYPE	REAR NUMBER PLATE TYPE	BODY TYPE	BASEPLATE	RARITY	BOX TYPE	VALUE	CHECK LIST
1	1989	Cream body, dark green chassis	Cream	Dark green	Solid chrome	Chrome	BAXTER'S	Acorn*	B	Closed	2	MATCHBOX © 1988 MACAU	D	J 1	£20	✓
2		Cream body, dark green chassis	Cream	Dark green	Solid chrome	Chrome	BAXTER'S	Streamline	B	Closed	2	MATCHBOX © 1988 MACAU		J 1	£10	

DIAGRAM 1 HEADLIGHTS

ACORN

STREAMLINE

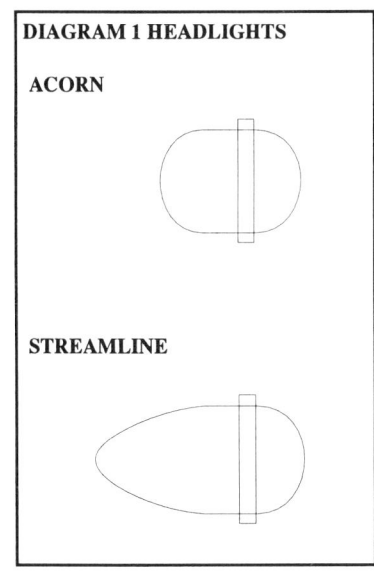

DIAGRAM 2 BONNET TYPES

TYPE A — RAISED BONNET

TYPE B — FLUSH BONNET

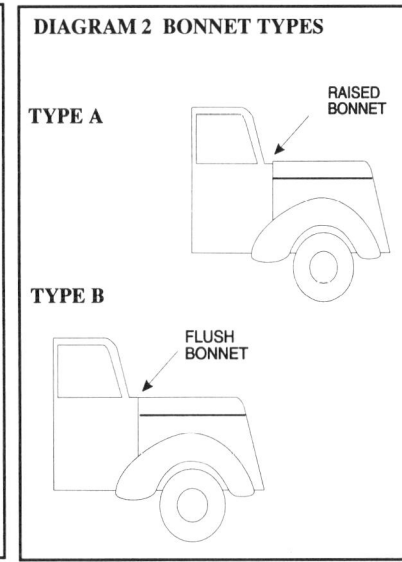

DIAGRAM 3 REAR NUMBER PLATE "OPEN TYPE"

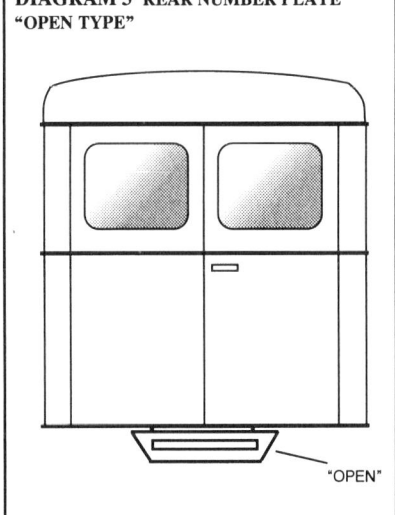

LIVERY GOBLIN
Tampo
Van sides. Red GOBLIN with gold outline above gold ELECTRIC CLEANERS above gold MANUFACTURED IN LONDON. All to the right of a gold goblin carrying a Union flag in red, white and blue.
Cab doors. Gold BRITISH VACUUM CLEANER AND ENG CO LTD LONDON SW6.

LIVERY BAXTER'S
Tampo
Van sides. Company logo, a stag and hind against a highland loch background in black, blue and green with black BAXTER'S above black SCOTTISH with tartan strips in black, blue and light green. Green thistles and pink flowers. Two emblems in black above side strips. All above black FAMOUS FOR, ROYAL GAME SOUP.
Cab doors. Black BAXTER'S above black W.A. BAXTER & SONS LIMITED FOCHABERS SCOTLAND.

INVESTMENT COMMENT
ORIGINAL PRICE
GOBLIN £5.75p BAXTER'S £7.95p

Goblin Issue 1 is certainly worth looking out for before this new variation is known amongst the trade. Issue 2 peaked in value in 1988 and has remained constant ever since.

BAXTER'S Issue 1 is the one to have. There appears to be plenty of Issue 2 on the market stalls.

NOTES

INVESTMENT COMMENT
ORIGINAL PRICE £8.99p
A popular livery in Australia where it sold well. It is believed that there are still quantities of unsold stock in the market place.

Y12-5 1937 GMC VAN   (CONTINUED)   Scale 1:45

GOANNA. It was planned to use the livery of the Singer Sewing Machine Company for the 1991 issue, but permission was not given by the trademark owner and so the Goanna logo, submitted by Matchbox Australia, was adopted. There was a mixed reaction by collectors to this eleventh hour substitution and as one 'wag' was heard to comment, "It's OK. if you have a sick bush"! Early production models were fitted with dark red wheels and the tampo colours were darker which resulted in a more striking orangey red effect. Later production models were fitted with wheels of a mid-red shade which appear to have an orangey tinge. The tampo colours were of a paler finish which gave a slightly less striking overall effect.

C : GOANNA

ISSUE	YEAR OF RELEASE	COLOURS	ROOF	SEATS	WHEELS	PLATED PARTS	LOGO	TAMPO DECORATION	HEAD LIGHTS	BONNET TYPE	BODY TYPE	THREADED SCREW HOLE	BASEPLATE	RARITY	BOX TYPE	VALUE	CHECK LIST
1	1991	Dark blue body gloss black chassis	Dark blue	Fawn	Dark red solid	Chrome	GOANNA	Bright red, dark blue & white	Streamline	B	2	Yes	MATCHBOX © 1988 CHINA		NI	£8	
2		Dark blue body gloss black chassis	Dark blue	Fawn	Mid red solid	Chrome	GOANNA	Mid red, mid blue & white	Streamline	B	2	Yes	MATCHBOX © 1988 CHINA		NI	£8	✓
3		Dark blue body gloss black chassis	Dark blue	Fawn	Mid red solid	Chrome	GOANNA	Orangey-red, pale blue & white	Streamline	B	2	Yes	MATCHBOX © 1988 CHINA		NI	£8	

LIVERY GOANNA

Tampo
Van sides. GOANNA in white with dark blue edging above white
THE AUSTRALIAN BUSH REMEDY above black ESTABLISHED 1910 in dark blue. On the left a sketch of a tin and lettering in white and blue; all on orangey red or red background.
Cab doors. HEALING PENETRATING SOOTHING with scroll-work, all in white.

NOTES
Compare with YPP08 and YFE10.

INVESTMENT COMMENT
ORIGINAL PRICE £0.12.5p

Curiously the many issues of this model still do not vary much in price. Values have been maintained over the last few years - it is still a popular First Series Yesteryear. Issue 3 remains extremely rare and has managed a small increase in value.

Y13-1 1862 AMERICAN "GENERAL" CLASS LOCOMOTIVE   Scale 1: 112

There were several easily identifiable modifications made to the Y13 Santa Fe. Early baseplates were in part secured to the chassis component by a rivet which passed through a hole in the baseplate and so this round rivet is dark red in colour. Later a much longer rivet cast on the underneath of the body was used to pass through the chassis and then the baseplate before being turned over ie a green rivet. The left hand side piston slots were also modified. Very early slots were well defined and clear (Type A). The second type incorporated partial filling in (Type B) and in some cases totally filled in. Although the driving wheels throughout production were in black with twelve spokes, early wheels were thicker than later wheels, and various minor shade differences exist ranging from black through to brown. One of the rarest of Santa Fe models is the short run of lighter green locomotives. These have proved most difficult to obtain, which is reflected in the premium often added to the price.

ISSUE	YEAR OF RELEASE	COLOURS	WHEELS	BASEPLATE RIVET	CONDENSER TOPS	HEAD LAMP LENSES	PISTON SLOT TYPE	BOILER WALKWAY EDGE	SMOKE STACK RIM	BELL	VALVE	BASEPLATE	RARITY	BOX TYPE	VALUE	CHECK LIST
1	1959	Dark green body, dark red chassis, black base	Driving black 12 spoke front black solid	Dark red	Gold	Silver	A	Gold	Gold	Dark green	Dark green	LESNEY ENGLAND		B/C	£95	
2		Dark green body, dark red chassis, black base	Driving black 12 spoke front black solid	Dark red	Gold	Silver	A	Dark green	Gold	Dark green	Dark green	LESNEY ENGLAND		B/C/D1	£95	
3		Light green* body, dark red chassis, black base	Driving black 12 spoke front black solid	Dark red	Gold	Silver	A	Light green*	Gold	Light Green*	Light green*	LESNEY ENGLAND	E R	C/D1	£800	
4		Dark green body, dark red chassis, black base	Driving black 12 spoke front black solid	Dark red	Gold	Silver	B	Dark green	Gold	Dark green	Dark green	LESNEY ENGLAND		C/D1	£90	✓
5		Dark green body, dark red chassis, black base	Driving black 12 spoke front black solid	Dark red	Gold	Dark red	B	Dark green	Gold	Dark green	Dark green	LESNEY ENGLAND		C/D1	£90	
6		Dark green body, dark red chassis, black base	Driving black 12 spoke front black solid	Dark red	Dark green	Dark red	B	Dark green	Gold	Dark green	Dark green	LESNEY ENGLAND		D1	£90	
7		Dark green body, dark red chassis, black base	Driving black 12 spoke front black solid	Dark red	Dark green	Dark red	B	Dark green	Dark red	Dark green	Dark green	LESNEY ENGLAND		D 2	£90	
8		Dark green body, dark red chassis, black base	Driving black 12 spoke front black solid	Dark green	Gold	Silver	B	Dark green	Gold	Dark green	Dark green	LESNEY ENGLAND		D1	£90	
9		Dark green body, dark red chassis, black base	Driving black 12 spoke front black solid	Dark green	Gold	Dark red	B	Dark green	Gold	Dark green	Dark green	LESNEY ENGLAND		D 2	£95	
10		Dark green body, dark red chassis, black base	Driving black 12 spoke front black solid	Dark green	Dark green	Dark red	B	Dark green	Gold	Dark green	Dark green	LESNEY ENGLAND		D2	£95	
11		Dark green body, dark red chassis, black base	Driving black 12 spoke front black solid	Dark green	Dark green	Dark red	B	Dark green	Dark red	Dark green	Dark green	LESNEY ENGLAND		D 2	£95	

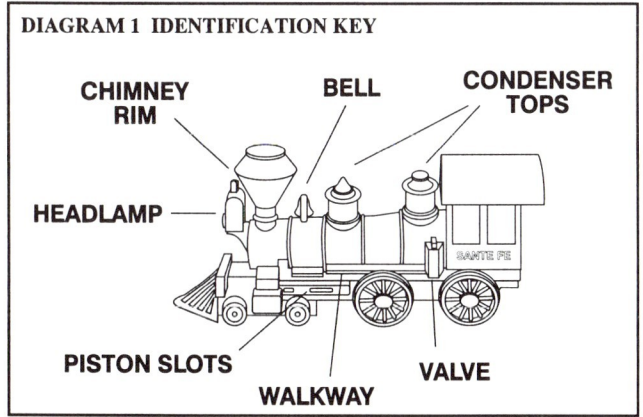

DIAGRAM 1 IDENTIFICATION KEY

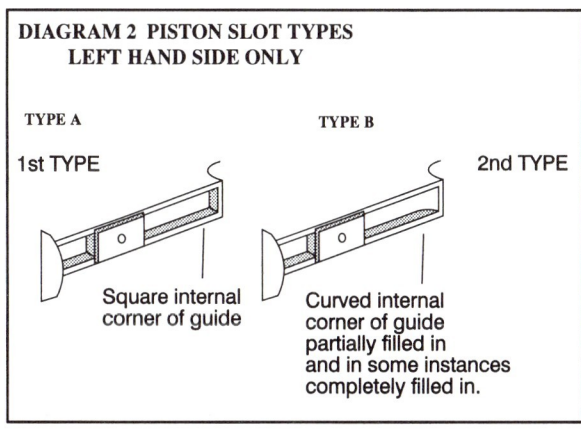

DIAGRAM 2 PISTON SLOT TYPES LEFT HAND SIDE ONLY

LIVERY

Transfers
SANTA FE in yellow with red outline on cab doors.

NOTES

The Yesteryear number, No. 13 is to be found above the rear axle.

INVESTMENT COMMENT
ORIGINAL PRICE £0.25p
An excellent model but its huge sales in the 1960s have limited dramatic growth. It remains a common model and one still easily obtainable on the collectors market. The black seated issues have continued to increase in value compared with the dark red seated issues.

Y13-2 1911 DAIMLER TYPE A12   Scale 1:45

This model is a typical example of Lesney's pursuance of producing perfect miniatures. The body and bonnet are separate components and the main body colour can vary from lemon to pale orange, various combinations can exist on any one model. Initially the steering wheel had five spokes and an advance/retard lever; but this was superseded by the more regular four spoke with no added detail. The five spoke steering wheel was fitted by locating it through the floor. This component also included two foot pedals. The four spoke steering wheel had no pedals and the two small holes in the floor were eventually deleted. The baseplate was changed/modified no less than seven times as a result of using this model in the plated Giftware Series with different methods of mounting on gift ware bases being adopted. Radiator grilles are not very well retained and can easily fall out. Grilles in green or red and grey tyres are the result of Lesney experiments/plastic trials and were not officially released by the factory. The black paint on the chassis can vary from a gloss to a matt finish. In 1984 the model was issued as part of the Connoisseurs Collection in a different livery and had mask-sprayed/tampo printed enhanced detailing.

ISSUE	YEAR OF RELEASE	COLOURS	SEATS	GRILLE	STEERING WHEEL	SPARE WHEEL RECESS TYPE	WHEELS	PLATED PARTS	BASEPLATE TYPE	BASEPLATE	RARITY	BOX TYPE	VALUE	CHECK LIST
1	1966	Yellow body, glossy black chassis	Black*	Black	5 spoke	1	Brass 26 spoke 13mm diameter	Brass	A	LESNEY ENGLAND	D	E	£50	
2		Yellow body, glossy black chassis	Dark red	Black	5 spoke	1	Brass 26 spoke 13mm diameter	Brass	A	LESNEY ENGLAND	D	E	£25	
3		Yellow body, glossy black chassis	Black*	Black	5 spoke	2	Brass 26 spoke 13mm diameter	Brass	A	LESNEY ENGLAND	D	E/E1	£50	
4		Yellow body, glossy black chassis	Dark red	Black	5 spoke	2	Brass 26 spoke 13mm diameter	Brass	A	LESNEY ENGLAND		E/E1	£20	
5	1967	Yellow body, glossy black chassis	Black*	Black	4 spoke	2	Brass 26 spoke 13mm diameter	Brass	A	LESNEY ENGLAND	D	E1	£50	
6		Yellow body, glossy black chassis	Dark red	Black	4 spoke	2	Brass 26 spoke 13mm diameter	Brass	A	LESNEY ENGLAND		E1	£18	
7		Yellow body, glossy black chassis	Dark red	Black	4 spoke	2	Brass 26 spoke 13mm diameter	Brass	B	LESNEY ENGLAND		E1/F	£18	
8		Yellow body, glossy black chassis	Dark red	Black	4 spoke	2	Brass 26 spoke 13mm diameter	Brass	C*	LESNEY ENGLAND	R	E1/F	£50	
9		Yellow body, glossy black chassis	Dark red	Black	4 spoke	2	Brass 26 spoke 13mm diameter	Brass	D	LESNEY ENGLAND		F	£18	
10		Yellow body, glossy black chassis	Dark red	Black	4 spoke	2	Brass 26 spoke 13mm diameter	Brass	E*	LESNEY ENGLAND	S	F/G	£40	
11		Yellow body, glossy black chassis	Dark red	Black	4 spoke	2	Brass 26 spoke 13mm diameter	Brass	F	LESNEY ENGLAND		F/G	£20	
12		Yellow body, glossy black chassis	Dark red	Black	4 spoke	2	Brass 26 spoke 13mm diameter	Brass	G*	LESNEY ENGLAND	S	G	£25	
13	1984	Mid blue body, powder blue chassis	Brown	Black	4 spoke	2	Silver 26 spoke 13mm diameter	Silver	H	MATCHBOX © 1984 ENGLAND	H	K	£95 The Set	

DIAGRAM 1 SPARE WHEEL RECESS TYPE

CLOSED IN SIDE   OPEN SIDE

TYPE 1   TYPE 2

NOTES

The Y13-2 seats were made using the same tools that made the Y2-3 Vauxhall seats.

Y13-2 1911 DAIMLER TYPE A 12   (CONTINUED)   Scale 1:45

BASEPLATE TYPES

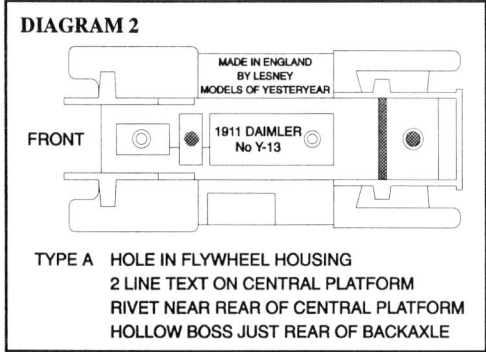

DIAGRAM 2

TYPE A HOLE IN FLYWHEEL HOUSING
2 LINE TEXT ON CENTRAL PLATFORM
RIVET NEAR REAR OF CENTRAL PLATFORM
HOLLOW BOSS JUST REAR OF BACKAXLE

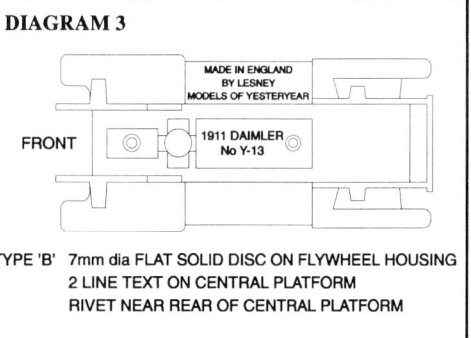

DIAGRAM 3

TYPE 'B' 7mm dia FLAT SOLID DISC ON FLYWHEEL HOUSING
2 LINE TEXT ON CENTRAL PLATFORM
RIVET NEAR REAR OF CENTRAL PLATFORM

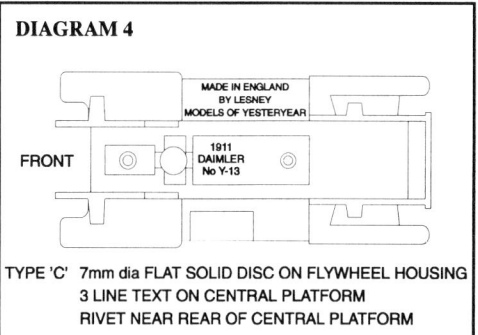

DIAGRAM 4

TYPE 'C' 7mm dia FLAT SOLID DISC ON FLYWHEEL HOUSING
3 LINE TEXT ON CENTRAL PLATFORM
RIVET NEAR REAR OF CENTRAL PLATFORM

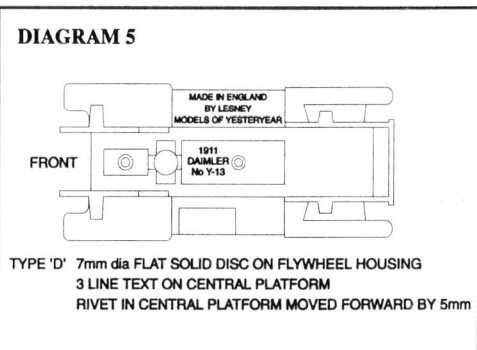

DIAGRAM 5

TYPE 'D' 7mm dia FLAT SOLID DISC ON FLYWHEEL HOUSING
3 LINE TEXT ON CENTRAL PLATFORM
RIVET IN CENTRAL PLATFORM MOVED FORWARD BY 5mm

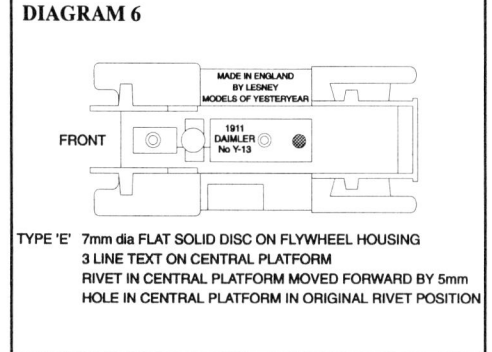

DIAGRAM 6

TYPE 'E' 7mm dia FLAT SOLID DISC ON FLYWHEEL HOUSING
3 LINE TEXT ON CENTRAL PLATFORM
RIVET IN CENTRAL PLATFORM MOVED FORWARD BY 5mm
HOLE IN CENTRAL PLATFORM IN ORIGINAL RIVET POSITION

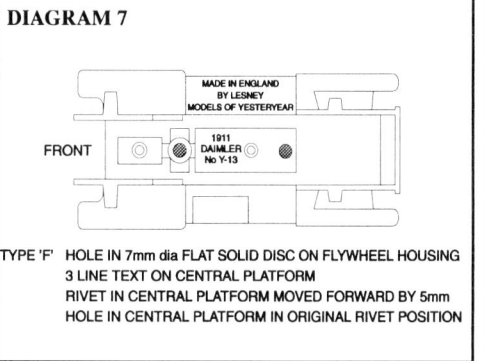

DIAGRAM 7

TYPE 'F' HOLE IN 7mm dia FLAT SOLID DISC ON FLYWHEEL HOUSING
3 LINE TEXT ON CENTRAL PLATFORM
RIVET IN CENTRAL PLATFORM MOVED FORWARD BY 5mm
HOLE IN CENTRAL PLATFORM IN ORIGINAL RIVET POSITION

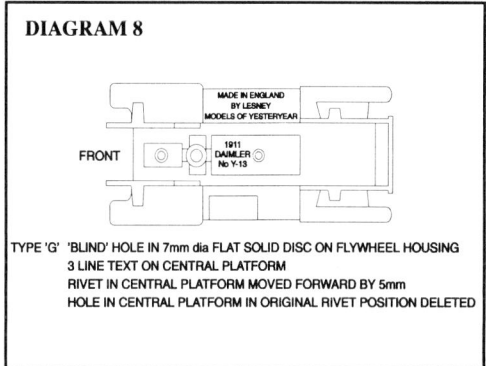

DIAGRAM 8

TYPE 'G' 'BLIND' HOLE IN 7mm dia FLAT SOLID DISC ON FLYWHEEL HOUSING
3 LINE TEXT ON CENTRAL PLATFORM
RIVET IN CENTRAL PLATFORM MOVED FORWARD BY 5mm
HOLE IN CENTRAL PLATFORM IN ORIGINAL RIVET POSITION DELETED

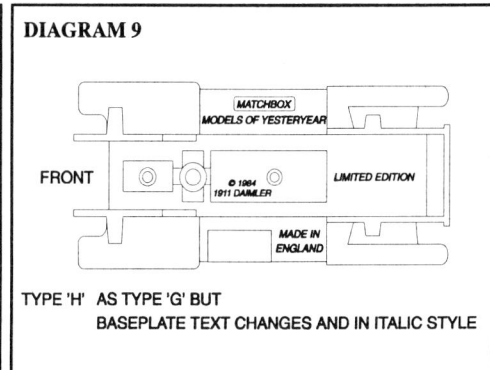

DIAGRAM 9

TYPE 'H' AS TYPE 'G' BUT
BASEPLATE TEXT CHANGES AND IN ITALIC STYLE

NOTES

Y13-3 1918 CROSSLEY

Scale 1:47

INVESTMENT COMMENT
ORIGINAL PRICE £1.25p

This model remains one of the more desirable models in the Woodgrain series; although values for standard releases have fallen away in recent years. Issues 14 and 15 have risen and there is further potential for growth.

Not an immediate success, this model is now a must for todays modern day collectors. This is due to the fact it was the first 'commercial' vehicle since 1959. Modifications were made to the chassis/base casting in quick succession and the first two types are very hard to find. These are not to be confused with pre-production types which had the copyright date incomplete i.e.197. Milky white seats are the norm, but dull dark red (actually half way between red and dark red) seats and green (lighter than those fitted to the metallic red Y8-3 Stutz) seats were fitted. The number of models reported with these less common colours indicates they were deliberate issues rather than the results of plastic trials etc. First type truck bodies had five small pips cast along the top edge of each side to represent rear canopy fixing cleats. These were reduced to just two very early in the production run because as they were obstructive to the application of the R.A.F. roundel label. The olive green canopies and grilles were made using plastic from the Battle King range. The final run of this model exhausted supplies of the more regular tan canopies and grilles, and a concession was given to the production line to use the components being made elsewhere at the Lesney Gift Ware factory. Whilst these canopies and grilles are regularly referred to as black, they are in fact very dark charcoal grey. Canopies and radiator grilles are easily switched/changed on this model and models have been reported with any combination of coloured components on one model.

A : R.A.F. AMBULANCE

ISSUE	YEAR OF RELEASE	COLOURS	CAB TILT	REAR CANOPY	RADIATOR GRILLE	SEATS	PLATED PARTS	WHEELS	TRUCK BODY TYPE	FRONT SPRINGS/MUD GUARDS TYPE	BASEPLATE TYPE	BASEPLATE	RARITY	BOX TYPE	VALUE	CHECK LIST
1	1975	R.A.F. blue body & chassis	Tan	Tan	Tan	Dull dark red	Brass	Chrome 24 spoke	A*	A*	A*	LESNEY © 1973 ENGLAND	E R	H	£400	
2		R.A.F. blue body & chassis	Tan	Tan	Tan	Milky white	Brass	Chrome 24 spoke	A*	A*	A*	LESNEY © 1973 ENGLAND	V R	H	£350	
3		R.A.F. blue body & chassis	Tan	Tan	Tan	Dull dark red	Brass	Chrome 24 spoke	B*	A*	A*	LESNEY © 1973 ENGLAND	V R	H	£300	
4		R.A.F. blue body & chassis	Tan	Tan	Tan	Milky white	Brass	Chrome 24 spoke	B*	A*	A*	LESNEY © 1973 ENGLAND	V R	H	£250	
5		R.A.F. blue body & chassis	Tan	Tan	Tan	Milky white	Brass	Chrome 24 spoke	B*	B	A*	LESNEY © 1973 ENGLAND	R	H	£75	
6		R.A.F. blue body & chassis	Tan	Tan	Tan	Milky white	Brass	Chrome 24 spoke	B	B	B	LESNEY © 1973 ENGLAND		H	£25	✓ 2x
7		R.A.F. blue body & chassis	Tan	Tan	Tan	Milky white	Brass	Chrome 12 spoke	B	B	B	LESNEY © 1973 ENGLAND		H	£30	
8		R.A.F. blue body & chassis	Tan	Tan	Tan	Dull dark red	Brass	Chrome 12 spoke	B	B	B	LESNEY © 1973 ENGLAND		H	£30	
9		R.A.F. blue body & chassis	Tan	Tan	Tan	Green*	Brass	Chrome 12 spoke	B	B	B	LESNEY © 1973 ENGLAND	R	H	£200	
10		R.A.F. blue body & chassis	Olive green*	Olive green*	Olive green*	Milky white	Brass	Chrome 12 spoke	B	B	B	LESNEY © 1973 ENGLAND	D	H	£70	
11		R.A.F. blue body & chassis	Olive green*	Olive green*	Olive green*	Milky white	Brass	Chrome 24 spoke	B	B	B	LESNEY © 1973 ENGLAND	D	H	£70	
12		R.A.F. blue body & chassis	Dark tan	Dark tan	Dark tan	Milky white	Brass	Chrome 24 spoke	B	B	B	LESNEY © 1973 ENGLAND		H	£30	
13		R.A.F. blue body & chassis	Dark tan	Dark tan	Dark tan	Milky white	Brass	Chrome 12 spoke	B	B	B	LESNEY © 1973 ENGLAND		H	£40	
14		R.A.F. blue body & chassis	Charcoal grey*	Charcoal grey*	Charcoal grey*	Milky white	Brass	Chrome 24 spoke	B	B	B	LESNEY © 1973 ENGLAND	V R	H	£300	
15		R.A.F. blue body & chassis	Charcoal grey*	Charcoal grey*	Charcoal grey*	Dull dark red	Brass	Chrome 24 spoke	B	B	B	LESNEY © 1973 ENGLAND	V R	H	£300	

DIAGRAM 1
TYPE A BASEPLATE
MADE IN ENGLAND
LESNEY PRODUCTS & Co LD
MATCHBOX
MODELS OF YESTERYEAR No Y-13
1918 CROSSLEY R.A.F. TENDER
© 1973
"& CO LD" COMPLETE

DIAGRAM 2
TYPE B BASEPLATE
MADE IN ENGLAND
LESNEY PRODUCTS & Co
MATCHBOX
MODELS OF YESTERYEAR No Y-13
1918 CROSSLEY R.A.F. TENDER
© 1973
"LD" DELETED

DIAGRAM 3 FRONT SPRINGS TYPES

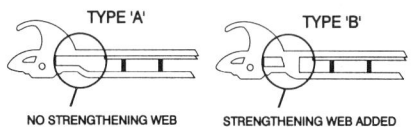

TYPE 'A' — NO STRENGTHENING WEB
TYPE 'B' — STRENGTHENING WEB ADDED

DIAGRAM 4 TRUCK BODY TYPES

TYPE A
5 CLEATS
RAISED EDGES (RELIEF) TO TOP & ENDS EDGES

TYPE B
2 CLEATS
RAISED EDGES (RELIEF) TO TOP & ENDS EDGES

LIVERY
Labels
Rear Canopy. Red cross on white square. Truckbody. Red white and blue roundels with R.A.F. in white on airforce blue background.

NOTES
BECKENHAM APPEAL MODEL. Beige body, bonnet & chassis, dark tan cab & rear canopy & grille, dull dark red seat, chrome 24 spoke wheels.
Livery "FIELD AMBULANCE".
N.B. No R.A.F. decals.
Some issued models were fitted with copper axles.

Y13-3 1918 CROSSLEY (CONTINUED) Scale 1:47

INVESTMENT COMMENT
ORIGINAL PRICE £1.50p
Produced in too many numbers and values have generally failed to appreciate. However issues 1 and 2 are at present good value.

EVANS BROS. After World War I, many ex-military Crossleys were adapted to civilian use and this model is such an example, being used for coal deliveries. The two body cleats on the truck body sides were deleted for this model and were never re-introduced; but a small number of bodies with the two cleats were used during the beginning of the production run. Similarly, the words 'R.A.F. Tender' were deleted from the baseplate; but a considerable quantity of Type B bases, with this inscription were also used during the early production run. Models have been reported with dark tan and olive green grilles and cab canopies and with milky white seats but it must be remembered that these components can be easily switched from the R.A.F. Tender, and this practise was commonplace during the late '70's and early '80's. Consequently these oddities have not been given separate listing. 'Evans Bros.' labels with a turquoise coloured background is the result of fading. The final issue of this model had a lighter, brighter red finish and the spare wheel was retained by a larger headed bright steel stud/rivet. This 'new' stud/rivet became the norm for all subsequent issues of the Crossley vehicle. All Crossleys made after the R.A.F. Tender run, had the "B" type front springs/mudguards area casting.

B : EVANS BROS

ISSUE	YEAR OF RELEASE	COLOURS	CAB TILT	SEATS	GRILLE	STEERING WHEEL	PLATED PARTS	WHEELS	REAR LOAD	TRUCK BODY TYPE	SPARE WHEEL RETAINING STUD/RIVET	BASEPLATE TYPE	BASEPLATE	RARITY	BOX TYPE	VALUE	CHECK LIST
1	1979	Dark red body gloss black chassis	Black	Black	Black	Black	Brass	Chrome 24 spoke	Black sacks & coal	B*	Small head grey metal	B	LESNEY © 1973 ENGLAND	R	I	£75	
2		Dark red body gloss black chassis	Black	Black	Black	Black	Brass	Red 12 spoke	Black sacks & coal	B*	Small head grey metal	B	LESNEY © 1973 ENGLAND	R	I	£75	
3		Dark red body gloss black chassis	Black	Black	Black	Black	Brass	Chrome 24 spoke	Black sacks & coal	C	Small head grey metal	B	LESNEY © 1973 ENGLAND		I	£15	
4		Dark red body gloss black chassis	Black	Black	Black	Black	Brass	Chrome 12 spoke	Black sacks & coal	C	Small head grey metal	B	LESNEY © 1973 ENGLAND		I	£15	
5		Dark red body gloss black chassis	Black	Black	Black	Black	Brass	Bright red 12 spoke	Black sacks & coal	C	Small head grey metal	B	LESNEY © 1973 ENGLAND		I	£15	
6		Dark red body gloss black chassis	Black	Black	Black	Black	Brass	Bright red 12 spoke	Black sacks & coal	C	Small head grey metal	C	LESNEY © 1973 ENGLAND		I	£10	
7		Dark red body gloss black chassis	Black	Black	Black	Black	Brass	Chrome 24 spoke	Black sacks & coal	C	Small head grey metal	C	LESNEY © 1973 ENGLAND		I	£15	
8		Dark red body gloss black chassis	Black	Black	Black	Black	Brass	Dark red 12 spoke	Black sacks & coal	C	Small head grey metal	C	LESNEY © 1973 ENGLAND		I	£10	✔
9	1982	Bright red body gloss black chassis	Black	Black	Black	Black	Brass	Bright red 12 spoke	Black sacks & coal	C	Large head chrome/steel*	C	LESNEY © 1973 ENGLAND	D	I	£20	

DIAGRAM 1
TYPE 'B' BASEPLATE

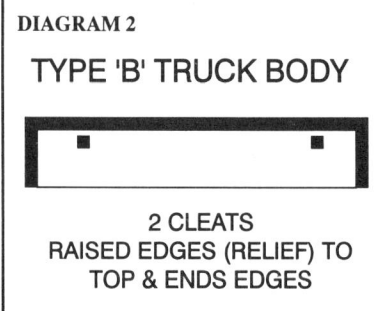

"LD" DELETED

DIAGRAM 2
TYPE 'B' TRUCK BODY

2 CLEATS
RAISED EDGES (RELIEF) TO TOP & ENDS EDGES

DIAGRAM 3
TYPE 'C' BASEPLATE

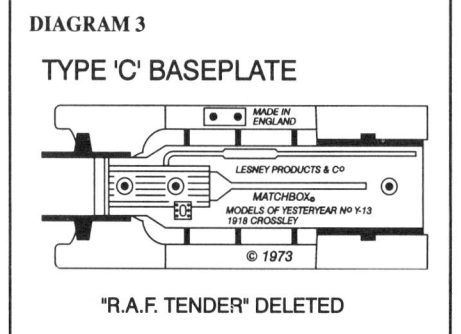

"R.A.F. TENDER" DELETED

DIAGRAM 4
TYPE 'C' TRUCK BODY

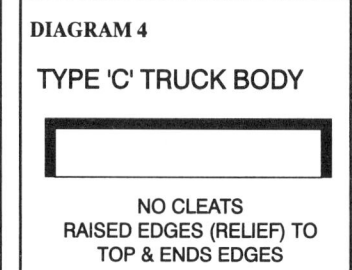

NO CLEATS
RAISED EDGES (RELIEF) TO TOP & ENDS EDGES

LIVERY
Label.
Truck sides. EVANS BROS COAL & COKE in white with bright red shadow effect on very dark red background.

NOTES
BECKENHAM APPEAL MODEL
1. Dark red body & bonnet, gloss black chassis, dark tan cab canopy, olive grille, white seat, 2 cleats on body sides, Type D base, chrome 24 spoke wheels.
2. Issue 9 also in 1982 Limited Edition pack of five models.

INVESTMENT COMMENT	# Y13-3 1918 CROSSLEY (CONTINUED) Scale 1:47
ORIGINAL PRICE £3.50p Still a poor performer but may see an upturn if exposed to new collectors especially those collecting to a theme such as beer.	Issued in 1983, this is the first model to have Lesney Products base text replaced by Matchbox Toys Ltd. text. However a small number of Type C bases left over from the 'Evans Bros.' run were used during the initial part of the Carlsberg run; but these issues are very hard to find. Examples have been reported with black grilles and seats, but due to the ease of switching these components and doubts of their authenticity, these variants have not been seperately listed. The standard colour was dull dark red seats with light green grille and canopies. Gold and chrome twelve spoke wheels were fitted, and models with a mixture of the two finishes on one axle are known to exist! The moulds for the rear canopy were modified to produce this component with smooth, raised rectangular panels to provide an even surface for the labels. Models with 'Ice Blue' grilles and cab and rear canopies, are probably 'lunch time' or 'Friday afternoon' specials (see glossary). Also milky white seats are the result of these components being switched from the R.A.F. Tender or the metallic blue Y8-3 Stutz. A production run in late 1983 sported darker green grilles, cab and rear canopies and maroon seats. The 1984 issue had the same colours of plastic components and had the E type baseplate with 'Y13/Y26' text denoting the commonality of this component between the Y13-3 and Y26-1.

C : CARLSBERG

ISSUE	YEAR OF RELEASE	COLOURS	CAB TILT	SEATS	GRILLE	STEERING WHEEL	PLATED PARTS	WHEELS	REAR CANOPY	TRUCK BODY TYPE	BASEPLATE TYPE	BASEPLATE	RARITY	BOX TYPE	VALUE	CHECK LIST
1	1983	Cream body & bonnet glossy black chassis	Light green	Dull dark red or black	Light green or black	Black	Brass	Chrome 12 spoke	Light green	C	C*	LESNEY © * 1973 ENGLAND	R	I	£45	
2		Cream body & bonnet glossy black chassis	Light green	Dull dark red or black	Light green or black	Black	Brass	Gold 12 spoke	Light green	C	C*	LESNEY © * 1973 ENGLAND	R	I	£45	
3		Cream body & bonnet glossy black chassis	Light green	Dull dark red or black	Light green or black	Black	Brass	Chrome 12 spoke	Light green	C	D	MATCHBOX © 1973 ENGLAND		I	£8	
4		Cream body & bonnet glossy black chassis	Light green	Dull dark red or black	Light green or black	Black	Brass	Gold 12 spoke	Light green	C	D	MATCHBOX © 1973 ENGLAND		I	£8	✗
5		Cream body & bonnet glossy black chassis	Darker green	Maroon	Darker green	Black	Brass	Chrome 12 spoke (W)	Darker green	C	D	MATCHBOX © 1973 ENGLAND		I	£8	
6		Cream body & bonnet glossy black chassis	Darker green	Maroon	Darker green	Black	Brass	Gold 12 spoke (W)	Darker green	C	D	MATCHBOX © 1973 ENGLAND		I	£8	✓
7	1984	Cream body & bonnet glossy black chassis	Darker green	Maroon	Darker green	Black	Brass	Gold 12 spoke	Darker green	C	E	MATCHBOX © 1973 ENGLAND		J	£8	
8		Cream body & bonnet glossy black chassis	Darker green	Maroon	Darker green	Black	Brass	Gold 12 spoke	Darker green	D	E	MATCHBOX © 1973 ENGLAND		J	£15	

DIAGRAM 1

TYPE D BASEPLATE

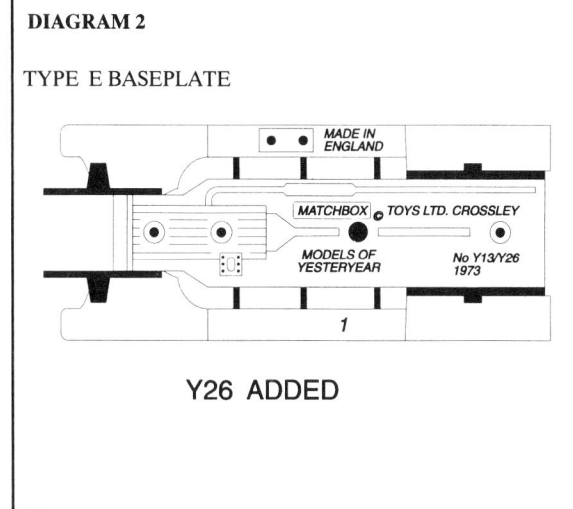

INSCRIPTION RE-ARRANGED. PROP-SHAFT INCOMPLETE WITH 3mm dia HOLE IN CENTRE

DIAGRAM 2

TYPE E BASEPLATE

Y26 ADDED

DIAGRAM 3 TRUCK BODY TYPE D

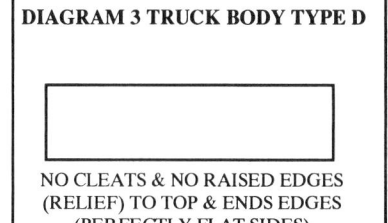

NO CLEATS & NO RAISED EDGES (RELIEF) TO TOP & ENDS EDGES (PERFECTLY FLAT SIDES)

LIVERY CARLSBERG

Labels.
Rear canopy. CARLSBERG in lemon on dark green background.

NOTES

The colour of the word Carlsberg can vary from pale to rich lemon and the dark green of the background can vary slightly.

Y13-3 1918 CROSSLEY CONTINUED   Scale 1:47

WARING & GILLOW. The 'Waring and Gillow' models were intended to have cream canopies with cream labels. However, the first batch of labels had white backgrounds. Matchbox quickly produced 5,000 white canopies to match the labels. The label suppliers were notified of their error and all subsequent batches had a cream background which suited the already manufactured cream canopies. Inevitably cream labels were affixed to white canopies and vice versa. It was soon noticed that the white labels have a gloss surface, but the cream labels have a matt surface. Switching of labels is possible, but if a label shows signs of "creasing", then it has definitely been interfered with. The raised relief on the truck body sides had been deleted for the Y26-1 Löwenbräu tampo decoration. The truck body is common between the Y13 & Y26, and this casting change was seen on both the Waring & Gillow and the Kohle & Koks.

KOHLE & KOKS. The Kohle & Koks was the first Y13-3 to be made after production was moved to Macau. The livery/logo was submitted by Matchbox Germany, but collectors gave it an indifferent reception due to its unlikely livery for a coal truck. The simulated coal load was a modified version of the 'Evans Bros.' component in that it had two more sacks of coal. Wheel variations are far less common on Macau models; but this is an exception. Produced simultaneously with the Macau version of the Y5-4 Talbot 'Roses', some of the dark green twelve spoke wheels intended for the 'Roses' were mistakenly fitted to some 'Kohle & Koks' models.

D : WARING & GILLOW

ISSUE	YEAR OF RELEASE	COLOURS	CAB TILT	SEATS	GRILLE	STEERING WHEEL	PLATED PARTS	WHEELS	TYRES	REAR CANOPY/LOAD	LABELS	TRUCK BODY TYPE	BASEPLATE TYPE	BASEPLATE	RARITY	BOX TYPE	VALUE	CHECK LIST
1	1985	Dark green body, gloss black chassis	White	Maroon	Black	Black	Brass	Gold 12 spoke	Black	White	White	D	E	MATCHBOX © 1973 ENGLAND		J	£9	
2		Dark green body, gloss black chassis	White	Maroon	Black	Black	Brass	Gold 12 spoke	Black	White	Cream	D	E	MATCHBOX © 1973 ENGLAND		J	£9	
3		Dark green body, gloss black chassis	Cream	Maroon	Black	Black	Brass	Gold 12 spoke	Black	Cream	White	D	E	MATCHBOX © 1973 ENGLAND		J	£10	✓
4		Dark green body, gloss black chassis	Cream	Maroon	Black	Black	Brass	Gold 12 spoke	Black	Cream	Cream	D	E	MATCHBOX © 1973 ENGLAND		J/L	£10	
5		Dark green body, gloss black chassis	Cream	Maroon	Black	Black	Brass	Chrome* 12 spoke	Black	Cream	Cream	D	E	MATCHBOX © 1973 ENGLAND	D	J	£15	

E : KOHLE & KOKS

ISSUE	YEAR OF RELEASE	COLOURS	CAB TILT	SEATS	GRILLE	STEERING WHEEL	PLATED PARTS	WHEELS	TYRES	REAR CANOPY/LOAD	LABELS	TRUCK BODY TYPE	BASEPLATE TYPE	BASEPLATE	RARITY	BOX TYPE	VALUE	CHECK LIST
1	1988	Dark lemon body, gloss black chassis	Black	Black	Black	Black	Brass	Black 12 spoke	Black	Black sacks & coal	-	D	F	MATCHBOX © 1973 MACAU		J	£10	✓
2		Dark lemon body, gloss black chassis	Black	Black	Black	Black	Brass	Dark green 12 spoke*	Black	Black sacks & coal	-	D	F	MATCHBOX © 1973 MACAU	D	J	£45	

DIAGRAM 1 BASEPLATE TYPE

TYPE 'F'

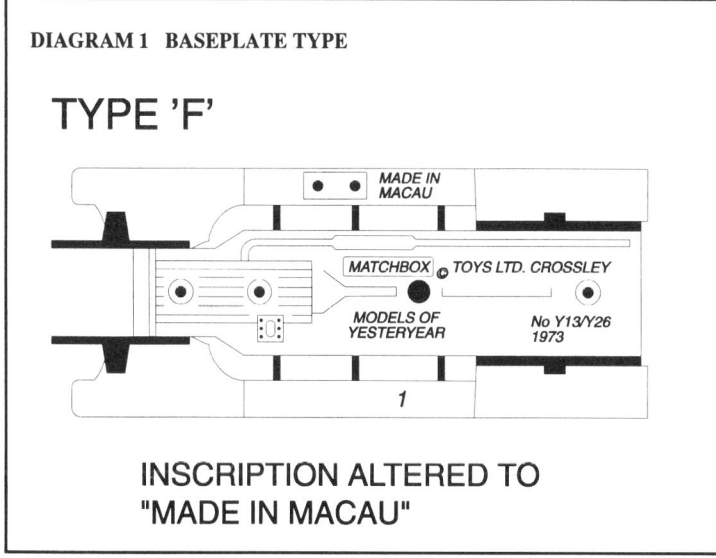

INSCRIPTION ALTERED TO "MADE IN MACAU"

DIAGRAM 2 TRUCK BODY TYPE

TYPE 'D'

NO CLEATS & NO RAISED EDGES (RELIEF) TO TOP & ENDS EDGES (PERFECTLY FLAT SIDES)

LIVERY WARING & GILLOW
Tampo
Truck sides. Gold WARING'S with black outline.
Labels. Canopy. LONDON W & G MADRID above PARIS in reddish brown on white or cream background.
N.B. White labels have a gloss surface and cream labels have a matt surface.

LIVERY   KOHLE & KOKS
Tampo
Truck sides. KOHLE & KOKS with crossed hammers in black.

INVESTMENT COMMENT
ORIGINAL PRICE, WARINGS £3.99p
KOHLE & KOKS £4.25p

WARING & GILLOW Upon release there was an immediate premium to be paid for all five issues but this growth has never progressed further. The possible reason could be the number of switched canopies and labels on the market.
KOHLE & KOKS Genuine examples of Issue 2 have enjoyed considerable growth. May have peaked!

NOTES
Issue 4 of the Warings model also sold in the 1986 '30 Years of Models of Yesteryear' boxed set of three models.

The production quantity of the Kohle & Koks models was 60,000 (E)

INVESTMENT COMMENT
ORIGINAL PRICE £0.14p

Although originally unpopular with Yesteryear collectors, the Y14 has maintained its market value during the last few years. It is still harder to find in mint condition than the Y13-1 Santa Fe.

Y14-1 1903 'DUKE OF CONNAUGHT' LOCOMOTIVE Scale 1:130

The major casting modification was to the model's sand boxes. Early models were issued with a gap between the boxes and the wheelarches. This was relatively quickly changed to a filled-in gap. Also there are two different types of baseplate; see diagram 3. The second type was modified to be mounted on a Wade ceramic ashtray and a hole for the attachment screw was located in the baseplate. Early models are easily recognised in that they have a brown rear baseplate rivet. Later, in an attempt to make the assembly of the model quicker, a long rivet was cast through the rear of the model, fitted through the brown chassis and onto the baseplate, before being peined over. Earlier models had separate wheels free running fitted to steel axles. Later the wheels were cast in pairs, including the axle, and instead of being free-running, were only capable of rotating together. The last production run with silver boiler doors has proved to be a not-too easy variation to find!

ISSUE	YEAR OF RELEASE	COLOURS	REAR RIVET COLOUR	SMALL WHEELS	DRIVING WHEELS	COMBINED WHEELS & AXLES	WHEEL COVER/SAND BOX	WALKWAY BOXES TRIM	AXLE BOX COVERS & CONDENSER DOME	BOILER DOOR	BASEPLATE TYPE	BASEPLATE	RARITY	BOX TYPE	VALUE	CHECK LIST
1	1959	Dark green body, dark brown chassis	Brown	Brown 12 spoke	Brown 16 spoke	No	Gap, Type 1	Gold *	Gold	Gold	Type A	LESNEY ENGLAND	D	B	£130	✓
2		Dark green body, dark brown chassis	Brown	Brown 12 spoke	Brown 16 spoke	No	Gap, Type 1	None	Gold	Gold	Type B *	LESNEY ENGLAND	S	B/C	£120	
3		Dark green body, dark brown chassis	Brown	Brown 12 spoke	Brown 16 spoke	No	Gap, Type 1	None	Gold	Gold	Type A	LESNEY ENGLAND		B/C	£90	
4		Dark green body, dark brown chassis	Brown	Brown 12 spoke	Brown 16 spoke	No	No gap, Type 2	None	Gold	Gold	Type A	LESNEY ENGLAND		C/D1	£90	
5		Dark green body, dark brown chassis	Green	Brown 12 spoke	Brown 16 spoke	Yes	No gap, Type 2	None	Gold	Gold	Type A	LESNEY ENGLAND		C/D1	£90	
6	1964	Dark green body, dark brown chassis	Green	Brown 12 spoke	Brown 16 spoke	Yes	No gap, Type 2	None	Gold	Silver*	Type A	LESNEY ENGLAND	S	D1	£120	

DIAGRAM 1 IDENTIFICATION KEY

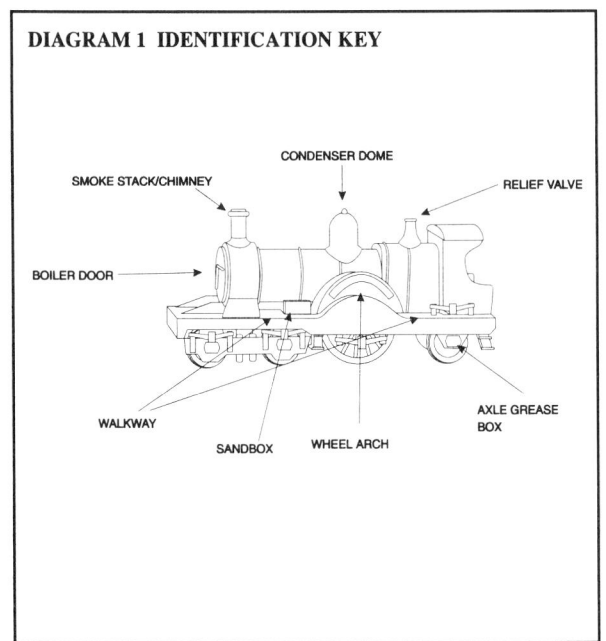

DIAGRAM 2 WHEEL ARCH TYPES

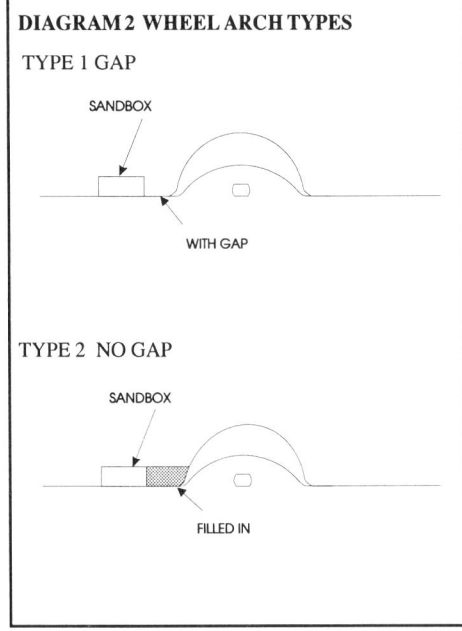

DIAGRAM 3 BASEPLATE TYPES

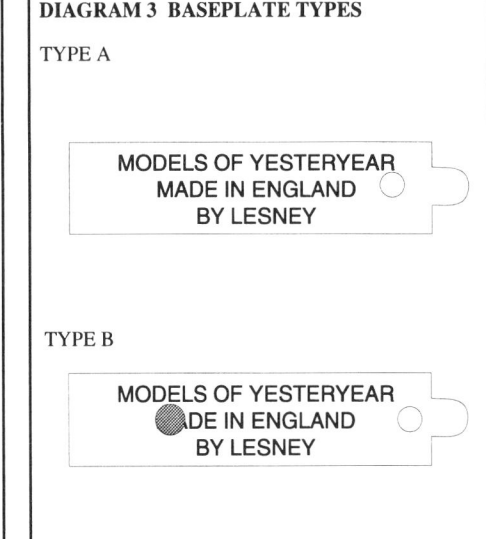

LIVERY

Transfers
Wheel arches. DUKE OF CONNAUGHT in yellow on red panels

NOTES

No gold trim to the axle grease boxes is a negative variation.

INVESTMENT COMMENT
ORIGINAL PRICE £0.19.5p

Produced in vast numbers for seven years and still a poor performer. However it affords the new collector the opportunity of buying a model which is thirty years old for around £20.

Y14-2 1911 MAXWELL ROADSTER   Scale 1:49

This simple model of the 1911 Maxwell Roadster Model G.A. was introduced in 1965, phased out eight years later; but re-issued as part of the 1984 Connoisseurs Set. The colour of turquoise varied little although as with many models of this era any combination of unplated parts could be found. Various modifications were made to the baseplate; initially because the Maxwell was released as part of the Lesney Giftware range. Minor modifications were made to the springs. It should be noted that bright red hoods, although on plated models, were not released on painted models and yellow hoods were only experimental colour trials. Models from the first production had brass plated petrol tanks although they were meant to have a copper coloured finish. Models could have brass or copper plated fire extinguishers and the brass finish is harder to find. Hoods and seats are easily interchangeable with the Y13-3, Y8-3, Y25-1 and Y26-1 models, so beware! The 1984 issue was given a considerable degree of enhanced detailing and the underside of the hood had 'Limited Edition' cast into it.

ISSUE	YEAR OF RELEASE	COLOURS	HOOD	SEATS	GRILLE	WHEELS	PLATED PARTS	PETROL TANK	FIRE EXTINGUISHER	BASEPLATE TYPE	BASEPLATE	RARITY	BOX TYPE	VALUE	CHECK LIST
1	1965	Turquoise body & chassis	Black smooth	Dark red	Black	Brass 12 spoke	Brass	Brass*	Copper	1	LESNEY NO 14 ENGLAND	R	D3	£75	
2		Turquoise body & chassis	Black smooth	Dark red	Black	Brass 12 spoke	Brass	Copper	Copper	1	LESNEY NO 14 ENGLAND		D3	£20	
3		Turquoise body & chassis	Black smooth	Dark red	Black	Brass 12 spoke	Brass	Copper	Copper	2	LESNEY NO 14 ENGLAND		D3/E1	£20	
4		Turquoise body & chassis	Black smooth	Dark red	Black	Brass 12 spoke	Brass	Copper	Brass*	2	LESNEY NO 14 ENGLAND	S	E1/F	£25	
5		Turquoise body & chassis	Black smooth	Black	Black	Brass 12 spoke	Brass	Copper	Copper	2	LESNEY NO 14 ENGLAND		E1/F	£20	
6		Turquoise body & chassis	Black smooth	Dark red	Black	Brass 12 spoke	Brass	Copper	Copper	3	LESNEY NO 14 ENGLAND		E1/F/G	£20	
7		Turquoise body & chassis	Black smooth	Dark red	Tan*	Brass 12 spoke	Brass	Copper	Copper	3	LESNEY NO 14 ENGLAND	R	E1/F/G	£40	
8		Turquoise body & chassis	Black textured	Dark red	Black	Brass 12 spoke	Brass	Copper	Copper	3	LESNEY NO 14 ENGLAND		G	£20	
9		Turquoise body & chassis	Black textured	Dark red	Black	Brass 12 spoke	Brass	Copper	Brass*	3	LESNEY NO 14 ENGLAND	S	G	£25	
10	1984	Dark cream body, dark green chassis	Black textured	Dark green	Black	Brass 12 spoke	Brass	Copper	Gold	4	MATCHBOX © 1984 LIMITED EDITION ENGLAND		K	£95 The Set	

DIAGRAM 1 BASEPLATE TYPE 1
TWO RAISED HOLLOW BOSSES; ONE IN SUMP, ONE AT REAR OF CAST PROP SHAFT

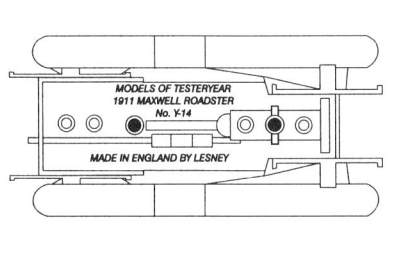

DIAGRAM 2 BASEPLATE TYPE 2
TWO RAISED BOSSES CAPPED (BLANKED OFF) WITH SMALL CENTRAL PIP ON TOP OF BOSSES; ONE IN SUMP, ONE AT REAR OF CAST PROP SHAFT

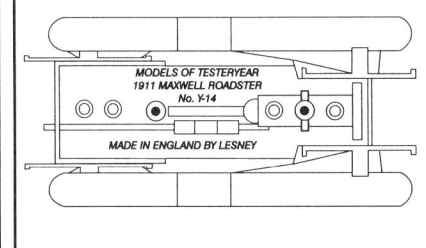

DIAGRAM 3 BASEPLATE TYPE 3
RAISED BOSSES DELETED. 7MM DIAMETER FLAT BOSS IN CENTRE OF SUMP. EJECTOR PIN IMPRESSION AT REAR OF CAST PROP SHAFT

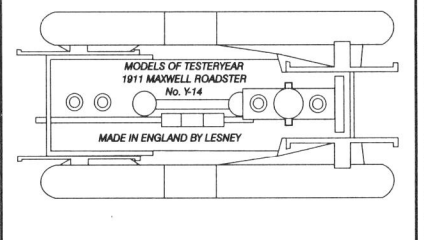

DIAGRAM 4 BASEPLATE TYPE 4
AS TYPE 3, BUT EJECTOR PIN IMPRESSION AT REAR OF CAST PROP SHAFT DELETED. DIFFERENT STYLE OF SCRIPT-UPSIDE DOWN COMPARED TO PREVIOUS TYPES, 'LIMITED EDITION' CAST.

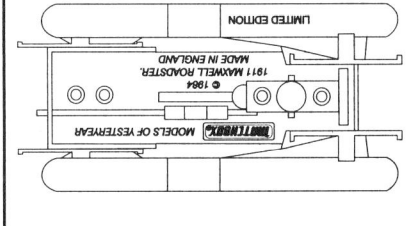

NOTES
It is known that one or two issues were fitted with wheels smaller in diameter that standard models. As yet we do not know which baseplate types are relevant.

Y14-3 1931 STUTZ BEARCAT

Scale 1:44

INVESTMENT COMMENT
ORIGINAL PRICE £1.25p
Very little to report — prices have been maintained and the Stutz remains a popular addition to any collection.

The Stutz is yet another fine example of 1930's flamboyant American styling. Originally scheduled for release in 1973, it didn't appear until 1974. The copyright date was originally cast on the underside of the right hand running board to read "1973", but was changed to 1974, to reflect the re-scheduled release date. A very small number of © 1973 bases were used in the initial production run, but the majority were © 1974. The rear bumper was modified quickly as the Type A tended to buckle and/or break during the fettling/tumbling process. A fourth vertical strut (Type B) was added and the centre struts were thickened, which solved the problem. Issue 3 models can be found with copper axles. On the 1979 issue, mask spraying was used to apply the paint to the top body panels. To overcome spray spreading problems, the body mould was modified so that a raised 'V' ridge was cast onto the boat tail. Different coloured plastic components to those listed were the result of trials and were never officially released by the factory. 1979 issues have been reported with red and chrome solid wheels, but their authenticity is doubtful. In 1990, this model was included in the "Great Motor Cars of the Century" mail order scheme in N. America and was packaged in plain white boxes with black text. It was simultaneously released world wide in the 'N' style boxes.

ISSUE	YEAR OF RELEASE	COLOURS	DOOR TOPS	CAST 'V' RIDGE ON BOAT TAIL	SEATS	GRILLE	PLATED PARTS	STEERING WHEEL	WHEELS	REAR BUMPER	AXLES	THREADED SCREW HOLE	BASEPLATE	RARITY	BOX TYPE	VALUE	CHECK LIST
1	1974	Metallic light green body, metallic dark green chassis	Metallic light green	No	Bright red	Bright red	Brass	Black	Chrome 24 spoke	Type A	Riveted	No	LESNEY © 1973 * ENGLAND	R	H	£150	
2		Metallic light green body, metallic dark green chassis	Metallic light green	No	Bright red	Bright red	Brass	Black	Chrome 24 spoke	Type B	Riveted	No	LESNEY © 1973 * ENGLAND	R	H	£150	
3		Metallic light green body, metallic dark green chassis	Metallic light green	No	Bright red	Bright red	Brass	Black	Chrome 24 spoke	Type B	Riveted	No	LESNEY © 1974 ENGLAND		H	£12	✓
4		Metallic light green body, metallic dark green chassis	Metallic light green	No	Dark red*	Bright red	Brass	Black	Chrome 24 spoke	Type B	Riveted	No	LESNEY © 1974 ENGLAND	S	H	£75	
5		Metallic lime* green body, metallic dark green chassis	Metallic lime green *	No	Dark red*	Bright red	Brass	Black	Chrome 24 spoke	Type B	Riveted	No	LESNEY © 1974 ENGLAND	S	H	£75	
6	1979	Cream body, bright red top panels, darker red chassis	Bright red	No	Bright red*	Bright red	Silver	Black	Chrome 24 spoke (WW)	Type B	Riveted	No	LESNEY © 1974 ENGLAND	S	I	£45	
7		Cream body, bright red top panels, darker red chassis	Bright red	No	Bright red*	Black	Silver	Black	Chrome 24 spoke (WW)	Type B	Riveted	No	LESNEY © 1974 ENGLAND	S	I	£45	
8		Cream body, bright red top panels, darker red chassis	Bright red	No	Black	Black	Silver	Black	Chrome 24 spoke (WW)	Type B	Riveted	No	LESNEY © 1974 ENGLAND		I	£10	
9		Cream body, bright red top panels, darker red chassis	Bright red	Yes	Bright red*	Black	Silver	Black	Chrome 24 spoke (WW)	Type B	Riveted	No	LESNEY © 1974 ENGLAND	S	I	£45	
10		Cream body, bright red top panels, darker red chassis	Bright red	Yes	Bright red*	Dark red	Silver	Black	Chrome 24 spoke (WW)	Type B	Riveted	No	LESNEY © 1974 ENGLAND	S	I	£45	
11		Cream body, bright red top panels, darker red chassis	Bright red	Yes	Black	Black	Silver	Black	Chrome 24 spoke (WW)	Type B	Riveted	No	LESNEY © 1974 ENGLAND		I	£10	

DIAGRAM 1 REAR BUMPER

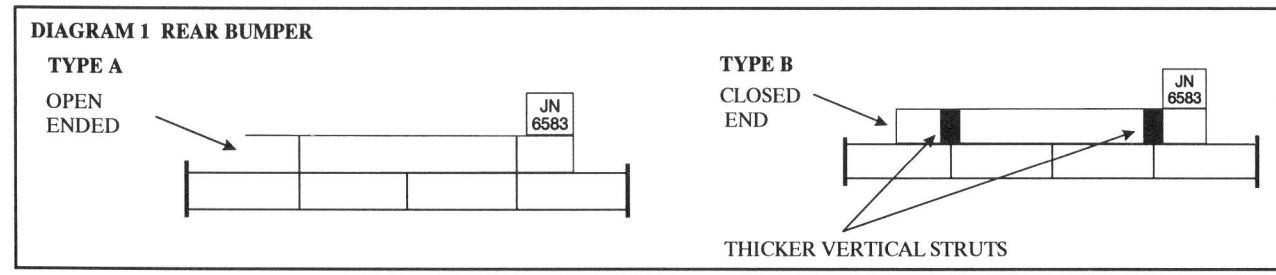

TYPE A — OPEN ENDED

TYPE B — CLOSED END — THICKER VERTICAL STRUTS

NOTES

BECKENHAM APPEAL MODEL
Maroon body and chassis, bright red seat and grille.
Chrome 24 spoke wheels.
Brass plated parts.

Y14-3 1931 STUTZ BEARCAT CONTINUED   Scale 1:44

In 1990 the baseplate text was changed to Matchbox Int. Ltd. and for obvious reasons the country of origin to 'Made in Macau'. However no logic explains the copyright date being changed from 1974 to 1979. Other noted changes to the baseplate at this time were raised perimeters to the front and rear rivet holes, a recessed rivet hole in the engine sump, and a square block between the engine and prop-shaft for the screw hole. Total production of Issues 19-21, was 29,553. The Stutz Bearcat was released again in 1995 as one of six re colours in the Grand Marques Series; similar in casting to the 1990 release. The enhanced detailing was more extensive. These sold for £12.50.

ISSUE	YEAR OF RELEASE	COLOURS	DOOR TOPS	CAST 'V' RIDGE ON BOAT TAIL	SEATS	GRILLE	PLATED PARTS	STEERING WHEEL	WHEELS	REAR BUMPER	AXLES	THREADED SCREW HOLE	BASEPLATE	RARITY	BOX TYPE	VALUE	CHECK LIST
12		Cream body, bright red top panels, darker red chassis	Cream	Yes	Black	Black	Silver	Black	Chrome 24 spoke (WW)	Type B	Riveted	No	LESNEY © 1974 ENGLAND		I	£10	
13		Cream body, bright red top panels, darker red chassis	Cream	Yes	Black	Dark red	Silver	Black	Chrome 24 spoke (WW)	Type B	Riveted	No	LESNEY © 1974 ENGLAND		I	£10	
14	1981	Cream body, emerald green chassis	Cream	Yes	Black	Dark red	Silver	Black	Chrome 24 spoke (WW)	Type B	Riveted	No	LESNEY © 1974 ENGLAND		I	£10	
15		Cream body, emerald green chassis	Cream	Yes	Black	Black	Silver	Black	Chrome 24 spoke (WW)	Type B	Riveted	No	LESNEY © 1974 ENGLAND		I / J	£10	✓
16		Cream body, emerald green chassis	Cream	Yes	Black	Black	Silver	Black	Red 12* spoke (WW)	Type B	Riveted	No	LESNEY © 1974 ENGLAND	D	I / J	£25	
17	1985	French blue body, battleship grey chassis	French blue	Yes	Tan	Black	Silver	Black	Chrome 24 spoke	Type B	Riveted	No	LESNEY © 1974 ENGLAND		J	£8	
18		French blue body, battleship grey chassis	French blue	Yes	Oatmeal pale tan	Black	Silver	Black	Chrome 24 spoke	Type B	Riveted	No	LESNEY © 1974 ENGLAND		J	£8	✓
19	1990	Dark blue body & top panels cream side panels, dark blue chassis	Dark blue	Yes	Dark red	Black	Bright silver	Tan with black spokes	Chrome 24 spoke (WF)	Type B	Press-fit	Yes	MATCHBOX © 1979 MACAU		P/N	£12	✓
20		Dark blue body & top panels cream side panels, dark blue chassis	Dark blue	Yes	Maroon	Black	Bright silver	Tan with black spokes	Chrome 24 spoke (WF)	Type B	Press-fit	Yes	MATCHBOX © 1979 MACAU		N	£10	
21		Dark blue body & top panels cream side panels, dark blue chassis	Dark blue	Yes	Maroon	Black	Bright silver	Light olive green with black spokes	Chrome 24 spoke (WF)	Type B	Press-fit	Yes	MATCHBOX © 1979 MACAU		N	£10	
22	1995	Bright red body and top panels, gloss black chassis	Bright red	Yes	Light tan	Black	Bright silver	Black with light tan spokes	Chrome 24 spoke (WF)	Type B	Press-fit	Yes	MATCHBOX © 1979 CHINA		N 2		

NOTES

1. All issues to 1985 have cast number plate digits 'JN6583'.
2. 1990 issues have blue on yellow tampo printed digits '88 86513'.
3. 1995 issue does not have digits.

Y14-4 1935 E.R.A "R.1.B"

Scale 1:35

INVESTMENT COMMENT
ORIGINAL PRICE £4.25p
Both colour schemes are seldom seen on sale. The black issue is harder to locate and has more potential than the yellow and blue models.

Originally intended to be a 1936 ERA, the recent death of its owner the Honorable Patrick Lindsay brought about the change to the 1935 Type R.1.B. as a mark of respect. Some pre-production examples do have 1936 cast on the base. The Type R.1.B. was owned by Patrick Marsh. In 1935, this was the first Type B and was purchased by Richard Seaman whose colours were black. In this guise, the Yesteryear model had a plastic chassis. After production moved to Macau, Matchbox released the recoloured version, which had been christened 'Romulus' by its owner Prince Bira of Siam (now known as Thailand). The recoloured Yesteryear model now had a diecast chassis. The R.1.B. version was one of the four racing cars launched in conjunction with Matchbox's decision to sponsor certain Formula One racing events. The sponsorship did not happen but the four car set was released. In 1991 when Yesteryear production was being carried out in China, the Romulus version was resurrected for a special order, together with five other models from the range for Poland. These six models are now known on the 'Chinese Six'! Due to economic and political factors however, the majority of this order was distributed through Woolworths and Tesco stores in the UK. No casting variations were noticed, although the wheels had been made in a paler yellow plastic. It was also one of the first Yesteryears to have press-fit axles.

ISSUE	YEAR OF RELEASE	COLOURS	SEATS/DASH BOARD	UNDERSIDE ENGINE/GEAR BOX	GRILLE	STEERING WHEEL	PLASTIC PARTS	WHEELS	BASEPLATE	RARITY	BOX TYPE	VALUE	CHECK LIST
1	1986	Glossy black body & chassis	Reddish brown	Light grey	Light grey	Light grey	Light grey	Bright chrome 24 spoke	MATCHBOX © 1986 ENGLAND		J	£15	✔
2		Glossy black body & chassis	Reddish brown	Light grey	Light grey	Light grey	Light grey	Aluminuim 24 spoke	MATCHBOX © 1986 ENGLAND		J	£15	
3	1988	French racing blue body, yellow chassis	Black	Grey	Grey	Grey	Grey	Yellow 24 spoke	MATCHBOX © 1986 MACAU		J1	£10	✔
4		French racing blue body, dark yellow chassis	Black	Grey	Grey	Grey	Grey	Yellow 24 spoke	MATCHBOX © 1986 MACAU		J1	£10	
5	1991	French racing blue body, yellow chassis	Black	Grey	Grey	Grey	Grey	Lighter yellow 24 spoke	MATCHBOX © 1986 CHINA*	S	J2	£15	
6		French racing blue body, dark yellow chassis	Black	Grey	Grey	Grey	Grey	Lighter yellow 24 spoke	MATCHBOX © 1986 CHINA*	S	J2	£15	

LIVERY ISSUES 1 & 2

Tampo
Racing number '7' in black on light grey disc both sides of tail.
Racing number '7' in black on radiator grille.

LIVERY ISSUES 3 to 6

Tampo
Racing number '4' in black on light grey disc, both sides of tail.
Racing number '4' in black on radiator grille.
Three small red, white, blue, white and red striped flags on both sides of tail and side of bonnet with red white and blue Union Flag off side of bonnet.

NOTES

Y15-1 1907 ROLLS ROYCE SILVER GHOST — Scale 1:55

INVESTMENT COMMENT
ORIGINAL PRICE £0.18p

A huge seller with an exceptionally lengthy production life. Most interest still remains with Issues 1 and 2 and the dark green seated issue. Good value exists in all issues, regarded by many collectors as a first series model.

This was the model which extended the Y numbers beyond the original cut-off figure of Y14. It also heralded the use of metallic effect paintwork and plastic seats. It started the policy of having at least one Rolls Royce current within the Yesteryear range, this example being modelled on the original Silver Ghost owned by Rolls Royce Motors. The overall livery can vary from very light (almost silver) green to mid-green and the gold paint on the radiator shell and sidelights can be omitted. Original road wheels were given a dull silver finish and had split rim bolt head detailing. A second production run saw these wheels with a brass finish; but all other runs had wheels with stepped, less detailed rims and which had either 2 or 4 triangular braces on the inside face. Models can be found with any combination of these later design wheels. This model was used extensively for the plated gift-ware series and this is reflected by the many changes made to the baseplate casting; no fewer than 4 different types. Issue 6 onwards had thicker sidelight arms than previous issues; and the detailing of the steering wheel boss, originally with a central pip, was changed to a domed shape. The spare tyre carrier altered only slightly in design; but later issues had a new design in as much that it had a "stepped" rim (Type B). This popular model was "retired" in 1968.

ISSUE	YEAR OF RELEASE	COLOURS	SEATS	WHEELS	WHEEL TYPE	TYRES	HEADLAMPS & FRONT NUMBER PLATE	RADIATOR SHELL & SIDELIGHTS	REAR NUMBER PLATE	REAR LIGHT	BASEPLATE TYPE	SPARE TYRE CARRIER	BASEPLATE	RARITY	BOX TYPE	VALUE	CHECK LIST
1	1960	Metallic light green body, bonnet & chassis	Black	Silver 12 spoke	Type A	Grey knobbly*	Silver	Gold	Silver*	Red*	A	A	LESNEY ENGLAND	R	C	£55	
2		Metallic light green body, bonnet & chassis	Black	Silver 12 spoke	Type A	Grey knobbly*	Silver	Gold	Metallic light green	Metallic light green	A	A	LESNEY ENGLAND	S	C	£55	
3		Metallic light green body, bonnet & chassis	Black	Silver 12 spoke	Type A	Black knobbly	Silver	Gold	Metallic light green	Metallic light green	A	A	LESNEY ENGLAND		C	£30	
4		Metallic light green body, bonnet & chassis	Black	Brass 12 spoke	Type A	Black knobbly	Silver	Gold	Metallic light green	Metallic light green	A	A	LESNEY ENGLAND		C/D1	£30	
5		Metallic light green body, bonnet & chassis	Black	Brass 12 spoke	Type A	Black knobbly	Silver	Gold	Metallic light green	Metallic light green	B	A	LESNEY ENGLAND		C/D1	£30	
6		Metallic light green body, bonnet & chassis	Black	Brass 12 spoke	Type B*	Black fine	Silver	Gold	Metallic light green	Metallic light green	B	A or B	LESNEY ENGLAND	D	D1/D2	£40	
7		Metallic light green body, bonnet & chassis	Black	Brass 12 spoke	Type B*	Black fine	Silver	Gold	Metallic light green	Metallic light green	C	A or B	LESNEY ENGLAND	D	D1/D2	£30	
8		Metallic light green body, bonnet & chassis	Black	Brass 12 spoke	Type C	Black fine	Silver	Gold	Metallic light green	Metallic light green	C	A or B	LESNEY ENGLAND		D2/D3/E	£30	2x✓✓
9		Metallic light green body, bonnet & chassis	Dark green*	Brass 12 spoke	Type C	Black fine	Silver	Gold	Metallic light green	Metallic light green	C	A or B	LESNEY ENGLAND	R	D3/E/E1	£70	
10		Metallic light green body, bonnet & chassis	Black	Brass 12 spoke	Type C	Black fine	Silver	Gold	Metallic light green	Metallic light green	D	B	LESNEY ENGLAND		E/F	£22	

BASEPLATES

TYPE A DOME HEADED BOSS AT REAR CROSS MEMBER WITH DOME IN CENTRE OF BASEPLATE

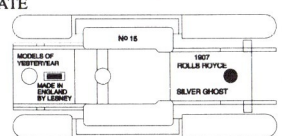

TYPE B AS 'A' FLAT HEADED BOSS AT REAR HOLE 7mm TO REAR OF FRONT RIVET

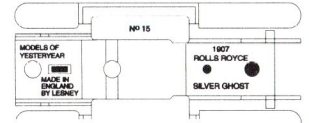

TYPE C AS 'B' BUT HOLLOW BOSS AT REAR OF BASEPLATE. NO GAPS BETWEEN RUNNING BOARDS/REAR MUDGUARDS/CHASSIS AREA

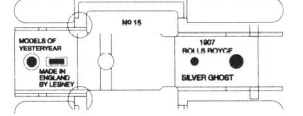

TYPE D AS 'B' BUT REAR PLATFORM EXTENDED FORWARD TO JOIN CENTRAL CROSS MEMBER HOLE TO REAR OF FRONT RIVET DELETED

NO GAPS BETWEEN RUNNING BOARDS/REAR MUDGUARDS & CHASSIS AREA

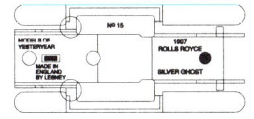

NOTES

Later issues with grey tyres have been reported but their authenticity is suspect!

ROAD WHEELS

TYPE A SILVER OR BRASS FINISH SPLIT RIM WITH BOLT HEAD DETAIL

TYPE B SILVER OR BRASS FINISH ONLY, SINGLE WIDTH RIM

TYPE C BRASS FINISH ONLY. STEPPED RIM WITH 2 OR 4 TRIANGULAR BRACES ON INSIDE FACE BETWEEN SPOKES & HUB

SPARE TYRE CARRIER TYPES

TYPE 'A' SINGLE WIDTH RIM

TYPE 'B' STEPPED RIM

INVESTMENT COMMENT
ORIGINAL PRICE £0.50p
It is still believed that most of the standard issues remain undervalued and that they have good growth potential.

Y15-2 1930 PACKARD VICTORIA   Scale 1:46

Introduced in 1969, this model was not withdrawn until 1987. Three main casting variations were made. Firstly the two triangular brackets both sides of the steering wheel hole in the dashboard were lengthened; Type 2. Secondly the two webs which were part of the base casting and were directly beneath or above the rear axle (whichever way you look at them) were deleted to allow the axles to be fitted easily; and thirdly the cast coachline on the top of the rear side panels was made deeper; Type B. All the plastic components, the grilles, hoods, seats and rear luggage trunks, are easily interchangeable which has accounted for countless permutations, some authentic, but many not. Plastic components in blue, grey, yellow, red, green, orange, pink and brown, mostly occuring on Issues 6 and 7 were the results of plastic trials and were never officially released by the factory. Several moulds were used for the front and rear bumpers, and the radiator/headlights components and minor differences can be detected, but are not worthy of separate codes. The model was only issued in four basic colour schemes, the lime gold being the most attractive. Issue 11 is a transitional model, and is extremely hard to find.

ISSUE	YEAR OF RELEASE	COLOURS	SIDE PANELS	SEATS	GRILLE	HOOD	REAR LUGGAGE TRUNK	PLATED PARTS	WHEELS	REAR PANELS CAST COACHLINE	REAR AXLE SUPPORT WEBS	STEERING WHEEL HOUSING BRACKETS	BASEPLATE	RARITY	BOX TYPE	VALUE	CHECK LIST
1	1969	Metallic brown/gold body & bonnet, dark brown chassis	Metallic brown/gold	Maroon*	Maroon*	Maroon textured	Maroon	Brass	Brass 24 spoke	Type 'A' thin	Cast	Type 1*	LESNEY © 1969 ENGLAND	S	G	£35	✓
2		Metallic brown/gold body & bonnet, dark brown chassis	Metallic brown/gold	Dark red	Bright red	Maroon textured	Maroon	Brass	Brass 24 spoke	Type 'A' thin	Cast	Type 1*	LESNEY © 1969 ENGLAND	D	G	£30	✓
3		Metallic brown/gold body & bonnet, dark brown chassis	Metallic brown/gold	Dark red	Bright red	Dark red textured	Dark red	Brass	Brass 24 spoke	Type 'A' thin	Cast	Type 2	LESNEY © 1969 ENGLAND		G	£18	
4		Metallic brown/gold body & bonnet, dark brown chassis	Metallic brown/gold	Dark red	Bright red	Dark red textured	Dark red	Brass	Brass 24 spoke	Type 'A' thin	Not cast*	Type 2	LESNEY © 1969 ENGLAND	D	G	£30	
5	1974	Metallic brown/gold body & bonnet, dark brown chassis	Metallic brown/gold	Dark red	Bright red	Dark red textured	Dark red	Brass	Chrome 24 spoke*	Type 'A' thin	Not cast*	Type 2	LESNEY © 1969 ENGLAND	S	H	£50	
6		Metallic lime gold body & bonnet, dark brown chassis	Metallic lime gold	Dark red	Bright red	Maroon textured	Maroon	Brass	Chrome 24 spoke	Type 'A' thin	Not cast	Type 2	LESNEY © 1969 ENGLAND		H	£15	
7		Metallic lime gold body & bonnet, dark brown chassis	Metallic lime gold	Dark red	Dark red	Dark red textured	Dark red	Brass	Chrome 24 spoke	Type 'A' thin	Not cast	Type 2	LESNEY © 1969 ENGLAND		H	£15	
8		Metallic lime gold body & bonnet, dark brown chassis	Metallic lime gold	Dark red	Dark red	Black textured	Black	Brass	Chrome 24 spoke	Type 'A' thin	Not cast	Type 2	LESNEY © 1969 ENGLAND		H	£15	
9		Metallic lime gold body & bonnet, dark brown chassis	Metallic lime gold	Dark red	Dark red	Black textured	Black	Brass	Chrome 12 spoke	Type 'A' thin	Not cast	Type 2	LESNEY © 1969 ENGLAND		H	£15	
10		Metallic lime gold body & bonnet, dark brown chassis	Metallic lime gold	Dark red	Dark red	Black textured	Black	Brass	Chrome 24 spoke	Type 'B' thick*	Not cast	Type 2	LESNEY © 1969 ENGLAND	S	H	£60	

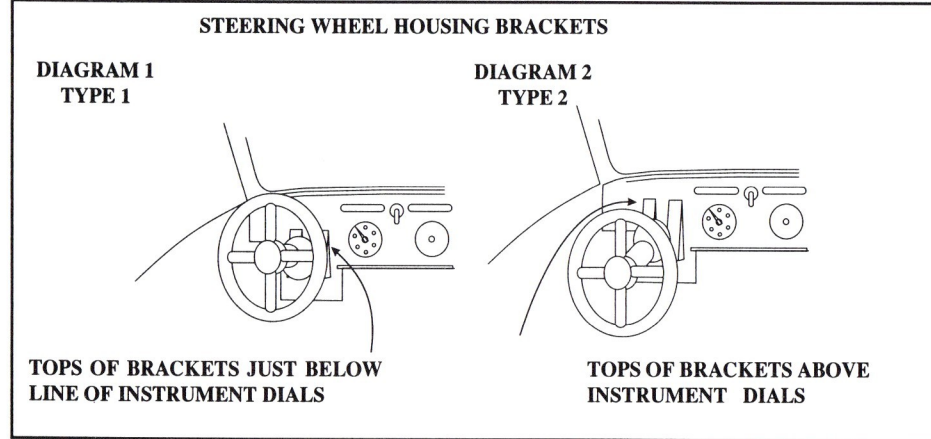

STEERING WHEEL HOUSING BRACKETS

DIAGRAM 1 TYPE 1 — TOPS OF BRACKETS JUST BELOW LINE OF INSTRUMENT DIALS

DIAGRAM 2 TYPE 2 — TOPS OF BRACKETS ABOVE INSTRUMENT DIALS

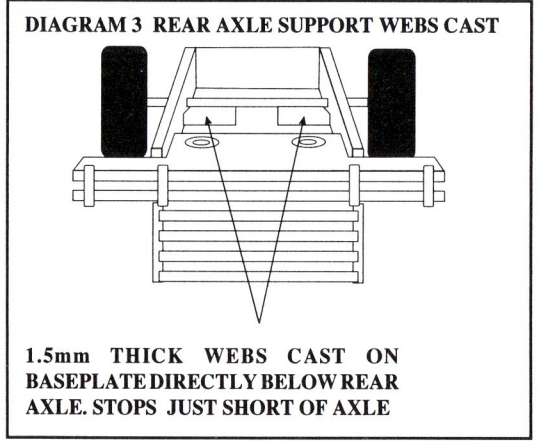

DIAGRAM 3 REAR AXLE SUPPORT WEBS CAST

1.5mm THICK WEBS CAST ON BASEPLATE DIRECTLY BELOW REAR AXLE. STOPS JUST SHORT OF AXLE

NOTES
BECKENHAM APPEAL MODEL
Pale grey body, dark grey chassis, dark red seats and trunk black hood. Bright red grille. Chrome 24 spoke wheels. Brass plated parts.

Y15-2 1930 PACKARD VICTORIA CONTINUED   Scale 1:46

ISSUE	YEAR OF RELEASE	COLOURS	SIDE PANELS	SEATS	GRILLE	HOOD	REAR LUGGAGE TRUNK	PLATED PARTS	WHEELS	REAR PANELS CAST COACHLINE	REAR AXLE SUPPORT WEBS	STEERING WHEEL HOUSING	BASEPLATE	RARITY	BOX TYPE	VALUE	CHECK LIST
11		Metallic lime gold body & bonnet, gloss black* chassis	Metallic lime gold	Dark red	Dark red	Black textured	Black	Brass	Chrome 24 spoke	Type 'B' thick	Not cast	Type 2	LESNEY © 1969 ENGLAND	V R	H	£250	
12	1979	Glossy black body bonnet & chassis	Red	Dark red	Black	Black textured	Black	Silver	Chrome solid (WW)	Type 'B' thick	Not cast	Type 2	LESNEY © 1969 ENGLAND		I	£10	
13		Glossy black body bonnet & chassis	Red	Dark red	Black	White textured	Black	Silver	Chrome 24 spoke (WW)	Type 'B' thick	Not cast	Type 2	LESNEY © 1969 ENGLAND		I	£10	
14		Glossy black body, bonnet & chassis	Red	Dark red	Black	White textured	Black	Silver	Chrome solid (WW)	Type 'B' thick	Not cast	Type 2	LESNEY © 1969 ENGLAND		I	£10	✓ 2x
15		Glossy black body, bonnet & chassis	Red	Dark red	Dark red	White textured	Dark red*	Silver	Chrome solid (WW)	Type 'B' thick	Not cast	Type 2	LESNEY © 1969 ENGLAND	D	I	£15	
16		Glossy black body, bonnet & chassis	Red	Bright red*	Black	White textured	Black	Silver	Chrome solid (WW)	Type 'B' thick	Not cast	Type 2	LESNEY © 1969 ENGLAND	S	I	£20	
17	1984	Dark sand/cream body & bonnet, dark brown chassis	Dark sand/cream	Dark red*	Black	Brown textured	Black	Silver	Bright red 24 spoke (WW)	Type 'B' thick	Not cast	Type 2	LESNEY © 1969 ENGLAND	S	J	£20	
18		Dark sand/cream body & bonnet, dark brown chassis	Dark sand/cream	Light tan	Black	Brown textured	Black	Silver	Bright red 24 spoke (WW)	Type 'B' thick	Not cast	Type 2	LESNEY © 1969 ENGLAND		J	£8	✓
19		Dark sand/cream body & bonnet, dark brown chassis	Dark sand/cream	Light tan	Black	Brown textured	Black	Silver	Red 12 spoke	Type 'B' thick	Not cast	Type 2	LESNEY © 1969 ENGLAND		J	£9	
20	1984	Dark sand/cream body & bonnet, dark brown chassis	Dark sand/cream	Light tan	Black	White textured	Black	Silver	Bright red 24 spoke (WW)	Type 'B' thick	Not cast	Type 2	LESNEY © 1969 ENGLAND		J	£8	
21		Dark sand/cream body & bonnet, dark brown chassis	Dark sand/cream	Light tan	Black	Orange brown* textured	Black	Silver	Bright red 24 spoke (WW)	Type 'B' thick	Not cast	Type 2	LESNEY © 1969 ENGLAND	R	J	£100	

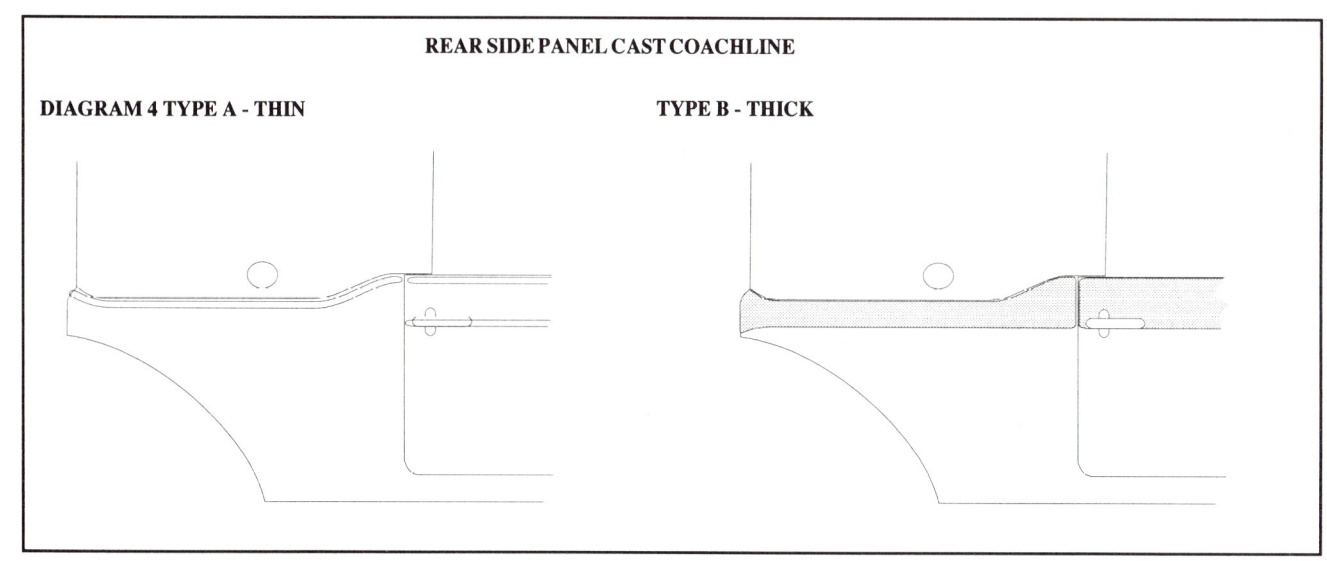

REAR SIDE PANEL CAST COACHLINE

DIAGRAM 4 TYPE A - THIN   TYPE B - THICK

NOTES

Y15-3 1920 PRESTON TRAM CAR   Scale 1:87

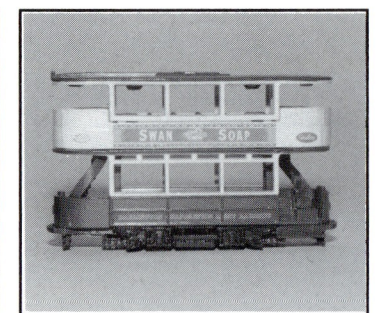

LONDON TRANSPORT. This was the second time that a tram had been featured in the Yesteryear range: the first being the Y3-1. Its large size meant that much more intricate detailing was possible than previously. The first issue was in London Transport livery. Early production models had a gap between the resistor box and passenger compartment, see Diagram 1; but during the casting process metal flow problems occured and the gap was partially filled in see Diagram 2. On all issues the upper deck had a large hole which corresponded with the hole in the lower deck ceiling. A second baseplate type was used which had the letter 'A' adjacent to the area of the rivet on the axle housing and wheel grid. The letter 'A' type baseplates have slightly larger axle housings than the non letter type. The wheel finishes can vary from matt bronze to glossy black. The London Transport livery was issued as part of the 1987 UK Passport Scheme, as well as a range model a little later. Only 8,000 models were released in framed cabinets worldwide.
DARLINGTON CORPORATION. This new livery was designated as being on a Preston type tram! There are no visible casting differences. The Darlington Corporation tram was not made with the first type resistor box castings. It was released in March 1988 as a Limited Edition, and a total of 51,070 models were made.

A : LONDON TRANSPORT

ISSUE	YEAR OF RELEASE	COLOURS	UPPER DECK BODY COLOUR	ROOF	SEATS	FLOOR/ STAIRS	WINDOW FRAMES	LOGO	RESISTOR BOX	SIDE FRAME	BASEPLATE TYPE	THREADED SCREW HOLE	BASEPLATE	RARITY	BOX TYPE	VALUE	CHECK LIST
1	1987	London Transport red body, dark grey chassis	London Transport red	Dark grey	Light brown	Light brown	White	SWAN VESTAS	Type 1	Type A	No "A"	No	MATCHBOX © 1987 MACAU		J1/M	£10/£70	✓
2		London Transport red body, dark grey chassis	London Transport red	Dark grey	Light brown	Light brown	White	SWAN VESTAS	Type 1	Type A	With "A"	No	MATCHBOX © 1987 MACAU		J1/M	£10/£70	
3		London Transport red body, dark grey chassis	London Transport red	Dark grey	Light brown	Light brown	White	SWAN VESTAS	Type 2*	Type A	No "A"*	No	MATCHBOX © 1987 MACAU	D	J1/M	£15/£80	
4		London Transport red body, dark grey chassis	London Transport red	Dark grey	Light brown	Light brown	White	SWAN VESTAS	Type 2	Type A	With "A"	No	MATCHBOX © 1987 MACAU		J1/M	£10/£70	

B : DARLINGTON CORPORATION

ISSUE	YEAR OF RELEASE	COLOURS	UPPER DECK BODY COLOUR	ROOF	SEATS	FLOOR/ STAIRS	WINDOW FRAMES	LOGO	RESISTOR BOX	SIDE FRAME	BASEPLATE TYPE	THREADED SCREW HOLE	BASEPLATE	RARITY	BOX TYPE	VALUE	CHECK LIST
1	1988	Royal blue body, grey chassis	Off-white	Royal blue	Light brown	Light brown	Off-white	SWAN SOAP	Type 2	Type A	No "A"*	No	MATCHBOX © 1987 MACAU	D	J	£15	
2		Royal blue body, grey chassis	Off-white	Royal blue	Light brown	Light brown	Off-white	SWAN SOAP	Type 2	Type A	With "A"	No	MATCHBOX © 1987 MACAU		J	£10	✓

DIAGRAM 1 RESISTOR BOX

TYPE 1

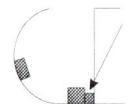

RESISTOR BOX (UNDER STAIRS) WITH GAP BETWEEN ITSELF & LOWER DECK PARTITION

VIEWED FROM ABOVE THE DRIVER'S POSITION

DIAGRAM 2 RESISTOR BOX

TYPE 2

GAP BETWEEN RESISTOR BOX & LOWER DECK PARTITION FILLED IN

VIEWED FROM ABOVE THE DRIVER'S POSITION

LIVERY LONDON TRANSPORT
Tampo
Lower deck panel. LONDON TRANSPORT in gold. Upper side panels. SWAN VESTAS adverts in red, yellow and green.
Upper deck curved panels. CEREBOS advert in blue & white, and HORLICKS MALTED MILK advert in blue & white Ornamental advertising grille in black on lower deck panels beneath stairway, both ends.

LIVERY DARLINGTON
Tampo
Lower deck panel. DARLINGTON CORPORATION LIGHT RAILWAYS in gold.
Upper side panels. SWAN SOAP adverts in pale cream & light & dark blue.
Upper deck curved panels CEREBOS advert in blue & pale cream, HORLICKS THE ORIGINAL MALTED MILK in blue and pale cream.

ORIGINAL PRICE, LONDON, £5.25p DARLINGTON £5.50
LONDON TRANSPORT The framed cabinet model is seldom seen offered for sale below £70. This attractively presented model enjoys worldwide popularity. A small production run and surely that means values will continue to increase.
DARLINGTON Not particularly attractive and little, or no interest has been recorded.

NOTES

Y15-3 1920 PRESTON TRAM CAR (CONTINUED)   Scale 1:87

PAISLEY DISTRICT. The third livery was that of 'Paisley District Tramways' and no doubt due to its attractive appearance sold extremely well. No new casting modifications have been noted and no examples with first type resistor box areas or baseplates without the letter 'A' have been reported. It is possible to find roof components fitted the wrong way round so that the passengers would be facing 'backward'; which also applies to the Darlington Corporation model. It was released as the standard range model in July 1989 and a total of 33,588 were produced.

NEWCASTLE CORPORATION. After Yesteryear production moved to the new factory in China, the Newcastle Corporation livery was one of the first models to be made there. All models were fitted with the second type resistor box bodies and with letter 'A' baseplates. However the base side frame comprising the axle boxes springs and side rail components on the chassis, had been redesigned; Type B. Pre-production examples have been seen with the Newcastle Corporation model attached to the unmodified side frame; Type A. The baseplate was amended to read 'Made in China' and a post was cast into the chassis. This was one of the first models to use this method of securing by a self tapping screw in the box. Also it was noted that the colours of the upper deck advert panels and the lower deck panels immediately below the window frames were finished in either yellow or orange colours.

C : PAISLEY DISTRICT

ISSUE	YEAR OF RELEASE	COLOURS	UPPER DECK BODY COLOUR	ROOF	SEATS	FLOOR/ STAIRS	WINDOW FRAMES	LOGO	TAMPO DECORATION LOWER PANELS	TAMPO DECORATION UPPER PANELS	RESISTOR BOX	SIDE FRAME	BASEPLATE TYPE	THREADED SCREW HOLE	BASEPLATE	RARITY	BOX TYPE	VALUE	CHECK LIST
1	1989	Orange body black chassis	Cream	Light grey	Light brown	Light brown	Cream	GOLDEN SHRED	No change	No change	Type 2	Type A	With 'A'	No	MATCHBOX © 1987 MACAU		J 1	£12	✓

D : NEWCASTLE CORPORATION

ISSUE	YEAR OF RELEASE	COLOURS	UPPER DECK BODY COLOUR	ROOF	SEATS	FLOOR/ STAIRS	WINDOW FRAMES	LOGO	TAMPO DECORATION LOWER PANELS	TAMPO DECORATION UPPER PANELS	RESISTOR BOX	SIDE FRAME	BASEPLATE TYPE	THREADED SCREW HOLE	BASEPLATE	RARITY	BOX TYPE	VALUE	CHECK LIST
1	1991	Dark brown body black chassis	Dark brown	Dark grey	Black	Black	Pale cream	ZEBRA GRATE POLISH	Yellow	Yellow	Type 2	Type B	With 'A'	Yes	MATCHBOX © 1987 CHINA		N 1	£10	✓
2		Dark brown body black chassis	Dark brown	Dark grey	Black	Black	Pale cream	ZEBRA GRATE POLISH	Orange	Yellow	Type 2	Type B	With 'A'	Yes	MATCHBOX © 1987 CHINA		N 1	£10	✓
3		Dark brown body black chassis	Dark brown	Dark grey	Black	Black	Pale cream	ZEBRA GRATE POLISH	Yellow	Orange	Type 2	Type B	With 'A'	Yes	MATCHBOX © 1987 CHINA		N 1	£10	
4		Dark brown body black chassis	Dark brown	Dark grey	Black	Black	Pale cream	ZEBRA GRATE POLISH	Orange	Orange	Type 2	Type B	With 'A'	Yes	MATCHBOX © 1987 CHINA		N 1	£10	

DIAGRAM 1 SIDE FRAMES

TYPE A

TYPE B

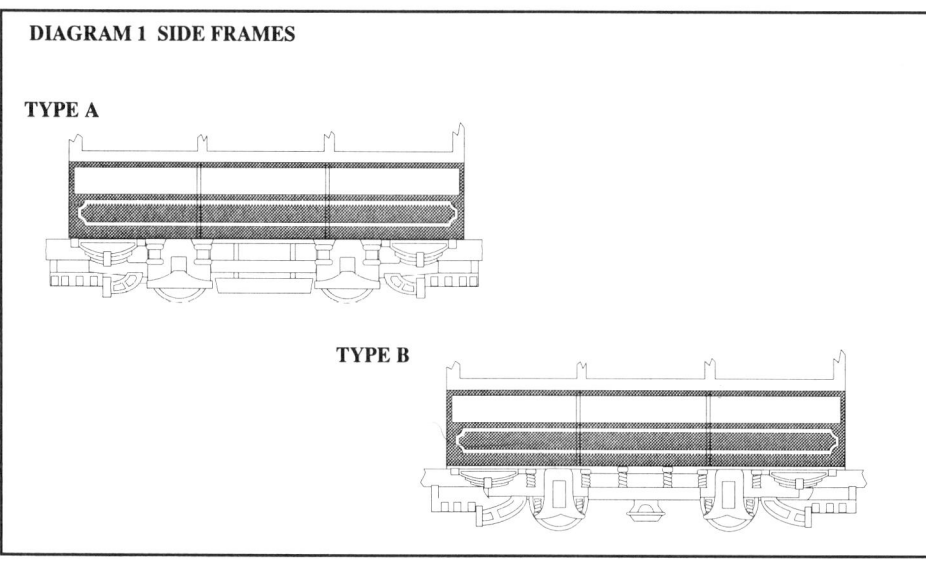

LIVERY PAISLEY DISTRICT
Tampo
Lower body panels. Orange PAISLEY DISTRICT TRAMWAYS with black shadow effect in light cream panel. All within black coachlining. All below centred black and red device within black decorated coachlining.
Upper body panels. Two blue, black, red and cream figures holding a blue panel with cream ROBERTSON'S and MARMALADE each side of blue PUT THE TASTE ON YOUR TOAST WITH, above dark blue outlined orange GOLDEN SHRED. All within dark blue coachlining.

LIVERY NEWCASTLE CORPORATION
Tampo
Lower body panels. Gold NEWCASTLE CORPORATION TRANSPORT with gold coachlining, below crest on yellow or orange panel with gold coachlining.
Upper body panels. Red ZEBRA GRATE POLISH with black shaodw effect. Black and white Zebra head on white square each end of panel. All within reddish-brown coachlining.
Upper curved panels. White DAILY SKETCH with black shadow effect on red panel each side of body panel.

INVESTMENT COMMENT
ORIGINAL PRICE, PAISLEY, £6.25p
NEWCASTLE, £7.25P

PAISLEY A relatively short production run which converts into potential for growth; but it may be slow in coming.
NEWCASTLE A drab colour scheme on the fourth Preston model resulted in a rather uninspiring release and has not attracted much attention.

NOTES

Y16-1 1904 SPYKER VETERAN AUTOMOBILE — Scale 1:45

INVESTMENT COMMENT
ORIGINAL PRICE £0.14.5p

Regarded by many collectors as being a true First Series models. Standard issues have maintained their values and Issues 5, 10 and 12 have appreciated. At present, prices represent good value with plenty of scope to increase.

The 1962 pocket catalogue showed an illustration of a pre-production Spyker in two tone green but this colour scheme was never released. Production models were initially for a short run only, finished in a very creamy pale yellow. Early models had wheels with bolt head detailing. They also had tyres with knobbly treads which were soon superseded by the more common smooth tread type. Gold paint was applied by hand to the radiator shell, the headlamp lens and sidelights. In later years this trim was not applied to the radiator shell. Models are known to exist with some or all of the gold trim omitted, especially on the maroon liveries. Paint used for the maroon parts of the Y13-1 Santa Fe was used on a small batch of Spykers. Towards the end of production the pale lemon yellow colour was replaced by a mustard yellow, which has been described as being a 'grubby' darker shade of yellow. The final run was in a 'cleaner' brighter dark yellow. Three different windscreen moulds were used throughout production. The brake/gear levers originally featured one of the levers with a curved stem but this was later replaced by a new component, with two straight levers. Also the steering wheel first had a detailed centre boss which eventually deteriorated to a flat dome. No particular year saw the deletion, or introduction of the levers, the windscreen frame or the steering wheel types and are impossible to list in chronological order. The listing of possible permutations is further complicated when the road wheels without the bolt head detail are considered, as these can have two, or four triangular braces on the inside face. Models have been seen with any combination of all three types of wheels on the one model! However separate listings have been given to the major casting modifications.

ISSUE	YEAR OF RELEASE	COLOURS	RADIATOR SHELL	WHEELS	WHEEL RIM BOLT HEAD DETAIL	TYRES	CHASSIS TO RUNNING BOARD PANEL TYPE	RUNNING BOARD SUPPORT PLATE	BASE PLATE TYPE	BASEPLATE	RARITY	BOX TYPE	VALUE	CHECK LIST
1	1961	Pale cream* yellow body & chassis	Gold	Brass 12 spoke	Yes	Grey knobbly*	1	1	A	LESNEY NO 16 ENGLAND	VR	D1	£350	
2		Pale lemon yellow body & chassis	Gold	Brass 12 spoke	Yes	Grey knobbly*	1	1	A	LESNEY NO 16 ENGLAND	R	D1	£70	
3		Pale lemon yellow body & chassis	Gold	Brass 12 spoke	Yes	Black knobbly*	1	1	A	LESNEY NO 16 ENGLAND	S	D1	£40	
4		Pale lemon yellow body & chassis	Gold	Brass 12 spoke	Yes	Black fine	1	1	A	LESNEY NO 16 ENGLAND		D1	£30	
5		Pale lemon yellow body & chassis	Gold	Brass 12 spoke	Yes	Black fine	1	1	B*	LESNEY NO 16 ENGLAND	R	D1	£100	
6		Maroon* body & chassis	Maroon*	Brass 12 spoke	Yes	Black knobbly	1	1	A	LESNEY NO 16 ENGLAND	ER	D1/D2	£1500	
7		Maroon* body & chassis	Maroon*	Brass 12 spoke	No	Black fine	1	1	A	LESNEY NO 16 ENGLAND	ER	D1	£1500	
8		Maroon* body & chassis	Maroon*	Brass 8 spoke*	No	Black knobbly	1	1	A	LESNEY NO 16 ENGLAND	ER	D2	£1500	
9		Pale lemon yellow body & chassis	Gold	Brass 12 spoke	No	Black fine	1	1	A	LESNEY NO 16 ENGLAND		D1/D2/D3	£25	
10		Pale lemon yellow body & chassis	Gold	Brass 12 spoke	No	Black fine	1	1	B*	LESNEY NO 16 ENGLAND	R	D2/D3/E	£100	
11		Pale lemon yellow body & chassis	Pale lemon yellow	Brass 12 spoke	No	Black fine	2	1	A	LESNEY NO 16 ENGLAND		D3/F	£25	
12		Pale lemon yellow body & chassis	Pale lemon yellow	Brass 12 spoke	No	Black fine	2	1	B*	LESNEY NO 16 ENGLAND	R	D3/E/E1	£100	

DIAGRAM 1 CHASSIS TO RUNNING BOARD PANELS

TYPE 1 — 2 PANEL EFFECT. GAPS BY MUDGUARDS

TYPE 2 — 4 PANEL EFFECT. NO GAPS

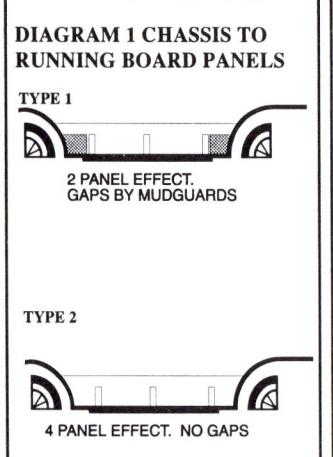

RUNNING BOARD SUPPORT PLATE

DIAGRAM 2
1st TYPE
0.5mm wide gap between baseplate and support plates.
*Diagram of chassis with 1st type running board panels

DIAGRAM 3
1st TYPE
*Diagram of chassis with 2nd type running board panels

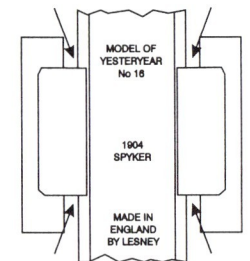

DIAGRAM 4
2nd TYPE
No gap between baseplate and support plates.
*This type only with 2nd type running boards

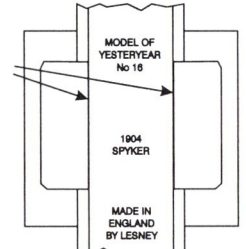

NOTES

Although there are too many possible combinations of variations for listing purposes, collectors should note that there are three windscreen types:-

a) The central strut joins the top and bottom members in a flush manner.

b) A rounder strut "overlaps" the members, and the side struts are thicker and rounder.

c) As (b) with strengthening wedges on both sides of the central strut base and also on the internal faces of the bases to the outer struts.

Y16-1 SPYKER VETERAN AUTOMOBILE CONTINUED Scale 1:45

The chassis to the running board panels was changed from a two panel effect to a four panel effect (Diagram 1). The second major alteration was to the running board support plates. Originally a gap existed on both sides of the baseplate area containing the text, rivets and the running board support plates. After the colour scheme was changed to mustard yellow, these two gaps were deleted (Diagrams 2, 3, and 4). The Spyker was also featured in the Giftware series and therefore the baseplate can have two hollow bosses; one of which deletes the text, Diagram 5. Finally the road wheels and twin levers can be found in bare metal. The seats were only released in dark green plastic.

ISSUE	YEAR OF RELEASE	COLOURS	RADIATOR SHELL	WHEELS	WHEEL RIM BOLT HEAD DETAIL	TYRES	CHASSIS TO RUNNING BOARD PANEL TYPE	RUNNING BOARD SUPPORT PLATE	BASEPLATE TYPE	BASEPLATE	RARITY	BOX TYPE	VALUE	CHECK LIST
13		Pale yellow body & chassis	Pale lemon yellow	Brass 12 spoke	No	Black fine	2	1	A	LESNEY NO 16 ENGLAND		D3/E/E1	£25	
14	1968	Mustard yellow body & chassis	Mustard yellow	Brass 12 spoke	No	Black fine	2	1	A	LESNEY NO 16 ENGLAND		D3/E/E1/F	£25	✓
15		Mustard yellow body & chassis	Mustard yellow	Brass 12 spoke	No	Black fine	2	2	A	LESNEY NO 16 ENGLAND		E1/F	£25	
16		Brighter yellow body & chassis	Brighter yellow	Brass 12 spoke	No	Black fine	2	2	A	LESNEY NO 16 ENGLAND		F	£25	

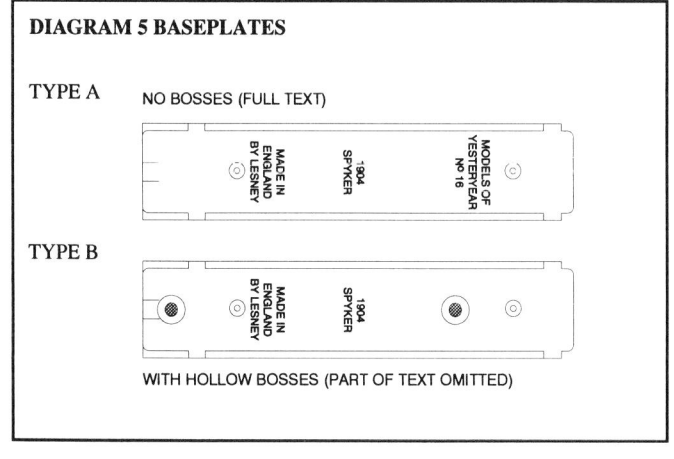

DIAGRAM 5 BASEPLATES

TYPE A NO BOSSES (FULL TEXT)

TYPE B WITH HOLLOW BOSSES (PART OF TEXT OMITTED)

NOTES

1. Although there are too many possible combinations of variations for listing purposes, collectors should note that there are three windscreen types:-
a. The central strut joins the top and bottom members in a flush manner.
b. A rounder strut "overlaps" the members, and the side struts are thicker and rounder.
c. As (b) with strengthening wedges on both sides of the central strut base and also on the internal faces of the bases to the outer struts.

INVESTMENT COMMENT
ORIGINAL PRICE £0.50p
Still a favourite model with collectors. A number of the two-tone green models have surfaced in the USA, and so the value of this popular issue has remained static. The two-tone blue model has fallen away slightly but should strengthen again, whereas the mid blue model with milky white panels has shown an increase.

Y16-2 1928 MERCEDES BENZ SS COUPE

Scale 1:45

One of the longest surviving models in the range; it was also one of the best sellers and produced several sought after variations. The first issue with cast rear differential is keenly sought after. Due to difficulties in fitting the rear axle, the cast differential housing was deleted early in the model's life. Also the rear luggage trunk was modified to have a textured finish. Collectors should beware of switching in relation to Issues 1 and 2. ie moving textured trunks to models with cast differentials. The Mercedes model initially had a separate full length exhaust pipe but due to distortion and breakages during the fettling process this component was replaced by a cast ridge on the baseplate to represent the exhaust pipe. The colour of the metallic lime green can vary from pale lime green to almost "grass" green. Models with a mixture of black and green grilles, hoods and seats have been reported; these of course can be genuine variations but could also arise due to switching between models! Because of the large number of possible permutations these have not been listed separately. To stimulate the US market, a batch of metallic lime green models were fitted with bases painted in the same dark metallic green as used on the first issues of the Y14-3 Stutz Bearcat. This variation should not be confused with the wide ranging tone differences to the lime green paints; which incidentally can fade with exposure to bright sunlight.

ISSUE	YEAR OF RELEASE	COLOURS	SIDE PANELS	STEERING WHEEL	SEATS	GRILLE	HOOD	REAR LUGGAGE TRUNK	PLATED PARTS	WHEELS	EXHAUST	REAR AXLE DIFFERENTIAL	AXLES	THREADED SCREW HOLE	BASEPLATE	RARITY	BOX TYPE	VALUE	CHECK LIST
1	1972	Silver body & bonnet, metallic red chassis	Silver	Black	Black	Black	Black textured	Black smooth*	Brass	Brass 24 spoke	Separate brass	Cast*	Riveted	No	LESNEY © 1972 ENGLAND	R	G	£125	
2		Silver body & bonnet, metallic red chassis	Silver	Black	Black	Black	Black textured	Black textured	Brass	Brass 24 spoke	Separate brass	Not cast	Riveted	No	LESNEY © 1972 ENGLAND		G	£45	
3		Silver body & bonnet, metallic red chassis	Silver	Black	Black	Black	Black textured	Black smooth*	Brass	Brass 24 spoke	Separate brass	Not cast	Riveted	No	LESNEY © 1972 ENGLAND	S	G	£35	
4	1974	Metallic lime green body & chassis	Metallic lime green	Black	Black	Black	Black textured	Black textured	Brass	Chrome 24 spoke	Separate brass	Not cast	Riveted	No	LESNEY © 1972 ENGLAND		H	£20	✓
5		Metallic lime green body & chassis	Metallic lime green	Black	Black	Black	Black textured	Black textured	Brass	Chrome 12 spoke*	Separate brass	Not cast	Riveted	No	LESNEY © 1972 ENGLAND	D	H	£30	
6		Metallic lime green body & chassis	Metallic lime green	Black	Dark green*	Dark green*	Dark green textured*	Dark green textured*	Brass	Chrome 12 spoke*	Separate brass	Not cast	Riveted	No	LESNEY © 1972 ENGLAND	S	H	£45	
7		Metallic lime green body & chassis	Metallic lime green	Black	Dark green*	Dark green*	Dark green textured*	Dark green textured*	Brass	Chrome 24 spoke	Separate brass	Not cast	Riveted	No	LESNEY © 1972 ENGLAND	S	H	£45	
8		Metallic lime green body & bonnet metallic dark (Stutz) green chassis*	Metallic lime green	Black	Black	Black	Black textured	Black textured	Brass	Chrome 24 spoke	Separate brass	Not cast	Riveted	No	LESNEY © 1972 ENGLAND	R	H	£225	
9		Metallic lime green body & chassis	Metallic lime green	Black	Dark green*	Dark green*	Dark green textured*	Dark green textured*	Brass	Chrome 24 spoke	Cast	Not cast	Riveted	No	LESNEY © 1972 ENGLAND	D	H	£35	
10		Metallic lime green body & chassis	Metallic lime green	Black	Black	Black	Black textured	Black textured	Brass	Chrome 24 spoke	Cast	Not cast	Riveted	No	LESNEY © 1972 ENGLAND		H	£20	
11		Metallic lime green body & chassis	Metallic lime green	Black	Black	Black	Black textured	Black textured	Brass	Dark green 12 spoke*	Cast	Not cast	Riveted	No	LESNEY © 1972 ENGLAND	S	H	£95	

DIAGRAM 1 REAR AXLE DIFFERENTIAL CAST

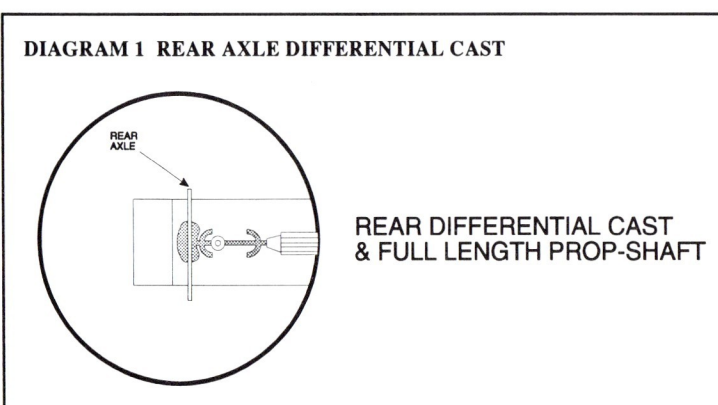

REAR DIFFERENTIAL CAST & FULL LENGTH PROP-SHAFT

DIAGRAM 2 REAR AXLE DIFFERENTIAL DELETED

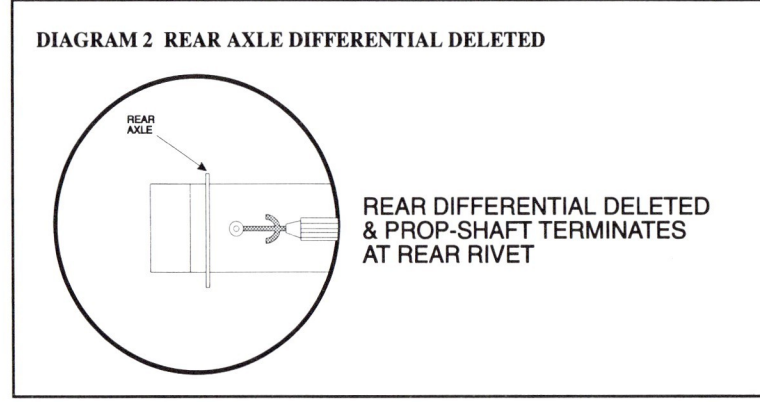

REAR DIFFERENTIAL DELETED & PROP-SHAFT TERMINATES AT REAR RIVET

NOTES

Y16-2 1928 MERCEDES BENZ SS COUPE CONTINUED Scale 1:45

A quick comparison with the Stutz will establish whether it is the real thing or not! Mercedes with Stutz green bodies on Stutz green or Mercedes green bases are lunch-time/Friday afternoon specials and as such are not listed. A very limited number of white bodies were assembled with gloss black chassis components and this is the rarest variant of this model. The 1981 issues of the mid blue liveried models produced the greatest number of colour variations due to paint supply shortages of the appropriate colour for the bonnet and the body side panels. The pale grey side panels were the scheduled colours for this issue; but various other colours were used to complete the projected issue quantities; the duck-egg blue side panels variant being the most sought after. The 1985 issue was the only model to feature the hood in the folded down position. The Mercedes was resurrected to be included in the Great Motor Cars of the Century mail order scheme in N. America and was issued in plain white boxes with black lettering. It was simultaneously released world wide in the 'N' style boxes; hence the need for the screw hole in the base. The 1990 livery was acclaimed as the best of all and sold extremely well. The total production of Issues 23 and 24 was 30,114.

ISSUE	YEAR OF RELEASE	COLOURS	SIDE PANELS	STEERING WHEEL	SEATS	GRILLE	HOOD	REAR LUGGAGE TRUNK	PLATED PARTS	WHEELS	EXHAUST	REAR AXLE DIFFERENTIAL	AXLES	THREADED SCREW HOLE	BASEPLATE	RARITY	BOX TYPE	VALUE	CHECK LIST
12	1979	White body & chassis	White	Black	Black	Black	Black textured	Black textured	Silver	Chrome 24 spoke (WW)	Cast	Not cast	Riveted	No	LESNEY © 1972 ENGLAND		I	£15	
13		White body & chassis	White	Black	Black	Black	Black textured	Black textured	Silver	Chrome solid	Cast	Not cast	Riveted	No	LESNEY © 1972 ENGLAND		I	£15	
14		White body, glossy black* chassis	White	Black	Black	Black	Black textured	Black textured	Silver	Chrome 24 spoke (WW)	Cast	Not cast	Riveted	No	LESNEY © 1972 ENGLAND	E R	I	£400	
15	1981	Mid blue body & chassis	Mid grey	Black	Black	Black	Black textured	Black textured	Silver	Chrome 24 spoke (WW)	Cast	Not cast	Riveted	No	LESNEY © 1972 ENGLAND		I	£8	
16		Mid blue body & chassis	Mid grey	Black	Black	Black	Black textured	Black textured	Silver	Red 12* spoke (WW)	Cast	Not cast	Riveted	No	LESNEY © 1972 ENGLAND	D	I	£20	
17		Mid blue body & chassis	Duck egg* blue	Black	Black	Black	Black textured	Black textured	Silver	Chrome 24 spoke (WW)	Cast	Not cast	Riveted	No	LESNEY © 1972 ENGLAND	S	I	£60	
18		Mid blue body & chassis	Milky white*	Black	Black	Black	Black textured	Black textured	Silver	Chrome 24 spoke (WW)	Cast	Not cast	Riveted	No	LESNEY © 1972 ENGLAND	R	I	£80	
19		Mid blue body & chassis	Fawn*	Black	Black	Black	Black textured	Black textured	Silver	Chrome 24 spoke (W)	Cast	Not cast	Riveted	No	LESNEY © 1972 ENGLAND	D	I	£18	
20		Mid blue body & chassis	Fawn*	Black	Black	Black	Black textured	Black textured	Silver	Chrome solid	Cast	Not cast	Riveted	No	LESNEY © 1972 ENGLAND	D	I	£18	
21	1985	Bright red body & bonnet silver chassis	Bright red	Black	Black	Black	Black folded down	Black textured	Silver	Red 24 spoke (WW)	Cast	Not cast	Riveted	No	LESNEY © 1972 ENGLAND		J	£10	
22		Bright red body & bonnet, silver chassis	Bright red	Black	Black	Black	Black folded down	Black textured	Silver	Red 12 spoke (WW)	Cast	Not cast	Riveted	No	LESNEY © 1972 ENGLAND		J	£10	
23	1990	Light pinky grey body & bonnet, glossy black chassis	Light pinky grey	Tan with black spokes	Black	Black	Black textured	Black textured	Silver	Chrome 24 spoke (WF)	Cast	Not cast	Press-fit	Yes	MATCHBOX © 1972 MACAU		N / P	£15	
24		Light pinky grey body & bonnet, glossy black chassis	Light pinky grey	Light olive green with black spokes	Black	Black	Black textured	Black textured	Silver	Chrome 24 spoke (WF)	Cast	Not cast	Press-fit	Yes	MATCHBOX © 1972 MACAU		N	£15	✓

NOTES

BECKENHAM APPEAL MODEL
1. Normal white body and chassis with black plastic components.
Silver plated parts.
Chrome 24 spoke wheels.

2. Some issues were fitted with copper axles.

INVESTMENT COMMENT
ORIGINAL PRICE £4.25p
Probably the least successful of the four racing cars introduced during 1986. Still a relatively poor performer.

Y16-3 1960 FERRARI DINO 246 / V12   Scale 1:35

This model has the distinction of being the "youngest" Yesteryear and was one of four models launched in conjunction with Matchbox Toys' decision to sponsor specific Grand Prix racing car events in 1985 and 1986, although the sponsorship did not materialise. The models which had already been manufactured were released as part of the 1986 range. Early production models had excessive sideway movement on the axles and to reduce this effect, one twenty thousandth of an inch was added to the brake drums; Type 2. Final production models were fitted with wheels in an aluminium finish, which collectors thought was more realistic than the chromed ones. Also it was one of the four racing cars which saw the introduction of press-fit axles; but four years elapsed before their use became the standard practice. Pre-production models have been recorded in blue or green, and some red models were decorated with the number '47' instead of number '17'.

ISSUE	YEAR OF RELEASE	COLOURS	EXHAUST PIPES	SEAT	GRILLE	STEERING WHEEL	ENGINE/COCKPIT INTERIOR	WINDSCREEN/ ENGINE COVER	WHEELS	BRAKE DRUMS	AXLES	BASEPLATE	RARITY	BOX TYPE	VALUE	CHECK LIST
1	1986	Red body & chassis	Light grey	Black	Light grey	Light grey	Light grey	Clear Perspex	Bright chrome 24 spoke	Grey type 1*	Press-fit	MATCHBOX © 1986 ENGLAND	S	J	£12	✓
2		Red body & chassis	Light grey	Black	Light grey	Light grey	Light grey	Clear Perspex	Bright chrome 24 spoke	Grey type 2	Press-fit	MATCHBOX © 1986 ENGLAND		J	£10	
3		Red body & chassis	Light grey	Black	Light grey	Light grey	Light grey	Clear Perspex	Aluminium 24 spoke*	Grey type 2	Press-fit	MATCHBOX © 1986 ENGLAND	D	J	£18	

LIVERY
Tampo
Racing number '17' in black on white disc on both tail panels and bonnet above grille.
Ferrari badge in gold and black both cockpit sides.

NOTES
Generally the colour of the chassis is brighter than the colour of the body and the body colour can vary from a dark red to an orangey red.

Y16-4 1922 SCANIA VABIS HALF TRACK POST BUS Scale 1:49

INVESTMENT COMMENT
ORIGINAL PRICE £17.49p

Possibly over-priced at its time of release in 1988. Its value has slowly crept up to the £20 level. Maybe, its value will be stimulated with the introduction of the 1995 release and with new collectors wishing to fill a gap in their collection.

This unusual model, a postal bus equipped for winter driving was overshadowed by the simultaneous release of the Diddler Trolley bus in late 1988. Originally the Post Bus was to have been issued with yellow spoked wheels; but a late decision saw them change to gold effect. In line with Matchbox Toys' policy, this Special Limited Edition, which retailed at £17.49, was limited to sixty thousand models worldwide and was issued in a superior gold and red box, Type 0. The packaging erroneously described the model as circa 1923 instead of 1922.

ISSUE	YEAR OF RELEASE	COLOURS	ROOF	SEATS / FLOOR	PLATED PARTS	GRILLE	WHEELS	HALF TRACK PONY WHEELS	CATERPILLAR TRACK	LIGHTS LENSES	PAINTED TRIM	SKIS	BASEPLATE	RARITY	BOX TYPE	VALUE	CHECK LIST
1	1988	Yellow body, gloss black chassis and half track supports	Metallic light grey	Brown		Gold	Black	Gold 12 spoke	Black solid	Black	Silver	Royal blue	Yellow	MATCHBOX © 1988 SPECIAL LIMITED EDITION MACAU		0	£20	✓

LIVERY

Tampo
Bus sides. Dark blue coachlines below window frames (except at vehicle front) and to roof edge.
Royal crowns in gold, red and blue above a horn outlined in dark blue with a light blue N21 below.

Labels.
Number plates, Z1089 in black on white.

NOTES

The windows have clear Perspex panes.
The roof finish is not smooth, but has a very slight roughened appearance.
Compare with YSC01-M and YET04-M.

Y16-5 1929 SCAMMELL 100 TON LOW LOADER Scale 1:64

INVESTMENT COMMENT
ORIGINAL PRICE £29.99p
An all time classic and regarded by many collectors as the best subject matter so far. In the early 1990s the Scammell was fetching £50. At present it is valued at £90 and soon could break through the £100 level. Keep watching this one!

Released in December 1989 this giant low loader and locomotive load was the largest, most expensive and most ambitious model made by Matchbox. Matchbox expressed reservations about how collectors would react to this magnificent but costly model. However within weeks of its release, such was the success of this model that most examples had been sold. The Research and Development Department were fortunate to get drawings of the tractor unit and trailer. Originally the model load was to have been a giant steam shovel excavator; but this was dropped in favour of the locomotive: G.E.R. E4 Class 2-4-0. This Y16 model saw the introduction of a moulded expanded polystyrene container for Special Limited Edition models, which was covered by a superior red and gold foil sleeve. Total worldwide production was 33,296. There are no reported variations.

TRACTOR UNIT

ISSUE	YEAR OF RELEASE	COLOURS	ROOF	DASHBOARD SEATS & FLOOR	STEERING WHEEL	PLATED PARTS	FRONT WHEELS	REAR WHEELS	TRANSMISSION DRIVE CHAINS	BASEPLATE	RARITY	BOX TYPE	TOTAL VALUE	CHECK LIST
1	1989	Dark blue body, bright red chassis	White	Light brown	Light brown	Chrome	Red 6 spoke	Red 6 mousehole 4 double sets	Black	MATCHBOX © 1989 SPECIAL LIMITED EDITION MACAU		0	THE SET £90	✓

LOW LOADER TRAILER

		COLOURS	ROOF	DASHBOARD SEATS & FLOOR	STEERING WHEEL	PLATED PARTS	FRONT WHEELS	REAR WHEELS	TRANSMISSION DRIVE CHAINS	BASEPLATE	RARITY	BOX TYPE	TOTAL VALUE	CHECK LIST
		Dark blue trailer & bogie	White	None	Black	None	N/A	Red 6 mousehole 8 double sets	None	MATCHBOX © 1989 SPECIAL LIMITED EDITION MACAU				✓

LOCOMOTIVE

		COLOURS	ROOF	CAB CONTROL PANEL & SEATS	STEERING WHEEL	PLATED PARTS	'PONY' WHEELS	DRIVING WHEELS	CONNECTING RODS	BASEPLATE	RARITY	BOX TYPE	TOTAL VALUE	CHECK LIST
		Gloss black smokebox & chimney, "G.E.R." dark navy blue boiler, cab & chassis	Black	Tan	N/A	Brass	Black 12 spoke	Black 16 spoke	Bright red	MATCHBOX © 1989 SPECIAL LIMITED EDITION MACAU				✓

LIVERY TRACTOR
Tampo
Cab sides. White PICKFORDS.
Header board. B.L.H. 21 in white on blue board above white PICKFORDS on blue board. All within blue coachlining.

LIVERY TRAILER
Tampo
Steerman's cab. 1679 in white within white coachlining.

LIVERY LOCOMOTIVE
Cab sides. Gold 490 on gold edged red plate.
Driving wheel arches. Dark red and gold coachlines.
Red coachlines to cab sides, boiler bands, walkways and driving wheel flanges and hubs.
Gold trim to front leaf spring shackles, front axle box covers, flue box door hinges and the central locking knob.

NOTES

INVESTMENT COMMENT
ORIGINAL PRICE £0.60p

Little, or no dramatic movement to be reported, although Issues 5 and 6 have made gains. The green issues were overproduced and are readily available on the collectors market. The 1990 release with its relatively short run and with so many variations, remains one for the future.

Y17-1 1938 HISPANO SUIZA

Scale 1:48

Now one of the longest surviving models in the range. The base of the Hispano Suiza has the copyright date of 1973, although the model wasn't released until 1975. Re-runs in new colour schemes were made in 1980, 1981, 1986, 1988 and 1995. The 1986 colours were then retained for 1988 after production had moved to Macau. The metallic red model has been reported with solid chrome wheels; but these are fakes because this type of wheel was not introduced until 1979 for the Y18 Cord. Plastic trial models have been seen with yellow, dark red, white and dark green roofs and seats. The Hispano Suiza Company's emblem of a flying stork is clearly visible on the boot lid. The 1986 and 1988 models were released with a contemporary plastic diarama road and backdrop and packaged in a larger carton. To comply with safety regulations, the bumpers tabs were modified and protective raised ridges were cast around the rivet holes. Because there were large stocks of unmodified bumpers both types were fitted indiscriminately. See Diagrams 1 and 2. So the possible permutations with the two tone green model are considerable and therefore have not been given separate listings. The 1990 models for worldwide release all had a card insert diarama in the new style boxes. The 1990 Hispano in two-tone green was issued as part of Matchbox Toys USA's programme in North America under the banner of 'Great Motor Cars of the Century' and were packaged in white boxes with black lettering. They were released simultaneously worldwide in the then new style 'N' type boxes. The rear number plates were made thicker to eliminate the cast digits and to create a flat surface to take the tampo printed number plate. Also for the same reason the front number plate was thickened. However, there were considerable quantities of the old type front number plate and these were indiscriminately fitted to the 1990 issues.

ISSUE	YEAR OF RELEASE	COLOURS	SIDE PANELS	SEATS	HOOD	WHEELS	AXLES	GRILLE	PLATED PARTS	FRONT NUMBER PLATE DIGITS	REAR NUMBER PLATE DIGITS	STEERING WHEEL	THREADED SCREW HOLE	BASEPLATE	RARITY	BOX TYPE	VALUE	CHECK LIST
1	1975	Metallic red body, glossy black chassis	Dark red	Black	Black	Chrome 24 spoke	Riveted	Black	Chrome	Cast	Cast	Black	No	LESNEY © 1973 ENGLAND		H	£15	✓✗
2		Metallic red body, black chassis	Dark red	Black	Black	Chrome 12*spoke	Riveted	Black	Chrome	Cast	Cast	Black	No	LESNEY © 1973 ENGLAND	S	H	£25	
3	1980	Pale metallic blue body & chassis	Powder blue	Black	Black	Chrome 24 spoke (WW)	Riveted	Black	Chrome	Cast	Cast	Black	No	LESNEY © 1973 ENGLAND		I	£12	
4		Pale metallic blue body & chassis	Powder blue	Black	Black	Chrome solid (WW)	Riveted	Black	Chrome	Cast	Cast	Black	No	LESNEY © 1973 ENGLAND		I	£12	
5	1980	Pale metallic blue body glossy black chassis	Powder blue	Black	Black	Chrome solid (WW)	Riveted	Black	Chrome	Cast	Cast	Black	No	LESNEY © 1973 ENGLAND		I	£12	✓
6		Pale metallic blue body, glossy black chassis	Powder blue	Black	Black	Chrome* 24 spoke	Riveted	Black	Chrome	Cast	Cast	Black	No	LESNEY © 1973 ENGLAND	S	I	£25	
7	1981	Silver metallic body* glossy black chassis	Powder blue	Black	Black	Chrome solid (WW)	Riveted	Black	Chrome	Cast	Cast	Black	No	LESNEY © 1973 ENGLAND	R	I	£125	
8		Silver metallic body & cvhassis*	Powder blue	Black	Black	Chrome solid (WW)	Riveted	Black	Chrome	Cast	Cast	Black	No	LESNEY © 1973 ENGLAND	R	I	£125	
9	1986	Emerald green body, dark green chassis	Emerald green	Black	Black	Gold 24 spoke	Riveted	Black	Gold	Cast	Cast	Black	No	LESNEY © 1973 ENGLAND		J	£14	✓
10		Emerald green body, dark green chassis	Emerald green	Black	Black	Gold 24 spoke	Riveted	Dark green*	Gold	Cast	Cast	Black	No	LESNEY © 1973 ENGLAND	D	J	£20	

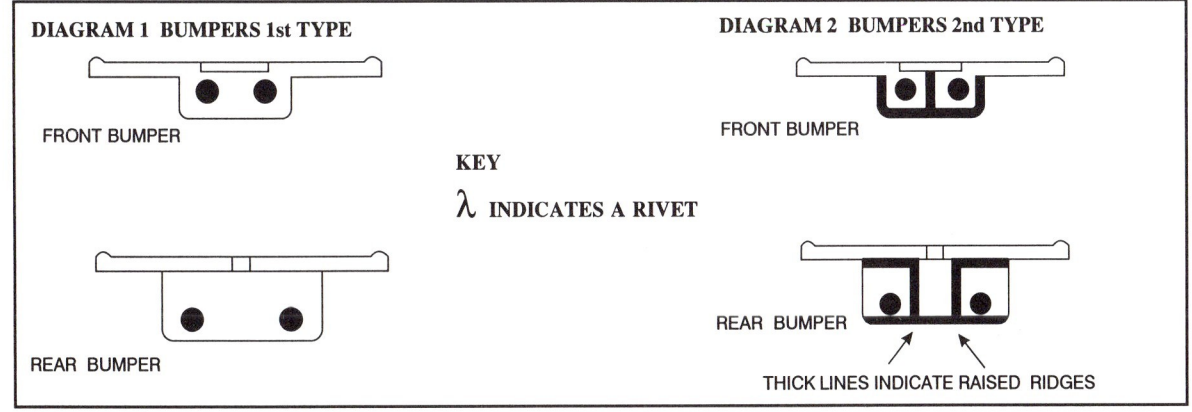

DIAGRAM 1 BUMPERS 1st TYPE — FRONT BUMPER / REAR BUMPER

DIAGRAM 2 BUMPERS 2nd TYPE — FRONT BUMPER / REAR BUMPER — THICK LINES INDICATE RAISED RIDGES

KEY
λ INDICATES A RIVET

NOTES

BECKENHAM APPEAL MODEL. Mustard yellow body and chassis, Black plastic components, Chrome plated parts 24 spoke wheels. Total production, Issues 1 to 19 was 34,020.

Y17-1 1938 HISPANO SUIZA   CONTINUED   Scale 1:48

The Hispano Suiza was re-issued in 1995 as a model in the Grand Marques series. Issue price was £12.50. Although now sold under the Matchbox Collectibles banner, little was different from the 1990 release except for a new livery and wheels. The wheels with white wall flanges had been replaced with white wall tyres. The underside of the engine gearbox etc were now all finished in gold. The bumpers were now Type 2. The colour scheme of dark blue with gold enhancement and gold plated parts ensured that the model was an immediate success.

ISSUE	YEAR OF RELEASE	COLOURS	SIDE PANELS	SEATS	HOOD	WHEELS	AXLES	GRILLE	PLATED PARTS	FRONT NUMBER PLATE DIGITS	REAR NUMBER PLATE DIGITS	STEERING WHEEL	THREADED SCREW HOLE	BASEPLATE	RARITY	BOX TYPE	VALUE	CHECK LIST
11		Emerald green body, dark green chassis	Emerald green	Black	Black	Gold 24 spoke	Riveted	Black	Gold	Cast	Cast	Black	No	MATCHBOX © 1973 ENGLAND	R	J/I	£50	
12	1988	Emerald green body, dark green chassis	Emerald green	Black	Black	Gold 24 spoke	Riveted	Black	Gold	Cast	Cast	Black	No	MATCHBOX © 1973 MACAU		J	£14	
13	1990	Metallic mid green body & chassis	Pale lime green	Pale cream	Pale cream	Chrome 24 spoke (WF)	Riveted	Black	Chrome	Cast*	Tampo	Light brown, black spokes	No*	MATCHBOX © 1973 MACAU	S	P*	£14	
14		Metallic mid green body & chassis	Pale lime green	Pale cream	Pale cream	Chrome 24 spoke (WF)	Riveted	Black	Chrome	Tampo	Tampo	Light brown, black spokes	No*	MATCHBOX © 1973 MACAU	S	P*	£14	
15		Metallic mid green body & chassis	Pale lime green	Pale cream	Pale cream	Chrome 24 spoke (WF)	Riveted	Black	Chrome	Cast*	Tampo	Light brown, black spokes	Yes	MATCHBOX © 1973 MACAU	D	N	£15	
16		Metallic mid green body & chassis	Pale lime green	Pale cream	Pale cream	Chrome 24 spoke (WF)	Riveted	Black	Chrome	Tampo	Tampo	Light brown, black spokes	Yes	MATCHBOX © 1973 MACAU		N	£12	✓
17		Metallic mid green body & chassis	Dark lime green	Pale cream	Pale cream	Chrome 24 spoke (WF)	Riveted	Black	Chrome	Cast*	Tampo	Light brown, black spokes	Yes	MATCHBOX © 1973 MACAU	D	N	£15	
18		Metallic mid green body & chassis	Dark lime green	Pale cream	Pale cream	Chrome 24 spoke (WF)	Riveted	Black	Chrome	Tampo	Tampo	Light brown, black spokes	Yes	MATCHBOX © 1973 MACAU		N	£10	
19		Metallic mid green body & chassis	Dark lime green	Pale cream	Pale cream	Chrome 24 spoke (WF)	Press-fit	Black	Chrome	Tampo	Tampo	Light brown, black spokes	Yes	MATCHBOX © 1973 MACAU		N	£10	
20		Metallic mid green body & chassis	Dark lime green	Pale cream	Pale cream	Chrome 24 spoke (WF)	Press-fit	Black	Chrome	Cast*	Tampo	Light brown, black spokes	Yes	MATCHBOX © 1973 MACAU	D	N	£15	
21	1995	Navy blue body & chassis	Navy blue	Light tan	Black	Gold 24 spoke (WW)	Press-fit	Black	Gold	Tampo	Tampo	Black, gold spokes	Yes	MATCHBOX © 1973 CHINA		N 2		

NOTES

Issue 21 was coded by Matchbox Collectibles as YY017 A/D on the box ends.

INVESTMENT COMMENT
ORIGINAL PRICE £1.50p
The plum red model remains relatively hard to find and the 1990 release in yellow has good potential in either box. Once newer collectors begin to search for earlier issues values may be stimulated by the release of the YY018 in 1995.

Y18-1 1937 CORD 812 SEDAN
Scale 1:48

The 1937 Cord 812 Supercharged Convertible Phaeton Sedan is a good example of the flamboyant styling of American cars of the 1930's. The Y18-1 model boasts three firsts. It was the first car model to have 'solid' wheels; the first to have white wall tyres and the first to have tyre walls in a colour other than black, or white i.e. lemon yellow on the 1990 version. One of the most famous pre-production colour trial Cord models is in white with a red plastic hood. No casting changes occurred on this model; but the red coloured livery can vary considerably. Collectors thought the red version was not realistic, however the plum red was eagerly purchased. The 1990 version in pale yellow was issued in North America via Matchbox Toys mail order scheme of the 'Great Motor Cars of the Century' and was packaged in a plain white box with black printing. It was given extensive enhanced detailing; which included silver trim to the radiator and bonnet side fins, exhaust pipes and the number plates in pale blue with lemon yellow numbers. It was released simultaneously worldwide in the then new 'N' style box. The total production for Issue 8 was 30,150. In 1995 the Cord was re issued as the Y018 as part of the "Grand Marques" series.

ISSUE	YEAR OF RELEASE	COLOURS	HOOD	SEATS	GRILLE	STEERING WHEEL	WHEELS	PLATED PARTS	AXLES	BASEPLATE	RARITY	BOX TYPE	VALUE	CHECK LIST
1	1979	Bright red body, bonnet, chassis and base	White	White	Bright red	Black	Chrome 24 spoke* (W W)	Chrome	Riveted	LESNEY © 1978 ENGLAND	D	I	£12	
2		Bright red body, bonnet, chassis and base	White	White	Bright red	Black	Red solid* (WW)	Chrome	Riveted	LESNEY © 1978 ENGLAND	D	I	£12	
3		Bright red body, bonnet, chassis and base	White	White	Bright red	Black	Chrome solid (WW)	Chrome	Riveted	LESNEY © 1978 ENGLAND		I	£8	✓
4		Bright red body, dark orange bonnet, chassis & base	White	White	Bright red	Black	Chrome solid (WW)	Chrome	Riveted	LESNEY © 1978 ENGLAND		I	£8	
5	1981	Dark* red body, bonnet, chassis & base	White	White	Dark red	Black	Chrome solid (WW)	Chrome	Riveted	LESNEY © 1978 ENGLAND	S	I	£12	
6	1983	Plum red body, bonnet, chassis & black base	White	White	Plum red	Black	Chrome solid (WW)	Chrome	Riveted	LESNEY © 1978 ENGLAND		I	£15	
7		Plum red body, bonnet, chassis & black base	White	White	Plum red	Black	Chrome 24 spoke* (WW)	Chrome	Riveted	LESNEY © 1978 ENGLAND	D	I	£15	
8	1990	Pale yellow body, bonnet, chassis & black base	Brown	Brown	Silver	Pale yellow	Chrome solid lemon walls	Chrome	Press-fit	MATCHBOX © 1978 MACAU	D	P*/N	£18	✓
9	1995	Rich cream body bonnet, chassis & base	Tan	Dark brown	Silver	Pale cream with silver spokes	Chrome solid (WW)	Chrome	Press-fit	MATCHBOX © 1978 CHINA		N 2		

NOTES

Number plates.
Issues 1 to 7 are cast, MB4036.
Issue 8 is tampo printed, 536-414.
Issue 9 is tampo printed, 761-494.

Y18-2 1918 ATKINSON MODEL 'D' STEAM WAGON Scale 1:60

LAKE GOLDSMITH. The 'Lake Goldsmith' livery was one of the first Yesteryear models to be aimed specifically at the collectors market. One of the first Limited Edition Yesteryears, the baseplate had the words Limited Edition. It was packaged in a superior red box and it sold at a premium price, £6.99, compared to the then normal RSP of £4.95. Early pre-production models were fitted with solid black tyres and late pre-production models featured rounded mudguards. It was believed that some production models were released with these rounded mudguards but this now is thought to be unlikely. Also very early pre-production models were fitted with two steering mechanisms at the front. On production models this was reduced to just one.

BLUE CIRCLE. The 'Lake Goldsmith' model had a watertank at the rear of the cab but for the 'Blue Circle' model and subsequent releases, this tank was at the rear of the back axle. The 'Blue Circle' issue encountered initial problems with the blue cab lines, but this was quickly rectified. Early issues, 5000 units, also appeared in a pale yellow which was darkened for issue 2 by applying a second coat of yellow paint. Total production for the 'Blue Circle Cement' model was 108,000.

A : LAKE GOLDSMITH

ISSUE	YEAR OF RELEASE	COLOURS	ROOF	MUDGUARDS	SEATS	TYRES	WHEELS	PLATED PARTS	TRANSMISSION CHAIN	PIPES & CYLINDERS	CAB LINE TYPE	BASEPLATE	RARITY	BOX TYPE	VALUE	CHECK LIST
1	1985	Emerald green body, bright red chassis	Emerald green	Black	Black	Light grey solid	Emerald green 8 spoke	Chrome	Black	Black	N/A	MATCHBOX © 1985 LIMITED EDITION ENGLAND		J	£20	✓

B : BLUE CIRCLE CEMENT

ISSUE	YEAR OF RELEASE	COLOURS	ROOF	MUDGUARDS	SEATS	TYRES	WHEELS	PLATED PARTS	TRANSMISSION CHAIN	PIPES & CYLINDERS	CAB LINE TYPE	BASEPLATE	RARITY	BOX TYPE	VALUE	CHECK LIST
1	1986	Pale yellow body, black chassis	Pale yellow	Black	Black	Light grey solid	Yellow 8 spoke	Chrome	Black	Black	Pale blue* A	MATCHBOX © 1986 ENGLAND	D	J	£7	
2		Deeper yellow body, black chassis	Deeper yellow	Black	Black	Light grey solid	Yellow 8 spoke	Chrome	Black	Black	Darker blue B	MATCHBOX © 1986 ENGLAND		J	£7	✓

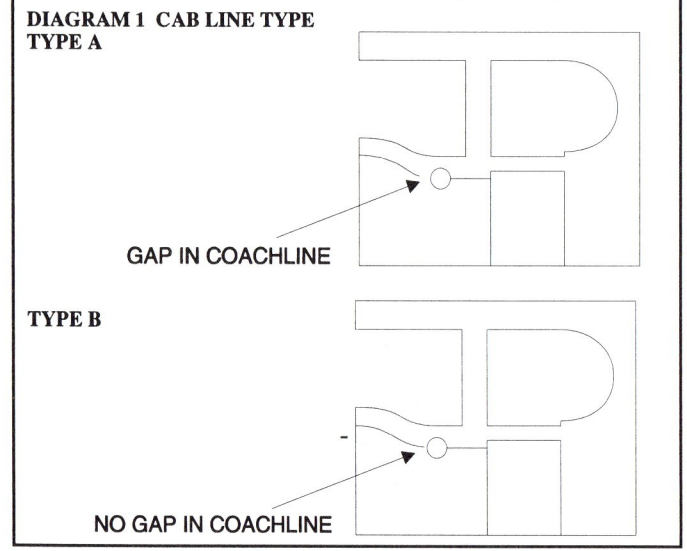

DIAGRAM 1 CAB LINE TYPE
TYPE A — GAP IN COACHLINE
TYPE B — NO GAP IN COACHLINE

LIVERY LAKE GOLDSMITH

Tampo
Truck sides. SAND & GRAVEL in pale yellow with brown shadow effect and knight's armour helmet in red, black & white within pale yellow rope circle with white decoration; on three panels with white & black coachlining.
Truck Tailboard. LAKE GOLDSMITH MINING PTY LTD. in pale yellow with brown shadow effect with white decoration and black & white coachlining.
Cab sides. White GOLDSMITH within white coachlining.
Cab doors. Pale yellow rope encircling white 12 with white coachlining.
Cab front panel. Pale yellow LAKE GOLDSMITH with red shadow effect above black MINING PTY LTD on pale yellow stripe above pale yellow AUSTRALIA with black shadow effect. All below black & white curved coachline with white decoration.

LIVERY BLUE CIRCLE CEMENT

Tampo
Truck sides. Blue BLUE CIRCLE PORTLAND CEMENT.
Cab side panels. Yellow PORTLAND CEMENT on blue ring around blue BLUE CIRCLE.
Cab doors. Blue No. 20
Cab front. Blue THE CEMENT MARKETING COMPANY LIMITED.
Coachline. Blue coachlining to cab.
N.B. No lines at bottom edge.

INVESTMENT COMMENT

ORIGINAL PRICE, LAKE GOLDSMITH £6.99p
BLUE CIRCLE £4.25p

Lake Goldsmith. This Special Limited Edition model has already trebled in value in ten years and is likely to continue to increase in value.

Blue Circle. Was unpopular at the time of release; overproduced and still readily available on the collectors market.

NOTES

Y18-2 1918 ATKINSON STEAM MODEL 'D' WAGON CONTINUED Scale 1:60

BASS & Co. Flat beds and chain lorries have proved popular with diecast collectors and the Y18-2 in 'Bass & Co.' livery issued in October 1987 as one of three Special Limited Edition models, proved no exception. The 'Bass & Co.' model normally retailed at £9.50 compared to the standard range price of £5.25. In all 60,000 models were released. There are no known variations.

BURGHFIELD MILLS. This livery was released in March 1988. Although most of the model was decorated by tampo printing, it was necessary to decorate the cab front with a label. Problems had arisen with an earlier livery, because the curve of the cab was too severe to enable the tampo printing pads to make a uniform contact. The 'Burghfield' livery was not particularly well received by collectors, due to its garish colour scheme and unrealistically coloured load of sacks. There are no known variations for this model.

C : BASS & CO

ISSUE	YEAR OF RELEASE	COLOURS	ROOF	MUD GUARDS	SEATS	TYRES	WHEELS	PLATED PARTS	TRANSMISSION CHAIN	PIPES & CYLINDERS	LOAD	WAGON CHAINS	BASEPLATE	RARITY	BOX TYPE	VALUE	CHECK LIST
1	1987	Royal blue body, black chassis	Royal blue	Black	Black	Black solid	Red 8 spoke	Chrome	Red	Red	7 Dark brown barrels/mid brown planked floor	Brass chain on 8 black posts	MATCHBOX © 1987 LIMITED EDITION MACAU		J1	£14	✓

D : BURGHFIELD MILLS

ISSUE	YEAR OF RELEASE	COLOURS	ROOF	MUD GUARDS	SEATS	TYRES	WHEELS	PLATED PARTS	TRANSMISSION CHAIN	PIPES & CYLINDERS	LOAD	WAGON CHAINS	BASEPLATE	RARITY	BOX TYPE	VALUE	CHECK LIST
1	1988	Bright red body, black chassis	Bright red	Black	Black	Light grey solid	Red 8 spoke	Chrome	Black	Black	Light yellow sacks	N/A	MATCHBOX © 1987 MACAU		J1	£8	✓

LIVERY BASS & CO
Tampo
Wagon sides. Gold BASS & CO BURTON ON TRENT between red decorative stripes. All below gold coachlines.
Cab sides. Red CELEBRATED BURTON FINE ALES on three gold and red scrolls. All within gold and red coachlines.
Cab doors. Gold No.1 in red, within gold and red coachlines.
Cab front panel. Red outlined gold BASS & CO above small red triangle above white ESTABLISHED 1777.

LIVERY BURGHFIELD MILLS
Tampo
Wagon sides. White BURGHFIELD MILLS READING
Cab sides. Yellow decorative scroll within yellow coachlining.
Cab doors. White No.18 below yellow scroll. All within yellow coachlining.
Label
Cab front panel. JAMES DEWE in white above white BURGHFIELD MILLS READING with yellow scroll decorations. All within yellow coachlining.

INVESTMENT COMMENT
ORIGINAL PRICE BASS £9.50p
BURGHFIELD MILL £5.75p
Bass. Surprisingly, this beautiful Special Limited Edition model has been slow to appreciate, but this may alter if it is found by "Great Beers of the World" collectors.

Burghfield. Has shown little growth and is not likely to, in the immediate future.

NOTES

Compare with YGB-03 and YAS06-M.

Y19-1 1936 AUBURN SPEEDSTER 851   Scale 1:42

INVESTMENT COMMENT
ORIGINAL PRICE £1.50p
All issues are abundant on the collectors market and this has tended to restrict growth.

Like the Y18-1 Cord, the 1936 Auburn Supercharged Speedster is an example of flamboyant American 1930's styling. First issue models have been reported fitted with brown, black, yellow, pink, grey and maroon seats which were the results of colour plastic trials. The issues released between 1979 and 1985 never sold well and it is known that private individuals swapped wheels from other Yesteryear models to stimulate interest in the Y19-1 Auburn. No casting variations are known to exist for this model and no variations have come to light for the 1985 and 1990 issues. The blue colour on the bonnet sides and on part of the doors for the 1985 issue was achieved by mask spraying. The 1990 version was issued in North America by mail order only through the 'Great Motor Cars of the Century' scheme and was packaged in a plain white box with black printing. It was released simultaneously worldwide in the 'N' style box. Collectors appreciated the extensive use of enhanced detailing which included extra trim to the steering wheel, silver central bonnet hinge and door handles, a silver engine underside, gearbox, prop-shaft and exhaust pipe. The number plate was also detailed (see livery). Total production for Issue 11 was 30,198.

ISSUE	YEAR OF RELEASE	COLOURS	RADIATOR SHELL	BONNET DOORS & TAIL TOPS	SEATS	GRILLE	STEERING WHEEL	WHEEL	AXLES	PLATED PARTS	THREADED SCREW HOLE	BASEPLATE	RARITY	BOX TYPE	VALUE	CHECK LIST
1	1979	Light beige body & bonnet sides, dark brown chassis	Light beige	Light brown	Orangey red	Chrome	Black	Cherry red solid (BW)	Riveted	Chrome	No	LESNEY © 1979 ENGLAND		I	£10	✓
2		Dark beige body & bonnet sides, dark brown chassis	Dark beige	Light brown	Orangey red	Chrome	Black	Cherry red solid (W)	Riveted	Chrome	No	LESNEY © 1979 ENGLAND		I	£10	
3		Dark beige body & bonnet sides, dark brown chassis	Dark beige	Light brown	Orangey red	Chrome	Black	Chrome solid (BW)	Riveted	Chrome	No	LESNEY © 1979 ENGLAND		I	£10	
4		Dark beige body & bonnet sides, dark brown chassis	Dark beige	Light brown	Orangey red	Chrome	Black	Red solid (BW)	Riveted	Chrome	No	LESNEY © 1979 ENGLAND		I	£10	
5		Dark beige body & bonnet sides, dark brown chassis	Dark beige	Light brown	Bright red	Chrome	Black	Red solid (BW)	Riveted	Chrome	No	LESNEY © 1979 ENGLAND		I	£10	
6		Dark beige body & bonnet sides, darker brown chassis	Dark beige	Light brown	Orangey red	Chrome	Black	Cherry red solid (BW)	Riveted	Chrome	No	LESNEY © 1979 ENGLAND		I	£12	
7	1983	Light* cream body & bonnet sides, glossy black chassis	Light cream	Light cream	Bright red	Chrome	Black	Red solid (BW)	Riveted	Chrome	No	LESNEY © 1979 ENGLAND	S	I	£15	
8		Creamy white body & bonnet sides, glossy black chassis	Creamy white	Cream white	Bright red	Chrome	Black	Red solid (BW)	Riveted	Chrome	No	LESNEY © 1979 ENGLAND		I	£10	✓
9		Creamy white body & bonnet sides, glossy black chassis	Creamy white	Cream white	Bright red	Chrome	Black	Red 12 spoke (BW)	Riveted	Chrome	No	LESNEY © 1979 ENGLAND		I	£10	
10	1985	White body, blue bonnet sides and doors, white chassis	White	White part blue doors	Blue	Chrome	Black	Blue 24 spoke (BW)	Riveted	Chrome	No	LESNEY © 1979 ENGLAND		J	£8	
11	1990	Dark tan body cream doors, side panels, dark tan chassis	Dark tan	Dark tan	Dark brown	Black* and chrome	Pale cream black spokes	Chrome 24 (WF)	Press-fit	Chrome	Yes	MATCHBOX © 1979 MACAU	D	P* /N	£15	✓

LIVERY

Tampo - 1990 Release
SUPERCHARGED in silver on black panel, above the exhaust manifold and offside grille.
Number plates. Lemon yellow SA 29582 on pale blue lemon edged plate (one line for front plate and two for the rear plate).

NOTES

On the 1990 release the black radiator grille is faced with a chrome chevron bar.

INVESTMENT COMMENT
ORIGINAL PRICE £14.99p

An immediate success in all the major markets. As a unique casting, this model is likely to continue to appreciate in value. Growth potential may be stimulated by the release of the YAS05-M.

Y19-2 1905 FOWLER B6 SHOWMANS ENGINE Scale 1:68

This beautiful Special Limited Edition model was released just before Christmas 1986. At one time Matchbox intended to issue it with a plastic roof but influenced by representations from MICA this component was changed to diecast. The engine comprises nineteen individual components and is today regarded as being a masterpiece of miniature toy production. There was extensive use of tampo printing in gold and red to decorate the model and although some components were produced in plastic most collectors accepted the manufacturer's reason that accurate detail would have been impossible if diecast had been used throughout. Limited to only 65,000 units worldwide the Y19-2 was sold in a superior type of red box. The red flock lining of the box can cause slight discolouration to the roof and collectors are advised to protect the model with a plastic covering or with acid-free tissue paper, if it is to be kept in the box.

ISSUE	YEAR OF RELEASE	COLOURS	SMOKE BOX/FRONT AXLE SUPPORT	GENERATOR PLATFORM	ROOF	SMOKE STACK	TYRES	WHEELS	ROOF SUPPORTS	BASEPLATE	RARITY	BOX TYPE	VALUE	CHECK LIST
1	1986	Royal blue body & boiler	Black	Black	White	Black	Dark grey solid	Red 12 spoke front red 18 spoke rear	Chrome	MATCHBOX ©1986 LIMITED EDITION ENGLAND	D	0	£35	
2		Royal blue body & boiler	Black	Black	Pale cream	Black	Dark grey solid	Red 12 spoke front red 18 spoke rear	Chrome	MATCHBOX © 1986 LIMITED EDITION ENGLAND	D	0	£35	✓?

LIVERY

Tampo
Roof fascias HEY-HO COME TO THE FAIR in gold on red panel. Flanked each end by NAMED SUNNY BOY II 1905 in gold on blue panel.
Gold highlights to outside faces of wheel spokes.
Extensive red and gold coachlining.

NOTES

In artificial light the colour of the roof supports can appear gold.
The boiler rings have a chrome finish.
Compare with YAS05-M. ✓

Y19-3 1929 MORRIS COWLEY VAN   Scale 1:39

BRASSO. The Morris van was one of the next Morris production vehicles following on from the success of Bullnose Cowley. Such vans were a common sight in many Commonwealth countries during the 1930's; being cheap and reliable to operate. During production of the Y19 a change was made to the roof component, to prevent distortion. During ejection from the mould, the roof component was still hot and tended to buckle. The areas to the outer side of the outer roof brackets were filled in to give the component extra strength (Roof Type 2). This new roof component was used for all subsequent Y19/3 production. In 1991 the 'Brasso' had a short production run at the new factory in China as a special order for Poland. However, due to Polish political and economic problems, the order was drastically reduced and Matchbox decided to distribute the models to Woolworths and Tesco stores in the United Kingdom.

MICHELIN. An attractive model which displayed different coloured designs on each side of the van body. Soon after release collectors noted that there were two distinct colours of yellow lettering used during the tampo printing. Early production models were issued with a bright yellow ink, whereas later models have a distinctively lemon yellow colour. All 'Michelin' models had the filled in Type 2 strengthened brackets underneath the cab/van roof, as first cast onto some of the 'Brasso' models. The total production of the Michelin model was 53,358.

A : BRASSO

ISSUE	YEAR OF RELEASE	COLOURS	ROOF	SEATS	GRILLE	PLATED PARTS	TOOL BOX TOP COVER	WHEELS	ROOF CASTING	WINDOWS	LOGO	TAMPO DECORATION	AXLE	BASE SCREW HOLE	BASEPLATE	RARITY	BOX TYPE	VALUE	CHECK LIST
1	1987	Dark blue body, glossy black chassis	White	Mid brown	Black	Chrome	Brass	Red 12 spoke	Type 1	Clear Perspex	BRASSO	Red disc yellow surround	Riveted	No	MATCHBOX © 1987 MACAU		J 1	£10	
2		Dark blue body, glossy black chassis	White	Mid brown	Black	Chrome	Brass	Chrome 12 spoke	Type 1	Clear Perspex	BRASSO	Red disc yellow surround	Riveted	No	MATCHBOX © 1987 MACAU		J 1	£10	
3		Dark blue body, glossy black chassis	White	Mid brown	Black	Chrome	Brass	Red 12 spoke	Type 2	Clear Perspex	BRASSO	Red disc yellow surround	Riveted	No	MATCHBOX © 1987 MACAU*	D	J 1	£10	✓
4	1991	Dark blue body, glossy black chassis	White	Darker* brown	Black	Chrome	Brass	Red 12 spoke	Type 2	Clear Perspex	BRASSO	Pale red disc* yellow surround	Press fit	Yes	MATCHBOX © 1987 CHINA*	D	J 2	£15	

B : MICHELIN

ISSUE	YEAR OF RELEASE	COLOURS	ROOF	SEATS	GRILLE	PLATED PARTS	TOOL BOX TOP COVER	WHEELS	ROOF CASTING	WINDOWS	LOGO	TAMPO DECORATION	AXLE	BASE SCREW HOLE	BASEPLATE	RARITY	BOX TYPE	VALUE	CHECK LIST
1	1988	Royal blue body, glossy black chassis	Deep yellow	Mid brown	Black	Chrome	Brass	Chrome 12 spoke	Type 2	Clear Perspex	MICHELIN	Michelin yellow	Riveted	No	MATCHBOX © 1987 MACAU		J 1	£10	✓
2		Royal blue body, glossy black chassis	Deep yellow	Mid brown	Black	Chrome	Brass	Chrome 12 spoke	Type 2	Clear Perspex	MICHELIN	Michelin lemon yellow	Riveted	No	MATCHBOX © 1987 MACAU		J 1	£10	

BRACKETS ON UNDERSIDE OF ROOF

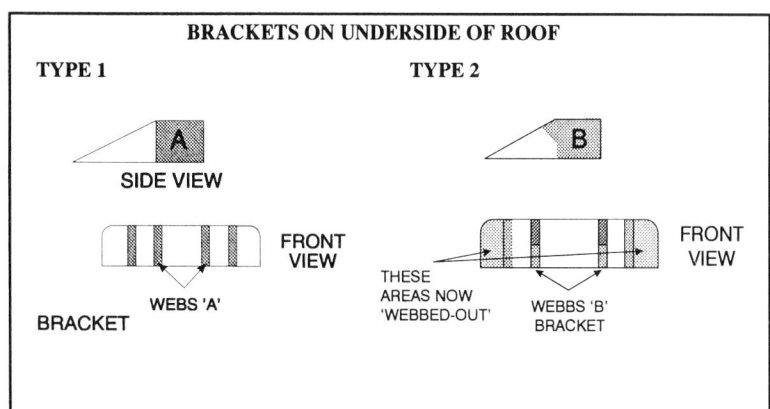

TYPE 1 — SIDE VIEW, BRACKET, FRONT VIEW, WEBS 'A'
TYPE 2 — THESE AREAS NOW 'WEBBED-OUT', WEBBS 'B' BRACKET, FRONT VIEW

LIVERY BRASSO

Tampo
Van sides. White BRASSO on red disc with yellow surround. All on white sun-burst effect covering the whole panel.
Cab doors. Yellow METAL POLISH.

LIVERY MICHELIN

Tampo
Van nearside. Yellow MICHELIN above black & white Michelin man with yellow box across his back with black TOO SMALL A TYRE IS SOON RUINED.
Van offside. Yellow MICHELIN above black & white Michelin man holding a yellow balloon with black PUMP UP EVERY FRIDAY.
Van rear doors. MICHELIN TYRES TECHNICAL DEPT NO CHARGE, MICHELIN TYRES in yellow above black & white Michelin man.
Cab doors. Yellow MICHELIN.

INVESTMENT COMMENT
ORIGINAL PRICE, BRASSO AND MICHELIN £5.25p

Brasso. The China manufactured model has, rather surprisingly, not appreciated as quickly as was originally thought.
Michelin. Although an attractive model with two differing panel decorations, there is little interest recorded.

NOTES
The production figure for the Brasso model was 75,000 (E).

Y19-3 1929 MORRIS COWLEY VAN CONTINUED Scale 1:39

INVESTMENT COMMENT
ORIGINAL PRICE £6.99p

Few now seen for sale. However, it is rather drab and does little to excite collectors. Brown coloured models seldom sell quickly.

SAINSBURY. Originally, the colour scheme selected had a dark blue main body. When shown to the J. Sainsbury management they asked that the colour be changed to an authentic dark brown; which has been well received by collectors. The rear doors were also decorated and clever use was made of the roof sides for additional advertising. Because the hole for the self-tapping screw was fitted amongst the words 'Models of Yesteryear', the baseplate inscription detail remained the same as for previous Y19 liveries. The production run was 60,000 (E).

C : SAINSBURY

ISSUE	YEAR OF RELEASE	COLOURS	ROOF	SEATS	WHEELS	PLATED PARTS	TOOL BOX TOP COVER	ROOF CASTING	SIDE WINDOW	LOGO	TAMPO DECORATION	AXLES	THREADED SCREW HOLE	BASEPLATE	RARITY	BOX TYPE	VALUE	CHECK LIST
1	1990	Dark brown body, glossy black chassis	White	Mid brown	Chrome 12 spoke	Chrome	Brass	Type 2	Clear Perspex	SAINSBURY	Roof lettering in dark navy blue	Press fit	Yes	MATCHBOX© 1987 MACAU		N	£10	✓
2		Dark brown body, glossy black chassis	White	Mid brown	Chrome 12 spoke	Chrome	Brass	Type 2	Clear Perspex	SAINSBURY	Roof lettering in blue	Press fit	Yes	MATCHBOX © 1987 MACAU		N	£10	

LIVERY

Tampo
Nearside roof panel. DELICIOUS DAIRY BUTTER in blue.
Offside roof panel. BLUE KADDY TEA in blue.
Van sides and rear doors. J SAINSBURY in gold with pale blue shadow effect.
66 WESTERN ROAD BRIGHTON and 632 in gold.

NOTES

1. Compare with Y47-1, YGB04 and YY047/SA.

INVESTMENT COMMENT
ORIGINAL PRICE £2.49
Values have remained static.

Y20-1 1937 MERCEDES BENZ 540K

Scale 1:45

This was the first car since the Y8-1 Morris Cowley to have an opening dickey seat. Many pre-production colour variations were produced; most notably in royal blue and black, metallic blue and silver and overall metallic red, before the classic silver and black livery was chosen for production. The driver's cockpit interior is a one piece component representing the seats, floor and door interior panels. Initially it was a loose fit; but later was widened by two millimetres which resulted in a much better fit. No casting variations have been noted; but different wheels were fitted during the four years that the silver and black version was issued. The white walling to the tyres can vary considerably in width and also plain black tyres can be found. The 1987 issue was packaged complete with a plastic diarama. The 1989/90 version was first released as part of the Great Motor Cars of the Century promotion. These issues were given considerable extra trim ; a black dashboard with chromed instrument panels, silver door handles, hinges and lamps and by using labels, the front and rear number plates not only had easily read letters and numbers, but also a black and orange German heraldic crest. Finally it should be noted that to accommodate the screw hole in the baseplate, the term '540k' was moved nearer to the rear axle. The total production for Issues 10 to 12, was 40,302 models. In 1995 the Mercedes was one of six models released in the "Grand Marques" series.

ISSUE	YEAR OF RELEASE	COLOURS	UNDER FRAME	BODY STRIPE	SEATS & COCKPIT INTERIOR	STEERING WHEEL	WHEELS	AXLES	PLATED PARTS	THREADED SCREW HOLE	BASEPLATE	RARITY	BOX TYPE	VALUE	CHECK LIST
1	1981	Silver body, glossy black chassis	Chrome	None	Red 28 mm*	Black	Chrome 24 spoke (WW)	Riveted	Chrome	No	LESNEY © 1979 ENGLAND	D	I	£15	✓
2		Silver body, glossy black chassis	Chrome	None	Red 30 mm	Black	Chrome 24 spoke (WW)	Riveted	Chrome	No	LESNEY © 1979 ENGLAND		I	£10	
3		Silver body, glossy black chassis	Chrome	None	Maroon 30 mm	Black	Chrome 24 spoke (WW)	Riveted	Chrome	No	LESNEY © 1979 ENGLAND		I	£10	
4		Silver body, glossy black chassis	Chrome	None	Amber 30 mm	Black	Chrome 24 spoke (WW)	Riveted	Chrome	No	LESNEY © 1979 ENGLAND		I	£10	
5		Silver body, glossy black chassis	Chrome	None	Red 30 mm	Black	Chrome solid (WW)	Riveted	Chrome	No	LESNEY © 1979 ENGLAND		I	£10	
6		Silver body, glossy black chassis	Chrome	None	Red 30 mm,	Black	Red 12 spoke (WW)	Riveted	Chrome	No	LESNEY © 1979 ENGLAND		I	£10	
7	1985	White body & chassis	Chrome	Red	Red 30 mm	Black	Red 24 spoke (BW)	Riveted	Chrome	No	LESNEY © 1979 ENGLAND		J	£8	✓
8	1987	Bright red body & chassis	Chrome	None	Mid brown 30 mm	Black	Chrome 24 spoke (WW)	Riveted	Chrome	No	MATCHBOX © 1979 MACAU		J 1	£9	✓
9	1990	Gloss black body & chassis	Chrome	Sliver	Maroon 30 mm	Light tan black spokes	Chrome 24 spoke (WW)	Riveted	Chrome	No*	MATCHBOX © 1979 MACAU	S	P*	£12	
10		Gloss black body & chassis	Chrome	Silver	Maroon 30 mm	Light tan black spokes	Chrome 24 spoke (WW)	Riveted	Chrome	Yes	MATCHBOX © 1979 MACAU		N	£8	
11		Gloss black body & chassis	Chrome	Silver	Maroon 30 mm	Light tan black spokes	Chrome 24 spoke (WF)	Press-fit	Chrome	Yes	MATCHBOX © 1979 MACAU		N	£8	✓
12		Gloss black body & chassis	Chrome	Silver	Maroon 30 mm	Light olive green black spokes	Chrome 24 spoke (WF)	Press-fit	Chrome	Yes	MATCHBOX © 1979 MACAU		N	£8	
13	1995	Gloss black body & chassis	Chrome	Silver	Bright red 30 mm	Black with silver spokes	Chrome 24 spoke (WF)	Press-fit	Chrome	Yes	MATCHBOX © 1979 CHINA		N 2		

NOTES

Issues 13 is coded as YY020-1 by Matchbox Collectibles and has extensive silver painted trim.
Some issues 1-12 have been found with copper axles.
Issues 1 to 8 no digits on number plates.
Issues 9-12 crest and 14654 tampo printed.
Issue 13 IT -147901 tampo printed.

Y21-1 1930 FORD MODEL "A" WOODY WAGON   Scale 1:40

INVESTMENT COMMENT
ORIGINAL PRICE £2.49p
All issues, except 4 and 5, are plentiful. Prices have remained on a par with the level reached in 1992.

In the 1930's the Woody Wagon was a common sight on American roads. This model was the first Yesteryear to feature an all plastic body. Many colour trial versions of the body were produced before the Research and Development Department were satisfied with the overall appearance of the production colour scheme. This model was produced for several years and ran concurrently with the Y21-2 'A & J' version. Consequently different coloured bonnets and seats from each livery got mixed during assembly; giving many variations. Initially the baseplate text changed from '1930 Ford A' to 'Ford Model A'. That was because the chassis component was used for the Y22-1 Ford 'A' van. Later, the base text was changed from 'Lesney Products & Co. Ltd.' to 'Matchbox Int'l Ltd.'; which resulted in yet more variations. In 1982 black chassis components intended for the Y22-1 'Oxo' model were used and are now a scarce variant. In 1983 bonnets which had already been painted yellow were over sprayed with a copper coloured paint which resulted in a metallic orange effect. Copper and acrylic dark orange coloured bonnets were fitted during the last two production runs.

ISSUE	YEAR OF RELEASE	COLOURS	BODY TRIM	ROOF	SEATS/FLOOR/STEERING WHEEL	WHEELS	PLATED PARTS	WINDSCREEN FRAME	BASEPLATE	RARITY	BOX TYPE	VALUE	CHECK LIST
1	1981	Bright yellow bonnet, dark brown chassis	Light brown panels, brown struts	Matt black	Red	Chrome 24 spoke	Chrome	Chrome	LESNEY ©1981 1930* FORD A ENGLAND	D	I	£15	
2		Bright yellow bonnet, dark brown chassis	Light brown panels, brown struts	Matt black	Red	Chrome 24 spoke	Chrome	Chrome	LESNEY © 1981 FORD MODEL A ENGLAND		I	£8	
3		Bright yellow bonnet, dark brown chassis	Light brown panels, brown struts	Matt black	Orange*	Chrome 24 spoke	Chrome	Brown*	LESNEY © 1981 1930* FORD A ENGLAND	S	I	£50	
4	1982	Bright yellow bonnet, glossy black* chassis	Light brown panels, brown struts	Matt black	Red	Chrome 24 spoke	Chrome	Chrome	LESNEY © 1981 FORD MODEL A ENGLAND	D	I	£30	
5		Bright yellow bonnet, glossy black* chassis	Light brown panels, brown struts	Matt black	Red	Chrome 24 spoke	Chrome	Chrome	MATCHBOX © 1981 FORD MODEL A ENGLAND	D	I	£30	
6	1983	Dark metallic orange bonnet, dark brown chassis	Light brown panels, brown struts	Matt black	Red	Chrome 12 spoke (BW)	Chrome	Chrome	LESNEY © 1981 FORD MODEL A ENGLAND		I	£8	
7		Metallic copper bonnet, dark brown chassis	Light brown panels, brown struts	Matt black	Red	Chrome 12 spoke (BW)	Chrome	Chrome	LESNEY © 1981 FORD MODEL A ENGLAND		I	£8	
8		Dark metallic orange bonnet, dark brown chassis	Light brown panels, brown struts	Matt black	Red	Chrome 12 spoke (BW)	Chrome	Chrome	MATCHBOX © 1981 FORD MODEL A ENGLAND		I	£8	
9		Metallic copper bonnet, dark brown chassis	Light brown panels, brown struts	Matt black	Red	Chrome 12 spoke (BW)	Chrome	Chrome	MATCHBOX © 1981 FORD MODEL A ENGLAND		I	£8	
10		Non* metalllic orange bonnet, dark brown chassis	Light brown panels, brown struts	Matt black	Red	Chrome 12 spoke (BW)	Chrome	Chrome	LESNEY © 1981 FORD MODEL A ENGLAND	D	I	£15	
11		Non* metallic orange bonnet, dark brown chassis	Light brown panels, brown struts	Matt black	Red	Chrome 12 spoke (BW)	Chrome	Chrome	MATCHBOX © 1981 FORD MODEL A ENGLAND	D	I	£15	

NOTES

The roof finish to all Y21-1 Ford 'A' models is a matt black imitation wood finish.
A batch of models were produced with copper coloured axles.

INVESTMENT COMMENT
ORIGINAL PRICE £3.50p

Prices have hardly fluctuated since last recorded. Issue 8 is the one to find.

Y21-2 1930 FORD MODEL 'A' TRADESMAN WOODY WAGON Scale 1:40

A & J BOX. The 'A & J Box' was the first of a series of commercial vans based upon light delivery vans. The sides of the model were altered to feature a new side panel in place of the windows. As explained in the introduction to the Y21-1 Woody Wagon, these liveries were produced concurrently and due to bonnet colours and baseplate inscription changes, several variations have been recorded. A small run of the 'A & J Box' had the windscreen frame hot-foil chrome plated, but because of the expense this was quickly abandoned. Bright yellow bonnets were taken from the Y21-1 Woody Wagon assembly line, possibly to keep production going rather than halt it and wait for the yellow bonnets to be oversprayed copper. Yellow bonnets from the Y21-1 run, oversprayed with copper paint gave a metallic orange finish and this variant is easily distinguishable from the pure copper type by the yellow painted bonnet rivets on the baseplate. Two types of baseplates can be found. The pale brown seats, issues 9 and 10, are a different colour to the light brown seats fitted to the Y21-2 'Carters'.

A : A & J BOX

ISSUE	YEAR OF RELEASE	COLOURS	BODY TRIM	ROOF	SEATS / FLOOR	STEERING WHEEL	WHEELS	PLATED PARTS	WINDSCREEN FRAME	LOGO	BASEPLATE	RARITY	BOX TYPE	VALUE	CHECK LIST
1	1983	Metallic copper bonnet, dark brown chassis	Light brown panels, brown struts	Matt black	Off-white	Off-white	Chrome 12 spoke (BW)	Chrome	Brown	A & J	LESNEY © 1981 FORD MODEL A ENGLAND		I	£8	
2		Metallic copper bonnet, dark brown chassis	Light brown panels, brown struts	Matt black	Off-white	Off-white	Chrome 12 spoke (BW)	Chrome	Chrome*	A & J	LESNEY © 1981 FORD MODEL A ENGLAND	D	I	£15	
3		Metallic orange bonnet, dark brown chassis	Light brown panels, brown struts	Matt black	Off-white	Off-white	Chrome 12 spoke (BW)	Chrome	Chrome*	A & J	LESNEY © 1981 FORD MODEL A ENGLAND	D	I	£15	
4		Dark orange bonnet, dark brown chassis	Light brown panels, brown struts	Matt black	Off-white	Off--white	Chrome 12 spoke (BW)	Chrome	Brown	A & J	LESNEY © 1981 FORD MODEL A ENGLAND		I	£8	
5		Metallic orange bonnet, dark brown chassis	Light brown panels, brown struts	Matt black	Off-white	Off-white	Chrome 12 spoke (BW)	Chrome	Brown	A & J	LESNEY © 1981 FORD MODEL A ENGLAND		I	£8	✓
6		Metallic orange bonnet, dark brown chassis	Light brown panels, brown struts	Matt black	White*	White*	Chrome 24 spoke (BW)	Chrome	Brown	A & J	LESNEY © 1981 FORD MODEL A ENGLAND	D	I	£15	
7		Bright yellow* bonnet, dark brown chassis	Light brown panels, brown struts	Matt black	Bright red*	Bright red*	Chrome 24 spoke (BW)	Chrome	Brown	A & J	LESNEY © 1981 1930 FORD A ENGLAND	S	I	£50	
8		Bright yellow* bonnet, black* chassis	Light brown panels, brown struts	Matt black	Off-white	Off-white	Chrome 24 spoke (BW)	Chrome	Brown	A & J	LESNEY © 1981 FORD MODEL A ENGLAND	S	I	£50	
9		Bright yellow* bonnet, black* chassis	Light brown panels, brown struts	Matt black	Pale brown*	Pale brown*	Chrome 24 spoke (BW)	Chrome	Brown	A & J	LESNEY © 1981 1930 FORD A ENGLAND	S	I	£40	
10		Dark orange bonnet, black chassis	Light brown panels, brown struts	Matt black	Pale brown*	Pale brown*	Chrome 12 spoke (BW)	Chrome	Brown	A & J	LESNEY © 1981 FORD MODEL A ENGLAND	S	I	£30	
11		Dark orange bonnet, dark brown chassis	Light brown panels, brown struts	Matt black	Off-white	Off-white	Chrome 12 spoke (BW)	Chrome	Brown	A & J	MATCHBOX © 1981 FORD MODEL A ENGLAND		I	£8	
12		Dark orange bonnet, dark brown chassis	Light brown panels, brown struts	Matt black	Bright red*	Bright red*	Chrome 12 spoke (BW)	Chrome	Brown	A & J	MATCHBOX © 1981 FORD MODEL A ENGLAND	S	I	£50	
13		Dark orange bonnet, dark brownchassis	Light brown panels, brown struts	Matt black	Off-white	Off-white	Chrome 24 spoke (BW)	Chrome	Brown	A & J	MATCHBOX © 1981 FORD MODEL A ENGLAND		I	£8	
14		Metallic copper bonnet, dark brown chassis	Light brown panels, brown struts	Matt black	Off-white	Off-white	Chrome 12 spoke (BW)	Chrome	Brown	A & J	MATCHBOX © 1981 FORD MODEL A ENGLAND		I	£8	

LIVERY

Tampo
Wagon panels. Gold A & J BOX GENERAL STORES.

NOTES

One batch of models was produced with copper coloured axles.

Y21-2 1930 FORD MODEL 'A' TRADESMAN WOODY WAGON   Scale 1:40

INVESTMENT COMMENT
ORIGINAL PRICE £3.50p

An unpopular model due to its visibly high plastic content. At present there does not appear to be any likelihood of a substantial price rise.

CARTERS. The 'Carters' livery in early 1985 became the standard livery for this vehicle. The overall appearance and the continued use of plastic ensured that it never sold particularly well. However as with previous liveries the fairly large range of variations kept the serious collector satisfied. A short run of 'Carters' were fitted with Lesney inscription baseplates and this variation is becoming increasingly difficult to find. Some models were fitted with copper coloured axles. Originally the 'Carters' was packaged in 'J' boxes marked Y22 Limited Edition! Also 'Carters' surplus stock was sold in the D301 twinpack.

B : CARTERS

ISSUE	YEAR OF RELEASE	COLOURS	BODY TRIM	ROOF	SEATS / FLOOR	STEERING WHEEL	WHEELS	PLATED PARTS	WINDSCREEN FRAME	LOGO	"CARTERS" COLOURS	BASEPLATE	RARITY	BOX TYPE	VALUE	CHECK LIST
1	1985	Royal blue bonnet glossy black chassis	Cream panels dark blue struts	Matt black	Brown	Brown	Chrome 12 spoke (BW)	Chrome	Cream	Carters	Blue	MATCHBOX © 1981 FORD MODEL A ENGLAND		J	£8	
2		Royal blue bonnet glossy black chassis	Cream panels dark blue struts	Matt black	Brown	Brown	Chrome 24 spoke (BW)	Chrome	Cream	Carters	Blue	MATCHBOX © 1981 FORD MODEL A ENGLAND		J	£8	
3		Royal blue bonnet glossy black chassis	White panels dark blue struts	Matt black	Light brown	Light brown	Chrome 12 spoke (BW)	Chrome	White	Carters	Pale Blue	MATCHBOX © 1981 FORD MODEL A ENGLAND		J	£10	
4		Royal blue bonnet glossy black chassis	Cream panels dark blue struts	Matt black	Brown	Brown	Chrome 12 spoke (BW)	Chrome	Cream	Carters	Blue	LESNEY © 1981* FORD MODEL A ENGLAND*	S	J	£20	✓
5		Royal blue bonnet glossy black chassis	Cream panels dark blue struts	Matt black	Off-white	Off-white	Chrome 12 spoke (BW)	Chrome	Cream	Carters	Blue	MATCHBOX © 1981 FORD MODEL A ENGLAND		J	£8	
6		Royal blue bonnet glossy black chassis	White panels dark blue struts	Matt black	Off-white	Off-white	Chrome 12 spoke (BW)	Chrome	White	Carters	Pale blue	MATCHBOX © 1981 FORD MODEL A ENGLAND		J	£10	✓
7		Light blue bonnet glossy black chassis	White panels light blue struts	Matt black	Light brown	Light brown	Chrome 12 spoke	Chrome	White	Carters	Pale blue	MATCHBOX © 1981 FORD MODEL A ENGLAND		J	£10	
8		Royal blue bonnet glossy black chassis	Off white panels dark blue struts	Matt black	Light brown	Light brown	Chrome 12 spoke	Chrome	Off-white	Carters	Pale blue	MATCHBOX © 1981 FORD MODEL A ENGLAND		J	£8	

LIVERY CARTERS

Tampo
Wagon panels. CARTERS TESTED SEEDS in blue scroll on white.

NOTES

INVESTMENT COMMENT
ORIGINAL PRICE £17.99p

A good seller for Matchbox. An example of Issue 2 sold at auction in 1992 for £401. However, since then "samples" of Issue 1 have been "leaked" onto the market from the Far East. These "pre-production" models, identical to Issue1, have affected market values.

Y21-3 1894 AVELING & PORTER STEAM ROLLER   Scale 1:60

One of three Special Limited Edition models released in November 1987. This, the second steam roller within the Yesteryear range, was based on an example located in the North of England Open Air Transport Museum at Beamish, County Durham, England. Early pre-production models had red rear wheel spokes, but these were changed to green and further spokes were added. A second inscription was incorporated under the roof as there was no more room left on the base. However, a small batch without any roof inscriptions were packaged and distributed and these are now rare. It has been noted that the colour of the light grey paint on the roofs can vary slightly but not enough to warrant separate codings. The retail sale price of this very attractive model was £17.99 in the UK. The run was limited to 60,000 models worldwide.

ISSUE	YEAR OF RELEASE	COLOURS	CANOPY	FIRE BOX	SMOKE BOX/FRONT ROLLER PIVOT	SMOKE STACK	PLATED PARTS	FRONT ROLLER HOUSING	FRONT ROLLERS-REAR WHEEL TYRES	FRONT ROLLER WHEELS	DRIVING WHEELS	INSCRIPTION UNDERSIDE CANOPY	BASEPLATE	RARITY	BOX TYPE	VALUE	CHECK LIST
1	1987	Emerald green body & boiler	Milky white*	Black	Black	Black with gold rim	Gold	Bright red	Pale* grey solid	Emerald green 5 spoke	Emerald green 16 spoke	None*	MATCHBOX © 1987	R	0	£250	
2		Emerald green body & boiler	Light grey	Black	Black	Black with gold rim	Gold	Bright red	Mid grey solid	Emerald green 5 spoke	Emerald green 16 spoke	None*	MATCHBOX © 1987	V R	0	£300	
3		Emerald green body & boiler	Light grey	Black	Black	Black with gold rim	Gold	Bright red	Mid grey solid	Emerald green 5 spoke	Emerald green 16 spoke	MATCHBOX LIMITED EDITION MACAU	MATCHBOX © 1987		0	£25	✓

LIVERY
Tampo
Canopy fascias. Yellow JAMES YOUNG & SONS EDINBURGH with yellow coachlining.
Roller pivot housing. Gold rampant horse above black INVICTA on gold chevron.
Cylinder housing. Black on gold inscription plates within yellow & black borders.
Coachlining. Yellow to roller support frame. Yellow and black borders to cab sides and outer spokes of the rear wheels.
Roller frame. Red with yellow coachlining.

NOTES
Compare with YAS03.

Y21-4 1957 BMW 507

Scale 1:38

INVESTMENT COMMENT
ORIGINAL PRICE £9.75p

Not popular with collectors even though a Special Limited Edition. In the early 1990s large numbers of unsold stock were "off-loaded" by UK wholesalers onto the collectors market and values ever since have been depressed.

Released in late 1988 as a Special Limited Edition, this BMW car became one of the "youngest dated" models in the Yesteryear range. At a scale of 1:38, it was considered too large to be included in the newly "revived" Dinky Collection. The model was unique in featuring an opening bonnet which revealed a detailed engine. Enhanced detailing was given to this model. This included tampo printed silver "inscription" on a black number plate; red rear stoplights; tampo printed BMW badges on the bonnet front and rear boot; a fully detailed black plastic steering wheel and an opening bonnet which revealed an engine finished in chrome and black. However, it was given a lukewarm reception by collectors; especially when it was discovered that a piece of "flash" had been filed off by hand to enable the bonnet to shut properly and that the filing marks had not been touched in with blue paint. Limited to just under 60,000 models, it was packaged in a superior red and gold box.

ISSUE	YEAR OF RELEASE	COLOURS	HOOD	SEATS	WHEELS	PLATED PARTS	AXLES	BASEPLATE	RARITY	BOX TYPE	VALUE	CHECK LIST
1	1988	Mid blue body, gloss black baseplate	Black	Bright red	Chrome solid (WW)	Chrome	Press-fit	MATCHBOX © 1988 SPECIAL LIMITED EDITION MACAU		J 1	£12	✔

NOTES

The front and rear number plates have silver ^B_R 681° - 313 on black plates with silver edging.
Please be aware that the red flock interior of the box can cause paintwork damage in time.

Y21-5 1926 FORD MODEL 'TT' VAN   Scale 1:41

OSRAM. This is a model of the first commercial vehicle built by Ford Motors. Before 1926 Model 'T' vans and tankers were originally Model 'T' cars with commercial bodies fitted by private companies. In the quest for maximum realism, Matchbox produced a component consisting of the rear axle, differential, prop-shaft, flywheel housing and axle stabilising subframe. Collectors considered the narrower section tyres to be more in scale than the normal wider version. The 10,000 Issue 1 models were made without the black tampo printing to the radiator grille; a marketing variation. After Issue 2 it was considered necessary to cast a strengthening lug under the roof directly above the seats. The total production of the Osram model was 92,850.
MY BREAD. With the introduction of the 'N' type boxes with the diarama background it was necessary to incorporate a screwhole into the base of the model. Therefore, the cast Matchbox registered trademark legend was removed from the base onto the underside of the van body, adjacent to the rear of the nearside step. There were two colours used for the overall livery, a sandy beige or a light beige. Because the van body, roof, bonnet and cab were painted separately before assembly, it is possible to find models with a mixture of colours. The colour of the transmission components, sub frame and the seats can be either, a mid grey or lilac grey. Later issues have darker shades of lilac and brown in the tampo decoration. Because of their press-fit axles, Issues 5 and 6 are easily recognised. These issues were distributed mainly in North America. The total production of the 'My Bread' model was 45,108.

A : OSRAM

ISSUE	YEAR OF RELEASE	COLOURS	ROOF	SEATS	GRILLE	WHEELS	PLATED PARTS	TRANSMISSION & UNDERFRAME	LUG UNDERSIDE CAB ROOF	LOGO	AXLES	THREADED SCREW HOLE	"MATCHBOX" LOCATION	BASEPLATE	RARITY	BOX TYPE	VALUE	CHECK LIST
1	1989	Dark green body and bonnet glossy black chassis	Bright red	Mid grey	Chrome*	Bright red 12 spoke	Chrome	Mid grey	No	OSRAM	Riveted	No	Baseplate	MATCHBOX © 1988 MACAU	D	J1	£15	
2		Dark green body and bonnet glossy black chassis	Bright red	Mid grey	Black	Bright red 12 spoke	Chrome	Mid grey	No	OSRAM	Riveted	No	Baseplate	MATCHBOX © 1988 MACAU		J1	£10	✓
3		Dark green body and bonnet glossy black chassis	Bright red	Mid grey	Black	Bright red 12 spoke	Chrome	Mid grey	Yes*	OSRAM	Riveted	No	Baseplate	MATCHBOX © 1988 MACAU	D	J1	£20	

B : MY BREAD

ISSUE	YEAR OF RELEASE	COLOURS	ROOF	SEATS	GRILLE	WHEELS	PLATED PARTS	TRANSMISSION & UNDERFRAME	LUG UNDERSIDE CAB ROOF	LOGO	AXLES	THREADED SCREW HOLE	"MATCHBOX" LOCATION	BASEPLATE	RARITY	BOX TYPE	VALUE	CHECK LIST
1	1990	Sandy beige body & bonnet, glossy black chassis	Sandy beige	Lilac grey	Black	Red 12 spoke	Chrome	Lilac grey	Yes	MY BREAD	Riveted	Yes	Van body underside	MATCHBOX © 1988 MACAU		N	£10	
2		Sandy beige body & bonnet, glossy black chassis	Sandy beige	Mid grey	Black	Red 12 spoke	Chrome	Lilac grey	Yes	MY BREAD	Riveted	Yes	Van body underside	MATCHBOX © 1988 MACAU		N	£10	✓
3		Sandy beige body & bonnet, glossy black chassis	Sandy beige	Mid grey	Black	Red 12 spoke	Chrome	Mid grey	Yes	MY BREAD	Riveted	Yes	Van body underside	MATCHBOX © 1988 MACAU		N	£10	
4		Light beige* body, sandy beige bonnet, glossy black chassis	Sandy beige	Mid grey	Black	Red 12 spoke	Chrome	Lilac grey	Yes	MY BREAD	Riveted	Yes	Van body underside	MATCHBOX © 1988 MACAU	S	N	£15	
5		Light beige body, & bonnet, glossy black chassis	Light beige	Mid grey	Black	Red 12 spoke	Chrome	Mid grey*	Yes	MY BREAD	Press-fit*	Yes	Van body underside	MATCHBOX © 1988 MACAU	D	N	£15	
6		Light beige body, & bonnet, glossy black chassis	Sandy* beige	Mid grey	Black	Red 12 spoke	Chrome	Lilac grey	Yes	MY BREAD	Press-fit*	Yes	Van body underside	MATCHBOX © 1988 MACAU	D	N	£15	

DIAGRAM 1 LUG UNDERSIDE CAB ROOF

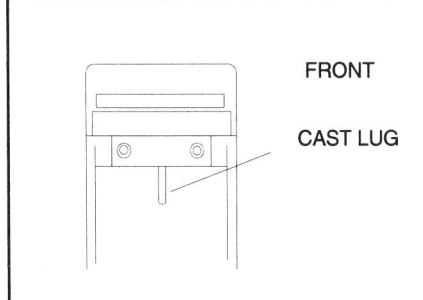

FRONT

CAST LUG

LIVERY OSRAM

Tampo
White outlined red O FOR AN OSRAM superimposed over a white edged yellow light bulb with black G.E.C.
White THE GENERAL ELECTRIC COMPANY at front corner.
White coachlining to oval side window. All within white coachlining.
Cab doors. Red 3 on white disc within white coachlining.

LIVERY MY BREAD

Tampo
Van sides. Brown edged lilac MY BREAD above brown edged lilac stripe. All to the right of a running man in lilac, brown & black; with black AHEAD OF THEM ALL. All above brown MY BREAD BAKING CO. on brown edged lilac stripe.
Rear doors. Smaller version of MY BREAD on van sides, above brown BAKING CO.
Cab doors. Dark lilac 33 in beige circle. All within lilac coachlining.

INVESTMENT COMMENT

ORIGINAL PRICE, OSRAM, £6.25p
MY BREAD £7.25p
OSRAM. An attractive and popular release. One for the future.
MY BREAD. A poor seller and still readily available on the collectors market.

NOTES

Compare with YGB02 and YGB13.

The Y12-4 Rocket will always remain as an incongruous item in the Yesteryear story but it remains an excellent model and one seldom undertaken by model car manufacturers. The Y12-5 GMC van although much more modern is somehow a more authentic looking vehicle - shame about the Singer livery wasn't it?

The Y13-2 Daimler is an excellent example of precision engineering and contains many minor variations, although it is the black seated version which attracts most interest. Lesney and Matchbox extracted great longevity out of the Y13-3 Crossley in a variety of guises. Also featured are the two colour types of the Y14-2 Maxwell.

The Y15-3 Tram has proved to be rather uninteresting visually, whilst the Y14-3 Stutz went through a number of colour schemes, each one more impressive than its predecessor. The most recent release can be seen on the MICA clock photograph! The Y14-4 ERA was deemed a poor model and the Y15-2 Packard has failed to generate any enthusiasm, apart from the colour variations of its plastic components.

The Y16-5 Scammell 100 Ton Tractor is undoubtedly one of the most impressive Yesteryears ever made and appeals to a much wider audience than just Yesteryear collectors. The Y16-4 Scania Bus. by way of contrast, didn't appear to appeal to many people at all! The Y16-2 Mercedes went through several colour schemes and of note is the two-tone green issue. The latest release can be found on the plate featuring some 1991 releases.

The Y17-1 Hispano Suiza benefited from its last colour scheme which finally set off its attractive lines. All issues of the Y18-1 Cord are popular with collectors. The Y18-2 Atkinson has only appeared in four releases, each time in a very different guise.

The Y19-2 Showmans Engine was a beautiful model which would possibly have sold in much higher quantities had it not been a Special Limited Edition. The Y21-3 Road Roller compliments the Showmans Engine. The Y21-4 BMW would have been better suited to the Dinky Collection. The Y19-1 Auburn is a strangely boring model of an exciting car, whereas the Y20-1 Mercedes is a stunning model in any colour scheme.

The Y21-1 Woody Wagon was not destined to excite the collectors market, not least because it was so unattractive; its derivative 'sister', the panelled Y21-2 van, was not much better. Commercial vans such as the Y21-5 Ford 'TT' are keenly collected. However, the Y22-1 Model 'A' van has been in the range too long and has outstayed its early welcome!

Of all the Y23-1 AEC Omnibus models, the most desirable is the red labelled Schweppes version. Becoming harder to find is the Maples version that only came in a gift set. The Y24-1 Bugatti has proved a popular addition to the Yesteryear range. The two Y23-2 tankers are substantial models, both having tanks made of diecast metal and not plastic.

Y21-5 1930 FORD MODEL "TT" VAN Scale 1:41

INVESTMENT COMMENT
ORIGINAL PRICE £8.99p

Drambuie. A good performer helped by a production run estimated to be around 35,000. Further growth potential, as few remain on the market.

DRAMBUIE. The world famous Drambuie Scotch Liqueur became the third logo (second recolour) to be featured on this model. Whilst the overall black livery was nothing unusual, the extremely attractive colours of the logo and the brass plating of the wheels, radiator, headlamps and windscreen framework all added to the overall appeal of the model which was eagerly bought by collectors and many shops were soon "sold out". The "Osram" and "My bread" versions were made in Macau, and although the Drambuie version was made in China, no casting changes were apparent. The cab ceiling lug was still visible but 'Drambuie' models have also been found without this lug. Because the model is still screwed on to the diarama by a screw, the hole is retained in the baseplate. The Matchbox registered trademark legend remains on the underside of the van body. The baseplate legend was amended to reflect the country of manufacture, ie. China. Axles were all press-fit. The production run was 35,000 (E).

C : DRAMBUIE

ISSUE	YEAR OF RELEASE	COLOURS	ROOF	SEATS	PLATED PARTS	GRILLE	WHEELS	TRANSMISSION & UNDERFRAME	LUG UNDERSIDE CAB ROOF	THREADED SCREWHOLE	"MATCHBOX" LOCATION	BASEPLATE	RARITY	BOX TYPE	VALUE	CHECK LIST
1	1992	Gloss black body and chassis	Gloss black	Grey	Brass	Black	Brass 12 spoke	Grey	Yes	Yes	Van body underside	MATCHBOX © 1988 CHINA		N1	£20	✓
2		Gloss black body and chassis	Gloss black	Grey	Brass	Black	Brass 12 spoke	Grey	No	Yes	Van body underside	MATCHBOX © 1988 CHINA		N1	£20	

LIVERY DRAMBUIE

Tampo
Van body. DRAMBUIE in red with gold edging, PRINCE CHARLES EDWARD'S LIQUEUR, 8/9 UNION STREET, EDINBURGH in gold. All within red coachline. Red outline to oval side windows.
Rear door. DRAMBUIE in red with gold edging and 8/9 UNION STREET, EDINBURGH in gold.
Cab doors. Company coat of arms in gold, red, white, green and black.

NOTES

Compare with YGB02 and YGB13

INVESTMENT COMMENT
ORIGINAL PRICE £2.99p

Issue 1 is seldom seen for sale and should continue to command a high premium. Issue 8 with its unique baseplate continues to appreciate in value.

Y22-1 1930 FORD MODEL "A" VAN   Scale 1:40

OXO. The attractive "Oxo" model was released in 1982. After the initial production run, the tools were modified to allow more metal into the cab roof area; which resulted in a raised, slightly textured rectangular panel (Type 2). The 'Oxo' van saw the introduction of a glazed clear Perspex window. Bright red plastic seat, dashboard and cab rear partition components had been used in pre-production trials and the remainder of those were used during the first production run. Due to density variations of the white ink, the colour of the word 'Oxo' and of the Oxo cube varies from white to pink.

A : OXO

ISSUE	YEAR OF RELEASE	COLOURS	VAN ROOF	CAB ROOF	SEATS	WHEELS	PLATED PARTS	LIVERY	BASEPLATE	RARITY	BOX TYPE	VALUE	CHECK LIST
1	1982	Red body, glossy black chassis	Matt black type A	Red type 1	Red*	Chrome 24 spoke (WW)	Chrome	OXO	LESNEY © 1981 Y21 ENGLAND	R	I	£125	
2		Red body, glossy black chassis	Matt black type A	Red type 1	Fawn	Chrome 24 spoke (WW)	Chrome	OXO	LESNEY © 1981 Y21 ENGLAND		I	£10	
3		Red body, glossy black chassis	Gloss* black type A	Red type 1	Fawn	Chrome 24 spoke (WW)	Chrome	OXO	LESNEY © 1981 Y21 ENGLAND	D	I	£20	
4		Red body, glossy black chassis	Matt black type A	Red type 2	Fawn	Chrome 24 spoke (WW)	Chrome	OXO	LESNEY © 1981 Y21 ENGLAND		I	£10	✓
5		Red body, glossy black chassis	Gloss* black type A	Red type 2	Fawn	Chrome 24 spoke (WW)	Chrome	OXO	LESNEY © 1981 Y21 ENGLAND	D	I	£20	
6		Red body, glossy black chassis	Matt black type A	Red type 2	Fawn	Chrome 12 spoke (WW)	Chrome	OXO	LESNEY © 1981 Y21 ENGLAND		I	£12	
7		Red body, glossy black chassis	Matt black type A	Red type 2	Fawn	Chrome solid* (WW)	Chrome	OXO	LESNEY © 1981 Y21 ENGLAND	R	I	£45	
8		Red body, glossy black chassis	Matt black type A	Red type 2	Fawn	Chrome 24 spoke (WW)	Chrome	OXO	MATCHBOX © 1981 Y21 ENGLAND*	S	I	£25	

DIAGRAM 1 VAN ROOF TYPES
TYPE A
TYPE B

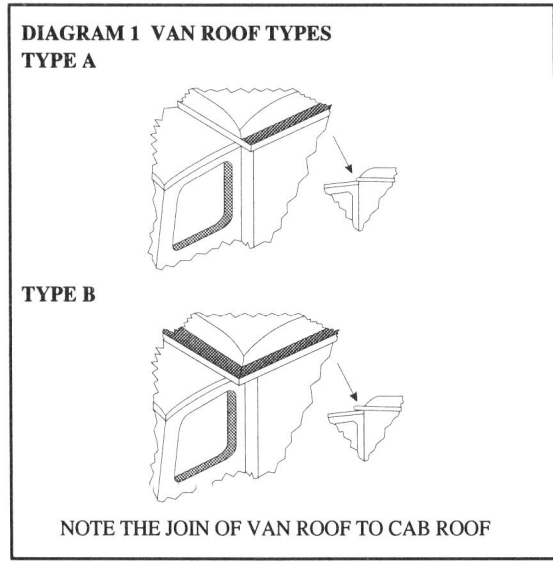

NOTE THE JOIN OF VAN ROOF TO CAB ROOF

DIAGRAM 2 CAB ROOF TYPES
TYPE 1 — SMOOTH CAB ROOF
TYPE 2 — "RAISED PANEL" EFFECT CAB ROOF

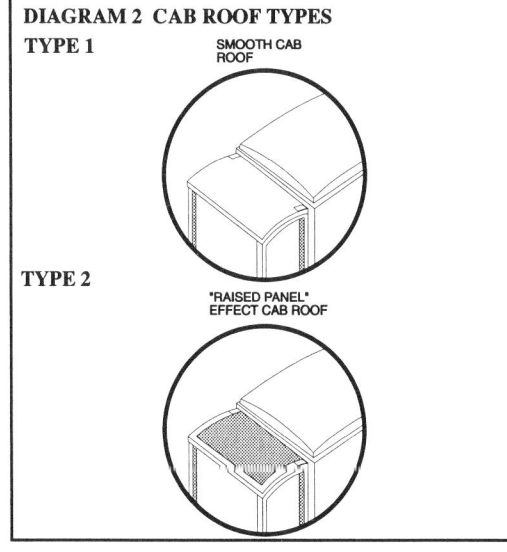

LIVERY OXO

Tampo
Van sides. White OXO with black surround and white IT'S MEAT AND DRINK TO YOU on blue panel.
Cab doors. White outline design of cube and white OXO CUBE CONCENTRATED BEEF + A MEAL IN A MOMENT.

NOTES

Y22-1 1930 FORD MODEL "A" VAN CONTINUED Scale 1:40

INVESTMENT COMMENT
ORIGINAL PRICE £3.50p

A popular model and still available on the obsolete market at reasonable prices. One to watch, especially those with Lesney Product bases. Good growth reported with issues 1 and 6.

MAGGIS. Problems were encountered when mask-spraying the van roof in red. Alterations were made to the tools which resulted in a one millimetre wide guideline ridge along the front edge of the roof (Type B). Two tampo printing plates had been made and although basically similar, there were noticeable differences to several letters in the words 'Suppen' and 'Spiesen'. On the last runs a darker ink was used. The Maggis Company took 14,000 models for their own promotion. Unbeknown to Lesney several thousand, believed to be six thousand, had the Maggis logo applied to the rear doors and were packed into a non Yesteryear box and are therefore classed as Code 3 models.

B : MAGGIS

ISSUE	YEAR OF RELEASE	COLOURS	VAN ROOF	CAB ROOF	SEATS	WHEELS	PLATED PARTS	LIVERY	SCRIPT TYPE	BASEPLATE	RARITY	BOX TYPE	VALUE	CHECK LIST
1	1984	Yellow body, glossy black chassis	Gloss red type A*	Yellow type 2	Fawn	Chrome 24 spoke (WW)	Chrome	MAGGIS	1	LESNEY* © 1981 Y21 ENGLAND	R	I	£40	2
2		Yellow body, glossy black chassis	Gloss red type A*	Yellow type 2	Fawn	Chrome 24 spoke (WW)	Chrome	MAGGIS	1	MATCHBOX © 1981 Y21 ENGLAND	R	I	£40	
3		Yellow body, glossy black chassis	Gloss red type B	Yellow type 2	Fawn	Chrome 24 spoke (WW)	Chrome	MAGGIS	2	LESNEY* © 1981 Y21 ENGLAND	D	I	£25	
4		Yellow body, glossy black chassis	Gloss red type B	Yellow type 2	Fawn	Chrome 24 spoke (WW)	Chrome	MAGGIS	2	MATCHBOX © 1981 Y21 ENGLAND		I	£8	✓ 2x
5		Yellow body, glossy black chassis	Gloss red type B	Yellow type 2	Fawn	Chrome 12 spoke (WW)	Chrome	MAGGIS	2	MATCHBOX © 1981 Y21 ENGLAND		I	£15	
6		Yellow body, glossy black chassis	Gloss red type B	Yellow type 2	Fawn	Red* 12 spoke (WW)	Chrome	MAGGIS	2	LESNEY* © 1981 Y21 ENGLAND	S	I	£30	
7		Yellow body, glossy black chassis	Gloss red type B	Yellow type 2	Fawn	Chrome 12 spoke (WW)	Chrome	MAGGIS	Thicker 2	MATCHBOX © 1981 Y21 ENGLAND		I	£8	

DIAGRAM 1 SCRIPT TYPES

TYPE 1 Suppen - & Speisen -

TYPE 2 Suppen - & Speisen -

LIVERY MAGGIS

Tampo
Van sides. Red MAGGIS, black SUPPEN & SPEISEN. Red WÜRZE, yellow MAGGI-GESELLSCHAFT on black panel.
Cab doors. Black star centring four yellow squares. Gold SCHUTZMARKE.

NOTES

Y22-1 1930 FORD MODEL "A" VAN CONTINUED   Scale 1:40

TOBLERONE. Body castings which had been painted red for the 'Oxo' run, then yellow for the 'Maggis' run were used again, this time overpainted in beige, for the initial run of the 'Toblerone' production. Consequently, these early models had the van roof without the front edge (Type A). Different brown colours were used during the tampo printing process and Issue 2 can have shadow effect to the 'Toblerone' lettering.

PALM TOFFEE. The introduction of the 'Palm Toffee' van revealed another change to the body component; a plastic van roof. This Type C roof can be found on all subsequent Y22 vans. Previous modifications had not solved the problem of the molten metal cooling before each casting was completed. Also, the mask spraying of the metal van roof components had never been to an acceptable standard. With the second production runs in 1985 an emerald green ink was used for the main logo and for the laurel wreaths on the cab doors.

C : TOBLERONE

ISSUE	YEAR OF RELEASE	COLOURS	VAN ROOF	SEATS	WHEELS	PLATED PARTS	LIVERY	TAMPO DECORATION	BASEPLATE	RARITY	BOX TYPE	VALUE	CHECK LIST
1	1984	Beige body, glossy dark brown chassis	Glossy red type A*	Beige	Chrome 24 spoke (W W)	Chrome	TOBLERONE	Brown boy & cab door letters	MATCHBOX © 1981 Y21 ENGLAND	S	J	£20	
2		Beige body, glossy dark brown chassis	Glossy red type B	Beige	Chrome 24 spoke (W W)	Chrome	TOBLERONE	Brown boy & cab door letters	MATCHBOX © 1981 Y21 ENGLAND		J	£8	✓
3		Beige body, glossy dark brown chassis	Glossy red type B	Beige	Chrome 24 spoke (WW)	Chrome	TOBLERONE	Dark brown boy & cab door letters	MATCHBOX © 1981 Y21 ENGLAND		J	£8	
4		Beige body, glossy dark brown chassis	Glossy red type B	Beige	Chrome 24 spoke (W W)	Chrome	TOBLERONE	Light brown boy & cab door letters	MATCHBOX © 1981 Y21 ENGLAND		J	£8	

D : PALM TOFFEE

ISSUE	YEAR OF RELEASE	COLOURS	VAN ROOF	SEATS	WHEELS	PLATED PARTS	LIVERY	TAMPO DECORATION	BASEPLATE	RARITY	BOX TYPE	VALUE	CHECK LIST
1	1984	Light cream body, bright red chassis	Red plastic type C	Beige	Gold 24 spoke	Pale brass	PALM TOFFEE	Dark green logo & laurels	MATCHBOX © 1981 Y21 ENGLAND		J	£8	✓
2	1985	Light cream body, bright red chassis	Red plastic type C	Beige	Gold 24 spoke	Pale brass	PALM TOFFEE	Emerald* green logo & laurels	MATCHBOX © 1981 Y21 ENGLAND	D	J	£12	
3		Light cream body, bright red chassis	Red plastic type C	Beige	Chrome 24* spoke (WW)	Chrome*	PALM TOFFEE	Dark green logo & laurels	MATCHBOX © 1981 Y21 ENGLAND	S	J	£15	

LIVERY   TOBLERONE

Tampo
Van sides. Red TOBLERONE, small boy in brown making a T with his fingers.
Cab doors. Brown CHOCOLAT TOBLER BERNE.

LIVERY   PALM TOFFEE

Tampo
Van sides. Red WALTERS DELICIOUS CREEMY. PALM TOFFEE outlined on green panel and green figure.
Cab doors. Red M.B. WALTERS, green PALM WORKS ACTON LONDON W3. and two green laurels.

INVESTMENT COMMENT

ORIGINAL PRICE TOBLERONE & PALM TOFFEE £3.50p

The Toblerone was probably over-produced. The Palm Toffee, Issue 2, is distinctively different from the other issues and is one to acquire, whilst prices are still reasonable.

NOTES

Y22-1 1930 FORD MODEL "A" VAN CONTINUED   Scale 1:40

CANADA POST. In 1984 the Canadian Post Corporation asked Matchbox for a special Yesteryear to sell through their branches. Those models were packed in a specially lettered box; 'Exclusively from Canada' and 'Exclusente De Postes Canada'. Eventually the model was sold on a worldwide basis in standard boxes.

SPRATT'S. The 'Spratt's' van was released in October 1986 as a Limited Edition with a total worldwide distribution of 85,000 models. The boxes for the 'Spratt's' model have a sticker attached advertising Models of Yesteryear Five Great Offers.

E : CANADA POST

ISSUE	YEAR OF RELEASE	COLOURS	VAN ROOF	SEATS	WHEELS	LIVERY	PLATED PARTS	BASEPLATE	RARITY	BOX TYPE	VALUE	CHECK LIST
1	1984	Post office red body, glossy black chassis	Black plastic type C	Fawn	Black 24 spoke	POSTES CANADA POST	Chrome	MATCHBOX © 1981 Y21 ENGLAND	D	J (CANADA*)	£15	
2		Post office red body, glossy black chassis	Black plastic type C	Fawn	Black 24 spoke	POSTES CANADA POST	Chrome	MATCHBOX © 1981 Y21 ENGLAND		J	£8	✔
3		Post office red body, glossy black chassis	Black plastic type C	Fawn	Chrome*24 spoke	POSTES CANADA POST	Chrome	MATCHBOX © 1981 Y21 ENGLAND	D	J	£15	
4		Post office red body, matt* black chassis	Black plastic type C	Fawn	Black 24 spoke	POSTES CANADA POST	Chrome	MATCHBOX © 1981 Y21 ENGLAND	S	J	£15	

F : SPRATT'S

ISSUE	YEAR OF RELEASE	COLOURS	VAN ROOF	SEATS	WHEELS	LIVERY	PLATED PARTS	BASEPLATE	RARITY	BOX TYPE	VALUE	CHECK LIST
1	1986	Reddish brown body, glossy dark brown chassis	White plastic type C	Light tan	Chrome 24 spoke	SPRATT'S	Chrome	MATCHBOX © 1981 ENGLAND		J	£8	✔
2		Reddish brown body, glossy dark brown chassis	White plastic type C	Light tan	Gold* 12 spoke	SPRATT'S	Chrome	MATCHBOX © 1981 ENGLAND	D	J	£20	

LIVERY CANADA POST
Tampo
Van sides. POSTES CANADA POST in white above multi-coloured royal crest, G. and R. in gold either side.

LIVERY SPRATT'S
Tampo
Van sides.
SPRATT'S, BONIO—OVALS—WEETMEET, all in white above four small black dogs on white panel with red border.
Cab doors. Black dog above red SPRATT'S DOG FOODS BUILD UP A DOG. All on white disc with red border.

INVESTMENT COMMENT
ORIGINAL PRICE, CANADA POST £3.50p
SPRATT'S £3.99p
CANADA POST. Issue 1 is hard to find and is seldom seen for sale. Issue 4 is still eagerly sought after but standard issues remain rather dormant.
SPRATT'S. Brown models never seem to sell well and the Spratt's is no exception, although Issue 2 with its wheel variation is the one to have.

NOTES

Y22-1 1930 FORD MODEL "A" VAN (CONTINUED) Scale 1:40

LYONS' TEA. In 1981, Lesney Products had considered releasing the first Y12-3 Model 'T' Van with a Lyons' Tea livery, but for various reasons it never happened. This Y22 with 'Lyons' Tea' livery was released in June 1987, and is notable as being one of the first models from the Macau factory. Issue 4 is one of the "Chinese Six" models.

CHERRY BLOSSOM. This livery was issued in August 1989, but in 1991 a further production run occurred at the new China factory using the now standard baseplate component for the Y35, the Y21 and the Y22 models. The new method of securing models within the boxes, by means of a self-tapping screw meant that an appropriate hole had to be cast into the baseplate. A total of 47,524 'Cherry Blossom' models were made excluding Issue 2, which is one of the "Chinese six" models.

G : LYONS' TEA

ISSUE	YEAR OF RELEASE	COLOURS	VAN ROOF	SEATS	WHEELS	PLATED PARTS	LIVERY	AXLES	THREADED SCREW HOLE	BASEPLATE	RARITY	BOX TYPE	VALUE	CHECK LIST
1	1987	Dark blue body, glossy black chassis	White plastic type C	Mushroom brown	Chrome 12 spoke	Chrome	LYONS' TEA	Riveted	No	MATCHBOX © 1981 Y7 Y21 Y22 MACAU		J 1	£10	✓
2		Dark blue body, glossy black chassis	White plastic type C	Mushroom brown	Gold* 12 spoke	Chrome	LYONS' TEA	Riveted	No	MATCHBOX © 1981 Y7 Y21 Y22 MACAU	D	J 1	£12	
3		Dark blue body, glossy black chassis	White plastic type C	Mushroom brown	Red 12 spoke	Chrome	LYONS' TEA	Riveted	No	MATCHBOX © 1981 Y7 Y21 Y22 MACAU		J 1	£10	
4	1991	Dark blue body, glossy black chassis	White plastic type C	Light brown*	Chrome 12 spoke	Chrome	LYONS' TEA	Press-fit*	Yes*	MATCHBOX © 1981 Y35 Y21 Y22 CHINA*	S	J 2	£20	

H : CHERRY BLOSSOM

ISSUE	YEAR OF RELEASE	COLOURS	VAN ROOF	SEATS	WHEELS	PLATED PARTS	LIVERY	AXLES	THREADED SCREW HOLE	BASEPLATE	RARITY	BOX TYPE	VALUE	CHECK LIST
1	1989	White body, glossy black chassis	Black plastic type C	Fawn	Red 12 spoke	Chrome	CHERRY BLOSSOM	Riveted	No	MATCHBOX © 1981 Y7 Y21 Y22 MACAU		J 1	£10	✓ 2x
2	1991	White body, glossy black chassis	Black plastic type C	Light brown*	Red 12 spoke	Chrome	CHERRY BLOSSOM	Press-fit*	Yes*	MATCHBOX © 1981 Y35 Y21 Y22 CHINA*	S	J 2	£20	

LIVERY LYONS' TEA
Tampo
Van sides. LYONS' TEA in white with orange and black outline.
Cab doors. 15 in white within white edged circle.

LIVERY CHERRY BLOSSOM
Tampo
Van sides. GIVES A QUICK AND LASTING SHINE in red. A tin of polish with CHERRY BLOSSOM BOOT POLISH in white, red and black.
Cab doors. CHISWICK PRODUCTS LTD CHISWICK LONDON W4 in black.

INVESTMENT COMMENT
ORIGINAL PRICE, LYONS' £5.25p
CHERRY BLOSSOM £6.75p

All issues of the Lyons' Tea have grown in value. Issue 4 is the one to find.

Issue 2 of the Cherry Blossom model is an interesting variation and can often be found for sale at a low price. Worth having.

NOTES

Y22-1 1930 FORD MODEL "A" VAN (CONTINUED) Scale 1:40

INVESTMENT COMMENT
ORIGINAL PRICE £8.99p

Few, if any, exist on the market. Several thousand models of unsold stock were converted into Code 2 models in 1995. Whether that will mean an increase in values remains to be seen.

PRATTS. 'Pratts' was the ninth livery displayed upon this type of model van. Pre-production versions of this model had much larger lettering on the cab doors; but this was not acceptable to the copyright holder. Packed in the then new 'N I' type box, the model was fitted with the new standard self-tapping screw holed baseplate. The production was 35,000 (E).

I : PRATTS

ISSUE	YEAR OF RELEASE	COLOURS	VAN ROOF	SEATS	WHEELS	PLATED PARTS	LIVERY	MAIN DECORATION COLOUR	AXLES	THREADED SCREW HOLE	BASEPLATE	RARITY	BOX TYPE	VALUE	CHECK LIST
1	1991	White body, glossy black chassis	Black plastic type C	Light brown	Orange solid (W W)	Chrome	PRATTS	Orange	Press-fit	Yes	MATCHBOX © 1981 Y35 Y21 Y22 CHINA		N I	£10	✔
2		White body, glossy black chassis	Black plastic type C	Light brown	Orange solid (WW)	Chrome	PRATTS	Red	Press-fit	Yes	MATCHBOX © 1981 Y35 Y21 Y22 CHINA		N I	£10	

LIVERY   PRATTS

Tampo
Van sides. Orange SUPREME IN THE AIR ON LAND AND WATER. All within black edged rectangle:
To the left of petrol pump symbol in orange white and black.
To the left of orange filled circle with black outline; containing black PRATTS with white outline and THE GUARANTEED MOTOR SPIRIT
Van rear doors. Orange filled circle with details similar th van sides.
Cab doors. Black ANGLO-AMERICAN OIL CO LTD.

NOTES

Compare with YGB01 and YFE12.

INVESTMENT COMMENT
ORIGINAL PRICE £3.50p
Issues 1, 2 and 3 have maintained their values. Some potential lies with the later issues such as issues 7 and 8.

Y23-1 1922 AEC OMNIBUS
Scale 1:72

SCHWEPPES Labels with red 'Schweppes' artwork, Type 1, had been produced but rejected and although these were not supposed to be issued a considerable quantity went to Hamleys Toy Shop in London, England. The colour was changed to black and these labels, Type 2, were fitted to the greater majority of models. When the Schweppes trademark owners were shown the black and white labels they were disappointed with the rather drab appearance and thought it was not authentic. A new label was designed about twice the height of the originals and was accepted by Schweppes, Type 3, However this meant that to accommodate the larger sized label the upperhand rail had to be redesigned. This, new, single hand rail became the standard component for all subsequent Y23 Omnibus models. All issues were fitted with black grilles. Many of the last run models left the factory with unplated radiator shells; a negative variation and as such not coded in this publication.

A : SCHWEPPES

ISSUE	YEAR OF RELEASE	COLOURS	UPPER BODY / STAIRS	SEATS / SAFETY BARS	RADIATOR SHELL	LOGO	SIDE PANEL LABEL COLOURS	UPPER DECK HANDRAIL	WHEELS	BASEPLATE	RARITY	BOX TYPE	VALUE	CHECK LIST
1	1983	"London General" red body, glossy black chassis	"London General" red	Light Tan	Silver	SCHWEPPES Type 1	Red & white*	Double	Red 12 spoke	LESNEY © 1982 ENGLAND	S	I	£100	
2		"London General" red body, glossy black chassis	"London General" red	Tan	Silver	SCHWEPPES Type 1	Red & white*	Double	Red 12 spoke	LESNEY © 1982 ENGLAND	S	I	£100	
3		"London General" red body, glossy black chassis	"London General" red	Dark brown	Silver	SCHWEPPES Type 1	Red & white*	Double	Red 12 spoke	LESNEY © 1982 ENGLAND	S	I	£100	
4		"London General" red body, glossy black chassis	"London General" red	Light tan	Silver	SCHWEPPES Type 2	Black & white	Double	Red 12 spoke	LESNEY © 1982 ENGLAND		I	£10	✓
5		"London General" red body, glossy black chassis	"London General" red	Tan	Silver	SCHWEPPES Type 2	Black & white	Double	Red 12 spoke	LESNEY © 1982 ENGLAND		I	£10	
6		"London General" red body, glossy black chassis	"London General" red	Dark brown	Silver	SCHWEPPES Type 2	Black & white	Double	Red 12 spoke	LESNEY © 1982 ENGLAND		I	£10	
7		"London General" red body, glossy black chassis	Light red*	Tan	Silver	SCHWEPPES Type 2	Black & white	Double	Red 12 spoke	LESNEY © 1982 ENGLAND	S	I	£25	
8		"London General" red body, glossy black chassis	Dark red*	Tan	Silver	SCHWEPPES Type 2	Black & white	Double	Red 12 spoke	LESNEY © 1982 ENGLAND	D	I	£15	
9		"London General" red body, glossy black chassis	"London General" red	Tan	Silver	SCHWEPPES Type 3	Yellow black & white	Single	Red 12 spoke	LESNEY © 1982 ENGLAND		I	£10	
10		"London General" red body, glossy black chassis	Dark red*	Tan	Silver	SCHWEPPES Type 3	Yellow black & white	Single	Red 12 spoke	LESNEY © 1982 ENGLAND		I	£10	

DIAGRAM 1 UPPER DECK HANDRAIL TYPES

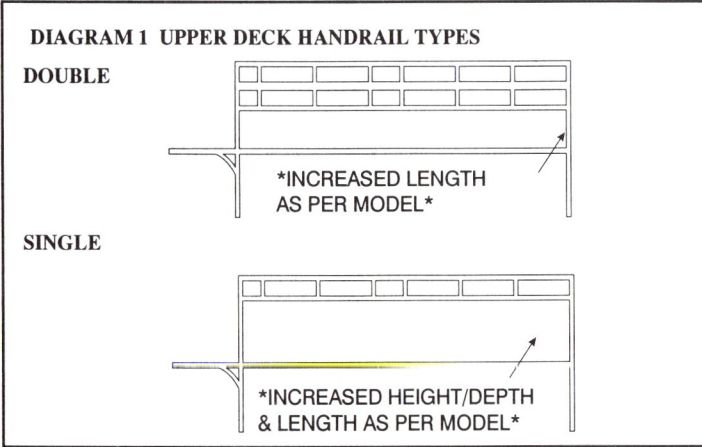

DOUBLE

INCREASED LENGTH AS PER MODEL

SINGLE

INCREASED HEIGHT/DEPTH & LENGTH AS PER MODEL

LIVERY
Labels
Front Destination Board - Central panel HITHER GRN STN, HARROW ROAD, PADDINGTON STN, VICTORIA STN, CAMBERWELL GRN, NEW + GATE, LEWISHAM, CATFORD. HUDSONS SOAP advertisement each side. All in black, blue and white on red background.
Stairway advertising panel. HORLICKS THE ORIGINAL MALTED MILK in blue on white. White OXO. White CEREBOS on blue oval. All above white PICCADILLY. All on diagonal red label.
Side upper panels. SCHWEPPES TONIC WATER with horizontal line above and below. Imitation scolloped edges. All in red on white panel.
Tampo
Side lower panel. GENERAL in gold with gold underlining between E and A.
Issues 4 to 8 All as above except upper side panels black on white labels.
Issue 9 & 10 All as above except upper side panels. Yellow labels with Purveyors to His Mastesty King George V in black. SCHWEPPES in white with black shadow effect. Encircled black R and SODA WATER DRY GINGER ALE Etc in black.

NOTES
Fake models exist of issues 1, 2 and 3. These are poorly cut on a matt paper with square ends. Genuine labels are on the same texture paper as the black and white labels. They should have a gloss finish with rounded "corners".

Y23-1 1922 AEC OMNIBUS (CONTINUED) Scale 1:72

RAC. Founded in 1897 the Royal Automobile Club is the first organisation specifically formed to cater for the needs of the motorist at a time when the first motor cars were very unreliable. Since then the RAC has become a UK national institution with its own famous club in Pall Mall, London, England. The Club organises the annual London to Brighton veteran car rally which commemorates the abolition of the "Man with the red flag" which prior to the event was a legal requirement for car drivers on UK roads. Matchbox Toys took particular care to accurately reproduce the multi coloured authentic liveried side panel labels. The design was taken from a bus at the National Motor Museum, Beaulieu, Hampshire, England. As with the earliest 'Schweppes' model a late production run was released without plated radiator shells.

MAPLES. Maples of Tottenham Court Road, London, is one of the four best known UK late 19th Century furniture design and manufacturing concerns; the others being Heals and Liberty, both of London and Warings & Gillow of Lancaster. This model is found only in the 1985 Father's Day Gift Set with the Y11-3 1938 Lagonda Drophead and the Y25-1 Renault Van 'Duckhams Oil' models. Only 40,000 sets were made for worldwide sales. As with the 'RAC' and 'Schweppes' models the 'Maples' was based on a London General Omnibus Company vehicle.

B : RAC

ISSUE	YEAR OF RELEASE	COLOURS	UPPER BODY / STAIRS	SEATS / SAFETY BARS	RADIATOR SHELL	LOGO	WHEELS	BASEPLATE	RARITY	BOX TYPE	VALUE	CHECK LIST
1	1985	"London General" red body, glossy black chassis	"London General" red	Tan	Silver	RAC	Red 12 spoke	LESNEY © 1982 ENGLAND		J	£10	✓

C : MAPLES

ISSUE	YEAR OF RELEASE	COLOURS	UPPER BODY / STAIRS	SEATS / SAFETY BARS	RADIATOR SHELL	LOGO	WHEELS	BASEPLATE	RARITY	BOX TYPE	VALUE	CHECK LIST
1	1985	"London General" red body, glossy black chassis	"London General "red	Tan	Silver	MAPLES	Red 12 spoke	LESNEY © 1982 ENGLAND		L	£30 The Set	
2		"London General" red body, glossy black chassis	Dark red*	Tan	Silver	MAPLES	Red 12 spoke	LESNEY © 1982 ENGLAND	S	L	£70 The Set	

LIVERY RAC

Labels
Front Destination Board.
HITHER GRN STN with HUDSONS SOAP in red, white, black & blue.
HARROW ROAD PADDINGTON STN, VICTORIA STN, CAMBERWELL GRN, NEW + GATE LEWISHAM CATFORD
Stairway panels.
HORLICKS THE ORIGINAL MALTED MILK, OXO, CEREBOS and PICCADILLY CIRCUS in white, red and blue.
Side Upper Panels
RAC in blue, THE SERVICE BEGAN RUNNING 25 (in yellow) YEARS BEFORE THIS BUS in orange, edged in blue, two RAC logos in white on blue.
Tampo
Side lower panels. Gold GENERAL

LIVERY MAPLES

Labels
Front Destination Board.
TO DOLLIS HILL in red, EDGWARE RD, MARYLEBONE RD, TOTTENHAM CT. RD. CHARING + WATERLOO BRIDGE, ELEPHANT, in black on white background above white MAPLES on green panel.
Stairway Panels.
HORLICKS THE ORIGINAL MALTED MILK, OXO, CEREBOS and PICCADILLY CIRCUS in white, red and blue.
Side Upper Panels
White MAPLES with black surround, ARTISTIC FURNITURE in white on green panel.
Tampo
Side lower panels. Gold GENERAL.

INVESTMENT COMMENT

ORIGINAL PRICE, RAC £3.99p

RAC. Never as popular as the Schweppes model and still readily available on the market.
MAPLES. Because it only came in a gift set of three models and in restricted numbers, prices have continued to rise. Presently these boxed sets sell in excess of £30 in the UK. Issue 2 is of course the one to find.

NOTES

Maples Issue 2-only three models have been reported so far!

Y23-1 1922 AEC OMNIBUS (CONTINUED)   Scale 1:72

HAIG. This model advertises one of the better known brands of Scottish Whisky and was the first non London General red Omnibus in the series. The dark brown and cream Express Omnibus Company's livery became the standard 1986 issue with a total production of 119,800 models. The colour of plastic associated with Issue 1 is sometimes referred to as light grey.

RICE KRISPIES. To celebrate sixty years of 'Rice Krispies' in 1987, Kellogg's commissioned Matchbox to produce an omnibus with Kellogg's advertisements. Initially the model was obtained via an "on-pack" offer run by Kellogg's. A light blue MB 38 Ford 'A' van was also offered! However, enough models were made to satisfy collectors worldwide. Issued in January 1988 the model became the best selling Yesteryear that year and the best all time selling Y23-1 Omnibus. The front destination board and rear stair advertising labels were changed to promote the Kellogg's product. There have been reports of 'Rice Krispies' models with England baseplates. These may well be factory pre-production models and it is unclear whether any were released for general sale. The main production facility was in the Far East at the newly opened factory in Macau.

D: HAIG

ISSUE	YEAR OF RELEASE	COLOURS	UPPER BODY/STAIRS	SEATS & SAFETY BARS	RADIATOR SHELL	LOGO	WHEELS	BASEPLATE	RARITY	BOX TYPE	VALUE	CHECK LIST
1	1986	Dark brown body, glossy black chassis	Off white	Dark brown	Silver	HAIG	Dark red 12 spoke	LESNEY © 1982 ENGLAND		J	£10	
2		Dark brown body, glossy black chassis	Light cream	Dark brown	Silver	HAIG	Dark red 12 spoke	LESNEY © 1982 ENGLAND		J	£10	✓
3		Dark brown body, glossy black chassis	Light cream	Dark brown	Silver	HAIG	Light red 12 spoke	LESNEY © 1982 ENGLAND		J	£10	
4		Dark brown body, glossy black chassis	Light cream	Mid brown	Silver	HAIG	Light red 12 spoke	LESNEY © 1982 ENGLAND		J	£10	
5		Dark brown body, glossy black chassis	Light cream	Mid brown	Silver	HAIG	Dark red 12 spoke	LESNEY © 1982 ENGLAND		J	£10	
6		Dark brown body, glossy black chassis	Dark cream	Dark brown	Silver	HAIG	Dark red 12 spoke	LESNEY © 1982 ENGLAND		J	£10	

E: RICE KRISPIES

ISSUE	YEAR OF RELEASE	COLOURS	UPPER BODY/STAIRS	SEATS & SAFETY BARS	RADIATOR SHELL	LOGO	WHEELS	BASEPLATE	RARITY	BOX TYPE	VALUE	CHECK LIST
1	1988	"London General" red body, glossy black chassis	"London General" red	Tan	Silver	RICE KRISPIES	Red 12 spoke	MATCHBOX © 1982 MACAU		J1	£10	✓

LIVERY HAIG
Labels
Front Destination Board.
Red STRAND with black ALDWYCH above BUSHEY PARK, WALDERGRAVE RD. RICHMOND RD. HAMMERSMITH BDY, KNIGHTSBRIDGE, HYDE PARK CORNER, PICCADILLY CIRCUS CHARING + in black on cream background.
Each side of board DON'T BE VAGUE ASK FOR HAIG in red with black outline on cream background.
Stairway Panels.
HORLICKS THE ORIGINAL MALTED MILK, OXO, CEREBOS and PICCADILLY CIRCUS in white, red and blue.
Side Upper Panels. HAIG in red outlined in blue DON'T BE VAGUE ASK FOR WHISKY AT IT'S BEST in black.
Tampo
Side Lower Panels. Gold EXPRESS.

LIVERY RICE KRISPIES
Labels
Front destination board.
Red Kellogg's RICE KRISPIES in black and the three Snap, Crackle and Pop characters in red, black, yellow, orange, brown and cream on white background.
Stairway Panels.
KELLOGG'S RICE KRISPIES in red on white.
Side Upper Panels
KELLOGG'S in red, RICE KRISPIES in black with the same three "characters" as on the destination board.
Tampo
Side Lower Panels   Gold GENERAL.

INVESTMENT COMMENT
ORIGINAL PRICE, HAIG and RICE KRISPIES £4.25p
HAIG. The Haig livery has been slow to appreciate, probably because of its 'brown' colour scheme and high production numbers.
RICE KRISPIES. A poor performer and one with little potential.

NOTES

| INVESTMENT COMMENT | # Y23-1 1922 AEC OMNIBUS (CONTINUED) | Scale 1:72 |

ORIGINAL PRICE £6.25p

LIFEBUOY Issue 1 now changes hands at three times its original price and is the one to search and find.

LIFEBUOY. Only the second colour change in the six years production of this bus, the model appeared in the livery of the East Surrey Omnibus Company in January 1989 as a Limited Edition. A mistake was made in printing the name of the town Copthorne, which was misspelt as "Coptworne". However, the mistake was soon rectified and models with new labels were released in May 1989. Matchbox Toys changed the grille to dark brown. The production run was 60,000 (E).

F : LIFEBUOY

ISSUE	YEAR OF RELEASE	COLOURS	UPPER BODY & STAIRS	SEATS & SAFETY BARS	GRILLE	RADIATOR	LOGO	WHEELS	DESTINATION BOARD	BASEPLATE	RARITY	BOX TYPE	VALUE	CHECK LIST
1	1989	Dark blue body, glossy black chassis	Light cream	Dark brown	Dark brown	Silver	LIFEBUOY	Cream 12 spoke	Coptworne*	MATCHBOX © 1982 MACAU	D	J 1	£20	✓
2		Dark blue body, glossy black chassis	Light cream	Dark brown	Dark brown	Silver	LIFEBUOY	Cream 12 spoke	Copthorne	MATCHBOX © 1982 MACAU		J 1	£10	

LIVERY LIFEBUOY
Labels.
Front Destination Board. HARTFIELD REDHILL EARLSWOOD SALFORDS HORLEY SMALLFIELD COPTWORNE (or COPTHORNE) FELBRIDGE E. GRINSTEAD ASHURST WOOD. All on white panel.
Upper side panels. White FOR SAVING LIFE TO CLEANSE above white LIFEBUOY SOAP on black panel with black outlined white lifebuoy with black ROYAL DISINFECTANT and white crest above black FOR PRESERVATION OF HEALTH TO PURITY. All on yellow panel.
Staircase panel. White LIFEBUOY SOAP on black panel with yellow.

NOTES

Compare with YET05.

Y23-2 1930 MACK TANKER
Scale 1:60

TEXACO. Originally scheduled to appear in May 1989, it wasn't until August 1989 that it did finally arrive. Initially the appearance was spoilt by the twin rear wheels being too wide and many designs of wheel were made before the R & D Department were satisfied with the general appearance. However, several models were found, mainly in Belgium and Australia, fitted with final pre-production front wheels, Type 1 which had not been intended to be fitted to production models. The normal production wheels, Type 2 for this model were also used for the Y9-4 Leyland Cub Fire Engine. Collectors were most impressed with the extensive amount of diecast metal used in the manufacture of the tanker which felt heavy and substantial. All baseplates had Y23 cast. Total production was 50,076.

CONOCO. The Conoco petrol tanker was released in April 1991. Matchbox Toys Ltd. had talked with the Budweiser corporation and at one time it appeared that this famous American brewer would be the second livery on the Y23. However, negotiations did not progress and with the 1991 selection meetings imminent, an alternative livery, that of 'Conoco', was sought and obtained. The end flaps of the box featured the number '23-B' - the letter B indicated that this was the first re-colour or change of livery to the Y23.

A : TEXACO

ISSUE	YEAR OF RELEASE	COLOURS	TANK	SEAT	HEADLIGHTS FIRE EXTINGUISHER	PETROL CANS DISCHARGE VALVES	REAR WHEELS	FRONT WHEEL TYPES	LOGO	THREADED SCREW HOLE	BASEPLATE	RARITY	BOX TYPE	VALUE	CHECK LIST
1	1989	Bright red body, glossy black chassis	Bright red	Fawn	Brass	Chrome	Red solid doubles	Red type 1*	TEXACO	No	Y23 MATCHBOX © 1985 MACAU	S	J 1	£25	✓
2		Bright red body, glossy black chassis	Bright red	Fawn	Brass	Chrome	Red solid doubles	Red type 2	TEXACO	No	Y23 MATCHBOX © 1985 MACAU		J 1	£12	

B : CONOCO

ISSUE	YEAR OF RELEASE	COLOURS	TANK	SEAT	HEADLIGHTS FIRE EXTINGUISHER	PETROL CANS DISCHARGE VALVES	REAR WHEELS	FRONT WHEEL TYPES	LOGO	THREADED SCREW HOLE	BASEPLATE	RARITY	BOX TYPE	VALUE	CHECK LIST
1	1991	Bright red body, glossy black chassis	White	Fawn	Brass	Chrome	Red solid doubles	Red type 2	CONOCO	Yes	Y23 MATCHBOX © 1985 CHINA		N 1	£10	✓

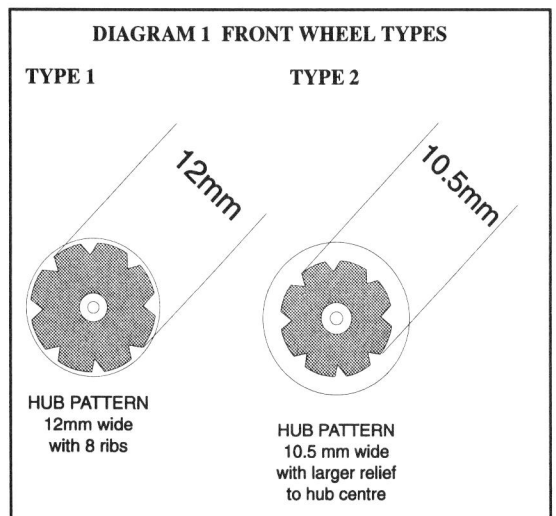

DIAGRAM 1 FRONT WHEEL TYPES

TYPE 1 — HUB PATTERN 12mm wide with 8 ribs

TYPE 2 — HUB PATTERN 10.5 mm wide with larger relief to hub centre

LIVERY TEXACO
Tampo
Truck body panels. White TEXACO PETROLEUM PRODUCTS MADE BY THE TEXACO COMPANY U.S.A. with two logos of white 'T' on red 5 pointed star with red "TEXACO" on white disk.
Tank rear panel. White company logo above white TEXACO.
Cab side panels. White company logo above white THE TEXAS COMPANY.
Bonnet front. Mack logo of white M on black disc within white coachlining.

LIVERY CONOCO
Tampo
Truck body panels. White CONTINENTAL OIL COMPANY with white coachlining.
Tank sides. Logo of red and white triangles with white CONOCO on red panel both sides of red CONOCO.
Tank rear panel. Red and white company logo.
Cab side panels. White coachlining.
Cab doors. Smaller version of company logo within white coachlining.
Bonnet front. Company's red and white logo with white coachlining above white CONOCO.

INVESTMENT COMMENT
ORIGINAL PRICE TEXACO £6.25p
CONOCO £7.25p

TEXACO. The Texaco model has proved popular especially Issue 1.

CONOCO. A very poor performer and likely to continue so.

NOTES
Compare with YFE11.

Y24-1 1928 BUGATTI T44

Scale 1:38

INVESTMENT COMMENT
ORIGINAL PRICE £3.50p

All values have remained as for 1992 and standard issues are still relatively easy to obtain on the obsolete market. Maybe the 1995 release will stimulate the market for earlier issues, which new collectors may seek to purchase.

Hugh Conway the well known automobile historian submitted photographs and drawings to Matchbox for use in the design of this model. Two design modifications were made. Firstly, the rear window was reduced in width from fifteen to thirteen millimetres. Secondly, once production had begun it was seen that the gaps between the inside edges of the rear mudguards and the rear number plate tended to fill with 'flash'. The tools were modified so that the gaps could be filled, Type 2. Originally, the doors and rear side panels were mask sprayed; but this meant that the horizontal bar immediately above the door handles could not be colour matched to the body, Issues 1-8. The problem was solved by tampo printing that area. Four different coloured seats were fitted to the 1983/84 issues. The 1987 issue 13, was packaged with a plastic diorama. The 1990 issue formed part of the 'Great Motor Cars of the Century' mail order promotion in the USA. Later the model was released worldwide and towards the end of the production period the model was made with the new style press-fit axles. The total production for Issues 14, 15, 16 and 17 was 33,156.

ISSUE	YEAR OF RELEASE	COLOURS	DOOR & REAR SIDE PANELS	DOOR STRIPE	STEERING WHEEL	SEATS	WHEELS	PLATED PARTS	LUGGAGE TRUNK	REAR WINDOW WIDTH	REAR MUDGUARD GAP	AXLES	THREADED SCREW HOLE	BASEPLATE	RARITY	BOX TYPE	VALUE	CHECK LIST
1	1983	Black body roof & chassis	Bright yellow	Bright yellow	Black	Beige	Chrome 24 spoke	Chrome	Black	15 mm	Type 1 open	Riveted	No	MATCHBOX © 1983 ENGLAND		I	£10	
2		Black body roof & chassis	Bright yellow	Bright yellow	Black	Brown*	Chrome 24 spoke	Chrome	Black	15 mm	Type 1 open	Riveted	No	MATCHBOX © 1983 ENGLAND	R	I	£150	
3		Black body roof & chassis	Bright yellow	Bright yellow	Black	Green*	Chrome 24 spoke	Chrome	Black	15 mm	Type 1 open	Riveted	No	MATCHBOX © 1983 ENGLAND	R	I	£150	
4		Black body roof & chassis	Bright yellow	Bright yellow	Black	White*	Chrome 24 spoke	Chrome	Black	15 mm	Type 1 open	Riveted	No	MATCHBOX © 1983 ENGLAND	S	I	£100	
5		Black body roof & chassis	Bright yellow	Bright yellow	Black	Beige	Chrome 24 spoke	Chrome	Black	13 mm*	Type 1 open	Riveted	No	MATCHBOX © 1983 ENGLAND	D	I	£50	
6	1983	Black body roof & chassis	Yellow*	Yellow	Black	White*	Chrome 24 spoke	Chrome	Black	15 mm*	Type 2 closed	Riveted	No	MATCHBOX © 1983 ENGLAND	D	I	£75	
7		Black body roof & chassis	Bright yellow	Bright yellow	Black	Beige	Chrome 24 spoke	Chrome	Black	15 mm*	Type 2 closed	Riveted	No	MATCHBOX © 1983 ENGLAND	D	I	£50	
8		Black body roof & chassis	Bright yellow	Bright yellow	Black	Beige	Chrome 24 spoke	Chrome	Black	13 mm	Type 2 closed	Riveted	No	MATCHBOX © 1983 ENGLAND		I/J	£10	✓
9	1984	Black body roof & chassis	Lemon yellow	Black	Black	Beige	Chrome 24 spoke	Chrome	Black	13 mm	Type 2 closed	Riveted	No	MATCHBOX © 1983 ENGLAND		J	£10	
10		Black body roof & chassis	Lemon yellow	Black	Black	White*	Chrome 24 spoke	Chrome	Black	13 mm	Type 2 closed	Riveted	No	MATCHBOX © 1983 ENGLAND	S	J	£30	

DIAGRAM 1 TYPE 1 OPEN GAPS — REAR MUDGUARDS TO REAR NUMBER PLATE — **DIAGRAM 2 TYPE 2 FILLED IN**

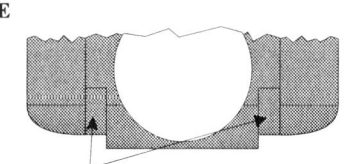

NOTES

Y24-1 1928 BUGATTI T44 (CONTINUED) Scale 1:38

The Bugatti was re-issued in 1995 as part of the "Grand Marques" series. Selling price was £12.50. The wheels were now devoid of the white wall flanges as found in Issues 14, 15 and 16. The doors and rear side panels brought admirable comments from collectors because of the exceptionally fine 'basket weave' effect tampo decoration.

ISSUE	YEAR OF RELEASE	COLOURS	DOOR & REAR SIDE PANELS	DOOR STRIPE	STEERING WHEEL	SEATS	WHEELS	PLATED PARTS	LUGGAGE TRUNK	REAR WINDOW WIDTH	REAR MUDGUARD GAP	AXLES	THREADED SCREW HOLE	BASEPLATE	RARITY	BOX TYPE	VALUE	CHECK LIST
11	1987	Black body roof & chassis	Lemon yellow	Black	Black	Black*	Chrome 24 spoke	Chrome	Black	13 mm	Type 2 closed	Riveted	No	MATCHBOX © 1983 ENGLAND	D	J	£15	
12	1987	Black body roof & chassis	Lemon yellow	Black	Black	Black*	Chrome 12* spoke	Chrome	Black	13 mm	Type 2 closed	Riveted	No	MATCHBOX © 1983 ENGLAND	S	J	£30	
13	1987	Light grey body and roof, red chassis	Dull red	Light grey	Black	Beige	Chrome solid	Chrome	Light grey	13 mm	Type 2 closed	Riveted	No	MATCHBOX © 1983 MACAU		J 1	£10	✓
14	1990	Black body roof & chassis	Dark red	Black	Black	Light brown	Chrome 24 spoke (WF)	Chrome	Light tan	13 mm	Type 2 closed	Riveted	Yes	MATCHBOX © 1983 MACAU	D	P/N	£15	
15		Black body roof & chassis	Red	Black	Black	Light brown	Chrome 24 spoke (WF)	Chrome	Light tan	13 mm	Type 2 closed	Riveted	Yes	MATCHBOX © 1983 MACAU		N	£10	
16		Black body roof & chassis	Red	Black	Black	Light brown	Chrome 24 spoke (WF)	Chrome	Light tan	13 mm	Type 2 closed	Press-fit	Yes	MATCHBOX © 1983 MACAU		N	£10	
17		Black body roof & chassis	Dark red	Black	Black	Light brown	Chrome 24 spoke (WF)	Chrome	Light tan	13 mm	Type 2 closed	Press-fit	Yes	MATCHBOX © 1983 MACAU		N	£12	✓
18	1995	Gloss black body, roof and chassis	Khaki wicker work	Khaki	Light tan with black spokes	Light tan	Chrome 24 spoke	Chrome	Black	13 mm	Type 2 closed	Press-fit	Yes	MATCHBOX © 1983 CHINA		N 2		

NOTES
Issue 18 is coded as YY024/A-D on the box by Matchbox Collectibles.

INVESTMENT COMMENT
ORIGINAL PRICE £3.50p

Issue 1 remains at the same value as reported previously but could start to climb. All other issues are stationary.

Y25-1 1910 RENAULT TYPE AG VAN   Scale 1:38

PERRIER. At first the Y25 'Perrier' van was released with fewer roof struts (Type one). However it was soon found that the plastic was weak and that these luggage rails broke easily. Also, the tools for the side lamp lens on the driver's side were altered. The modified lens was used on all subsequent models of the Y25. Due to the easy interchangeability of the seat component with the Y14 Maxwell and Y13/Y26 Crossley models, no premium should be attached to seat colour variations. A problem occurred with the windscreen mould tooling which resulted in the grab handles being filled in during the James Neale run. Several thousand of these components were produced before the fault was rectified. The majority of the closed grab handle windscreens were fitted to the James Neale vans, but some were also fitted to later runs of the Perrier, the Duckhams, Eagle Pencil and the Tunnocks.

A : PERRIER

ISSUE	YEAR OF RELEASE	COLOURS	BONNET & CAB FLOOR	HOLE IN CAB FLOOR	ROOF	SEATS	RIGHT HAND LENS	WHEELS	PLATED PARTS	GRAB HANDLES	LOGO	BASEPLATE	RARITY	BOX TYPE	VALUE	CHECK LIST
1	1983	Bright green body, dark green chassis	Dark green	No	White type A*	White	Type 1	Gold 12 spoke	Brass	Open	PERRIER	MATCHBOX © 1983 ENGLAND	V R	I	£250	
2		Bright green body, dark green chassis	Dark green	No	White type B	White	Type 1	Gold 12 spoke	Brass	Open	PERRIER	MATCHBOX © 1983 ENGLAND		I	£10	
3		Bright green body, dark green chassis	Dark green	No	White type B	White	Type 1	Bright red 12 spoke (BW)	Brass	Open	PERRIER	MATCHBOX © 1983 ENGLAND		I	£10	
4		Bright green body, dark green chassis	Dark green	No	White type B	White	Type 1	Dark red 12 spoke	Brass	Open	PERRIER	MATCHBOX © 1983 ENGLAND		I	£10	
5		Bright green body, dark green chassis	Dark green	No	White type B	Dark red	Type 1	Gold 12 spoke	Brass	Open	PERRIER	MATCHBOX © 1983 ENGLAND		I/J	£8	
6		Bright green body, dark green chassis	Dark green	No	White type B	White	Type 2	Gold 12 spoke	Brass	Open	PERRIER	MATCHBOX © 1983 ENGLAND		I/J	£8	✓
7		Bright green body, dark green chassis	Dark green	No	White type B	White	Type 2	Chrome 12 spoke	Brass	Open	PERRIER	MATCHBOX © 1983 ENGLAND		I/J	£8	
8	1985	Bright green body, dark green chassis	Dark green	No	White type B	White	Type 2	Gold 12 spoke	Brass	Closed*	PERRIER	MATCHBOX © 1983 ENGLAND	R	I/J	£75	

DIAGRAM 1 ROOF TYPES

DIAGRAM 2 LENS TYPES

TYPE 1   TYPE 2

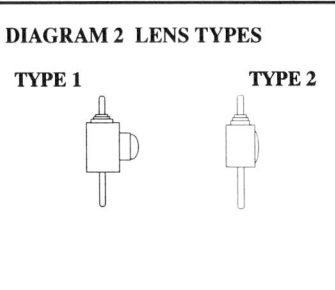

DIAGRAM 3 GRAB HANDLES

OPEN   CLOSED

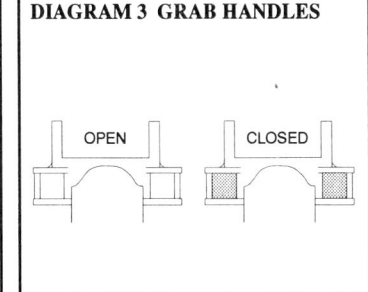

LIVERY PERRIER
Tampo
Van sides. PERRIER in white with black shadow effect and small white R in white circle. Above red, and white Perrier logo. All within white frame. All within white frame. All above white MISE EN BOUTEILLE A LA SOURCE VERGEZE (GARD) FRANCE.
Header board. Black PERRIER and two scrolls.

NOTES

Y25-1 1910 RENAULT TYPE AG VAN CONTINUED Scale 1:38

INVESTMENT COMMENT
ORIGINAL PRICE £15.00p
Although standard issues have retreated somewhat, there is still plenty of interest in the later issues.

JAMES NEALE As an inducement the Y25 'James Neale' models were offered to U.K. wholesalers who had ordered the Connoisseur set of six models which were proving difficult to sell. Wholesalers were invited to order a further 50% of their previous order. It was intended that the van should be given free with Connoisseur sets. However this did not happen; instead the dealers with few exceptions, sold the vans at a premium price of around £15.
30,000 James Neale vans were produced, of which 5,000 were sent to Australia. Differing yellow coloured wheels were produced at the Rochford factory. Models have been reported with a mixture of yellow, dark yellow and orangey yellow on the one model! Final issues of the van had chassis and wing components painted with the blue used on the concurrently produced 'Duckhams' van. Because ejector pins stuck in the moulds, some models have a hole in the cab floor.

B : JAMES NEALE

ISSUE	YEAR OF RELEASE	COLOURS	BONNET & CAB FLOOR	HOLE IN CAB FLOOR	ROOF	SEATS	RIGHT LENS	WHEELS	PLATED PARTS	GRAB HANDLES	LOGO	BASEPLATE	RARITY	BOX TYPE	VALUE	CHECK LIST
1	1985	Yellow body, royal blue chassis	Yellow	No	White type B	Black	Type 2	Dark yellow 12 spoke	Brass	Closed	JAMES NEALE	MATCHBOX © 1983 ENGLAND		J	£20	
2		Yellow body, royal blue chassis	Yellow	No	White type B	Black	Type 2	Light yellow 12 spoke	Brass	Closed	JAMES NEALE	MATCHBOX © 1983 ENGLAND		J	£20	
3		Yellow body, royal blue chassis	Yellow	Yes*	White type B	Black	Type 2	Light yellow 12 spoke	Brass	Closed	JAMES NEALE	MATCHBOX © 1983 ENGLAND	D	J	£30	
4		Yellow body, royal blue chassis	Yellow	No	White type B	Black	Type 2	Orangey yellow 12 spoke	Brass	Closed	JAMES NEALE	MATCHBOX © 1983 ENGLAND		J	£30	✓
5		Yellow body, royal blue chassis	Yellow	Yes*	White type B	Black	Type 2	Orangey yellow 12 spoke	Brass	Closed	JAMES NEALE	MATCHBOX © 1983 ENGLAND	D	J	£30	
6		Yellow body, royal blue chassis	Yellow	Yes	White type B	Black	Type 2	Dark yellow 12 spoke	Brass	Closed	JAMES NEALE	MATCHBOX © 1983 ENGLAND		J	£20	
7		Yellow body, royal blue chassis	Yellow	No	White type B	Black	Type 2	Dark yellow 12 spoke	Brass	Open*	JAMES NEALE	MATCHBOX © 1983 ENGLAND	S	J	£30	
8		Yellow body, navy* blue chassis	Yellow	Yes	White type B	Black	Type 2	Dark yellow 12 spoke	Brass	Open*	JAMES NEALE	MATCHBOX © 1983 ENGLAND	S	J	£30	
9		Yellow body, navy* blue chassis	Yellow	No	White type B	Black	Type 2	Dark yellow 12 spoke	Brass	Closed	JAMES NEALE	MATCHBOX © 1983 ENGLAND	R	J	£40	
10		Yellow body, navy* blue chassis	Yellow	No	White type B	Black	Type 2	Dark yellow 12 spoke	Brass	Open*	JAMES NEALE	MATCHBOX © 1983 ENGLAND	R	J	£45	
11		Yellow body, navy* blue chassis	Yellow	No	White type B	Black	Type 2	Orangey yellow 12 spoke	Brass	Open*	JAMES NEALE	MATCHBOX © 1983 ENGLAND	R	J	£45	

DIAGRAM 1 GRAB HANDLES

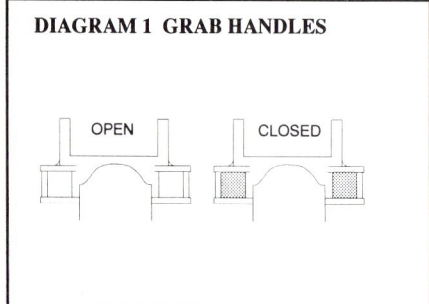

DIAGRAM 2 HOLE IN CAB FLOOR

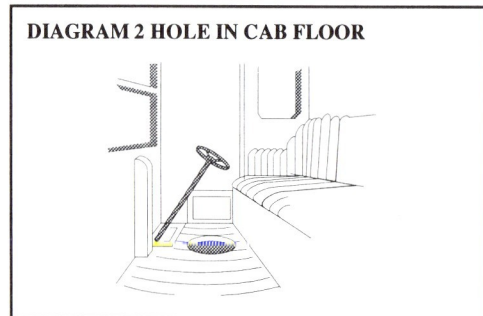

LIVERY   JAMES NEALE

Van sides. JAMES NEALE & SONS in gold with blue outline above LIMITED and two scrolls in yellow with black outline. All above dark blue MAKERS OF above dark blue FINE VEHICLE EQUIPMENT above dark blue SINCE 1849. All within dark blue coachlining. Header board. VEHICLE to left of RAYDYOT to right of EQUIPMENT with a scroll on each side. All in black.

NOTES

Y 25-1 1910 RENAULT TYPE AG VAN (CONTINUED)   Scale 1:38

DUCKHAM'S. This livery was only released in the 1985 Yesteryear Limited Edition Gift Set of which 40,000 were produced. The other two models in the set were the Y23 Omnibus 'Maples' and the all red Y11-3 1938 Lagonda Drophead. Because the 'Duckham's' Y25 model was made at the same time as the 'James Neale' there was the inevitable use of both types of grab handle components. By now all lens were of the Type 2 category.
EAGLE PENCILS. During the 1985 Toy and Hobby Fair at Earl's Court in London one of the Matchbox Toys management discovered, at one of the stationery stalls, a picture of the Eagle Pencil Co. logo. Subsequently its authenticity and accuracy was verified by the Research and Development Department at Matchbox Toys and a decision was made to use the livery for a future Y25 Renault van. The 'Eagle Pencil' has the same colour baseplate as the 'Duckham's Oil' van. In late 1986 a further production run of 'Eagle Pencil' was produced for a special box made for Christmas 1986 celebrating '30 Years of Models of Yesteryear'. The colour of the eagle on the van side was much lighter i.e. Issues 3 to 6. Generally these later models were fitted with the Y25 Ambulance baseplates, and were also available as individually boxed models.

C : DUCKHAM'S

ISSUE	YEAR OF RELEASE	COLOURS	BONNET & CAB FLOOR	SEATS	HOLE IN CAB FLOOR	ROOF TYPE	WHEELS	PLATED PARTS	GRAB HANDLES	LOGO	BASEPLATE	RARITY	BOX TYPE	VALUE	CHECK LIST
1	1985	Metallic silver grey, body navy blue chassis	Metallic silver grey	Dark red	No	White type B	Red 12 spoke	Brass	Open	DUCKHAM'S	MATCHBOX © 1983 ENGLAND		L	£12	
2		Metallic silver grey, body navy blue chassis	Metallic silver grey	Dark red	No	White type B	Red 12 spoke	Brass	Closed*	DUCKHAM'S	MATCHBOX © 1983 ENGLAND	S	L	£50	

D : EAGLE PENCIL

ISSUE	YEAR OF RELEASE	COLOURS	BONNET & CAB FLOOR	SEATS	HOLE IN CAB FLOOR	ROOF TYPE	WHEELS	PLATED PARTS	GRAB HANDLES	LOGO	BASEPLATE	RARITY	BOX TYPE	VALUE	CHECK LIST
1	1985	Mid blue body, navy blue chassis	Mid blue	Dark red	No	White type B	Gold 12 spoke	Brass	Open	EAGLE PENCIL (Dark gold)	MATCHBOX © 1983 ENGLAND		J / L	£10	✓
2		Mid blue body, navy blue chassis	Mid blue	Dark red	No	White type B	Gold 12 soke	Brass	Closed*	EAGLE PENCIL (Dark Gold)	MATCHBOX © 1983 ENGLAND	R	J	£60	
3	1986	Mid blue body, navy blue chassis	Mid blue	Dark red	No	White type B	Gold 12 spoke	Brass	Open	EAGLE PENCIL (Light Gold)	MATCHBOX © 1986 ENGLAND LIMITED EDITION*	D	J	£15	
4		Mid blue body, navy blue chassis	Mid blue	Dark red	No	White type B	Gold 12 spoke	Brass	Open	EAGLE PENCIL (Light Gold)	MATCHBOX © 1983 ENGLAND		J / L	£10	
5		Mid blue body, navy blue chassis	Mid blue	Dark red	No	White type B	Chrome 12 spoke	Brass	Open	EAGLE PENCIL (Light Gold)	MATCHBOX © 1983 ENGLAND		J	£10	
6		Mid blue body, navy blue chassis	Mid blue	Dark red	No	White type B	Gold 12 spoke	Brass	Open	EAGLE PENCIL (Light Gold)	MATCHBOX © 1986* ENGLAND	D	J	£15	

LIVERY DUCKHAM'S

Tampo
Van sides. DUCKHAM'S OIL in black and four round pictures of green and gold, red and gold oil logos above PERFECTION IN LUBRICATION in black.
Header board. Black DUCKHAM'S OILS.

LIVERY EAGLE PENCIL

Tampo
Van sides. THE EAGLE PENCIL CO in red with black shadow effect below a flying eagle logo in gold, black, blue and white above TOTTENHAM LONDON N17 in black.
Header board. Red EAGLE PENCILS.

INVESTMENT COMMENT
ORIGINAL PRICE EAGLE PENCIL £3.99p

Duckhams. The Duckham's model was only released in a gift set of three models. At present these boxed sets sell in excess of £30 in the UK. Surprisingly Issue 2 has dropped back a little since 1992.

Eagle Pencil. A popular model and a steady performer.

NOTES

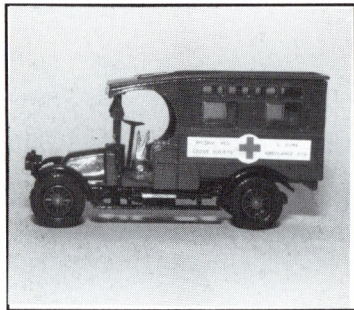

Y25-1 1910 RENAULT TYPE AG VAN (CONTINUED)   Scale 1:38

BRITISH RED CROSS. This Special Limited Edition 'Ambulance' was released worldwide in December 1986 with a production of 30,000. The roof component was made without the luggage rails and windows were incorporated into the body. Originally the plastic roof was to have been black but it was decided that it would be more appropriate to match the body colour of "Army", sometimes referred to as "Field Green". As a military vehicle Matchbox restricted the use of plating. The windscreen was finished in green and the headlamp case was only in black.

TUNNOCK. This highly acclaimed model was released in February 1987 as a standard model within the range. The new body colour of red adding a new colour dimension to the basic model. The Research and Development Department contacted the Thomas Tunnock Company to confirm the authenticity of the Y25 livery. Due to the recurrence of an ejector pin sticking in the mould, some 'Tunnock' models have a hole in the cab floor. The 'Tunnock' van was the last Yesteryear to be made at the Rochford factory. There has been one unconfirmed report of a model with the headboard lettering in maroon, not red!

E: BRITISH RED CROSS

ISSUE	YEAR OF RELEASE	COLOURS	BONNET & FLOOR	HOLE IN FLOOR	ROOF TYPE	SEATS	WHEELS	PLATED PARTS	GRAB HANDLES	LOGO	BASEPLATE	RARITY	BOX TYPE	VALUE	CHECK LIST
1	1986	Army green body glossy black chassis	Army green	No	Green Type C	Dark beige	Green 12 spoke	Brass	Open	BRITISH RED CROSS	MATCHBOX © 1986 LIMITED EDITION ENGLAND		J	£18	✓ 2x
2		Army green body glossy black chassis	Army green	No	Green Type C	Dark beige	Green 12 spoke	Brass	Open	BRITISH RED CROSS	MATCHBOX © 1986 ENGLAND		J	£18	

F: TUNNOCK

ISSUE	YEAR OF RELEASE	COLOURS	BONNET & FLOOR	HOLE IN FLOOR	ROOF TYPE	SEATS	WHEELS	PLATED PARTS	GRAB HANDLES	LOGO	BASEPLATE	RARITY	BOX TYPE	VALUE	CHECK LIST
1	1987	Bright red body glossy black chassis	Bright red	No	White Type B	White	Black 12 spoke	Brass	Open	TUNNOCK	MATCHBOX © 1983 ENGLAND		J	£8	
2		Bright red body glossy black chassis	Bright red	Yes*	White Type B	White	Black 12 spoke	Brass	Open	TUNNOCK	MATCHBOX © 1983 ENGLAND	S	J	£20	
3		Bright red body glossy black chassis	Bright red	No	White Type B	White	Black 12 spoke	Brass	Open	TUNNOCK	MATCHBOX © 1986 ENGLAND		J	£8	✓
4		Bright red body glossy black chassis	Bright red	No	White Type B	White	Black 12 spoke	Silver* N.B.	Open	TUNNOCK	MATCHBOX © 1986 ENGLAND	R	J	£50	
5		Bright red body glossy black chassis	Bright red	No	White Type B	White	Gold 12 spoke*	Brass	Open	TUNNOCK	MATCHBOX © 1986 ENGLAND	D	J	£15	
6		Bright red body glossy black chassis	Bright red	No	Cream* Type B	White	Black 12 spoke	Brass	Open	TUNNOCK	MATCHBOX © 1986 ENGLAND	R	J	£50	
7		Bright red body glossy black chassis	Bright red	No	White Type B	White	Black 12 spoke	Brass	Open	TUNNOCK	MATCHBOX © 1986 LIMITED EDITION* ENGLAND		J	£15	
8		Bright red body glossy black chassis	Bright red	No	White Type B	White	Black 12 spoke	Brass	Closed*	TUNNOCK	MATCHBOX © 1986 ENGLAND	S	J	£25	

LIVERY BRITISH RED CROSS

Tampo
Van sides. BRITISH RED CROSS SOCIETY, an International Red Cross symbol, ST JOHN AMBULANCE ASSN in red on white banner. Rear doors. Red Cross symbol on white background. Front part of roof. Red Cross symbol on white background.

LIVERY TUNNOCK

Tampo
Van sides. YES! GO TO TUNNOCK'S in white with black shadow effect, above BAKER & CONFECTIONER, T. TUNNOCK UDDINGSTON & BOTHWELL in red with black outline and gold shadow effect. All within white oval with black surround. White PHONE 50 UDDINGSTON and PHONE 28 BOTHWELL. All within white coachlining.
Cab doors. Black edged gold T and ROOM with white coachlining. Header board. Red TUNNOCK'S

INVESTMENT COMMENT

ORIGINAL PRICE, TUNNOCK, £5.25p
BRITISH RED CROSS £6.50p

Red Cross. Although a Special Limited Edition it has proved a disappointment. Values are rising, albeit very slowly.

Tunnock. Released with several noticeable variations, all of which fetch a premium.

NOTES

Tunnock model issue 4: Headlight assembly only in silver, other plated parts in brass.

Y25-1 1910 RENAULT TYPE AG VAN (CONTINUED)   Scale 1:38

DELHAIZE. To help celebrate their 120th anniversary, the Belgian firm of 'Delhaize' asked Matchbox to make a van with their livery. Two differing liveries were used on the van sides; one in Flemish and the other in French. The model was released in November 1987 and the last production issue was fitted with thicker braces between the back of the number plates and the underside of the van. (Type 2). Surplus stocks of the 'Delhaize' were repackaged and sold in the D301 twin pack. The production run was 90,000 (E).

SUCHARD. Released in May 1989 and fitted with the thicker braces. No models in either Suchard or Delhaize liveries have been found with the ejector pin hole in the cab floor. The production run was 45,000 (E).

G : DELHAIZE

ISSUE	YEAR OF RELEASE	COLOURS	BONNET & FLOOR	ROOF	SEATS	WHEELS	PLATED PARTS	GRAB HANDLES	LOGO	REAR NUMBER PLATE	BASEPLATE	RARITY	BOX TYPE	VALUE	CHECK LIST
1	1987	Dark green body, glossy black chassis	Dark green	White type B	Dark red	Gold 12 spoke	Brass	Open	DELHAIZE	Type 1	MATCHBOX © 1986 MACAU	D	J 1	£12	
2		Dark green body, glossy black chassis	Dark green	White type B	Dark red	Gold 12 spoke	Brass	Open	DELHAIZE	Type 2	MATCHBOX © 1986 MACAU		J 1	£10	✓

H : SUCHARD

ISSUE	YEAR OF RELEASE	COLOURS	BONNET & FLOOR	ROOF	SEATS	WHEELS	PLATED PARTS	GRAB HANDLES	LOGO	REAR NUMBER PLATE	BASEPLATE	RARITY	BOX TYPE	VALUE	CHECK LIST
1	1989	Pale lilac body, glossy black chassis	Pale lilac	White type B	Dark brown	Gold 12 spoke	Brass	Open	SUCHARD	Type 2	MATCHBOX © 1986 MACAU		J 1	£10	✓ 2✗

DIAGRAM 1
REAR NUMBER PLATE BRACES VIEWED FROM UNDERNEATH

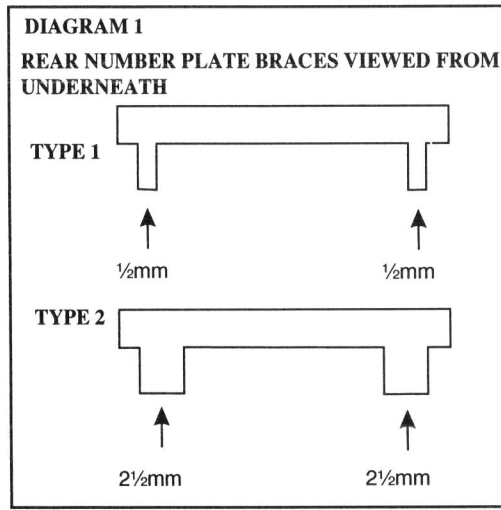

TYPE 1 — ½mm, ½mm
TYPE 2 — 2½mm, 2½mm

LIVERY DELHAIZE

Tampo
Nearside van sides.
GEBRS DELHAIZE & CIE DE LEEUW 1867 1987 in gold with black shadow effect. Gold and black crown with golden rays and prone lion in gold and black. OVERAL IN BELGIE in black on black outlined plinth with gold scrolls all on greyish white panel.
Cab sides. No3 in gold with black shadow effect with gold scrolls.
Offside van sides.
DELHAIZE FRERES & CIE DE LION 1867 1987 in gold with black shadow effect.
Gold and black crown with golden rays and prone lion in gold and black.
PARTOUT EN BELGIQUE in black on black outlined plinth with gold scrolls all on greyish white panel.
Cab side. No.3 in gold with black shadow effect.
Header board. Green DELHAIZE LE LION with gold shadow effect.

LIVERY SUCHARD

Tampo
Van sides. Black shadow effect gold SUCHARD and light brown CHOCOLAT. A mountain scene in black and white with a St Bernard dog, in brown, gold, black and white.
Header board. SUCHARD in black.

INVESTMENT COMMENT

ORIGINAL PRICE, DELHAIZE, £5.25p
SUCHARD £6.25p

Delhaize. Little or no interest recorded.

Suchard. The same applies to the Suchard.

NOTES

Compare with YPP01, and YGB07.

INVESTMENT COMMENT
ORIGINAL PRICE £3.50p

Löwenbräu. Although the standard issues are rather dormant, the rarer issues have generally performed well.

Y26-1 1918 CROSSLEY DELIVERY TRUCK Scale 1:47

LÖWENBRÄU. Originally scheduled to be a Y13-3 model but because the load was to be a number of barrels it was designated Y26. During the initial production assembly some Y25-1 Renault baseplate components were mistakenly used. Also baseplates, with only No. Y13 were used. However, because the baseplate was common to the Y13-3 and the Y26-1 models, the baseplate text had to be changed to No. Y13/Y26. No other modifications have been reported. During the life of the "Löwenbräu" livery the colour of the plastics used for the tilt and barrels changed. The schedule below is based on Matchbox's records and it must be appreciated that these components are easily interchanged. The raised relief to the top and end edges of the truck body were deleted for tampo printing purposes. Thus all Y26-1 Crossleys have Type "D" bodies. (Diagram 4 below) Red plastic barrels are not officially released components. The transverse barrel has the 'Löwenbräu' crest on one end and can be fitted either next to the cab; or to the rear of the truck body.

A: LÖWENBRÄU

ISSUE	YEAR OF RELEASE	COLOURS	CAB TILT	SEATS	GRILLE	WHEELS	PLATED PARTS	COLOUR OF BARRELS	LOGO	BASEPLATE TYPE	BASEPLATE	RARITY	BOX TYPE	VALUE	CHECK LIST
1	1984	Powder blue body, glossy black chassis	Tan	Ruby red	Black	Red solid	Brass	Brown	LÖWENBRÄU	R*	MATCHBOX © 1983 Y25* ENGLAND	VR	J	£80	
2		Powder blue body, glossy black chassis	Tan	Ruby red	Black	Red solid	Brass	Brown	LÖWENBRÄU	D*	MATCHBOX © 1973 Y13* ENGLAND	S	J	£50	
3		Powder blue body, glossy black chassis	Tan	Ruby red	Black	Red solid	Brass	Brown	LÖWENBRÄU	E	MATCHBOX © 1973 Y13/Y26 ENGLAND		J	£8	✓
4		Powder blue body, glossy black chassis	Light tan	Ruby red	Black	Red solid	Brass	Brown	LÖWENBRÄU	E	MATCHBOX © 1973 Y13/Y26 ENGLAND		J	£10	
5		Powder blue body, glossy black chassis	Light tan	Ruby red	Black	Red 12 spoke*	Brass	Brown	LÖWENBRÄU	E	MATCHBOX © 1973 Y13/Y26 ENGLAND	D	J	£20	
6	1986	Powder blue body, glossy black chassis	Cream	Ruby red	Black	Red solid	Brass	Dark brown	LÖWENBRÄU	E	MATCHBOX © 1973 Y13/Y26 ENGLAND		J	£8	
7		Powder blue body, glossy black chassis	Light olive tan*	Ruby red	Black	Red solid	Brass	Dark brown	LÖWENBRÄU	E	MATCHBOX © 1973 Y13/Y26 ENGLAND	D	J	£15	

DIAGRAM 1 — BASEPLATE TYPE R

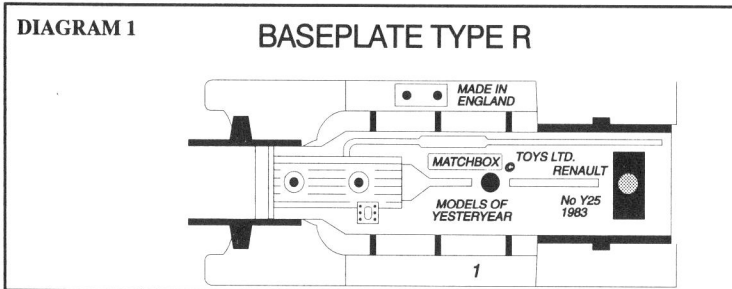

DIAGRAM 2 — BASEPLATE TYPE E

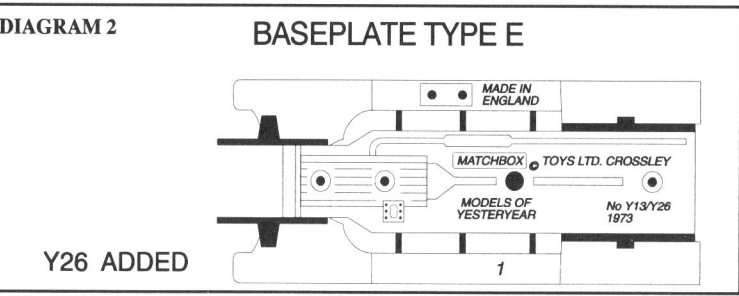

Y26 ADDED

LIVERY LÖWENBRÄU

Tampo
Truck sides. White LÖWENBRÄU with company crest in dark blue and gold within gold coachline. Company crest in black and gold on one end of transverse barrel.

DIAGRAM 3 — BASEPLATE TYPE D

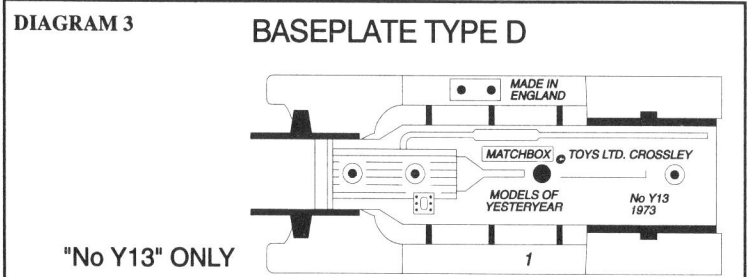

"No Y13" ONLY

DIAGRAM 4 — TRUCK BODY TYPE
TYPE D

NO CLEATS & NO RAISED EDGES
(RELIEF) TO TOP & ENDS EDGES
(PERFECTLY FLAT SIDES)

NOTES

Y26-1 1918 CROSSLEY DELIVERY TRUCK (CONTINUED) Scale 1:47

ROMFORD BREWERY. Issued as a Limited Edition; the livery is that of a brewery in Romford which in 1986 was not far from the Matchbox factory. The colour of the barrels is identical to the final 'Löwenbräu' issue. A small batch of 'Romford Brewery' models which were distributed through Woolworth and Tesco stores in the UK. had ruby red seats with either black or ruby red radiator grilles. The total production of all 'Romford Brewery' issues was 96,000.

GONZALEZ BYASS. The 'Gonzalez Byass' succeeded the 'Löwenbräu' livery as the standard model in the range. The Gonzalez Company had requested that the word 'Sherry' be on the barrels; but production started without the word being printed on the barrels. The Research and Development Department soon noted the omission and it was corrected. A limited number of models were fitted with chrome twelve spoke wheels instead of the more usual gold twelve spoke type. Examples of the 'Gonzalez Byass' model have been reported with tilts, radiator grilles and seats in the colours made for the 'Löwenbräu' and 'Romford Brewery' models. Due to the ease with which those components could be swapped around, their authenticity is extremely doubtful and therefore have not been listed.

B: ROMFORD BREWERY

ISSUE	YEAR OF RELEASE	COLOURS	CAB TILT	SEATS	GRILLE	WHEELS	PLATED PARTS	COLOUR OF BARRELS	LOGO	BASEPLATE TYPE	BASEPLATE	RARITY	BOX TYPE	VALUE	CHECK LIST
1	1986	Glossy black body, ochre brown chassis	Black	Light brown	Black	Gold 12 spoke	Brass	Dark brown	ROMFORD	E	MATCHBOX © 1973 Y13/Y26 ENGLAND		J	£10	✔
2		Glossy black body, ochre brown chassis	Black	Light brown	Black	Gold 12 spoke	Brass	Dark brown	ROMFORD	F*	MATCHBOX © 1973 Y13/Y26 ENGLAND	R	J	£60	
3		Glossy black body, ochre brown chassis	Black	Ruby red*	Black	Gold 12 spoke	Brass	Dark brown	ROMFORD	E	MATCHBOX © 1973 Y13/Y26 ENGLAND	D	J	£20	
4		Glossy black body, ochre brown chassis	Black	Ruby red*	Ruby red*	Gold 12 spoke	Brass	Dark brown	ROMFORD	E	MATCHBOX © 1973 Y13/Y26 ENGLAND	D	J	£20	

C: GONZALEZ BYASS

ISSUE	YEAR OF RELEASE	COLOURS	CAB TILT	SEATS	GRILLE	WHEELS	PLATED PARTS	COLOUR OF BARRELS	BARREL DECORATION	LOGO	BASEPLATE TYPE	BASEPLATE	RARITY	BOX TYPE	VALUE	CHECK LIST
1	1987	White body, ruby red chassis	Ruby red	Ruby red	Ruby red	Gold 12 spoke	Brass	Dark brown	No	GONZALEZ	E	MATCHBOX © 1973 Y13/Y26		J	£10	
2		White body, ruby red chassis	Ruby red	Ruby red	Ruby red	Gold 12 spoke	Brass	Dark brown	Yes	GONZALEZ	E	MATCHBOX © 1973 Y13/Y26		J	£10	
3		White body, ruby red chassis	Ruby red	Ruby red	Ruby red	Chrome 12* spoke	Brass	Dark brown	Yes	GONZALEZ	E	MATCHBOX © 1973 Y13/Y26	D	J	£20	✔

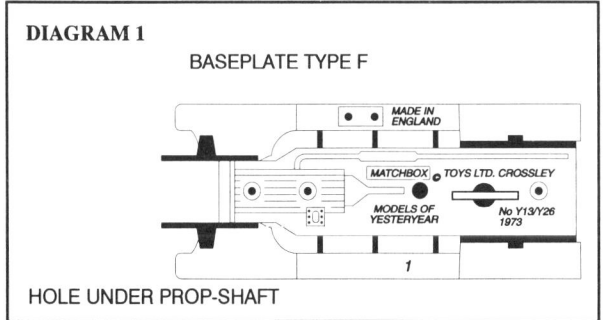

DIAGRAM 1
BASEPLATE TYPE F
HOLE UNDER PROP-SHAFT

LIVERY ROMFORD
Tampo
Truck sides. Gold ROMFORD BREWERY CO. within gold coachline.
Company crest in black and gold on one end of transverse barrel.

LIVERY GONZALEZ BYASS
Tampo
Truck sides. Red GONZALEZ BYASS with black outline. SHERRY in white on side of two barrels.
Company logo of sherry bottle and guitar in black, white and red and lime on off side of transverse barrel.

INVESTMENT COMMENT
ORIGINAL PRICE ROMFORD £3.50p GONZALEZ £4.25p
Romford. Issue 2 is still hard to find and issues with ruby red plastic S still prove popular.
Gonzalez. A poor performer, probably overproduced.
NOTES

Y 27-1 1922 FODEN STEAM WAGON   Scale 1:72

PICKFORDS. After the initial run it was noted by one of the production managers that there was a casting weakness in the area between the cab and the body (Issue one). Modifications were made to the tools. The production run continued; but the modification proved inadequate. The tools were modified again and this time the front cross rib was extended downwards to cover over the corner of the casting (Issue three onwards). The second run (Issue two) was very brief and only about two hundred castings were made. In 1986 the tools were modified again so that in order to achieve a more satisfactory contact during tampo printing, the depth of the struts on the lorry sides were reduced. Originally some 'Pickfords' models were to have been 'Frasers' models and had either hook plates, or a hook rivet at the rear of the baseplate. The 'Pickfords' Foden was always made at the Rochford factory, Essex, and all models have boilers, fire box, piston housing and connecting rods in black plastic. The hook shank was embossed 'Limited Edition' and obviously where the model has a hook, the hook rivet boss is obscured. Two different moulds may have made the flywheel. One has a raised edge, four dots and a raised inner circular ridge. The other is without this inner raised circular ridge. Both types are common to all Y27-1 releases. Or it may just be which way round the flywheel was fitted!

HÖVIS. This livery was released in October 1985 as a Limited Edition. At one time the canopy was to have been replaced by a load of grain sacks but this idea was shelved until 1990. When it appeared on the 'Joseph Rank' model. Total production of the 'Hövis' was 100,000. From the 'Hövis' livery onwards, all Y27 Fodens have Type "C" body/cab castings.

A : PICKFORDS

ISSUE	YEAR OF RELEASE	COLOURS	CAB ROOF	SEAT	BODY CANOPY	WHEELS	PLATED PARTS	LOGO	BODY TYPE	BODY PANEL STRUTS	HOOK RIVET	HOOK	BASEPLATE	RARITY	BOX TYPE	VALUE	CHECK LIST
1	1984	Blue body glossy red chassis	Light grey	Black	Light grey	Red daisy	Gold	PICKFORDS	A*	Deep	No	No	MATCHBOX © 1984 ENGLAND	S	J	£25	
2		Blue body glossy red chassis	Light grey	Black	Light grey	Red daisy	Gold	PICKFORDS	B*	Deep	No	No	MATCHBOX © 1984 ENGLAND	R	J	£80	
3		Blue body glossy red chassis	Light grey	Black	Light grey	Red daisy	Gold	PICKFORDS	C	Deep	No	No	MATCHBOX © 1984 ENGLAND		J	£10	✓
4		Blue body glossy red chassis	Dark grey*	Black	Dark grey*	Red daisy	Gold	PICKFORDS	C	Deep	No	No	MATCHBOX © 1984 ENGLAND	D	J	£15	
5	1986	Blue body glossy red chassis	Light grey	Black	Light grey	Red daisy	Gold	PICKFORDS	C	Shallow	No	No	MATCHBOX © 1986 ENGLAND		J	£10	
6		Blue body glossy red chassis	Light grey	Black	Light grey	Red daisy	Gold	PICKFORDS	C	Shallow	Yes	Yes*	MATCHBOX © 1986 ENGLAND	D	J	£15	
7		Blue body glossy red chassis	Dark grey	Black	Dark grey	Red daisy	Gold	PICKFORDS	C	Shallow	Yes	Yes*	MATCHBOX © 1986 ENGLAND	D	J	£15	
8		Blue body glossy red chassis	Dark grey	Black	Dark grey	Red daisy	Gold	PICKFORDS	C	Shallow	No	No	MATCHBOX © 1986 ENGLAND		J	£10	
9		Blue body glossy red chassis	Light grey	Black	Light grey	Red daisy	Gold	PICKFORDS	C	Shallow	Yes*	No	MATCHBOX © 1986 ENGLAND	R	J	£100	
10		Blue body glossy red chassis	Dark grey	Black	Dark grey	Red daisy	Gold	PICKFORDS	C	Shallow	Yes*	No	MATCHBOX © 1986 ENGLAND	R	J	£100	

B : HÖVIS

ISSUE	YEAR OF RELEASE	COLOURS	CAB ROOF	SEAT	BODY CANOPY	WHEELS	PLATED PARTS	LOGO	BODY TYPE	BODY PANEL STRUTS	HOOK RIVET	HOOK	BASEPLATE	RARITY	BOX TYPE	VALUE	CHECK LIST
1	1985	Dark brown body glossy black chassis	Yellowy cream	Black	Yellowy cream	Yellowy cream daisy	Gold	HÖVIS	C	Deep	No	No	MATCHBOX © 1984 ENGLAND		J	£10	✓
2		Dark brown body glossy black chassis	Light yellowy cream	Black	Light yellowy cream	Light yellowy cream daisy	Gold	HÖVIS	C	Deep	No	No	MATCHBOX © 1984 ENGLAND		J	£10	
3		Dark brown body glossy black chassis	Tan*	Black	Tan*	Creamy brown daisy*	Gold	HÖVIS	C	Deep	No	No	MATCHBOX © 1984 ENGLAND	S	J	£12	

DIAGRAM 1 BODY TYPES

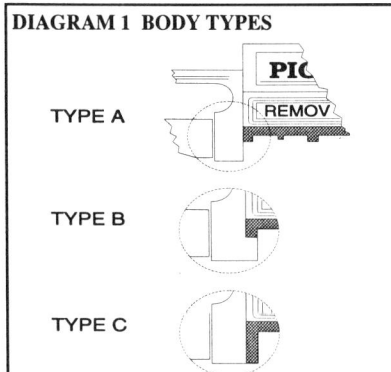

TYPE A

TYPE B

TYPE C

DIAGRAM 2 REAR CHASSIS TYPES

A. WITH "HOOK" SHANK

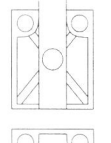

B. WITH "HOOK" SHANK RIVET

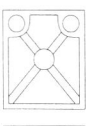

C. WITHOUT "HOOK" SHANK OR RIVET BOSS

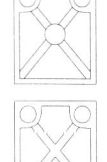

LIVERY PICKFORDS
Labels
Canopy sides. PICKFORDS in white on blue panel with white edges.
Tampo
Wagon sides. REMOVALS STORAGE in white all within white surrounds.
Cab doors. White No.3 within white surround.

LIVERY HÖVIS
Labels
Canopy sides. HÖVIS in white on brown oval.
Tampo
Wagon sides. HÖVIS WEEKLY BULLETIN in white on brown and ENTICES & SUFFICES in brown on white and brown and white crossroads sign post.
Cab doors. White HÖVIS.

INVESTMENT COMMENT
ORIGINAL PRICE PICKFORDS & HÖVIS £4.25p

Pickfords. Large quantities were withdrawn from the market by Code 3 producers. The Pickfords remains a popular model and growth is recorded in some on the non standard issues.
Hövis. A 'brown' model and a poor performer.

NOTES
Pickford models have been reported with a mixture of light and dark grey cab roofs and rear canopies. Please beware of 'switching'.

Y 27-1 1922 FODEN STEAM WAGON (CONTINUED) Scale 1:72

TATE & LYLE'S. This livery was issued in June 1986. After the initial run it was noticed that the tampo printing on the wagon side panels was not of an acceptable standard; therefore the struts on the truck body sides were made less pronounced. It should be noted that it was only because further production runs of the "Pickfords" occurred, after the Tate & Lyle's runs, that the "Pickfords" had this modified body panel. A total of 122,000 models were produced.

FRASERS'. The 'Frasers" wagon and trailer was released as a Limited Edition in December 1986. Surplus castings with either the hookplate attached or with the hook rivet were later used for the 'Pickfords' or 'Spillers' models. From the 'Frasers' onwards, all Y27 Fodens had, as standard, the shallow body panel struts/ribs. The 'Frasers' trailer has the same baseplate wording as the wagon except that the words "'C' Type Steam Wagon" have been omitted. All Foden models continued to have the boiler, fire box, piston housing and connecting rods in black plastic. The majority of 'Frasers" boxes have a black and gold sticker advertising five Matchbox offers including the 1987 Yesteryear calendar and M.I.C.A. Because no variations are known seperate listing for the trailer has not been included in this book.

C : TATE & LYLE'S

ISSUE	YEAR OF RELEASE	COLOURS	CAB ROOF	SEAT	BODY CANOPY	WHEELS	PLATED PARTS	LOGO	BODY PANEL STRUTS	HOOK RIVET	TOWING HOOK	BASEPLATE	RARITY	BOX TYPE	VALUE	CHECK LIST
1	1986	Red brown body, glossy black chassis	Black	Black	Black	Red daisy	Gold	TATE & LYLE'S	Deep*	No	No	MATCHBOX © 1984 ENGLAND	S	J	£35	✔
2		Red brown body, glossy black chassis	Black	Black	Black	Red daisy	Gold	TATE & LYLE'S	Shallow	No	No	MATCHBOX © 1984 ENGLAND		J	£8	
3		Red brown body, glossy black chassis	Black	Black	Black	Red daisy	Gold	TATE & LYLE'S	Shallow	No	No	MATCHBOX © 1986 ENGLAND		J	£8	

D : FRASERS'

ISSUE	YEAR OF RELEASE	COLOURS	CAB ROOF	SEAT	BODY CANOPY	WHEELS	PLATED PARTS	LOGO	BODY PANEL STRUTS	HOOK RIVET	TOWING HOOK	BASEPLATE	RARITY	BOX TYPE	VALUE	CHECK LIST
1	1986	Dark green body, glossy red chassis	White	Black	White	Red daisy	Gold	FRASERS'	Shallow	Yes	Yes	MATCHBOX © 1986 LIMITED EDITION		J	£25	
2		Dark green body, glossy black chassis	White	Black	Off white	Red daisy	Gold	FRASERS'	Shallow	Yes	Yes	MATCHBOX © 1986 LIMITED EDITION		J	£25	

LIVERY TATE & LYLE'S
Tampo
Wagon sides. ASK FOR with two scrolls. TATE & LYLE'S PACKET SUGAR. All in gold with blue and white shadow effect.
Cab sides. Gold PEASE & SON WANDLE WHARF WANDSWORTH S.W.18. PHONE PUTNEY 2420.

LIVERY FRASERS'
Tampo
Wagon sides. White HOUSE FURNISHERS IPSWICH with gold TELEGRAMS MEN, TELEPHONE No 36. All with gold coachlining.
Cab sides. White FRASERS' IPSWICH within gold coachlining.
Canopy sides. FRASERS' in dark green with red shadow effect.
Trailer sides. White DEPOSITORIES 8 STRONG ROOMS IPSWICH with gold TELEGRAMS MEN and No 6. All within gold coachlining.
Trailer canopy sides. FRASERS' in dark green with red shadow effect.
Front panel. White ESTBD 1833 REMOVALS TO ALL PARTS ESTIMATES FREE.

INVESTMENT COMMENT
ORIGINAL PRICE £4.95p FRASERS' £10.00
Tate & Lyle's. Issue 1 has proved to be a sound investment with very limited quantities compared with issues 2 and 3.
Frasers'. This model has begun to enjoy considerable growth recently, maybe because it is a unique double casting.

NOTES

Y27-1 1922 FODEN STEAM WAGON (CONTINUED) Scale 1:72

SPILLERS. When the Limited Edition "Spillers" appeared in March 1987 it was noted that a quantity had a rivet on the rear of the baseplate. This had been cast to facilitate the fixing of the towing hook on the "Frasers'". Baseplates left over from the "Frasers'" run, plus baseplates with rivets too short for attaching the hook, were used up in the initial run of "Spillers". Different shades of green were recorded on the wagon panels. The 1987 issues are in a dark green similar to the roof colour; or a green similar to the chassis colour, or even a very dark green, nearly black! For the second production run in 1988 all baseplate components with tow hook rivets had been exhausted; and the tampo print was a bright emerald green. Please note that the differing shades of green in the tampo printing effect both the truck body sides and the "Spillers" logo on the cab sides. Surplus stock were also sold in the D301 twin pack.

GUINNESS. The 'Guinness' Foden was released as part of a Guinness promotion in June 1989; but it was also released by Matchbox Toys to all the major markets in July, that year. The body tools were modified to provide two holes in the floor of the lorry body to which the false floor, and the barrels were fitted. Unused 'Guinness' body castings were later fitted to in the early runs of the 'Joseph Rank' model. The production run was 60,000 (E).

E : SPILLERS

ISSUE	YEAR OF RELEASE	COLOURS	CAB ROOF	SEAT	LOAD	WHEELS	PLATED PARTS	LOGO	WAGON PANEL COLOURS	TOW HOOK RIVET	BODY FLOOR HOLES	BASEPLATE	RARITY	BOX TYPE	VALUE	CHECK LIST
1	1987	Pale cream body, green chassis	Dark green	Black	Dark cream sacks	Red daisy	Gold	SPILLERS	Dark green	Yes*	N/A	MATCHBOX © 1986 ENGLAND	D	J	£15	
2		Pale cream body, green chassis	Dark green	Black	Dark cream sacks	Red daisy	Gold	SPILLERS	Green	Yes*	N/A	MATCHBOX © 1986 ENGLAND	D	J	£15	
3		Pale cream body, green chassis	Dark green	Black	Dark cream sacks	Red daisy	Gold	SPILLERS	Dark green	No	N/A	MATCHBOX © 1986 ENGLAND		J	£8	✔
4		Pale cream body, green chassis	Dark green	Black	Dark cream sacks	Red daisy	Gold	SPILLERS	Darker green	No	N/A	MATCHBOX © 1986 ENGLAND		J	£8	
5	1988	Pale cream body, green chassis	Dark green	Black	Dark cream sacks	Red daisy	Gold	SPILLERS	Emerald green	No	N/A	MATCHBOX © 1986 ENGLAND		J	£8	

F : GUINNESS

ISSUE	YEAR OF RELEASE	COLOURS	CAB ROOF	SEAT	LOAD	WHEELS	PLATED PARTS	LOGO	WAGON PANEL COLOURS	TOW HOOK RIVET	BODY FLOOR HOLES	BASEPLATE	RARITY	BOX TYPE	VALUE	CHECK LIST
1	1989	Dark blue body, black chassis	Black	Black	Brown barrels	Red daisy	Gold	GUINNESS	N/A	No	Yes	MATCHBOX © 1986 MACAU		J1	£20	✔

LIVERY SPILLERS

Tampo
Wagon sides. Pale cream SPILLERS CATTLE PIG & POULRTY FOODS on green panel.
Cab sides. Green SPILLERS.

LIVERY GUINNESS

Tampo
Wagon sides and rear panels. gold GUINNESS within gold coachlining.
Cab doors and sides. Gold coachlining.
Cab front panels. GUINNESS logo in black and yellow within gold coachlining.

INVESTMENT COMMENT

ORIGINAL PRICE SPILLERS £4.95p GUINNESS £6.25p

Spillers. Issues 1 and 2 evoke the most interest and sell for a slight premium.

GUINNESS. In short supply, due to the attentions of Code 3 producers as well as being an attractive internationally renown livery. Possible further growth potential.

NOTES

Y27-1 1922 FODEN STEAM WAGON (CONTINUED) Scale 1:72

JOSEPH RANK. With the introduction of press-fit axles the wheel hubs were thickened, which in turn blanked off the axle holes on the outside face. However, early models had wheels with axle holes all the way through the hubs. Early production models were fitted with truck bodies left over from the "Guinness" run, which had two cast rivet holes in the bed of the truck body. The production run of the 'Joseph Rank' model was 42,390.

McMULLEN. This famous Hertfordshire brewery became the second Y27 Foden with a load of 5 beer barrels. Unlike the Guinness all 5 barrel tops were tampo decorated. This obviously added to the overall effect and the model was keenly appreciated by collectors worldwide and sold out in many areas soon after release, although many were bought by private concerns to alter to their own designs, which created an artificial shortage. The false floor section on which the barrels are mounted was used again and although they can't be seen, the rivet holes in the truck body bed were re-instated to secure the false floor. The production run was 35,000 (E).

G : JOSEPH RANK

ISSUE	YEAR OF RELEASE	COLOURS	CAB ROOF	SEAT	LOAD	WHEELS	PLATED PARTS	LOGO	BODY FLOOR HOLES	WHEEL HUB	THREADED SCREW HOLE	BASEPLATE	RARITY	BOX TYPE	VALUE	CHECK LIST
1	1990	Dark green body, light brown chassis	Brown	Black	Off-white sacks	Dark green daisy	Gold	JOSEPH RANK	Yes*	Type 1	Yes	MATCHBOX © 1986 MACAU	S	N	£15	✔
2		Dark green body, light brown chassis	Dark brown	Black	Off-white sacks	Dark green daisy	Gold	JOSEPH RANK	Yes*	Type 1	Yes	MATCHBOX © 1986 MACAU	S	N	£15	
3		Dark green body, light brown chassis	Dark brown	Black	Off-white sacks	Dark green daisy	Gold	JOSEPH RANK	None	Type 1*	Yes	MATCHBOX © 1986 MACAU	D	N	£12	
4		Dark green body, light brown chassis	Brown	Black	Off-white sacks	Darker green daisy	Gold	JOSEPH RANK	None	Type 2	Yes	MATCHBOX © 1986 MACAU		N	£10	
5		Dark green body, light brown chassis	Dark brown	Black	Off-white sacks	Darker green daisy	Gold	JOSEPH RANK	None	Type 2	Yes	MATCHBOX © 1986 MACAU		N	£10	
6		Dark green body, tan chassis*	Brown	Black	Off-white sacks	Darker green daisy	Gold	JOSEPH RANK	None	Type 2	Yes	MATCHBOX © 1986 MACAU	D	N	£15	
7		Dark green body, tan chassis*	Dark brown	Black	Off-white sacks	Darker green daisy	Gold	JOSEPH RANK	None	Type 2	Yes	MATCHBOX © 1986 MACAU	D	N	£15	

H : McMULLEN

ISSUE	YEAR OF RELEASE	COLOURS	CAB ROOF	SEAT	LOAD	WHEELS	PLATED PARTS	LOGO	BODY FLOOR HOLES	WHEEL HUB	THREADED SCREW HOLE	BASEPLATE	RARITY	BOX TYPE	VALUE	CHECK LIST
1	1992	Black body, bright red chassis	Pale cream	Black	5 Dark brown barrels	Bright red daisy	Gold	McMULLEN	Yes	Type 2	Yes	MATCHBOX © 1986 CHINA		N 1	£25	✔

DIAGRAM 1 WHEEL HUB TYPES

TYPE 1
(END OF AXLE VISIBLE)

TYPE 2
(AXLE HOLE BLANKED OFF & EXTENDED HUB)

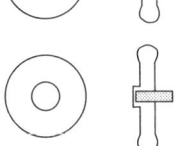

LIVERY JOSEPH RANK
Tampo
Wagon sides. JOSEPH RANK LTD, PREMIER FLOUR MILLS LONDON in gold with gold coachlines.
Cab sides. gold THE WORLD'S CHOICEST FLOUR.
Rear panels. Gold JOSEPH RANK LTD with gold coachlines.
Four rear sacks highlighted in black with black JOSEPH RANK LTD.

LIVERY McMULLENS
Tampo
Wagon sides. McMULLEN & SONS LTD THE HERTFORD BREWERY, BRILLIANT AK ALES with scroll work all in gold within double gold coachlines.
Rear panels McMULLEN & SONS LTD. THE HERTFORD BREWERY in gold.
Cab sides. Company crest in gold, white, red and green. ESTABLISHED 1827 in gold.
Company crest in gold on tops of all 5 barrels.

INVESTMENT COMMENT
ORIGINAL PRICE J. RANK £6.99p
McMULLEN £8.99p

J Rank. Issues 1 and 2 are still sought after and have good potential. Issues 6 and 7 have further promise.
McMullen. 'Sold-out' within weeks of release in most markets — but additional stock was found in a Matchbox warehouse and were put onto the market. Values fell from a high of £30 down to just below £20. Should come back!

NOTES
Compare with YY027/SA and YAS02-M.

INVESTMENT COMMENT
ORIGINAL PRICE £3.50p
Not a great performer to date. Issues 1, 2 and 3 have proved rather disappointing. Issue 11 is hard to find in most markets. A good one to watch?

Y28-1 1906 UNIC TAXI

Scale 1:42

Although described on the box as a 1907 taxi, the Y28 was modelled on a 1906 Taxi owned by the London Taxi Preservation Society. There were several casting changes made to early red models. The rear lights were strengthened by webbing out the mould to provide a stronger attachment (rear light Type 2). The second casting change was to improve the poor fit of the hood to the body. Originally the hood had been fixed by three locating lugs on the hood. The revised method was to have two pins on the body and to locate the hood by means of two small holes. Also in 1985 because the plastic fare meter did not fit properly and was fragile a metal component was substituted. Standard models had silver "pram" tensioning arms, tampo printed side window frames and with tampo printed 'London General Cab Company Ltd.' beneath the windows; however sometimes one or more of these details are missing and are negative variations only. In 1987 the livery changed to a dark blue and pre-production models were produced with the old style body components without the body pins. Although Matchbox dispensed with the tampo decoration, all blue models should have silver hood tensioning arms. In 1991 the body colour became white. Trials of pre-production blue bodies or white bodied models had been made at the Macau factory; but none were released. White models with the screw hole in the baseplate were produced at the new factory in China. All Y28 Unic Taxis were fitted with black plastic grilles, and black textured hoods.

ISSUE	YEAR OF RELEASE	COLOURS	SEATS	HOOD TENSIONING ARMS	HOOD BODY PINS	WHEELS	REAR LIGHTS	PLATED PARTS	FARE METER	CAB FLOOR/TOOL BOX	LOGO ON PASSENGER DOORS	THREADED SCREW HOLE	PASSENGER WINDOWS DECORATION	BASEPLATE	RARITY	BOX TYPE	VALUE	CHECK LIST
1	1984	Dark red body, glossy black chassis	Brown	Silver	None	Bright red 12 spoke	Type 1	Gold	Gold plastic	Silver	LONDON GENERAL CAB COMPANY LTD	None	Yes	MATCHBOX © 1984 ENGLAND		J	£10	
2		Dark red body, glossy black chassis	Brown	Silver	None	Gold 12 spoke	Type 1	Gold	Gold plastic	Silver	LONDON GENERAL CAB COMPANY LTD	None	Yes	MATCHBOX © 1984 ENGLAND		J	£12	
3		Dark red body, glossy black chassis	Brown	Silver	None	Bright red 12 spoke	Type 2	Gold	Gold plastic	Silver	LONDON GENERAL CAB COMPANY LTD	None	Yes	MATCHBOX © 1984 ENGLAND		J	£10	✓
4		Dark red body, glossy black chassis	Brown	Silver	Yes	Bright red 12 spoke	Type 1	Gold	Gold metal	Silver	LONDON GENERAL CAB COMPANY LTD	None	Yes	MATCHBOX © 1984 ENGLAND		J	£10	
5		Dark red body, glossy black chassis	Brown	Silver	Yes	Bright red 12 spoke	Type 2	Gold	Gold metal	Silver	LONDON GENERAL CAB COMPANY LTD	None	Yes	MATCHBOX © 1984 ENGLAND		J	£8	
6		Dark red body, glossy black chassis	Brown	Silver	Yes	Dull red 12 spoke	Type 2	Gold	Gold metal	Silver	LONDON GENERAL CAB COMPANY LTD	None	Yes	MATCHBOX © 1984 ENGLAND		J	£8	
7		Dark red body, glossy black chassis	Brown	Silver	Yes	Maroon 12 spoke	Type 2	Gold	Gold metal	Silver	LONDON GENERAL CAB COMPANY LTD	None	Yes	MATCHBOX © 1984 ENGLAND		J	£8	
8	1987	Dark blue body, glossy black chassis	Brown	Silver	Yes	Maroon 12 spoke	Type 2	Gold	Gold metal	Silver	None	None	None	MATCHBOX © 1984 ENGLAND		J	£10	✓
9		Dark blue body, glossy black chassis	Brown	Silver	Yes	Dull red 12 spoke	Type 2	Gold	Gold metal	Silver	None	None	None	MATCHBOX © 1984 ENGLAND		J	£10	
10		Dark blue body, glossy black chassis	Brown	Silver	Yes	Chrome 12 spoke	Type 2	Gold	Gold metal	Silver	None	None	None	MATCHBOX © 1984 ENGLAND		J	£10	
11	1991	White body, glossy black chassis	Black	Silver	Yes	Gold 12 spoke	Type 2	Gold	Gold metal	Silver	LONDON	Yes	None	MATCHBOX © 1984 CHINA		N 1	£15	✓

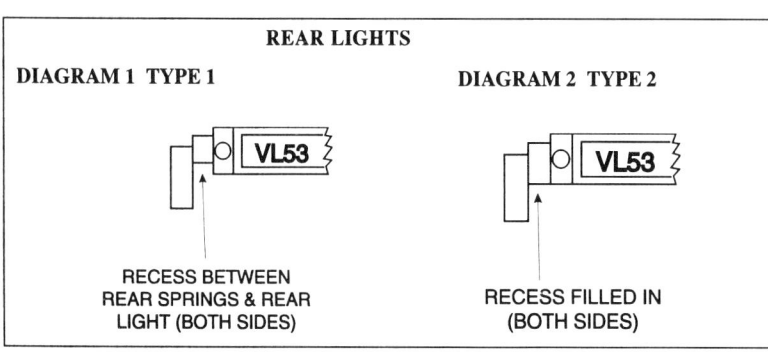

REAR LIGHTS

DIAGRAM 1 TYPE 1 — RECESS BETWEEN REAR SPRINGS & REAR LIGHT (BOTH SIDES)

DIAGRAM 2 TYPE 2 — RECESS FILLED IN (BOTH SIDES)

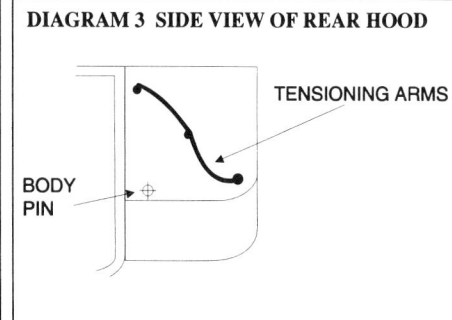

DIAGRAM 3 SIDE VIEW OF REAR HOOD — TENSIONING ARMS, BODY PIN

LIVERY

Tampo
Issues with logos have very very small upper case letters coloured reddish brown and located on the horizontal panels above the door handles. Passenger window decoration is in reddish brown lines around door window reveal. VL5372 in white on black panel at front of hood.
1991 issue: LONDON in black beneath passenger windows. Black coachlines on body sides.

NOTES

Y29-1 1919 WALKER ELECTRIC VAN   Scale 1:51

HARRODS. In 1984 this internationally known department store asked Matchbox to produce a new model, for which Harrods would pay the tooling costs. Matchbox agreed that the Y29 in 'Harrods Ltd.' livery would be sold only by Harrods. Because two colours of plastic were used to make the canopy and the battery boxes were finished in two distinct colours; there are a number of variations. A very limited number of models were released which accidentally had the word 'Walker' printed upside down. These have not been included in the listing as they are a negative variation. Only the 'Harrods' and 'Harrods Bread' models have a white plastic front to the maintenance record card holder at the bottom right hand corner of the front panel. The box for the 'Harrods' model is specially coloured in Harrods green with gold lettering. It was also sold in the D301 twin pack.
JOSEPH LUCAS. Released on 17th March 1986 with a production run of 103,000. Although slight differences to the appearance of the lettering 'King of the Road' have been noted; these can be attributed to the pressure applied by the tampo printing pads. Canopy and tilt components were made from self coloured plastic and later issues have a mottled appearance. Whether this mottled finish was intended, or not is not known, but when compared to the normal smooth finish is quite apparent.

A : HARRODS

ISSUE	YEAR OF RELEASE	COLOURS	CANOPY &TILT	SEATS	WHEELS	BATTERY BOXES	LOGO	LIVERY CHANGES	BASEPLATE	RARITY	BOX TYPE	VALUE	CHECK LIST
1	1985	Army green body black chassis	Dark cream	Pinky beige	Dark green solid	Army green black surround	Harrods	Harrods Ltd in gold	MATCHBOX © 1985 ENGLAND		J	£8	
2		Army green body black chassis	Pale cream	Pinky beige	Dark green solid	Army green black surround	Harrods	Harrods Ltd in light gold	MATCHBOX © 1985 ENGLAND		J	£8	
3		Army green body black chassis	Dark cream	Pinky beige	Dark green solid	Olive green black surround	Harrods	Harrods Ltd in gold	MATCHBOX © 1985 ENGLAND		J/L	£8	✓
4		Army green body black chassis	Pale cream	Pinky beige	Dark green solid	Olive green black surround	Harrods	Harrods Ltd in light gold	MATCHBOX © 1985 ENGLAND		J	£8	✓

B : JOSEPH LUCAS

ISSUE	YEAR OF RELEASE	COLOURS	CANOPY &TILT	SEATS	WHEELS	BATTERY BOXES	LOGO	LIVERY CHANGES	BASEPLATE	RARITY	BOX TYPE	VALUE	CHECK LIST
1	1986	Bright green body black chassis	Smooth bright green	Pinky beige	Red solid	Black	Joseph Lucas	None	MATCHBOX © 1985 ENGLAND		J	£10	
2		Bright green body black chassis	Mottled bright green	Pinky beige	Red solid	Black	Joseph Lucas	None	MATCHBOX © 1985 ENGLAND		J	£10	✓

LIVERY HARRODS
Tampo
Canopy sides. Gold HARRODS LTD above Royal Crest in blue, gold and red with gold by SPECIAL APPOINTMENT.
Van side panels. Gold BROMPTON ROAD S.W.1. Gold 524 within a gold circle above cab windows.
Van rear doors. Gold HARRODS LTD.
Van front panel. Gold HARRODS LTD above white outlined black panel with white HCVC 1919 WALKER above black plate with white LW6737 above black plate with gold WALKER beneath main panel.

LIVERY JOSEPH LUCAS
Tampo
Canopy sides. White JOSEPH LUCAS LTD FORMANS RD BIRMINGHAM with company logo in black, red and white. All within white coachlining.
Van side panels. White KING OF THE ROAD.
Van front panel. Smaller verison of canopy side livery above black plate with white BB 5345, above black plate with gold WALKER beneath main panel.

INVESTMENT COMMENT
ORIGINAL PRICE HARRODS £3.99p
JOSEPH LUCAS £4.25p
Harrods. Remains a poor performer and likely to continue as such. Still for sale in Harrods.
J Lucas. Another poor performer.

NOTES
Issue 3 Harrods also sold in the "30 Years of Models of Yesteryear" boxed set of three models, released in 1986.

Y29-1 1919 WALKER ELECTRIC VAN (CONTINUED) Scale 1:51

HIS MASTER'S VOICE. Released as a Limited Edition model 1988. Pre-production models were made in a red colour, but none were offically released. This was because the trade mark owners had pointed out that the red colour was not authentic. No casting variations have been reported.

HARRODS SPECIAL BREAD. Issued in July 1989 using the remainder of the castings for the 'Harrods Ltd.' model which had not sold nearly as well as the Y12 Model 'T' 'Harrods' van. The two distinctly different shades of green used for the battery boxes decoration were quite apparent and two differing colours had been used for the side panel decoration on the body tilt. Once again the model was sold in a special green coloured box.

C : HIS MASTER'S VOICE

ISSUE	YEAR OF RELEASE	COLOURS	SEATS	CANOPY & TILT	WHEELS	BATTERY BOXES	LOGO	TAMPO DECORATION	BASEPLATE	RARITY	BOX TYPE	VALUE	CHECK LIST
1	1988	Dark blue body black chassis	Pinky beige	Mid grey	Dark blue solid	Black	HIS MASTER'S VOICE	N/A	MATCHBOX © 1985 MACAU		J 1	£8	1/2x

D : HARRODS SPECIAL BREAD

ISSUE	YEAR OF RELEASE	COLOURS	SEATS	CANOPY & TILT	WHEELS	BATTERY BOXES	LOGO	TAMPO DECORATION	BASEPLATE	RARITY	BOX TYPE	VALUE	CHECK LIST
1	1989	Army green body, black chassis	Red-brown	Dark green	Dark green solid	Army green, black surround	HARRODS BREAD	Very pale lemon yellow panels	MATCHBOX © 1985 ENGLAND		J	£12	
2		Army green body, black chassis	Red-brown	Dark green	Dark green solid	Army green, black surround	HARRODS BREAD	Light beige panels	MATCHBOX © 1985 ENGLAND		J	£12	
3		Army green body, black chassis	Red-brown	Dark green	Dark green solid	Olive green, black surround	HARRODS BREAD	Very pale lemon yellow panels	MATCHBOX © 1985 ENGLAND		J	£12	
4		Army green body, black chassis	Red-brown	Dark green	Dark green solid	Olive green, black surround	HARRODS BREAD	Light beige panels	MATCHBOX © 1985 ENGLAND		J	£12	

LIVERY HIS MASTER'S VOICE
Tampo
Canopy sides. HMV logo of a "listening" dog and wind-up gramophone with "horn" in gold, brown and white on dark blue with brown edging.
Van side panels. White HIS MASTER'S VOICE.
Van front panel. White HIS MASTER'S VOICE. Black plate with gold WALKER beneath main panel.

LIVERY HARRODS SPECIAL BREAD
Tampo
Canopy sides. Dark green HARRODS SPECIAL BREAD DELIVERY with gold shaodw effect. All on very pale lemon or light beige panel.
Van side panels. Gold BROMPTON ROAD S.W.1. Gold 524 within a gold circle above cab windows.
Van rear doors. Gold HARRODS LTD.
Van front panel. Gold HARRODS LTD above white outlined black panel with white HCVC 1919 WALKER above black plate with white LW6737 above black plate with gold WALKER beneath main panel.

INVESTMENT COMMENT
ORIGINAL PRICE, HMV & HARRORDS SPECIAL BREAD £6.25p

HMV. Has yet to demonstrate any great growth.

Harrods Special Bread. Seldom seen for sale and is beginning to appreciate, albeit slowly.
NOTES

Y30-1 1920 AC MACK TRUCK

Scale 1:60

ACORN. The Y30 Mack Truck in 'Acorn Storage' livery was released in 1985. The basic colour scheme has been found in three blue tones ; 'Cambridge blue' for early issues, a slightly darker blue for the 1986 issues and finally a paler blue, known by Matchbox as 'Aqua blue' for the 1987 issues. It has been recorded that issue 10 which was a factory trial model, was released only into the Far East market and probably no more than two hundred or so models were made. Issue 2 is noticeable because a much paler ink was used during the tampo printing process for the gold lettering and coachlining on the truck's side panels. The 'Consolidated' model was fitted with a windscreen component and a small lug was cast on the underside of the cab roof against which the top of the windscreen was located. This tool modification meant that all subsequent issues of the Mack truck, including later issues of the 'Acorn' had this lug. Total production was 60,000 (E).

CONSOLIDATED. This livery was released in late 1985 as a Limited Edition of 65,000 models. The truck body was redesigned with a drop side body, a tilt, a cab windscreen and cab doors. It has been recorded that in 1987 there was a large increase in the availability of 'Consolidated' models on the U.K. market. It is believed that stock was found at the Rochford factory during its closure. Amongst this stock several cartons were found fitted with olive-khaki coloured tilts. These were sold through U.K. based wholesalers. The rest of this stock were of the darker yellow body colour fitted with a regular dark tan tilt; but with wheels in a slightly duller red than normal. Many colour trial tilts have been recorded including peppermint green, reddish brown and yellow but none were released on production models.

A : ACORN STORAGE

ISSUE	YEAR OF RELEASE	COLOURS	CAB & ROOF	VAN ROOF OR TILT	SEATS	WHEELS	PLATED PARTS	FRONT MUDGUARD STEPS & FLOOR	LOGO	TAMPO DECORATION	CAB ROOF LUG	BASEPLATE	RARITY	BOX TYPE	VALUE	CHECK LIST
1	1985	Cambridge blue body, dark blue chassis	Dark grey	Dark grey	Dark red	Light brown 5 spoke	Gold	Dark blue	ACORN STORAGE	Gold	No	MATCHBOX © 1984 ENGLAND Y30		J	£8	
2		Cambridge blue body, dark blue chassis	Dark grey	Dark grey	Dark red	Light brown 5 spoke	Gold	Dark blue	ACORN STORAGE	Pale gold*	No	MATCHBOX © 1984 ENGLAND Y30	D	J	£10	
3		Cambridge blue body, dark blue chassis	Dark grey	Dark grey	Dark red	Light brown 5 spoke	Gold	Dark blue	ACORN STORAGE	Gold	Yes*	MATCHBOX © 1984 ENGLAND Y30	D	J	£15	✓
4		Cambridge blue body, dark blue chassis	Dark grey	Dark grey	Dark red	Light brown 5 spoke	Gold	Dark blue	ACORN STORAGE	Gold	No*	MATCHBOX © 1985 ENGLAND Y30	D	J	£12	
5		Cambridge blue body, dark blue chassis	Dark grey	Dark grey	Dark red	Light brown 5 spoke	Gold	Dark blue	ACORN STORAGE	Gold	Yes	MATCHBOX © 1985 ENGLAND Y30		J	£8	
6	1986	Darker blue body, dark blue chassis	Dark grey	Dark grey	Dark red	Light brown 5 spoke	Gold	Dark grey*	ACORN STORAGE	Gold	No	MATCHBOX © 1984 ENGLAND Y30	D	J	£15	
7		Darker blue body, dark blue chassis	Dark grey	Dark grey	Dark red	Light brown 5 spoke	Gold	Dark grey*	ACORN STORAGE	Gold	Yes	MATCHBOX © 1984 ENGLAND Y30	D	J	£15	
8		Darker blue body, dark blue chassis	Dark grey	Dark grey	Dark red	Light brown 5 spoke	Gold	Dark grey*	ACORN STORAGE	Gold	Yes	MATCHBOX © 1985 ENGLAND Y30	D	J	£15	
9		Darker blue body, dark blue chassis	Dark grey	Dark grey	Dark red	Light brown 5 spoke	Gold	Dark grey*	ACORN STORAGE	Gold	Yes	MATCHBOX © 1985 ENGLAND Y30	D	J	£20	
10	1987	Aqua blue body, dark blue chassis	Pale grey*	Charcoal grey*	Dull dark red*	Light brown 5 spoke	Gold	Dark blue	ACORN STORAGE	Gold	Yes	MATCHBOX © 1985 MACAU* Y30	V R	J 1	£200	

B : CONSOLIDATED

ISSUE	YEAR OF RELEASE	COLOURS	CAB & ROOF	VAN ROOF OR TILT	SEATS	WHEELS	PLATED PARTS	FRONT MUDGUARD STEPS & FLOOR	LOGO	TAMPO DECORATION	CAB ROOF LUG	BASEPLATE	RARITY	BOX TYPE	VALUE	CHECK LIST
1	1985	Yellow body, dark brown chassis	Yellow	Dark tan	Dark red	Bright red 5 spoke	Gold	Dark brown	CONSOLIDATED	N / A	Yes	MATCHBOX © 1985 LIMITED EDITION ENGLAND Y30		J	£10	
2		Yellow body, dark brown chassis	Yellow	Pale olive	Dark red	Bright red 5 spoke	Gold	Dark brown	CONSOLIDATED	N / A	Yes	MATCHBOX © 1985 LIMITED EDITION ENGLAND Y30	S	J	£40	
3		Darker yellow body, dark brown chassis	Dark yellow	Dark tan	Dark red	Bright red 5 spoke	Gold	Dark brown	CONSOLIDATED	N / A	Yes	MATCHBOX © 1985 LIMITED EDITION ENGLAND Y30		J	£10	✓

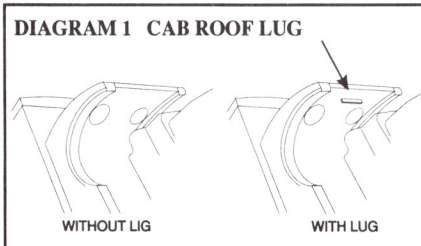

DIAGRAM 1 CAB ROOF LUG

WITHOUT LUG   WITH LUG

LIVERY ACORN STORAGE
Tampo
Truck sides. ACORN STORAGE CO PACKING AND SHIPPING in white above gold LOCAL AND LONG DISTANCE MOVING WAREHOUSE 304-306 W. 48th STREET MANHATTAN. An acorn in brown, gold and white within white oval. All within gold coachlining.

LIVERY CONSOLIDATED
Tampo
Truck sides. CONSOLIDATED in reddish brown with black outline with MOTOR LINES LTD in black on black lined strip, all on reddish brown square with black MOTOR TRANSPORT all within reddish brown scroll.
Cab doors. MOTOR TRANSPORT in black and reddish brown square.
Cab rear panels. Red coachlines.
Bonnet front. Mack logo in black within red coachline.

INVESTMENT COMMENT
ORIGINAL PRICE ACORN STORAGE £4.25 CONSOLIDATED £5.95
Acorn Storage. Still readliy available in most markets. Issues 6 to 9 attracted an immediate premium, but have grown very little since. Issue 10 has become a 'blue chip' investment.
Consolidated. Little growth so far, probably due to large stocks being released two years after its first release. Issue 2 is likely to further appreciate the most, due to its very restricted production figures.
NOTES
Compare with YGB08.

Y30-1 1920 AC MACK TRUCK (CONTINUED)   Scale 1:60

ARCTIC ICE CREAM. This livery is significant as being the first officially made Yesteryear at the Macau factory. In December 1986 the Rochford factory was closed and all the useable tools were sea freighted to the Far East. On the box the Artic is described as a 'Ltd Edition'

KIWI. Because the truck sides were too large to use the tampo printing process, labels were used instead. Three differing sets of labels were used which resulted in different brown colours for the Kiwi bird etc. Total production was 50,000 (E).

C : ARCTIC ICE CREAM

ISSUE	YEAR OF RELEASE	COLOURS	CAB & ROOF	VAN ROOF	SEATS	WHEELS	PLATED PARTS	FRONT MUDGUARDS STEPS & FLOOR	LOGO	LABEL DECORATION	CAB ROOF LUG	BASEPLATE	RARITY	BOX TYPE	VALUE	CHECK LIST
1	1987	Cream body, dark green chassis	Cream	Beige	Dark cream	Cream 5 spoke	Gold	Dark green	ARCTIC ICE CREAM	None	Yes	MATCHBOX © 1985 MACAU Y30		J 1	£8	✓

D : KIWI

ISSUE	YEAR OF RELEASE	COLOURS	CAB & ROOF	VAN ROOF	SEATS	WHEELS	PLATED PARTS	FRONT MUDGUARDS STEPS & FLOOR	LOGO	LABEL DECORATION	CAB ROOF LUG	BASEPLATE	RARITY	BOX TYPE	VALUE	CHECK LIST
1	1988	Bright red body, black chassis	Bright red	Beige	Dark cream	Brown 5 spoke	Gold	Bright red	KIWI	Kiwi & arch in very dark brown	Yes	MATCHBOX © 1985 MACAU Y30		J 1	£10	✓
2		Bright red body, black chassis	Bright red	Beige	Dark cream	Brown 5 spoke	Gold	Bright red	KIWI	Kiwi & arch in mid brown	Yes	MATCHBOX © 1985 MACAU Y30		J 1	£10	
3		Bright red body, black chassis	Bright red	Beige	Dark cream	Brown 5 spoke	Gold	Bright red	KIWI	Kiwi & arch in light brown	Yes	MATCHBOX © 1985 MACAU Y30		J 1	£10	

LIVERY ARCTIC
Tampo
Truck sides. ARCTIC ICE CREAM CO. ICE CREAM in red with gold shadow effect. POLAR BRAND in black with gold shadow effect. All within red coachlines.
Cab sides. Red coachlines.

LIVERY KIWI
Labels
Truck sides. White Kiwi outlined in black on white and black outlined red panels. THOROUGHLY and WATERPROOF in black on yellow scrolls above black on white BOOT POLISH in black outlined red panel with centrally placed brown arch segments above a brown Kiwi bird on black and yellow background and TRADE-MARK in black.
Cab sides. White 132 within white coachlining.
Cab front panels. White coachlining.
Bonnet front. Mack logo in black and white within white coachlining.

INVESTMENT COMMENT
ORIGINAL PRICE, ARCTIC £4.95p

Due to quite large production quantities for both models, no sign yet of any appreciation but they are not so readily available on the market now.

NOTES
Compare with Y33-1, YFE01 and YGB09.

Y31-1 1931 MORRIS COURIER

Scale 1:59

KEMP'S. The introduction of this model broke many years of tradition by extending the Y number beyond that of Y30. The scaling down of this large vehicle, lack of steering wheel and glazed windows caused initial disappointment. Nevertheless the model proved to be popular with collectors. Late pre-production bodies had the two horizontal recessed lines running the full length of the van (Type 1 body) but these proved to be a hindrance during the tampo printing process. The mould was modified so that the lines stopped 2mm short of the vertical cast lines (Type 2 body). However, a small number of the unmodified models were released. These Issue 1 models are finished in a slightly darker red than the Issue 2 releases. Total production was 48,438.
WEETABIX. By now, Yesteryear production had moved to China and consequently no Type 1 van bodies were fitted to the Weetabix models. However problems occured during pre-production trials with the tampo printing of the Weetabix logo on the van body sides. To overcome these problems, the positioning of the logo was slightly altered, and the two horizontal recesses on the van body sides were reduced in depth by about half, (Type 3 body). Also a quantity of these models were ordered by Weetabix to use in an on-pack offer redemption scheme in the UK. All Kemps & Weetabix models had chrome plated parts, press fit axles and base screw holes. Total production run was 40,000 (E).

A : KEMP'S

ISSUE	YEAR OF RELEASE	COLOURS	ROOF	SEATS	WHEELS	PLATED PARTS	LOGO	VAN SIDE HORIZONTAL CAST LINES	BASEPLATE	RARITY	BOX TYPE	VALUE	CHECK LIST
1	1990	Bright red body, black chassis	Off white	Black	Dark red solid	Chrome	KEMP'S	Type 1 *	MATCHBOX © 1989 MACAU	V R	N	£75	
2		Bright red body, black chassis	Off white	Black	Dark red solid	Chrome	KEMP'S	Type 2	MATCHBOX © 1989 MACAU		N	£12	✓

B : WEETABIX

ISSUE	YEAR OF RELEASE	COLOURS	ROOF	SEATS	WHEELS	PLATED PARTS	LOGO	VAN SIDE HORIZONTAL CAST LINES	BASEPLATE	RARITY	BOX TYPE	VALUE	CHECK LIST
1	1992	Deep yellow body, black chassis	Deep yellow	Black	Dark red solid	Chrome	WEETABIX	Type 3	MATCHBOX © 1989 CHINA		N 1	£10	
2	1992	Deep yellow body, black chassis	Deep yellow	Black	Red solid	Chrome	WEETABIX	Type 3	MATCHBOX © 1989 CHINA		N 1	£10	✓

VAN SIDES HORIZONTAL LINES
DIAGRAM 1

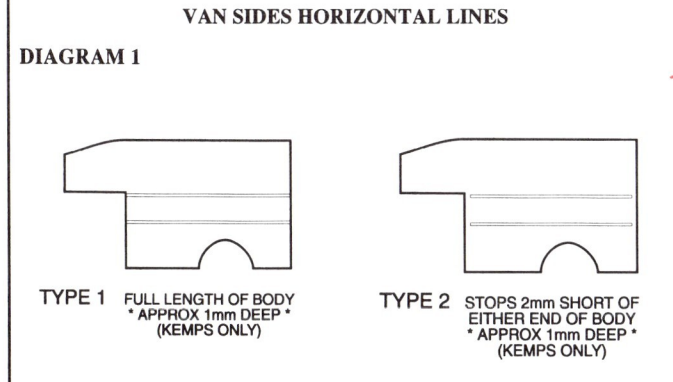

TYPE 1 FULL LENGTH OF BODY
* APPROX 1mm DEEP *
(KEMPS ONLY)

TYPE 2 STOPS 2mm SHORT OF EITHER END OF BODY
* APPROX 1mm DEEP *
(KEMPS ONLY)

LIVERY KEMP'S
Tampo
Van sides. Black edged gold KEMP'S BISCUITS above gold KELCEDA WORKS LONDON N.7.
Van rear doors. Smaller version of van sides.
Van front panel. Black edged gold KEMP'S with gold coachlining.
Cab doors. Gold BISCUITS OF REAL GOODNESS.

LIVERY WEETABIX
Tampo
Van sides. Black WEETABIX with red outline above black REGISTERED. All above MORE THAN A BREAKFAST FOOD in black. All above black MADE IN ENGLAND.
Van rear doors. Smaller version of van sides but no Made in England.
Van front panels. Weetabix box with green edging and red edged WEETABIX, black MORE THAN A BREAKFAST FOOD with a sketch of a large Weetabix.
Cab doors. Black WEETABIX LIMITED, BURTON LATIMER.

INVESTMENT COMMENT
ORIGINAL PRICE KEMP'S & WEETABIX £8.99p
Kemps. Issue 1 has been a good performer as the supply was extremely limited and will never satisfy demand.
Surely further potential.
Weetabix. A very good seller but still readily available. However, at present represents good value.

NOTES
Compare with YGB18 and YPP02.

INVESTMENT COMMENT

ORIGINAL PRICE £6.99p
This model was a popular release. The Y32 bases of issues 3 and 4 already attract a small premium.

Y32-1 1917 YORKSHIRE STEAM WAGON TYPE WA. Scale 1:61

The 'Samuel Smith Old Brewery (Tadcaster)' was released in June 1990. It was initially confused with the Y8 'Samuel Smith's Victoria Corn Mills of Sheffield' model. The Tadcaster model was fitted with the load of barrels and false floor section used originally with the Y27 'Guinness'. During production of the Y32, two baseplates were used because Matchbox had modified the number to read either Y8 or Y32. There were substantial quantities of both types. The total production was 44,280.

A : SAMUEL SMITH

ISSUE	YEAR OF RELEASE	COLOURS	ROOF	SEATS	WHEELS	LOGO	LOAD	BASEPLATE	RARITY	BOX TYPE	VALUE	CHECK LIST
1	1990	Maroon body & black chassis	White Type B	Black	White 6 spoke	SAMUEL SMITH	5 Brown barrels	MATCHBOX © 1987 MACAU Y8		N	£10	✓
2		Maroon body & black chassis	Light cream Type B	Black	White 6 spoke	SAMUEL SMITH	5 Brown barrels	MATCHBOX © 1987 MACAU Y8		N	£10	
3		Maroon body & black chassis	White Type B	Black	White 6 spoke	SAMUEL SMITH	5 Brown barrels	MATCHBOX © 1987 MACAU Y32		N	£12	
4		Maroon body & black chassis	Light cream Type B	Black	White 6 spoke	SAMUEL SMITH	5 Brown barrels	MATCHBOX © 1987 MACAU Y32		N	£12	

DIAGRAM 1   CAB ROOF RIVETS

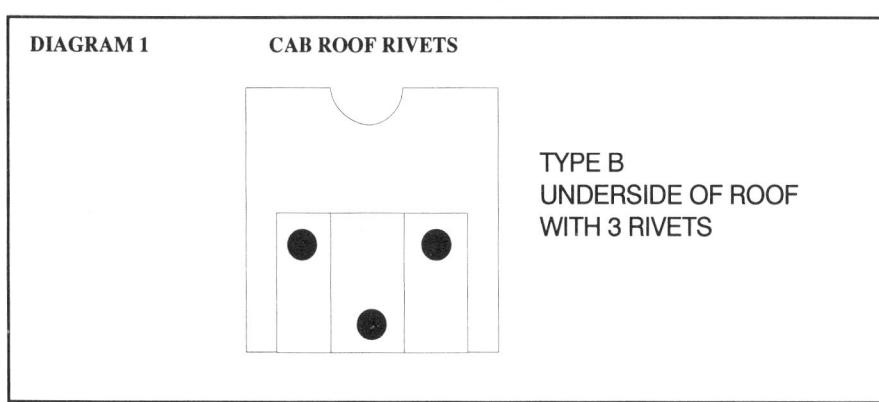

TYPE B
UNDERSIDE OF ROOF
WITH 3 RIVETS

LIVERY

Tampo
Wagon side panels. Gold SAMUEL SMITH OLD BREWERY (TADCASTER). All in gold coachlining.
Wagon rear panels. Gold SAMUEL SMITH within gold coachlining.
Cab doors. Gold edged diamond with signatures and THE OLD BREWERY, TADCASTER. in maroon.
Front panel boiler support. Gold SAMUEL SMITH OLD BREWERY (TADCASTER).
Solid coachlining to boiler bands and boiler support brackets with gold company diamond on top of two barrels.

NOTES

The Type A roof with two rivets as used on the Y8-5 was never used on the Y32-1.

The Y25-1 Renault range of models are thought to be the most attractive of all the Yesteryear vans. The Y26-1 Crossley beer lorries continue to prove popular with collectors.

Taxis such as these Y28-1 models are nice additions to any collection. The Y27-1 Fodens have continued to be appreciated, especially the Frasers which is becoming steadily scarcer.

The Y29-1 Walker Electric van was not highly regarded as a model, even though it was accurately based upon the van used by Harrod's department store. The Y30-1 has produced some attractive liveries especially this Kiwi design. The Y31-1 Morris has already proved popular. Also featured is the Y32-1 Yorkshire Steam Wagon.

Some 1990 issues: The Y39-1 Passenger Coach was an unusual and intricate model. The Y34-1 Cadillac has so far only appeared in these two liveries. The Y37-1 Chubbs wagon has produced a highly collectable casting variation. Other models illustrated here Y35-1; Y36-1 and Y38-1, unlike the Y33-1 Good Year which we forgot to include!

Some 1991 issues: Nice detail was incorporated into the two Special Limited Editions - the Y46-1 Merryweather and the Y45-1 Busch. Note the two versions of the Y44-1 Renault bus. How can the Y45-1 Bugatti Royale be authentically re-liveried? Other models seen are Y42-1; Y41-1; Y40-1; Y47-1; from 1990; the last issue of the Y16-2 Mercedes, and from 1992 the latest Y27-1 Foden.

Some 1992 issues: These later production models are all characterised by very high levels of detail, far removed from the original concepts of the range. The Y61-1 Fire Engine has proved very popular. The Y63-1 Bedford was also well received and sold out within three months of its launch. The opposite is true of the Y66 State Coach, regarded by enthusiasts as an outright error. The Y65-1 set of three Austins filled a long awaited gap in the market. The Y6-5 lorry was withdrawn from the 1992 range in this livery! Other models illustrated here are the Y62-1 and the Y64-1.

The first three Special Edition Yesteryears of 1993 have proved to be popular and consistent sellers. The Taste of France Citroën was the first themed set to emerge in the same year.

Powers of the Press. A 1995 set of eight vans themed to reflect famous newspapers and the first production livery of the Dodge Routemaster van.

INVESTMENT COMMENT	# Y33-1 1930 MACK A C TRUCK	Scale 1:60

ORIGINAL PRICE £6.99p

Possibly overlooked by collectors because of its similarity to the Y30 Acorn model. Issue 1 is worth acquiring from a less-informed vendor.

The 'Goodyear' livery had been scheduled to become the Y30-1 Mack Truck but when Goodyear found that the Y30 model had solid tyres, permission was refused, on the grounds that Goodyear pioneered the pneumatic tyre. No casting modifications have been noted; although it is of interest that the Y33 incorporates the windscreen components used on the Y30 'Consolidated' model, and has the lug on the underside of the cab roof. Unlike the Y30, the Y33 has the chassis springs and drive chassis in diecast instead of plastic. Initially the truck body was painted in an almost identical colour to that of the 'Cambridge blue' used for the Y30 'Acorn' model, Issue 6. The majority of Y33 Mack Trucks, in 'Goodyear' livery were painted in 'Aqua blue'. It should be noted that the colour of the wheels are 'Cambridge blue' and not 'Aqua blue' as originally described in The Collection. The total production was 41,202.

A : GOODYEAR

ISSUE	YEAR OF RELEASE	COLOURS	CAB & ROOF	VAN ROOF	SEATS	WHEELS	PLATED PARTS	FRONT MUDGUARDS/ CAB & FLOOR	LOGO	BASE SCREW HOLE	BASEPLATE	RARITY	BOX TYPE	VALUE	CHECK LIST
1	1990	Cambridge blue body* dark blue chassis	Dark grey	Dark grey	Dark muddy maroon	Solid Cambridge blue	Gold	Dark blue	GOODYEAR	Yes	MATCHBOX © 1985 MACAU Y23	S	N	£30	✓
2		Aqua blue body, dark blue chassis	Dark grey	Dark grey	Dark muddy maroon	Solid Cambridge blue	Gold	Dark blue	GOODYEAR	Yes	MATCHBOX © 1985 MACAU Y23		N	£8	

LIVERY
Tampo
Truck sides. TRANSCONTINENTAL MOTOR EXPRESS, GOOD YEAR, the Goodyear trademark, AKRON VIA LINCOLN HIGHWAY in white. BOSTON SAN FRANCISCO in white on dark grey panel. A white vertical rectangle with slate blue L and slate blue LINCOLN below red strip, and above slate blue HIGHWAY and slate blue strip.
Truck front. White GOODYEAR.
Bonnet front. Mack logo in white on a black panel within white coachline. White coachlines on the cab rear panels, the cab doors and the front panels.

NOTES
Compare with Y30-1, and YGB-09.

INVESTMENT COMMENT
ORIGINAL PRICE £6.99p

A popular release. Issues 1 to 3 with their relatively low production runs have potential. The 1992 release which originally sold for £8.99 is becoming hard to find.

Y34-1 1933 CADILLAC 452 V16   Scale 1:46

Released in September 1990, this model proved to be immensely popular with Yesteryear and car model collectors. It was finished to the 'enhanced detailing' standard with all relevant embellishments highlighted by mask spraying, or tampo printing. The chromed sub base and rear hood tensioning arms with gold hinges being particularly well detailed. Other enhanced detailing included: a chrome 'flying' figure on the radiator cap, chromed side flashes to the bonnet, chromed treads on the running boards and coachlining to the doors, door handles, hinges, side lamps, silver bonnet ridge and rear lights with red lenses. The hood was made in both light cream and pure white plastic; the latter version being the less easy to find. The wheels are the type with flanges on the outside face for whitewall decoration, with press-fit axles. The threaded screw hole was standard to all issues. The total production of the Y34 in navy blue was 49,662. 1992 saw the first recolour of the Cadillac, carried out at the China factory. The base bore the YY46, Y61 numbers which had superseded the original Y34 number when the chassis component was used for the Y61 Cadillac Fire Engine. The production of Issue 4 was 30,000 (E).

ISSUE	YEAR OF RELEASE	COLOURS	HOOD	SEAT	STEERING WHEEL	WHEELS	PLATED PARTS	BASEPLATE	RARITY	BOX TYPE	VALUE	CHECK LIST
1	1990	Navy blue body & chassis	White *	Pinky tan	Light olive green, black spokes	Chrome 24 spoke (W F)	Chrome	MATCHBOX © 1990 MACAU Y34	S	P */N	£30	
2		Navy blue body & chassis	Cream	Pinky tan	Light olive green, black spokes	Chrome 24 spoke (W F)	Chrome	MATCHBOX © 1990 MACAU Y34		N	£10	✓
3		Navy blue body & chassis	Cream	Pinky tan	Brown, black spokes	Chrome 24 spoke (W F)	Chrome	MATCHBOX © 1990 MACAU Y34		N	£10	
4	1992	White body, navy blue chassis	Black	Black	Black	Chrome 24 spoke (W F)	Chrome	MATCHBOX © 1990 CHINA YY46,Y61		N1	£12	

NOTES
Compare with YFE03 and Y61-1.

Y35-1 1930 FORD MODEL 'A' PICK-UP TRUCK Scale 1:40

CLIFFORD. This model is similar to the Y7-4 Breakdown truck except that the crane/winch gear was replaced by a load of 5 milk churns; one of which is rather precariously hanging over the edge of the floor section because the rear tail board is in the 'dropped' position. The base had the 'Y35,Y21,Y22' legend cast indicating its commonality; but surprisingly, no Y7 number is featured. The model is based on photographs submitted to the R&D dept and the first livery of "W. Clifford & Sons" was copied from a wooden milk cart located at the Milk Museum in Reading, Berkshire, England. It received a rather indifferent reception from collectors. The oval disc on the cab doors and 'Fresh Farm Milk' on the body sides can be in, either bright red, or orange. The base had a cast hole for the self tapping screw. The production run of the Clifford model was 40482.

AMBROSIA. The second livery, Ambrosia, was more enthusiastically received, most likely due to its more attractive colour and livery. It was orginally planned to issue it with a dark coffee coloured body with a rich cream chassis. However, the Ambrosia company were quick to point out that the production livery of mid blue and cream was the authentic colour scheme of that period. No variations were apparent, casting or otherwise from the W.Clifford version; except of course for the country of manufacture being changed to Made In China. The production was 35,000 (E).

A : W. CLIFFORD & SONS

ISSUE	YEAR OF RELEASE	COLOURS	ROOF	SEAT/ FLOOR & DASH	FRONT BUMPER	PLATED PARTS	WHEELS	LOAD	LOGO	BASEPLATE	RARITY	BOX TYPE	VALUE	CHECK LIST
1	1990	Cream cab & body gloss black chassis	Black plastic	Brown	Cream plastic	Chrome	Yellow solid (WW)	5 milk churns	W. CLIFFORD (RED)	MATCHBOX © 1981 Y35 Y21 Y22 MACAU		N	£8	✓
2		Cream cab & body gloss black chassis	Black plastic	Brown	Cream plastic	Chrome	Yellow solid (WW)	5 milk churns	W. CLIFFORD (ORANGE)	MATCHBOX © 1981 Y35 Y21 Y22 MACAU		N	£8	

B : AMBROSIA

ISSUE	YEAR OF RELEASE	COLOURS	ROOF	SEAT/ FLOOR & DASH	FRONT BUMPER	PLATED PARTS	WHEELS	LOAD	LOGO	BASEPLATE	RARITY	BOX TYPE	VALUE	CHECK LIST
1	1992	Mid blue cab & body cream chassis	Cream plastic	Light orangey brown	Mid blue plastic	Chrome	Cream solid (WW)	5 milk churns	AMBROSIA	MATCHBOX © 1981 Y35 Y21 Y22 CHINA		N I	£15	✓

LIVERY W. CLIFFORD & SONS
Tampo
Body sides. FRESH FARM MILK in red or orange.
Cab doors. W. CLIFFORD & SONS ESTABLISHED 1874 and scroll work in yellow with white DAIRYMEN. All on red or orange oval.

LIVERY AMBROSIA
Tampo
Body sides. Pale lemon AMBROSIA above TM REGD. All within pale lemon coachlines.
Cab doors. Pale lemon FROM OUR DEVON CREAMERY within pale lemon coachlines.
Bonnet offside panel. Pale lemon EST 1907. All within pale lemon coachlines.
Bonnet near side panel. Pale lemon coachlines.

INVESTMENT COMMENT
ORIGINAL PRICE, CLIFFORD £6.99p
AMBROSIA £8.99p
The Ambrosia may be a 'sleeper'. The Clifford has been a disappointment.
NOTES

Y36-1 1926 ROLLS-ROYCE PHANTOM 1 — Scale 1:46

INVESTMENT COMMENT
ORIGINAL PRICE £6.99p

Both issues were well received by collectors. The blue coloured model sold out quickly and few remain on the collectors market.

This was the first regular (non Special Edition) Yesteryear to be made at the China factory. Collectors were somewhat bemused to read on the box that the first livery was based on Rudyard Kipling's car, when in fact this was not the case. Permission was not forthcoming from R. Kipling's estate to use his livery, but the chassis and coachwork were identical to this car. The first colour scheme was taken from photos of another Phantom. The dark red liveried model formed part of 'The Great Motor Cars of the Century' mail order scheme in N. America and was packaged in a plain white box with black lettering. It was simultaneously released world-wide in the 'N' style box. The total production of the red Y36 model was 48,942. 1992 saw the model finally issued in Rudyard Kipling's colours of mid blue and black. It was an immediate success with Yesteryear and car collectors. No casting changes have been noted, although slightly more enhanced detailing was applied to Issue 2 models e.g., running board treads picked out in silver and silver bonnet hinges. The production of the mid blue Phantom was 16,506. In 1994 the model was re-run as part of the "Grand Classic's" Collection. The dark red was duller and the seats were made from a dark brown plastic.

ISSUE	YEAR OF RELEASE	COLOURS	ROOF/HOOD	SEATS CAR INTERIOR	RADIATOR & GRILLE	STEERING WHEEL	WHEELS	PLATED PARTS	RUNNING BOARD TREADS	BASEPLATE	RARITY	BOX TYPE	VALUE	CHECK LIST
1	1990	Dark red body, bonnet gloss black chassis	Black	Dark red	Chrome	Black	Chrome solid	Chrome	Black	MATCHBOX © 1990 CHINA		P/N1	£15	✓
2	1992	Mid blue body, bonnet gloss black chassis	Black	Maroon	Chrome	Black	Chrome solid	Chrome	Silver	MATCHBOX © 1990 CHINA		N1	£12	✓
3	1994	Dull dark red body, bonnet gloss black chassis	Black	Dark brown	Chrome	Black	Chrome solid	Chrome	Black	MATCHBOX © 1990 CHINA		N2		

NOTES
The original price of Issue 2 was £7.25 and the original price of Issue 3 was £12.50

Y37-1 1929 GARRETT STEAM WAGON   Scale 1:59

CHUBB'S. The actual Garrett on which this model was based is located at Ware in Hertfordshire, England. It is a coal merchant's wagon with a truck body and the water tank mounted between the rear of the cab and the truck body. However, photographs had showed that to increase the load carrying area this vehicle could be fitted with the water tank behind the rear axle. Therefore most steam lorries had their water tanks moved from behind the cab to under the chassis. The 'Chubb's' livery was also taken from photographs. Because the two components were painted separately the van body colour varies slightly from that of the cab. The curved cab front panel was too acute for tampo printing and therefore a label had to be used. Late preproduction bases with the word 'Garrett' misspelt were released as production models. Production was 42,138 models.

MILKMAID. The first re-livery of the Garrett, Milkmaid Brand Milk was an immediate 'hit' with collectors and stocks were sold out within weeks in many areas of the world. R&D had thought it might be necessary to use a label on the van body sides due to the intricacy of the milkmaid, but tampo printing was used throughout and the effect of all the tampo printed surfaces is a masterpiece in itself. However the curved front nearside corner of the cab neccessitated a transparent label, as the curve was too acute for the tampo plates to make a smudge-free contact. Slight disappointment was expressed that no tampo decoration had been applied to the rear doors of the van body. Production was 30,000 models (E).

A : CHUBB'S

ISSUE	YEAR OF RELEASE	COLOURS	CAB ROOF	VAN ROOF	SEATS	FRONT WHEELS	REAR WHEELS	PLATED PARTS	TRANSMISSION CHAIN PIPES & CYLINDERS	LOGO	BASEPLATE	RARITY	BOX TYPE	VALUE	CHECK LIST
1	1990	Pale blue body, navy blue chassis	White	Cream	Black	Pale blue 6 spoke	Pale blue daisy	Chrome	Black	CHUBB'S	MATCHBOX© 1990 MACAU, GARRTT*	V R	N	£90	
2		Pale blue body, navy blue chassis	White	Cream	Black	Pale blue 6 spoke	Pale blue daisy	Chrome	Black	CHUBB'S	MATCHBOX © 1990 MACAU, GARRETT		N	£10	✓

B : MILKMAID

ISSUE	YEAR OF RELEASE	COLOURS	CAB ROOF	VAN ROOF	SEATS	FRONT WHEELS	REAR WHEELS	PLATED PARTS	TRANSMISSION CHAIN PIPES & CYLINDERS	LOGO	BASEPLATE	RARITY	BOX TYPE	VALUE	CHECK LIST
1	1992	Cream body, navy blue cab & chassis	Navy blue	White	Black	Red 6 spoke	Red daisy	Chrome	Black	MILKMAID	MATCHBOX © 1990 CHINA, GARRETT		N 1	£25	

LIVERY CHUBB'S

Tampo
Van sides. White CHUBB'S SAFE DEPOSITS with black shadow effect and white scroll with black shadow effect.
Van rear doors. White CHUBB'S LOCKS with black shadow effect above white SAFE MAKERS LONDON.
Cab nearside rear panel. White CHUBB'S SAFES LONDON. All within white coachlining.
Cab near side door. White coachline.
Cab off side rear panel. Garrett's logo on oval in black, red, white and yellow; above white CHUBB'S LOCKS with black shadow effect. White coachlining.
Cab off side front panel. White coachlining.
Cab frontleft panel. White CHUBB'S SAFE MAKERS LONDON within white coachline.
Label
Cab curved panel. Small version of van sides. All within white coachline.

LIVERY MILKMAID

Tampo
Van sides. Picture of milkmaid in blue, red, white, cream and black; above black TRADE MARK. All to the left of dark blue MILKMAID BRAND and LARGEST SALE IN THE WORLD.
Cab near side panel. Multi-coloured milkmaid picture and lemon TRADEMARK. All within lemon coachlines.
Cab off side rear panel. Milkmaid's picture and trademark as per near side above lemon MILKMAID BRAND MILK. All within lemon coachlines.
Cab off side front panel. Lemon LARGEST SALE IN THE WORLD. All within lemon coachlines.
Cab front left hand panel. Smallest picture of multi-coloured milkmaid and trademark. All within lemon coachlines.
Label
Cab curved panel. Lemon MILKMAID MILK to left of an oval with Garrett's logo in black, red, white and yellow. All within lemon coachlines.

INVESTMENT COMMENT

ORIGINAL PRICE, CHUBB'S £7.99p MILK MAID £8.99p

Chubb's Issue 1 has grown quickly in value and is an issue well worth finding.

Milkmaid has made rapid progress. Any stock holdings have been reduced to zero and there is plenty of scope for further growth.

NOTES
Compare with YGB15.

Y38-1 1920 ROLLS-ROYCE ARMOURED CAR Scale 1:48

INVESTMENT COMMENT
ORIGINAL PRICE £14.99p

Regarded as a rather uninspiring subject, this Special Limited Edition recently started to grow in value. One to watch.

This model was released as a Special Limited Edition in August 1990. Although the Y13-3 RAF Tender and the Y25-1 Renault Ambulance were military vehicles this model broke years of Yesteryear tradition; by being the first "aggressively armed" vehicle. Whilst two distinctly different khaki colours have been found, no other differences have been recorded. Collectors were disappointed with the poor match between the khaki livery and the colour of the headlamps. Final pre-production samples had headlamps in a coloured polymer similar to the khaki livery, whereas on production models the colour had changed to a pinky-beige. The total production was 35,880.

ISSUE	YEAR OF RELEASE	COLOURS	TURRET	GUN	HEAD LAMPS	WHEELS	ENGINE UNDERSIDE ARMOUR PLATING	BASEPLATE	RARITY	BOX TYPE	VALUE	CHECK LIST
1	1990	Light khaki	Light khaki	Black	Pinky beige	Dark khaki solid	Dark khaki	MATCHBOX © 1990 SPECIAL LIMITED EDITION MACAU		0	£20	✓
2		Darker khaki	Darker khaki	Black	Pinky beige	Dark khaki solid	Dark khaki	MATCHBOX © 1990 SPECIAL LIMITED EDITION MACAU		0	£20	

LIVERY

Logo - Tampo
"HMAC" "AJAX" in black both bonnet sides.
Red white and blue roundel, both front body sides and turret top slopes.

NOTES

INVESTMENT COMMENT
ORIGINAL PRICE £29.95p

A good performer already, and one to watch closely.

Y39-1 1820 PASSENGER COACH & HORSES Scale 1:43

This model was based on a coach located at the Science Museum in London, England. Originally it was to have been a Royal Mail Coach but this would have meant that Matchbox would have had to pay royalties and the Company refused to do so, and so the Royal Mail logo was not used. As a rule Matchbox do not pay royalties and if they had, the Company would have been concerned that the model would have had to be even more expensive than the approximate U.K. price of £30. Some comments were expressed regarding Queen Victoria's royal cypher on the coach doors, because she didn't succeed to the crown until 1837. However it was pointed out that the coach was built to an 1820 design, many years later. Being a Special Limited Edition, the model was packaged in a special container which was a two piece moulded polystyrene holder within a bright red, maroon and gold finished cardboard sleeve. Initially, after a slow start it soon became a best seller! The total production quantity was 39,880.

ISSUE	YEAR OF RELEASE	COLOURS	LOWER PANELS / DOORS	ROOF	SEATS	EXTERNAL SEATS	REAR GUARD	LUGGAGE	DRAW BAR	FIGURES	HORSES	HORSE TACKLE & TRACES	PLATED PARTS	WHEELS	BASEPLATE	RARITY	BOX TYPE	VALUE	CHECK LIST
1	1990	Gloss black body, bright red chassis	Maroon	Black	Brown	Black	Bright red	Brown	Bright red	6	4	Black	Gold	Bright red 12 spoke front Bright red 14 spoke rear	MATCHBOX © 1990 CHINA		0	£40	✓

LIVERY

Tampo
"VR" in gold both front side panels within gold coachlines.
"No. 14" in gold both rear side panels all within gold coachlines.
Gold coachlines to maroon door panels and panel beneath door window openings.

NOTES

Y40-1 1931 MERCEDES BENZ 770   Scale 1:48

INVESTMENT COMMENT
ORIGINAL PRICE £8.99p

A unique model with no recolours and a popular addition to the range.

The vehicle upon which this model is based is in the Mercedes Benz Museum at Stuttgart Germany to which the Research and Development team of engineers went to photograph and measure the actual vehicle. The huge car weighs 3.5 tonnes and the model accurately reflects its imposing presence. The colour scheme has been reproduced as faithfully as modern technology allows. The livery depicted is at the time of Kaiser Willhelm II who was exiled in Holland in November 1918. It was well received by collectors who appreciated the degree of detailing such as the silver door handles and hinges, the dividing glass screen between the driver's and passenger compartments, and the 'three dimensional' tensioning arms to the rear portion of the roof. The model also has a hole in the baseplate for a self tapping screw. In 1994, the model was re-run as part of the "Grand Classics" collection.

ISSUE	YEAR OF RELEASE	COLOURS	ROOF	SEATS & CAR INTERIOR	WHEELS	PLATED PARTS	BASEPLATE	RARITY	BOX TYPE	VALUE	CHECK LIST
1	1991	Grey body & chassis	Dark blue	Maroon	Chrome solid	Chrome	MATCHBOX © 1990 CHINA		N 1	£15	✓
2	1994	Lighter grey body & chassis	Dark blue	Maroon	Chrome solid	Chrome	MATCHBOX © 1990 CHINA		N 2	£15	

NOTES

Y41-1 1932 MERCEDES BENZ L5 LORRY   Scale 1:69

INVESTMENT COMMENT
ORIGINAL PRICE £8.99p
Issue 2 is still readily available on the market, and is often sold without a premium. Over production is likely to stifle immediate growth.

HOWALDTSWERKE A.G. The 'Howaldtswerke' company logo was submitted by Matchbox Toys Germany for inclusion in the range. This firm was still in existence in 1991 and operated this type of lorry in the 1930's. Only black and white photographs existed of the firm's livery; but the colour scheme was selected after consulting the Howaldtswerke management. It had been planned to produce the false planked body floor in diecast but the expense meant that instead this component was made in a mid brown coloured plastic. The unusual load of a huge diesel engine cylinder block was unique and was well received. Although minor changes were made to the baseplate to include the threaded screw hole for packaging purposes and the new "Made in China" legend it is surprising that the baseplate still has only the Y6 number of the earlier 'Hofbräu' model. The only variation is the finish of the radiator shell, which is a separate component from the headlamps. Total production was 48,222.

A : HOWALDTSWERKE A. G.

ISSUE	YEAR OF RELEASE	COLOURS	MUDGUARDS / STEPS	ROOF	SEATS	GRILLE	WHEELS	PLATED PARTS	RADIATOR SHELL	LOGO	LOAD	BASEPLATE	RARITY	BOX TYPE	VALUE	CHECK LIST
1	1991	Dark green body, dark grey chassis	Glossy black	Light grey	Light grey	Black	Red 6 spoke	Chrome	Matt* silver	HOWALDTSWERKE	Light grey cylinder block	MATCHBOX © 1988 CHINA	D	N 1	£15	✓
2		Dark green body, dark grey chassis	Glossy black	Light grey	Light grey	Black	Red 6 spoke	Chrome	Bright chrome	HOWALDTSWERKE	Light grey cylinder block	MATCHBOX © 1988 CHINA		N 1	£9	

LIVERY
Tampo
Lorry sides. HOWALDTSWERKE A.G. KIEL in gold.
Cab doors. Company logo in gold and red.

NOTES
Compare with Y6-5, YFE05 and YPP03.

INVESTMENT COMMENT

ORIGINAL PRICE £8.99p

Not popular with collectors and still available on the market.

Y42-1 1939 ALBION 10 TON CX27 LORRY   Scale 1 : 60

LIBBY'S. Chosen by the Research and Development Department quite simply because they wanted a 'flat fronted' i.e. cab over engine design lorry. Also it was the first regular Yesteryear to be of a Heavy Goods Vehicle classification and to have more than two axles on a rigid vehicle. At first the factory encountered tampo printing difficulties with the word 'Libby's'; the script lettering was thickened before production. Also the factory found it hard to match the colour of the blue wheels to the blue of the flat bed. Pre-production samples have wheel hubs in a much paler blue than the colour of the flat bed. The only variation of note is with regards to the radiator shell which can be found in bright chrome or matt silver. The production run was 38,682.

A : LIBBY'S

ISSUE	YEAR OF RELEASE	COLOURS	CAB	CAB INTERIOR & SEATS	MUDGUARDS	WHEELS	LOAD	LOGO	HEADLAMPS	RADIATOR SHELL	BASEPLATE	RARITY	BOX TYPE	VALUE	CHECK LIST
1	1991	Mid blue body, navy blue chassis	White	Blue	Dark blue	Mid blue	28 bright chrome milk churns	LIBBY'S	Bright chrome	Matt silver	MATCHBOX © 1991 CHINA		N 1	£15	✓
2		Mid blue body, navy blue chassis	White	Blue	Dark blue	Mid blue	28 bright chrome milk churns	LIBBY'S	Bright chrome	Bright chrome	MATCHBOX © 1991 CHINA		N 1	£10	

LIVERY LIBBY'S

Tampo
Cab sides. Red LIBBY'S.

NOTES

Y43-1 1905 BUSCH SELF PROPELLED FIRE ENGINE Scale 1:43

INVESTMENT COMMENT
ORIGINAL PRICE £34.95p

An instant "sell out" in every market. Both issues have recorded good growth and likely to continue. Always check for Issue 1.

This Special Limited Edition model of a self propelled steam fire engine is a replica of the vehicle in the Feuer Wehr Museum at Basel in Switzerland, which is also a working fire station. Although copper plated boiler pipes and collars had been specified, production models had these components brass plated. However, it has been reported that some models with copper pipes and collars did leave the factory. Initially this imposing model received a mixed reception from collectors which, probably, was due to the colour of the authentic livery, being dark green, instead of the more usual red. However, the model was soon appreciated for the amount of detail and excellent quality workmanship; an example being the finely sculpted firemen. The production run was 34,198.

ISSUE	YEAR OF RELEASE	COLOURS	STOKER'S PLATFORM	BOILER	SEATS	FRONT HOSE REEL	GAS CYLINDERS	WHEELS	BOILER PIPES & BOTTOM COLLARS	CHIMNEY COLLAR	CREW	SIDE HOSES / CONTROL HANDLES	CREWS FOOTPLATE	PLATED PARTS	BASEPLATE	RARITY	BOX TYPE	VALUE	CHECK LIST
1	1991	Dark green body & crew area	Black	Metallic powder blue	Black	Green with grey hose	3 Green	Bright red 14 spoke	Copper* plated effect	Copper painted effect	5	Grey	Silver	Brass	MATCHBOX © 1991 CHINA	V R	0	£85	
2		Dark green body & crew area	Black	Metallic powder blue	Black	Green with grey hose	3 Green	Bright red 14 spoke	Brass plated effect	Copper painted effect	5	Grey	Silver	Brass	MATCHBOX © 1991 CHINA	D	0	£45	✔

LIVERY BUSCH

Tampo
Front seat sides. FEUERWEHR BASEL 1905 in red with gold edging surrounding company shield in white gold and red.

NOTES

The column heading 'STOKER'S PLATFORM', includes the firebox, underframe and mudguards.

The crew men have blue uniforms, gold helmets. Thier hands and faces have a flesh coloured "effect". One man, the leading fireman, has a red cap instead of a helmet.

Y44-1 1910 RENAULT BUS

Scale 1:38

INVESTMENT COMMENT
ORIGINAL PRICE £8.99p
Good growth has already been recorded on issues 3 and 4. Issue 3 sold at auction in the UK in June 1994 for £75.00. Likely to continue even further upwards.

V. FONTAINE. When the Matchbox Research and Development team visited the Schlumpf Collection in France they were shown a privately built bus body fitted to a light van chassis. It was decided that such a body would fit nicely to the Y25-1 Renault AG Van chassis and so the Renault bus Yesteryear model was conceived. Many hotels in the early part of the 20th Century would commission the local coachbuilder to construct such vehicles which were used as a courtesy coach for local patrons. The chassis, baseplate, bonnet, windscreen, radiator and driver's seat components were from the Y25-1 1910 Renault van. The realistic narrow section tyres were first used on the Y16-4 Scania-Vabis Post Bus and more recently on the Y21-5 1926 Ford Model "TT" van. Whilst the majority of the Renault models had the standard black roof; 1900 were fitted with dark red roofs. Very few, if any, of these were released in Australia or the U.S.A. The majority of them were bought by a U.K. wholesaler who in turn sold a large number to a German wholesaler. Two noticeable shades of yellow have been recorded. All issues were released with press-fit axles and a hole in the baseplate for a self tapping screw. Total production of all issues was 29,530.

A : VINCENT FONTAINE

ISSUE	YEAR OF RELEASE	COLOURS	ROOF	SEATS	REAR STEP	WHEELS	PLATED PARTS	WINDOWS	BASEPLATE	RARITY	BOX TYPE	VALUE	CHECK LIST
1	1991	Bright yellow body, gloss black chassis	Black	Mid brown	Mid brown	Red 12 spoke	Brass	Clear Perspex	MATCHBOX © 1986 Y44 Y25 CHINA		N1	£15	✓
2		Darker yellow body, gloss black chassis	Black	Mid brown	Mid brown	Red 12 spoke	Brass	Clear Perspex	MATCHBOX © 1986 Y44 Y25 CHINA		N1	£15	
3		Bright yellow body, gloss black chassis	Red*	Mid brown	Mid brown	Red 12 spoke	Brass	Clear Perspex	MATCHBOX © 1986 Y44 Y25 CHINA	R	N1	£90	
4		Darker yellow body, gloss black chassis	Red*	Mid brown	Mid brown	Red 12 spoke	Brass	Clear Perspex	MATCHBOX © 1986 Y44 Y25 CHINA	R	N1	£90	

LIVERY VINCENT FONTAINE
Tampo
Body sides. Gold WESSERLING - BUSSANG on narrow red stripe.
Body rear panels. Gold BUSSANG on the left and No15 on the right. Both on narrow red stripes.
Rear door. Gold TELEPHONE on narrow red stripe above red VINCENT FONTAINE.
Cab sides. Red VINCENT FONTAINE.

NOTES
Compare with Y25-1, YGB07, YPP01 and YET06.

INVESTMENT COMMENT
ORIGINAL PRICE £8.99p

An excellent seller and very popular with collectors. Few remain on the market and although growth has not been dramatic, it is one to watch closely.

Y45-1 1930 BUGATTI ROYALE NAPOLEON   Scale 1:46

Housed in Le Museé National de L'Automobile (Schlumpf Collection) in France. Because the first was Bugatti's personal vehicle the 'Napoleon' is probably the most exclusive of all Bugatti cars. Seven other almost identical cars were meticulously made virtually by hand and used by the Bugatti family. Being a one off car, collectors wondered how Matchbox Toys were going to release it later as a recolour! However, collectors were delighted with the fine diecasting, especially the enhanced headlights, door handles, ribbed pads to the runningboards, Bugatti nameplate on the radiator shell etc. The Y45 Bugatti was the first Yesteryear to have the scale endorsed on the chrome baseplate. The production quantity was 32,022. In 1994 it was re-run as part of the Grand Classics Collection.

ISSUE	YEAR OF RELEASE	COLOURS	BONNET SIDE PANELS	PART FRONT DOOR PANELS	ROOF	SEATS	GRILLE	STEERING WHEEL	WHEELS	PLATED PARTS	BASEPLATE	RARITY	BOX TYPE	VALUE	CHECK LIST
1	1991	Black body & chassis	Dark blue	Dark blue	Black	Dark blue	Black	Black, lemon spokes	Chrome solid	Chrome	MATCHBOX © 1991 CHINA		N 1	£15	✓
2	1994	Black body & chassis	Dark blue	Dark blue	Black	Lilac blue	Black	Black, lemon spokes	Chrome solid	Chrome	MATCHBOX © 1991 CHINA		N 2		

NOTES

Y 46-1 1880 MERRYWEATHER FIRE ENGINE   Scale 1:43

INVESTMENT COMMENT
ORIGINAL PRICE £34.95p

Not as successful as the Y43 Busch but as a Special Limited Edition now beginning to show growth.

This beautiful Special Limited Edition was the only horse drawn fire engine to be featured in the range since the 1960, Y4-2 Shand Mason and was eagerly bought by Yesteryear and Fire Engine collectors. It is a faithful replica of the 'Greenwich' type Merryweather Engine; an original of which was located at the West of England Steam Engine Society. When the Research and Development team went to photograph and measure that vehicle, it was undergoing a complete restoration. Whilst this was advantageous for measuring it was difficult to envisage how it would look assembled. The Society has records and pictures to show that the vehicle had been privately owned and operated by the owners of Tehidy House, in Cornwall England. The moulds for the horses with the Y39 Stage Coach were used again for the Y46 model. The draw bar has been seen in two distinct colours. Initially it was assumed that this component was the same as that for the Stage Coach. However, with this model it is longer and is of a different shape where it locates onto the turntable. The Y46 comes with four firemen crew, all with flesh coloured faces and hands and clad in dull blue uniforms with brass decoration and gold helmets. The total production of this Special Limited Edition was 31,608.

ISSUE	YEAR OF RELEASE	COLOURS	BOILER	DRIVERS SEAT	HOSES	PUMP	WHEELS	REAR WHEEL BRAKES	CREW	DRAW BAR	HORSES	HORSE COLLARS & TRACES	BASEPLATE	RARITY	BOX TYPE	VALUE	CHECK LIST
1	1991	Bright pinky red body	Brass	Black	White	Black & brass	Red 12 spoke front Red 16 spoke rear	Black	4	Pale red *	Two, white with grey details	Black	MATCHBOX © 1991 CHINA	S	0	£60	
2		Bright pinky red body	Brass	Black	White	Black & brass	Red 12 spoke front Red 16 spoke rear	Black	4	Dark red	Two, white with grey details	Black	MATCHBOX © 1991 CHINA		0	£40	✓

LIVERY

Tampo
Gold TEHIDY HOUSE on driver's seat support frame within gold coachlines.
Black MERRYWEATHER 1908 ENGINEERS LONDON on gold oval, within two raised gold coachlines, all on hose reel container panel.
Gold coachlines to top of seat, foot rests and outer rims of wheels.
Merryweather plate on both boiler sides.

NOTES

INVESTMENT COMMENT
ORIGINAL PRICE £8.99p
Although not a popular model at its time of release, there are few on the collectors market all of which are selling at a premium.

Y 47-1 1929 MORRIS COWLEY LIGHT VAN Scale 1:39

LINDT. This is a development of the Y19-3 1929 Morris Light Van with oval side windows, just to the rear of the cab doors omitted. Whilst researching the Y19-3 'Sainsbury' livery the Research and Development team noticed that various photographs showed this type of van with or without, the oval side windows. The decision to delete these windows was taken so as to give a larger surface area for the livery decoration. Due to alignment problems with the tampo machine, which could not give a perfect print of the intricate shadow effect to the main wording, labels were used. However, the lettering on the cab doors is tampo printed. It should be noted that in 1991 Matchbox Toys U.K. gave to the British Broadcasting Corporation, six relabelled vans in the 'Antiques Road Show Going Live' livery as prizes for a competition run on television. In all, twenty four vans were made, the balance being allocated to members of the Matchbox Marketing and the Research and Development Departments. The Y47 was fitted with the baseplate screw hole and press-fit axles. The production run of the Y47-1 'Lindt' was 31,536.

A : LINDT

ISSUE	YEAR OF RELEASE	COLOURS	ROOF	ROOF CASTING TYPE	SEATS & CAB INTERIOR	CAB WINDOWS	GRILLE	WHEELS	PLATED PARTS	LOGO	BASEPLATE	RARITY	BOX TYPE	VALUE	CHECK LIST
1	1991	Black body & chassis	Bright yellow	2	Light brown	Clear Perspex	Black	Chrome 12 spoke	Chrome but brass tool box cover	LINDT	MATCHBOX © 1987 CHINA		N 1	£15	✓

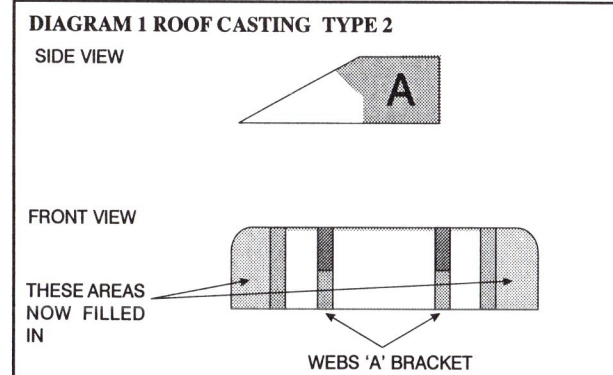

DIAGRAM 1 ROOF CASTING TYPE 2
SIDE VIEW
FRONT VIEW
THESE AREAS NOW FILLED IN
WEBS 'A' BRACKET

LIVERY LINDT
Labels
Van sides. White LINDT & SPRUNGLI, above CHOCOLAT LINDT in bright yellow with darker yellow shadow effect, above white LE VERITABLE THE GENUINE, all within bright yellow coachlining.
Tampo
Cab doors. White MARQUE ROD, LINDT FILS BERNE.

NOTES
Compare with Y19-3, YGB04 and YY047/SA.

Y61-1 1933 CADILLAC FIRE ENGINE — Scale 1:46

INVESTMENT COMMENT
ORIGINAL PRICE £8.99p

A good seller for Matchbox and few if any remain on the market. Even more collectable with the introduction of the Fire Engine series.

Whilst researching the Y43 Busch Fire Engine at the Feuerwehr Museum at Basel in Switzerland, the R & D team saw this vehicle amongst the many fire vehicles on display. As luck would have it, the chassis was virtually identical to the Y34 Cadillac town car. The Y34 chassis was used for this model, but the rest of the main construction was completely new. The ladder is the same design as the ones used on the Y6-4 Rolls Royce Fire Engine which was scaled at 1:48 and the wheels are common to those on the Y12-5 GMC van. Whilst many fire engines have appeared as Yesteryears, this is the first time the range has featured, what in reality is a fire-support vehicle. If in fact, it could pump water, its capability to do so would be extremely limited. The production run was 20,502.

ISSUE	YEAR OF RELEASE	COLOURS	LADDERS	SEATS	GRILLE	STEERING WHEEL	WHEELS	PLATED PARTS	LADDER RACK	ENHANCED DETAILING	LOGO	BASEPLATE	RARITY	BOX TYPE	VALUE	CHECK LIST
1	1992	Bright red body bonnet & chassis	Light brown	Black	Black with chrome bars	Black	Chrome solid	Chrome	Red	Yes	FEUERWEHR AARAU	MATCHBOX © 1990 CHINA YY46 Y61		N 1	£20	✓

LIVERY
Tampo
Front doors. FEUEWEHR AARAU in black on gold background over black, red and white "spread eagle" shield.

White 'F' tampo printed onto lens of ladder rack lamp.

NOTES

Compare with Y34-1 and YFE03.

INVESTMENT COMMENT
ORIGINAL PRICE £8.99p

A popular addition to the range and a good seller. Few left on the market. Likely to increase in value especially as variation collectors will want both chassis types.

Y 62-1 1932 MODEL 'AA' FORD 1½ TON TRUCK   Scale: 1:46

With an extended and strengthened chassis as well as a more powerful engine this delightful delivery truck was the workhorse based on the internationally famous Ford Model 'A' car. These trucks were used all over the world and were built in the U.S.A., Britain, and in Russia. After discussions with Peacocks the logo of the firm G. W. Peacock was chosen, a photograph of which had been sent to Matchbox by an avid collector. Collectors were most impressed with the cast detailing on the sides and rear of the body and like the Y21-5 "TT" Ford Van, full rear axle housing, prop shaft front and rear axle struts were fitted to this model. However there was disappointment that some of the chassis was made in plastic. Two different tools were used to make the plastic part of the chassis. Consequently there are differences to the nearside rear springs and the chassis member ends. Type A and Type B. The spare wheel carrier beneath the body was the first of its type on a Yesteryear model. All models were issued with press-fit axles and with a screw hole in the base. The production run of the 'Peacock' model was 23,526.

A : PEACOCK

ISSUE	YEAR OF RELEASE	COLOURS	ROOF	SEAT	GRILLE	WINDOWS	WHEELS	PLATED PARTS	LOAD	CHASSIS TYPE	LOGO	BASEPLATE	RARITY	BOX TYPE	VALUE	CHECK LIST
1	1992	Pale green body , black chassis	Light grey	Black	Black with chrome bar	Clear Perspex	Red solid	Chrome	Light brown sacks	A	PEACOCK	MATCHBOX © 1991 CHINA		N 1	£15	
2		Pale green body , black chassis	Light grey	Black	Black with chrome bar	Clear Perspex	Red solid	Chrome	Light brown sacks	B	PEACOCK	MATCHBOX © 1991 CHINA		N 1	£15	✓

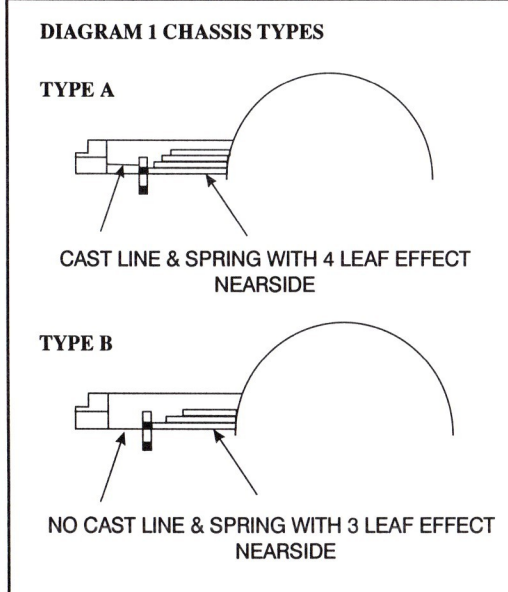

DIAGRAM 1 CHASSIS TYPES

TYPE A — CAST LINE & SPRING WITH 4 LEAF EFFECT NEARSIDE

TYPE B — NO CAST LINE & SPRING WITH 3 LEAF EFFECT NEARSIDE

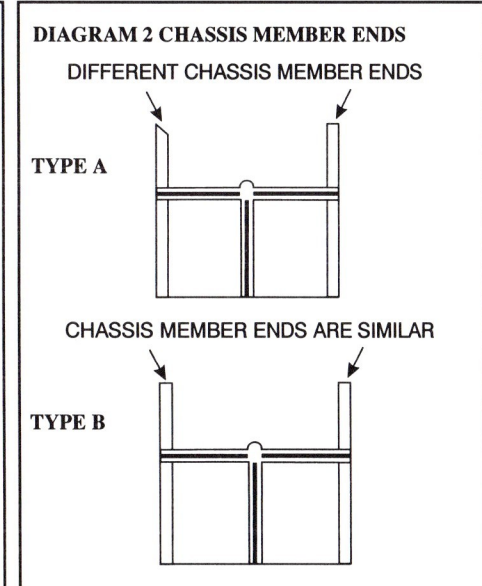

DIAGRAM 2 CHASSIS MEMBER ENDS

TYPE A — DIFFERENT CHASSIS MEMBER ENDS

TYPE B — CHASSIS MEMBER ENDS ARE SIMILAR

LIVERY PEACOCK
Tampo
Truck sides and tailboard. Dark red coachlining.
Cab doors. White G.W. PEACOCK above ST IVES (CAMBS) 68129 in white. All within dark red coachlines.
Bonnet rear panels. White G.W.P. within dark red circle inside dark red coachlines.

NOTES
Compare with YGB05, YGB16, YFE06, YFE09 and YPP05.

Y63-1 1939 BEDFORD TYPE "KD" TRUCK   Scale 1:46

INVESTMENT COMMENT
ORIGINAL PRICE £8.99p
A "sell out" in all markets. A very popular release. Further growth potential expected.

Introduced by Bedford in 1939, this small lorry was a true workhorse which soon began to appear in virtually every Commonwealth country. This version of the K range of vehicles was given the designation of KD, the D referring to the drop side nature of the truck body. Yesteryear collectors were most impressed with the amount of fine detail given to this model, especially the prop-shaft, rear axle housing and spare wheel carrier; similar to its excellent stablemate, the Y62 Ford Model AA Truck. The model was packaged with a separate bag of real stones, but collectors are advised that if the stones are unpacked and placed in the truck body, they could cause a damaging reaction between the stone and the paintwork. Early pre-production models have several words misspelt on the baseplate. A second mould was made with the correct spelling and is identified by the 'Y63-1' legend. However, the spelling mistakes on the original mould were corrected and this is recognised by the 'Y63-2' legend. The location of certain words and letters differs between the two bases and the dimensions of the cab steps differ very slightly. The production run was 26,700.

A : G FARRAR

ISSUE	YEAR OF RELEASE	COLOURS	SEATS	CAB	RADIATOR GRILLE	PLATED PARTS	WHEELS	LOGO	LOAD	BASEPLATE	RARITY	BOX TYPE	VALUE	CHECK LIST
1	1992	Light brown body, black chassis	Black	Bright red	Black with silver bars	Chrome	Chrome solid	G FARRAR	Light brown York stones	MATCHBOX © 1991 CHINA Y63-2*	S	N 1	£50	
2		Light brown body, black chassis	Black	Bright red	Black with silver bars	Chrome	Chrome solid	G FARRAR	Light brown York stones	MATCHBOX © 1991 CHINA Y63-1	D	N 1	£35	✓

LIVERY
Tampo
Truck sides. GEORGE FARRAR YORKSHIRE STONE in white with black shadow effect. All within white coachlining.
Tailboard. GEORGE FARRAR in white with black shadow effect above white KEIGHLEY YORKSHIRE. All within white coachlining.
Cab doors. GEORGE FARRAR KEIGHLEY YORKSHIRE in white. All within coachlining. White coachlined lower panels.
Hoarding board. GEORGE FARRAR in white with black shadow effect.

NOTES
Compare with YFE04 and YFE04/B.

Y64-1 1938 LINCOLN ZEPHYR   Scale 1:43

INVESTMENT COMMENT
ORIGINAL PRICE £8.99p

A new model in 1992; rarely modelled by other diecast manufacturers and eagerly bought by the car fraternity. Potential may possibly be increased by the release in 1995 of the "Grand Marques" model. Look out for both issues.

The first Lincoln Zephyr was lauched in 1935, and at the time was hailed by the Museum of Modern Art " as the first successfully designed streamlined car in America". Whether you agree or disagree with those sentiments, it is certainly an excellent stable mate for the Y18-1 Cord and the Y19-1 Auburn, although the enhanced detailing tends to put the Y18 and Y19 in the shade slightly. Enthusiastically received by collectors, disappointment was expressed at the "unfinished" state of the rear panel of the back of the front seat and the rather chunky appearance of the windscreen framework. The Zephyr saw two firsts on a Yesteryear. The headlamps were made of clear Perspex and featured chrome rims and a totally new wheel, tyre and hub cap design was used. The Zephyr was the first car with a separate casting representing the axle and transmission componets. In 1995 the Lincoln was re-issued as one of the models in the Grand Marques series. Production of Issue 1 was 35,000(E).

ISSUE	YEAR OF RELEASE	COLOURS	AXLES & TRANSMISSION	SEATS	INTERIOR TRIM /FLOOR	FOLDED HOOD	STEERING WHEEL	PLATED PARTS	PAINTED TRIM	WHEELS	BASEPLATE	RARITY	BOX TYPE	VALUE	CHECK LIST
1	1992	Cream body & chrome chassis, black running boards	Black plastic	Brown	Brown	Dark cream	Cream, brown spokes	Chrome	Silver & red	Chrome solid (W W)	MATCHBOX © 1992 CHINA		N1	£25	✓
2	1995	Maroon body & chrome chassis, silver running boards	Black plastic	Light brown	Tan. Highlights in light brown, silver & black	Off white	Yellow silver spokes	Chrome	Silver	Chrome solid (W W)	MATCHBOX © 1992 CHINA		N2		

LIVERY
ISSUE 1. NUMBER PLATES
Tampo
Black with lemon yellow border and UK 92.

LIVERY
ISSUE 2. NUMBER PLATES
Tampo
White with black C780.

NOTES
The 1995 release was coded as YY064-1 by Matchbox Collectibles. Original price was £12.50

Y65-1 1928 AUSTIN 7 : BMW : ROSENGART   Scale 1:43

Released in September 1992, this special edition set took the collecting world by storm by being the first time the Austin 7 had been mass produced by a major toy manufacturer. It was also the first time a single Yesteryear issue had contained 3 individual versions of one model. Herbert Austin introduced the Austin 7 in 1927 as the first truly affordable motor car to compete with the growing motorcycle and cycle-car market. So successful was his strategy that by 1928, BMW of Germany and Lucien Rosengart of France were building their versions under licence from Austin. This set contains an example of all 3 versions. The van is the commercial version as made by Austin in England; the open tourer is the BMW version; and the saloon is the Rosengart version. The minor differences to the body work (e.g. the doors, radiators) are faithfully captured by these superb models. Whilst they appear rather small, they were just that; the roof height being just chest height on a 6 foot tall person! A restored example of an Austin 7 located at King's Lynn in Norfolk, England was used as the basis for this special edition issue. Total production was 35,000 sets (E).

AUSTIN 7 VAN

ISSUE	YEAR OF RELEASE	COLOURS	ROOF	FOLDED HOOD	SEATS & FLOOR	PLATED PARTS	WHEELS	SOLID WHEEL TRIMS	TYRES	LOGO	THREADED SCREW HOLE	BASEPLATE	RARITY	BOX TYPE	SET VALUE	CHECK LIST
1	1992	Bright red body gloss black chassis	Bright red	N/A	Brown	Chrome	Chrome 18 spoke	N/A	Black	"CASTROL"	Yes	MATCHBOX © 1992 CHINA	O			✓

ROSENGART

ISSUE	YEAR OF RELEASE	COLOURS	ROOF	FOLDED HOOD	SEATS & FLOOR	PLATED PARTS	WHEELS	SOLID WHEEL TRIMS	TYRES	LOGO	THREADED SCREW HOLE	BASEPLATE	RARITY	BOX TYPE	SET VALUE	CHECK LIST
1	1992	Blue body gloss black chassis	Textured black plastic	N/A	Brown	Chrome	Chrome 18 spoke	Yes	Black	N/A	Yes	MATCHBOX © 1992 CHINA				✓

B M W DIXIE

ISSUE	YEAR OF RELEASE	COLOURS	ROOF	FOLDED HOOD	SEATS & FLOOR	PLATED PARTS	WHEELS	SOLID WHEEL TRIMS	TYRES	LOGO	THREADED SCREW HOLE	BASEPLATE	RARITY	BOX TYPE	SET VALUE	CHECK LIST
1	1992	White body gloss black chassis	N/A	Black	Brown	Chrome	Chrome 18 spoke	N/A	Black	N/A	Yes	MATCHBOX © 1992 CHINA			£50	✓

LIVERY CASTROL
Tampo
Van body sides. CASTROL in black on white panel with black edging on orange circle with black WAKEFIELD MOTOR OIL. and white C.C. WAKEFIELD & CO LTD.
Cab doors. White WAKEFIELD HOUSE CHEAPSIDE LONDON
Bonnet sides. White ESTD 1899.

INVESTMENT COMMENT
ORIGINAL PRICE £34.95p
An excellent seller and a set which now only sells with a considerable premium. Good growth potential.

NOTES
Compare with YCC01 and YCC02.
All baseplates are marked Special Limited Edition.

INVESTMENT COMMENT
ORIGINAL PRICE £24.99p
Not a popular release with Yesteryear collectors. Overproduced and many collectors considered that it was 'not a real Yesteryear'. However, values which at one time dropped considerably, have begun to ascend. One to watch.

Y66 1762 GOLD STATE COACH

Scale 1:105

The Gold State Coach was built in 1762 and was first used by King George III to travel to Parliament. Since the coronation of George IV in 1821, it has been used for the coronation of every sovereign of the U.K. Matchbox released this model to commemorate the 40th anniversary of Queen Elizabeth II's accession to the throne in February 1952, and was officially endorsed by the Royal Anniversary Trust. For each purchase, a donation was made to the Trust's Charitable Fund. The release of this model as a Yesteryear caused much controversy amongst the collecting fraternity who, because of its scale and choice of subject, were quite outspoken in their opposition to it being given the status of a Yesteryear. It was released as one of 1992's Special Limited Editions in a special red flock lined box which was completely different to the usual Special Limited Edition boxes. In 1994 unsold coaches were repacked by Matchbox with three miniature models; a bus, a black taxi and a model 'T' van. This set was known as 'Britain in Miniature'. It did not sell particularly well either at £14.95.

ISSUE	YEAR OF RELEASE	COACH & DRAWBAR	WINDOWS	FRONT WHEELS	REAR WHEELS	HORSES	HORSEMEN	BASEPLATE/DRAWBAR	RARITY	BOX TYPE	VALUE	CHECK LIST
1	1992	Gold	Blue	Gold 10 spoke	Gold 12 spoke	8 white with red manes & maroon tackle	4 with red jackets, white pants & black caps & boots	MATCHBOX © 1992 CHINA Y66		0	£7	✓

NOTES

INVESTMENT COMMENT
ORIGINAL PRICE £9.95
Too early to comment.

YTF- 01 1947 CITROËN TYPE 'H' VAN "EVIAN" Scale 1:43

Originally developed to become part of the Matchbox Dinky Collection, the newly created Matchbox Collectibles division of Tyco Toys, decided to include it as part of the Yesteryear range. The Citroën van had been very rarely modelled by a major diecast manufacturer in the past and although this version was far superior in all aspects to its predecessors, many Yesteryear collectors gave it a rather icy reception. However as the series progressed, more collectors returned to the 'fold' and within eighteen months, hardly any Taste of France models were seen for sale. The models were mounted via two screws onto a plastic plinth with a plastic protective "bridge" to eliminate transit damage to the model. Also, for the first time a common theme was to feature on a range model. Being a French vehicle, what would be more appropriate than "A Taste of France," which was to be a series of six vans featuring six different famous French products. The first featured product was Evian Mineral Water, one of the world's oldest and best known brand names. The "Evian" was painted in a rather shocking pale pink, but it was soon noticed that some examples had been painted a darker, more regular shade of pink. Although the Citroën van, by its very simple construction, has few endearing features, collectors were pleased to note that the model had been given enhanced detailing, the chrome highlighting of the radiator grille being particulary fine. Hinges and light lenses were also highlighted in appropriate colours. True to scale wheels and tyres on press fit axles completed a very fine model. The total quantity produced was 25,000.

EVIAN

ISSUE	YEAR OF RELEASE	COLOURS	CAB & VAN ROOF	CAB INTERIOR	NUMBER PLATE	PAINTED TRIM	WHEEL	BODY TYPE	SERIES NUMBER	BASEPLATE	RARITY	BOX TYPE	VALUE	CHECK LIST
1	1993	Pink* body, matt black chassis	Pink*	Pale grey	4765 AY-33	Silver & red	Cream solid	1	Cast YTF 1	MATCHBOX COLLECTIBLES ® 1993 CHINA	S	Q	£30	
2	1993	Pale pink body with matt black chassis	Pale pink	Pale grey	4765 AY-33	Silver & red	Cream solid	1	Cast YTF 1	MATCHBOX COLLECTIBLES ® 1993 CHINA		Q		✔

DIAGRAM 1

1st Type body casting Near side.

Spare wheel panel with no buttons-catches.

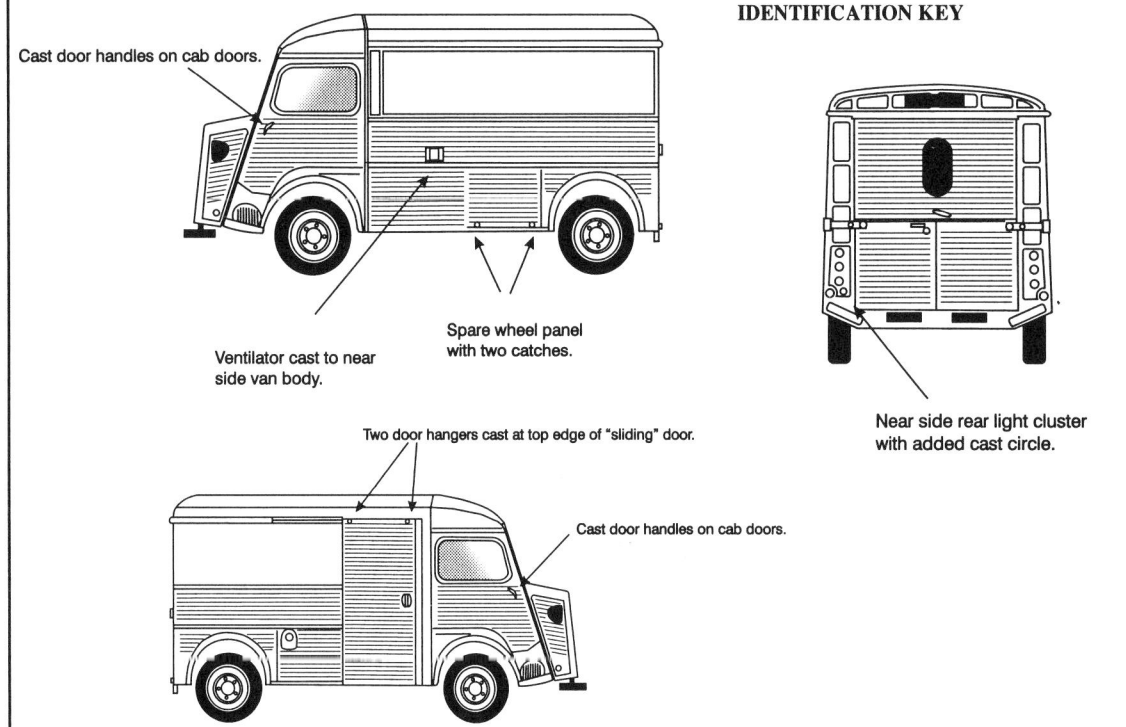

IDENTIFICATION KEY

- Cast door handles on cab doors.
- Ventilator cast to near side van body.
- Spare wheel panel with two catches.
- Two door hangers cast at top edge of "sliding" door.
- Cast door handles on cab doors.
- Near side rear light cluster with added cast circle.

LIVERY EVIAN

Tampo
Van body sides. An impression of an Alpine range in blue and white above EVIAN in red above EAU MINERALE NATURELLE SOURCE CACHAT in blue.
Cab doors. EVIAN, a mineral bottle and two glasses, all in red. All within red surround.
Number plates. Silver 4765 AY-33 on black plate.

NOTES

1. All six models in the Taste of France series have pale grey seats, a black left hand steering wheel, black plastic headlights with silver lenses, rear red lights, a black plastic radiator grille with chrome foil stamped detail, chrome cab steps, a black front bumper and clear Perspex windows.

INVESTMENT COMMENT	# YTF-02 1947 CITROËN TYPE 'H' VAN "MARTELL" Scale 1:43

INVESTMENT COMMENT
ORIGINAL PRICE £9.95

Too early to comment.

YTF-02 1947 CITROËN TYPE 'H' VAN "MARTELL"   Scale 1:43

The Citroën Company had a policy of making the Type 'H' van according to each individual customers requirements. Fully aware of this Matchbox Collectibles decided to make minor alterations to the tooling for the van bodies for each of the six different liveries. These subtle changes are known as "marketing variations"; the object being to generate more interest, especially with collectors who like variations. In their promotional literature for the Taste of France series, Matchbox Collectibles stated that this series was "unique" in that "only six vans had been commisioned to display the unique design… in this mini series. Production quantities will remain the same for each model in this limited series and when the last model runs off the assembly line the dies (tooling) will be destroyed". Collectors soon realised the implications of this statement i.e. the possibilty of cross-over casting variations between liveries on a model which would never again appear as a Model of Yesteryear. Two small pips had been cast onto the left hand lower panel to represent button-catches on the spare wheel compartment panel: also unaltered bodies appeared in "Martell" colours. The cast baseplate legend "YTF" was altered to indicate the progressive numbering for each livery. The total quantity produced was 25,000.

MARTELL

ISSUE	YEAR OF RELEASE	COLOURS	CAB & VAN ROOF	CAB INTERIOR	NUMBER PLATE	PAINTED TRIM	WHEEL	BODY TYPE	SERIES NUMBER	BASEPLATE	RARITY	BOX TYPE	VALUE	CHECK LIST
1	1993	Navy blue body with dark cream upper panels & matt black chassis	Dark cream	Pale grey	4766AY-33	Silver & red	Cream solid	1*	Cast YTF 2	MATCHBOX COLLECTIBLES ® 1993 CHINA	R	Q	£35	
2		Navy blue body with dark cream upper panels & matt black chassis	Dark cream	Pale grey	4766AY-33	Silver & red	Cream solid	2*	Cast YTF 2	MATCHBOX COLLECTIBLES ® 1993 CHINA		Q		✓
3		Navy blue body with dark cream upper panels & matt black chassis	Cream	Pale grey	4766AY-33	Silver & red	Cream solid	2*	Cast YTF 2	MATCHBOX COLLECTIBLES ® 1993 CHINA	D	Q	£25	

DIAGRAM 1

1st Type body casting
Near side

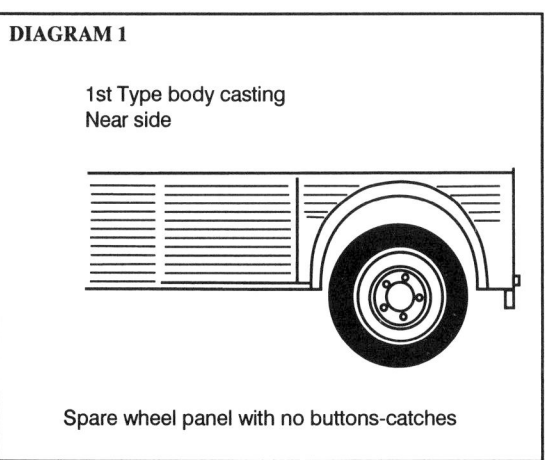

Spare wheel panel with no buttons-catches

DIAGRAM 2

2nd Type body casting
Nearside

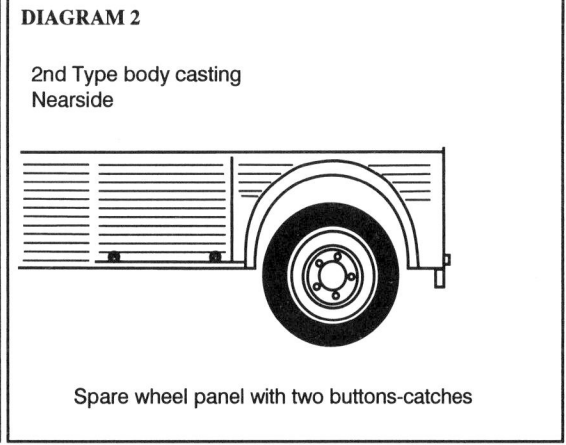

Spare wheel panel with two buttons-catches

LIVERY MARTELL
Tampo
Upper van body sides.
MARTELL in cream with gold shadow effect on dark blue panel with double gold border below a golden swift.
Lower van body sides.
JF MARTELL above CORDON BLEU above CLASSIC COGNAC in gold. All over a vertical blue ribbon (ie. Cordon Bleu).
Cab doors. FONDEE EN 1715 in gold with a company crest in gold and navy blue.
Number plates. White 4766 AY-33 on black plate.

NOTES

1. All six models in the Taste of France series have pale grey seats, a black left hand steering wheel, black plastic headlights with silver lenses, rear red lights, a black plastic radiator grille with chrome foil stamped detail, chrome cab steps, a black front bumper and clear Perspex windows.

INVESTMENT COMMENT
ORIGINAL PRICE £9.95

Too early to comment.

YTF-03 1947 CITROËN TYPE 'H' VAN "YOPLAIT" Scale 1:43

The Citroën Company made each type 'H' van by hand; with a marketing slogan of "To each his H." Matchbox Collectibles literature stated, "Just as in the production of the Citroën vans, no two models in this collection are alike". This third livery "Yoplait" has three different body types and a distinct colour difference for the tampo decoration. "Yoplait" models with Type 1 and 2 bodies are rare. Regarding the tampo printed livery, the colour was intended to be bright red; however for a short run a dark cherry red ink was used. Because there are very few Authorised Matchbox Collectible Centres in collectors of variations were quite frustrated in their quest for each type. The majority of collectors receive their models by post and so it is pure luck as to which variation arrived! "Yoplait" is a French manufacturer of a diverse range of yoghurt and dairy products and many collectors thought the livery to be a rather modern design; but Matchbox Collectibles assured them that it was appropriate for the vintage of the van. The total quantity produced was 25,000.

YOPLAIT

ISSUE	YEAR OF RELEASE	COLOURS	CAB & VAN ROOF	CAB INTERIOR	NUMBER PLATE	TAMPO COLOUR VARIATION	PAINTED TRIM	WHEELS	BODY TYPE	SERIES NUMBER	BASEPLATE	RARITY	BOX TYPE	VALUE	CHECK LIST
1	1993	White body with bright light green lower panels & matt black chassis	Bright light green with white strip between	Pale grey	4767 AY-33	Dark cherry red	Silver and red	Bright light green solid	1*	Cast YTF 3	MATCHBOX COLLECTIBLES ® 1993 CHINA	R	Q	£35	
2		White body with bright light green lower panels & matt black chassis	Bright light green with white strip between	Pale grey	4767 AY-33	Dark cherry red	Silver and red	Bright light green solid	2*	Cast YTF 3	MATCHBOX COLLECTIBLES ® 1993 CHINA	R	Q	£35	✓
3		White body with bright light green lower panels & matt black chassis	Bright light green with white strip between	Pale grey	4767 AY-33	Dark cherry red	Silver and red	Bright light green solid	3	Cast YTF 3	MATCHBOX COLLECTIBLES ® 1993 CHINA		Q		
4		White body with bright light green lower panels & matt black chassis	Bright light green with white strip between	Pale grey	4767 AY-33	Bright red	Silver and red	Bright light green solid	3	Cast YTF 3	MATCHBOX COLLECTIBLES ® 1993 CHINA		Q		

DIAGRAM 1

3rd Type body casting
Near side rear light cluster.

Cast circle added.

LIVERY YOPLAIT

Tampo
Van body sides. Black YOPLAIT almost surrounded with an oval in bright red, or dark red with an orange and bright red or dark red petalled flower. An orange with two green leaves and two dark cherries with green stems and leaf to the left. An orange with two green leaves and two strawberries with green stalks to the right.
Van rear door top panel. Smaller version of YOPLAIT and oval with flowers, all as per van sides.
Cab doors. Medium sized version of YOPLAIT and oval with flowers, all as per van sides.
Number plates. White 4767 AY-33 on black plate.

NOTES

1. All six models in the Taste of France series have pale grey seats, a black left hand steering wheel, black plastic headlights with silver lenses, rear red lights, a black plastic radiator grille with chrome foil stamped detail, chrome cab steps, a black front bumper and clear Perspex windows.

YTF-04 1947 CITROËN TYPE 'H' VAN "MARCILLAT"
Scale: 1:43

INVESTMENT COMMENT
ORIGINAL PRICE £9.95
Too early to comment.

By now collectors were really appreciating this model for its uniqueness and as each new model arrived, they were closely scrutinised to see what had been added to make it different from the previous issue. As with the "Yoplait" with its additional cast circle in the rear light cluster, some changes were not immediately obvious. In the case of the "Marcillat", the addition of cab door handles were more easily spotted. Naturally enough a few models appeared without the handles. As one writer commented "How did the occupants get in or out of the vans which had no cab handles? Perhaps they had to use the rear doors!" This livery produced another first, namely, the use of a metallic finish ink. A beautiful grass green metallic finish had been applied to the van body upper panels which did vary slightly, but not significantly enough to warrant separate listings. Marcillat is a famous name associated with a large range of cheese products. Brie is a very soft cheese and "Marcillat" has been famous for its version since the evolution of this brand in 1931. The total quantity produced was 25,000 models.

MARCILLAT

ISSUE	YEAR OF RELEASE	COLOURS	CAB & VAN ROOF	CAB INTERIOR	NUMBER PLATE	PAINTED TRIM	WHEEL	BODY TYPE	SERIES NUMBER	BASEPLATE	RARITY	BOX TYPE	VALUE	CHECK LIST
1	1993	Cream body with matt black chassis	Cream	Pale grey	4768 AY-33	Silver	Red solid	3*	Cast YTF 4	MATCHBOX COLLECTIBLES ® 1993 CHINA	R	Q	£35	
2		Cream body with matt black chassis	Cream	Pale grey	4768 AY-33	Silver	Red solid	4	Cast YTF 4	MATCHBOX COLLECTIBLES ® 1993 CHINA		Q		✓

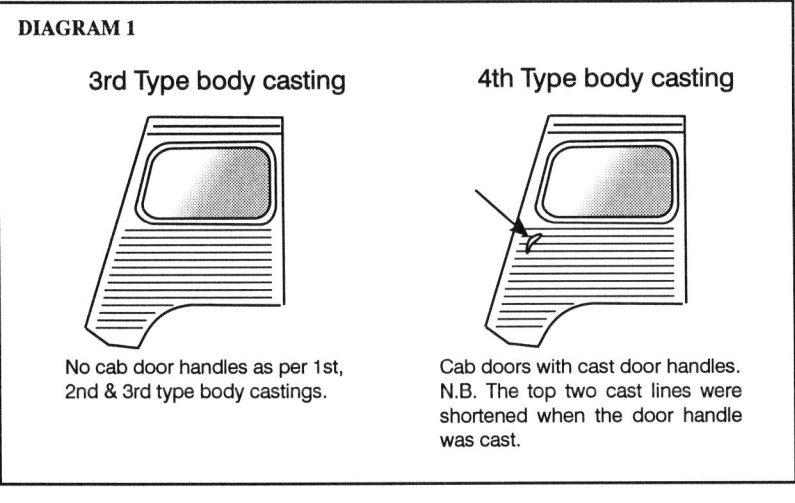

DIAGRAM 1

3rd Type body casting — No cab door handles as per 1st, 2nd & 3rd type body castings.

4th Type body casting — Cab doors with cast door handles. N.B. The top two cast lines were shortened when the door handle was cast.

LIVERY MARCILLAT
Tampo
Upper van body side panels. BRIE in red above MARCILLAT in black with pale gold shadow effect, on a very light grey panel with pale gold, black and red rope effect edging, all on dark metallic green panel.
Van body centre panels. FABRIQUE EN FRANCE MARCILLAT 88430 CORCIEUX in red.
Cab doors. The company crest of crown in pale gold, and red with black rope effect edging surrounding red BRIE above black MARCILLAT with gold shadow effect.
Number plates. White 4768 AY-33 on black plate.

NOTES
1. All six models in the Taste of France series have pale grey seats, a black left hand steering wheel, black plastic headlights with silver lenses, rear red lights, a black plastic radiator grille with chrome foil stamped detail, chrome cab steps, a black front bumper and clear Perspex windows.

INVESTMENT COMMENT	# YTF-05 1947 CITROËN TYPE 'H' VAN "TAITTINGER"
ORIGINAL PRICE £9.95	**Scale: 1:43**
Too early to comment.	The fifth livery in this series was "Taittinger" one of the worlds truly great champagnes. Initial reaction was mixed due to the rather dull and uninspiring colour scheme. However, some felt it rather refreshing to see at least one of this series in a finish that was an excellent representation of the natural finish of the metal used in the vans' construction. As the metal of the model is an aluminum colour, a single coat of paint was sufficent to achieve the desired finish; and in turn this allowed more of the cast detail to be fully appreciated. This time the additional detail to the casting was the inclusion of a small vent on the near side of the van body, just above the lower front panel. As with the other liveries, some "Taittingers" appeared without the vent and it would appear that a "Taittingers" with a 4th type body is one of the harder to find variations in this series. As the series progressed, the number plates changed in that the fourth digit advanced by one (eg 4766;4767;4768). Because this was the fifth model, collectors assumed the "Taittinger" would be numbered 4769, but in fact it had jumped two to 4770. Somewhat confusing, but the "Taittinger" was the fifth model and the baseplates are endorsed YTF5. The total quantity produced was 25,000.

TAITTINGER

ISSUE	YEAR OF RELEASE	COLOURS	CAB & VAN ROOF	CAB INTERIOR	NUMBER PLATE	TAMPO COLOUR VARIATION	PAINTED TRIM	WHEELS	BODY TYPE	SERIES NUMBER	BASEPLATE	RARITY	BOX TYPE	VALUE	CHECK LIST
1	1993	Aluminum body with black matt chassis	Maroon with aluminum strip between	Pale grey	4770 AY-33	Beige panel background	Dark grey	Maroon solid	4*	Cast YTF 5	MATCHBOX COLLECTIBLES ® 1993 CHINA	R	Q	£35	
2	1993	Aluminum body with black matt chassis	Maroon with aluminum strip between	Pale grey	4770 AY-33	Cream panel background	Dark grey	Maroon solid	5	Cast YTF 5	MATCHBOX COLLECTIBLES ® 1993 CHINA		Q		✓

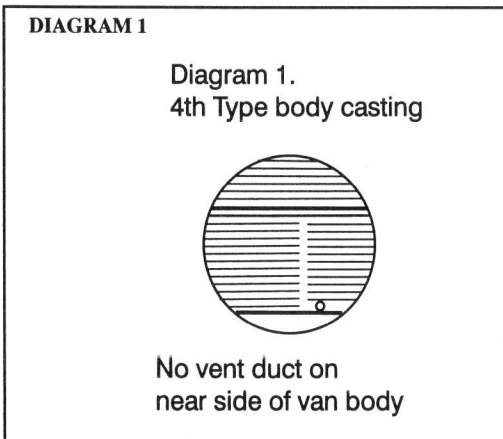

Diagram 1.
4th Type body casting

No vent duct on near side of van body

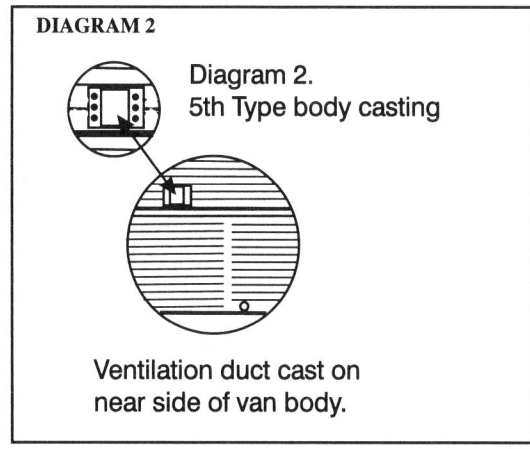

Diagram 2.
5th Type body casting

Ventilation duct cast on near side of van body.

LIVERY TAITTINGER
Tampo
Upper body sides. CHAMPAGNE TAITTINGER ANCIENNE MAISON FOURMEAUX FOREST ET SUX in black with company crest in dark red and gold on cream.
Cab doors. REIMS FRANCE in black.
Rear doors. CHAMPAGNE TAITTINGER FONDE EN 1734 in black.
Number plates. White 4770 AY-33 on black plate.

NOTES
1. All six models in the Taste of France series have pale grey seats, a black left hand steering wheel, black plastic headlights with silver lenses, rear red lights, a black plastic radiator grille with chrome foil stamped detail, chrome cab steps, a black front bumper and clear Perspex windows.

INVESTMENT COMMENT	YTF-06 1947 CITROËN TYPE 'H' VAN "POMMERY"	Scale 1:43

ORIGINAL PRICE £9.95

Too early to comment.

YTF-06 1947 CITROËN TYPE 'H' VAN "POMMERY" — Scale 1:43

Moutarde de Meaux Pommery is exported to over thirty-nine countries. It has remained a traditionally made mustard since 1632. Designed by Pierre Franchiset and produced in 1947, the Citroën 'H' type was to become known by Citroën dealers as the 'H Bomb'. Although the last of the series, this model had the most variations. The final difference to the casting included hangers at the top edge of the sliding door on the offside just behind the cab door. Also, more than one body type has been used for the YTF 06. In addition the position of the tampo decoration on the rear doors could be either high, or low (diagram 3). The Taste of France series received a mixed reception from collectors. There was the immediate recognition that the Citroën was more suited to the Dinky Collection; and being the first themed collection, the more experienced and dedicated collectors had difficulties in accepting the need to buy six "identical" castings at the same time. In time, all six models will be appreciated, because as they do form a very fine 'set' with just the right amount of change in appearance, from one model to another, to hold one's interest. The total quantity of the YTF06 was 25,000.

ISSUE	YEAR OF RELEASE	COLOURS	CAB & VAN ROOF	CAB INTERIOR	NUMBER PLATE	REAR DOOR TAMPO	PAINTED TRIM	WHEELS	BODY TYPE	SERIES NUMBER	BASEPLATE	RARITY	BOX TYPE	VALUE	CHECK LIST
1	1993	Cream body with matt black chassis	Bright red with cream body strip between	Pale grey	4769 AY-33	High	Silver	Dark red solid	4*	Cast YTF 6	MATCHBOX COLLECTIBLES ® 1993 CHINA	V R	Q	£45	
2		Cream body with matt black chassis	Bright red with cream body strip between	Pale grey	4769 AY-33	High	Silver	Dark red solid	5*	Cast YTF 6	MATCHBOX COLLECTIBLES ® 1993 CHINA	D	Q	£20	✓
3		Cream body with matt black chassis	Bright red with cream body strip between	Pale grey	4769 AY-33	Low	Silver	Dark red solid	5*	Cast YTF 6	MATCHBOX COLLECTIBLES ® 1993 CHINA	D	Q	£20	
4		Cream body with matt black chassis	Bright red with cream body strip between	Pale grey	4769 AY-33	High	Silver	Dark red solid	6	Cast YTF 6	MATCHBOX COLLECTIBLES ® 1993 CHINA		Q		
5		Cream body with matt black chassis	Bright red with cream body strip between	Pale grey	4769 AY-33	Low	Silver	Dark red solid	6	Cast YTF 6	MATCHBOX COLLECTIBLES ® 1993 CHINA		Q		

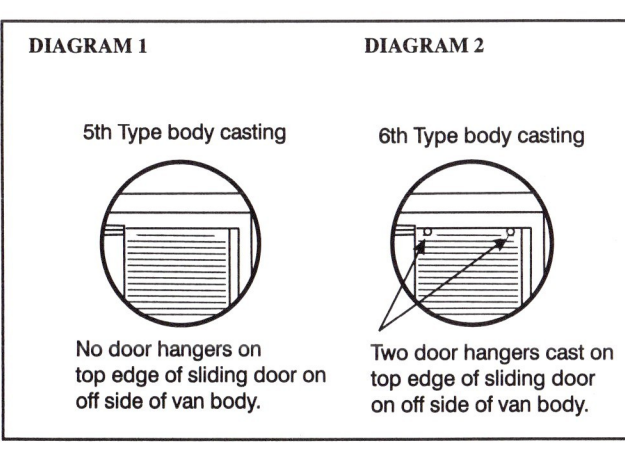

DIAGRAM 1 — 5th Type body casting. No door hangers on top edge of sliding door on off side of van body.

DIAGRAM 2 — 6th Type body casting. Two door hangers cast on top edge of sliding door on off side of van body.

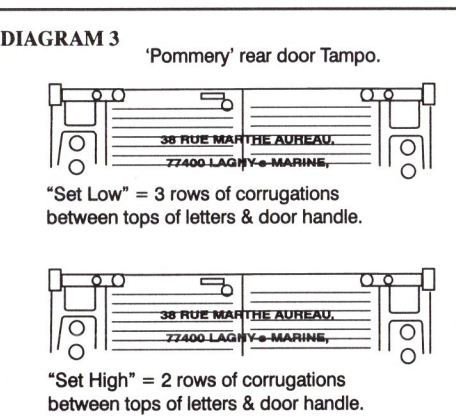

DIAGRAM 3 — 'Pommery' rear door Tampo.

"Set Low" = 3 rows of corrugations between tops of letters & door handle.

"Set High" = 2 rows of corrugations between tops of letters & door handle.

LIVERY POMMERY

Tampo
Upper body sides. MOUTARDE DE MEAUX in gold with black outline and black ®. All above POMMERY in red with black ®. Company crest of crown and two rampant lions in gold and black. All within black and gold rectangle.
N.B. Offside panel is smaller.
Cab doors. A jar of mustard in black, red and gold.
Rear doors. 38, RUE MARTHE-AUREAU 77400 LAGNY-s-MARNE, FRANCE in red.
Number plates. White 4769 AY-33 on black plate.

NOTES

1. All six models in the Taste of France series have pale grey seats, a black left hand steering wheel, black plastic headlights with silver lenses, rear red lights, a black plastic radiator grille with chrome foil stamped detail, chrome cab steps, a black front bumper and clear Perspex windows.

INVESTMENT COMMENT
ORIGINAL PRICE £32.95

Although a beautiful model, it was probably overproduced as Matchbox Collectibles still offer it for sale from time to time, albeit at a selling price of £40.

YSH-1 1900 GYPSY CARAVAN

Scale: 1:43

This authentically decorated caravan is typical of the caravans used by Romanies and gypsies in Europe at the turn of the century. The YSH-1 is a reproduction of the popular Reading wagon or 'Kite' as it was nicknamed because of its flared sides. Collectors were pleased with the amount of diecast detailing and the extensive tampo decoration. The coachlining on the wheels was particularly fine and was typical of the beautiful artwork that the Romanies afforded their horse-drawn caravans. The only variation noted is the colour of the chassis, rear wheels, turntable and front wheels, which can be beige or a darker beige.

Released in December 1993 the YSH-1 was a Special Edition, and was limited to 20,000 models only.

ISSUE	YEAR OF RELEASE	COLOURS	DRAWBAR & REAR STEPS	HORSES	WINDOWS	FRONT WHEELS	REAR WHEELS	FRONT FIGURES	REAR FIGURES	ROOF	CHIMNEY	SERIES NUMBER	BASEPLATE	RARITY	BOX TYPE	VALUE	CHECK LIST
1	1993	Red caravan body with beige chassis, springs & swivel	Cream	White & brown	Clear Perspex	12 spoke beige	14 spoke beige	Man & woman with child	Boy, girl & dog	White	Chrome	Cast YSH1	MATCHBOX COLLECTIBLES © 1993 CHINA		Q4	£40	✓
2		Red caravan body with beige chassis, springs & swivel	Cream	White & brown	Clear Perspex	12 spoke dark beige	14 spoke dark beige	Man & woman with child	Boy, girl & dog	White	Chrome	Cast YSH1	MATCHBOX COLLECTIBLES © 1993 CHINA		Q4	£40	

NOTES
1. The plastic roof is not a secure fit and collectors should avoid lifting the models up by the roof.
2. Originally there was to be a small pony included but although prototype examples were made, none were ever included with the YSH-1.

INVESTMENT COMMENT
ORIGINAL PRICE £32.95
Models are still available from Matchbox Collectibles at £39.90 plus postage.

YSH-2 1886 LONDON OMNIBUS

Scale: 1:43

The YSH-2 Special Edition model was released in December 1993. This was the second time that a horse-drawn bus had been included in the range: the first being the much smaller and less sophisticated Y12-1 1899 London Bus released in 1959.

The YSH-2 model was typical of many Omnibus vehicles seen in British cities in the 19th Century and features authentic advertising posters of the time. A mixture of coloured and clear labels were used. Of the main components, the upper compartment sides, the rear stairs and the advertising hoarding boards were made from plastic. The animation of the horses and the inclusion of the crew and passengers really brought the model to life. No variations have been recorded. The production run was 20,000 models worldwide.

ISSUE	YEAR OF RELEASE	COLOURS	SEATS & LOWER DECK FLOOR	DRAWBAR & DRIVERS SEAT	FRONT WHEELS	REAR WHEELS	CREW	PASSENGERS	HORSES	TACKLE & TRACES	SERIES NUMBER	BASEPLATE	RARITY	BOX TYPE	VALUE	CHECK LIST
1	1993	Light cream lower deck, chocolate brown upper decks & rear stairs. Yellow chassis springs & swivel	Mid brown	Buttercup Yellow	12 spoke buttercup yellow	16 spoke buttercup yellow	Driver & conductor	2 women	1 white, 1 mid brown	Black	Cast YSH2	MATCHBOX COLLECTIBLES ® 1993 CHINA		Q4	£40	✓

LIVERY
Labels
Left-hand upper deck. OAKEYS in yellow, WELLINGTON KNIFE POLISH in white. All on blue background.
Left-hand lower deck. CC-A in black on white rectangle. OXFORD ST, REGENT ST, PICCADILLY STRAND in blue with black shadow effect on pale yellow rectangle. LONDON GENERAL OMNIBUS COMPANY LIMITED in yellow with black shadow effect, and BAKER ST & WATERLOO in pale yellow with blue shadow effect. STATIONS in white. All on brown panel.
Right-hand upper deck. SAVOY in red, LAST WEEK FOR in black. THEATRE, A MIDSUMMER NIGHT'S DREAM in blue. PRESENTED BY GRANVILLE BARKER in black. All on white background.
Right-hand lower deck. The same detailing as on the left-hand lower deck.
Rear upper deck panel. Milkmaid Milk advert in blue and white with multi-coloured Milkmaid figure.
Rear stairs panel. Brasso advert in yellow, blue, white and red. Robin Starch advert in red, white, yellow and brown.
Zebra Grate Polish advert in yellow, red, white, blue and black.
Rear stairs lower panel. OVER-WATERLOO BRIDGE in yellow with black shadow effect.
Beneath rear staircase. Van Houten's advert in white and brown.
Rear footplate. Black 1,638 on white rectangle.
Rear left-hand body panel. LONDON GENERAL OMNIBUS COMPANY LIMITED in yellow and white with red and black shadow effect
Either side of driver. Hudson's Soap adverts in black, yellow, red, white and blue.
Driver's foot platform. Nestle's Milk advert in red, white and blue.
BS & W BAKER ST & WATERLOO in black on white rectangle. OXFORD CIRCUS OVER WESTMINSTER-BRIDGE in yellow with black shadow effect.

NOTES

INVESTMENT COMMENT	YSH-3 1875 WELLS FARGO STAGECOACH — Scale: 1:43
ORIGINAL PRICE £32.95 Still available from Matchbox Collectibles priced at £39.90	Wells Fargo is the best known stagecoach operator. The company played such an important part in opening up the American 'west'. This particular coach was a Concord type built for Wells Fargo in Concord, New Hampshire, USA, and was capable of carrying nine passengers. The working Mine Museum at Broken Hill in Victoria, Australia, has a similar version of this coach and gives rides to fare paying passengers. Although the detailing and animation was of the highest standard, the uniqueness of the YSH-3 was affected by being one of the three horse-drawn models, all released in December 1993. Some consolation was afforded by the weight of the model, which reflected a high proportion of diecast with plastic kept to a minimum. Originally the driver was to be issued with a whip, but Wells Fargo pointed out to Matchbox Collectibles that their drivers never used whips and requested that the whip be deleted. The production quantity was 20,000 models.

ISSUE	YEAR OF RELEASE	COLOURS	DRAW BAR	HORSES	TACKLE & TRACES	FRONT WHEELS	REAR WHEELS	CREW	PASSENGERS	LUGGAGE	SERIES NUMBER	BASEPLATE	RARITY	BOX TYPE	VALUE	CHECK LIST
1	1993	Dark red coach body with black roof, rear compartment & springs, mid brown chassis & swivel	Mid brown	2 chestnut & 2 dark brown	Black	12 spoke primrose yellow	14 spoke primrose yellow	Driver & shotgun guard	Man & woman	Orangey brown with black straps	Cast YSH3	MATCHBOX COLLECTIBLES ® 1993 CHINA		Q4	£40	

LIVERY
Tampo
Crew members seat. US MAIL in yellow
Coach panels. WELLS, FARGO & COMPANY in yellow with yellow coachlining and scrollwork. With dark brown raised strutts

Label
Cab doors. A picture of a landscape.

NOTES
1. The handrail adjacent to the shotgun guard is thin and can easily break.

COLLECTORS' NOTES:

Y _____

ISSUE	YEAR OF RELEASE	COLOURS				BASEPLATE	RARITY	BOX	VALUE

COMMENTS

PLEASE PHOTOCOPY AND SEND TO THE PUBLISHERS WITH YOUR ADDITIONAL INFORMATION; UNCODED ISSUES, MARKET VALUES etc

A PAGE AT A GLANCE

INVESTMENT COMMENT:

This gives the original UK retail selling price, quoted in sterling but not in the pounds, shillings and pence which was paid for earlier models. There may be some regional variations in prices. The figures mentioned do not include postage, packaging or insurance costs. The comments on the market situation are subjective and should not be read as anything more than a general guide.

MAIN HEADING AND INFORMATION:

The Y number or Yesteryear number is shown at the top of the page. Also, a brief history of the model and explanations for the variations recorded. The scale of the model is shown.

THE SCHEDULE:

Each model is recorded under headed columns, which name the various 'parts' of a model and other relevant information. The heading descriptions change with the type of model. The Issue column numbers each model variation as it progresses through its production life. Starting when it was first released with a 1 against its year of release. Any amount of issue numbers may or may not appear in one year. Should an issued variation be manufactured in the succeeding year, then the appropriate Issue number will be found adjacent to that year. The information recorded under the Colours column is kept to the basic colours with adjectives to 'subjectively' describe colour shades and tones. In the Rarity column where it is relevant, we use one of five ratings. In most instances these would link with the small asterisks (*) used in the schedule. These indicate the changes on a model, justifying allocating one of the rarity ratings, eg a new colour, a new inscription, or a change in the design of a 'component'.

THE LIVERY:

Usually, this is relevant only to commercial vehicles, ie those with advertising. However, there are a few models, eg racing cars, with a small amount of 'decoration' and these have been recorded. In most instances the lettering has been set-out in upper case (capital) letters. This has been done even when the lettering of the model is in lower case. This presentation should make the description easier to record and to read. Also, the position of the livery on the model vehicle has been indicated and whether it has been produced by tampo printing or by a transfer, or is a label.

DIAGRAMS:

These are not scaled drawings but are accurate enough to give an adequate indication of the various points which need explanation.

NOTES:

This is additional data which may amplify the main text, or which is not suitable for inclusion. For instance, details of the Beckenham Appeal Models. Also, since the release of the 1993/94/95 models, many of which may have been made from existing tools, cross references with other models have been included.

BLACK AND WHITE PHOTOGRAPHS:

These are intended to be used for guide reference identification and should be read in conjunction with the many colour pages in this book.

Some of the Great Beers of the World models. Of special interest is the extremely rare Steinlager model on the left. Also note the two types of Castlemaine XXXX and Becks models.

Later Great beers of the World models adopt ever more complex and intricate liveries, making them extremely attractive.

The Fire Engine series has proved to be a big success with collectors. Note the two types of wheel hubs available on the Land Rover.

The Christmas Treasures sets of 1994 and 1995 are novel although not released in large quantities annually. Also shown are the models in the Grand Marques Collection.

A selection of Yesteryear models. The Scania, top shelf, was notable for having two types of tree. The Y12-3 Taystee Bread and the Stutz Bearcat are included because they were omitted from the first 'White' book. The remaining models are a selection of short run Code 1 models produced for private customers.

Ten models in pre-production form. Two of the Citroën vans were not progressed. The pink Evian is a shocker! Please note the whip in the stagecoach driver's hand which was not approved by Wells Fargo. The Gypsy Caravan originally was planned to be released with this small pony.

This, and the next plate, are devoted to pre-production and colour trial Yesteryears. The Y7-2 Mercer Raceabout is designated as a Y6 on the baseplate! Only a handful of the two-tone green Y16-1 Spykers or the metallic green Y6-2 Bugattis are known to exist. The Y10-2 Mercedes is a colour trial based on a plated casting. The Y11-3 Lagonda is a striking example of a colour trial that was rightfully rejected.

More pre-production and colour trial Yesteryears. The Y9-4 Cub is only one of a small batch produced before the brass-plating was changed to chrome. The Y12-5 Singer van nearly happened but was stopped because of a trademark dispute.

INVESTMENT COMMENT	YPP01 1910 RENAULT A G VAN 'LE FIGARO' Scale 1:38
ORIGINAL PRICE £12.50 Too soon to comment.	1995 saw the launch of the Powers of the Press series featuring famous newspaper titles from around the world. The first in this series was France's most popular paper, Le Figaro, which was featured on the only current French commercial vehicle in the range, the Renault. The model is basically similar to the YGB07 in the livery of "Kronenbourg", except that the series number on the underside of the right running board was no longer cast, but tampo printed. On first impressions, collectors thought it a rather non-inspiring colour scheme. However, extensive enhanced detailing helped to make the model more interesting.

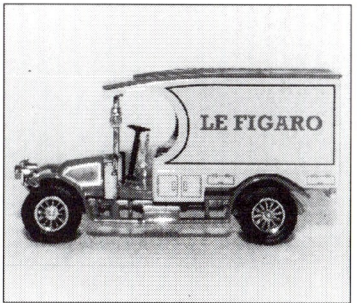

ISSUE	YEAR OF RELEASE	COLOURS	ROOF	SEAT	WHEELS	PLATED PARTS	PAINTED TRIM	RUNNING BOARD TRIM	SERIES NUMBER	BASEPLATE	RARITY	BOX TYPE	VALUE	CHECK LIST
1	1995	Yellow body, light blue floor, bonnet & chassis	Bright red Type C	Dark brown	Gold 12 spoke	Gold	Silver	Gold	Tampo YPP01	MATCHBOX COLLECTIBLES 1993 CHINA		Q		✓

LIVERY. LE FIGARO

Tampo
Van sides. LE FIGARO in bright red with black coachlining.
Rear Doors. LE FIGARO in bright red with black coachlining on rear of body.
Header board. LE FIGARO in bright red with black scrollwork.

NOTES

1. There are no © or ® marks on the baseplate. It would appear that a central ejector. pin impression in the gearbox area has obliterated any such marks.
2. Compare with Y25-1, Y44-1 and YGB07.

INVESTMENT COMMENT	YPP02 1931 MORRIS VAN 'THE TIMES'	Scale 1:59
ORIGINAL PRICE £12.50 Too early to comment.	Appearing almost simultaneously with the YGB18 Cascade, the Morris, with its all new van body, this time featured the leading British quality newspaper, The Times. Established in 1785, The Times is still the most prestigious daily newspaper and covers news from all round the world. Collectors were a little disappointed with the bland livery and logo, but purists were delighted with the weightiness of the model, signifying extensive use of diecast metal. The roof suffered somewhat with blemishes to the paintwork. At the time of writing, the Research & Development department are experimenting with suitable glazing plastics, so any future use of the Morris van may see it fitted with glazed cab windows.	

ISSUE	YEAR OF RELEASE	COLOURS	ROOF	SEATS	WHEELS	PLATED PARTS	PAINTED TRIM	RADIATOR	SERIES NUMBER	BASEPLATE	RARITY	BOX TYPE	VALUE	CHECK LIST
1	1995	Cream body, bonnet & cab with dark grey front & rear mudguards & matt black chassis	Dark grey	Dark grey	Light cream solid, Doubles at rear	Chrome	Silver & red	Chrome shell & black grille	Tampo YPP02	MATCHBOX COLLECTIBLES © 1994 CHINA		Q		✓

LIVERY THE TIMES
Tampo.
THE TIMES, PRINTING HOUSE SQUARE, LONDON, E C 4 in black.
Rear doors. Smaller version of side panels.
Brown horizontal line on both sides of van body

NOTES
1. Compare with Y31-1 and YGB18

INVESTMENT COMMENT	YPP03 1932 MERCEDES BENZ L5 TRUCK 'BERLINER MORGENPOST'
ORIGINAL PRICE £12.50	Scale 1:69
Too early to comment.	

YPP03 1932 MERCEDES BENZ L5 TRUCK 'BERLINER MORGENPOST'
Scale 1:69

The third in this series featured one of Germany's best known daily newspapers, "Berliner Morgenpost", established in 1898. Only World War II interrupted continuous publication. The L5 lorry has been in the range several times before, but this was the first time it had been fitted with an entirely diecast van body. Provision was also made to allow the fitting of a diesel fuel tank. Although a separate component from the van body, the fuel filler cap detail had been cast into the van body. The glazing for the cab windows, first featured on the YFE05 closely followed by the YGB17, was retained. As with all the Powers of the Press models, the baseplate featured two holes for self-tapping screws which became redundant by the introduction of the thin plastic formers holding the model within the Q style boxes.

ISSUE	YEAR OF RELEASE	COLOURS	CAB ROOF	SEATS	WHEELS	RADIATOR	PLATED PARTS	PAINTED TRIM	CAB STEP SUPPORTS	SERIES NUMBER	BASEPLATE	RARITY	BOX TYPE	VALUE	CHECK LIST
1	1995	Green body, cab & bonnet. Cream van roof. Gloss black cab steps & mudguards. Matt grey chassis	Cream	Black	Chrome 6 spoke. Doubles at rear	Chrome shell with black grille. Chrome Mercedes symbol & DIESEL	Chrome	Silver, red & black	Black Type B	Tampo YPP03	MATCHBOX COLLECTIBLES © 1993 CHINA		Q		✓

LIVERY BERLINER MORGENPOST
Tampo
Truck sides. BERLINER in black, above black MORGENPOST with grey edging within grey coachlines above brown horizontal line
Rear doors. Smaller version of grey outlined black MORGENPOST.
Cab doors and side panels. Company insignia of grey and black crown above 40 on grey shield. All within grey coachlining.

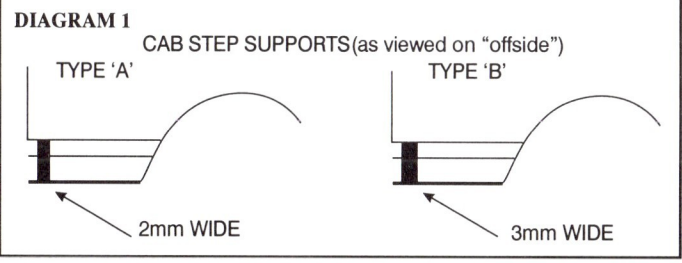

NOTES
Compare with Y6-5, Y41-1, YGB06, YGB17 and YFE05.

INVESTMENT COMMENT	
ORIGINAL PRICE £12.50	

Too early to comment.

YPP04 1948 DODGE ROUTE VAN 'THE NEW YORK TIMES'

This model was the first new model in the range, other than the Special Limited Editions and the Citroën. This was also the first model in the Yesteryear range to be "researched and developed" in the Far East, a task previously only carried out by the Matchbox Research and Development department in the UK. As such no-one knows what scale the Dodge van is! It was originally to have been decorated with the "Washington Post" livery and preproduction models do exist. Instead, the Washington Post was changed to the 1930 Model 'A' Ford van. Although the Dodge was a widely used vehicle in the USA, few were used elsewhere; which was probably one reason why experienced Yesteryear collectors viewed it somewhat apprehensively. However, it certainly added interest to the Power of the Press series. Purists were pleased that the use of plastic had been kept to an absolute minimum. And what more fitting livery for this model than that of the New York Times? Founded in 1851, the New York Times has received more Pulitzer prizes than any other newspaper, and it certainly lives up to its motto of 'All the news that's fit to print'.

ISSUE	YEAR OF RELEASE	COLOURS	SEAT & CAB INTERIOR	WHEELS	RADIATOR	PLATED PARTS	PAINTED TRIM	WINDOWS	SERIES NUMBER	BASEPLATE	RARITY	BOX TYPE	VALUE	CHECK LIST
1	1995	Royal blue body, matt black baseplate & rear bumper	Off-white	Chrome solid	Royal blue with silver bars	Chrome	Silver & orange	Clear Perspex with black seals	Tampo YPP04	MATCHBOX COLLECTIBLES © 1994 CHINA		Q		✓

LIVERY NEW YORK TIMES

Tampo
Van sides. THE NEW YORK TIMES in white above New York skyline in white, black, yellow and turquoise green.
Rear doors. ALL THE NEWS THAT'S FIT TO PRINT in white.

NOTES

1. The two baseholes are unused as the model was secured by thin plastic formers. The cab interior is a one-piece component which extends through the van body floor and inner wheel arches.

INVESTMENT COMMENT	YPP05 1932 FORD 'AA' 1 ½ TON TRUCK 'LOS ANGELES TIMES'
ORIGINAL PRICE £12.50	Scale 1:46

Too early to comment.

The Los Angeles Times was founded in 1881 and is still the number one choice of newspaper in California, USA. Boasting several Pulitzer prize winning reporters, it held the position of being the No. 1 metropolitan daily newspaper in 1992. Collectors, especially diecast purists, were delighted that the new truck body and tarpaulin cover was all metal. Although the 'AA' truck had been issued three times before in the range, this was the first time it had been fitted with a new truck body. The detail of the high-sided body is particularly fine, even if the "representative" tarpaulin cover looks a little ungainly. Securing ropes were part of the truck body detailing. No casting modifications have been reported.

ISSUE	YEAR OF RELEASE	COLOURS	CAB ROOF	TARPAULIN	SEATS	RADIATOR	WHEELS	PLATED PARTS	PAINTED TRIM	CHASSIS NUMBER	SERIES	BASEPLATE	RARITY	BOX TYPE	VALUE	CHECK LIST
1	1995	Dark blue cab, bonnet, mudguards & cab steps white truck body. Black sub-chassis	White	Light brown	Black	Chrome shell & centre bar. Black grille	Chrome solid	Chrome	Silver	A	Tampo YPP05	MATCHBOX COLLECTIBLES © 1993 CHINA		Q		
2	1995	Dark blue cab, bonnet, mudguards & cab steps white truck body. Black sub-chassis	White	Light brown	Black	Chrome shell & centre bar. Black grille	Chrome solid	Chrome	Silver	B	Tampo YPP05	MATCHBOX COLLECTIBLES © 1993 CHINA		Q		

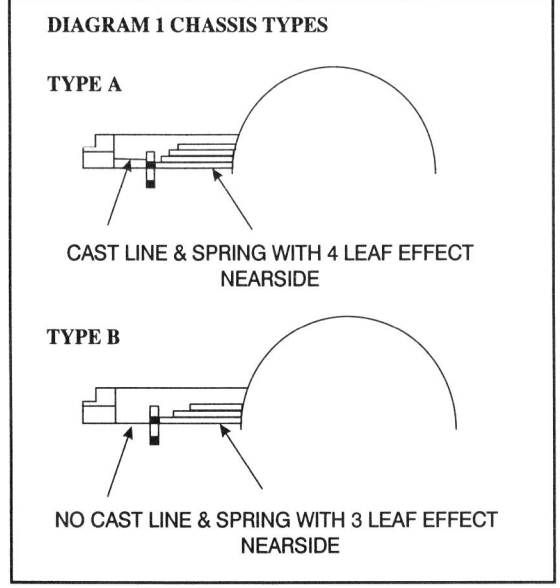

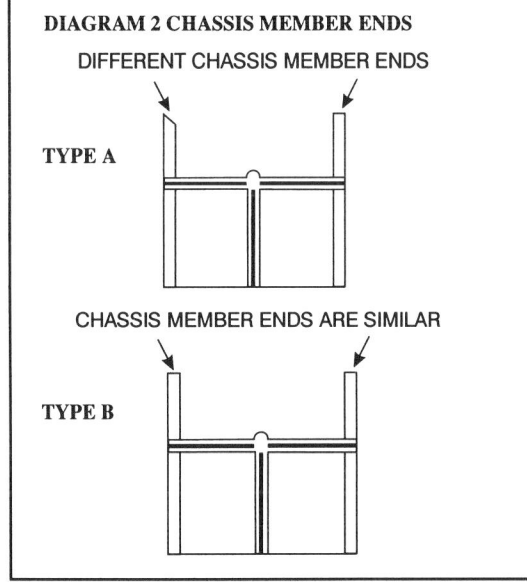

LIVERY LOS ANGELES TIMES
Tampo
Truck sides and rear panel. LOS ANGELES TIMES in blue with blue coachlining. Brown securing ropes and black cleats on both sides of truck body.
Cab doors. TIMES MIRROR SQUARE, LOS ANGELES, CALIFORNIA in white within white coachline.
Bonnet. White coachlining, and white louvres.

NOTES

Compare with Y62-1, YGB05, YGB16, YFE06 and YFE09

INVESTMENT COMMENT	YPP06 1923 AC MACK TRUCK 'PRAVDA'	Scale 1:60

ORIGINAL PRICE £12.50

Too early to comment

YPP06 1923 AC MACK TRUCK 'PRAVDA' — Scale 1:60

"Pravda" (meaning the truth) was established in 1912 as the official voice of the Communist Party in Russia. Collectors were bemused by the choice of an American truck to bear the Pravda livery! No casting alterations were evident since the Mack appeared as YGB09 in the livery of "Moosehead Beers", except that the series number was no longer cast, but tampo printed on the baseplate. This was the first time that the Mack had been produced with solid tyres on spoked wheels since 1988 as Y30-1 in the livery of "Kiwi". The wheel hub centres had been extended to blank-off the axle holes and it was also the first time a bronze coloured plastic had been used for the wheels. So although the Pravda didn't exactly make the front page headlines, a couple of firsts and if one adds the use of cyrillic letters a third gives it a certain claim to fame!

ISSUE	YEAR OF RELEASE	COLOURS	CAB ROOF	VAN ROOF	SEATS	WHEELS	PLATED PARTS	PAINTED TRIM	SERIES NUMBER	BASEPLATE	RARITY	BOX TYPE	VALUE	CHECK LIST
1	1995	Bright red body, cab, bonnet front, mudguards & cab steps. Dark grey chassis	Bright red	White	Light tan	Bronze 5 spoke	Gold	Gold & silver	Tampo YPP06	MATCHBOX COLLECTIBLES © 1994 CHINA		Q		✓

LIVERY PRAVDA

Tampo
Truck sides. PRAVDA in Russian capitals and two lines of Russian wording in black, two double horizontal coachlines and Pravda insignia in black and white
Bonnet. Gold coachlining and Mack logo.

NOTES

1. Compare to Y30-1, Y33-1, YGB09.

INVESTMENT COMMENT
ORIGINAL PRICE £12.50
Too early to comment.

YPP07 1937 GMC VAN 'THE AUSTRALIAN' Scale 1: 45

For anyone who lives in, or has visited, Australia, one would expect that the geography and huge distances to be an insurmountable obstacle to anyone proposing to publish a national daily newspaper. "The Australian" newspaper was originally printed in Canberra and flown all over the country but today's technology allows it to be printed simultaneously in every Australian capital city. It is the only national daily. The livery, however, is not as powerful as other liveries within the Powers of the Press series. Also, despite various modifications in the past, the white overall colour only served to "show up" the ill-fitting bonnet top cover, and exaggerates the seemingly over-spacious front wheel arches. No casting changes were apparent between the YGB08 and the YPP07, except for the series number now being tampo printed and repositioned adjacent to the rear axle.

ISSUE	YEAR OF RELEASE	COLOURS	ROOF	SEATS	WHEELS	PLATED PARTS	PAINTED TRIM	HEADLIGHTS	BONNET TYPE	BODY TYPE	SERIES NUMBER	BASEPLATE	RARITY	BOX TYPE	VALUE	CHECK LIST
1	1995	White body, cab, bonnet & mudguards. Matt black running boards & baseplate	White	Dark red	Chrome solid	Chrome	Silver	Streamline	B	2	Tampo YPP07	MATCHBOX COLLECTIBLES © 1993 CHINA		Q		✓

LIVERY THE AUSTRALIAN
Tampo

Van sides. THE AUSTRALIAN in black on dark orange map of Australia and Tasmania.
Rear doors. THE AUSTRALIAN AUSTRALIA'S ONLY NATIONAL DAILY NEWSPAPER in black.
Cab doors. Smaller version of rear door lettering.

NOTES

Compare with Y12-5 and YGB08.

INVESTMENT COMMENT
ORIGINAL PRICE £12.50
Too early to comment.

YPP08 1930 MODEL 'A' FORD VAN 'WASHINGTON POST'

Scale: 1:40

The "Washington Post" is one of the leading American newspapers. It was included in the Powers of the Press series along with the models featuring the "New York Times" and the "Los Angeles Times", to further stimulate the ever growing North American Yesteryear market. The new Type C van roof was now standard. Since 1984 the van body roof had been cast as a separate component in plastic to overcome over-spraying problems. With better technology at the factory, Matchbox Collectibles stipulated that the plastic roof be replaced and upgraded with a smooth diecast roof. The two cast unthreaded baseplate bosses were still in place, although they were not used; instead thin black plastic 'formers' were used to keep the YPP08 secure in its box. The cast series number was deleted and replaced by one in tampo print. Because all the radiators and van bodies with cast number plate digits had been used during the initial 'Castlemaine' run, no Washington Post models have been found with number plate variations.

ISSUE	YEAR OF RELEASE	COLOURS	CAB ROOF	VAN ROOF	SEATS	WHEELS	PLATED PARTS	PAINTED TRIM	SERIES NUMBER	BASEPLATE	RARITY	BOX TYPE	VALUE	CHECK LIST
1	1995	Blue body, cab, bonnet & chassis	Blue	Blue Type C	Grey	Chrome 12 spoke	Chrome	Silver	Tampo YPP08	MATCHBOX COLLECTIBLES ® 1993 CHINA		Q		✓

LIVERY WASHINGTON POST
TAMPO
Van sides. WASHINGTON POST in black on white panel above skyline of Washington DC in white, black, pale blue and light gold.
Cab doors. White 1150 15th St NW WASHINGTON DC
Bonnet. Double white coachlining
Number plates. Yellow 56-311M:SS 1930 on dark blue

NOTES

Compare with Y21-1, Y22-1, Y35-1 and YGB01.

INVESTMENT COMMENT
ORIGINAL PRICE £9.95
Too early to comment.

YGB01 1930 FORD MODEL 'A' VAN 'CASTLEMAINE XXXX
Scale 1:40

This was the first model in the theme series "Great Beers of the World". It is in the livery of the Australian company, Castlemaine Brewery. Their XXXX (4 X) beer has been brewed since 1878 and is now sold worldwide. Because the model had to be held onto a plastic display platform by two self tapping screws, the baseplate of the Y22-1 Ford 'A' van was altered to accommodate two raised open bosses in lieu of one open hole. Also, the model description details were moved to the rear of the baseplate and YGB01 substituted for Y35, Y21, Y22. The inscription was altered to read © 1993 MATCHBOX COLLECTIBLES. The front and rear number plates were tampo printed and to provide a suitable surface, the cast digits on the plates were removed. Although all issues should have smooth number plates, some models were released with the tampo printed over the cast digits. These components are from unused stock at the factory. Also, varying shade differences in the deep yellow paint have been noted, but are not listed as variations. In late 1995 a further production run had the new style diecast van roof. The roof was still a separate component, but was now cast in metal instead of being in plastic and had a smooth finish (Type C) instead of a textured one. Also the finish to the number plates was further improved.

ISSUE	YEAR OF RELEASE	COLOURS	CAB ROOF	VAN ROOF	SEATS	WHEELS	PLATED PARTS	PAINTED TRIM	CAST DIGITS FRONT No PLATE	CAST DIGITS REAR No PLATE	SERIES NUMBER	BASEPLATE	RARITY	BOX TYPE	VALUE	CHECK LIST
1	1993	Deep yellow body, cab & bonnet gloss black chassis	Deep yellow Type B	Matt red Type B	Brown	Red 12 spoke (WW)	Chrome	Silver	Yes*	Yes*	Cast YGB01	MATCHBOX COLLECTIBLES ©1993 CHINA	VR	Q	£50	✓
2		Deep yellow body, cab & bonnet gloss black chassis	Deep yellow Type B	Matt red Type B	Brown	Red 12 spoke (WW)	Chrome	Silver	No*	Yes*	Cast YGB01	MATCHBOX COLLECTIBLES ©1993 CHINA	R	Q	£30	
3		Deep yellow body, cab & bonnet gloss black chassis	Deep yellow Type B	Matt red Type B	Brown	Red 12 spoke (WW)	Chrome	Silver	Yes*	No*	Cast YGB01	MATCHBOX COLLECTIBLES ©1993 CHINA	R	Q	£30	
4		Deep yellow body, cab & bonnet gloss black chassis	Deep yellow Type B	Matt red Type B	Brown	Red 12 spoke (WW)	Chrome	Silver	No	No	Cast YGB01	MATCHBOX COLLECTIBLES ©1993 CHINA		Q		
5	1995	Deep yellow body, cab & bonnet gloss black chassis	Deep yellow Type B	Red Type C	Brown	Red 12 spoke (WW)	Chrome	Silver	No	No	Cast YGB01	MATCHBOX COLLECTIBLES ©1993 CHINA		Q		

LIVERY CASTLEMAINE XXXX
Tampo
Van sides. Red CASTLEMAINE with black shadow effect on white cloud effect panel, above red and gold sketch of brewery; all above four large red X's each with black edging and white shadow effect with a black R in a black circle, all within red coachlining.
Closed rear doors. Red CASTLEMAINE with black shadow effect on white panel above black QUEENSLAND AUSTRALIA, all within red coachlining.
Cab doors, BREWED SINCE 1878 in black all within red coachlining
Van bonnet, red coachlining to top and to side louvres. Red encircled red 22 on right side.

NOTES

1. Eagle eyed collectors will have noticed that the method of riveting the front bumper to the base has been altered from roughly finished black coloured heads to ones with a chrome dome.
2. Compare with Y21-1, Y22-1, Y35-1 and YPP08.

INVESTMENT COMMENT
ORIGINAL PRICE £9.95
Too early to comment.

YGB02 1926 MODEL 'TT' FORD VAN 'BECK & CO'
Scale: 1:41

Manufactured between 1926 and 1930 ie up to the time that Ford Motors introduced the Model 'A' van, the Model 'TT' was the first commercial vehicle wholly built by Ford Motors. The YGB02 displays the livery of one of the world's oldest brewers, Beck & Co., which was established in 1553 and now is Germany's biggest beer exporter. Basically, the model is similar to that of the Y21-5 "Drambuie" release. The difference being, the removal of the transmission prop-shaft and the square open boss to accommodate the two raised open bosses with their strengthening webs, which are used for the self tapping screws. Also, the text was transferred to the base of the van body. The red tampo livery colour can either be that of the roof, or a more strawberry red tone. In late 1995 the model was re-run by Matchbox Collectibles. The small oval windows in the van sides were deleted and the cast series number replaced with tampo printed digits.

ISSUE	YEAR OF RELEASE	COLOURS	ROOF	SEATS	RADIATOR	WHEELS	PLATED PARTS	PAINTED TRIM	OVAL WINDOW	TRANSMISSION & UNDER FRAME	LUG UNDER CAB ROOF	TAMPO COLOUR VARIATION	SERIES NUMBER	BASEPLATE	RARITY	BOX TYPE	VALUE	CHECK LIST
1	1993	Sandy cream cab & bonnet with mid green chassis & mudguards	Red	Dark grey	Gold shell with black grille	Red 12 spoke	Chrome	Silver	Yes	Dark grey	No	BECK & CO (bright red)	Cast YGB02	MATCHBOX COLLECTIBLES © 1993 CHINA		Q		
2	1993	Sandy cream cab & bonnet with mid green chassis & mudguards	Red	Dark grey	Gold shell with black grille	Red 12 spoke	Chrome	Silver	Yes	Dark grey	No	BECK & CO (strawberry red)	Cast YGB02	MATCHBOX COLLECTIBLES © 1993 CHINA		Q		
3	1995	Sandy cream cab & bonnet with mid green chassis & mudguards	Red	Dark grey	Gold shell with black grille	Red 12 spoke	Chrome	Silver	No	Dark grey	No	BECK & CO (bright red)	Tampo YGB02	MATCHBOX COLLECTIBLES © 1993 CHINA		Q		✓

LIVERY BACK & CO.
Tampo
Van sides. Red encircled red 39 to the left of the company crest in red, white, black and silver, above red BECKS on white banner. To the left of BECK & CO in black above red EXPORTBRAUEREI, above red BREMEN. All within red coachlining.
Red outlined oval window (Issues 1 and 2).
Closed rear doors. BECK & CO. above EXPORTBRAUEREI above BREMEN, all in red. Two red outlined oval windows. All within red coachlining.
Cab doors. Red BECK & CO above EXPORTBRAUEREI above BREMEN, all in red, all within red coachlining.
Bonnet top. Red coachlining.
Bonnet Louvres in silver.

NOTES

1. Compare with Y21-5 and YGB13.
2. The colour of the van roof for issue 3 is very slightly darker red than those for issues 1 and 2. Most likely, this is due to the two year gap in the production; resulting in a different batch of paint being used.

INVESTMENT COMMENT
ORIGINAL PRICE £9.95
Too early to comment.

YGB03 1918 ATKINSON STEAM WAGON 'SWAN BREWERY'

Scale: 1:60

The Atkinson Steamer was made between 1918 and 1924 and when fully loaded had a top speed of 20 k.h.p. (12 m.p.h.). The YGB03 carries the livery of Australia's Swan Brewery. Established in 1887 it is renowned for its range of lagers. The company's insignia depicts the beautiful Western Australia Black Swan. The model has a cab body and base similar to those of the Y18-2 Atkinson except for the provision of a central rib to the cab roof luggage area; the installation of one hollow boss and one base hold for the self tapping screw and the alteration to the text to read MADE IN CHINA © 1993 MATCHBOX COLLECTIBLES and its position on the baseplate. The word MATCHBOX was moved to beneath the rear axle and YGB03 1918 ATKINSON STEAM WAGON put onto the bottom of the water tank. The van container is similar to that of the Y37-1 Garrett wagon. Regarding the tampo decoration, the colour of the water upon which the swan swims can be either a powder blue or a very pale powder blue.

ISSUE	YEAR OF RELEASE	COLOURS	CAB ROOF	VAN ROOF	SEATS	WHEELS	PLATED PARTS	TRANSMISSION CHAIN PIPES & CYLINDERS	SERIES NUMBER	BASEPLATE	RARITY	BOX TYPE	VALUE	CHECK LIST
1	1993	Dark green body & cab, black chassis	Dark green	Red	Black	Red 8 spoke	Chrome	Black	Cast YGB03	MATCHBOX COLLECTIBLES © 1993 CHINA		Q		

LIVERY SWAN BREWERY
Tampo
Van sides. Black swan on blue water, with black and bluish white background in an oval, edged in black and gold; with gold decoration each side. All above gold THE SWAN BREWERY CO LTD with red shadow effect. All within gold coachlining.
Closed rear doors. Smaller version of van side panels, but without gold side decoration.
Cab. Gold decoration and coachlining to rear side panels. SINCE 1867 in gold with red shadow effect within gold coachlining to cab doors.
Label
Curved cab front. Smaller version of van side panels; but with THE SWAN BREWERY CO LTD on one line with red shadow effect.

NOTES

1. Compare with Y18-2 and Y37-1.

YGB04 1929 MORRIS LIGHT VAN 'FULLER'S'   Scale: 1:39

INVESTMENT COMMENT
ORIGINAL PRICE £ 9.95
Too early to comment.

The model displays the livery of the well known British firm, Fuller's Griffin Brewery. Founded in 1845 at Chiswick, London, it has remained an independent family business producing prize-winning beers. The YGB04 has a modified Y47-1 "Lindt" livery baseplate. The centrally placed open hole has been replaced with a blind hole and two raised bosses have been added to accommodate self tapping screws. An additional layer of diecast has been added to obscure the original cast inscription. This layer stops short of the differential and so forms a distinctive change of levels across the baseplate. The revised wording ® 1993 MATCHBOX COLLECTIBLES is repositioned under the near side running board; the word MATCHBOX is under the other running board. The centre of the baseplate has 1929 MORRIS LIGHT VAN YGB04 MODELS OF YESTERYEAR cast in three lines. Like the "Lindt" model, the body does not have oval side windows. Two distinctive finishes, gold or copper are applied to the plated components and wheels.

ISSUE	YEAR OF RELEASE	COLOURS	ROOF	ROOF CASTING	SEATS & CAB INTERIOR	CAB WINDOWS	GRILLE	WHEELS	PLATED PARTS	PAINTED TRIM	PAINTED SIDE LIGHTS	RUNNING BOARD TREADS	DOOR HANDLES	SERIES NUMBER	BASEPLATE	RARITY	BOX TYPE	VALUE	CHECK LIST
1	1993	Light bottle green body, cab & bonnet, bright red chassis, mudguards & running boards	Bright red	Type 2	Light brown	Clear Perspex	Black	Gold 12 spoke	Gold	Gold	Gold	Bright red	Silver	Cast YGB04	MATCHBOX COLLECTIBLES ® 1993 CHINA		Q		
2		Light bottle green body, cab & bonnet, bright red chassis, mudguards & running boards	Bright red	Type 2	Light brown	Clear Perspex	Black	Copper 12 spoke	Copper with gold edging to tool box lid	Gold	Gold	Bright red	Silver	Cast YGB04	MATCHBOX COLLECTIBLES ® 1993 CHINA		Q		✓

LIVERY 'FULLER'S'
Tampo
Van sides. Gold and black Griffin symbol above gold edged ribbon with GRIFFIN BREWERY in gold all above white, black and gold edged, red panel with FULLER'S in white with black and gold shadow effect. All above CHISWICK in gold with faint black coachlining. All within gold coachlining.
Closed rear doors. Black, white and gold edged red shield surmounted with gold Griffin on black background over red rectangle with white FULLER'S above gold CHISWICK above white LONDON PRIDE with black shadow effect, black edged white BEST BITTER on gold background. All above gold EST 1845 with dark red shadow effect. All within gold coachlining.
Cab doors. Smaller version of rear door shield. All within gold coachlining.
Bonnet. Gold coachlining to top and gold louvres both sides. Gold encircled gold 6 above tool box.
Toolbox. Black finish to top panel within gold edging.

NOTES
1. Compare with Y47-1 and YY047/SA.

INVESTMENT COMMENT
ORIGINAL PRICE £9.95
Too early to comment.

YGB05 1932 MODEL AA FORD 1½ TON TRUCK 'CARLSBERG'

Scale: 1:46

Based on the Ford Model 'A' car, this truck has an extended and strengthened chassis and a more powerful engine. The Carlsberg Brewery was founded in 1847 as the result of the amalgamation of two older businesses owned separately by a brewer and his son. The YGB05 is basically similar to the Y62-1 "Peacock" liveried truck; but with an additional hole for the second self tapping screw. Also, the inscription has been altered to read: MATCHBOX COLLECTIBLES and YGB05 ® 1993. Like the Y62-1 there are two types of chassis castings, ie Type A and Type B. The canopy is a new component for the Yesteryear range; being the first to have a "closed" rear part. The moulding impressions represent two flaps which can be attached together to form a closed end to the canopy. The model has some enhancement details including coachlining, silver door handles and running board treads.

ISSUE	YEAR OF RELEASE	COLOURS	CAB ROOF	CANOPY	SEAT	RADIATOR	WHEELS	PLATED PARTS	PAINTED TRIM	CHASSIS TYPE	SERIES NUMBER	BASEPLATE	RARITY	BOX TYPE	VALUE	CHECK LIST
1	1993	Dark green body, cab & bonnet, black chassis & mudguards	Dark cream	Light cream	Light grey	Chrome shell & centre bar with black grille	Red solid	Chrome	Silver	A	Cast YGB05	MATCHBOX COLLECTIBLES ® 1993 CHINA		Q		
2		Dark green body, cab & bonnet, black chassis & mudguards	Dark cream	Light cream	Light grey	Chrome shell & centre bar with black grille	Red solid	Chrome	Silver	B	Cast YGB05	MATCHBOX COLLECTIBLES ® 1993 CHINA		Q		✔

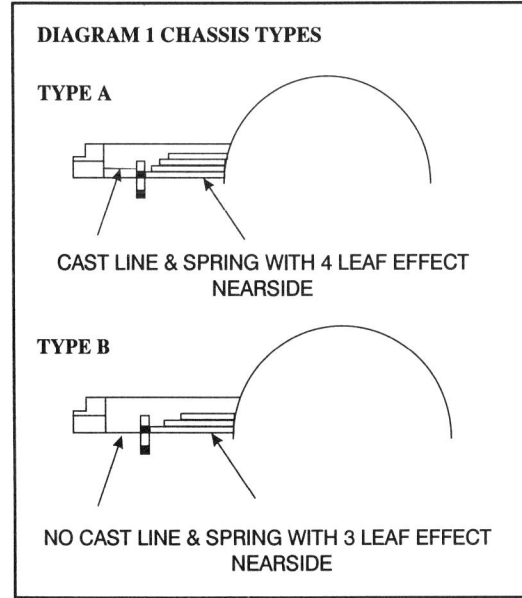

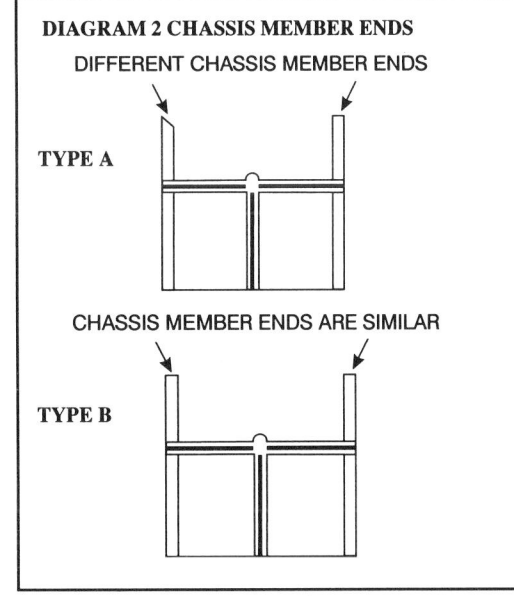

LIVERY CARLSBERG
Tampo
Canopy sides. Black outlined gold CARLSBERG PILSNER. All within red coachlining.
Canopy rear. Green and gold Carlsberg shield edged in black surmounted with gold crown, black CARLSBERG BRYGGERIERNE all within red coachlining.
Truck body. Two gold coachlined rectangles each side and on the tailboard.
Cab doors. Gold crown above gold CARLSBERG PILSNER on black oval. All within gold coachlining.
Bonnet. Rear side panels. Black encircled black 62 all within gold coachlining and gold coachlining to bonnet top.

NOTES
1. The two types of numbering under the top of the canopy signify, only, that two tools were used and therefore do not warrant separate codings. Because the surface to the underside is rough it is difficult to see the revised numbers and letters.
2. Compare with Y62-1, YGB16, YPP05 and YFE09
3. For transport purposes a clear plastic "keeper" band has been placed around the canopy and the lorry. Collectors are advised to retain this band to stop the two components coming apart

INVESTMENT COMMENT	YGB06 1932 MERCEDES BENZ "LS" LORRY 'HOLSTEN' Scale: 1:69
ORIGINAL PRICE £9.95 Too early to comment.	Originally intended to be a white Y41-1 model with white tarpaulin for 1992; its proposed commissioning coincided with Tyco Toys buying the Universal Matchbox Group and production did not start at that time. The model carries the livery of yet another well known Germany brewery, Holsten, which was established in Hamburg in 1879 and the black knight seated upon a black charger symbol is known, in many countries, as the sign for top quality beer. Basically, the chassis and the cab are similar to those of the Y41-1 "Howaltdswerke A.G.", except that on the baseplate the centrally placed screw hole has been blanked-off and two open holes provided for self tapping screws. This meant that the inscription had to be moved towards the rear and the revised wording reads MATCHBOX COLLECTIBLES, YGB06 ® 1993. Like the YGB05 "Carlsberg" model, the canopy has a closed rear end.

ISSUE	YEAR OF RELEASE	COLOURS	CAB ROOF	SEATS	WHEELS	RADIATOR	PLATED PARTS	PAINTED TRIM	CANOPY	TRUCK PLANKING EFFECT	CAB STEP SUPPORTS	SERIES NUMBER	BASEPLATE	RARITY	BOX TYPE	VALUE	CHECK LIST
1	1993	Cream body & cab with matt black chassis & gloss mudguards	Cream	Black	Dark red 6 spoke. Doubles at rear	Chrome shell with black grille with chrome Mercedes symbol & DIESEL	Chrome	Silver	Orange	Shallow	Black Type B	Cast YGB06	MATCHBOX COLLECTIBLES © 1993 CHINA		Q		✓

LIVERY HOLSTEN
Tampo
Canopy sides. Black and blue Knight with blue, black, white and red shield mounted on white highlighted black charger with brown tackle in front of black edged cream banner with black HOLSTEN BRAUEREL. Black HAMBURG to left or horse and black SEIT 1879 to the right.
Canopy rear. Black HOLSTEN on black edged cream banner above SEIT 1879.
Lorry sides. Black HOLSTEN-BIER above black HERVORRAGENDE QUALITAT with black coachlining.
Lorry tailboard. Black outline of Knight on charger all on red 'wax' style seal with black encircled black 32 in right corner. All within black coachlining.
Cab doors. Black outline of knight on charger on red 'wax' style seal. All within black coachlining.
Bonnet. Black coachlining to the top and to the side louvres.

NOTES
1. The two types of numbering under the top of the canopy only signify that two tools were used and therefore do not warrant separate codes
2. For transit purposes a clear plaastic "keeper" band has been placed around the canopy and the lorry. Collectors are advised to retain this band to stop the two components coming apart
3. Compare with Y6-5, Y41-1, YGB17, YPP03 and YFE05
4. The YGB06 does not have clear Perspex cab windows

INVESTMENT COMMENT
ORIGINAL PRICE £9.95
Too early to comment.

YGB07 1910 RENAULT A.G. VAN 'KRONENBOURG'

Scale: 1:38

Established in 1664 at Strasburg, the Kronenbourg brewery produces half the beer drunk in France. The model carrying the "Kronenbourg" livery is a modification of the Y25-1 Ambulance. The ambulance type roof has been retained, even with the slight defects on the top surface! The body does not have the windows or the extra cast lines; but does retain the horizontal cast line indicating the position of the bottom edge to the original van sides. The rear door panel has shallower cast lines and the edge and bottom ridges are smaller. The prominent cast rear number plate digits have been deleted to give a smooth surface for the new tampo printed number plate, as is the case with the front number plate. The baseplate propshaft has been altered to accommodate two bosses for self tapping screws. The centre rivet now has two raised segments around it. The inscription has been altered so that the words now read MADE IN CHINA under the near side running boards, MODELS OF YESTERYEAR under the other board and on the central part, 1993 MATCHBOX COLLECTIBLES YGB07. Collectors expressed their disappointment over the following: Why was the redundant spare wheel recess in the off-side running board retained? Why wasn't the tool box moved so that the lid could be "accessible"?

ISSUE	YEAR OF RELEASE	COLOURS	ROOF	SEAT	WHEELS	PLATED PARTS	TOOL BOX LID & RUNNING BOARD TRIM	SERIES NUMBER	BASEPLATE	RARITY	BOX TYPE	VALUE	CHECK LIST
1	1994	White body & floor, dark blue bonnet & chassis	Red type C	Light maroon	Copper 12 spoke	Gold	Gold	Cast YGB07	MATCHBOX COLLECTIBLES 1993 CHINA		Q		✓

LIVERY KRONENBOURG

Tampo
Van sides. Small company crest in white, red, gold with black outline overlapping two red rectangles, all above very dark blue KRONENBOURG with gold shadow effect above dark blue INTERNATIONAL BEER. All within dark blue coachlining.
Van rear. Smaller version of van sides. All above black registration plate with white numbers and letters, KY520.
Front black registration plate with white numbers and letters, KY520.

NOTES

1. Compare with Y25-1, Y44-1 and YPP01.
2. The copyright mark © and registration mark ® are not easily identifiable on the baseplate.

INVESTMENT COMMENT	# YGB08 1937 GMC VAN 'STEINLAGER'	Scale: 1:45

INVESTMENT COMMENT
ORIGINAL PRICE £9.95
Issue 2 is obviously the one to find and has considerable potential.

YGB08 1937 GMC VAN 'STEINLAGER'

Scale: 1:45

This van with its 86 b.h.p. engine could carry a ton load and was particularly suitable for conditions in New Zealand. The YGB08 displays the livery of the New Zealand Brewers Ltd, producers of "Steinlager" beer. Brewed as a direct result of the New Zealand government's threat to ban imported beer, the Steinlager brand has become so well known that it now represents 98% of New Zealand's beer exports. The model is similar to the Y12-5 "Goanna" model; except that the baseplate open hole has been replaced with two bosses for self tapping screws. Also the baseplate wording has been altered and repositioned. There are two known livery types. Type B went into initial production prior to final Steinlager approval. A limited 200 were made of Type B prior to Steinlager approval. The approval called for modification into what has become the common Type A of the 200 Type B, most were changed into the Type A. However, 72 Type B were produced and shipped, it is believed to the USA. These are extremely rare. The type of paint with which the body is painted is very unusual. It is dark bottle green with a very faint metallic 'stardust' effect for the background. Enhancement includes silver sidelights, door handles, hinges, bonnet hinge and louvres.

ISSUE	YEAR OF RELEASE	COLOURS	ROOF	SEATS	WHEELS	PLATED PARTS	PAINTED TRIM	HEAD LIGHTS	BONNET TYPE	PANEL DECORATION TYPE	BODY TYPE	SERIES NUMBER	BASEPLATE	RARITY	BOX TYPE	VALUE	CHECK LIST
1	1994	Dark metallic green body cab & bonnet, gloss black chassis	Dark metallic green	Fawn	Dark red solid	Chrome	Silver	Streamline	B	A	2	Cast YGB08	MATCHBOX COLLECTIBLES © 1993 CHINA		Q		✓
2		Dark metallic green body cab & bonnet, gloss black chassis	Dark metallic green	Fawn	Dark red solid	Chrome	Silver	Streamline	B	B*	2	Cast YGB08	MATCHBOX COLLECTIBLES © 1993 CHINA	ER	Q	£250	

DIAGRAM 1 PANEL DECORATION TYPE A

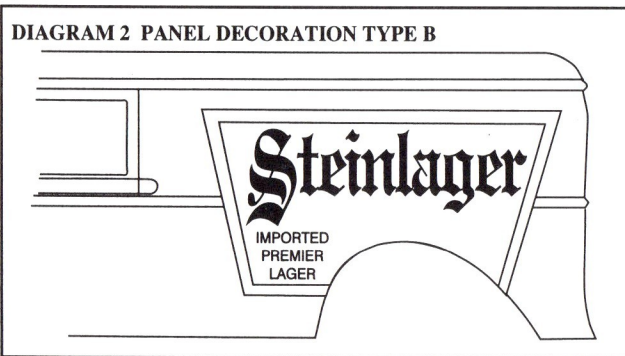

DIAGRAM 2 PANEL DECORATION TYPE B

LIVERY STEINLAGER
Tampo
TYPE B
Van sides. White STEINLAGER on large red background with black IMPORTED PREMIUM LAGER below all within gold edging.
TYPE A
Van sides. White STEINLAGER on red background, all within gold edging, adjacent to small white encircled white R.
All above white NEW ZEALAND'S FINEST BEER.
BOTH TYPES
Van doors. Company crest of black outlined barley sheaf on white background within red and white rings; with gold lion each side standing on a gold and black base. All above white PRODUCT OF NEW ZEALAND.
Van rear doors. Smaller version of company's crest above white NEW ZEALAND BREWERIES LTD, 368, KHYBER PASS ROAD AUCKLAND NEW ZEALAND.

NOTES
1. Compare with Y12-5 and YPP07.

INVESTMENT COMMENT
ORIGINAL PRICE £9.95
Too early to comment.

YGB09 1920 MACK A.C. TRUCK 'MOOSEHEAD'   Scale: 1:60

The forerunner of this truck was designed in 1914; of which many vehicles were used by the Allies during World War I. Because of the 7.7 litre engine and the three speed gear box, this type of vehicle was ideal for civil engineering contracts, where its ruggedness could be exploited. The YGB09 carries the livery of Canada's oldest independent brewery, "Moosehead", which since 1867 has been owned by the one family. Basically similar to the Y33-1 "Goodyear" truck, the baseplate has an additional boss, just forward of the centre rivet, to accommodate the extra self tapping screw. The baseplate wording has also been altered and rearranged to read © 1994 MATCHBOX COLLECTIBLES YGB09, with MADE IN CHINA at the rear.

ISSUE	YEAR OF RELEASE	COLOURS	CAB ROOF	VAN ROOF	SEATS	WHEELS	PLATED PARTS	SERIES NUMBER	BASEPLATE	RARITY	BOX TYPE	VALUE	CHECK LIST
1	1994	Dark green body, cab, steps & mudguards with bright red chassis	Dark green	Black	Cream	Solid red	Gold extinguisher, light copper lamps	Cast YGB09	MATCHBOX COLLECTIBLES ©1994 CHINA		Q		✓

LIVERY MOOSEHEAD
Tampo
Van sides. Gold outlined pale blue MOOSEHEAD BEER above gold and black, right facing head of a moose with chocolate brown oval above gold CANADIAN LAGER on chocolate brown scroll, all within gold coachlining.
Van rear doors. Smaller version of company's crest above white MOOSEHEAD BREWERIES LTD SAINT JOHN NEW BRUNSWICK & DARTMOUTH NOVA SCOTIA CANADA
Cab. Gold coachlining to doors, front and rear panels.
Bonnet. Gold coachlining to top and front. Gold louvres and radiator cap. White Mack symbol on gold 'dotted' disc background.

NOTES
1. Compare with Y30-1, Y33-1 and YPP06.

INVESTMENT COMMENT
ORIGINAL PRICE £9.95
Too early to comment.

YGB10 1927 TALBOT VAN 'SOUTH PACIFIC' Scale: 1:47

This van with its 14 b.h.p. engine has a custom built body which was the normal arrangement for tradesmen's vehicles in the '20s and '30s. The model carries the striking livery of the Papua New Guinea, South Pacific Breweries. Basically similar to the Y5-4 "Lyle's Golden Syrup" van; however the inscription on the baseplate had to be repositioned to accommodate the two bosses for the self tapping screws. Also, the inscription now reads MADE IN CHINA © 1993 MATCHBOX COLLECTIBLES YGB10. The details of the roof's internal downward projecting flange has reverted to the "no hole" type which was standard before the Macau production of the "Roses" and "Lyle's" models, which have two holes in the flange. The colour scheme of the YGB10 was well received by collectors. Advanced tampo printing achieved a greater number of colours and different shades of one colour. This quality was so good that many thought that the decoration had been achieved by a label.

ISSUE	YEAR OF RELEASE	COLOURS	ROOF	SEAT	WHEELS	PLATED PARTS	TOOL BOX LID	SERIES NUMBER	BASEPLATE	RARITY	BOX TYPE	VALUE	CHECK LIST
1	1994	Chocolate brown body cab & bonnet, gloss black chassis	Cream	Pale beige	Red 12 spoke	Light copper	Gold	Cast YGB10	MATCHBOX COLLECTIBLES © 1993 CHINA		Q		✓
2	1994	Chocolate brown body cab & bonnet, gloss black chassis	Darker cream	Pale beige	Red 12 spoke	Light copper	Gold	Cast YGB10	MATCHBOX COLLECTIBLES © 1993 CHINA		Q		

LIVERY SOUTH PACIFIC
Tampo

Van sides. Company insignia of red over red, orange, green and yellow Bird of Paradise with multi-coloured tropical background; standing on a yellow edged red banner. White with yellow shadow effect EXPORT. White SOUTH PACIFIC LAGER on a green ring with thin black, yellow and brown inner rings and yellow outer ring with black edge. All within yellow coachlining and decoration.
Van rear doors. Yellow SOUTH PACIFIC EXPORT LAGER within yellow coachlining and decoration.
Cab doors. Yellow SOUTH PACIFIC BREWERY LTD, PORT MORESBY PAPUA NEW GUINEA
Bonnet top. Yellow coachlining and decoration.

NOTES
Compare with Y5-4.

INVESTMENT COMMENT
ORIGINAL PRICE £9.95
Too early to comment.

YGB11 1922 FODEN TYPE 'C' STEAM WAGON 'WHITBREAD'S' Scale: 1:72

In the UK during the '20s to '50s period, this was a popular wagon for carrying beer, flour and other heavy loads. The "Whitbread" livery is the ninth on this Foden model which gives a good representation of the various uses to which that vehicle with its double crank compound engine developing 23 b.h.p. was put. This well known English brewery has been making ale since 1742. Basically the YGB11 is similar to the Y27-1 "McMullen" model, but the baseplate now has the one screwhole filled in and the provision of two bosses for the self tapping screws. Also the baseplate inscription has been rearranged and altered to read © 1994 MATCHBOX COLLECTIBLES YGB11. Like the Y27-1 "McMullen" wagon, the YGB11 still has the two holes in the wagon floor, originally needed to fix the false floor supporting the beer barrels on the earlier Y27-1 "Guinness" model.

ISSUE	YEAR OF RELEASE	COLOURS	CAB ROOF	SEAT	CANOPY	WHEELS	PLATED PARTS	2 BODY FLOOR HOLES	WHEELS HUBS	SERIES NUMBER	BASEPLATE	RARITY	BOX TYPE	VALUE	CHECK LIST
1	1994	Chocolate brown body & cab, gloss black chassis & mudguards	Pale cream	Black	Pale cream	Red daisy	Light copper	Yes	Type 2	Cast YGB11	MATCHBOX COLLECTIBLES ©1994 CHINA		Q		✔

LIVERY WHITBREAD'S
Tampo
Body sides. Deep cream WHITBREAD'S within white coachlining
Cab rear panels. The "By Royal Appointment Prince of Wales" three feather plumes in off-white on red shield outlined in white and black, over deep cream encircled deep cream 3.
Tailgate. Deep cream WHITBREAD'S over white ALE & STOUT within white coachlining.
Cab front panels. White WHITBREAD & CO LTD. LONDON all within white coachlining.
Header board. Deep cream WHITBREAD.
Canopy sides. Company emblem of deep cream and black stag's head over white WHITBREAD & CO LTD LONDON all on blue oval with black WHITBREAD'S LIGHT BEER on black and white edged deep cream oval band with narrow black edge on both sides of red WHITBREAD'S ALE & STOUT.

NOTES
1. Compare with Y27-1 and YY027/SA
2. For transport purposes a clear plastic "keeper" band has been placed around the canopy and the lorry. Collectors are advised to retain this band to stop the two components coming apart
3. Because the cab roof has a 'flat' gloss finish and the canopy is slightly textured, the two components appear to be different colours

INVESTMENT COMMENT
ORIGINAL PRICE £9.95
Too early to comment.

YGB12 1917 YORKSHIRE TYPE W.A. STEAM WAGON 'LÖWENBRÄU'
Scale: 1:61

This wagon is one of seven types built between 1903-1937 by the Yorkshire Patent Steam Wagon Co. Ltd. Yorkshire wagons shared the UK's heavy haulage trade with four other steam wagon companies, models of which are in the range. The "Löwenbräu" lion symbol commemorates the 1383 Tavern Brewery sited adjacent to the Bavarian Duke's lion's cage. This is the second model in the range which displays the "Löwenbräu" livery; the other being the Y26-1 Crossley Truck. Also, it is the fifth time that the Yorkshire wagon has appeared in the range. Basically the YGB12 is similar to the Y8-5 "Fyffe's" model. However, an additional boss for a self tapping screw has been fitted between the front axle and the gear box drive shaft. The baseplate inscription has also been rearranged and altered to YGB12 ©1994 MATCHBOX COLLECTIBLES.

ISSUE	YEAR OF RELEASE	COLOURS	CAB ROOF	CANOPY	SEATS	ROOF SUPPORT & REAR BULKHEAD	WHEELS	BOILER BANDS	WATER TANK, GEARBOX ASHCAN, CHIMNEY & BOILER ENDS	SERIES NUMBER	BASEPLATE	RARITY	BOX TYPE	VALUE	CHECK LIST
1	1994	Royal blue body, cab & boiler body	White	White	Black	Light brown	Red 6 spoke	Gold	Black	Cast YGB12	MATCHBOX COLLECTIBLES ©1994 CHINA		Q		✓

LIVERY 'LOWENBRÄU'
Tampo
Wagon sides. Gold lion on a gold edged blue plaque above gold outlined blue LÖWENBRÄU. All within gold coachlining.
Wagon tailgate. Gold outlined LÖWENBRÄU within gold coachlining.
Cab sides and doors. LÖWENBRÄU A.G. BRAUER VON QUALITATSBIEREN SEIT 1383. All within gold coachlining.
Boiler supports. Gold outlined blue LÖWENBRÄU within gold coachlining and gold coachlining to boiler base ends.
Canopy sides. Square panel of angled and alternating lines of white and blue diamonds each side of gold lion on a gold edged blue plaque above gold outlined blue LÖWENBRÄU.

NOTES
1. Compare with Y8-5.
2. For transport purposes a clear plastic "keeper" band has been placed around the canopy and the lorry. Collectors are advised to retain this band to stop the two components coming apart.

INVESTMENT COMMENT	# YGB13 1926 MODEL 'TT' FORD VAN 'ANCHOR' Scale: 1:41
ORIGINAL PRICE £9.95 Too early to comment.	This is the second time that the 'TT' van has been in the 'Great Beers of the World' series; the first being the YGB02 "Beck & Co". The model shows the livery of the very small but well known San Francisco, USA, company, Anchor Brewery, which has been in existence since 1896. Some difficulties were encountered in representing the Anchor livery to a high enough standard acceptable to the brewery. Basically, similar to the Beck's model. However, the side oval windows were removed and cast digits YGB02 were replaced by tampo printed YGB13. Also, the tampo printed MADE IN CHINA and 1926 FORD 'TT' descriptions have been omitted.

ISSUE	YEAR OF RELEASE	COLOURS	ROOF	SEATS	RADIATOR	WHEELS	PLATED PARTS	PRINTED TRIM	OVAL WINDOW	TRANSMISSION & UNDER FRAME	LUG UNDER CAB ROOF	SERIES NUMBER	BASEPLATE	RARITY	BOX TYPE	VALUE	CHECK LIST
1	1995	Dark blue body cab & bonnet with black chassis & mudguards	Cream	Grey	Gold shell with black grille	Gold 12 spoke	Gold	Gold	No	Grey	No	Tampo YGB13	MATCHBOX COLLECTIBLES © 1993 CHINA		Q		✔

LIVERY ANCHOR
Tampo
Van sides. SINCE, in gold to left of 1896 in gold to right of multi-coloured company's anchor crest, all above black MADE IN SAN FRANCISCO 1896. All the above under BREWED & BOTTLED BY ANCHOR BREWING CO. SAN FRANCISCO, CALIFORNIA. Very small copyright symbol and date in black. All in light cream oval. All within gold coachlining.
Van rear doors. Gold SAN FRANCISCO'S ORIGINAL above off-white outlined light blue ANCHOR STEAM, all within gold coachlining.
Cab sides. Gold rope entwined anchor above gold SAN FRANCISCO.
Bonnet. Gold coachlining to top and to the side louvres.

NOTES
1. Compare with Y21-5 and YGB02.

INVESTMENT COMMENT
ORIGINAL PRICE £9.95
Too early to comment.

YGB14 1912 FORD MODEL 'T' VAN 'KIRIN' Scale: 1:35

Starting with the "Coca-Cola" in 1979, this is the nineteenth time that the model 'T' van has been in the range. The livery of the YGB14 is that of the Japanese Kirin Brewery Co. Ltd., which was founded in 1888. The decorative livery features that ancient harbinger of good luck, the legendary half-dragon, half-deer called the Kirin. The YGB14 is similar to the Y12-3 "Rosella" Matchbox based model, in that the baseplate supporting the running board treads is tapered for the rearmost 10 mm so that each side ends 1 mm narrower than the remainder. The base has been altered to accommodate the two bosses needed for the self tapping screws. The two bosses on the underside of the van body section of the roof introduced when two holes were cast into the roof to accommodate the Heinz gherkin and still in evidence during the production of the Rosella models, have been removed. Slight defects on the top of the roof are visible on some models. The running boards have been enhanced with a gold finish.

ISSUE	YEAR OF RELEASE	COLOURS	ROOF	SEAT	RADIATOR	WHEELS	PLATED PARTS	PAINTED TRIM	REAR DOORS	REAR LIGHTS	BASE HOLE AT REAR OF BODY	UNDERSIDE ROOF BOSSED	SERIES NUMBER	BASEPLATE	RARITY	BOX TYPE	VALUE	CHECK LIST
1	1995	Imperial red body, cab & bonnet with black chassis	Cream	Black	Gold shell with black grille	Light copper 12 spoke	Gold	Gold	Type 3	Gold	Yes	No	Cast YGB14	MATCHBOX COLLECTABLES © 1995 CHINA		Q		✓

LIVERY KIRIN
Tampo
Van sides. White KIRIN BREWERY COMPANY LIMITED with green shadow effect, above white outlined gold and green Kirin animal above white outlined gold edged banner with green shadow effect white KIRIN LAGER.
Cab doors. White KIRIN BREWERY COMPANY LIMITED. Gold coachlining and decoration around van sides, oval side windows and cab doors.
Rear doors. White outlined gold edged banner with green shadow effect, white KIRIN LAGER with gold coachlining and decoration.
Bonnet. Gold coachlining and decoration to top, sides and to the louvres.

NOTES
1. Compare with Y12-3 and YCH01

YGB15 1929 GARRETT 6 TON STEAM WAGON 'FLOWER & SONS'

Scale: 1:59

INVESTMENT COMMENT
ORIGINAL PRICE £9.95
Too early to comment.

Founded in the late 18th century, Garrett is a well known English engineering company, which built their first steam wagon in 1904. After many developments, the firm designed and built a powerful and smooth running engine. Unusually, the driver is now positioned at one side of the boiler. The YGB15 displays the livery of that exceptionally fine ale brewery "Flower & Sons" which was established in 1831 at Stratford-upon-Avon, England. Basically the same as the Y37-1 "Chubb" and "Milkmaid" wagons, the YGB15 has an amended baseplate; the single screw hole has been replaced with a boss and an additional boss cast adjacent to the front axle, for self tapping screws. The inscription has been altered to read © 1995 MATCHBOX COLLECTABLES, MADE IN CHINA and YGB15

ISSUE	YEAR OF RELEASE	COLOURS	CAB ROOF	VAN ROOF	SEATS	FRONT WHEELS	REAR WHEELS	PLATED PARTS	PAINTED TRIM	MUDGUARDS, TRANSMISSION CHAIN, PIPES & CYLINDERS	SERIES NUMBER	BASEPLATE	RARITY	BOX TYPE	VALUE	CHECK LIST
1	1995	Matt primrose yellow body & cab with bright red chassis	Matt primrose yellow	Matt primrose yellow	Black	Pale red 6 spoke	Pale red daisy	Chrome	Silver	Black	Cast YGB15	MATCHBOX COLLECTABLES © 1995 CHINA		Q		✓

LIVERY FLOWER & SONS
Tampo
Van sides. Multi-coloured bust of Shakespeare in centre of primrose yellow oval below black FLOWERS with black accentuated edges above black TRADEMARK. All above black FINE ALES. To the left of the bust FLOWER in black and to the right & SONS in black. Black scroll decoration both sides of oval, all within red coachlining.
Van rear doors. Smaller version of side panel oval over black accentuated black FLOWER & SONS. All within red coachlining.
Cab off-side rear panel. Black FINE ALES above black FLOWER & SONS THE BREWERY EST 1831. All within red coachlining and decoration.
Cab nearside rear panel. FLOWER & SONS THE BREWERY in white within red coachlining.
Cab near-side door. Black No7, within red coachlining and decoration.
Cab front off-side panel. Multi-coloured bust of Shakespeare below black FLOWERS and TRADEMARK; all above black FINE ALES all within red coachlining and decoration.
Cab front centre panel. Black GARRETT symbol.
Label
Cab corner panel. Black FLOWER & SONS THE BREWERY EST 1831 all within red coachlining and decoration.

NOTES
1 Compare with Y37-1.
2. Because the cab roof has a matt gloss finish and van roof is self coloured plastic there is a slight difference of colour.

INVESTMENT COMMENT
ORIGINAL PRICE £9.95
Too early to comment.

YGB16 1932 MODEL AA FORD 1½ TON TRUCK 'CORONA' Scale: 1:46

This was the third appearance of the 1932 1½ Ton Ford in the range and the second time in the YGB series. The livery is that of "Corona" beer produced by the Grupo Modelo Brewery which, although only established in 1925, is Mexico's premier brewery. Although the YGB16 is basically similar to the YGB05, the baseplate has been altered. Both chassis types have been used (Types A&B). The cast YGB05 under the offside running board has been removed and replaced with a tampo printed YGB16. The canopy and cab roof have been combined and the new diecast component has a rear opening with a rolled up "blind". The sloping portion over the cab is secured by two rivets in the cab ceiling. Nice touches are the gold checker-board footplates to the cab steps and the gold finish cab door handles. Thus the vehicle has a much "smarter" appearance than the YGB05 'Carlsberg' model.

ISSUE	YEAR OF RELEASE	COLOURS	CAB ROOF & CANOPY	SEAT	RADIATOR	WHEELS	PLATED PARTS	PAINTED TRIM	CHASSIS TYPE	SERIES NUMBER	BASEPLATE	RARITY	BOX TYPE	VALUE	CHECK LIST
1	1995	Dark blue body, cab & bonnet, black sub chassis & mudguards	White with grey blind & black straps	Light grey	Gold shell & centre bar with black grille	Gold solid	Gold	Gold	A	Tampo YGB16	MATCHBOX COLLECTIBLES ® 1993 CHINA		Q		
2		Dark blue body, cab & bonnet, black sub chassis & mudguards	White with grey blind & black straps	Light grey	Gold shell & centre bar with black grille	Gold solid	Gold	Gold	B	Tampo YGB16	MATCHBOX COLLECTIBLES ® 1993 CHINA		Q		✓

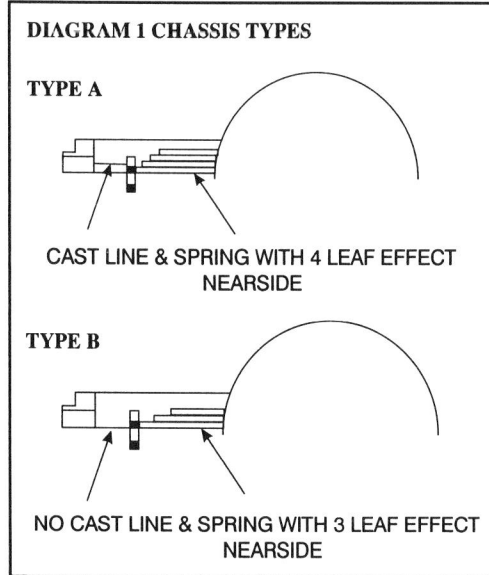

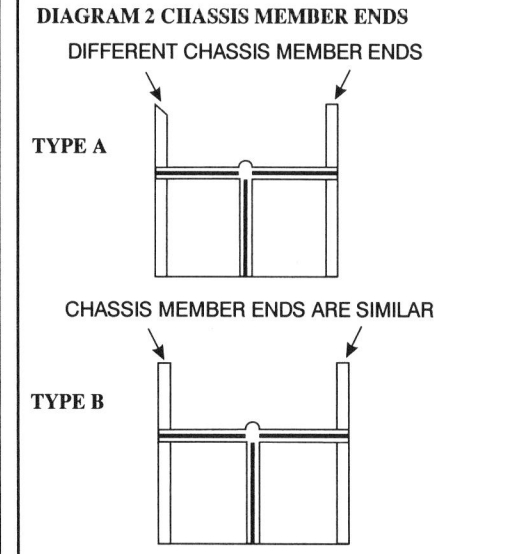

LIVERY CORONA
Tampo
Truck sides and tailgate. Two gold coachlined rectangles.
Cab doors. Company insignia of white barrel in front of a red cougar. All surrounded by black CERVECERIA MODELO, S.A. DE C.V. MEXICO on white ring.
Bonnet panels. Gold coachlined rectangle and gold coachlining to top and to side louvres.
Canopy sides. Rich yellow crown with small T.M in blue above dark blue CORONA EXTRA. All within red coachlining.
Sloping van roof. Smaller version of canopy side decoration.

NOTES
1. Compare with Y62-1, YGB05, YFE06, YFE09 and YPP05.
2. For transport purposes a clear plastic "keeper" band has been placed around the canopy and the lorry. Collectors are advised to retain this band to stop the two components coming apart.

INVESTMENT COMMENT
ORIGINAL PRICE £9.95
Too early to comment.

YGB17 1932 MERCEDES BENZ "LS" LORRY 'HENNINGER'

Scale: 1:69

Four other models of this lorry are in the range, the Y6-5 "Stuttgarter", the Y41-1 "Howaldtswerke" the YGB06 "Holsten" and the YPP03 "Berliner Morgenpost". The livery carried is that of the Henninger Brewery which, in 1665, was established in Frankfurt, Germany and which has a worldwide trade. The brewery's well known very tall landmark tower forms part of the company's insignia. Basically similar to the YGB06 Holsten model it has a modified baseplate. The cast YGB06 has been replaced by a tampo YGB17 printed centrally between the two screwholes. The three rivets holding the body to the baseplate have the new standard "spun" ends. Near to the tailgate are the small holes used for rivets to hold down the two barrels. The tarpaulin and its framework are the same size as used in the Y6-5 Stutgarter model. However, the rear horizontal framework has been deleted and the locating legs are slightly slimmer. The result is a less secure component. Some silver enhancement has been given to the running board treads, top of the tool box, cab door hinges and handles and to the bonnet side louvres. This was the first time that the 'L5' lorry had been fitted with glazed cab windows.

ISSUE	YEAR OF RELEASE	COLOURS	CAB ROOF	SEATS	WHEELS	RADIATOR	PLATED PARTS	PAINTED TRIM	TARPAULIN	TARPAULIN FRAME	TRUCK PLANKING EFFECT	CAB STEPS SUPPORTS	SERIES NUMBER	BASEPLATE	RARITY	BOX TYPE	VALUE	CHECK LIST
1	1995	White body & cab with red chassis & black gloss mudguards	Bright red	Light grey	Chrome 6 spoke. Doubles at rear	Chrome black grille	Chrome	Silver	Red covering 2 dark brown barrels	Black	Shallow	Black Type B	Tampo YGB17	MATCHBOX COLLECTIBLES © 1993 CHINA		Q		✓

LIVERY HENNINGER
Tampo
Body sides and tailgate. Red HENNINGER BRAU with gold shadow effect.
Cab doors. Red BRAUERI HENNINGER FRANKFURT above red W.20
Bonnet. Red coachlining and decoration to the top and to the sides.
Tarpaulin sides. Gold HB with gold representation of brewery tower.

NOTES
1. The YY32 on the tarpaulin framework is only a factory production code.
2. Compare with Y6-5, Y41-1, YGB06, YPP03.
3. For transport purposes a clear plastic 'keeper' band has been placed around the canopy and the lorry. Collectors are advised to retain this band to stop the two components coming apart.
4. The YGB17 has cab glazing.

INVESTMENT COMMENT
ORIGINAL PRICE £9.95
Too early to comment.

YGB-18 1931 MORRIS VAN 'CASCADE'   Scale: 1:50

After an absence of three years, the Morris Courier van reappeared in 1995 in the livery of Cascade as part of the third series of Great Beers of the World. Established in 1824 in Tasmania, Cascade is Australia's oldest brewery. Collectors were very impressed with the eye-catching livery and the superb logo reproduction. As with the YPP02 'The Times', the van body was a totally new component. The gentle upsweep of the lower edge of the van body aft of the rear mudguards and rear door detail, indicate that this component is totally new rather than an adaptation of a Y31-1 body to accept the differently shaped roof. The shape and height of the roof is so obviously different to the Y31-1. Purists were delighted with the fact that, not only the van body but the roof also was cast in metal. This was in line with Matchbox Collectibles' stated policy of using diecast instead of plastic wherever practically possible. Some silver painted enhancement has been given to the cab door handles, rear door handles and lock, and the petrol filler cap. Also, the four rear lights are 'picked out' in red.

ISSUE	YEAR OF RELEASE	COLOURS	ROOF	SEATS	WHEELS	PLATED PARTS	PAINTED TRIM	RADIATOR	SERIES NUMBER	BASEPLATE	RARITY	BOX TYPE	VALUE	CHECK LIST
1	1995	Dark green body & cab, beige front & rear wings. Matt black chassis	Beige	Beige	Beige solid. Doubles at rear	Chrome	Silver & red	Chrome shell & grille	Tampo YGB18	MATCHBOX COLLECTIBLES © 1994 CHINA		Q		✔

LIVERY CASCADE
TAMPO
Van sides. A multi-coloured country scene in orange, black, brown, gold and green of two animals facing left in a gold bordered landscape with a pale yellow background, surmounted by PREMIUM LAGER in pale yellow on an ochre band.
Rear doors. CASCADE in pale yellow on an ochre coloured circle. BREWED IN TASMANIA in gold
Front roof section. BREWED IN TASMANIA in gold, ochre and green
Cab doors. CASCADE BREWING CASCADE ROAD SOUTH HOBBART TAS. 7004 in gold
Gold coachlining to cab doors, bonnet and side panels

NOTES

1. Compare with Y31-1 and YPP02
2. A single horizontal cast line runs the full length of the new van body

INVESTMENT COMMENT
ORIGINAL PRICE £17.50

YFE01 1920 MACK AC FIRE ENGINE   Scale: 1:60

The first of a new group of models called 'The Fire Engine Series' in which each model was faithful to the original appearance and was seen and approved for historical accuracy by the Fire Brigade Society. The series was based on old castings but so many extra details were added that it is difficult to identify the original. The YFE01 Mack fire engine used the same base components as the YGB09 and the Y30-1. The YFE01 has a new upper body section but uses dark brown ladders of the same pattern as on the Y61-1 and the Y6-4 fire engine models. A small number of models were released with YGB09 cast on the baseplate. These are rare. The vast majority of first issue models have YFE01 cast on the baseplate.

Due to its popularity a second production run commenced in 1995. The cast YFE01 number was then replaced by one tampo printed in white. The ® mark after the words MODELS OF YESTERYEAR was repositioned and given better definition. Also, the third issue YFE01 models were packaged in moulded thin plastic formers.

ISSUE	YEAR OF RELEASE	COLOURS	SEATS	WHEELS	PLATED PARTS	PAINTED TRIM	FIRE EXTINGUISHER	BELL	FUEL TANK	FILLER CAPS	SIDE PRESSURE HOSES	OTHER HOSES	LADDERS	SERIES NUMBER	BASEPLATE	RARITY	BOX TYPE	VALUE	CHECK LIST
1	1994	Bright red body & chassis	Black	Chrome solid	Chrome	Silver	Gold	Gold	Bronze	Gold	Black	White	Dark brown	Cast YGB09*	MATCHBOX COLLECTIBLES © 1994 CHINA	R	Q	£35	
2		Bright red body & chassis	Black	Chrome solid	Chrome	Silver	Gold	Gold	Bronze	Gold	Black	White	Dark brown	Cast YFE01	MATCHBOX COLLECTIBLES © 1994 CHINA		Q		
3	1995	Bright red body & chassis	Black	Chrome solid	Chrome	Silver	Gold	Gold	Bronze	Gold	Black	White	Dark brown	Tampo YFE01	MATCHBOX COLLECTIBLES © 1994 CHINA		Q		

NOTES

1. Due to the unpopularity of the plastic plinths to hold the model during transportation, the YFE01 was first packaged in bubble wrap
2. Compare with YGB09, Y30-1, Y33-1, Y23-2 and YPP06

INVESTMENT COMMENT	# YFE02 1952 LANDROVER AUXILIARY	Scale: 1:43

ORIGINAL PRICE £17.50

Too early to comment.

A newcomer to the Models of Yesteryear range although it had been released twice as a 1948 Landrover in the Dinky Collection. However the trailer was a new casting. The combination was most successful; the Landrover sold well to those who remembered private fire brigades worldwide using such vehicles around factory complexes or in remote rural areas.

Due to being a sell out, Matchbox Collectibles re-ran the YFE02; the logo WORKS FIRE SERVICE was deleted and the red solid wheels replaced with bright chrome ones. All 1994 releases were accompanied with a Certificate of Approval from the Fire Brigade Society. These certificates did not appear with 1995 releases. On the 1995 re-run models, the © 1994 mark has been moved from the right side of the front rivet to the left side.

ISSUE	YEAR OF RELEASE	COLOUR	SEATS	WHEELS	PLATED PARTS	PAINTED TRIM	BONNET DETAIL	HOSES	COUNTER BALANCE	LADDER	LOGO	SERIES NUMBER	BASEPLATE	RARITY	BOX TYPE	VALUE	CHECK LIST
1	1994	Bright red body & trailer with matt black chassis	Black	Red solid	Chrome	Silver	Grey	Black	Off-white	Mid brown	WORKS FIRE SERVICE	Cast YFE02	MATCHBOX COLLECTIBLES©1994 CHINA		Q		
2	1995	Bright red body & trailer with matt black chassis	Black	Chrome solid	Chrome	Silver	Grey	Black	Off-white	Mid brown		Cast YFE02	MATCHBOX COLLECTIBLES©1994 CHINA		Q		

LIVERY
Tampo
Cab doors. White WORKS FIRE SERVICE.

NOTES
1. Compare with DY-9 Landrover and to YFE02/B.
2. The trailer baseplate has both Matchbox Collectibles and Matchbox Int'l cast.

INVESTMENT COMMENT
ORIGINAL PRICE £25.00
Within weeks of release the YFE02/B was selling with a considerable premium. One to watch very closely.

YFE02/B 1952 LAND ROVER FIRE TRUCK 'LONDONDERRY'   Scale 1:43

This second regional fire appliance closely followed the Belrose and was released in Australia in January 1996. Londonderry is a small town about 35 miles north west of Sydney, Australia. The Bush Fire Brigade was formed in the 1950s using World War II vehicles. This Land Rover was purchased from the Australian Army in 1972 for $400 AUS., jointly by the New South Wales Fire Brigade and the local Parish Council. The Londonderry Brigade fitted the vehicle out with suitable fire fighting equipment but kept it in its original yellow livery and it stayed in service until 1984.

A donation was made from the sale of each model by Automodels Pty Ltd to the Brigade 'To help them in their selfless and often dangerous work'. The model components are the same as the YFE02 except for some small details. The tow hook has been slightly reduced as have the rear lights and the ©1994 mark has been moved from the right side to the left side on the trailer chassis. The Londonderry model bears only one number plate, on the trailer, the index numbers being the same as the YFE02 models. Total production was 3,000 models.

ISSUE	YEAR OF RELEASE	LAND ROVER COLOURS	TRAILER COLOURS	CAB ROOF	SEATS	WHEELS	RADIATOR GRILLE	PLATED PARTS	PAINTED TRIM	LADDER	COUNTER BALANCE	LADDER RACK	TAIL LIGHTS	HEAD LIGHTS	SERIES NUMBER	BASEPLATE	RARITY	BOX TYPE	VALUE	CHECK LIST
1*	1996	Yellow body, matt black chassis	Yellow body, white chassis	White	Black	Yellow solid	Black	Chrome	Black	Brown	Dark cream	White	Orange	Silver	Cast YFE-2	MATCHBOX COLLECTIBLES © 1994 CHINA	S	Q	£40	

LIVERY
Tampo
Truck sides and trailer rear panel red LONDONDERRY.
Cab doors. N.S.W. BUSH FIRE BRIGADES and a crescent roundel badge in red, white, green, purple, gold and black.
Trailer rear panel. Red LONDONDERRY.
Trailer number plate. Black LOP652 on black edged yellow plate.

NOTES
1. Compare with YFE02 and DY9.

INVESTMENT COMMENT
ORIGINAL PRICE £17.50
Too early to comment.

YFE03 1933 CADILLAC V16 FIRE WAGON   Scale: 1:46

Based on the Y61-1, the YFE03 was fitted with a vast array of fire fighting equipment. The right hand spare wheel was replaced with a hose reel, searchlight and bell; the rear side windows were filled in and fire fighting equipment added; the rear doors were cut out to allow for the mounted pumping gear; water hoses were fixed to the front radiator shell and the roof rack was re-designed to hold a detailed ladder. All enhancement was in silver.

The YFE03 was first released in February 1995 and was bubble wrapped for internal packaging. A further production run was completed in May and these models were packed in the moulded formers.

ISSUE	YEAR OF RELEASE	COLOURS	SEATS	RADIATOR	WHEELS	PLATED PARTS	PAINTED TRIM	HOSES & ROLLOVERS	LADDER RACK	LADDER	REAR STEPS & FRONT BUMPER IRONS	SERIES NUMBER	BASEPLATE	RARITY	BOX TYPE	VALUE	CHECK LIST
1	1995	Bright red body & bonnet with chrome sub chassis	Black	Chrome shell & grille	Chrome solid	Chrome	Silver	Light tan with silver & black fittings	Chrome	Dark brown with silver trim	Black	Cast YFE03	MATCHBOX COLLECTIBLES © 1994 CHINA		Q		

NOTES.
Compare with Y61-1 and Y34-1.

| INVESTMENT COMMENT | # YFE04 1939 BEDFORD WATER TANKER | Scale: 1:46 |

ORIGINAL PRICE £17.50
Too early to comment.

Mistakenly described by Matchbox Collectibles as a 'Green Goddess'; which caused embarrassment and confusion. The "Green Goddesses" were later Bedford vehicles from the 1950s and 1960s. The 1939 Bedford is a forerunner of those later vehicles. The YFE04 is an authentic replica of a water-carrying vehicle, that saw service throughout the Second World War. The only components of this model which have appeared before, are the cab, wheels and chassis from the Y63-1 Bedford KD Truck. However, the YFE04 chassis is diecast, whereas the Y63-1 was plastic. The tank, side panels and the stopcocks at each end of the YFE04 are re-worked components from the Y23-2 Mack Tanker. All enhanced detailing was in silver. The Bedford Tanker was the first model in the Fire Engine series to be packaged in the moulded plastic formers.

ISSUE	YEAR OF RELEASE	COLOURS	SEATS	GRILLE	WHEELS	PLATED PARTS	PAINTED TRIM	HOSES	HEAD LIGHTS	SPOT LIGHT	LADDER	HOSE TROLLEY WHEELS & HANDLE	SERIAL NUMBER	BASEPLATE	RARITY	BOX TYPE	VALUE	CHECK LIST
1	1995	Bright red cab, bonnet, body, mudguards and tank with gloss black chassis	Black	Bright red with silver bars	Chrome solid	Chrome	Silver	White with silver ends & black straps	Black with silver lenses	Black with chrome lens	Brown	Bright 16 spoke with black handle. White hose	Cast YFE04	MATCHBOX COLLECTIBLES © 1994 CHINA		Q		

Notes

1. Compare with Y63-1 and YFE04/B.

INVESTMENT COMMENT
ORIGINAL PRICE £25 This model was only obtainable through Matchbox Collectibles and Collectible Centres in Australia and many Yesteryear collectors were unaware of its release. With so few models produced there is further growth potential.

YFE04/B BELROSE FIRE ENGINE   Scale: 1:46

Similar to the YFE-04 except for the black side mounted hoses and new tampo decoration. This model was commissioned by Automodels Pty Ltd of Australia, a toy and model retail shop. A donation of Aus $5 from the sale of each model produced was given to the Belrose Volunteer Bus Fire Brigade, which was formed in 1951.

The digits YFE04 were still cast on the baseplate and the model was packaged in a 'Q' style box with end flaps decorated as the regular YFE series but with specially designed main panel artwork. Total production was 3,000.

ISSUE	YEAR OF RELEASE	COLOURS	SEATS	GRILLE	WHEELS	PLATED PARTS	PAINTED TRIM	HOSES	HEAD LIGHTS	SPOT LIGHT	LADDER	TRANSIT WHEELS & HANDLE	SERIAL NUMBER	BASEPLATE	RARITY	BOX TYPE	VALUE	CHECK LIST
1*	1995	Bright red, cab, bonnet, body, mudguards & tank with gloss black chassis	Black	Bright red with silver bars	Chrome solid	Chrome	Silver	Black with silver ends & straps	Black with silver lenses	Black with chrome lens	Brown	Bright red 16 spoke with black handle. White hose	Cast YFE04	MATCHBOX COLLECTIBLES © 1994 CHINA	S	Q1	£80	

LIVERY BELROSE
Tampo
Water tank sides. Black BELROSE VOLUNTEER BUSH FIRE BRIGADE
Cab doors, rear tank compartment and rear locker door. Red, white, green and gold New South Wales Bush Fire Brigade badge topped by a gold, black and white King George VI crown.

NOTES
1. Compare with YG3-1 and YFE04.

INVESTMENT COMMENT
ORIGINAL PRICE £17.50

YFE05 1932 MERCEDES BENZ LADDER TRUCK Scale: 1:69

This Type L5 diesel lorry was equipped with a twenty-two metre turntable escape ladder that had to be constructed in three sections. Most effective in rescuing people from tall buildings! Despite the small scale of the YFE05, the reworking and superb detail ensured its popularity with not only Yesteryear collectors, but fire fighting model enthusiasts. Although the cab was common to the earlier Y6-5 and Y41-1 models, the rear extension and one piece roof was new. A new platform running the full length of the model was made to support a three-piece diecast and plastic silver ladder. The ladder is on a fully rotating turntable which has a friction pad to prevent the ladder dropping. All enhancement detail was silver. The YFE05 was only packaged in the moulded plastic formers.

ISSUE	YEAR OF RELEASE	COLOURS	ROOF	SEATS	WHEELS	RADIATOR	PLATED PARTS	PAINTED TRIM	HOSES	SEARCH LIGHT	HOSE TROLLEY WHEEL & HANDLE	LADDER	SERIES NUMBER	BASEPLATE	RARITY	BOX TYPE	VALUE	CHECK LIST
1	1995	Bright red body & cab with black chassis & front mudguards	Bright red & silver ladder supports	Light grey	Chrome 6 spoke. Doubles at rear	Chrome shell with black grille, chrome Mercedes symbol & DIESEL	Chrome	Silver & black	White	Black with silver lens	Red 5 spoke with black handle & silver ends	Silver	Tampo YFE05	MATCHBOX COLLECTIBLES ® 1993 CHINA		Q		

NOTES
1. Compare with Y6-5, Y41-1, YGB06, YGB17, YPP03 and YFE07
2. The YFE05 has cab window glazing

INVESTMENT COMMENT
ORIGINAL PRICE £17.50
Too early to comment.

YFE06 1932 FORD AA FIRE ENGINE   Scale: 1:46

This American fire fighter carried a front mounted pump that could delivery 400 gallons of water per minute. It was so effective that the Russians copied the design. Another superbly detailed model based on the earlier Y62-1 using that model's cab, (excluding the roof) base and chassis, the YFE06 has a new rear section of fire fighting equipment. This increased the weight of the model from 110 grammes to 170 grammes! Although shown in Matchbox Collectibles literature as having red wheels, all released models to date have chrome solid wheels. Much of the model has been enhanced with silver detailing. The YFE06 was only issued in the moulded plastic formers.

ISSUE	YEAR OF RELEASE	COLOURS	CAB ROOF HOSE	LADDERS	SEAT	RADIATOR	WHEELS	PLATED PARTS	PAINTED TRIM	CHASSIS TYPE	SIDE HOSES	FLAT BED HOSES	DRUM HOSES	SERIES NUMBER	BASEPLATE	RARITY	BOX TYPE	VALUE	CHECK LIST
1	1995	Bright red body & chassis, black sub chassis & transmission	Black with silver straps	Dark brown, silver trim	Light grey	Chrome shell & centre bar with black grille	Chrome solid	Chrome	Silver and red	A	White plastic, silver ends & straps	White metal	Light tan with red 8 spoke ends in plastic	Tampo YFE06	MATCHBOX COLLECTIBLES ® 1993 CHINA		Q		
2		Bright red body & chassis, black sub chassis & transmission	Black with silver straps	Dark brown, silver trim	Light grey	Chrome shell & centre bar with black grille	Chrome solid	Chrome	Silver and red	B	White plastic, silver ends & straps	White metal	Light tan with red 8 spoke ends in plastic	Tampo YFE06	MATCHBOX COLLECTIBLES ® 1993 CHINA		Q		✓

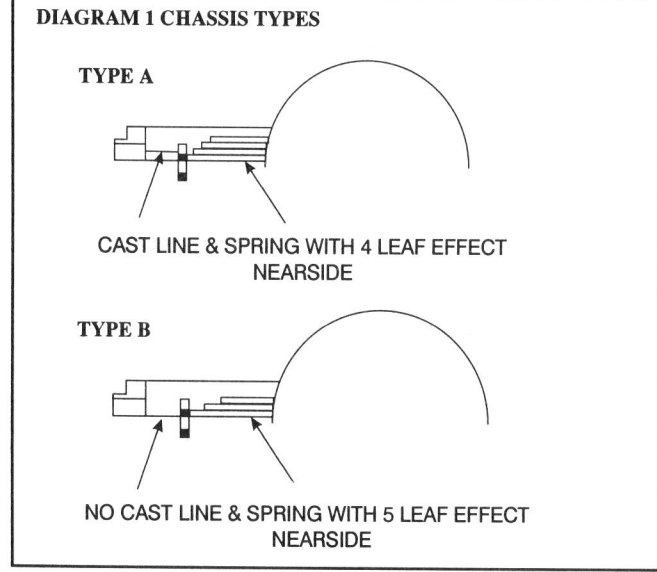

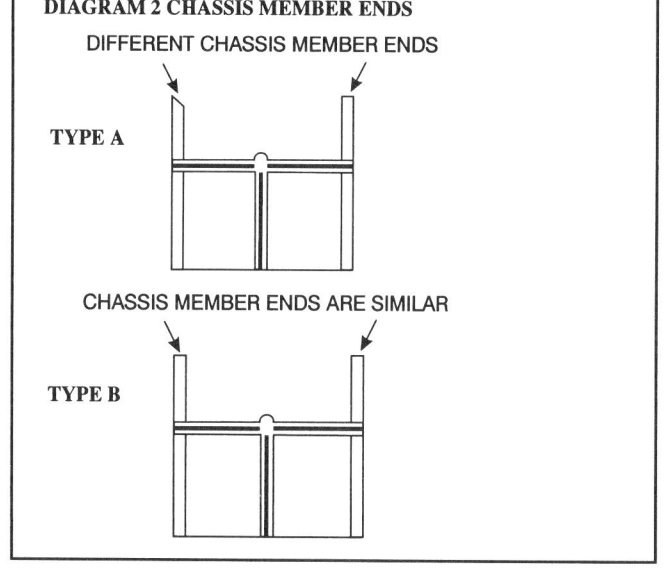

NOTES

1. Compare with Y62-1, YFB05 and YPP05

INVESTMENT COMMENT		
ORIGINAL PRICE £17.50		
Too early to comment.		

YFE-07 1938 MERCEDES KS15 FIRE TRUCK Scale 1:69

This nine ton fire fighting vehicle was based on the chassis of the Mercedes Benz LOD 3750. The 7.3 litre 6 cylinder engine could provide 100 horsepower to drive a 400 gallon per minute water pump or deliver up to 15 fire fighters at a top speed of 40 mph to the fire scene. Initial reaction to this model was that it is very similar to the previously released Mercedes L5 models. In fact, the only common component is the radiator and chassis, on which two cast bars have been added to delete the original text and the rear hole is now blind. A new sub-chassis, on which the new body is mounted, now has the base text under the running boards. The radiator surround has had the headlights removed and the rear transit hose is only common to the YFE05. A buff coloured fire blanket with black straps is fitted above the transit hose reel. There is a blue painted lens to the pump mounted lamp and chrome lenses to the headlamps and spot lamp. The wheels are of a new design but tend to "lose" their detail within the chrome finish. All enhancement detail is silver. The YFE07 was only packaged in the moulded plastic formers. It was released in January 1996.

ISSUE	YEAR OF RELEASE	COLOURS	CAB ROOF	SEATS	WHEELS	RADIATOR	PLATED PARTS	PAINTED TRIM	HOSES	TRANSIT HOSE WHEELS & HANDLE	LADDER	SERIES NUMBER	BASEPLATE	RARITY	BOX TYPE	VALUE	CHECK LIST
1	1996	Red body with white sub chassis & wings, black chassis & running boards	White	Light brown	Chrome solid at front, chrome dished doubles at rear	Black with encirlced 3 point star & DIESEL in chrome	Chrome	Silver. Black.	White	Red 5 spoke with black handle & silver nozzles	Brown	Cast YFE07	MATCHBOX COLLECTIBLES ® 1995 CHINA		Q		

NOTES

1. Compare with Y6-5, Y41-1, YGB06, YGB17, YPP02 and YFE05.

INVESTMENT COMMENT
ORIGINAL PRICE £39
Too early to comment.

YFE08 and YSFE02 1936 LEYLAND CUB FK-7 FIRE ENGINE
Scale: 1:49

Used by many fire services around the world, the Leyland Cub was probably one of the greatest fire engine vehicles of all time. Powered by a 4.7 litre engine, it was most efficient and it protected a crew of twelve with steel lined inner bodywork, transverse seating and safety glass. Knowing that the Y9-4 had sold out quickly in 1989, Matchbox Collectibles decided to re-issue the Cub as part of the Fire Engine series. Various changes were made to the existing tools. A new window was fitted, new faucets and hose termini were installed and a short ladder was fitted to the reworked roof panel. The words WORKS FIRE SERVICE are omitted and on the baseplate FIRE ENGINE has been added. Also the word MODELS is omitted from under the nearside running board. With its extra extensive gold decoration and darker shade of red, the Y9-4 in comparison to the YFE08, is rather drab. A small number of the YFE08 were released with a plinth and these Leyland models were coded as YSFE02. No holes were cast into either the YFE08 or YSFE02 as it was never intended to be screwed to the plinth.

ISSUE	YEAR OF RELEASE	COLOURS	ROOF	SEATS	RADIATOR	PLATED PARTS	PAINTED TRIM	HOSES	WHEELS	CHAINS	ESCAPE LADDER & WHEELS	SERIES NUMBER	BASEPLATE	RARITY	BOX TYPE	VALUE	CHECK LIST
1	1995	Bright red body, bonnet & chassis with chrome underframe	Fine textured matt black	Brown	Chrome shell & grille	Chrome	Gold	White	Chrome solid, doubles at rear	Gold	Dark brown with top pulley wheels in white, lower wheels in silver	Tampo YFE08	MATCHBOX COLLECTIBLES © 1995 CHINA		Q3		

LIVERY LEYLAND
Tampo
Body sides. LEYLAND in gold with black shadow effect.
Gold with black decoration to three corners of coachlining.
Double gold and white coachlining to door panels, body sides, toolbox, hose lockers, rear panel and bonnet.
Bonnet louvers, handles, hinges and side lights painted gold.

NOTES

1. Compare YFE08/YSFE02 to Y9-4.
2. Both Leyland Cub models were packaged in moulded formers.

INVESTMENT COMMENT
ORIGINAL PRICE £17.50
Too early to comment.

YFE-09 1932 FORD AA OPEN CAB FIRE ENGINE   Scale 1:46

Powered by the well known V8 engine, this small fire vehicle was quick to arrive at the fire scene where 500 gallons of water per minute could be pumped. The flatbed carries a 100 gallon water storage tank and for the 1930s, modern fire fighting equipment needed to reach isolated areas. Matchbox Collectibles have used the bonnet, front wings and sub-chassis of previous Ford AA models as well as substantial amounts of new cast components to produce this open cab version. Notably, the steering wheel is now to the left-hand side, a new front bumper with "irons" has been fitted. The radiator shell now has a horn cast to one side and the rear section is completely new except for the ladder and fire axe and shovel. Baseplate details are that of the YFE06 except for the series number. Much of the model has been enhanced with silver detailing. The YFE09 was only issued in the moulded plastic formers and was released in late January 1996.

ISSUE	YEAR OF RELEASE	COLOURS	WATER TANK HOSE	LADDER	SEAT	RADIATOR	WHEELS	PLATED PARTS	PAINTED TRIM	CHASSIS TYPE	SIDE HOSE	FLAT BED HOSES	DRUM HOSE	SERIES NUMBER	BASEPLATE	RARITY	BOX TYPE	VALUE	CHECK LIST
1	1996	Red body and chassis with black sub chassis	Black within 8 rung red drum	Dark brown	Black	Chrome shell & centre bar with black grille	Chrome solid	Chrome	Silver	Type A	Black chrome ends	White	White chrome ends	Cast YFE09	MATCHBOX COLLECTIBLES ® 1993 CHINA		Q		
2		Red body and chassis with black sub chassis	Black within 8 rung red drum	Dark brown	Black	Chrome shell & centre bar with black grille	Chrome solid	Chrome	Silver	Type B	Black chrome ends	White	White chrome ends	Cast YFE09	MATCHBOX COLLECTIBLES ® 1993 CHINA		Q		

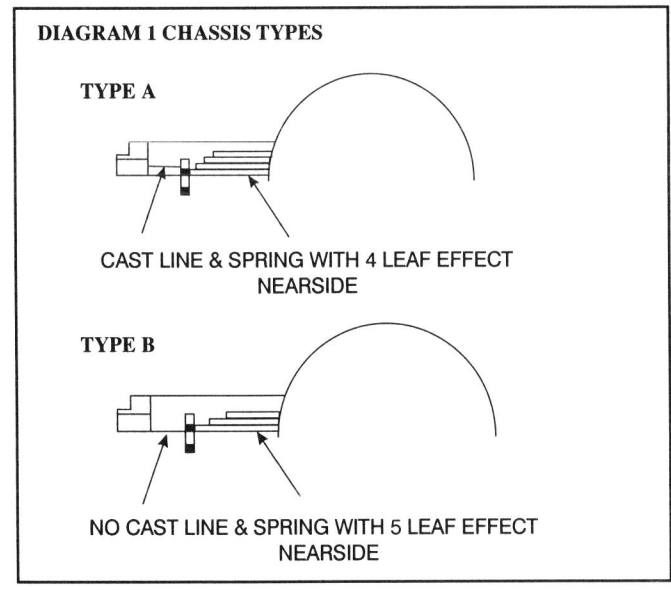

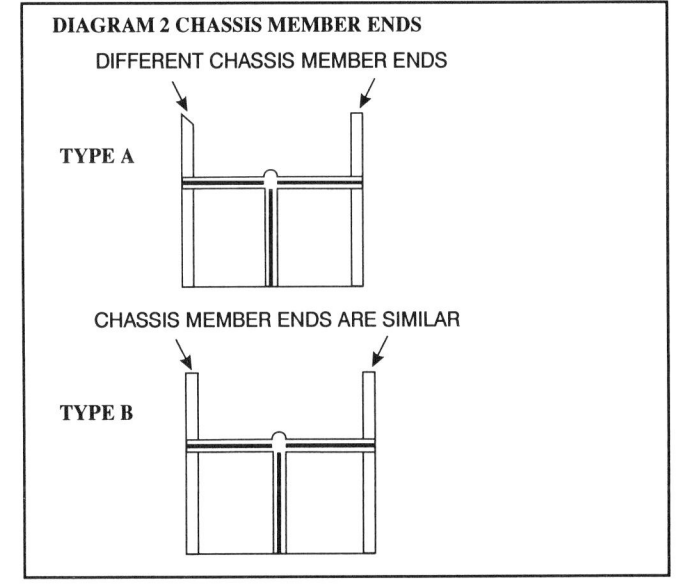

NOTES

1. Compare with YFE06, YPP05, YGB16, YGB05 and Y62-1.
2. Beware of breakages. The searchlight staunchion is fragile.

INVESTMENT COMMENT
ORIGINAL PRICE £59.95
Too early to comment.

YSFE-01 1930 AHRENS-FOX QUAD FIRE ENGINE
Scale 1:43

This Special Edition model released in December 1994 is an accurate replica of the original vehicle housed at the Hall of Flame in Phoenix, Arizona, USA. Known as the "Four Star General" of great fire engines, the Fox Quad could not be equalled with its pumping capacity; it had enormous water storage tanks, booster hoses and very long ladders. Another Ahrens-Fox model had been sold a few years earlier by Franklin Mint at a considerably higher price than the £59.95 asked by Matchbox Collectibles.

Despite the large amount of detailed components made in plastic, the overall weight of the YSFE01 is substantial mainly because the body and chassis is made in diecast. The Fox Quad was released with a black plinth and a Certificate of Authority from the Hall of Flame Antique Fire Engine Museum. Much of the model has been enhanced with silver and gold paint; considerably more trim was used when compared with the pre-production model shown in Matchbox Collectibles literature.

ISSUE	YEAR OF RELEASE	COLOURS	CAB FLOOR & REAR FOOT PLATE	SEATS	WHEELS	PLATED PARTS	COACH LINING	SIDE HOSES	FLAT BED HOSES	REAR HOSE REEL	REAR FOOT PLATE BASE	LADDERS	SERIES NUMBER	BASEPLATE	RARITY	BOX TYPE	VALUE	CHECK LIST
1	1994	Bright red body, bonnet, wings & chassis with gloss black running boards	Gloss black with silver trim	Black	Red solid	Chrome	Gold	Black	White	Red with silver hose pipe	Maroon	Dark brown	Cast YSFE-01	MATCHBOX COLLECTIBLES © 1994 CHINA		Q3		

NOTES

INVESTMENT COMMENT
ORIGINAL PRICE £12.99

With such a restrictive distribution, many Yesteryear collectors were unaware of this release. One to watch closely!

YY027/SA 1922 FODEN TYPE 'C' STEAM WAGON 'FULLER'S'   Scale: 1:72

This was the second of two specially commissioned Fuller's models to celebrate the brewery's 150th anniversary. Unlike the YY047/SA Morris van which was a re-run of the YGB04, this was the first time that the Fuller's livery had adorned the 1922 Yesteryear Foden. Its attractive colour scheme of red and black with gold decoration was an immediate hit with Yesteryear and steam vehicle enthusiasts alike. The baseplate was is similar to the YGB11 'Whitbread' model except that the cast digits YGB11 had been deleted and replaced with white tampo printed YY027/SA; 1922 FODEN was also printed in white transversely between the rear axle rear hangers. This model was packaged in an 'N' style box in an overall black colour. A clear label with gold lettering was applied to the right hand side front and top panels; the front and top of the box was decorated with Fuller's logos and inscriptions. The rear box panel gave a brief history of the Fuller's Griffin Brewery and showed a sepia reproduction of a Foden loaded with beer crates, an attendant driver and two yardsmen. Only one of the two screwhole bosses was used to secure the model to the card diarama insert. The total production of the YY027/SA worldwide was 7,000.

ISSUE	YEAR OF RELEASE	COLOURS	CAB ROOF	SEAT	LOAD	WHEELS	PLATED PARTS	2 BODY FLOOR HOLES	WHEEL HUBS	SERIES NUMBER	BASEPLATE	RARITY	BOX TYPE	VALUE	CHECK LIST
1	1995	Gloss black body & cab. Bright red chassis & mudguards	Bright red	Black	5 dark brown barrels	Pale red daisy	Gold	Yes	Type 2	Tampo YY027/SA	MATCHBOX COLLECTIBLES © 1994 CHINA		N3		

LIVERY FULLER'S
Tampo
Wagon body sides and tail gate. 150 YEARS OF BREWING EXCELLENCE in gold above gold Griffin and GRIFFIN BREWERY between 1845 and 1995 in gold within gold scrollwork, all above FULLER'S in white with gold edging and black shadow effect on red panel with gold and white border, all within gold coachline.
Cab front panels. FULLER, SMITH & TURNER, GRIFFIN BREWERY, CHISWICK in gold within gold coachlining.
Cab doors and rear cab panels. Gold coachlining.

NOTES
1. Compare with YGB11 and Y27-1.
2. The suffix 'SA' in the coding means that the 'S' is for special livery. and the 'A' shows it to be the first special livery.

YY047/SA 1929 MORRIS LIGHT VAN 'FULLER'S' LONDON PRIDE

Scale 1:39

INVESTMENT COMMENT
ORIGINAL PRICE £12.99

With such a short production run, many Yesteryear collectors were unaware of this release. Sure to appreciate in value.

This model is virtually identical to the YGB04. However, it was one of two specially commissioned Fuller's models to celebrate the brewery's 150th anniversary. The Fuller's London Pride model was available via the brewery or from Matchbox Collectibles Centres. It was noted that the copper plating was slightly lighter as was the shade of the red roof and chassis compared with the YGB04. Also, the small side lights on top of the front wings were now silver and the running board ridges were highlighted in silver. The baseplate inscription was similar, except that the cast digits YGB04, had been deleted and YY047/SA tampo printed instead. Only one screwhole boss was used to secure the model to the card diarama insert. An 'N' style window box had been used to package the YY047/SA; and is in an overall green colour with Fuller's logos and inscriptions. The cream rear box panel gives a brief history of the Fuller's Griffin brewery. The total production run was 7,000.

ISSUE	YEAR OF RELEASE	COLOURS	ROOF	ROOF CASTING	SEATS & CAB INTERIOR	CAB WINDOWS	GRILLE	WHEELS	PLATED PARTS	PAINTED TRIM	PAINTED SIDE LIGHTS	RUNNING BOARD TREADS	DOOR HANDLES	SERIES NUMBER	BASEPLATE	RARITY	BOX TYPE	VALUE	CHECK LIST
1	1995	Light bottle green body, cab & bonnet bright red chassis, mudguards & running boards	Bright red	Type 2	Light brown	Clear perspex	Black	Copper 12 spoke	Light copper	Gold	Silver	Bright red with silver ridges	Silver	Tampo YY047/SA	MATCHBOX COLLECTIBLES ® 1993 CHINA		N3		✓

LIVERY FULLER'S LONDON PRIDE
Tampo
Van sides. Gold and black Griffin symbol above gold edged ribbon with GRIFFIN BREWERY in gold all above white, black and gold edged, red panel with FULLER'S in white with black and gold shadow effect. All above CHISWICK in gold with faint black coachlining. All within gold coachlining.
Closed rear doors. Black, white and gold-edged red shield surmounted with gold Griffin on black background over red rectangle with white FULLER'S above gold CHISWICK above white LONDON PRIDE with black shadow effect, black edged white BEST BITTER on gold background. All above gold EST 1845, with dark red shadow effect. All within gold coachlining.
Cab doors. Smaller version of rear door shield. All within gold coachlining.
Bonnet. Gold coachlining on top and gold louvres both sides. Gold encircled gold 6 above tool box.
Toolbox. Black finish to top panel within gold edging.

NOTES
1. Compare with Y47-1 and YGB04.

INVESTMENT COMMENT
ORIGINAL PRICE £22.99
With Matchbox Collectibles stating "only 5,000 of this unique collectible will ever be available", future growth is a realistic forecast. It sold out very quickly.

YSC01-M 1922 SCANIA VABIS HALF TRACK POST BUS Scale 1:64

First issued by Matchbox as a Special Limited Edition in 1988 as the Y16-4. The Scania Post Bus was reissued for Christmas 1995, and was featured in the Matchbox Collectibles Christmas Catalogue. Although described as a post-bus, the YSC01-M bore the livery of Hemavan Lodge, a Swedish ski resort. The finish of 'pearlescent white' was one of several new paints introduced by Matchbox Collectibles. The roof mounted spruce trees were finely detailed and were made in Stoke-on-Trent, England, using the 'cold cast' technique. See Matchbox Terminology. The 'trees' were exported to China for assembly. A quantity arrived damaged and it was necessary to have 1,236 replacements made in China. These replacement trees (Type 2) are some 5% smaller in size. There are many colour shades associated with both types of tree. In comparison to the Y16-4, modifications were made to the wheel hubs and to the baseplate text. Total production of the YSC01-M was 5,004.

ISSUE	YEAR OF RELEASE	COLOURS	LOAD	SEATS / FLOOR	PLATED PARTS	GRILLE	WHEELS	HALF TRACK PONY WHEELS	CATERPILLAR TRACK	FRONT LIGHT LENSES	PAINTED TRIM	SKIS	SERIES NUMBER	BASEPLATE	RARITY	BOX TYPE	VALUE	CHECK LIST
1	1995	Pearlescent white body, roof, chassis & half track supports	Green tree Type 1	Brown	Light copper	Black	Light copper 12 spoke	Light copper solid	Black	Silver	Gold	Brown with pearlescent white frames	Tampo YSC01	MATCHBOX © 1988 CHINA		Q2	£30	
2		Pearlescent white body, roof, chassis & half track supports	Green tree Type 2*	Brown	Light copper	Black	Light copper 12 spoke	Light copper solid	Black	Silver	Gold	Brown with pearlescent white frames	Tampo YSC01	MATCHBOX © 1988 CHINA	S	Q2	£50	

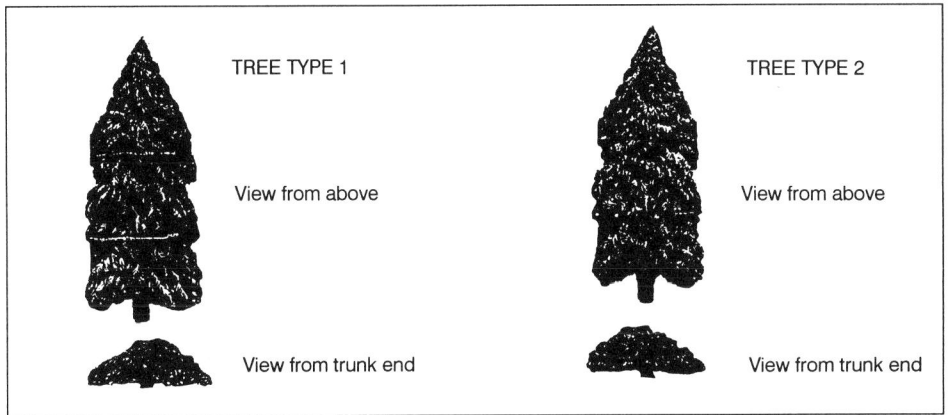

LIVERY
Tampo

Offside lower body panel. Gold HEMAVAN LODGE above heraldic shield in gold and pearlescent white.
Number plates. White with black edge and black Z1090.
Red tail light.
Edge of roof. Dark gold coachlining.

NOTES

1. The windows have clear Perspex panes.
2. Compare with Y16-4 and YET04.

INVESTMENT COMMENT
ORIGINAL PRICE £14.00
This model was only obtainable through Matchbox Collectibles and Collectible Centres in Australia and many Yesteryear collectors were unaware of this release. With so few models produced and with such a well-known livery, there is further growth potential.

YCH01 1912 MODEL 'T' VAN
Scale: 1:35

RONALD McDONALD HOUSE

Because the Beckenham Appeal models are Code 4, the YCH01 model is the first Code 1 specifically produced to support a charity. The Australian Ronald McDonald Children's Charities (RMCC) support Ronald McDonald's Houses and their social programmes to help sick and disabled children to live happier, healthier and productive lives. These Houses provide family accommodation for children having treatment for serious and life-threatening illnesses. AUS $5.00 donation to the RMCC was made from the sale of each model. The YCH01 is basically similar to the YGB14 "Kirin" model except that the baseplate inscription has been modified to show that it is a McDonald's charity model and is a limited edition.
The YCH01 sold well. The total production was 5,112.

ISSUE	YEAR OF RELEASE	COLOURS	ROOF	SEAT	RADIATOR	WHEELS	PLATED PARTS	PAINTED TRIM	REAR DOORS	REAR LIGHTS	BASE HOLE AT REAR OF BODY	UNDERSIDE ROOF BOSSED	SERIES NUMBER	BASEPLATE	RARITY	BOX TYPE	VALUE	CHECK LIST
1	1995	Bright yellow body, cab & bonnet. Orangey red chassis	Orangey* red	Black	Gold shell with black grille	Copper 12 spoke	Gold	Gold	Type 3	Orangey red	Yes	No	Tampo YCH01	MATCHBOX COLLECTABLES © 1995 CHINA	R	Q1	£100	
2		Bright yellow body, cab & bonnet. Orangey red chassis	Red*	Black	Gold shell with black grille	Copper 12 spoke	Gold	Gold	Type 3	Red	Yes	No	Tampo YCH01	MATCHBOX COLLECTABLES © 1995 CHINA	R	Q1	£100	

LIVERY RONALD McDONALD HOUSE
Tampo
Van body sides. Black RONALD McDONALD CHILDREN'S CHARITIES OF AUSTRALIA with two clasped hands and lower arms, one in flesh colour and one in yellow, red and white; all on white rectangle with orangey-red border. Above RONALD McDONALD HOUSE ® in white with blue surround and a red heart, above blue THE HOUSE THAT LOVE BUILT ® ....
Rear doors. White RONALD McDONALD HOUSE with blue surround and a red heart and blue ®
Cab doors. Outline of a house with a smile and a smoking chimney, all in blue.

NOTES
1. Compare with Y12-3 and YGB14.

YCC01 CHRISTMAS TREASURES 1994

Scale 1:43

Leading up to Christmas 1994, Matchbox Collectibles stated in their brochure, "In the spirit of Christmas we have assembled our first ever set of Chritmas ornaments." This is a specal Limited Edition issue set of four models; all of which are tampo dated 1994. All four Austin 7 vans are displayed in a special red marble effect box measuring 19 cms x 14 cms x 3.5 cms. Basically the same casting as the 1928 Austin 7 van from the Y65 set issued in 1992. All of the vans were fitted with clear Perspex windscreens with a transome line to indicate the opening section. The baseplate screwhole has been retained although the baseplate description now reads YCC01. The worldwide production run of the 1994 Christmas Treasures was 5,000 sets.

ISSUE	YEAR OF RELEASE	MESSAGE	COLOURS	ROOF	SEATS	FLOOR & PARTITION	PLATED PARTS	PAINTED TRIM	RADIATOR	WHEELS	SERIES NUMBER	BASEPLATE	RARITY	BOX TYPE	VALUE	CHECK LIST
1	1994	HAPPY HOLIDAY	Pearlescent white body, metallic blue upper panels, gloss black base & aluminium sub chassis	White with chrome eyelet	Royal blue	Royal blue	Chrome	Silver	Chrome shell with black honeycomb grille	Chrome 18 spoke	Cast YCC01	MATCHBOX © 1992 CHINA				
		MERRY CHRISTMAS	Red body, gloss black base & aluminium sub chassis	Red with chrome eyelet	White	White	Chrome	Silver	Chrome shell with black honeycomb grille	Chrome 18 spoke	Cast YCC01	MATCHBOX © 1992 CHINA				
		PEACE ON EARTH	Pale blue body, gloss black base & aluminium sub chassis	Pale blue with chrome eyelet	White	White	Chrome	Silver	Chrome shell with black honeycomb grille	Chrome 18 spoke	Cast YCC01	MATCHBOX © 1992 CHINA				
		SEASONS GREETINGS	Metallic stardust green body. Gloss black base & aluminium sub chassis	Metallic stardust green with chrome eyelet	Off-white	Off-white	Chrome	Silver	Chrome shell with black honeycomb grille	Chrome 18 spoke	Cast YCC01	MATCHBOX © 1992 CHINA		02	THE SET £30	

LIVERY: CHRISTMAS TREASURES 1994
Tampo
HAPPY HOLIDAY
Upper panels. Multi-coloured three wise men figures on camels; with gold star of Bethlehem.
Lower panels. Black HAPPY HOLIDAY.
Cab doors. Black 1994.
Number plates. White 1994 on black plate.

MERRY CHRISTMAS
Upper panels. Father Christmas figure clad in red and white robe on yellow and blue sledge with coloured parcels. All on snowy blue and white edged hemispherical background.
Lower panels. White MERRY CHRISTMAS.
Cab doors. White 1994.
Number plates. White 1994 on black plate.

PEACE ON EARTH
Upper panels. Three white doves, one with green holly leaf on stained glass window effect background in pale yellow, dark yellow, orange and black within black edged white hemispherical frame.
Lower panels. White PEACE ON EARTH
Cab doors. White 1994.
Number plates. White 1994 on black plate.

SEASONS GREETINGS
Upper panels. Brown, cream and black reindeer on white, yellow, green and black snow scene, within black and white oval.
Lower panels. White SEASONS GREETINGS
Cab door. White 1994.
Number plates. White 1994 on black plate.

INVESTMENT COMMENT
ORIGINAL PRICE £19.95

Whether these four models will be as popular as the Y65-1 Austin 7 set has yet to be proved. Because they could be considered complementary to that set, and with a low production run, they may well do so.

NOTES
1. Some radiator grilles may appear to have a chrome honeycomb similar to that of the van in the Y65-1 set, with a black background. This is due to the quality of the black paintwork, which has left some chrome showing.
2. Compare with Y65-1 Austin 7 set and the YCC02.

YCC02 CHRISTMAS TREASURES 1995

Scale: 1:43

In 1995 Matchbox Collectibles released a second Special Limited Edition of Austin 7 van Christmas tree ornaments. Boxed in a manner similar to the YCC01 1994 models, the box now had a green marble effect to the lid; on the back of which was a gold and black Matchbox Collectibles advertising device. The casting is similar to that of the YCC01 1994 van; however, the cast YCC01 and the 1:43 inscription have been replaced with a white tampo printed YCC02. The scale indication has been omitted. The remainder of the model is similar to the 1994 casting. Limited to 9,492 sets worldwide, the YCC02 sold quickly, appealing not only to Yesteryear collectors, but to collectors of Christmas 'goods', eg cards and Christmas decorations.

ISSUE	YEAR OF RELEASE	MESSAGE	COLOURS	ROOF	SEATS	FLOOR & PARTITION	PLATED PARTS	PAINTED TRIM	RADIATOR	WHEELS	SERIES NUMBER	BASEPLATE	RARITY	BOX TYPE	VALUE	CHECK LIST
1	1994	HAPPY HOLIDAY	Pearlescent white body, gloss black base & aluminium sub chassis	Pearlescent white with chrome eyelet	Blue	Blue	Chrome	Silver	Chrome shell with black honeycomb grille	Chrome 18 spoke	Tampo YCC02	MATCHBOX © 1992 CHINA				
		MERRY CHRISTMAS	Red body, gloss black base & aluminium sub chassis	Red with chrome eyelet	White	White	Chrome	Silver	Chrome shell with black honeycomb grille	Chrome 18 spoke	Tampo YCC02	MATCHBOX © 1992 CHINA				
		PEACE ON EARTH	Metallic stardust yellow body, gloss black base & aluminium sub chassis	Metallic stardust yellow with chrome eyelet	White	White	Chrome	Silver	Chrome shell with black honeycomb grille	Chrome 18 spoke	Tampo YCC02	MATCHBOX © 1992 CHINA				
		SEASONS GREETINGS	Metallic stardust green body. Gloss black base & aluminium sub chassis	Metallic stardust green with chrome eyelet	White	White	Chrome	Silver	Chrome shell with black honeycomb grille	Chrome 18 spoke	Tampo YCC02	MATCHBOX © 1992 CHINA		02		

LIVERY: CHRISTMAS TREASURES 1995
Tampo
HAPPY HOLIDAY
Upper panels. Golden haloed Virgin and Child figures clad in dark blue, light blue and white with flesh coloured faces and hands. All as part of a multi-coloured stained glass window
Lower panels. Black HAPPY HOLIDAY
Cab doors. Black 1995.
Number plates. White 1995 on black plate.
MERRY CHRISTMAS
Upper panels. Father Christmas figure clad in red and white robe carrying a sack of multi-coloured parcels; above white snow on the top of a white jointed red brick chimney, with blue sky background. All within orange part-hoop frame.
Lower panels. White MERRY CHRISTMAS. Cab doors. White 1995.
Number plates. White 1995 on black plate.
PEACE ON EARTH
Upper panels. Two white winged yellow clad Angels with yellow halos; all as part of a multi-coloured stained glass window
Lower panels. White PEACE ON EARTH. Cab doors. White 1995.
Number plates. White 1995 on black plate.
SEASONS GREETINGS
Upper panels. Seated brown and orange toy bear with a red bow, with a red ribboned orange parcel and three green holly sprigs with red berries, all within orange part-hoop frame.
Lower panels. White SEASONS GREETINGS.
Cab doors. White 1995.
Number plates. White 1995 on black plate.

INVESTMENT COMMENT
ORIGINAL PRICE £19.95

Too early to comment.

NOTES

1. Some radiator grilles may appear to have a chrome honeycomb similar to that of the van in the Y65-1 set, with a black background. This is due to the quality of the black paintwork which has some chrome showing.
2. Compare with the Y65-1 Austin 7 set and the YCC01.

INDEX

INDEX AND CHECK LIST BY
MODEL TYPE IN ALPHABETICAL ORDER

Y6-1	1916	AEC 'Y' Type Lorry "Osram Lamps"	☒	
Y23-1	1922	AEC Omnibus "Haig"	☒	
Y23-1	1922	AEC Omnibus "Lifebuoy"	☒	
Y23-1	1922	AEC Omnibus "Maples"	☐	
Y23-1	1922	AEC Omnibus "RAC"	☒	
Y23-1	1922	AEC Omnibus "Rice Krispies"	☒	
Y23-1	1922	AEC Omnibus "Schweppes"	☒	
YET-05	1922	AEC Omnibus "Kennedys"	☒	
YSFE01	1930	Ahrens Fox Quad	☐	
Y42-1	1939	Albion 10 Ton CX27 Lorry "Libby's"	☒	
Y1-1	1925	Allchin Traction Engine	☒	2x
Y13-1	1862	American General Class Locomotive "Santa Fe"	☒	
Y18-2	1918	Atkinson Model 'D' Steam Wagon "Bass & Co."	☒	
Y18-2	1918	Atkinson Model 'D' Steam Wagon "Blue Circle Cement"	☒	
Y18-2	1918	Atkinson Model 'D' Steam Wagon "Burghfield Mills"	☒	
Y18-2	1918	Atkinson Model 'D' Steam Wagon "Lake Goldsmith"	☒	
YGB03	1918	Atkinson Model 'D' Steam Wagon "Swan Brewery Co"	☒	
YGB22	1918	Atkinson Model 'D' Steam Wagon "Beamish"	☒	
YAS-06	1918	Atkinson " " " "Logger"	☒	
Y19-1	1936	Auburn Speedster 851	☒	3x
Y65-1	1928	Austin 7 : BMW : Rosengart: Castrol.	☒	
YCC01	1928	Austin 7 Vans Christmas Treasures, 1994	☐	
YCC02	1928	Austin 7 Vans Christmas Treasures, 1995	☐	
Y21-3	1894	Aveling & Porter Steam Roller grün	☒	
Y11-1	1920	Aveling & Porter Steam Roller grün	☒	
YAS-03	1920	Aveling + Porter Steam Roller blau	☒	
Y63-1	1939	Bedford Type 'KD' Truck "Farrar"	☒	
YFE04	1939	Bedford Water Tanker	☐	
YGB24	1939	Bedford Stake BED Truck "Tooheys"	☒	

YFE04/B	1939	Bedford "Belrose" Fire Engine	☐
Y2-4	1930	Bentley, 4½ Litre	☒
Y5-2	1929	Bentley, 4½ Litre	☒
Y5-1	1929	Bentley, Le Mans	☒
Y3-2	1910	Benz Limousine	☒
YMS02-M	*1910*	*Benz Limousine 40 Johre Matchbox*	☒
Y21-4	1957	BMW 507	☒
Y45-1	1930	Bugatti Royale Napoleon	☒
Y11-5	1924	Bugatti Type 35	☒
Y6-2	1926	Bugatti Type 35	☒
Y24-1	1928	Bugatti T44	☒ 3x
Y11-4	1932	Bugatti Type 51	☒
Y43-1	1905	Busch Self Propelled Fire Engine	☒
Y6-3	1913	Cadillac	☒
Y34-1	1933	Cadillac 452 V16	☒
Y61-1	1933	Cadillac Fire Engine	☒
YFE03	1933	Cadillac V16 Fire Wagon	☐
YTF1	1947	Citroën 'H' Van "Evian"	☒
YTF4	1947	Citroën 'H' Van "Marcillat"	☒
YTF2	1947	Citroën 'H' Van "Martell"	☒
YTF6	1947	Citroën 'H' Van "Pommery Mustard"	☒
YTF5	1947	Citroën 'H' Van "Taittinger Champagne"	☒
YTF3	1947	Citroën 'H' Van "Yoplait"	☒
YFE13	*1947*	*Citroen H Van Sapeur Pompiers de Longueville*	☒
Y18-1	1937	Cord 812 Sedan	☒
Y13-3	1918	Crossley "Carlsberg"	☒
~~Y13-3~~	~~1918~~	~~Crossley Coal and Coke~~	☒

Y13-3	1918	Crossley "Evans Bros"	☒
Y13-3	1918	Crossley "Kohle & Koks"	☒
Y13-3	1918	Crossley "Waring & Gillow"	☒
Y26-1	1918	Crossley Delivery Truck "Gonzalez Byass"	☒
Y26-1	1918	Crossley Delivery Truck "Löwenbräu"	☒
Y26-1	1918	Crossley Delivery Truck "Romford Brewery"	☒
Y13-3	1918	Crossley R.A.F. Tender	☒
YMS05-M	*1911*	*Daimler Type A12 40 Jahre Matchbox*	☒
Y13-2	1911	Daimler Type A12	☐
Y10-5	1931	Diddler Trolley Bus	☒
YET-03M	*1931*	*Diddler Trolley Bus*	☒
YPP04	1948	Dodge Route Van "New York Times"	☒
Y4-4	1930	Duesenberg Model J Town Car	☒
Y14-1	1903	Duke of Connaught Locomotive	☒
Y14-4	1935	ERA R.1.B.	☒
Y16-3	1960	Ferrari Dino 246/V12	☒
Y27-1	1922	Foden Steam Wagon "Frasers"	☐
YY027/SA	1922	Foden Steam Wagon "Fullers"	☐
Y27-1	1922	Foden Steam Wagon "Guinness"	☒
Y27-1	1922	Foden Steam Wagon "Hovis"	☒
Y27-1	1922	Foden Steam Wagon "Joseph Rank"	☒
Y27-1	1922	Foden Steam Wagon "McMullens"	☒
Y27-1	1922	Foden Steam Wagon "Pickfords"	☒
Y27-1	1922	Foden Steam Wagon "Spillers"	☒
Y27-1	1922	Foden Steam Wagon "Tate & Lyle's"	☒
YAS-02		*" " " Coal Truck*	☒
YY027/SC		*" " " "F. Parker u. Co"*	☒

YGB11	1922	Foden Steam Wagon "Whitbread"	☒
Y7-4	1930	Ford Breakdown Truck "Barlow Motor Sales"	☒
Y7-4	1930	Ford Breakdown Truck "Shell"	☒
Y35-1	1930	Ford Model 'A' Pick-up truck "Ambrosia"	☒
Y35-1	1930	Ford Model 'A' Pick-up truck "Clifford & Sons"	☒
YJC-01		Ford Model 'A' Van "Penneys" (Kanada)	☒
Y21-2	1930	Ford Model 'A' Tradesman Woody Wagon "A & J Box"	☒
Y21-2	1930	Ford Model 'A' Tradesman Woody Wagon "Carters"	☒
Y22-1	1930	Ford Model 'A' Van "Canada Post"	☒
YGB01	1930	Ford Model 'A' Van "Castlemaine"	☒
Y22-1	1930	Ford Model 'A' Van "Cherry Blossom"	☒
Y22-1	1930	Ford Model 'A' Van "Lyons' Tea"	☒
Y22-1	1930	Ford Model 'A' Van "Maggis"	☒
Y22-1	1930	Ford Model 'A' Van "Oxo"	☒
Y22-1	1930	Ford Model 'A' Van "Palm Toffee"	☒
Y22-1	1930	Ford Model 'A' Van "Pratts"	☒
Y22-1	1930	Ford Model 'A' Van "Spratt's"	☒
Y22-1	1930	Ford Model 'A' Van "Toblerone"	☒
YPP08	1930	Ford Model 'A' Van "Washington Post"	☒
Y21-1	1930	Ford Model 'A' Woody Wagon	☐
YY21A/SA-M	1930	Ford Model A Woody Wagon Pepsi-Cola Pepsioldtimer 1932	☒
YGB05	1932	Ford Model 'AA' 1 ½ Ton Truck "Carlsberg"	☒
YGB16	1932	Ford Model 'AA' 1 ½ Ton Truck "Corona"	☒
YPP05	1932	Ford Model 'AA' 1 ½ Ton Truck "Los Angeles Times"	☒
Y62-1	1932	Ford Model 'AA' 1 ½ Ton Truck "Peacock"	☒
YFE06	1932	Ford Model 'AA' Fire Engine	☒
YFE09	1932	Ford Model 'AA' Open Cab Fire Engine	☐
YGB20	1932	Ford Model AA Delivery Van "Stroh's"	☒
Y1-2	1911	Ford Model 'T' Car	☒
YMS-01	1911	Ford Model T Car 40year yesteryears	☒
Y3-4	1912	Ford Model 'T' Tanker "BP"	☒
Y3-4	1912	Ford Model 'T' Tanker "Carnation"	☒
Y3-4	1912	Ford Model 'T' Tanker "Castrol"	☒

Code	Year	Model	✓
Y3-4	1912	Ford Model 'T' Tanker "Express Dairy"	☒
Y3-4	1912	Ford Model 'T' Tanker "Mobiloil"	☒
Y3-4	1912	Ford Model 'T' Tanker "Red Crown"	☒
Y3-4	1912	Ford Model 'T' Tanker "Shell"	☒
Y3-4	1912	Ford Model 'T' Tanker "Zerolene"	☐
Y12-3	1912	Ford Model 'T' Van "Arnott's Biscuits"	☐
Y12-3	1912	Ford Model 'T' Van "Bird's Custard"	☒
Y12-3	1912	Ford Model 'T' Van "Captain Morgan"	☒
Y12-3	1912	Ford Model 'T' Van "Cerebos"	☒
Y12-3	1912	Ford Model 'T' Van "Coca-Cola"	☒
Y12-3	1912	Ford Model 'T' Van "Colman's"	☒
Y12-3	1912	Ford Model 'T' Van "Harrods"	☐
Y123	1912	Ford Model 'T' Van "Heinz"	☒
Y12-3	1912	Ford Model 'T' Van "Hoover"	☒
YGB14	1912	Ford Model 'T' Van "Kirin Lager"	☒
Y12-3	1912	Ford Model 'T' Van "Motor 100"	☐
Y12-3	1912	Ford Model 'T' Van "Pepsi-Cola"	☒
YCH01	1912	Ford Model 'T' Van "Ronald McDonald"	☐
Y12-3	1912	Ford Model 'T' Van "Rosella"	☒
Y12-3	1912	Ford Model 'T' Van "Royal Mail"	☒
Y12-3	1912	Ford Model 'T' Van "Silver Jubilee, 25 Years"	☒
Y12-3	1912	Ford Model 'T' Van "Smith's Crisps"	☐
Y12-3	1912	Ford Model 'T' Van "Sunlight Seife"	☒
Y12-3	1912	Ford Model 'T' Van "Suze"	☐
Y12-3	1912	Ford Model 'T' Van "Taystee"	☐
YGB19M	1912	Ford Model 'T' Van "Yuengling"	☒
Y12-3	1912	Ford Model 'T' Pick-up truck "Imbach"	☒
Y	1912	Ford Model T Van „USHER'S"	☒
YGB13	1926	Ford Model 'TT' Van "Anchor Steam"	☒
YGB02	1926	Ford Model 'TT' Van "Becks"	☒
Y21-5	1926	Ford Model 'TT' Van "Drambuie"	☒
Y21-5	1926	Ford Model 'TT' Van "My Bread"	☒
Y21-5	1926	Ford Model 'TT' Van "Osram"	☒
YJC13	1926	Ford Model TT Van "J.C Penney Co" (kanada)	☒
YRS06	1955	Ford F 100 Route US 66	☒

Y9-1	1924	Fowler "Big Lion" Showman's Engine	☒	Code 1+2
Y19-2	1905	Fowler B6 Showman's Engine	☐	
YAS-OSM	1905	Fowler "Sophie" Showman's Engine	☒	
Y37-1	1929	Garrett Steam Wagon "Chubb's"	☒	
YGB15	1929	Garrett Steam Wagon "Flowers"	☒	
Y37-1	1929	Garrett Steam Wagon "Milk Maid"	☐	
YPP07	1937	GMC Van "Australian"	☒	
Y12-5	1937	GMC Van Baxter's	☒	
Y12-5	1937	GMC Van Goanna	☒	
Y12-5	1937	GMC Van Goblin	☒	
YGB08	1937	GMC Van Steinlager	☒	
YJC 08	1937	GMC Van JC Penney (Kanada)	☒	
Y66-1	1762	Gold State Coach	☒	
YSH1	1900	Gypsy Caravan	☒	
Y17-1	1938	Hispano Suiza	☒	
YSH3	1875	Horse Drawn Carriage Wells Fargo	☐	
Y1-3	1936	Jaguar, SS100	☒	
Y11-3	1938	Lagonda Drophead Coupe	☒	
YFE02	1948	Land Rover Auxiliary & Trailer	☐	
YFE02/B	1952	Land Rover and Trailer "Londonderry"	☐	
Y9-4	1936	Leyland Cub Fire Engine FK-7	☒	
YSFE02/ YFE08	1936	Leyland Cub Fire Engine FK-7	☐	
Y9-3	1920	Leyland Lorry, 3 Ton Luff & Sons	☒	
Y5-5	1929	Leyland Titan Bus City of Coventry	☒	

Code	Year	Description	Check
Y5-5	1929	Leyland Titan Bus Southdown	☒
Y5-5	1929	Leyland Titan Bus Ashton-under-Lyne	☐
Y7-1	1918	Leyland Van, 4 Ton "Jacob's"	☐
YET-02 M	1930	Leyland Titan Bus "Van Houten's Cocoa"	☒
Y64-1	1938	Lincoln Zephyr	☒
Y3-1	1907	London 'E' Class Tramcar "News of the World"	☒
Y2-1	1911	London Bus, B Type "Dewar's"	☒
Y12-1	1899	London Horse Drawn Bus "Lipton's Tea"	☒
YSH2	1886	London Omnibus "Oakey's Knife Polish"	☒
YFE01	1920	Mack Fire Engine	☐
Y23-2	1930	Mack Tanker "Conoco"	☒
Y23-2	1930	Mack Tanker "Texaco"	☒
Y30-1	1920	Mack Truck " Acorn Storage"	☒
Y30-1	1920	Mack Truck "Arctic Ice Cream"	☒
Y30-1	1920	Mack Truck "Consolidated"	☒
Y33-1	1930	Mack Truck "Goodyear"	☒
Y30-1	1920	Mack Truck "Kiwi"	☒
YGB09	1920	Mack Truck "Moosehead"	☒
YPP06	1923	Mack Truck "Pravda"	☒
YGB 23	1920	Mack AC Tsingtao Beer	☒
YFE 11	1923	Mack AC Water Tanker	☒
YJC 09	1920	Mack AC Penney's (Kanada)	☒
Y10-4	1957	Maserati 250F	☒
Y14-2	1911	Maxwell Roadster gold	☒
Y14-2	1911	Maxwell Roadster	☐
YMS06	1911	Maxwell Roadster 40 Jahre Matchbox	
YFE05	1932	Mercedes Benz 'L5' Ladder Truck	☐
YGB17	1932	Mercedes Benz 'L5' Lorry "Henninger-Brau"	☒
YGB06	1932	Mercedes Benz 'L5' Lorry "Holsten"	☒
Y41-1	1932	Mercedes Benz 'L5' Lorry "Howaldtswerke"	☒
YPP03	1932	Mercedes Benz 'L5' Lorry "Morgenpost"	☒
Y6-5	1932	Mercedes Benz 'L5' Lorry "Stuttgarter Hofbrau"	☒
YGB 21	1932	Mercedes " " " "DAB" Pils	☒

Y10-2	1928	Mercedes Benz 36-220	☐
Y20-1	1937	Mercedes Benz 540K	☒
Y40-1	1931	Mercedes Benz 770	☒
Y16-2	1928	Mercedes Benz SS Coupe	☒
Y10-1	1908	Mercedes, Grand Prix	☐
YMS02-M			
Y7-2	1913	Mercer Raceabout Type 35J	☒
			☐
Y46-1	1880	Merryweather Fire Engine	☐
			☐
Y8-4	1945	MG TC	☒
Y31-1	1931	Morris Courier "Kemp's"	☒
YPP02	1931	Morris Courier "London Times"	☒
Y31-1	1931	Morris Courier "Weetabix"	☒
Y8-1	1926	Morris Cowley "Bullnose"	☐
Y47-1	1929	Morris Cowley "Light Van Lindt"	☒
Y19-3	1929	Morris Cowley Van "Brasso"	☒
YGB18	1931	Morris Cowley Van "Cascade	☒
YGB04	1929	Morris Cowley Van "Fullers"	☒
YY047/SA	1929	Morris Cowley Van "Fullers London Pride"	☐
Y19-3	1929	Morris Cowley Van "Michelin"	☒
Y19-3	1929	Morris Cowley Van "Sainsbury"	☒
YCH-04	1929	Morris "Light Van" RSPCA	☒
Y4-3	1909	Opel Coupe silber	☒
Y4-3	1909	Opel Coupe	☒
YMS03	1909	Opel Coupe 40 Jahre yesteryear	☒
Y15-2	1930	Packard Victoria	☒
Y11-2	1912	Packard Landaulet	☒ 2x
YMS04-M	1912	Packard Landaulet 40 Jahre Matchbox	☒
Y39-1	1820	Passenger Coach & Horses	☒
			☒
Y5-3	1907	Peugeot	☒

Y15-3	1920	Preston Tram Car "Golden Shread"	☒
Y15-3	1920	Preston Tram Car "Swan Soap"	☒
Y15-3	1920	Preston Tram Car "Swan Vestas"	☒
Y15-3	1920	Preston Tram Car "Zebra Grate Polish"	☒
YET-01M	1920	Preston Tram Car "Yorkshire Relish"	☒
Y2-3	1914	Prince Henry Vauxhall	☒
YMS07M	1914	Prince Henry Vauxhall 40 Jahre Machbox	☒
Y44-1	1910	Renault Bus	☒
Y2-2	1911	Renault Two Seater	☒
Y25-1	1910	Renault Type AG Van "British Red Cross"	☒
Y25-1	1910	Renault Type AG Van "Delhaize"	☒
Y25-1	1910	Renault Type AG Van "Duckham's"	☐
Y25-1	1910	Renault Type AG Van "Eagle Pencil"	☒
Y25-1	1910	Renault Type AG Van "James Neale"	☒
YGB07	1910	Renault Type AG Van "Kronenbourg"	☒
YPP01	1910	Renault Type AG Van "Le Figaro"	☒
Y25-1	1910	Renault Type AG Van "Perrier"	☒
Y25-1	1910	Renault Type AG Van "Suchard"	☒
Y25-1	1910	Renault Type AG Van "Tunnock"	☒
YET-06M	1910	Renault Bus "Paris"	☒
Y3-3	1934	Riley MPH	☒
Y10-3	1906	Rolls Royce Silver Ghost	☒
Y7-3	1912	Rolls Royce	☒
Y38-1	1920	Rolls Royce Armoured Car	☒
Y6-4	1920	Rolls Royce Fire Engine	☒ 2x
Y36-1	1926	Rolls Royce Phantom 1	☒
Y15-1	1907	Rolls Royce Silver Ghost	☒
Y16-5	1929	Scammell 100 ton Low Loader	☒

Code	Year	Description	☐
Y16-4	1922	Scania Vabis Half Track Post Bus	☒
YSC01-M	1922	Scania Vabis Half Track Post Bus (with Christmas tree)	☐
YET-04M	*1922*	*Scania Vabis Post Bus "Stockholm"*	☒
Y4-1	1928	Sentinel Steam Wagon Sand & Gravel Supplies	☒
Y4-2	1905	Shand Mason Horse Drawn Fire Engine Kent/London	☒
Y9-2	1912	Simplex	☒
YMS-08	*1912*	*Simplex 40 years yesteryear*	☒
Y16-1	1904	Spyker Veteran Automobile	☒
Y12-4	1829	Stephenson's Rocket	☒
YAS01-M		*Stephenson's Rocket*	☒
Y14-3	1931	Stutz Bearcat	☒
Y8-3	1914	Stutz Type 4E Roadster	☒
Y8-2	1914	Sunbeam Motorcycle with Milford Sidecar	☐
Y5-4	1927	Talbot Van "Chivers"	☒
Y5-4	1927	Talbot Van "Dunlop"	☐
Y5-4	1927	Talbot Van "Ever Ready"	☒
Y5-4	1927	Talbot Van "Lipton's Tea" (City Road)	☐
Y5-4	1927	Talbot Van "Lipton's Tea" (with Crest)	☒
Y5-4	1927	Talbot Van "Lyle's"	☒
Y5-4	1927	Talbot Van "Menier"	☒
Y5-4	1927	Talbot Van "Nestle's"	☐
Y5-4	1927	Talbot Van "Rose's"	☒
YGB10	1927	Talbot Van "South Pacific"	☒
Y5-4	1927	Talbot Van "Taystee"	☒
Y5-4	1927	Talbot Van "Wright's"	☒
Y12-2	1909	Thomas Flyabout	☒ 3x

Y28-1	1907	Unic taxi	☒	3x
Y29-1	1919	Walker Electric Van "Harrods"	☒	
Y29-1	1919	Walker Electric Van "Harrods Special Bread"	☐	
Y29-1	1919	Walker Electric Van "His Master's Voice"	☒	
Y29-1	1919	Walker Electric Van "Joseph Lucas"	☒	
Y8-5	1917	Yorkshire Steam Wagon "Fyffes"	☒	
Y8-5	1917	Yorkshire Steam Wagon "Johnnie Walker"	☒	
YGB12	1917	Yorkshire Steam Wagon "Lowenbrau"	☒	
Y8-5	1917	Yorkshire Steam Wagon "Samuel Smith"	☐	
Y8-5	1917	Yorkshire Steam Wagon "William Prichard"	☒	
Y32-1	1917	Yorkshire Steam Wagon Type WA "Samuel Smith of Tadcaster"	☒	
YAS-04		Yorkshire " " The de Selby Quarries	☒	

COLLECTORS' NOTES:

Y _____

ISSUE	YEAR OF RELEASE	COLOURS				BASEPLATE	RARITY	BOX	VALUE

COMMENTS

PLEASE PHOTOCOPY AND SEND TO THE PUBLISHERS WITH YOUR ADDITIONAL INFORMATION; UNCODED ISSUES, MARKET VALUES etc

COLLECTORS' NOTES:

Y _____

ISSUE	YEAR OF RELEASE	COLOURS				BASEPLATE	RARITY	BOX	VALUE

COMMENTS

PLEASE PHOTOCOPY AND SEND TO THE PUBLISHERS WITH YOUR ADDITIONAL INFORMATION; UNCODED ISSUES, MARKET VALUES etc

COLLECTORS' NOTES:

Y _____

ISSUE	YEAR OF RELEASE	COLOURS				BASEPLATE	RARITY	BOX	VALUE

COMMENTS

PLEASE PHOTOCOPY AND SEND TO THE PUBLISHERS WITH YOUR ADDITIONAL INFORMATION; UNCODED ISSUES, MARKET VALUES etc

COLLECTORS' NOTES:

Y _____

ISSUE	YEAR OF RELEASE	COLOURS				BASEPLATE	RARITY	BOX	VALUE

COMMENTS

PLEASE PHOTOCOPY AND SEND TO THE PUBLISHERS WITH YOUR ADDITIONAL INFORMATION; UNCODED ISSUES, MARKET VALUES etc

COLLECTORS' NOTES:

Y _____

ISSUE	YEAR OF RELEASE	COLOURS				BASEPLATE	RARITY	BOX	VALUE

COMMENTS

PLEASE PHOTOCOPY AND SEND TO THE PUBLISHERS WITH YOUR ADDITIONAL INFORMATION; UNCODED ISSUES, MARKET VALUES etc

COLLECTION SUMMARY 1996

OWNER:..**MICA MEMBERSHIP NUMBER** __/___/__

JANUARY TO MARCH 1996

- Number of Code One mint and boxed issues
- Number of Code One mint issues
- Number of Code One non mint or unboxed issues
- Number of unlisted Code One issues
- Number of pre-production/colour trials
- Number of Code Two mint and boxed issues
- Most valuable issues

  (a)_____ (a)_____
  (b)_____ (b)_____
  (c)_____ (c)_____
  (d)_____ (d)_____
  (e)_____ (e)_____

- Current book value
- Estimated value of non priced issues
- Amount covered for insurance

Date......................Signed............................

JULY TO SEPTEMBER 1996

- Number of Code One mint and boxed issues
- Number of Code One mint issues
- Number of Code One non mint or unboxed issues
- Number of unlisted Code One issues
- Number of pre-production/colour trials
- Number of Code Two mint and boxed issues
- Most valuable issues

  (a)_____ (a)_____
  (b)_____ (b)_____
  (c)_____ (c)_____
  (d)_____ (d)_____
  (e)_____ (e)_____

- Current book value
- Estimated value of non priced issues
- Amount covered for insurance

Date......................Signed............................

APRIL TO JUNE 1996

- Number of Code One mint and boxed issues
- Number of Code One mint issues
- Number of Code One non mint or unboxed issues
- Number of unlisted Code One issues
- Number of pre-production/colour trials
- Number of Code Two mint and boxed issues
- Most valuable issues

  (a)_____ (a)_____
  (b)_____ (b)_____
  (c)_____ (c)_____
  (d)_____ (d)_____
  (e)_____ (e)_____

- Current book value
- Estimated value of non priced issues
- Amount covered for insurance

Date......................Signed............................

OCTOBER TO DECEMBER 1996

- Number of Code One mint and boxed issues
- Number of Code One mint issues
- Number of Code One non mint or unboxed issues
- Number of unlisted Code One issues
- Number of pre-production/colour trials
- Number of Code Two mint and boxed issues
- Most valuable issues

  (a)_____ (a)_____
  (b)_____ (b)_____
  (c)_____ (c)_____
  (d)_____ (d)_____
  (e)_____ (e)_____

- Current book value
- Estimated value of non priced issues
- Amount covered for insurance

Date......................Signed............................

COLLECTION SUMMARY 1997

OWNER:......................................MICA MEMBERSHIP NUMBER __/___/__

JANUARY TO MARCH 1997

- Number of Code One mint and boxed issues
- Number of Code One mint issues
- Number of Code One non mint or unboxed issues
- Number of unlisted Code One issues
- Number of pre-production/colour trials
- Number of Code Two mint and boxed issues
- Most valuable issues

  (a)_____   (a)_____
  (b)_____   (b)_____
  (c)_____   (c)_____
  (d)_____   (d)_____
  (e)_____   (e)_____

- Current book value
- Estimated value of non priced issues
- Amount covered for insurance

Date........................Signed..

JULY TO SEPTEMBER 1997

- Number of Code One mint and boxed issues
- Number of Code One mint issues
- Number of Code One non mint or unboxed issues
- Number of unlisted Code One issues
- Number of pre-production/colour trials
- Number of Code Two mint and boxed issues
- Most valuable issues

  (a)_____   (a)_____
  (b)_____   (b)_____
  (c)_____   (c)_____
  (d)_____   (d)_____
  (e)_____   (e)_____

- Current book value
- Estimated value of non priced issues
- Amount covered for insurance

Date........................Signed..

APRIL TO JUNE 1997

- Number of Code One mint and boxed issues
- Number of Code One mint issues
- Number of Code One non mint or unboxed issues
- Number of unlisted Code One issues
- Number of pre-production/colour trials
- Number of Code Two mint and boxed issues
- Most valuable issues

  (a)_____   (a)_____
  (b)_____   (b)_____
  (c)_____   (c)_____
  (d)_____   (d)_____
  (e)_____   (e)_____

- Current book value
- Estimated value of non priced issues
- Amount covered for insurance

Date........................Signed..

OCTOBER TO DECEMBER 1997

- Number of Code One mint and boxed issues
- Number of Code One mint issues
- Number of Code One non mint or unboxed issues
- Number of unlisted Code One issues
- Number of pre-production/colour trials
- Number of Code Two mint and boxed issues
- Most valuable issues

  (a)_____   (a)_____
  (b)_____   (b)_____
  (c)_____   (c)_____
  (d)_____   (d)_____
  (e)_____   (e)_____

- Current book value
- Estimated value of non priced issues
- Amount covered for insurance

Date........................Signed..

COLLECTION SUMMARY 1998

OWNER:..MICA MEMBERSHIP NUMBER __ / ___ / __

JANUARY TO MARCH 1998

- Number of Code One mint and boxed issues
- Number of Code One mint issues
- Number of Code One non mint or unboxed issues
- Number of unlisted Code One issues
- Number of pre-production/colour trials
- Number of Code Two mint and boxed issues
- Most valuable issues

    (a)_____   (a)_____
    (b)_____   (b)_____
    (c)_____   (c)_____
    (d)_____   (d)_____
    (e)_____   (e)_____

- Current book value
- Estimated value of non priced issues
- Amount covered for insurance

Date........................Signed........................

APRIL TO JUNE 1998

- Number of Code One mint and boxed issues
- Number of Code One mint issues
- Number of Code One non mint or unboxed issues
- Number of unlisted Code One issues
- Number of pre-production/colour trials
- Number of Code Two mint and boxed issues
- Most valuable issues

    (a)_____   (a)_____
    (b)_____   (b)_____
    (c)_____   (c)_____
    (d)_____   (d)_____
    (e)_____   (e)_____

- Current book value
- Estimated value of non priced issues
- Amount covered for insurance

Date........................Signed........................

JULY TO SEPTEMBER 1998

- Number of Code One mint and boxed issues
- Number of Code One mint issues
- Number of Code One non mint or unboxed issues
- Number of unlisted Code One issues
- Number of pre-production/colour trials
- Number of Code Two mint and boxed issues
- Most valuable issues

    (a)_____   (a)_____
    (b)_____   (b)_____
    (c)_____   (c)_____
    (d)_____   (d)_____
    (e)_____   (e)_____

- Current book value
- Estimated value of non priced issues
- Amount covered for insurance

Date........................Signed........................

OCTOBER TO DECEMBER 1998

- Number of Code One mint and boxed issues
- Number of Code One mint issues
- Number of Code One non mint or unboxed issues
- Number of unlisted Code One issues
- Number of pre-production/colour trials
- Number of Code Two mint and boxed issues
- Most valuable issues

    (a)_____   (a)_____
    (b)_____   (b)_____
    (c)_____   (c)_____
    (d)_____   (d)_____
    (e)_____   (e)_____

- Current book value
- Estimated value of non priced issues
- Amount covered for insurance

Date........................Signed........................